Introduction to Formal Languages, Automata Theory and Computation

Introduction to Formal Languages, Automata Theory and Computation

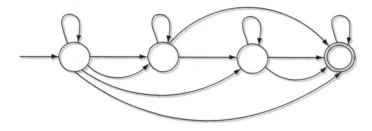

Kamala Krithivasan
Rama R
Indian Institute of Technology Madras

PEARSON

ISBN 978-81-317-2356-2

First Impression, 2009

Published by Pearson India Education Services Pvt.Ltd,CIN:U72200TN2005PTC057128.

Head Office: 15th Floor, Tower-B, World Trade Tower, Plot No. 1, Block-C, Sector 16, Noida 201 301, Uttar Pradesh, India.

Registered Office: The HIVE, 3rd Floor, Metro zone, No 44, Pilliayar Koil Street, Jawaharlal Nehru Road, Anna Nagar, Chennai, Tamil Nadu 600040.
Phone: 044-66540100, Website: in.pearson.com, Email: companysecretary.india@pearson.com

Digitally Printed in India by Repro Books Limited, Thane in the year of 2020.

Dedicated to

Goddess Sri Abhirami
Goddess Sri Mahalakshmi

About the Authors

Kamala Krithivasan received her PhD from the University of Madras, and she joined the Indian Institute of Technology Madras (IITM) in 1975. With more than 30 years of teaching and research experience at IITM, she is currently Professor at the Department of Computer Science and Engineering, in which she served as Chairman in 1992–1995. Her research interests include formal language theory and unconventional models of computing like DNA computing, membrane computing and discrete tomography. A recipient of the Fulbright fellowship in 1986, Professor Kamala is also a Fellow of the Indian National Academy of Engineering.

Rama R. was awarded a doctoral degree by Anna University in 1989. She taught in the College of Engineering, Anna University, before joining the Department of Mathematics, Indian Institute of Technology Madras (IITM), as Assistant Professor in 1996. She was subsequently elevated as Professor in 2006 and has been in that position ever since. Professor Rama has 20 years of teaching and research experience, and has guided four research students in their PhD theses. Her domain of interest is in the area of formal languages and automata, and natural computing. She is also a life member of the Indian Society for Technical Education.

Contents

Chapter 6   Variants of Finite Automata

Chapter 7   Pushdown Automata

Chapter 8   Context-Free Grammars-Properties and Parsing

Chapter 9   Turing Machines

Chapter 10   Variations of Turing Machines

Chapter 11   Universal Turing Machine and Decidability

Chapter 12   Time and Space Complexity

Chapter 13   Recent Trends and Applications

Chapter 14   New Models of Computation

Preface

Introduction to Formal Languages, Automata Theory and Computation presents the basic concepts of formal languages, automata, and computability theory to the students, with methods to solve problems in these topics.

Formal languages and automata theory emerged in the 1950's, when Noam Chomsky gave mathematical definitions of grammars for formal languages. One of his definitions coincided with the definition of the Backus Naur Form (BNF), used for the ALGOL 60 compiler. At about the same time, the concept of finite state automaton was introduced. While studying the application of compilers, the pushdown automaton was also defined and studied.

The theory of computation started with A. M. Turing's paper on computability in 1936. He defined a Turing machine as a model computing device, and his definition is considered a benchmark in the field of computation. His concept of computability has stood the test of time, while his work on undecidability is considered one of the major breakthroughs in mathematics in the first half of the twentieth century, since it has thrown much light on many problems in computability theory.

Over the decades, significant developments have taken place after the advent of Turing machines. New models of automata were defined and studied. The concept of intractable problems, concerned with the efficiency of algorithms, is another evolving area. These topics have applications in many branches of computer science, including compilers, computer networks, data bases and image processing. With the recent onset of DNA computing, more theoretical models of computation have been defined and studied.

Automata and language theory is offered as a core subject in the undergraduate program of computer science and engineering in almost all universities. It is prescribed for MCA, B Tech (IT) and M Sc (CS) courses; and is suitable for the students majoring in mathematics at the UG and PG level. Advanced topics in this subject are presented as electives in selected postgraduate programs.

Though several books are available on this topic today, the number of books that deal with both preliminary as well as advanced topics is limited. This book starts from the basics, and builds upon the subject over fourteen chapters, with the last two chapters turning to advanced topics that would be of interest to the research student.

We have banked on our teaching experience spanning several years to address the persistent difficulties faced by students in learning this subject. The book has been written assuming less by way of prerequisites from the student, and hence provides more details of arguments to elucidate the concepts as clearly as possible. A person embarking on research in this area usually finds it difficult to determine where the starting point of his groundwork should be. We have provided a simplified version of advanced topics in Chapters 6, 13 and 14 to encourage students to start their research in these areas.

Chapter 1 covers the preliminaries and gives the student an insight into the basic tenets governing the subject. Chapter 2 introduces the concept of grammars and explains the idea of context-free grammar. Chapters 3–5 deal with finite state automata. Chapter 6 probes some of the variants of finite state automata (FSA). Chapter 7 explains the pushdown automaton, while Chapter 8 discusses additional topics in context-free grammar. Chapters 9–12 are devoted to Turing machines and computability. While the former two of the aforesaid chapters talk about basic models, techniques and variations, Chapter 11 describes the idea of decidability. Chapter 12 is an introduction to complexity theory, and broaches on the concepts of time and space complexity, and NP-completeness.

Chapters 13 and 14 are intended for post-graduates and researchers. Chapter 13 gives an overview of some of the recent fields of interest such as regulated rewriting systems, contextual grammar and grammar systems. Chapter 14, the last chapter of the book, surveys the contemporary topics of DNA computing and membrane computing.

This book contains a rich and extensive pedagogy for almost all chapters. We believe that practice is the best way to acquaint oneself with the topics embodied in a typical course on automata. Hence, at the end of each chapter (except Chapters 13 and 14) we have provided problems accompanied by solutions. In addition, there are exercises for which solutions are accessible through the book's Web page at www.pearsoned. co.in/kamalakrithivasan. At the end of the book, there are two sets of multiple-choice questions sequenced according to their level of complexity. The problems in the first set are simple, while those in the second set are relatively harder. Some of these problems have appeared in GATE examinations.

We give in the following table, the importance, level of difficulty and usefulness of each chapter.

Chapter	Introductory UG	Core UG/PG	Senior UG/PG/Research
1	*		
2	2.1, 2.2	*	
3	*	*	
4		*	
5		*	
6		*	
7	*	*	
8		8.1, 8.2	8.3 – 8.9
9	*	*	
10		*	
11		*	
12		*	*
13			*
14			*

We hope that students would make good use of this book for learning the subject. We also believe that course instructors will find this book handy to expound on the subject in the class room. We have made every effort to make this book as error-free as possible, and would welcome comments and feedback on the topics discussed in the text.

Acknowledgements

We express our gratitude to the authorities of IIT Madras for enabling us to write this book under the golden jubilee scheme of the institute. We thank our research scholars and undergraduate students, especially P. Harsha, L. Jeganathan, S. N. Krishna, M. Madhu, S. V. Ramasubramanian, Rita Brata, M. Shakthibalan and Y. Sivasubramanian who have contributed to this book. We are obliged to the Heads of our respective departments, and our colleagues for their encouragement and support. We are indebted to E. Boopal, who was very helpful in the preparation of the manuscript. We acknowledge the contribution of our publishers, Pearson Education, India, in bringing out the book in its present form. Last, though not the least, we gratefully place on record the love and affection of our families. Work on this book would not have progressed successfully had it not been for their understanding support, encouragement and patience.

Kamala Krithivasan
Rama R

Preliminaries

In this chapter, we review some basic concepts required for understanding the contents of this book.

1.1 Sets, Relations, and Functions

Sets

A set is a collection of well-defined objects. Usually the elements of a set have common properties. For example, all the students who enroll for a course 'Computability' make up a set. Formally,

Definition 1.1 *A set is an unordered collection of objects.*

Note that the definition of a set is intuitive in nature and was stated by the German mathematician Cantor in 1895. The objects in a set are called the elements or members of the set.

Example 1.1 The set E of even positive integers less than 20 can be expressed by:

$$E = \{2, 4, 6, 8, 10, 12, 14, 16, 18\}$$

or

$$E = \{ x | x \text{ is even and } 0 < x < 20\}$$

A set is finite if it contains a finite number of elements and is infinite otherwise. The empty set has no elements and is denoted by ϕ. Cardinality of a set A is the number of elements in A and is denoted by $\#A$ or $|A|$. For example, if $A = \{2, 4, 6, 8\}$, then $\#A = 4$. Note that $\#\phi = 0$. If a set is infinite, one can not list all its elements. This set can be specified by providing a property that all members of the set must satisfy.

For example, $A = \{x | x \text{ is a positive integer divisible by 3}\}$. The general format of such specification is $A = \{x | P(x) \text{ is a property that } x \text{ must satisfy}\}$.

Sets can be represented by either set builder form or by explicitly listing its elements. Sets can be defined using an inductive definition also. An inductive definition of a set has three components. They are:

1. The basis or basis clause that lists some elements in the set (which are basic building blocks).

2. The induction or inductive clause which states how to produce new elements from the existing elements of the set.

3. The extremal clause which asserts that no object is a member of the set unless its being so follows from a finite number of applications of the basis and inductive clauses.

Example 1.2   Let W denote the set of well-formed parentheses. It can be defined inductively as follows:

Basis clause: $[\,] \in W$
Inductive clause: if $x, y \in W$, $xy \in W$ and $[x] \in W$
Extrenal clause: No object is a member of W unless its being so follows from a finite number of applications of the basis and the inductive clauses.

A set A is a subset of a set B if each element of A is also an element of B and is denoted by $A \subseteq B$. We also say that A is included in B. If A is a subset of B and A is not same as B, then we say that A is a proper subset B and is denoted by $A \subset B$. ϕ is a subset of every set. Two sets A and B are equal if every element of A is also an element of B and vice versa. We denote equal sets by $A = B$.

Two sets can be combined to form a third set by various set operations. They are union, intersection, and difference. The union of two sets has as elements, the elements of one of the two sets and possibly both. Union is denoted by the symbol $\cup$ so that $A \cup B = \{x | x \in A \text{ or } x \in B\}$.

The intersection of two sets is the collection of all elements of the two sets which are common and is denoted by $\cap$. For two sets A, B, $A \cap B = \{x | x \in A \text{ and } x \in B\}$.

The difference of two sets A and B denoted by $A - B$ is the set of all elements that are in the set A but not in the set B. For the sets A and B, $A - B = \{x | x \in A \text{ and } x \notin B\}$.

Let U be the universal set and $A \subseteq U$. The complement of A with respect to U is defined as $\overline{A} = U - A$.

The power set of set S is the set of all subsets of S and is denoted by $\mathbb{P}(S)$. If $S = \{a, b, c\}$ then,

$$\mathbb{P}(S) = \{\phi, \{a\}, \{b\}, \{c\}, \{a, b\}, \{b, c\}, \{a, c\}, \{a, b, c\}\}.$$

Sequences and Tuples

A sequence of objects is a list of objects in some order. For example, the sequence 7, 14, 21 would be written as $(7, 14, 21)$. In a set, the order does not matter but in a sequence it does. Also, repetition is not permitted in a set but is allowed in a sequence. For example, $(7, 7, 14, 21, 21)$ is a sequence whereas $\{7, 14, 21\}$ is a set. Like sets, sequences may be finite or infinite. Finite sequences are called tuples. A sequence of k elements is called a k-tuple. For example, $(2, 4)$ is a 2-tuple, $(7, 14, 21)$ is a 3-tuple.

If A and B are two sets, the Cartesian product or cross product of A and B written as $A \times B$ is the set of all pairs where the first component is a member of the set A and second component is a member of the set B. For example, if

$$A = \{0, 1\}, B = \{x, y, z\}, A \times B = \{(0, x), (0, y), (0, z), (1, x), (1, y), (1, z)\}$$

One can also write the Cartesian product of k-sets $A_1, A_2, \ldots, A_k$ in a similar fashion.

Relations and Functions

A binary relation on two sets A and B is a subset of $A \times B$. For example, if $A = \{1, 3, 9\}$, $B = \{x, y\}$, then $\{(1, x), (3, y), (9, x)\}$ is a binary relation on 2-sets. Binary relations on k-sets $A_1, A_2, \ldots, A_k$ can similarly be defined.

Another basic concept on sets is function. A function is an object that sets up an input-output relationship. That is, a function takes an input and produces the required output. For a function f, with input x, the output y, we write $f(x) = y$. We also say that f maps x to y. For example, addition is a function which produces the sum of the numbers that are input. The set of possible inputs to a function is called its "domain." The output of a function comes from a set called its "range." Let D be the domain and R be the range of a function f. We denote this description of a function as "$f: D \rightarrow R$". For example, f is a function with domain Z and range Z, we write it as $f: Z \rightarrow Z$. A function that uses all the elements of the range is said to be onto (surjective). A function "$f: D \rightarrow R$" is said to be one-to-one or 1–1 (injective) if for any two distinct elements $a, b \in D$, $f(a) \neq f(b)$. A function which is both one-to-one and onto is called a bijective function.

A binary relation $K \subseteq A \times B$ has an inverse, say $K^{-1} \subseteq B \times A$ defined as $(b, a) \in K^{-1}$ if and only if $(a, b) \in K$. For example,

$K = \{(x, y) | x \in S, y \in T, x$ is the student of $y\}$

$K^{-1} = \{(y, x) | x \in S, y \in T, y$ is the teacher of $x\}$

Note that the inverse of a function need not be a function. A function $f: A \rightarrow B$ may not have an inverse if there is some element $b \in B$ such that $f(a) = b$ for no $a \in A$. But every bijective 'f' possesses an inverse f^{-1} (say), and $f^{-1}(f(a)) = a$ for each $a \in A$.

A binary relation R is an equivalence relation if R satisfies the following conditions:

- R is reflexive i.e., for every x, $(x, x) \in R$.
- R is symmetric i.e., for every x and y, $(x, y) \in R$ implies $(y, x) \in R$.
- R is transitive i.e., for every x, y and z, $(x, y) \in R$ and $(y, z) \in R$ implies $(x, z) \in R$.

Equivalence relation on a set A partitions A into equivalence classes. The number of equivalence classes is called the index or rank of an equivalence relation. Index can be finite or infinite.

Example 1.3   Let N be the set of non-negative integers. The relation $\equiv$ is defined as follows: a $\equiv$ b if and only if a and b leave the same remainder when divided by 3. This can be easily seen to be an equivalence relation of index 3.

An equivalence relation induces a partition on the underlying set. In the above example, the set of non-negative integers is partitioned into three equivalence classes:

$$E_{11} = \{0, 3, 6, \ldots\},$$
$$E_{12} = \{1, 4, 7, \ldots\},$$
$$E_{13} = \{2, 5, 8, \ldots\},$$

An equivalence relation E_2 is a refinement of an equivalence relation E_1 if every equivalence class of E_2 is contained in an equivalence class of E_1. For example, let E_1 denote the mod 3 equivalence relation defined in Example 1.3. Let E_2 be an equivalence relation on the set of non-negative integers such that aE_2b if a and b leave the same remainder when divided by 6. In this case there are 6 equivalence classes.

$$E_{21} = \{0, 6, 12, \ldots\}$$
$$E_{22} = \{1, 7, 13, \ldots\}$$
$$E_{23} = \{2, 8, 14, \ldots\}$$
$$E_{24} = \{3, 9, 15, \ldots\}$$
$$E_{25} = \{4, 10, 16, \ldots\}$$
$$E_{26} = \{5, 11, 17, \ldots\}$$

It can be seen that every E_{2j} is completely included in an E_{1k}, $1 \leq j \leq 6$, $1 \leq k \leq 3$. Hence, E_2 is a refinement of E_1.

Ordered Pairs

Ordered pairs of natural numbers can be represented by a single natural number. That is we are not only interested in encoding ordered pairs into natural numbers, but also in decoding the natural numbers into ordered pairs. That is, we are interested to get a 1–1 mapping from N^2 to N. One of the simplest form of bijection from N^2 to N is as below:

Cantor-numbering scheme: Let $\pi^2 : N^2 \rightarrow N$ be such that

$$\pi^2(x, y) = \frac{(x + y)(x + y + 1)}{2} + x$$

$\pi^2(x, y)$ is called the Cantor number of the ordered pair (x, y). For example, the Cantor number of (2, 4) is 23. The following table lists some Cantor numbers for some pairs.

$x \backslash y$	0	1	2	3	4	5
0	0	1	3	6	10	15
1	2	4	7	11	16	22
2	5	8	12	17	23	30
3	9	13	18	–	–	–
4	14	19	–	–	–	–
5	20	26	–	–	–	–

This bijection is required in some computer science applications. This method can be used to enumerate ordered triples, as $\pi^3(x_1, x_2, x_3)$ can be looked as $\pi^2(\pi^2(x_1, x_2), x_3)$ and also to enumerate higher-order tuples.

Closures

Closure is an important relationship among sets and is a general tool for dealing with sets and relations of many kinds.

Let R be a binary relation on a set A. Then the reflexive (symmetric, transitive) closure of R is a relation R' such that:

1. R' is reflexive (symmetric, transitive)

2. $R' \supseteq R$

3. If R'' is a reflexive (symmetric, transitive) relation containing R, then $R'' \supseteq R'$.

The reflexive, transitive closure of R is denoted by R^*. Reflexive, transitive closure of a binary relation R is only one of the several possible closures. R^+ is a transitive closure of R which need not be reflexive, unless R itself happens to be reflexive.

Finite and Infinite Sets

A finite set contains finite number of elements. The size of the set is its basic property. The set which is not finite is said to be infinite. Two sets A and B have equal number of elements, or is said to be equinumerous if there is a one-to-one, onto function $f: A \rightarrow B$. In general, a set is finite if it is equinumerous with the set $\{1, 2, 3, \ldots, n\}$ for some natural number n. A set is said to be countably infinite if it is equinumerous with N, the set of natural numbers. A set which is not countable is said to be uncountable.

1.2   Methods of Proof

Here we introduce three basic methods of proofs:
(i) mathematical induction, (ii) pigeonhole principle, and (iii) diagonalization.

Mathematical Induction

Let A be a set of natural numbers such that:
  i. $0 \in A$

  ii. for each natural number n, if $\{0, 1, 2, ..., n\} \in A$, then $n + 1 \in A$. Then $A = N$. In particular, induction is used to prove assertions of the form "For all $n \in N$, the property P is valid." i.e.,

  1. In the basis step, one has to show that $P(0)$ is true i.e., the property is true for 0.

  2. P holds for n will be the assumption.

  3. Then one has to prove the validity of P for $n + 1$.

Example 1.4   Property $P : 1 + 2 + 3 + \cdots + n = \dfrac{n(n+1)}{2}$ for all $n \geq 0$. To see the validity of P for all $n \geq 0$, we employ mathematical induction.

  i. P is true for $n = 0$ as left-hand side and right-hand side of P will be 0.

  ii. Assume P to be true for some $n \geq 0$, with $1 + 2 + 3 + \cdots + n = \dfrac{n(n+1)}{2}$.

  iii. Consider

$$1 + 2 + 3 + \cdots n + (n+1) = (1 + 2 + 3 + \cdots + n) + (n+1)$$

$$= \frac{n(n+1)}{2} + n + 1$$

$$= \frac{(n+1)(n+2)}{2}$$

which is $P(n+1)$.

Sometimes a property $P(x)$ may hold for all $n \geq t$. In this case for basis clause one must prove $P(t)$.

Strong Mathematical Induction

Another form of proof by induction over natural numbers is called strong induction. Suppose we want to prove that $P(n)$ is true for all $n \geq t$. Then in the induction step, we assume that $P(j)$ is true for all $j, t \leq j < k$. Then using this, we prove $P(k)$. In ordinary induction (called weak induction) in the induction step, we assume $P(k-1)$ to prove $P(k)$. There are some instances, where the result can be proved easily using strong induction. In some cases, it will not be possible to use weak induction and one has to use strong induction.

Let us give some examples.

Example 1.5 $P(n)$: sum of the interior angles of an n-sided convex polygon is $(2n - 4)\pi/2$.

Basis: $P(3)$: Interior angles of a triangle sum upto $180° = (2 * 3 - 4)\pi/2$.

Induction Step: Let the result be true for all n upto k, $3 \leq n \leq k$.

To prove $P(k+1)$: Sum of the interior angles of a $(k+1)$-sided polygon is to be computed. Let the polygon be,

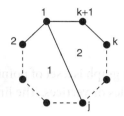

To compute the sum, join vertex numbered '1' with vertex numbered j, ($j \neq 2$ or $k+1$). Now, the interior angle sum will be the sum of interior angles of two convex polygons '1' and '2'. Polygon '1' has j sides and polygon '2' has $k + 3 - j$ sides. The sum of interior angles of polygon '1' is $(2j - 4)\pi/2$ and the sum of interior angles of polygon '2' is $(2(k+3-j)-4)\pi/2$.

Hence, sum of the interior angles of the $(k + 1)$-sided polygon is $(2(k+1)-4)\pi/2$.

Pigeonhole Principle

If A and B are two non-empty finite sets with $\#A > \#B$, then there exists no 1–1 function from A to B. i.e., if we attempt to pair the elements of A with the elements of B, sooner or later, we have to put more than one element of A in the already paired group.

Example 1.6 Among any group of 367 people, there must be at least two with the same birthday, because there are only 366 possible birthdays.

Diagonalization Principle

Let R be a binary relation on a set A and let $D = \{a | a \in A, \text{ and } (a, a) \notin R\}$. For each $a \in A$, let $R_a = \{b | b \in A, \text{ and } (a, b) \in R\}$. Then D is distinct from R_a for all $a \in A$.

Example 1.7 Let $A = \{a,b,c,d\}$ and $R = \{(a,b), (a,d), (b,b), (b,c), (c,c), (d,b)\}$. R can be represented as a square array as below:

	a	b	c	d
a		X		X
b		X	X	
c			X	
d		X		

$R_a = \{b, d\}, R_b = \{b, c\}, R_c = \{c\}, R_d = \{b\}, D = \{a, d\}$

Clearly, $D \neq R_a; R_b; R_c; R_d.$

Remark   The diagonalization principle holds for infinite sets as well.

1.3 Graphs

An undirected graph or simply a graph is a set of points with lines connecting some points. The points are called nodes or vertices. The lines are called edges.

Example 1.8   The number of edges at a particular vertex is the degree of the vertex. In Figure 1.1, degree of 1 is 3. No more than one edge is allowed between any two vertices. We label the vertices for convenience, and call the graph as labeled graph.

An induced subgraph H of a graph G is a graph with nodes of H being a subset of the nodes of G, and edges of H being the edges of G on the corresponding nodes. A path in a graph is a sequence of nodes connected by edges. A simple path is a path that does not repeat any node. A graph is connected if any two nodes have a path between them. A path is a cycle if it starts and ends in the same node. A simple cycle is one that does not repeat any node except the first and the last. A tree graph is a connected graph that has no simple cycle. The nodes of degree 1 in a tree are called the leaves of the tree.

A directed graph has directed lines between the nodes. The number of arrows pointing from a particular node is the outdegree of that node and the number of arrows to a particular node is the indegree.

Example 1.9   In the following directed graph (Figure 1.2) the indegree of node labeled 2 is 3 and its outdegree is 1.

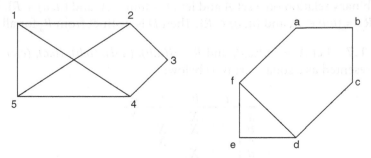

Figure 1.1.   Examples of undirected graphs

Graph 9

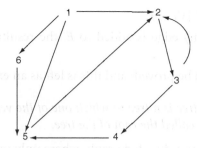

Figure 1.2. An example of a directed graph

Definition 1.2

1. *An undirected graph is connected if every pair of vertices is connected by a path. A path in a graph is a contiguous sequence of its vertices.*

2. *In any graph G, a path forms a cycle if its starting vertex and end vertex are same.*

3. *A connected, acyclic, undirected graph is a tree.*

Example 1.10 Consider the following graphs:

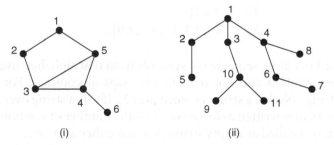

Graphs (i) and (ii) are connected.

1 2 3 4 6 is a path in Graph (i)

Graph (i) contains a cycle 1 2 3 4 5 1.

Graph (ii) is a tree.

The following are the observations about a tree.

Let $G = (V, E)$ be an undirected graph. Then the following statements are equivalent.

1. G is a tree.

2. Any two vertices in G are connected by a unique simple path.

3. G is connected, but if any edge is removed from E, the resulting graph is disconnected.

4. G is connected and $|E| = |V| - 1$.

5. G *is acyclic and* $|E| = |V| - 1$.

6. G is acyclic, but if any edge is added to E, the resulting graph contains a cycle.

All the above properties can be proved; and this is left as an exercise.

Definition 1.3 *A rooted tree is a tree in which one of the vertices is distinguished from others. Such a vertex is called the root of the tree.*

It can also be looked at as a directed graph, where only one node has indegree 0 (root). All other nodes have indegree 1. If the outdegree is 0, the node is a leaf.

1.4 Languages: Basic Concepts

Basic data structure or input to grammars or automaton are strings. Strings are defined over an alphabet which is finite. Alphabet may vary depending upon the application. Elements of an alphabet are called symbols. Usually we denote the basic alphabet set either as Σ or T. For example, the following are a few examples of an alphabet set.

$$\Sigma_1 = \{a, b\}$$
$$\Sigma_2 = \{0, 1, 2\}$$
$$\Sigma_3 = \{0, 1, 2, 3, 4, 5, 6, 7, 8, 9\}.$$

A string or word is a finite sequence of symbols from that alphabet, usually written as concatenated symbols and not separated by gaps or commas. For example, if $\Sigma = \{a, b\}$, a string *abbab* is a string or word over Σ. If w is a string over an alphabet Σ, then the length of w written as *len(w)* or $|w|$ is the number of symbols it contains. If $|w| = 0$, then w is called as empty string denoted either as λ or ε.

For any word w, $w\varepsilon = \varepsilon w = w$. For any string $w = a_1 \ldots a_n$ of length n, the reverse of w is written as w^R which is the string $a_n a_{n-1} \ldots a_1$, where each symbol a_i belongs to the basic alphabet Σ. A string z that is appearing consecutively within another string w is called a substring or subword of w. For example, *aab* is a substring of *baabb*.

The set of all strings over an alphabet Σ is denoted by Σ^* which includes the empty string ε. For example, for $\Sigma = \{0, 1\}$, $\Sigma^* = \{\varepsilon, 0, 1, 00, 01, 10, 11, \ldots\}$. Note that Σ^* is a countably infinite set. Also, Σ^n denotes the set of all strings over Σ whose length is n. Hence, $\Sigma^* = \Sigma^0 \cup \Sigma^1 \cup \Sigma^2 \cup \Sigma^3 \ldots$ and $\Sigma^+ = \Sigma^1 \cup \Sigma^2 \cup \Sigma^3 \ldots$. Subsets of Σ^* are called languages.

For example, if $\Sigma = \{a, b\}$, the following are languages over Σ

$L_1 = \{\varepsilon, a, b\}$
$L_2 = \{ab, aabb, aaabbb, \ldots\}$
$L_3 = \{w \varepsilon \Sigma^* | \text{ number of } a\text{'s and number of } b\text{'s in } w \text{ are equal.}\}$

In the above example, L_1 is finite, and L_2 and L_3 are infinite languages. ϕ denotes an empty language.

We have the following inductive definition of Σ^+ and Σ^*, where Σ is any basic alphabet set.

Definition 1.4 *Let Σ be any alphabet set. Σ^+ is a set of non-empty strings over Σ defined as follows:*

1. **Basis:** *If $a \in \Sigma$, then $a \in \Sigma^+$.*
2. **Induction:** *If $\alpha \in \Sigma^+$ and $a \in \Sigma$, αa, $a\alpha$ are in Σ^+.*
3. *No other element belongs to Σ^+.*

Clearly, the set Σ^+ contains all strings of length n, $n \geq 1$.

Example 1.11 Let $\Sigma = \{0,1,2\}$. Then

$$\Sigma^+ = \{0, 1, 2, 00, 01, 02, 10, 11, 12, 20, 21, 22, \ldots\}$$

Suppose we wish to include 'ε' in Σ^+, we modify the above definition as given below.

Definition 1.5 *Let Σ be any alphabet set. Σ^* is defined as follows:*

1. **Basis:** $\varepsilon \in \Sigma^*$.
2. **Induction:** *If $\alpha \in \Sigma^*$, $\alpha \in \Sigma$, then $a\alpha$, $\alpha a \in \Sigma^*$.*
3. *No other element is in Σ^*.*

Since languages are sets, one can define the set-theoretic operations of union, intersection, difference, and complement in the usual fashion.

The following operations are also defined for languages. If $x = a_1 \ldots a_n$, $y = b_1 \ldots b_m$, the concatenation of x and y is defined as $xy = a_1 \ldots a_n b_1 \ldots b_m$. The catenation (or concatenation) of two languages L_1 and L_2 is defined by, $L_1 L_2 = \{w_1 w_2 | w_1 \in L_1 \text{ and } w_2 \in L_2\}$.

Note that concatenation of languages is associative because concatenation of strings is associative. Also $L^0 = \{\varepsilon\}$ and $L\phi = \phi L = \phi$, $L\varepsilon = \varepsilon L = L$.

The concatenation closure (Kleene closure) of a language L, in symbols L^* is defined to be the union of all powers of L:

$$L^* = \bigcup_{i=0}^{\infty} L^i$$

Also $L^+ = \bigcup_{i=1}^{\infty} L^i$.

The right quotient and right derivative are the following sets, respectively.

$$L_1 \backslash L_2 = \{y | yz \in L_1 \text{for some } z \in L_2\}$$

$$\partial_z^r L = L \backslash \{z\} = \{y | yz \in L\}$$

Similarly, left quotient of a language L_1 by a language L_2 is defined by

$$L_2/L_1 = \{z|yz \in L_1 \text{ for some } y \in L_2\}.$$

The left derivative of a language L with respect to a word y is denoted as $\partial_y^l L$ which is equal to $\{z|yz \in L\}$.

The mirror image (or reversal) of a language is the collection of the mirror images of its words and $mir\ (L) = \{mir\ (w)|w \in L\}$ or $L^R = \{w^R|w \in L\}$.

The operations, substitutions and homomorphisms are defined as follows.

For each symbol a of an alphabet Σ, let $\sigma(a)$ be a language over Σ_a. Also, $\sigma(\varepsilon) = \varepsilon$, $\sigma(\alpha\beta) = \sigma(\alpha).\sigma(\beta)$ for $\alpha,\ \beta \in \Sigma^+$. σ is a mapping from Σ^* to 2^{v^*} or use $\mathbb{P}\ (v^*)$ where V is the union of the alphabets Σ_a, is called a substitution. For a language L over Σ, we define:

$$\sigma(L) = \{\alpha|\alpha \in \sigma(\beta) \text{ for some } \beta \in L\}.$$

A substitution is ε-free if and only if none of the language $\sigma(a)$ contains ε. A family of languages is closed under substitution if and only if whenever L is in the family and σ is a substitution such that $\sigma(a)$ is in the family, then $\sigma(L)$ is also in the family.

A substitution σ such that $\sigma(a)$ consists of a single word w_a is called a homomorphism. It is called ε-free homomorphism if none of $\sigma(a)$ is ε.

Algebraically, one can see that Σ^* is a free semigroup with ε as its identity. The homomorphism which is defined above agrees with the customary definition of homomorphism of one semigroup into another.

Inverse homomorphism can be defined as follows:

$$h^{-1}(w) = \{x|h(x) = w\}$$
$$h^{-1}(L) = \{x|h(x) \text{ is in } L\}$$

It should be noted that $h(h^{-1}(L))$ need not be equal to L. Generally $h(h^{-1}(L)) \subseteq L$ and $h^{-1}(h(L)) \supseteq L$.

Asymptotic Behavior of Functions

The time taken to execute any algorithm depends upon the machine on which it is implemented and also on the algorithm. Hence, efficiency of any algorithm is measured by the amount of time it takes and also the space it needs for execution on the machine. Comparison of algorithms has become an important topic. We give here a mathematical basis for comparing algorithms.

A complexity function f is a function of n, the size of the problem or parameter on which the problem is dependent. That is, $f(n)$ is either a measure of the time required to execute an algorithm on a problem of size n or the measure of memory space. If $f(n)$ is describing the measure of time, then $f(n)$ is called the time-complexity function; if $f(n)$ is describing the measure of space, then it is called space-complexity function.

We have the following important definitions of complexity functions.

Definition 1.6

1. Let f and g be two functions from N to R. Then g asymptotically dominates f or is an asymptotic upper bound for f or f is asymptotically dominated by g if there exist $k \geq 0$ and $c \geq 0$ such that $f(n) \leq cg(n)$ for all $n \geq k$.

2. The set of all functions which are asymptotically dominated by a given function g is denoted by $O(g)$ and read as 'big-oh' of g. That is $f \in O(g)$, then f is said to be in $O(g)$.

Example 1.12

1. Let $f(n) = n$, $g(n) = n^2$. Then clearly $f \in O(g)$ as $n \leq 1.n^2$, whereas $g \notin O(f)$.
2. $O(1) \subset O(logn) \subset O(n) \subset O(nlogn) \subset O(n^2) \subset O(c^n) \subset O(n!)$.

Definition 1.7

1. Let f and g be two functions from N to R. Then g is asymptotically tight bound for $f(n)$ if there exist positive constants c_1, c_2 and k such that $0 \leq c_1 g(n) \leq f(n) \leq c_2 g(n)$ for all $n \geq k$.

2. The set of all functions for which g is asymptotically tight bound is denoted by $\theta(g)$.

Example 1.13   If $f(n) = an^3 + bn^2 + cn + d$, where a, b, c, d are constants and $a > 0$. Then $f(n) \in \theta(n^3)$.

Definition 1.8

1. Let f and g be any two functions from N to R. Then g is said to be asymptotic lower bound for f if there exist positive constants c and k such that $0 \leq cg(n) \leq f(n)$ for all $n \geq k$.

2. The set of all functions for which g is asymptotic lower bound is denoted by $\Omega(g)$.

Example 1.14 $f(n) = an^2 + bn + c$, a, b, c, are constants, $a > 0$, belongs to $\Omega(n^2)$.

Problems and Solutions

Problem 1   *It is known that at the university 60 percent of the professors play tennis, 50 percent of them play bridge, 70 percent jog, 20 percent play tennis and bridge, 30 percent play tennis and jog, and 40 percent play bridge and jog. If someone claimed that 20 percent of the professors jog and play bridge and tennis, would you believe this claim? why?*

Solution.

Let T denote the percentage of professors who play tennis.

Let B denote the percentage of professors who play bridge.

Let J denote the percentage of professors who jog.

Given that $|T| = 60, |B| = 50, |J| = 70,$

$|T \cap B| = 20, |T \cap J| = 30, |B \cap J| = 40.$

$|T \cap B \cap J| = |T \cup B \cup J| - |T| - |B| - |J| + |T \cap B| + |T \cap J| + |B \cap J|.$

$|T \cap B \cap J| = 100 - 60 - 50 - 70 + 20 + 30 + 40 = 10.$ Given claim is wrong.

Problem 2   *Use mathematical induction to prove for all positive integers n, $n(n^2 + 5)$ is an integer multiple of 6.*

Solution.

Base: $n = 1, 1(1 + 5) = 6,$ is an integer multiple of 6.

Hypothesis: Let us assume that it is true for n.

Induction Step: We need to prove that it is true for $n + 1$. Consider $(n+1)((n+1)^2+5) = (n + 1)(n^2 + 1 + 2n + 5) = n(n^2 + 5) + (n^2 + 2n^2 + 3n + 6) = n(n^2 + 5) + 6 (\frac{n^2}{2} + \frac{n}{2} + 1) = n(n^2 + 5) + 6 (\frac{n(n+1)}{2} + 1).$ By hypothesis we know that $n(n^2 + 5)$ is divisible by 6. Clearly the last expression is divisible by 6. Therefore for all n, $n(n^2 + 5)$ is an integer multiple of 6.

Problem 3   *Suppose that we have a system of currency that has \$3 and \$5 bills. Show that any debt of \$n can be paid with only \$3 and \$5 bills for each integer $n \geq 8$. Do the same problem for \$2 and \$7 bills and $n \geq 9$.*

Solution.

Base: $n = 8$, clearly it can be paid with \$3 and \$5 bills.

Hypothesis: Assume that debt of \$n can be with \$3 and \$5 bills.

Induction Step:

Consider a debt of \$n + 1. Let $n = 3k_1 + 5k_2$

1. If $k_1 \geq 3$, then $n + 1 = (k_1 - 3) 3 + (k_2 + 2) 5.$
2. If $k_1 = 2$, then $n + 1 = 4 \times 3 + (k_2 - 1) 5.$
3. If $k_1 = 1$, then $n + 1 = 3 \times 3 + (k_2 - 1) 5.$
4. If $k_1 = 0$, then $n + 1 = 2 \times 3 + (k_2 - 1) 5.$

(Note that $k_2 \geq 1$ in cases 2, 3 and 4 as we need to prove only for $n \geq 8$.)

Hence $n + 1 = k_3. 3 + k_4. 5$ where k_3 and k_4 are integers. Hence the result.

Problem 4 *Let A be a set with n distinct elements. How many different binary relations on A are there?*

    a. *How many of them are reflexive?*
    b. *How many of them are symmetric?*
    c. *How many of them are reflexive and symmetric?*
    d. *How many of them are total ordering relation?*

Solution.
There are n^2 elements in the cross product $A \times A$. Since relation is a subset of cross product, the number of different binary relations on A are 2^{n^2}.

    a. There are 2^{n^2-n} reflexive relations.
    b. There are $2^{n(n+1)/2}$ symmetric relations.
    c. There are $2^{\frac{n(n-1)}{2}}$ relations which are both reflexive and symmetric.
    d. There are $n!$ total ordering relations.

Problem 5 *Let R be a symmetric and transitive relation on set A. Show that if for every 'a' in A there exists 'b' in A, such that (a, b) is in R, then R is an equivalence relation.*

Solution.
Given that R is a symmetric and transitive relation on A. To prove that R is an equivalence relation, we need to prove that R is reflexive. By hypothesis we know that $\forall a \exists b (a, b \in A \land (a, b) \in R)$. Since R is symmetric, it follows that if $(a, b) \in R$ then $(b, a) \in R$. Also given that R is transitive, it follows that $(a, a) \in R$. This implies that $\forall a \in A, (a, a) \in R$. This proves that R is reflexive. Therefore, R is an equivalence relation.

Exercises

1. Out of a total of 140 students, 60 are wearing hats to class, 51 are wearing scarves, and 30 are wearing both hats and scarves. Of the 54 students who are wearing sweaters, 26 are wearing hats, 21 are wearing scarves, and 12 are wearing both hats and scarves. Every one wearing neither a hat nor a scarf is wearing gloves.

    a. How many students are wearing gloves?
    b. How many students not wearing a sweater are wearing hats but not scarves?
    c. How many students not wearing a sweater are wearing neither a hat nor a scarf?

2. Among 100 students, 32 study mathematics, 20 study physics, 45 study biology, 15 study mathematics and biology, 7 study mathematics and physics, 10 study physics and biology, and 32 do not study any of the three subjects.

    a. Find the number of students studying all three subjects.
    b. Find the number of students studying exactly one of the three subjects.

3. At a family group meeting of 30 women, 17 are descended from George, 16 are descended from John, and 5 are not descended from George or John. How many of the 30 women are descended from both George and John?

4. 80 children went to a park where they can ride on three games namely A, B and C. It is known that 20 of them have taken all three rides, and 55 of them have taken at least two of the three rides. Each ride costs \$0.50, and the total receipt of the park was \$70. Determine the number of children who did not try any of the rides.

5. Use Induction to prove the following: If $a_n = 5a_{n-1} - 6a_{n-2}$ for $n \geq 2$ and $a_0 = 12$ and $a_1 = 29$ then $a_n = 5(3^n) + 7(2^n)$.

6. Use induction to prove for each integer $n \geq 5$, $2^n > n^2$.

7.

a. Show that $\frac{1}{1.2} + \frac{1}{2.3} + \frac{1}{3.4} + \ldots + \frac{1}{n(n+1)} = \frac{n}{n+1}$

b. Show that $\frac{1}{1.3} + \frac{1}{3.5} + \frac{1}{5.7} + \ldots + \frac{1}{(2n-1)(2n+1)} = \frac{n}{2n+1}$

c. Show that $\frac{1}{1.4} + \frac{1}{4.7} + \frac{1}{7.10} + \ldots + \frac{1}{(3n-2)(3n+1)} = \frac{n}{3n+1}$

8. Show that for any integer n, $(11)^{n+2} + (12)^{2n+1}$ is divisible by 133.

9. For each of the following check whether 'R' is reflexive, symmetric, anti-symmetric, transitive, an equivalence relation.

a. $R = \{(a, b)|a - b$ is an odd positive integer$\}$.

b. $R = \{(a, b)|a = b^2$ where $a, b \in I^+\}$.

c. Let P be the set of all people. Let R be a binary relation on P such that (a, b) is in R if a is a brother of b.

d. Let R be a binary relation on the set of all strings of 0's and 1's, such that $R = \{(a, b)|a$ and b are strings that have same number of 0's$\}$.

10. Let A be a set with n elements.

a. Prove that there are 2^n unary relations on A.

b. Prove that there are 2^{n^2} binary relations on A.

c. How many ternary relations are there on A?

11. Let R_1 and R_2 be arbitrary relations on A. Prove or Disprove the following assertions.

a. if R_1 and R_2 are reflexive, then $R_1 R_2$ is reflexive.

b. if R_1 and R_2 are irreflexive, then $R_1 R_2$ is irreflexive.

c. if R_1 and R_2 are symmetric, then $R_1 R_2$ is symmetric.

d. if R_1 and R_2 are antisymmetric, then $R_1 R_2$ is antisymmetric.

e. if R_1 and R_2 are transitive, then $R_1 R_2$ is transitive.

12. Find a set A with n-elements and a relation R on A such that R^1, R^2, ..., R^n are all distinct. This establishes the bound $t(R) = \cup_{i=1}^n R^i$

13. Let R_1 and R_2 be equivalence relations on a set A. Then $R_1 \cap R_2$ is an equivalence relation. Is $R_1 \cup R_2$ an equivalence relation?

14. Prove that the universal relation on any set A is an equivalence relation. What is the rank of this relation?

15. Suppose $A = \{a, b, c, d\}$ and π_1 is the following partition of A:

$$\pi_1 = \{\{a, b, c\}, \{d\}\}$$

a. List the ordered pairs of the equivalence relation induced by π_1.
b. Do the same for the partitions

$$\pi_2 = \{\{a\}, \{b\}, \{c\}, \{d\}\}$$
$$\pi_3 = \{\{a, b, c, d\}\}$$

16. Name five situations (Games, activities, real-life problems etc.,) that can be represented by means of graphs. Explain what the vertices and the edges denote.

17. Prove that in a group of n-people there are two who have the same number of acquaintances in the group.

18. Let $A = \{\varepsilon, a\}$, $B = \{ab\}$. List the elements of the following sets.

a. A^2
b. B^3
c. AB
d. A^+
e. B^*

19. Under what conditions is the length function which maps Σ^* to N a bijection?

20. Let A and B finite sets. Suppose $|A| = m$, $|B| = n$. State the relationship which must hold between 'm' and 'n' for each of the following to be true.

a. There exists an injection from A to B.
b. There exists an surjection from A to B.
c. There exists an bijection from A to B.

CHAPTER 2

Grammars

The idea of a grammar for a language has been known in India since the time of Panini (about 5th century B.C). Panini gave a grammar for the Sanskrit language. His work on Sanskrit had about 4000 rules (Sutras). From that, it is clear that the concept of recursion was known to the Indians and was used by them in very early times.

In 1959, Noam Chomsky tried to give a mathematical definition for grammar. The motivation was to give a formal definition for grammar for English sentences. He defined four types of grammar viz., type 0, type 1, type 2, and type 3. At the same time, the programming language ALGOL was being considered. It was considered as a block-structured language and a grammar was required which could describe all syntactically correct programs. The definition given was called Backus Normal Form or Backus-Naur Form (BNF). This definition was found to be the same as the definition given by Chomsky for type 2 grammar.

Consider the following two sentences in English and their parse trees (Figures 2.1 and 2.2).

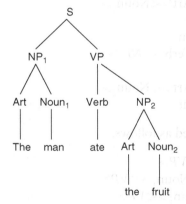

Figure 2.1.   Parse tree for an English sentence

We can see that the internal nodes of the parse trees are syntactic categories like article, noun, noun phrase, verb phrase etc. (Figures 2.1 and 2.2). The leaves of the tree are words from these two sentences.

'The man ate the fruit'
'Venice is a beautiful city.'

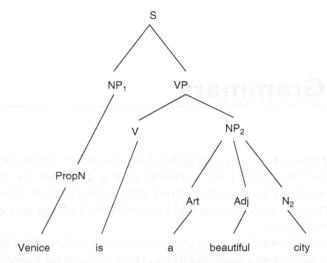

Figure 2.2. Parse tree for another English sentence

The rules of the grammar for a sentence can be written as follows:

S – sentence
NP – noun phrase
VP – verb phrase
Art – article

$$
\begin{aligned}
<S> &\rightarrow <NP_1><VP> \\
<NP_1> &\rightarrow <Art><Noun_1> \\
<Art> &\rightarrow \text{the} \\
<Noun_1> &\rightarrow \text{man} \\
<VP> &\rightarrow <Verb><NP_2> \\
<Verb> &\rightarrow \text{ate} \\
<NP_2> &\rightarrow <Art><Noun_2> \\
<Noun_2> &\rightarrow \text{fruit}
\end{aligned}
$$

The sentence can be derived as follows:

$$
\begin{aligned}
<S> &\Rightarrow <NP_1><VP> \\
&\Rightarrow <Art><Noun_1><VP> \\
&\Rightarrow \text{The } <Noun_1><VP> \\
&\Rightarrow \text{The man } <VP> \\
&\Rightarrow \text{The man } <Verb><NP_2> \\
&\Rightarrow \text{The man ate } <NP_2> \\
&\Rightarrow \text{The man ate } <Art><Noun_2> \\
&\Rightarrow \text{The man ate the } <Noun_2> \\
&\Rightarrow \text{The man ate the fruit}
\end{aligned}
$$

The rules for grammar for sentence 2 are as follows:

$<S>$ $\rightarrow$ $<NP_1><VP>$
$<NP_1>$ $\rightarrow$ $<PropN>$
$<PropN>$ $\rightarrow$ Venice
$<VP>$ $\rightarrow$ $<Verb><NP_2>$
$<Verb>$ $\rightarrow$ is
$<NP_2>$ $\rightarrow$ $<Art><adj><N_2>$
$<Art>$ $\rightarrow$ a
$<adj>$ $\rightarrow$ beautiful
$<N_2>$ $\rightarrow$ city

We find that the grammar has syntactic categories such as <verb phrase> which are rewritten further; it has words occurring at the leaves which cannot be rewritten further. We shall call them as non-terminals and terminals, respectively. The derivation always starts with the start or sentence symbol, and there are rules by which the non-terminals are rewritten.

2.1   Definitions and Classification of Grammars

We now formally define the four types of grammars:

Definition 2.1   *A phrase-structure grammar or a type 0 grammar is a 4-tuple $G = (N, T, P, S)$, where N is a finite set of non-terminal symbols called the non-terminal alphabet, T is a finite set of terminal symbols called the terminal alphabet, $S \in N$ is the start symbol and P is a set of productions (also called production rules or simply rules) of the form $u \rightarrow v$, where $u \in (N \cup T)^* N (N \cup T)^*$ and $v \in (N \cup T)^*$.*

The left-hand side of a rule is a string of the total alphabet $N \cup T$, which contains at least one non-terminal and the right-hand side is a string of the total alphabet.

Derivations are defined as follows:

If $\alpha u \beta$ is a string in $(N \cup T)^*$ and $u \rightarrow v$ is a rule in P, from $\alpha u \beta$ we get $\alpha v \beta$ by replacing u by v. This is denoted as $\alpha u \beta \Rightarrow \alpha v \beta$, where $\Rightarrow$ is read as 'directly derives.'

If $\alpha_1 \Rightarrow \alpha_2$, $\alpha_2 \Rightarrow \alpha_3, \ldots, \alpha_{n-1} \Rightarrow \alpha_n$, the derivation is denoted as $\alpha_1 \Rightarrow \alpha_2 \Rightarrow \ldots \Rightarrow \alpha_n$ or $\alpha_1 \overset{*}{\Rightarrow} \alpha_n$, where $\overset{*}{\Rightarrow}$ is the reflexive, transitive closure of $\Rightarrow$.

Definition 2.2   *The language generated by a grammar $G = (N, T, P, S)$ is the set of terminal strings derivable in the grammar from the start symbol.*

$$L(G) = \{w | w \in T^*, S \overset{*}{\Rightarrow} w\}$$

Example 2.1   Consider the grammar $G = (N, T, P, S)$ where $N = \{S, A\}$, $T = \{a, b, c\}$, production rules in P are:

1. $S \rightarrow aSc$
2. $S \rightarrow aAc$
3. $A \rightarrow b$

A typical derivation in the grammar is:

$$S \Rightarrow aSc$$
$$\Rightarrow aaScc$$
$$\Rightarrow aaaAccc$$
$$\Rightarrow aaabccc$$

The language generated is:

$$L(G) = \{a^n bc^n | n \geq 1\}$$

Rule 1 generates an equal number of a's and c's by repeated application. When we apply rule 2, one a and one c are generated. The derivation terminates by applying rule 3.

By putting restrictions on the form of production rules, we get type 1 grammar, type 2 grammar, and type 3 grammar.

Definition 2.3   *If the rules are of the form $\alpha A \beta \rightarrow \alpha \gamma \beta$, α, $\beta \in (N \cup T)^*$, $A \in N$, $\gamma \in (N \cup T)^+$, the grammar is called context-sensitive grammar (CSG).*

Definition 2.4   *If in the rule $u \rightarrow v$, $|u| \leq |v|$, the grammar is called length-increasing grammar.*

It can be shown that Definitions 2.3 and 2.4 are equivalent in the sense that the language class generated is the same in both the cases. These types of grammars are called type 1 grammars and the languages generated are called type 1 languages or context-sensitive languages (CSL).

Note: It should be noted that, by definition ε cannot be in any CSL language. To make an exception to include ε in a CSL, we can allow for a rule $S \rightarrow \varepsilon$ (S–start symbol) and make sure that S does not appear on the right-hand side of any production. we give below an example of type 1 grammar and language.

Example 2.2   Let $G = (N, T, P, S)$ where $N = \{S, B\}$, $T = \{a, b, c\}$, P has the following rules:

1. $S \rightarrow aSBc$
2. $S \rightarrow abc$
3. $cB \rightarrow Bc$
4. $bB \rightarrow bb$

The above rules satisfy the condition that the length of the right-hand side is greater or equal to the length of the left-hand side. Hence, the grammar is length-increasing or type 1.

Let us consider the language generated. The number appearing above $\Rightarrow$ denotes the rule being used.

$S \overset{2}{\Rightarrow} abc$; here $abc \in L(G)$

$S \overset{1}{\Rightarrow} aSBc$

$\overset{2}{\Rightarrow} aabcBc$

$\overset{3}{\Rightarrow} aabBcc$

$\overset{4}{\Rightarrow} aabbcc,\ a^2b^2c^2 \in L(G)$

Similarly,

$S \overset{1}{\Rightarrow} aSBc$

$\overset{1}{\Rightarrow} aaSBcBc$

$\overset{2}{\Rightarrow} aaabcBcBc$

$\overset{3}{\Rightarrow} aaabBccBc$

$\overset{3}{\Rightarrow} aaabBcBcc$

$\overset{3}{\Rightarrow} aaabBBccc$

$\overset{4}{\Rightarrow} aaabbBccc$

$\overset{4}{\Rightarrow} aaabbbccc,\ a^3b^3c^3 \in L(G)$

In general, any string of the form $a^nb^nc^n$ will be generated.

$S \overset{*}{\Rightarrow} a^{n-1} S(Bc)^{n-1}$ (by applying rule 1 (n − 1) times)

$\Rightarrow a^nbc(Bc)^{n-1}$ (rule 2 once)

$\overset{*}{\Rightarrow} a^nbB^{n-1}c^n$ (by applying rule 3 $\dfrac{n(n-1)}{2}$ times)

$\overset{*}{\Rightarrow} a^nb^nc^n$ (by applying rule 4, (n − 1) times)

Hence, $L(G) = \{a^nb^nc^n | n \geq 1\}$. This is a type 1 language.

Definition 2.5   *If in a grammar, the production rules are of the form, $A \to \alpha$, where $A \in N$ and $\alpha \in (N \cup T)^*$, the grammar is called a type 2 grammar or context-free grammar (CFG). The language generated is called a type 2 language or context-free language (CFL). Example 2.1 gives a CFG and language.*

Definition 2.6   *If the rules are of the form $A \to \alpha B$, $A \to \beta$, $A, B \in N$, $\alpha, \beta \in T^*$, the grammar is called a right-linear grammar or type 3 grammar and the language generated is called a type 3 language or regular set. We can even put the restriction that the rules can be of the form $A \to aB$, $A \to b$, where $A, B \in N$, $a \varepsilon T$, $b \varepsilon T \cup \varepsilon$. This is possible because a rule $A \to a_1 \ldots a_k B$ can be split into $A \to a_1B_1$, $B_1 \to a_2B_2, \ldots, B_{k-1} \to a_kB$ by introducing new non-terminals $B_1, \ldots, B_{k-1}$.*

Example 2.3 Let $G = (N, T, P, S)$, where $N = \{S\}$, $T = \{a, b\}$ P consists of the following rules.

1. $S \rightarrow aS$
2. $S \rightarrow bS$
3. $S \rightarrow \varepsilon$

This grammar generates all strings in T^*.
For example, the string abbaab is generated as follows:

$S \Rightarrow aS$ (rule 1)

$\Rightarrow abS$ (rule 2)

$\Rightarrow abbS$ (rule 2)

$\Rightarrow abbaS$ (rule 1)

$\Rightarrow abbaaS$ (rule 1)

$\Rightarrow abbaabS$ (rule 2)

$\Rightarrow abbaab$ (rule 3)

Derivation Trees

We have considered the definition of a grammar and derivation. Each derivation can be represented by a tree called a derivation tree (sometimes called a parse tree).

A derivation tree for the derivation considered in Example 2.1 will be of the form as given in Figure 2.3.

A derivation tree for the derivation of *aaaaaa* considered in Example 2.3 will have the form as given in Figure 2.4.

Derivation trees are considered for type 2 and type 3 grammars only. In the first section also, we have considered some English sentences and their parse trees.

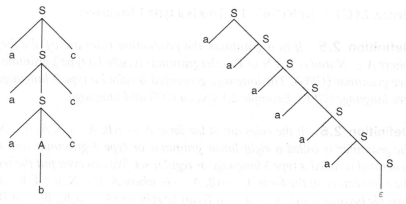

Figure 2.3. Derivation tree for a^3bc^3 **Figure 2.4.** Derivation tree for a^6

Example 2.4   Consider the following *CFG*, $G = (N, T, P, S)$, $N = \{S, A, B\}$,

$T = \{a, b\}$. *P* consists of the following productions:

1. $S \rightarrow aB$
2. $B \rightarrow b$
3. $B \rightarrow bS$
4. $B \rightarrow aBB$
5. $S \rightarrow bA$
6. $A \rightarrow a$
7. $A \rightarrow aS$
8. $A \rightarrow bAA$

The derivation tree for *aaabbb* is as follows (Figure 2.5):

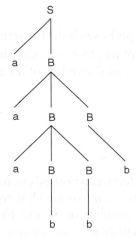

Figure 2.5.   Derivation tree for a^3b^3

The derivation tree has the structure of a rooted directed tree. Each node has a label. The labels of internal nodes are non-terminals and the labels of leaves are terminal symbols. The labels of the leaves of the tree read from the left to right gives the string generated, which is called the result or yield of the tree.

If $A \rightarrow B_1 \ldots B_m$ is a rule, when this is applied, the node with label A has sons with labels $B_1, \ldots, B_m$ in that order. A is the father of $B_1, \ldots, B_m$ and $B_1, \ldots, B_m$ are the sons of A. The words ancestor and descendant are used in a similar manner as for directed rooted trees. The root has the label which is the start symbol. A non-terminal node with label A with all its descendants is called the subtree rooted at A. Let us consider an example.

The language generated by the grammar in Example 2.4 consists of strings having equal number of *a*'s and *b*'s.

Proof   It can be proved by induction.

Induction hypothesis:

1. $S \overset{*}{\Rightarrow} w$ if and only if w has equal number of a's and b's.
2. $A \overset{*}{\Rightarrow} w$ if and only if w has one more a than, it has b's.
3. $B \overset{*}{\Rightarrow} w$ if and only if w has one more b than, it has a's.

Basis

The minimum length of the string derivable from S is $2(ab$ or $ba)$, $S \Rightarrow aB \Rightarrow ab$ and $S \Rightarrow bA \Rightarrow ba$. It has one a and one b.

The minimum of length of the string derivable from A is one and it is a $(A \Rightarrow a)$. It has one a and no b's. Similarly, the minimum length of the string derivable from B is one and it is $b(B \Rightarrow b)$. The next longer string derivable from A or B is of length 3. So, the result holds for $n = 1$ and 2, n denoting the length of the string.

Induction

Assume that the induction hypotheses hold for strings of length up to k, show that the result holds for string of length $k + 1$. Consider $S \overset{*}{\Rightarrow} w$ and $|w| = k + 1$. It should be shown that w has equal number of a's and b's. The first step of the derivation of w is:

$S \Rightarrow aB$ or $S \Rightarrow bA$

and the derivation is:

$S \Rightarrow aB \overset{*}{\Rightarrow} aw_1$ or $S \Rightarrow bA \overset{*}{\Rightarrow} bw_2$

where $|w_1| = |w_2| = k$ and by inductive hypothesis w_1 has one more b than a's and w_2 has one more a than b's and so $w = aw_1$ (or bw_2) has equal number of a's and b's.

Conversely, if w has equal number of a's and b's, we should prove that it is derivable from S. In this case, either $w = aw_1$ or $w = bw_2$ where w_1 has one more b than it has a's and w_2 has one more a than it has b's. By inductive hypothesis, $B \overset{*}{\Rightarrow} w_1$ and $A \overset{*}{\Rightarrow} w_2$. Using the first or the fifth rule, we get a derivation:

$S \Rightarrow aB \overset{*}{\Rightarrow} aw_1 = w$

$(or)\ S \Rightarrow bA \overset{*}{\Rightarrow} bw_2 = w.$

Similarly, consider $A \overset{*}{\Rightarrow} w$ and $|w| = k + 1$. It should be proved that w has one more a than it has b's. If $A \overset{*}{\Rightarrow} w$, the derivation either begins with $A \Rightarrow aS$ or $A \Rightarrow bAA$ if $|w| \geq 2$. In the former case, we have a derivation $A \Rightarrow aS \overset{*}{\Rightarrow} aw_1$, where w_1 has equal number of a's and b's by inductive hypothesis. Hence, $w = aw_1$ has one more a than it has b's. In the latter case,

$A \Rightarrow bAA \overset{*}{\Rightarrow} bw_3 A \overset{*}{\Rightarrow} bw_3 w_4.$

w_3 and w_4 are derivable from A and have length less than k. So, they have one more a than b's. Therefore, $w = bw_3 w_4$ has one more a than b's.

Conversely, if w has one more a than it has b's, then w is derivable from A. w either begins with a or b. If w begins with a, then $w = aw_1$, where w_1 has equal number of a's and b's. By inductive hypothesis $S \stackrel{*}{\Rightarrow} w_1$. Using the rule $A \to aS$, we have $A \Rightarrow aS \stackrel{*}{\Rightarrow} aw_1 = w$. On the other hand, if w begins with a b, w can be written in the form bw_3w_4, where w_3 and w_4 have one more a than b's. (This way of writing (decomposition) need not be unique). Hence, using $A \to bAA$, we have $A \Rightarrow bAA \stackrel{*}{\Rightarrow} bw_3A \stackrel{*}{\Rightarrow} bw_3w_4 = w$. Hence, w is derivable from A. A similar argument can be given for $B \stackrel{*}{\Rightarrow} w$, if and only if w has one more b than it has a's.

Consider the derivation of the string $aaabbb$.

$$S \stackrel{1}{\Rightarrow} aB$$
$$\stackrel{4}{\Rightarrow} aaBB$$
$$\stackrel{4}{\Rightarrow} aaaBBB$$
$$\stackrel{2}{\Rightarrow} aaabBB$$
$$\stackrel{2}{\Rightarrow} aaabbB$$
$$\stackrel{2}{\Rightarrow} aaabbb$$

The derivation tree is given in Figure 2.5.

In the above derivation, the leftmost non-terminal in the sentential form is always replaced. Such a derivation is called a leftmost derivation. If the rightmost non-terminal in a sentential form is always replaced, such a derivation is called a rightmost derivation. There can be derivations which are neither leftmost nor rightmost

$$S \stackrel{1}{\Rightarrow} aB$$
$$\stackrel{4}{\Rightarrow} aaBB$$
$$\stackrel{2}{\Rightarrow} aaBb$$
$$\stackrel{4}{\Rightarrow} aaaBBb$$
$$\stackrel{2}{\Rightarrow} aaabBb$$
$$\stackrel{2}{\Rightarrow} aaabbb$$

is a derivation which is neither leftmost nor rightmost.

$$S \stackrel{1}{\Rightarrow} aB$$
$$\stackrel{4}{\Rightarrow} aaBB$$
$$\stackrel{2}{\Rightarrow} aaBb$$
$$\stackrel{4}{\Rightarrow} aaaBBb$$
$$\stackrel{2}{\Rightarrow} aaaBbb$$
$$\stackrel{2}{\Rightarrow} aaabbb$$

represents a rightmost derivation. All these derivations are represented by the same tree given in Figure 2.5. Hence, we find that when a string is generated in a grammar, there can be many derivations (leftmost, rightmost, and arbitrary) which can be represented by the same derivation tree. Thus, correspondence between derivation trees and derivations is not one-one (bijection). But, we can easily see that the correspondence between leftmost derivations and derivation trees is a bijection.

The sequence of rules applied in the leftmost derivation in the above example is 144222 which gives a 'left parse' for the string *aaabbb*. In general, the sequence of rules applied in a leftmost derivation is called 'left parse' for the string generated. The reversal of the sequence of rules applied in a rightmost derivation is called a 'right parse'. In the above example, the sequence of rules applied in a rightmost derivation is 142422. The right parse is 224241. $\qquad\Box$

Example 2.5 Consider the grammar $G = (\{S\}, \{a,b\}, \{S \to SaSbS, S \to SbSaS, S \to \varepsilon\}, S)$. The language generated by this grammar is the same as the language generated by the grammar in Example 2.3, except that ε, the empty string is also generated here.

Proof It is not difficult to see that any string generated by this grammar will have equal number of a's and b's. If we apply rule 1 or 2, one a and one b will be generated. When we use rule 3, no symbol is generated. Hence, any string generated in the grammar will have equal number of a's and b's. The proof of the converse is slightly involved.

Consider a string w having equal number of a's and b's. We use induction.

Basis

$|w| = 0, S \Rightarrow \varepsilon$

$|w| = 2$, it is either ab or ba, then

$S \Rightarrow SaSbS \overset{*}{\Rightarrow} ab$

$S \Rightarrow SbSaS \overset{*}{\Rightarrow} ba$

Induction

Assume that the result holds up to strings of length $k - 1$. Prove that the result holds for strings of length k. Draw a graph, where the x axis represents the length of the prefixes of the given string. y axis represents the number of a's - number of b's. For the string *aabbabba*, the graph will appear as given in Figure 2.6.

For a given string w with equal number of a's and b's, there are three possibilities:

1. The string begins with 'a' and ends with 'b'.

2. The string begins with 'b' and ends with 'a'.

3. Other two cases (begins with a and ends with a, begins with b and ends with b)

In the first case, $w = aw_1 b$ and w_1 has equal numbers of a's and b's. So, we have $S \Rightarrow SaSbS \Rightarrow aSbS \Rightarrow aSb \overset{*}{\Rightarrow} aw_1 b$ as $S \overset{*}{\Rightarrow} w_1$ by inductive hypotheses. A similar

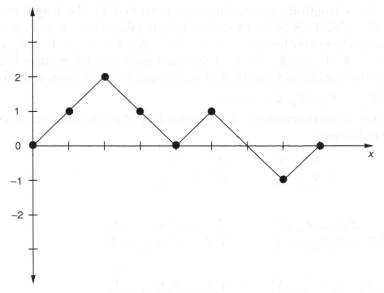

Figure 2.6.   The graph for the string *aabbabba* referred to in Example 2.5

argument holds for case 2. In case 3, the graph mentioned above will cross the *x* axis.

Consider $w = w_1 w_2$ where w_1, w_2 have equal number of *a*'s and *b*'s. Let us say w_1 begins with *a*, and w_1 corresponds to the portion where the graph touches the *x* axis for the first time. In the above example, $w_1 = aabb$ and $w_2 = abba$.

In this case, we can have a derivation as follows:

$$S \xRightarrow{1} SaSbS$$
$$\xRightarrow{3} aSbS$$
$$\xRightarrow{*} aw_1' bS \ (w_1 = aw_1' b)$$
$$\xRightarrow{*} aw_1' bw_2$$
$$\xRightarrow{*} w_1 w_2.$$

$S \xRightarrow{*} w$ follows from inductive hypothesis.   □

The difference between Example 2.5 and Example 2.4 is that in the former example, ε is not generated, whereas it is generated in Example 2.5.

We recall the definition of CSG and length-increasing grammar from Definition 2.3 and Definition 2.4, respectively.

Theorem 2.1   *Every CSL is length increasing and conversely.*

Proof   That every CSL is length-increasing can be seen from definitions.

That every length-increasing language is context-sensitive can be seen from the following construction.

Let L be a length-increasing language generated by the length-increasing grammar $G = (N, T, P, S)$. Without loss of generality, one can assume that the productions in P are of the form $X \to a$, $X \to X_1 \ldots X_m$, $X_1 \ldots X_m \to Y_1 \ldots Y_n$, $2 \le m \le n$, X, $X_1, \ldots, X_m$, $Y_1, \ldots, Y_n \in N$, $a \in T$. Productions in P which are already context-sensitive productions are not modified. Hence, consider a production of the form:

$$X_1 \ldots X_m \to Y_1 \ldots Y_n, \; 2 \le m \le n$$

(which is not context-sensitive). It is replaced by the following set of context-sensitive productions:

$$
\begin{aligned}
X_1 \ldots X_m &\to Z_1 X_2 \ldots X_m \\
Z_1 X_2 \ldots X_m &\to Z_1 Z_2 X_3 \ldots X_m
\end{aligned}
$$

$$\vdots$$

$$
\begin{aligned}
Z_1 Z_2 \ldots Z_{m-1} X_m &\to Z_1 Z_2 \ldots Z_m Y_{m+1} \ldots Y_n \\
Z_1 Z_2 \ldots Z_m Y_{m+1} \ldots Y_n &\to Y_1 Z_2 \ldots Z_m Y_{m+1} \ldots Y_n
\end{aligned}
$$

$$\vdots$$

$$
Y_1 Y_2 \ldots Y_{m-1} Z_m Y_{m+1} \ldots Y_n \to Y_1 Y_2 \ldots Y_m Y_{m+1} \ldots Y_n
$$

where Z_k, $1 \le k \le m$ are new non-terminals.

Each production that is not context-sensitive is to be replaced by a set of context-sensitive productions as mentioned above. Application of this set of rules has the same effect as applying $X_1 \ldots X_m \to Y_1 \ldots Y_n$. Hence, a new grammar G' thus obtained is context-sensitive that is equivalent to G. $\quad\square$

Example 2.6 Let $L = \{a^n b^m c^n d^m \mid n, m \ge 1\}$.

The type 1 grammar generating this CSL is given by $G = (N, T, P, S)$ with $N = \{S, A, B, X, Y\}$, $T = \{a, b, c, d\}$ and P.

$$
\begin{aligned}
S &\to a A B \mid a B \\
A &\to a A X \mid a X \\
B &\to b B d \mid b Y d \\
Xb &\to bX \\
XY &\to Yc \\
Y &\to c.
\end{aligned}
$$

Sample Derivations

$S \Rightarrow aB \;\; \Rightarrow abYd \Rightarrow abcd.$

$S \Rightarrow aB \;\; \Rightarrow abBd \Rightarrow abbYdd \Rightarrow ab^2cd^2.$

$S \Rightarrow aAB \Rightarrow aaXB \Rightarrow aaXbYd$
$ \Rightarrow aabXYd$
$ \Rightarrow aabYcd$
$ \Rightarrow a^2bc^2d.$

$S \Rightarrow aAB \Rightarrow aaAXB$
$ \Rightarrow aaaXXB$

$$\Rightarrow aaaXXbYd$$
$$\Rightarrow aaaXbXYd$$
$$\Rightarrow aaabXXYd$$
$$\Rightarrow aaabXYcd$$
$$\Rightarrow aaabYccd$$
$$\Rightarrow aaabcccd.$$

Example 2.7 Let $L = \{ww \mid w \in \{0, 1\}^+\}$. The above CSL is generated by the type 1 grammar $G = (N, T, P, S)$, where $N = \{S, X_0, X_1, L_0, L_1, R_0, R_1\}$, $T = \{0, 1\}$ and P consists of the following rules:

1. $S \rightarrow 0SX_0$, $S \rightarrow 1SX_1$.

2. $S \rightarrow L_0R_0$, $S \rightarrow L_1R_1$.

3. $R_0X_0 \rightarrow X_0R_0$.
   $R_0X_1 \rightarrow X_1R_0$.
   $R_1X_0 \rightarrow X_0R_1$.
   $R_1X_1 \rightarrow X_1R_1$.

4. $R_0 \rightarrow 0, R_1 \rightarrow 1$.

5. $L_0X_0 \rightarrow L_0R_0$.
   $L_0X_1 \rightarrow L_0R_1$.
   $L_1X_0 \rightarrow L_1R_0$.
   $L_1X_1 \rightarrow L_1R_1$.

6. $L_0 - 0, L_1 \rightarrow 1$.

Sample derivations

1. $S \Rightarrow 0SX_0 \Rightarrow 01SX_1X_0$
   $\Rightarrow 01L_0R_0X_1X_0$
   $\Rightarrow 01L_0X_1R_0X_0$
   $\Rightarrow 01L_0X_1X_0R_0$
   $\Rightarrow 01L_0R_1X_0R_0$
   $\Rightarrow 01L_0X_0R_1R_0$
   $\Rightarrow 01L_0R_0R_1R_0$
   $\overset{*}{\Rightarrow} 010010.$

2. $S \Rightarrow 0SX_0 \Rightarrow 00SX_0X_0$
   $\Rightarrow 001SX_1X_0X_0$
   $\Rightarrow 001L_0R_0X_1X_0X_0$
   $\Rightarrow 001L_0X_1R_0X_0X_0$

$$\Rightarrow 001L_0X_1X_0R_0X_0$$
$$\Rightarrow 001L_0X_1X_0X_0R_0$$
$$\Rightarrow 001L_0R_1X_0X_0R_0$$
$$\Rightarrow 001L_0X_0R_1X_0R_0$$
$$\Rightarrow 001L_0R_0R_1X_0R_0$$
$$\Rightarrow 001L_0R_0X_0R_1R_0$$
$$\Rightarrow 001L_0X_0R_0R_1R_0$$
$$\Rightarrow 001L_0R_0R_0R_1R_0$$
$$\overset{*}{\Rightarrow} 00100010.$$

Example 2.8   Consider the length-increasing grammar given in Example 2.2. All rules except rule 3 are context-sensitive. The rule $cB \rightarrow Bc$ is not context-sensitive. The following grammar is a CSG equivalent to the above grammar.

$$S \rightarrow aSBC$$
$$S \rightarrow abc$$
$$C \rightarrow c$$
$$CB \rightarrow DB$$
$$DB \rightarrow DC$$
$$DC \rightarrow BC$$
$$bB \rightarrow bb.$$

2.2 Ambiguity

Ambiguity in CFL is an important concept. It has applications to compilers. Generally, when a grammar is written for an expression or a programming language, we expect it to be unambiguous and during compiling, a unique code is generated. Consider the following English statement: "They are flying planes." It can be parsed in two different ways.

In Figure 2.7, 'They' refers to the planes, and in Figure 2.8 'They' refers to the persons on the plane. The ambiguity arises because we are able to have two different parse trees for the same sentence.

Now, we define ambiguity formally.

Definition 2.7   *Let $G = (N, T, P, S)$ be a CFG. A word w in $L(G)$ is said to be ambiguously derivable in G, if it has two or more different derivation trees in G.*

Since the correspondence between derivation trees and leftmost derivations is a bijection, an equivalent definition in terms of leftmost derivations can be given.

Definition 2.8   *Let $G = (N, T, P, S)$ be a CFG. A word w in $L(G)$ is said to be ambiguously derivable in G, if it has two or more different leftmost derivations in G.*

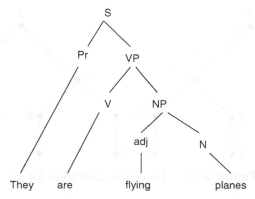

Figure 2.7. Parse tree 1

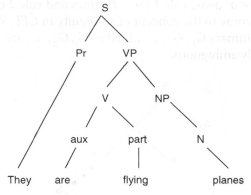

Figure 2.8. Parse tree 2

Definition 2.9 *A CFG is said to be ambiguous if there is a word w in L(G) which is ambiguously derivable. Otherwise, it is unambiguous.*

Example 2.9 Consider the *CFG G* with rules: 1.*S* → *aSb* and 2. *S* → *ab* where *S* is the non-terminal and *a, b* are terminal symbols. $L(G) = \{a^n b^n | n \geq 1\}$. Each $a^n b^n$ has a unique derivation tree as given in Figure 2.12.

There is a unique leftmost derivation where rule 1 is used $(n - 1)$ times and rule 2 is used once in the end. Hence, this grammar is unambiguous.

Example 2.10 Consider the grammar *G* with rules: 1.*S* → *SS* and 2.*S* → *a* where *S* is the non-terminal and a is the terminal symbol. $L(G) = \{a^n | n \geq 1\}$. This grammar is ambiguous as a^3 has two different derivation trees as follows: (Figure 2.9).

It should be noted that eventhough the grammar in Example 2.10 is ambiguous, language $\{a^n | n \geq 1\}$ can be generated unambiguously.

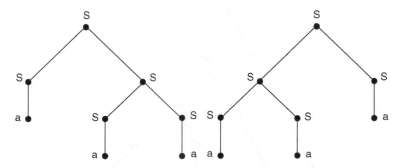

Figure 2.9. Two derivation trees for a^3

Example 2.11 $\{a^n | n \geq 1\}$ can be generated by: $1. S \to aS$ and $2. S \to a$. Each string has a unique derivation tree as shown in Figure 2.10. There is a unique leftmost derivation for a^n using rule 1 ($n - 1$) times and rule 2 once in the end.

So, now we have come to the concept of ambiguity in CFL. We see that a CFL L may have several grammars $G_1, G_2, \ldots$. If all of $G_1, G_2, \ldots$ are ambiguous, then L is said to be inherently ambiguous.

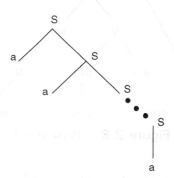

Figure 2.10. Unique derivation tree for a^n

Definition 2.10 *A CFL L is said to be inherently ambiguous if all the grammars generating it are ambiguous or in other words, there is no unambiguous grammar generating it.*

Example 2.12 $L = \{a^n b^m c^p | n, m, p \geq 1, n = m \text{ or } m = p\}$.
This can be looked at as $L = L_1 \cup L_2$

$L_1 = \{a^n b^n c^p | n, p \geq 1\}$
$L_2 = \{a^n b^m c^m | n, m \geq 1\}$.

L_1 and L_2 can be generated individually by unambiguous grammars, but any grammar generating $L_1 \cup L_2$ will be ambiguous. Since, strings of the form $a^n b^n c^n$ will have two different derivation trees, one corresponding to L_1 and another corresponding to L_2. Hence, L is inherently ambiguous.

It should be noted that the above argument is informal. A rigorous proof should be given to prove the result. This will be a slightly lengthy process.

Examples of some other inherently ambiguous CFL are:

1. $L = \{a^n b^n c^m d^m | n, m \geq 1\} \cup \{a^n b^m c^m d^n | n, m \geq 1\}$.
2. $L = \{a^n b^m c^n d^p | n, m, p \geq 1\} \cup \{a^n b^m c^q d^m | n, m, q \geq 1\}$.
3. $L = \{a^i b^j c^k | i, j \geq 1, \ k \leq i\} \cup \{a^i b^j c^k | i, j \geq 1, \ k \leq j\}$.
4. $L = \{a^i b^i c^j d^j e^k | i, j, k \geq 1\} \cup \{a^i b^i c^j d^k e^k | i, j, k \geq 1\}$.

Now the question arises: how do we find out whether a grammar is ambiguous or not, or a language is inherently ambiguous or not. Though for particular cases, it may be easy to find out, the general problem is undecidable. We shall see the proofs of these theorems in later chapters.

Theorem 2.2 *It is undecidable to determine whether a given CFG G is ambiguous or not.*

This means we cannot have an algorithm for this problem.

Theorem 2.3 *It is undecidable in general to determine whether a CFL L is inherently ambiguous or not.*

But for particular subclass it is decidable.

Definition 2.11 *A CFL L is bounded, if there exists strings $w_1, \ldots, w_k$ such that $L \subseteq w_1^* w_2^* \ldots w_k^*$.*

Theorem 2.4 *There exists an algorithm to find out whether a given bounded CFL is inherently ambiguous or not.*

Next we consider the concept of degree of ambiguity.

Consider the grammar G having rules: $1. S \to SS$ and $2. S \to a$. We have earlier seen that a^3 has two different derivation trees. a^4 has 5 and a^5 has 14. As the length of the string increases, the number of derivation trees also increases. In this case, we say that the degree of ambiguity is not bounded or infinite. On the other hand, consider the following grammar $G = (N, T, P, S)$ generating $\{a^n b^m c^p | n, m, p \geq 1, n = m \text{ or } m = p\}$, where $N = \{S, A, B, C, D\}$, $T = \{a, b, c\}$, P has rules

$$
\begin{aligned}
S &\to AB \\
S &\to CD \\
A &\to aAb \\
A &\to ab \\
B &\to cB \\
B &\to c \\
C &\to aC \\
C &\to a
\end{aligned}
$$

$$D \rightarrow bDc$$
$$D \rightarrow bc.$$

Any string of the form $a^n b^n c^p$ has a derivation starting with $S \rightarrow AB$. Any string of the form $a^n b^m c^m$ has a derivation starting with $S \rightarrow CD$. A string of the form $a^n b^n c^n$ will have two different leftmost derivations, one starting with $S \rightarrow AB$ and another with $S \rightarrow CD$. So, any string will have one derivation tree or at most two different derivation trees. No string has more than two different derivation trees. Here, we say that the degree of ambiguity is 2.

Definition 2.12 *Let $G = (N, T, P, S)$ be a CFG then the degree of ambiguity of G is the maximum number of derivation trees a string $w \in L(G)$ can have in G.*

We can also use the idea of power series and find out the number of different derivation trees a string can have. Consider the grammar with rules $S \rightarrow SS$, $S \rightarrow a$, write an equation $S = SS + a$. Initial solution is $S = a$, $S_1 = a$.

Using this in the equation for S on the right-hand side

$$S_2 = S_1 S_1 + a$$
$$= aa + a.$$
$$S_3 = S_2 S_2 + a$$
$$= (aa + a)(aa + a) + a$$
$$= a^4 + 2a^3 + a^2 + a.$$
$$S_4 = S_3 S_3 + a$$
$$= (a^4 + 2a^3 + a^2 + a)^2 + a$$
$$= a^8 + 4a^7 + 6a^6 + 6a^5 + 5a^4 + 2a^3 + a^2 + a.$$

We can proceed like this using $S_i = S_{i-1} S_{i-1} + a$. In S_i, upto strings of length i, the coefficient of the string will give the number of different derivation trees it can have in G. For example, in S_4 coefficient of a^4 is 5 and a^4 has 5 different derivation trees in G. The coefficient of a^3 is 2–the number of different derivation trees for a^3 is 2 in G.

In arithmetic expression, it is better to avoid ambiguity.

$E \rightarrow E + E, E \rightarrow E * E$
$E \rightarrow id$

will generate $id + id * id$ which will have two different derivation trees (Figure 2.11).

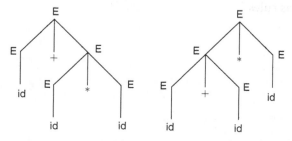

Figure 2.11. Two parse trees for $id + id * id$

We would like to have the first one rather than the second (as * has higher precedence than $+$). Evaluation according to the second one will give a wrong answer. Hence in many cases, it is advantageous to have unambiguous grammars.

2.3   Simplification of CFGs

Context-free grammars can be put in simple forms. The simplification is done on productions and symbols of the grammar. Such simplified grammars should be equivalent to the original grammars started with. Such simplifications on CFGs are important as CFGs have wide applications in compilers.

A given CFG may have rules and symbols which do not contribute ultimately to its language. Hence, one can modify the grammar by removing such rules and symbols. Another issue is the presence of ε-rules in the productions. One may want to have a ε-free set of context-free rules in the grammar whenever the underlying CFL does not contain the empty string. We also give a simplified CFG that has no unit rules, which are of the form $A \rightarrow B$ where A and B are non-terminal symbols.

Removing Useless Productions

We now introduce the definition of useful and useless symbols in any CFG. We give an algorithm to obtain an equivalent CFG that has only useful symbols.

Definition 2.13   *Let $G = (N, T, P, S)$ be a CFG. A variable X in N is said to be useful, if and only if there is at least a string $\alpha \in L(G)$ such that:*

$$S \overset{*}{\Rightarrow} \alpha_1 X \alpha_2 \overset{*}{\Rightarrow} \alpha,$$

where $\alpha_1,\ \alpha_2 \in (N \cup T)^*$ i.e., X is useful because it appears in at least one derivation from S to a word α in $L(G)$. Otherwise X is useless. Consequently, the production involving X is useful.

One can understand the 'useful symbol' concept in two steps.

Step 1 For a symbol $X \in N$ to be useful, it should occur in some derivation starting from S, i.e., $S \overset{*}{\Rightarrow} \alpha_1 X \alpha_2$.

Step 2 Also X has to derive a string $\alpha \in T^*$ i.e., $X \overset{*}{\Rightarrow} \alpha$.

These two conditions are necessary. But they are not sufficient. These two conditions maybe satisfied still α_1 or α_2 may contain a non-terminal from which a terminal string cannot be derived. So, the usefulness of a symbol has to be tested in two steps as above.

Lemma 2.1   *Let $G = (N, T, P, S)$ be a CFG such that $L(G) \neq \phi$. Then there exists an equivalent CFG $G' = (N', T', P', S)$ that does not contain any useless symbol or productions.*

Proof   The CFG G' is obtained by the following elimination procedures:

I. First eliminate all those symbols X, such that X does not derive any string over T^*. Let $G_2 = (N_2, T, P_2, S)$ be the grammar thus modified. As $L(G) \neq \phi$, S will not be eliminated. The following algorithm identifies symbols that need not be eliminated.

Algorithm GENERATING

Step 1 Let $GEN = T$;

Step 2 If $A \rightarrow \alpha$ and every symbol of α belongs to GEN, then add A to GEN.

Remove from N all those symbols that are not in the set GEN and all the rules using them.

Let the resultant grammar be $G_2 = (N_2, T, P_2, S)$.

II. Now eliminate all symbols in the grammar G_2 that are not occurring in any derivation from 'S.' i.e., $S \overset{*}{\Rightarrow} \alpha_1 X \alpha_2$.

Algorithm REACHABLE

Let $REACH = \{S\}$.

If $A \in REACH$ and $A \rightarrow \alpha \in P$ then add every symbol of α to $REACH$.

The above algorithm terminates as any grammar has only finite set of rules. It collects all those symbols which are reachable from S through derivations from S.

Now in G_2 remove all those symbols that are not in $REACH$ and also productions involving them. Hence, one gets the modified grammar $G' = (N', T', P', S)$, a new CFG without useless symbols and productions using them.

The equivalence of G with G' can easily be seen since only symbols and productions leading to derivation of terminal strings from S are present in G'. Hence, $L(G) = L(G')$.   □

Theorem 2.5   *Given a CFG $G = (N, T, P, S)$. Procedure I of Lemma 2.1 is executed to get $G_2 = (N_2, T, P_2, S)$ and procedure II of Lemma 2.1 is executed to get $G' = (N', T', P', S)$. Then G' contains no useless symbols.*

Proof   Suppose G' contains a symbol X (say) which is useless. It is easily seen that $N' \subseteq N_2$, $T' \subseteq T'$, $P' \subseteq P_2$. Since X is obtained after execution of II, $S \overset{*}{\Rightarrow} \alpha_1 X \alpha_2$, $\alpha_1, \alpha_2 \in (N' \cup T')^*$. Every symbol of N' is also in N_2. Since G_2 is obtained from by execution of I, it is possible to get a terminal string from every symbol of N_2 and hence from N': $\alpha_1 \overset{*}{\Rightarrow} w_1$ and $\alpha_2 \overset{*}{\Rightarrow} w_2$, $w_1, w_2 \in T^*$. Thus, $S \overset{*}{\Rightarrow} \alpha_1 X \alpha_2 \overset{*}{\Rightarrow} w_1 X w_2 \overset{*}{\Rightarrow} w_1 w w_2$.

Clearly, X is not useless as supposed. Hence G' contains only useful symbols.   □

Example 2.1   Let $G = (N, T, P, S)$ be a *CFG* with

$$
\begin{aligned}
N &= \{S, A, B, C\} \\
T &= \{a, b\} \text{ and} \\
P &= \{S \to Sa|A|C, A \to a, B \to bb, C \to aC\}
\end{aligned}
$$

First 'GEN' set will be $\{S, A, B, a, b\}$. Then $G_2 = (N_2, T, P_2, S)$ where

$$
\begin{aligned}
N_2 &= \{S, A, B\} \\
P &= \{S - Sa \mid A, A \to a, B \to bb\}
\end{aligned}
$$

In G_2, REACH set will be $\{S, A, a\}$. Hence $G' = (N', T', P', S)$ where

$$
\begin{aligned}
N' &= \{S, A\} \\
T' &= \{a\} \\
P' &= \{S \to Sa \mid A, A \to a\} \\
L(G) &= L(G') = \{a^n | n \geq 1\}.
\end{aligned}
$$

ε-rule Elimination Method

Next simplification of CFG is to remove ε-rules when the language is ε-free.

Definition 2.14   *Any production of the form $A \to \varepsilon$ is called a ε-rule. If $A \overset{*}{\Rightarrow} \varepsilon$, then we call A a nullable symbol.*

Theorem 2.6   *Let $G = (N, T, P, S)$ be a CFG such that $\varepsilon \notin L(G)$. Then there exists a CFG without ε-rules generating $L(G)$.*

Proof   Before modifying the grammar one has to identify the set of nullable symbols of G. This is done by the following procedure.

Algorithm NULL

1. Let $NULL := \phi$,

2. If $A \to \varepsilon \in P$, then $A \in NULL$ and

3. If $A \to B_1 \dots B_t \in P$, and each B_i is in $NULL$, then $A \in NULL$.

Run algorithm $NULL$ for G and get the $NULL$ set.

The modification of G to get $G' = (N, T, P', S)$ with respect to $NULL$ is given below.

If $A \to A_1 \dots A_t \in P$, $t \geq 1$ and if n ($n < t$) of these A_is are in $NULL$. Then P will contain 2^n rules where the variables in $NULL$ are either present or absent in all possible combinations. If $n = t$ then remove $A \to \varepsilon$ from P. The grammar $G' = (N, T, P', S)$ thus obtained is ε-free.

To prove that a word $w \in L(G)$, if and only if $w \in L(G')$. As G and G' do not differ in N and T, one can equivalently show that:

$$
A \overset{*}{\Rightarrow}_G w
$$

if and only if,

$$A \overset{*}{\Rightarrow}_{G'} w$$

for $A \in N$.

Clearly, $w \neq \varepsilon$. Let $A \overset{n}{\Rightarrow}_G w$. $n = 1$, $A \overset{*}{\Rightarrow}_G w$ then $A \rightarrow w$ is in P and hence in P'. Then $A \overset{*}{\Rightarrow}_{nG'} w$. Assume the result to be true for all derivations from A of length $n - 1$. Let $A \overset{*}{\Rightarrow}_G w$ i.e., $A \underset{G}{\Rightarrow} Y_1 \ldots Y_k \overset{n-1}{\Rightarrow}_G w$.

Let $w = w_1 \ldots w_k$ and let $X_1, X_2, \ldots, X_m$ be those Y_j's in order such that $Y_j \overset{*}{\Rightarrow} w_j$, $w_j \neq \varepsilon$. Clearly, $k \geq 1$ as $w \neq \varepsilon$. Hence, $A \rightarrow X_1 \ldots X_m$ is a rule in G'.

We can see that $X_1 \ldots X_m \overset{*}{\Rightarrow}_G w$ as some Y_j derive only ε. Since each $Y_j \overset{*}{\Rightarrow} w_j$, w_j takes fewer than n steps, by induction, $Y_j \overset{*}{\Rightarrow} w_j$, for $w_j \neq \varepsilon$. Hence, $A \underset{G}{\Rightarrow} X_1 \ldots X_m \overset{*}{\Rightarrow} w$.

Conversely, if $A \overset{*}{\Rightarrow}_{G'} w$, then to show that $A \overset{*}{\Rightarrow}_G w$ also. Again the proof is by induction on the number of derivation steps.

Basis

If $A \underset{G'}{\Rightarrow} w$, then $A \rightarrow w \in G'$. By the construction of G', one can see that there exists a rule $A \rightarrow \alpha$ in G such that α and w differ only in nullable symbols. Hence $A \underset{G}{\Rightarrow} \alpha \overset{*}{\Rightarrow}_G w$ where for $\alpha \overset{*}{\Rightarrow} w$ only ε-rules are used.

Induction

Assume $A \overset{n}{\Rightarrow}_{G'} w$ $n > 1$. Then let $A \underset{G'}{\Rightarrow} Y_1 \ldots Y_k \overset{*}{\Rightarrow}_G w$. For $A \underset{G'}{\Rightarrow} Y_1 \ldots Y_k$ the corresponding equivalent derivation by G will be $A \underset{G}{\Rightarrow} X_1 \ldots X_m \overset{*}{\Rightarrow}_G Y_1 \ldots Y_k$ as some of the X_i's are nullable. Hence, $A \overset{*}{\Rightarrow}_G Y_1 \ldots Y_k \overset{*}{\Rightarrow}_G w_1 \ldots w_k = w$ by induction hypothesis. Hence $A \overset{*}{\Rightarrow}_G w$. Hence $L(G) = L(G')$.

Example 2.13 Consider $G = (N, T, P, S)$ where $N = \{S, A, B, C, D\}$, $T = \{0, 1\}$ and

$$P = \{S \rightarrow AB0C, A \rightarrow BC, B \rightarrow 1|\varepsilon, C \rightarrow D|\varepsilon, D \rightarrow \varepsilon\}$$ The set $NULL = \{A, B, C, D\}$. Then G' will be with
$$P' = \{S \rightarrow AB0C|AB0|A0C|B0C|A0|B0|0C|0, A \rightarrow BC|B|C, B \rightarrow 1, C \rightarrow D\}.$$

Procedure to Eliminate Unit Rules

Definition 2.15 *Any rule of the form $X \rightarrow Y$, X, $Y \in N$ is called a unit rule. Note that $A \rightarrow a$ with $a \in T$ is not a unit rule.*

In simplification of CFGs, another important step is to make the given CFG unit rule free i.e., to eliminate unit rules. This is essential for the application in compilers. As the compiler spends time on each rule used in parsing by generating semantic routines, having unnecessary unit rules will increase compile time.

Lemma 2.2 *Let G be a CFG, then there exists a CFG G' without unit rules such that $L(G) = L(G')$.*

Proof   Let $G = (N, T, P, S)$ be a *CFG*. First, find the sets of pairs of non-terminals (A, B) in G such that $A \overset{*}{\Rightarrow} B$ by unit rules. Such a pair is called a unit-pair.

Algorithm UNIT-PAIR

1. $(A, A) \in UNIT\text{-}PAIR$, for every variable $A \in N$.

2. If $(A, B) \in UNIT\text{-}PAIR$ and $B \rightarrow C \in P$ then $(A, C) \in UNIT\text{-}PAIR$

Now construct $G' = (N, T, P', S)$ as follows. Remove all unit productions. For every unit-pair (X, Y), if $Y \rightarrow \alpha \in P$ is a non-unit rule, add to P', $X \rightarrow \alpha$. Thus G' has no unit rules.

Let us consider leftmost derivations in G and G'.

If $w \in L(G')$, then $S \overset{*}{\Rightarrow}_{G'} w$. Clearly, there exists a derivation of w from S by G where zero or more applications of unit rules are used. Hence, $S \overset{*}{\Rightarrow}_G w$ whose length may be different from $S \overset{*}{\Rightarrow}_{G'} w$.

If $w \in L(G)$, then one can consider $S \overset{*}{\Rightarrow}_{G'} w$ by G. A sequence of unit-productions applied in this derivation is to be written by a non-unit production. Since this is a leftmost derivation, for such sequence there exists one rule in G' doing the same job. Hence, one can see the simulation of a derivation of G with G'. Hence $L(G) = L(G')$.

Example 2.14   Let $G = (N, T, P, S)$ be a CFG, where $N = \{X, Y\}$, $T = \{a, b\}$ and

$P = \{X \rightarrow aX|Y|b, \ Y \rightarrow bK|K|b, \ K \rightarrow a\}$
$\quad UNIT\text{-}PAIR = \{(X, X), (Y, Y), (K, K), (X, Y), (Y, K), (X, K)\}$

Then $G' = (N, T, P', S)$, where $P' = \{X \rightarrow aX|bK|b|a, \ Y \rightarrow bK|b|a, \ K \rightarrow a\}$.

Remark   Since removal of ε-rule can introduce unit productions, to get a simplified *CFG* to generate $L(G) - \{\varepsilon\}$, the following steps have to be used in the order given.

1. Remove ε-rules;

2. Remove unit-rules and

3. Remove useless symbols.

   i. Remove symbols not deriving terminal strings.

   ii. Remove symbols not reachable from S.

Example 2.15   It is essential that steps 3(i) and 3(ii) have to be executed in that order. If step 3(ii) is executed first and then step 3(i), we may not get the required reduced grammar.

Consider CFG $G = (N, T, P, S)$ where $N = \{S, A, B, C\}$, $T = \{a, b\}$ and
$P = \{S \rightarrow ABC|a, A \rightarrow a, C \rightarrow b\}$
$\quad L(G) = \{a\}$

Applying step 3(ii) first removes nothing. Then apply step 3(i) which removes B and $S \rightarrow ABC$ leaving $S \rightarrow a$, $A \rightarrow a$, $C \rightarrow b$. Though A and C do not contribute to the set $L(G)$, they are not removed.

On the other hand applying step 3(i) first, removes B, $S \rightarrow ABC$. Afterwards apply step 3(ii), removes A, C, $A \rightarrow a$, $C \rightarrow b$. Hence $S \rightarrow a$ is the only rule left which is the required result.

2.4 Normal Forms

We have seen in Section 2.3, how a given CFG can be simplified. In this section, we see different normal forms of CFG i.e., one can express the rules of the CFG in a particular form. These normal form grammars are easy to handle and are useful in proving results. The most popular normal forms are Weak Chomsky Normal Form (WCNF), Chomsky Normal Form (CNF), Strong Chomsky Normal Form (SCNF), and Greibach Normal Form (GNF).

Weak Chomsky Normal Form

Definition 2.16 Let $G = (N, T, P, S)$ be a CFG. If each rule in P is of the form $A \rightarrow \Delta$, $A \rightarrow a$ or $A \rightarrow \varepsilon$, where $A \in N$, $\Delta \in N^+$, $a \in T$, then G is said to be in WCNF.

Example 2.16 Let $G = (N, T, P, S)$ be a CFG, where $N = \{S, A, B\}$, $T = \{a, b\}$ and $P = \{S \rightarrow ASB \mid AB, A \rightarrow a, B \rightarrow b\}$. G is in WCNF.

Theorem 2.7 For any CFG $G = (N, T, P, S)$ there exists a CFG G' in WCNF such that $L(G) = L(G')$.

Proof Let $G = (N, T, P, S)$ be a CFG. One can construct an equivalent CFG in WCNF as below. Let $G' = (N', T', P', S')$ be an equivalent CFG where $N' = N \cup \{A_a / a \in T\}$, none of A_a's belong to N.

$P' = \{A \rightarrow \Delta \mid A \rightarrow \alpha \in P$ and every occurrence of a symbol from T present in α is replaced by A_a, giving $\Delta\} \cup \{A_a \rightarrow a \mid a \in T\}$. Clearly, $\Delta \in N'^+$ and P' gets the required form. G' is in WCNF. That G and G' equivalent can be seen easily.

Chomsky Normal Form

Definition 2.17 Let $\varepsilon \notin L(G)$ and $G = (N, T, P, S)$ be a CFG. G is said to be in CNF, if all its productions are of the form $A \rightarrow BC$ or $A \rightarrow a$, $A, B, C \in N$, $a \in T$.

Example 2.17 The following CFGs are in CNF.

1. $G_1 = (N, T, P, S)$, where $N = \{S, A, B, C\}$, $T = \{0, 1\}$ and
   $P = \{S \rightarrow AB \mid AC \mid SS, C \rightarrow SA, A \rightarrow 0, B \rightarrow 1\}$.

2. $G_2 = (N, T, P, S)$ where $N = \{S, A, B, C\}$, $T = \{a, b\}$ and
$P = \{S \rightarrow AS \mid SB, A \rightarrow AB \mid a, B \rightarrow b\}$.

Remark   No CFG in CNF can generate ε. If ε is to be added to $L(G)$, then a new start symbol S' is to be taken and $S' \rightarrow \varepsilon$ should be added. For every rule $S \rightarrow \alpha$, $S' \rightarrow \alpha$ should be added, which make sure that the new start symbol does not appear on the right-hand side of any production.

Theorem 2.8   *Given CFG G, there exists an equivalent CFG G'in CNF.*

Proof   Let $G = (N, T, P, S)$ be a CFG without ε rules, unit-rules and useless symbols and also $\varepsilon \notin L(G)$. Modify G to G' such that $G' = (N', T, P', S)$ is in WCNF. Let $A \rightarrow \Delta \in P$. If $|\Delta| = 2$, such rules need not be modified. If $|\Delta| \geq 3$, the modification is as below:

If $A \rightarrow \Delta = A_1 A_2 A_3$, the new set of equivalent rules will be:
$A \rightarrow A_1 B_1$
$B_1 \rightarrow A_2 A_3$.
Similarly, if $A \rightarrow A_1 A_2 \ldots A_n \in P$, it is replaced by
$A \quad \rightarrow A_1 B_1$
$B_1 \quad \rightarrow A_2 B_2$
$\vdots$
$B_{n-2} \rightarrow A_{n-1} A_n$.

Let P'' be the collection of modified rules and $G'' = (N'', T, P'', S)$ be the modified grammar which is clearly in CNF. Also $L(G) = L(G'')$.

Example 2.18   Let $G = (N, T, P, S)$ be a CFG where $N = \{S, A, B\}$,
$T = \{a, b\}$
$P = \{S \rightarrow SAB \mid AB \mid SBC, A \rightarrow AB \mid a, B \rightarrow BAB \mid b, C \rightarrow b\}$.
Clearly, G is not in CNF but in WCNF. Hence, the modification of rules in P are as below:

For $S \rightarrow SAB$, the equivalent rules are $S \rightarrow SB_1$, $B_1 \rightarrow AB$.
For $S \rightarrow SBC$, the equivalent rules are $S \rightarrow SB_2$, $B_2 \rightarrow BC$.
For $B \rightarrow BAB$, the equivalent rules are $B \rightarrow BB_3$, $B_3 \rightarrow AB$.

Hence $G'' = (N'', T, P'', S)$ will be with $N'' = \{S, A, B, C, B_1, B_2, B_3\}$, $T = \{a, b\}$
$P'' = \{S \rightarrow SB_1 \mid SB_2 \mid AB, B_1 \rightarrow AB, B_2 \rightarrow BC, B_3 \rightarrow AB,$
$\quad A \rightarrow AB \mid a, B \rightarrow BB_3 \mid b, C \rightarrow b\}$.

Clearly, G'' is in *CNF*.

Strong Chomsky Normal Form

Definition 2.18   *A CFG $G = (N, T, P, S)$ is said to be in SCNF when rules in P are only of the forms $A \rightarrow a$, $A \rightarrow BC$ where $A, B, C \in N$, $a \in T$ subject to the following conditions:*

1. *if $A \to BC \in P$, then $B \neq C$.*
2. *if $A \to BC \in P$, then for each rule $X \to DE \in P$, we have $E \neq B$ and $D \neq C$.*

Theorem 2.9   *For every CFG $G = (N, T, P, S)$ there exists an equivalent CFG in SCNF.*

Proof   Let $G = (N, T, P, S)$ be a CFG in CNF. One can construct an equivalent CFG, $G' = (N', T, P', S')$ in SCNF as below.

$N' = \{S'\} \cup \{A_L, A_R | A \in N\}$

$T = T$

$P' = \{A_L \to B_L C_R, A_R \to B_L C_R | A \to BC \in P\}$
$\cup \{S' \to X_L Y_R | S \to XY \in P\}$
$\cup \{S' \to a | S \to a \in P\}$
$\cup \{A_L \to a, A_R \to a | A \to a \in P, a \in T\}$.

Clearly, $L(G) = L(G')$ and G' is in SCNF.

Example 2.19   Let $G = (N, T, P, S)$ be a CFG where $N = \{S, A, B\}, T = \{0, 1\}$ and $P = \{S \to AB | 0, B \to BA | 1, A \to AB | 0\}$. Then $G' = (N', T, P', S')$ in SCNF will be with

$N' = \{S' S_L, S_R, A_L, A_R, B_L, B_R\}$

$T = \{0, 1\}$

$P' = \{S' \to A_L B_R | 0, S_L \to A_L B_R | 0,$
$S_R \to A_L B_R | 0, A_L \to A_L B_R | 0,$
$A_R \to A_L B_R | 0, B_L \to B_L A_R | 1,$
$B_R \to B_L A_R | 1\}.$

Greibach Normal Form

Definition 2.4   *Let $\varepsilon \notin L(G)$ and $G = (N, T, P, S)$ be a CFG. G is said to be in GNF, if each rule in P rewrites a variable into a word in TN^* i.e., each rule will be of the form $A \to a\alpha, a \in T, \alpha \in N^*$.*

Before we proceed to construct a CFG in GNF, we prove the following techniques.

Technique 1

For any CFG $G = (N, T, P, S)$ with a A-production $A \to \alpha_1 B \alpha_2 \in P$, and B-productions $B \to y_1 | y_2 | \ldots y_n$, there exists an equivalent CFG with new A-productions

$A \to \alpha_1 y_1 \alpha_2 | \alpha_1 y_2 \alpha_2 | \ldots \alpha_n y_n \alpha_n$, i.e., $G' = (N, T, P', S)$ with

$P' = \{P - \{A \to \alpha_1 B \alpha_2\}\} \cup \{A \to \alpha_1 y_i \alpha_2, 1 \leq i \leq n\}$. How is $L(G') = L(G)$?

$A \to \alpha_1 B \alpha_2$ is a production in P. Whenever this production is used, the subsequent application of rules will be B-rules. Hence in G, $A \Rightarrow \alpha_1 B \alpha_2 \Rightarrow \alpha_1 y_i \alpha_2$

whereas in G', $A \Rightarrow \alpha_1 y_i \alpha_2$. Conversely, if $A \Rightarrow \alpha_1 y_i \alpha_2$, then the rules used for reaching $\alpha_1 y_i \alpha_2$ are $A - \alpha_1 B \alpha_2$ and $B \rightarrow y_i$ in G.

Technique 2

Let $G = (N, T, P, S)$ be a CFG with A-productions,

$A \rightarrow Ax_1 | Ax_2 | \ldots | Ax_n | y_1 | \ldots | y_m$ where y_i's do not start with A.

Let $G' = (N \cup \{Z\}, T, P', S)$ where P' is defined to include the following set of rules.

1. $A \rightarrow y_1 | y_2 | \ldots | y_m$.

   $A \rightarrow y_1 Z | y_2 Z | \ldots | y_m Z$.

2. $Z \rightarrow x_1 | x_2 | \ldots | x_n$

   $Z \rightarrow x_1 Z | x_2 Z | \ldots | x_n Z$.

3. Remaining rules of P excluding original A-productions.

Then G' and G are equivalent. Left recursion is removed by introducing right recursion. If $w \in L(G)$, $S \overset{*}{\Rightarrow}_{lm} w$.

If $A \Rightarrow Ax_{i_n} \Rightarrow Ax_{i_{n-1}} x_{i_n} \Rightarrow \ldots \Rightarrow Ax_{i1} x_{i2} \ldots x_{i_n} \Rightarrow y_j x_{i1} \ldots x_{i_n}$ is a derivation in G, the corresponding derivation in G' will be:

$A \Rightarrow y_j Z \Rightarrow y_j x_{i1} Z \Rightarrow y_j x_{i1} x_{i2} Z \Rightarrow \ldots \Rightarrow y_j x_{i1} x_{i2} \ldots x_{i_{n-1}} Z \Rightarrow y_j x_{i1} \ldots x_{i_{n-1}} x_{i_n}$

Theorem 2.4   *For every CFL L with $\varepsilon \notin L$, there exists a CFG in GNF such that* $L(G) = L$.

Proof   Let $G = (N, T, P, S)$ be a CFG without ε rules and *WCNF*. A *CFG* in *GNF* is constructed in five-steps.

   Step 1   Rename all the variables as $\{A_1, A_2, \ldots, A_n\}$ with $S = A_1$.

   Step 2   To obtain productions either in the form $A \rightarrow aw$ or $A_i \rightarrow A_j w$ where $j > i$ where the construction is by induction on i.

Basis

For A_1-productions, using Technique 1 and Technique 2 one can get equivalent A_1-rules which are clearly either in the form $A_1 \rightarrow aw$ or $A_1 \rightarrow A_j w$, $j > 1$. The A_1 rules which are already in the required form will be retained.

Induction

Consider A_{i+1} productions assuming that all A_j productions $1 \leq j \leq i$ are put in the required form. Productions already in the required form are not modified. Hence, consider $A_{i+1} \rightarrow A_l w$ where l is the least index among such symbols occurring on the right-hand side of A_{i+1} rules. If $l > i + 1$, one need not modify the rule. Otherwise, apply induction hypothesis to A_l rules where $l \leq i$. By Technique 1, one can convert these rules to the required form. Then modify $A_{i+1} \to A_j w$, $j \leq i + 1$, to reach the form $A_{i+1} \to A_l w$, $l \geq i + 1$, $A_{i+1} \to aw$, $a \in T$. Rules of the form $A_{i+1} \to A_{i+1} w$ can be modified by Technique 2.

Step 3 Convert all A_n rules to the form $A_n \to aw$ using Technique 2. Now all A_n rules are in GNF form.

Step 4 Modification in Step 3 for A_n rules is to be propagated to A_{n-1} rules to convert them to GNF form and so on upto A_1 rules. At the end of this step all A_i rules will be in GNF.

Step 5 For each Z_i rules introduced by application of Technique 2 the required form is reached via substitution of A_i rules. (Technique 1).

Hence G_1 is in GNF.

$L(G) = L(G')$ because during the conversion only Techniques 1 and 2 are used which do not affect the language generated. □

Remark (i) If G is in CNF, then any A-rule will be of the form $A \to a$, $A \to BC$, $A \to AD$. By Technique 1 or 2 as in step 2, new equivalent A-rules can be obtained which are $A \to aw$ or $A \to w'$ where $w \in N^*$, $w' \in N^+$, $a \in T$. Steps 3–5 modify the A-rule to $A \to aw$ or $Z \to bw'$ where, $a, b \in T$, w, $w' N^*$.

(ii) When $\varepsilon \in L$, the previous construction works for $L - \{\varepsilon\}$ and subsequently ε rules can be added to the modified grammar without affecting the other rules as mentioned earlier.

Example 2.5 Consider a CFG $G = (N, T, P, S)$ where $N = \{S\}$, $T = \{a, b\}$ and

$$P = \{S \to SS, S \to aSb, S \to ab\}.$$

The equivalent CFG in WCNF will be

$$G' = (N', T, P', S) \text{ where } N = \{S, A, B\}, T = \{a, b\} \text{ and}$$
$$P' = \{S \to ASB, S \to AB, A \to a, B \to b, S \to SS\}.$$

The conversation of this to GNF is as shown below:

Step 1 $S = A_1$, $A = A_2$, $B = A_3$.
Rules now become:

1. $A_1 \to A_1 A_1$
2. $A_1 \to A_2 A_1 A_3$
3. $A_1 \to A_2 A_3$
4. $A_2 \to a$
5. $A_3 \to b$.

Step 2 Convert the A_i rules such that they are of the form $A_i \to aw$ or $A_i \to A_j w$ $j > i$. Taking rules 1, 2, and 3 they can be replaced by the following 6 rules:

7. $A_1 \rightarrow A_2 A_1 A_3$

8. $A_1 \rightarrow A_2 A_3$

9. $A_1 \rightarrow A_2 A_1 A_3 Z$

10. $A_1 \rightarrow A_2 A_3 Z$

11. $Z \rightarrow A_1 Z$

12. $Z \rightarrow A_1$.

A_2, A_3 rules are already in GNF.

Step 3   is not necessary here.

Step 4   Convert A_i rules into GNF. Starting from A_n and going up to A_1,

$A_3 \rightarrow b$

$A_2 \rightarrow a$ are in GNF

A_1 rules become

7′. $A_1 \rightarrow a A_1 A_3$

8′. $A_1 \rightarrow a A_3$

9′. $A_1 \rightarrow a A_1 A_3 Z$

10′. $A_1 \rightarrow a A_3 Z$

Step 5   Convert the Z rules into GNF

11   is replaced by the 4 rules

13. $Z \rightarrow a A_1 A_3 Z$

14. $Z \rightarrow a A_3 Z$

15. $Z \rightarrow a A_1 A_3 Z Z$

16. $Z \rightarrow a A_3 Z Z$

12   is replaced by the 4 rules

13′. $Z \rightarrow a A_1 A_3$

14′. $Z \rightarrow a A_3$

15′. $Z \rightarrow a A_1 A_3 Z$

16′. $Z \rightarrow a A_3 Z$

Note that 15′ and 16′ are repetition of 13 and 14.
So we end up with:

$A_1 \rightarrow a A_1 A_3$

$A_1 \rightarrow a A_3$

$A_1 \rightarrow a A_1 A_3 Z$

$A_1 \rightarrow a A_3 Z$

$A_2 \rightarrow a$

$A_3 \rightarrow b$

13. $Z \rightarrow aA_1 A_3 Z$

14. $Z \rightarrow aA_3 Z$

15. $Z \rightarrow aA_1 A_3 ZZ$

16. $Z \rightarrow aA_3 ZZ$

13′. $Z \rightarrow aA_1 A_3$

14′. $Z \rightarrow aA_3$.

Useless symbols and rules can be removed afterwards (e.g. $A_2 \rightarrow a$).

Problems and Solutions

Problem 1. Give CFG for the following:

a. $\{a^n b^n | n \geq 1\}$

Solution. $G = (N, T, P, S)$

$N = \{S\}$, $T = \{a, b\}$, P consists of the following rules:

$$\{1.S \rightarrow aSb, \text{ and } 2.S \rightarrow ab\}$$

Whenever rule 1 is applied, one 'a' is generated on the left and one 'b'; on the right. The derivation terminates by using rule 2. A sample derivation and derivation tree are given below (Figure 2.12).

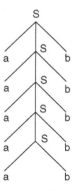

Figure 2.12. A sample derivation tree

$S \Rightarrow aSb$

$\Rightarrow aaSbb$

$\Rightarrow aaaSbbb$

$\Rightarrow aaaaSbbbb$

$\Rightarrow aaaaa\,bbbbb$

b. $\{a^n b^m c^n | n, m \geq 1\}$

Solution. The grammar $G = (N, T, P, S), N = \{S, A\}, T = \{a, b, c\}$ P is given as follows:

1. $S \rightarrow aSc$
2. $S \rightarrow aAc$
3. $A \rightarrow bA$
4. $A \rightarrow b$

Rule 1 and 2 generate equal number of a's and c's; rule 2 makes sure at least one a and one c are generated. Rule 3 and 4 generate b's in the middle. Rule 4 makes sure at least one b is generated. It is to be noted that a's and c's are generated first and b's afterwards.

c. $\{a^n b^n c^m | n, m \geq 1\}$

Solution. $G = (N, T, P, S), N = \{S, A, B\}, T = \{a, b, c\}$ P is given as follows:

1. $S \rightarrow A B$
2. $A \rightarrow aAb$
3. $A \rightarrow ab$
4. $B \rightarrow cB$
5. $B \rightarrow c$

Rule 2 and 3 generate equal number of a's and b's. Rule 4 and 5 generate c's. Rule 1 is applied first so that equal number of a's and b's are followed by a string of c's.

In the following solutions, only the rules are given. Capital letters stand for non-terminals and small letters stand for terminals.

d. $\{a^n b^n c^m d^m | n, m \geq 1\}$

Solution.

1. $S \rightarrow A B$
2. $A \rightarrow aAb$
3. $A \rightarrow ab$
4. $B \rightarrow cBd$
5. $B \rightarrow cd$

e. $\{a^n b^m c^m d^n | n, m \geq 1\}$

Solution.

1. $S \rightarrow aSd$
2. $S \rightarrow aAd$
3. $A \rightarrow bAc$
4. $A \rightarrow bc$

f. $\{a^n b^m | n, m \geq 1, n > m\}$

Solution.

  1. $S \rightarrow aSb$
  2. $S \rightarrow aAb$
  3. $A \rightarrow aA$
  4. $A \rightarrow a$

g. $\{a^n b^m | n, m \geq 1, n \neq m\}$

Solution. $\{a^n b^m | n, m \geq 1, n \neq m\} = \{a^n b^m | n, m \geq 1, n > m\} \cup \{a^n b^m | n, m \geq 1, m > n\}$ Rules are:

  1. $S \rightarrow aSb$
  2. $S \rightarrow aAb$
  3. $A \rightarrow aA$
  4. $A \rightarrow a$
  5. $S \rightarrow aBb$
  6. $B \rightarrow bB$
  7. $B \rightarrow b$

Rules 1, 2, 3, and 4 generate more a's than b's. Rules 1, 5, 6, and 7 generate more b's than a's.

h. $\{wcw^R | w \in \{a, b\}^*\}$

Solution. Rules are:

  1. $S \rightarrow aSa$
  2. $S \rightarrow bSb$
  3. $S \rightarrow c$

i. $\{w | w \in \{(,)\}^+, w$ is a well-formed string of parenthesis$\}$

Solution. $\{w | w \in \{(,)\}^+, w$ is a well-formed string of parenthesis$\}$ Rules are:

  1. $S \rightarrow SS$
  2. $S \rightarrow (S)$
  3. $S \rightarrow ()$

The following grammar generates the same language plus the empty string:

  1. $S \rightarrow SaSbS$
  2. $S \rightarrow \varepsilon$

Problem 2. Give regular grammars for

a. $\{a^n | n \geq 1\}$

Solution. $G = (N, T, P, S)$, $N = \{S\}$, $T = \{a\}$
P has the following rules:

   1. $S \rightarrow aS$
   2. $S \rightarrow a$

b. $\{a^n b^m | n, m \geq 1\}$

Solution.   We give below the rules only. Capital letters stand for non-terminals.

   1. $S \rightarrow aS$
   2. $S \rightarrow aA$
   3. $A \rightarrow bA$
   4. $A \rightarrow b$

c. $\{a^{2n} | n \geq 1\}$

Solution.

   1. $S \rightarrow aA$
   2. $A \rightarrow aS$
   3. $A \rightarrow a$

d. $\{(ab)^n | n \geq 1\}$

Solution.

   1. $S \rightarrow aA$
   2. $A \rightarrow bS$
   3. $A \rightarrow b$

e. $\{a^n b^m c^p | n, m, p \geq 1\}$

Solution.

   1. $S \rightarrow aS$
   2. $S \rightarrow aA$
   3. $A \rightarrow bA$
   4. $A \rightarrow bB$
   5. $B \rightarrow cB$
   6. $B \rightarrow c$

f. $\{(abc)^n | n \geq 1\}$

Solution.

   1. $S \rightarrow aA$
   2. $A \rightarrow bB$
   3. $B \rightarrow cS$
   4. $B \rightarrow c$

Exercises

1. Find a CFG for the languages over $\{0, 1\}$ consisting of those strings in which the ratio of the number of 1's to the number of 0's is three to two.

2. Define CFGs that generate the following languages.
   a. The set of odd length string S in $\{0, 1\}^*$ with middle symbol 1
   b. $\{a^i b^j c^k \mid j > i + k\}$.

3. Prove that the following CFGs do not generate
   $$L = \{x \in \{0, 1\}^* \mid \#_0(x) = \#_1(x)\}$$
   a. $S \rightarrow S01S \mid S10S \mid \varepsilon$
   b. $S \rightarrow 0S1 \mid 1S0 \mid 01S \mid S01 \mid S10 \mid \varepsilon$.

4. Show that the CFG $S \rightarrow SS \mid a \mid b$ is ambiguous.

5. Convert the following to CNF.
   $$S \rightarrow ABA$$
   $$A \rightarrow aA \mid \varepsilon$$
   $$B \rightarrow bB \mid \varepsilon$$

6. Which of the following grammars are ambiguous? Are the languages generated inherently ambiguous?
   a. 1. $S \rightarrow \varepsilon$
      2. $S \rightarrow aSb$
      3. $S \rightarrow SS$
   b. 1. $S \rightarrow \varepsilon$
      2. $S \rightarrow aSb$
      3. $S \rightarrow bSa$
      4. $S \rightarrow SS$
   c. 1. $S \rightarrow bS$
      2. $S \rightarrow Sb$
      3. $S \rightarrow \varepsilon$
   d. 1. $S \rightarrow SaSa$
      2. $S \rightarrow b$
   e. 1. $S \rightarrow Sb$
      2. $S \rightarrow aSb$
      3. $S \rightarrow Sa$
      4. $S \rightarrow a$
   f. 1. $S \rightarrow a$
      2. $S \rightarrow aaS$
      3. $S \rightarrow aaaS$

g. 1. $S \rightarrow A$
2. $S \rightarrow aSb$
3. $S \rightarrow bS$
4. $A \rightarrow Aa$
5. $A \rightarrow a$

h. 1. $S \rightarrow AA$
2. $A \rightarrow AAA$
3. $A \rightarrow bA$
4. $A \rightarrow Ab$
5. $A \rightarrow a$

7. Consider L^2 where $L = \{ww^R \mid w \in \{a, b\}^*\}$. Give an argument that L^2 is inherently ambiguous.

8. Give an unambiguous grammar for
$L = \{w \mid w \in \{a, b\}^+, w$ has equal number of a's and b's$\}$

9. Consider the grammars over the terminal alphabet $\Sigma = \{a, b\}$ with rules

a. $S \rightarrow wSS$

b. $S \rightarrow aSS$

   $S \rightarrow a$

   $S \rightarrow bSS$

   $S \rightarrow b$

   $S \rightarrow w$

where w is some string over Σ. Show that each of these grammars is always ambiguous whatever w may be.

10. Consider the grammar $S \rightarrow aS|aSbS|\varepsilon$. Prove that the grammar generates all and only the strings of a's and b's such that every prefix has at least as many a's as b's. Show that the grammar is ambiguous. Find an equivalent unambiguous grammar.

11. Consider the following grammar. $E \rightarrow +EE| * EE| - EE|x|y$. Show that the grammar is unambiguous. What is the language generated?

12. Which of the following CFLs you think are inherently ambiguous? Give arguments.

a. $\{a^i b^j c^k d^l | i, j, k, l \geq 1, i \neq j$ and $k \neq l\}$
b. $\{a^i b^j c^k d^l | i, j, k, l \geq 1, i = k$ or $j = l\}$
c. $\{a^i b^j c^k d^l | i, j, k, l \geq 1, i = j$ and $k = l$ or $i = l$ and $j = k\}$
d. $\{a^i b^j c^k d^l | i, j, k, l \geq 1, i \neq j$ or $k \neq l\}$

13. Remove the useless symbols from the following CFGs.

a. 1. $S \rightarrow ABB$
2. $S \rightarrow CAC$
3. $A \rightarrow a$
4. $B \rightarrow Bc$
5. $B \rightarrow ABB$

6. $C \rightarrow bB$

7. $C \rightarrow a$

b. 1. $S \rightarrow aSASb$

2. $S \rightarrow Saa$

3. $S \rightarrow AA$

4. $A \rightarrow caA$

5. $A \rightarrow Ac$

6. $B \rightarrow bca$

7. $A \rightarrow \varepsilon$

14. Consider the following CFGs. Construct equivalent CFGs without ε-productions.

a. $S \rightarrow bEf$

$E \rightarrow bEc$

$E \rightarrow GGc$

$G \rightarrow b$

$G \rightarrow KL$

$K \rightarrow cKd$

$K \rightarrow \varepsilon$

$L \rightarrow dLe$

$L \rightarrow \varepsilon$

b. $S \rightarrow eSe$

$S \rightarrow GH$

$G \rightarrow cGb$

$G \rightarrow \varepsilon$

$H \rightarrow JHd$

$H \rightarrow \varepsilon$

$J \rightarrow bJ$

$J \rightarrow f$

15. Remove unit production from the following grammar:

a. $S \rightarrow cBA$

b. $S \rightarrow B$

c. $A \rightarrow cB$

d. $A \rightarrow AbbS$

e. $B \rightarrow aaa$

16. Find a CFG with six productions (including ε productions) equivalent to the following grammar:

$S \rightarrow b \mid bHF \mid bH \mid bF$

$H \rightarrow bHc \mid bc$

$F \rightarrow dFe \mid de \mid G$

$G \rightarrow dG \mid d$

17. Given two grammars G and G'

G

a. $S \rightarrow EFG$

b. $E \rightarrow bEc$

c. $E \rightarrow \varepsilon$

d. $F \rightarrow cFd$

e. $F \rightarrow \varepsilon$

f. $G \rightarrow dGb$

g. $G \rightarrow \varepsilon$

G'

$1' \ S \rightarrow EQ$

$2' \ Q \rightarrow FG$

(b)–(g) as in G'.

Give an algorithm for converting a derivation in G' of a terminal string into a derivation in G of the same terminal string.

18. Let G and G' be CFGs where

G

$S \rightarrow bSc$

$S \rightarrow bc$

$S \rightarrow bSSc$

G'

$S \rightarrow bJ$

$J \rightarrow bJc$

$J \rightarrow c$

$J \rightarrow bJbJc$

a. Give an algorithm for converting a derivation in G of a terminal string into a derivation in G' of the same terminal string

b. Give an algorithm for converting a derivation in G' of a terminal string into a derivation in G.

19. Suppose G is a CFG and $w \in L(G)$ and $|w| = n$. How long is a derivation of w in G if:

    a. G is in CNF

    b. G is in GNF

20. Show that every CFL without ε is generated by a CFG whose productions are of the form $A \rightarrow a$, $A \rightarrow aB$ and $A \rightarrow aBC$.

21. An operator CFG represents an ε-free context-free grammar such that no production has two consecutive non-terminals on its right-hand side. That is, an ε-free CFG, $G = (N, T, P, S)$, is an operator CFG if for all $p \in P$, $rhs(p) \notin (N \cup T)^* NN(N \cup T)^*$. Prove that for every CFG G there exists an operator CFG, G', such that $L(G) = L(G')$.

22. Find CNF and GNF equivalent to the following grammars:

a.	$S \rightarrow S \wedge S$	b.	$E \rightarrow E + E$
	$S \rightarrow S \vee S$		$E \rightarrow E * E$
	$S \rightarrow \neg S$		$E \rightarrow (E)$
	$S \rightarrow (S)$		$E \rightarrow a$
	$S \rightarrow p$		
	$S \rightarrow q$		

23. A grammar $G = (N, T, P, S)$ is said to be self-embedding if there exists a non-terminal $A \in N$ such that $A \overset{*}{\Rightarrow} \alpha A \beta$, $\alpha, \beta \in (N \cup T)^+$. If a grammar is non-self-embedding, it generates a regular set. Prove.

24. A CFG $G = (N, T, P, S)$ is said to be invertible if $A \rightarrow \alpha$ and $B \rightarrow \alpha$ implies $A = B$. For each CFG G, there is an invertible CFG G' such that $L(G) = L(G')$. Prove.

25. For each CFG $G = (N, T, P, S)$ there is an invertible CFG, $G' = (N', T, P', S')$ such that $L(G) = L(G')$. Moreover

    a. $A \rightarrow \varepsilon$ is in P' if and only if $\varepsilon \in L(G)$ and $A = S'$

    b. S' does not appear on the right-hand side of any rule in P'

26. Let L be a CFL. Then show that L can be generated by a CFG $G = (N, T, P, S)$ with the rules of the following forms:

    $S \rightarrow \varepsilon$

    $A \rightarrow a, a \in T$

    $A \rightarrow B, B \in N - \{S\}$

    $A \rightarrow \alpha BC\beta$, $\alpha, \beta \in ((N \cup T) - \{S\})^*$, $B, C \in (N \cup T) - \{S\}$ and either $B \in T$ or $C \in T$.

Finite State Automata

A language is a subset of the set of strings over an alphabet. In Chapter 2, we have seen how a language can be generated by a grammar. A language can also be recognized by a machine. Such a device is called a recognition device. Hence, a language can have a representation in terms of a generative device as a grammar as well as in terms of a recognition device which is called an acceptor. The simplest machine or recognition device is the finite state automaton which we discuss in this chapter and in the next two chapters. Apart from these two types of representation, there are other representations like regular expressions, which is also discussed in this chapter.

Consider a man watching a TV in his room. The TV is in 'on' state. When it is switched off, the TV goes to 'off' state. When it is switched on, it again goes to 'on' state. This can be represented by the following Figure.

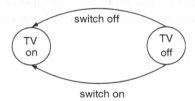

Figure 3.1. An example of FSA

The above Figure 3.1 is called a state diagram.

Consider another example, a set of processes currently on a single processor. Some scheduling algorithm allots them time on the processors. The states in which a system can be are 'wait,' 'run,' 'start,' 'end.' The connections between them can be brought out by the following figure (Figure 3.2).

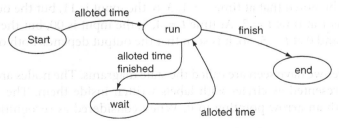

Figure 3.2. Another example of FSA

When the schedule allots time, the process goes from 'start' state to 'run' state. When the allotted time is finished, it goes from 'run' state to 'wait' state. When the job is finished, it goes to the 'end' state.

As another example, consider a binary serial adder. At any time it gets two binary inputs x_1 and x_2. The adder can be in any one of the states 'carry' or 'no carry.' The four possibilities for the inputs $x_1 x_2$ are 00, 01, 10, and 11. Initially, the adder is in the 'no carry' state. The working of the serial adder can be represented by the following figure (Figure 3.3).

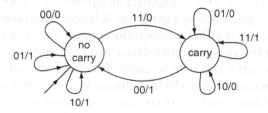

Figure 3.3. A binary serial adder

$p \xrightarrow{x_1 x_2 / x_3} q$ denotes that when the adder is in state p and gets input $x_1 x_2$, it goes to state q and outputs x_3. The input and output on a transition from p to q is denoted by i/o. It can be seen that suppose the two binary numbers to be added are 100101 and 100111.

Time 6 5 4 3 2 1
     1 0 0 1 0 1
     1 0 0 1 1 1

The input at time $t = 1$ is 11 and the output is 0, and the machine goes to 'carry' state. The output is 0. Here at time $t = 2$, the input is 01; the output is 0 and the machine remains in 'carry' state. At time $t = 3$, it gets 11 and outputs 1 and remains in 'carry' state. At time $t = 4$, the input is 00; the machine outputs 1 and goes to 'no carry' state. At time $t = 5$, the input is 00; the output is 0 and the machine remains in 'no carry' state. At time $t = 6$, the input is 11; the machine outputs 0 and goes to 'carry' state. The input stops here. At time $t = 7$, no input is there (and this is taken as 00) and the output is 1.

It should be noted that at time $t = 1, 3, 6$, the input is 11, but the output is 0 at $t = 1, 6$ and is 1 at time $t = 3$. At time $t = 4, 5$, the input is 00, but the output is 1 at time $t = 4$ and 0 at $t = 5$. So, it is seen that the output depends both on the input and the state.

The figures we have seen are called the state diagrams. The nodes are the states. They are represented as circles with labels written inside them. The initial state is marked with an arrow pointing to it. When considered as recognition devices, the final states are represented as double circles. The transition from one state to another is represented by directed edge.

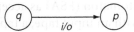

Figure 3.4.   Representation of a transition

The above figure (Figure 3.4) indicates that in state q when the machine gets input i, it goes to state p and outputs o.

Let us consider one more example of a state diagram given in Figure 3.5. The input and output alphabets are $\{0, 1\}$. For the input 011010011, the output is 001101001 and machine is in q_1 state. It can be seen that the first is 0 and afterwards, the output is the symbol read at the previous instant. It can also be noted that the machine goes to q_1 after reading a 1 and goes to q_0 after reading a 0. It should also be noted that when it goes from state q_0 it outputs a 0 and when it goes from state q_1, it outputs a 1. This machine is called a one-moment delay machine.

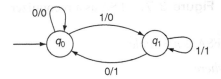

Figure 3.5.   One-moment delay machine

One can try to construct two-moment delay machine and three-moment delay machines. The idea for such construction is that for two-moment delay machine last two inputs must be remembered and for three-moment delay machine, last three inputs should be remembered.

For example, construct a finite state machine which reads a binary string and outputs a 0, if the number of 1's it has read is even and 1 if the number of 1's is odd. Such a machine is called a parity checker.

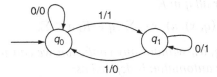

Figure 3.6.   Parity checker

The above state diagram represents such a machine (Figure 3.6).

3.1 Deterministic Finite State Automaton (DFSA)

So far we have considered the finite state machine as an input/output device. We can also look at the finite state automaton (FSA) as accepting languages, i.e., sets of strings. We can look at the FSA with an input tape, a tape head, and a finite control (which denotes the state) (Figure 3.7).

The input string is placed on the input tape. Each cell contains one symbol. The tape head initially points to the leftmost symbol. At any stage, depending on the state and the symbol read, the automaton changes its state and moves its tape head one cell to the right. The string on the input tape is accepted, if the automaton goes to one of the designated final states, after reading the whole of the input. The formal definition is as follows.

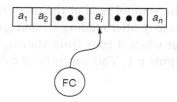

Figure 3.7.   FSA as a recognizer

Definition 3.1   *A DFSA is a 5-tuple*

$M = (K, \Sigma, \delta, q_0, F)$, *where*

- *K is a finite set of states*
- Σ *is a finite set of input symbols*
- q_0 *in K is the start state or initial state*
- $F \subseteq K$ *is set of final states*
- δ, *the transition function is a mapping from $K \times \Sigma$ to K.*

$\delta(q, a) = p$ *means, if the automaton is in state q and reading a symbol a, it goes to state p in the next instant, moving the pointer one cell to the right. δ is extended as $\hat{\delta}$ to $K \times \Sigma^*$ as follows:*

- $\hat{\delta}(q, \varepsilon) = q$ *for all q in K*
- $\hat{\delta}(q, xa) = \delta(\hat{\delta}(q, x), a), x \in \Sigma^*, q \in K, a \in \Sigma.$

Since $\hat{\delta}(q, a) = \delta(q, a)$, without any confusion we can use δ for $\hat{\delta}$ also. The language accepted by the automaton is defined as:

- $T(M) = \{w | w \in T^*, \delta(q_0, w) \in F\}.$

Example 3.1   Let a *DFSA* have state set $\{q_0, q_1, q_2, D\}$; q_0 is the initial state; q_2 is the only final state. The state diagram of the DFSA is in Figure 3.8.

The behavior of the machine on string aaabb can be represented as follows:

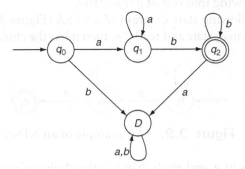

Figure 3.8. DFSA accepting $\{a^n b^m \mid n, m \geq 1\}$

$a\,a\,a\,b\,b$
↑
q_0

$a\,a\,a\,b\,b$
  ↑
  q_1

$a\,a\,a\,b\,b$
    ↑
    q_1

$a\,a\,a\,b\,b$
      ↑
      q_1

$a\,a\,a\,b\,b$
        ↑
        q_2

$a\,a\,a\,b\,b$
          ↑
          q_2

After reading *aaabb*, the automaton reaches a final state. It is easy to see that

$$T(M) = \{a^n b^m \mid n, m \geq 1\}$$

There is a reason for naming the fourth state as D. Once the control goes to D, it cannot accept the string, as from D the automaton cannot go to a final state. On further reading, for any symbol the state remains as D. Such a state is called a dead state or a sink state.

3.2 Non-deterministic Finite State Automaton (NFSA)

In Section 3.1, we have seen what is meant by a DFSA. If the machine is in a particular state and reads an input symbol, the next state is uniquely determined.

In contrast, we can also have a non-deterministic FSA (NSFA), where the machine has the choice of moving into one of a few states.

Consider the following state diagram of a NFSA (Figure 3.9).

If the machine is in q_0 state and reads 'a,' then it has the choice of going to q_0 or q_1.

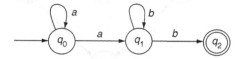

Figure 3.9. An example of an NFSA

If the machine is in q_1 and reads 'b,' it has the choice of going to q_1 or q_2. Hence, the machine is non-deterministic. It is not difficult to see that the language accepted is $\{a^n b^m | n, m \geq 1\}$. On a string $aaabb$, the transition can be looked at as follows:

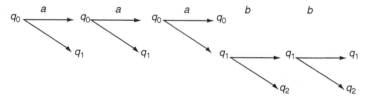

Figure 3.10. Transition sequences for $aaabb$

Starting on the input tape with $aaabb$ in state q_0, after reading a, the automaton can be in q_0 or q_1. From q_0, after reading the second a, it can be in state q_0 or q_1. From q_1, it cannot read a. From Figure 3.10, it can be seen that after reading $aaabb$, the automaton can be in state q_1 or q_2. If there is a sequence of moves which takes the automaton to a final state, then the input is accepted. In this example, the sequence is:

$$q_0 \xrightarrow{a} q_0 \xrightarrow{a} q_0 \xrightarrow{a} q_1 \xrightarrow{b} q_1 \xrightarrow{b} q_2 \qquad (3.1)$$

Now, we give the formal definition of NFSA.

Definition 3.2   A NFSA is a 5-tuple $M = (K, \Sigma, \delta, q_0, F)$, where $K, \Sigma, \delta, q_0, F$ are as given for DFSA and δ, the transition function is a mapping from $K \times \Sigma$ into finite subsets of K.

The mappings are of the form $\delta(q, a) = \{p_1, \ldots, p_r\}$, which means if the automaton is in state q and reads 'a' then it can go to any one of the states $p_1, \ldots, p_r$, δ is extended as $\hat{\delta}$ to $K \times \Sigma^*$ as follows:

$$\hat{\delta}(q, \varepsilon) = \{q\} \quad \text{for all } q \text{ in } K.$$

If P is a subset of K,

$$\delta(P, a) = \bigcup_{p \in P} \delta(p, a)$$

$$\hat{\delta}(q, xa) = \delta(\hat{\delta}(q, x), a)$$

$$\hat{\delta}(P,x) = \bigcup_{p \in P} \hat{\delta}(p,x)$$

Since $\delta(q. a)$ and $\hat{\delta}(q. a)$ are equal for $a \in \Sigma$, we can use the same symbol δ for $\hat{\delta}$ also.

The set of strings accepted by the automaton is denoted by $T(M)$.

$T(M) = \{w | w \in T^*, \delta(q_0, w)$ contains a state from $F\}$.

The automaton can be represented by a state table also. For example, the state diagram given in Figure 3.9 can be represented as the state table given in Figure 3.11.

There is a row corresponding to each state and a column corresponding to each input symbol. The initial state is marked with an arrow and the final state with a circle. In the case of NFSA, each cell contains a subset of states and in the case of DFSA each cell contains a single state.

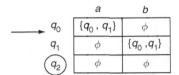

Figure 3.11. State table

Example 3.2 The state diagram of an NFSA which accepts binary strings which have at least one pair '00' or one pair '11' is in Figure 3.12.

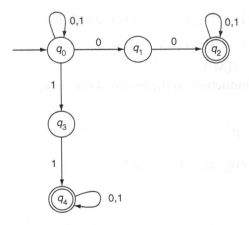

Figure 3.12. State diagram for Example 3.2

Example 3.3 The state diagram of an NFSA which accepts binary strings which end with '00' or '11' is in Figure 3.13.

By making the automaton non-deterministic do we get any additional power? The answer is negative. It is seen that NFSA are equivalent to deterministic automata in language accepting power.

Theorem 3.1   *If L is accepted by a NFSA then L is accepted by a DFSA*

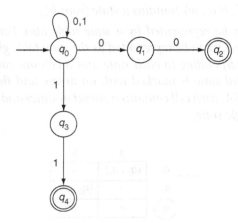

Figure 3.13.   State diagram for Example 3.3

Proof   Let L be accepted by a NFSA $M = (K, \Sigma, \delta, q_0, F)$. Then, we construct a DFSA $M' = (K', \Sigma, \delta', q'_0, F')$ as follows: $K' = P(K)$, power set of K. Corresponding to each subset of K, we have a state in $K'. q'_0$ corresponds to the subset containing q_0 alone. F' consists of states corresponding to subsets having at least one state from F. We define δ' as follows:

$$\delta'([q_1, \ldots, q_k], a) = [r_1, r_2, \ldots, r_s] \text{ if and only if}$$

$$\delta(\{q_1, \ldots, q_k\}, a) = \{r_1, r_2, \ldots, r_s\}.$$

We show that $T(M) = T(M')$.

We prove this by induction on the length of the string.

We show that:

$$\delta'(q'_0, x) = [p_1, \ldots, p_r]$$

if and only if $\delta(q_0, x) = \{p_1, \ldots, p_r\}.$

Basis

$|x| = 0$ *i.e.*, $x = \varepsilon$

$\delta'(q'_0, \varepsilon) = q'_0 = [q_0]$

$\delta(q_0, \varepsilon) = \{q_0\}$

Induction

Assume that the result is true for strings x of length upto m. We have to prove for string of length $m + 1$. By induction hypothesis

$$\delta'(q'_0, x) = [p_1, \ldots, p_r]$$

if and only if $\delta(q_0, x) = \{p_1, \ldots, p_r\}$.

$$\delta'(q'_0, xa) = \delta'([p_1, \ldots, p_r], a),$$

$$\delta(q_0, xa) = \bigcup_{p \in P} \delta(p, a),$$

where $P = \{p_1, \ldots, p_r\}$.

Suppose $\bigcup_{p \in P} \delta(p, a) = \{s_1, \ldots, s_m\}$

$$\delta(\{p_1, \ldots, p_r\}, a) = \{s_1, \ldots, s_m\}.$$

By our construction

$$\delta'([p_1, \ldots, p_r], a) = [s_1, \ldots, s_m] \text{ and hence,}$$

$$\delta'(q'_0, xa) = \delta'([p_1, \ldots, p_r], a) = [s_1, \ldots, s_m].$$

In M', any state representing a subset having a state from F is in F'. So, if a string w is accepted in M, there is a sequence of states which takes M to a final state f and M' simulating M will be in a state representing a subset containing f. Thus, $L(M) = L(M')$.

Example 3.4   Let us construct the DFSA for the NFSA given by the table in Figure 3.11. We construct the table for DFSA.

$$\delta'([q_0, q_1], a) = [\ \delta(q_0, a) \cup \delta(q_1, a)] \tag{3.2}$$

$$= [\{q_0, q_1\} \cup \phi] \tag{3.3}$$

$$= [q_0, q_1] \tag{3.4}$$

$$\delta'([q_0, q_1], b) = [\delta(q_0, b) \cup \delta(q_1, b)] \tag{3.5}$$

$$= [\varphi \cup \{q_1, q_2\}] \tag{3.6}$$

$$= [q_1, q_2] \tag{3.7}$$

The state diagram is given in Figure 3.14.

Other states $[q_1]$, $[q_2]$, $[q_0, q_2]$, $[q_0, q_1, q_2]$ are not accessible from $[q_0]$ and hence the transitions involving them are not shown.

Note the similarity between the Figure 3.8 and Figure 3.14.

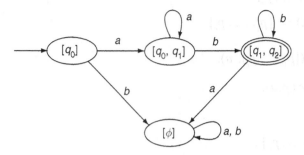

Figure 3.14. DFSA for the NFSA in Figure 3.9

NFSA with ε-transitions

Having defined NFSA, we now try to include ε-transition to NFSA. We allow the automaton to change state without reading any symbol. This is represented by an ε-transition (Figure 3.15).

Figure 3.15. ε-transition

Example 3.5

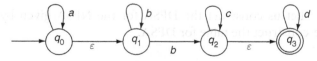

Figure 3.16. An example of NFSA with ε-transitions

In Figure 3.16, q_0 is the initial state and q_3 is final state. There is an ε-transition from q_0 to q_1 and another from q_2 to q_3. It is not difficult to see that the set of strings which take the automaton from q_0 to q_3 can be represented by $\{a^n b^m c^p d^q / m \geq 1, n, p, q \geq 0\}$.

By adding ε-transition do we get an additional power? The answer is negative. For any NFSA with ε-transition, we can construct an NFSA without ε-transitions.

Definition 3.3 *An NFSA with ε-transition is a 5-tuple $M = (K, \Sigma, \delta, q_0, F)$, where K, Σ, q_0, F are as defined for NFSA and δ is a mapping from $K \times (\Sigma \cup \{\varepsilon\})$ into finite subsets of K.*

δ can be extended as $\hat{\delta}$ to $K \times \Sigma^*$ as follows. First, we define the ε-closure of a state q. It is the set of states which can be reached from q by reading ε only. Of course, ε-closure of a state includes itself.

$\hat{\delta}(q, \varepsilon) = \varepsilon$-closure$(q)$.

For w in Σ^* and a in Σ,

$\hat{\delta}(q, wa) = \varepsilon$-closure$(P)$, where $P = \{p |$ for some r in $\hat{\delta}(q, w)$, p is in $\delta(r, a)\}$. Extending δ and $\hat{\delta}$ to a set of states, we get:

$$\delta(Q, a) = \bigcup\nolimits_{q \ in \ Q} \delta(q, a)$$

$$\hat{\delta}(Q, w) = \bigcup\nolimits_{q \ in \ Q} \hat{\delta}(q, w)$$

The language accepted is defined as:

$T(M) = \{w | \hat{\delta}(q_0, w)$ contains a state in $F\}$.

Theorem 3.2   Let L be accepted by a NFSA with ε-moves. Then L can be accepted by a NFSA without ε-moves.

Proof   Let L be accepted by a NFSA with ε-moves $M = (K, \Sigma, \delta, q_0, F)$. Then, we construct a NFSA $M' = (K, \Sigma, \delta', q_0, F')$ without ε-moves for accepting L as follows.

$F' = F \cup \{q_0\}$ if ε-closure of q_0 contains a state from F.

$\quad = F$ otherwise.

$\delta'(q, a) = \hat{\delta}(q, a)$.

We should show $T(M) = T(M')$.

We wish to show by induction on the length of the string x accepted that $\delta'(q_0, x) = \hat{\delta}(q_0, x)$.

We start the basis with $|x| = 1$ because for $|x| = 0$, i.e., $x = \varepsilon$ this may not hold. We may have $\delta'(q_0, \varepsilon) = \{q_0\}$ and $\hat{\delta}(q_0, \varepsilon) = \varepsilon$-closure of q_0 which may include other states.

Basis

$|x| = 1$. Then x is a symbol of Σ say a, and $\delta'(q_0, a) = \hat{\delta}(q_0, a)$ by our definition of δ'.

Induction

$|x| > 1$. Then $x = ya$ for some $y \in \Sigma^*$ and $a \in \Sigma$.
Then $\delta'(q_0, ya) = \delta'(\delta'(q_0, y), a)$.
By the inductive hypothesis $\delta'(q_0, y) = \hat{\delta}(q_0, y)$.
Let $\hat{\delta}(q_0, y) = P$.

$$\delta'(P,a)= \bigcup_{p\in P}\delta'(p,a)=\bigcup_{p\in P}\hat{\delta}(p,a)$$

$$\bigcup_{p\in P}\hat{\delta}(p,a)=\hat{\delta}(q_0,ya)$$

Therefore $\delta'(q_0,ya)=\hat{\delta}(q_0,ya)$

It should be noted that $\delta'(q_0,x)$ contains a state in F' if and only if $\hat{\delta}(q_0,x)$ contains a state in F.

For ε, this is clear from the definition. For $x=ya$, if $\hat{\delta}(q_0,x)$ contains a state from F, then surely $\delta'(q_0,x)$ contains the same state in F'. Conversely, if $\delta'(q_0,x)$ contains a state from F' other than q_0, then $\delta'(q_0,x)$ contains this state of F. The only case the problem can arise is when $\delta'(q_0,x)$ contains q_0 and q_0 is not in F. This can happen if ε-closure of q_0 contains some other states. In this case $\hat{\delta}(q_0,x)=\varepsilon$-closure of $\delta(\hat{\delta}(q_0,y),a)$. Some state of q other than q_0 must have been reached from q_0 and this must be in $\hat{\delta}(q_0,x)$.

Example 3.6 Consider the ε-NFSA of Example 3.5. By our construction, we get the NFSA without ε-moves given in Figure 3.17.

ε-closure of $(q_0)=\{q_0,q_1\}$
ε-closure of $(q_1)=\{q_1\}$
ε-closure of $(q_2)=\{q_2,q_3\}$
ε-closure of $(q_3)=\{q_3\}$

It is not difficult to see that the language accepted by the above NFSA $=\{a^n b^m c^p d^q \mid m\geq 1, n, p, q\geq 0\}$.

3.3 Regular Expressions

Regular expressions are another way of specifying regular sets.

Definition 3.4 *Let Σ be an alphabet. For each a in Σ, **a** is a regular expression representing the regular set $\{a\}$. ϕ is a regular expression representing the empty set. ε is a regular expression representing the set $\{\varepsilon\}$.*

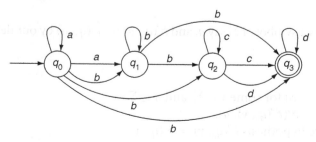

Figure 3.17. NFSA without ε-moves for Example 3.5

If r_1 and r_2 are regular expressions representing the regular sets R_1 and R_2 respectively, then $r_1 + r_2$ is a regular expression representing $R_1 \cup R_2$. $r_1 r_2$ is a regular expression representing $R_1 R_2$. r_1^* is a regular expression representing R_1^*.

Any expression obtained from ϕ, ε, $a(a \in \Sigma)$, using the above operations and parentheses where required, is a regular expression.

Example 3.7 $(ab)^* abcd$ represent the regular set:

$$\{(ab)^n cd \mid n \geq 1\}$$

Example 3.8 $(a + b)^*(c + d)(a + b)^*$ is a regular expression representing the regular set:

$$\{w_1 c w_2 \mid w_1, w_2 \text{ are strings of } a's \text{ and } b's \text{ including } \varepsilon\} \cup$$

$$\{w_1 d w_2 \mid w_1, w_2 \text{ are strings of } a's \text{ and } b's \text{ including } \varepsilon\}$$

Now, we shall see how to construct an NFSA with ε-moves from a regular expression and also how to get a regular expression from a DFSA.

Theorem 3.3 *If r is a regular expression representing a regular set, we can construct an NFSA with ε-moves to accept r.*

Proof r is obtained from a, $(a \in \Sigma)$, ε, ϕ by finite number of applications of $+$, $\cdot$ and $*$ ($\cdot$ is usually left out).

For ε, ϕ and a we can construct NFSA with ε-moves as given in Figure 3.18.

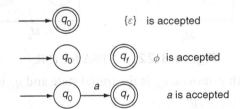

Figure 3.18.   NFSA for ε, ϕ, and a

Let r_1 represent the regular set R_1 and R_1 is accepted by the NFSA M_1 with ε-transitions (Figure 3.19).

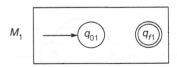

Figure 3.19. M_1 accepting R_1

Without loss of generality, we can assume that each such NFSA with ε-moves has only one final state.

R_2 is similarly accepted by an NFSA M_2 with ε-transition (Figure 3.20).

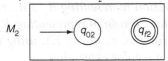

Figure 3.20. M_2 accepting R_2

Now, we can easily see that $R_1 \cup R_2$ (represented by $r_1 + r_2$) is accepted by the NFSA given in Figure 3.21.

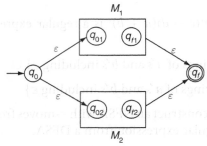

Figure 3.21. NFSA for $R_1 \cup R_2$

For this NFSA, q_0 is the 'start' state and q_f is the 'end' state.

$R_1 R_2$ represented by $r_1 r_2$ is accepted by the NFSA with ε-moves given in Figure 3.22.

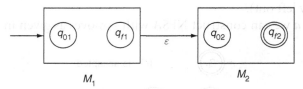

Figure 3.22. NFSA for $R_1 R_2$

For this NFSA with ε-moves, q_{01} is the initial state and q_{f2} is the final state.

$$R_1^* = R_1^0 \cup R_1^1 \cup R_1^2 \cup \ldots \cup R_1^k \cup \ldots$$

$R_1^0 = \{\varepsilon\}$ and $R_1^1 = R_1$.

R_1^* represented by r_1^* is accepted by the NFSA with ε-moves given in Figure 3.23.

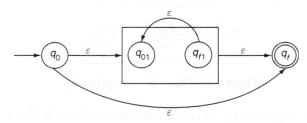

Figure 3.23. NFSA for R_1^*

For this NFSA with ε-moves, q_0 is the initial state and q_f is the final state. It can be seen that R_1^* contains strings of the form $x_1 x_2 \ldots x_k$ each $x_i \in R_1$. To accept this string, the control goes from q_0 to q_{01} and then after reading x_1 and reaching q_{f1}, it goes to q_{01}, by an ε-transition. From q_{01}, it again reads x_2 and goes to q_{f1}. This can be repeated a number (k) of times and finally the control goes to q_f from q_{f1} by an ε-transition. $R_1^0 = \{\varepsilon\}$ is accepted by going to q_f from q_0 by an ε-transition.

Thus, we have seen that for a given regular expression one can construct an equivalent NFSA with ε-transitions. ☐

We know that we can construct an equivalent NFSA without ε-transitions from this, and can construct a DFSA. (Figure 3.24).

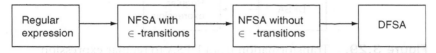

Figure 3.24. Transformation from regular expression to DFSA

Example 3.9 Consider a regular expression aa^*bb^*. a and b are accepted by NFSA with ε-moves given in Figure 3.25.

Figure 3.25. NFSA for a and b

a^* and b^* are accepted by NFSA with ε-moves given in Figure 3.26.

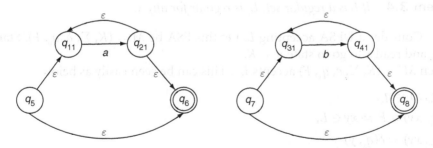

Figure 3.26. NFSA for a^* and b^*

aa^*bb^* will be accepted by NFSA with ε-moves given in Figure 3.27.

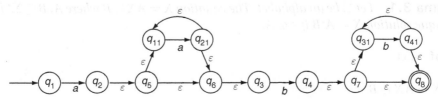

Figure 3.27. NFSA for aa^*bb^*

But we have already seen that a simple NFSA can be drawn easily for this as in Figure 3.28.

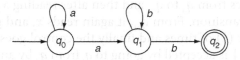

Figure 3.28. Simple NFSA for aa^*bb^*

Next, we see that for a given DFSA how the corresponding regular expression can be found. (Figure 3.29).

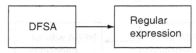

Figure 3.29. Transformation from DFSA to regular expression

This along with the diagram in Figure 3.24 brings out the equivalence between DFSA, NFSA, NFSA with ε-moves and regular expressions.

Definition 3.5 *Let $L \subseteq \Sigma^*$ be a language and x be a string in Σ^*. Then the derivative of L with respect to x is defined as:*

$$L_x = \{y \in \Sigma^* / xy \in L\}.$$

It is sometimes denoted as $\partial_x L$.

Theorem 3.4 *If L is a regular set, L_x is regular for any x.*

Proof Consider a DFSA accepting L. Let this FSA be $M = (K, \Sigma, \delta, q_0, F)$. Start from q_0 and read x to go to state $q_x \in K$.

Then $M' = (K, \Sigma, \delta, q_x, F)$ accepts L_x. This can be seen easily as below.

$\delta(q_0, x) = q_x,$

$\delta(q_0, xy) \in F \Leftrightarrow xy \in L,$

$\delta(q_0, xy) = \delta(q_x, y)$

$\delta(q_x, y) \in F \Leftrightarrow y \in L_x$

$\therefore M'$ accepts L_x. $\qquad\square$

Lemma 3.1 *Let Σ be an alphabet. The equation $X = AX \cup B$ where $A, B \subseteq \Sigma^*$ has a unique solution $X = A^*B$ if $\varepsilon \notin A$.*

Proof Let

$X = AX \cup B$

$\quad = A(AX \cup B) \cup B$

$\quad = A^2X \cup AB \cup B$

$$= A^2 (AX \cup B) \cup AB \cup B$$
$$= A^3X \cup A^2B \cup AB \cup B$$
$$\vdots$$
$$= A^{n+1}X \cup A^nB \cup A^{n-1}B \cup \cdots \cup AB \cup B \tag{3.8}$$

Since $\varepsilon \notin A$, any string in A^k will have minimum length k. To show $X = A^*B$. Let $w \in X$ and $|w| = n$. We have:

$$X = A^{n+1}X \cup A^nB \cup \cdots \cup AB \cup B \tag{3.9}$$

Since any string in $A^{n+1}X$ will have minimum length $n + 1$, w will belong to one of A^kB, $k \leq n$. Hence, $w \in A^*B$.

On the other hand, let $w \in A^*B$. To prove $w \in X$.
Since $|w| = n$, $w \in A^kB$ for some $k \leq n$. Therefore from Equation (3.9) $w \in X$.
Hence, we find that the unique solution for $X = AX + B$ is $X = A^*B$.

Note: If $\varepsilon \in A$, the solution will not be unique. Any A^*C, where $C \supseteq B$, will be a solution.

Next we give an algorithm to find the regular expression corresponding to a *DFSA*.

Algorithm

Let $M = (K, \Sigma, \delta, q_0, F)$ be the DFSA.
$\Sigma = \{a_1, a_2, \ldots, a_k\}$, $K = \{q_0, q_1, \ldots, q_{n-1}\}$.

Step 1 Write an equation for each state in K.

$q = a_1 q_{i1} + a_2 q_{i2} + \cdots + a_k q_{ik}$
if q is not a final state and $\delta(q, a_j) = q_{ij}$ $1 \leq j \leq k$
$q = a_1 q_{i1} + a_2 q_{i2} + \cdots + a_k q_{ik} + \lambda$
if q is a final state and $\delta(q, a_j) = q_{ij}$ $1 \leq j \leq k$.

Step 2 Take the n equations with n variables q_i, $1 \leq i \leq n$, and solve for q_0 using Lemma 3.1 and substitution.

Step 3 Solution for q_0 gives the desired regular expression.

Let us execute this algorithm for the following DFSA given in Figure 3.30.

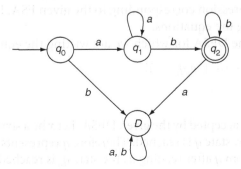

Figure 3.30. DFSA for aa^*bb^*

Step 1

$$q_0 = aq_1 + bD \tag{3.10}$$

$$q_1 = aq_1 + bq_2 \tag{3.11}$$

$$q_2 = aD + bq_2 + \lambda \tag{3.12}$$

$$D = aD + bD \tag{3.13}$$

Step 2

From Equation (3.13), Solving for q_0.

$$D = (a + b) D + \phi$$

Using Lemma 3.4.1

$$D = (a + b)^* \phi = \phi. \tag{3.14}$$

Using Equation (3.14) in Equations (3.10) and (3.12)

$$q_0 = aq_1 \tag{3.15}$$

$$q_1 = aq_1 + bq_2 \tag{3.16}$$

$$q_2 = bq_2 + \lambda \tag{3.17}$$

Note that we have got rid of one equation and one variable. In Equation (3.17) using Lemma 3.4.1, we get

$$q_2 = b^* \tag{3.18}$$

Now using Equation (3.18) in Equation (3.16)

$$q_1 = aq_1 + bb^* \tag{3.19}$$

We now have Equations (3.15) and (3.19). Again, we eliminated one equation and one variable.

Using Lemma 3.4.1 in Equation (3.19), we obtain:

$$q_1 = a^*bb^* \tag{3.20}$$

Using Equation (3.20) in Equation (3.15), we obtain:

$$q_0 = aa^*bb^* \tag{3.21}$$

This is the regular expression corresponding to the given FSA. Next, we see how we are justified in writing the equations.

Let q be the state of the DFSA for which we are writing the equation,

$$q = a_1 q_{i_1} + a_2 q_{i_2} + \cdots + a_k q_{i_k} + Y. \tag{3.22}$$

$$Y = \lambda \text{ or } \phi.$$

Let L be the regular set accepted by the given DFSA. Let x be a string such that starting from q_0, after reading x, state q is reached. Therefore q represents L_x, the derivative of L with respect to x. From q after reading a_j, the state q_{ij} is reached.

$$L_x = q = a_1 L_{xa_1} + a_2 L_{xa_2} + \cdots + a_k L_{xa_k} + Y. \tag{3.23}$$

$a_j L_{xa_j}$ represents the set of strings in L_x beginning with a_j. Hence, Equation (3.23) represents the partition of L_x into strings beginning with a_1, a_2, and so on. If L_x contains ε, then $Y = \varepsilon$ otherwise $Y = \phi$. It should be noted that when L_x contains ε, q is a final state and so $x \in L$.

It should also be noted that considering each state as a variable q_j, we have n equation in n variables. Using Lemma 3.1, and substitution, each time one equation is removed while one variable is eliminated. The solution for q_0 is $L_\varepsilon = L$. This gives the required regular expression.

In this chapter, we have considered the definition of *DFSA*, *NFSA*, *NFSA* with ε-moves and regular expressions, and shown the equivalence among them.

Problems and Solutions

Problem 1.   Construct DFSA for the following sets of strings.

a. The set of strings over $\{a, b\}$ having an even number of a's and odd number of b's.

Solution. It should be noted that the set of strings over $\Sigma = \{a, b\}$ can be divided into four classes.

  1. having even number of a's and even number of b's.

  2. having even number of a's and odd number of b's.

  3. having odd number of a's and even number of b's.

  4. having odd number of a's and odd number of b's.

Strings in class (i) take the machine to q_0, class (ii) to q_3, class (iii) to q_1, and class (iv) to q_2 (Figure 3.31).

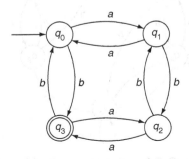

Figure 3.31.   Solution to Problem 1.a

b. The set of strings over {*a*, *b*} whose length is divisible by 4 (Figure 3.32).

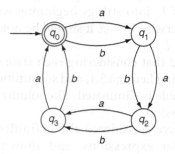

Figure 3.32. Solution to Problem 1.b

c. The set of strings over {*a*, *b*, *c*} having *bca* as substring (Figure 3.33).

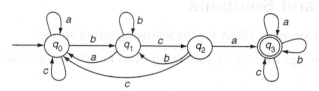

Figure 3.33. Solution to Problem 1.c

d. The set of strings over {*a*, *b*, *c*} in which the substring *abc* occurs an even number of times (possibly zero) (Figure 3.34).

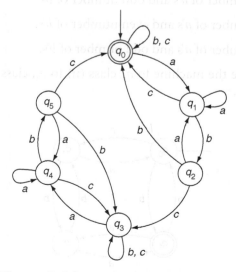

Figure 3.34. Solution to Problem 1.d

Problem 2.

a. Describe the language accepted by the following DFSA in Figure 3.35.

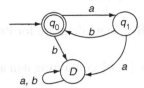

Figure 3.35. State diagram for Problem 2.a

Solution. $L = \{(ab)^n | n \geq 0\}$.

b. Describe the language accepted by the following DFSA in Figure 3.36.

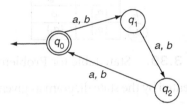

Figure 3.36. State diagram for Problem 2.b

Solution. $L =$ set of strings in $(a, b)^*$ whose length is divisible by 3.

c. Describe the language accepted by the following DFSA in Figure 3.37.

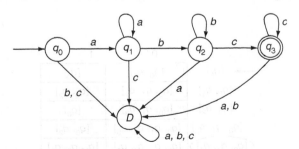

Figure 3.37. State diagram for Problem 2.c

Solution. $L = \{a^n b^m c^p | n, m, p \geq 1\}$.

d. Describe the language accepted by the following DFSA in Figure 3.38.

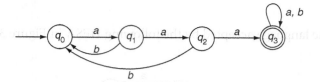

Figure 3.38. State diagram for Problem 2.d

Solution. Set of strings over $\{a, b\}$ containing aaa as a substring.

Problem 3.

a. For the following NFSA find equivalent DFSA (Figure 3.39).

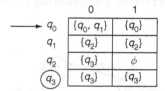

	0	1
q_0	$\{q_0, q_1\}$	$\{q_0\}$
q_1	$\{q_2\}$	$\{q_2\}$
q_2	$\{q_3\}$	ϕ
q_3	$\{q_3\}$	$\{q_3\}$

Figure 3.39. State table for Problem 3.a

The state table can be represented by the state diagram as given below (Figure 3.40).

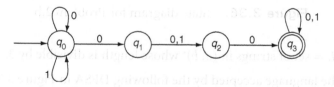

Figure 3.40. State diagram for Problem 3.a

Solution.

	0	1
$[q_0]$	$[q_0, q_1]$	$[q_0]$
$[q_0, q_1]$	$[q_0, q_1, q_2]$	$[q_0, q_2]$
$[q_0, q_2]$	$[q_0, q_1, q_3]$	$[q_0]$
$[q_0, q_1, q_2]$	$[q_0, q_1, q_2, q_3]$	$[q_0, q_2]$
$[q_0, q_1, q_3]$	$[q_0, q_1, q_2, q_3]$	$[q_0, q_2, q_3]$
$[q_0, q_1, q_2, q_3]$	$[q_0, q_1, q_2, q_3]$	$[q_0, q_2, q_3]$
$[q_0, q_2, q_3]$	$[q_0, q_1, q_3]$	$[q_0, q_3]$
$[q_0, q_3]$	$[q_0, q_1, q_3]$	$[q_0, q_3]$

Figure 3.41. Solution to Problem 3.a

b. For the following NFSA find equivalent DFSA (Figure 3.42).

	0	1
$\rightarrow q_0$	$\{q_0, q_1\}$	$\{q_0, q_3\}$
q_1	$\{q_2\}$	ϕ
(q_2)	ϕ	ϕ
q_3	ϕ	$\{q_4\}$
(q_4)	ϕ	ϕ

Figure 3.42. State table for Problem 3.b

The state table can be represented by the state diagram given in Figure 3.13.

Solution.

	0	1
$\rightarrow [q_0]$	$[q_0, q_1]$	$[q_0, q_3]$
$[q_0, q_1]$	$[q_0, q_1, q_2]$	$[q_0, q_3]$
$[q_0, q_3]$	$[q_0, q_1]$	$[q_0, q_3, q_4]$
$([q_0, q_1, q_2])$	$[q_0, q_1, q_2]$	$[q_0, q_3]$
$([q_0, q_3, q_4])$	$[q_0, q_1]$	$[q_0, q_3, q_4]$

Figure 3.43. Solution to Problem 3.b

c. For the following NFSA find equivalent DFSA (Figure 3.44).

	0	1
$\rightarrow q_0$	$\{q_0, q_1\}$	$\{q_0, q_3\}$
q_1	$\{q_2\}$	ϕ
(q_2)	$\{q_2\}$	$\{q_2\}$
q_3	ϕ	$\{q_4\}$
(q_4)	$\{q_4\}$	$\{q_4\}$

Figure 3.44. State table for Problem 3.c

The state table can be represented by the state diagram given in Figure 3.12.

	0	1
$\rightarrow [q_0]$	$[q_0, q_1]$	$[q_0, q_3]$
$[q_0, q_1]$	$[q_0, q_1, q_2]$	$[q_0, q_3]$
$[q_0, q_3]$	$[q_0, q_1]$	$[q_0, q_3, q_4]$
$([q_0, q_1, q_2])$	$[q_0, q_1, q_2]$	$[q_0, q_2, q_3]$
$([q_0, q_3, q_4])$	$[q_0, q_1, q_4]$	$[q_0, q_3, q_4]$
$([q_0, q_2, q_3])$	$[q_0, q_1, q_2]$	$[q_0, q_2, q_3, q_4]$
$([q_0, q_1, q_4])$	$[q_0, q_1, q_2, q_4]$	$[q_0, q_3, q_4]$
$([q_0, q_2, q_3, q_4])$	$[q_0, q_1, q_2, q_4]$	$[q_0, q_2, q_3, q_4]$
$([q_0, q_1, q_2, q_4])$	$[q_0, q_1, q_2, q_4]$	$[q_0, q_2, q_3, q_4]$

Figure 3.45. Solution to Problem 3.c

d. For the following NFSA find equivalent DFSA (Figure 3.46).

	0	1
→ q_0	$\{q_0, q_1\}$	$\{q_0\}$
q_1	$\{q_2\}$	$\{q_2\}$
q_2	$\{q_3\}$	$\{q_3\}$
((q_3))	ϕ	ϕ

Figure 3.46. State table for Problem 3.d

The state table can be represented by the state diagram given below (Figure 3.47:).

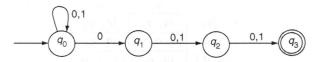

Figure 3.47. State diagram for Problem 3.d

Solution.

	0	1
→ $[q_0]$	$[q_0, q_1]$	$[q_0]$
$[q_0, q_1]$	$[q_0, q_1, q_2]$	$[q_0, q_2]$
$[q_0, q_2]$	$[q_0, q_1, q_3]$	$[q_0, q_3]$
$[q_0, q_1, q_2]$	$[q_0, q_1, q_2, q_3]$	$[q_0, q_2, q_3]$
$([q_0, q_1, q_3])$	$[q_0, q_1, q_2, q_3]$	$[q_0, q_2]$
$([q_0, q_3])$	$[q_0, q_1]$	$[q_0]$
$([q_0, q_1, q_2, q_3])$	$[q_0, q_1, q_2, q_3]$	$[q_0, q_2, q_3]$
$([q_0, q_2, q_3])$	$[q_0, q_1, q_3]$	$[q_0, q_3]$

Figure 3.48. Solution to Problem 3.d

Note: The language accepted is the set of strings over $\{0, 1\}$, where the third symbol from the end is a '0.' We note that the *DFSA* requires $2^3 = 8$ states. In general for a language over $\Sigma = \{0, 1\}$, if the *nth* element from the end is fixed, we can have a NFSA with $n + 1$ states, but the DFSA requires 2^n states.

Problem 4. Write regular expression for each of the following languages over the alphabet $\{a, b\}$.

1. The set of strings containing *ab* as a substring.

2. The set of strings having at most one pair of consecutive *a*'s and at most one pair of consecutive *b*'s.

3. The set of strings whose length is divisible by 6.

4. The set of strings whose 5*th* last symbol (5*th* symbol from the end) is *b*.

Solution.

1. $A = (a + b)^* ab(a + b)^*$

2. One pair of *a*'s but no pair of *b*'s $B_1 = (b + \varepsilon)(ab)^* aa(ba)^*(b + \varepsilon)$ One pair of *b*'s but no pair of *a*'s $B_2 = (a + \varepsilon)(ba)^* bb(ab)^*(a + \varepsilon)$ $B = B_1 + B_2$

   aa occurring before *bb*

   $C = (b + \varepsilon)(ab)^* \, aa(ba)^* \, bb(ab)^* \, (a + \varepsilon)$

   bb occurring before *aa*

   $D = (a + \varepsilon)(ba)^* \, bb(ab)^* \, aa(ba)^* \, (b + \varepsilon)$

   No pair of *a*'s and *b*'s

   $E = (b + \varepsilon)(ab)^* \, (a + \varepsilon)$

   Required regular expression is $B + C + D + E$

3. $[(a + b)^6]^*$

4. $(a + b)^* b(a + b)^4$

Exercises

1. The following are the state diagrams of two DFSA's M_1 and M_2. Answer the following questions about these machines (Figure 3.49)

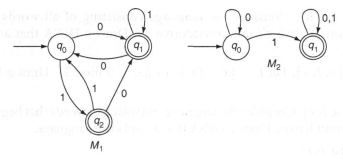

Figure 3.49.   State diagrams for Exercise 1

a. What is the start state of M_1?

b. What are the accepting states of M_1?

c. What is the start state of M_2?

d. What is the sequence of states does M_1 go through on input 0000111?

e. Does. M_1 accept 00001111?

f. Does M_2 accept ε?

2. Construct DFSA to accept the following languages.

   a. $\{a, b\}^+$

   b. $\{a, b\}^*$

   c. $\{(ab)^n | n \geq 1\}$

   d. $\{a^n b^m c^p | n, m, p \geq 1\}$

   e. $\{w | w \in \{a, b\}^*, w$ has an even number of a's and even number of b's$\}$

3. Find a DFSA for each of the following languages.

   a. $L = \{w | w$ is a binary string containing both substrings 010 and 101$\}$.

   b. For any fixed integer $k \geq 0$, $L = \{0^i w 1^i | w$ is a binary string and $0 \leq i \leq k\}$.

4. Suppose we restrict DFSA's so that they have at most one accepting state. Can any regular language L be recognized by this restricted form of DFSA? Justify your answer.

5. Design deterministic finite automata for each of the following sets:

   a. the set of all strings in $\{1, 2, 3\}^*$ containing 231 as substring.

   b. the set of strings $x \in \{0, 1\}^*$ such that $\#_0(x)$ is even and $\#_1(x)$ is a multiple of three.

   c. the set of strings in $(a)^*$ whose length is divisible by either 2 or 7.

6. Let $\Sigma = \{0, 1, 2, 3, 4, 5, 6, 7, 8, 9\}$. Consider the base 10 numbers formed by strings from Σ^*. 15 represents fifteen, 408 represents four hundred, and eight and so on. Let $L = \{x \in \Sigma^* |$ the numbers represented by x is exactly divisible by 7$\} = \{\epsilon, 0, 00, 000, ..., 7, 07, 007, ..., 14, 21, 28, 35, ...\}$. Find a DFSA that accepts L.

7. Let $\Sigma = \{a, b\}$. Consider the language consisting of all words that have neither consecutive a's nor consecutive b's. Draw a DFSA that accepts this language.

8. Let $\Sigma = \{a, b, c\}$. Let $L = \{x \in \{a, b, c\}^* || x| = 0 \mod 5\}$. Draw a DFSA that accepts L.

9. Let $\Sigma = \{a, b, c\}$. Consider the language consisting of words that begin and end with different letters. Draw a DFSA that accepts this language.

10. Let $\Sigma = \{a, b, c\}$.

    a. Draw a DFSA that rejects all words for which the last two letters match.

    b. Draw a DFSA that rejects all words for which the first two letters match.

11. Suppose we alter the definition of a DFSA so that once the automaton leaves its start state, it cannot return to its start state. For such a DFSA, if an input w causes it to take a transition from a state p to its start state q_0, where $p \neq q_0$, then the DFSA immediately halts and rejects w. Call this new type of DFSA as no-return-DFSA.

Prove that the class of languages recognized by no-return-DFSA is the class of regular languages.

12. Construct a NFSA for each of the languages given in problem no. 1,3,5,6,7,8,9.

13. Given a non-deterministic finite automaton M without ε-transitions, show that it is possible to construct a NFSA with ε-transitions M' such that:

   a. M' has exactly one start state and one end state

   b. $L(M) = L(M')$.

14. What is the language accepted by the NFSA M (Figure 3.50)?

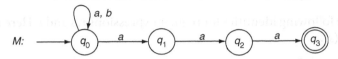

Figure 3.50.   State diagram for Exercise 14

15. Let $\Sigma = \{a, b\}$. Find a NFSA for each of the following languages:

   a. $\{x|x$ contains an even number of a's$\}$.

   b. $\{x|x$ contains an odd number of b's$\}$.

   c. $\{x|x$ contains an even number of a's and an odd number of b's$\}$

   d. $\{x|x$ contains an even number of a's or an odd number of b's$\}$

16. Suppose we alter the definition of an NFSA so that we now identify two types of states in its state set Q: the good states $G \subseteq Q$, and the bad states $B \subseteq Q$ where $G \cap B = \phi$. (Note that a state in Q may be neither good nor bad, but no state is both good and bad). The automata accepts input w if, considering all possible computations on w, some computation ends in G and no computation ends in B. Call this new type of NFSA as a good-bad NFSA.

Prove that the class of languages recognized by good-bad NFSAs is the class of regular languages.

17. In the questions below, given a language L we describe how to form a new language from the strings in L. Prove that if L is regular then the new languages are regular by constructing an NFSA for the new languages.

   a. $skip(L) = \{xy|xcy \in L$, where x and y are strings, c is a letter$\}$

   b. $suffix(L) = \{y|xy \in L, x, y$ are strings$\}$.

18. Convert the following two NFSA to equivalent DFSA using subset construction method (Figure 3.51).

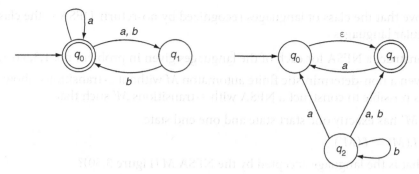

Figure 3.51. State diagrams for Exercise 18

19. Prove the following identities for regular expressions r, s and t. Here $r = s$ means $L(r) = L(s)$.

    a. $r + s = s + r$

    b. $\phi^* = \varepsilon$

    c. $(r^*s^*)^* = (r + s)^*$

    d. $(rs)^* r = r(sr)^*$

20. Construct a NFSA accepting the language denoted by the following regular expressions. Also convert the NFSA to an equivalent DFSA.

    a. $a^*ba^*ab^*$

    b. $a^*bb^*(a + b)ab^*$

    c. $b((aab^* + a^4)b)^*a$

21. Given the following DFSAs, construct equivalent regular expressions (Figure 3.52).

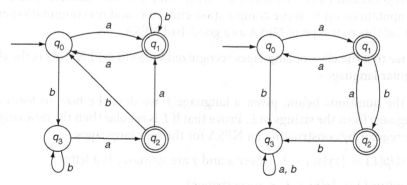

Figure 3.52. State diagrams for Exercise 21

22. Give an NFSA with four states equivalent to the regular expression $(01 + 011 + 0111)^*$. Convert this automaton to an equivalent DFSA using subset construction.

23. Give regular expressions that describe each of the following languages, which are over the alphabet $\{0, 1\}$. Explain how you constructed your regular expressions.

    a. $\{w|\ w$ contains substrings 010 and 101$\}$

    b. $\{w|w$ does not contain substring 0110$\}$

    c. $\{w|\ w$ has an even number of 0's and an even number of 1's$\}$

    d. $\{w|w$ has the same number of occurrences of 10 and 01$\}$

    Note that in (a) and (d) occurrences can overlap.

24. For each of the following languages, give two strings that are members and two strings that are not members – a total of four strings for each part. Let $\Sigma = \{a, b\}$ in all parts.

    a. a^*b^*

    b. $a(ba)^*b$

    c. $a^* \cup b^*$

    d. $(aaa)^*$

    e. $\Sigma^*a\Sigma^*b\Sigma^*a\Sigma^*$

    f. $aba \cup bab$

    g. $(\Sigma \cup a)b$

    h. $(a \cup ba \cup bb)\ \Sigma^*$

25. Let $\Sigma = \{a, b\}$. Give (if possible) a regular expression that describes the set of all even-length words in Σ^*.

26. Give examples of sets that demonstrate the following inequalities. Here, r_1, r_2, r_3 are regular expressions.

    a. $r_1 + \epsilon \neq r_1$

    b. $r_1 \cdot r_2 \neq r_2 \cdot r_1$

    c. $r_1 \cdot r_1 \neq r_1$

    d. $r_1 + (r_2 \cdot r_3) \neq (r_1 + r_2) \cdot (r_1 + r_3)$

    e. $(r_1 \cdot r_2)^* \neq (r_1^* \cdot r_2^*)^*$

27. Find examples of sets that show the following expressions maybe equal under some conditions. Here, r_1, r_2, r_3 are regular expressions.

    a. $r_1 + \epsilon = r_1$

    b. $r_1 \cdot r_2 = r_2 \cdot r_1$ (even if $r_1 \neq r_2$)

    c. $r_1 \cdot r_1 = r_1$

    d. $r_1 + (r_2 \cdot r_3) = (r_1 + r_2) \cdot (r_1 + r_3)$ (even if $r_1 \neq r_2$ and $r_3 = r_1$)

28. Solve the following language equations for X_1, X_2, and X_3 by eliminating X_3 and then eliminating X_2. Solve for X_1 and then back-substitute to find X_2 and X_3.

$$X_1 = \phi + \phi X_1 + (0 + 1)X_2 + \phi X_3$$
$$X_2 = \epsilon + 0X_1 + 1X_2 + \phi X_3$$
$$X_3 = \phi + \phi X_1 + (0 + 1) X_2 + \phi X_3.$$

Finite State Automata: Characterization, Properties, and Decidability

In this chapter, the equivalence between right linear grammars and finite state automata (FSA) is proved. The pumping lemma for regular sets is considered, and is used to give a method for showing a language not to be regular. We also consider some basic closure properties and decidability results.

4.1 FSA and Regular Grammars

Theorem 4.1 *If a language L is accepted by a finite non-deterministic automaton, then L can be accepted by a right linear grammar and conversely.*

Proof Let L be a language accepted by a finite non-deterministic automaton $M = (K, \Sigma, \delta, q_0, F)$ where $K = \{q_0, \ldots, q_n\}$. If $w \in L$, then w is obtained by the concatenation of symbols corresponding to different transitions starting from q_0 and ending at a finite state. Hence, for each transition by M while reading a symbol of w, there must be a correspondence to a production of a right linear grammar G. The construction is as shown below:

$$G = (\{S_0, S_1, \ldots, S_n\}, \Sigma, P, S_0)$$

where productions in P are

    1. $S_i \to a S_j$ if $\delta(q_i, a)$ contains q_j for $q_j \notin F$
    2. $S_i \to a S_j$ and $S_i \to a$ if $\delta(q_i, a)$ contains q_j, $q_j \in F$.

To prove $L(G) = L = L(M)$.

From the construction of P, one is able to see that $S_i \Rightarrow a S_j$, if and only if $\delta(q_i, a)$ contains q_j and $S_i \Rightarrow a$, if and only if $\delta(q_i, a) \in F$. Hence, if $S_0 \Rightarrow a_1 S_1 \Rightarrow a_1 a_2 S_2 \Rightarrow \cdots \Rightarrow a_1 \ldots a_n$ if and only if $\delta(q_0, a_1)$ contains q_1, $\delta(q_1, a_2)$ contains $q_2, \ldots, \delta(q_{n-1}, a_n)$ contains q_n where $q_n \in F$.

Hence, $w \in L(G)$ if and only if $w \in L(M)$.

Let $G = (N, T, P, S)$ be a right linear grammar. An equivalent non-deterministic finite state automaton (NFSA) with ε-moves is constructed as below:

Let $M = (K, T, \delta, [S], [\varepsilon])$, where

$K = \{[\alpha] | \alpha$ is S or suffix of some right-hand side of a production in P, the suffix need not be proper$\}$.

The transition function δ is defined as follows:

1. $\delta([A], \varepsilon) = \{[\alpha] | A \to \alpha \in P\}$
2. If $a \in T$ or $\alpha \in T^*N$, then $\delta([a\alpha], a) = \{[\alpha]\}$. Clearly, $[\alpha] \in \delta([S], w)$ if and only if $S \stackrel{*}{\Rightarrow} xA \Rightarrow xy\alpha$ where $A \to y\alpha \in P$ and $xy = w$. If $w \in L(M)$, then $\alpha = \varepsilon$. M accepts w if and only if $S \stackrel{*}{\Rightarrow} xA \Rightarrow xy = w$, $w \in T^*$. Hence the converse follows. □

Example 4.1   Let $G = (\{S, A\}, \{0, 1\}, \{S \to 0A, A \to 10A/\varepsilon\}, S)$ be a regular grammar. The corresponding *NFSA* will be (Figure 4.1):

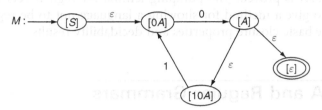

Figure 4.1.   NFSA for Example 4.1

Clearly, $L(G) = L(M) = 0(10)^*$.

Example 4.2   Consider the finite automaton $M = (K, \Sigma, \delta, A, F)$ where $K = \{A, B, C, D\}$

$\Sigma = \{0, 1\}$

$F = \{B\}$

$\delta: \{\delta(A, 0) = B, \delta(B, 0) = D, \delta(C, 0) = B, \delta(A, 1) = D, \delta(B, 1) = C,$
$\delta(C, 1) = D, \delta(D, 0) = D, \delta(D, 1) = D\}$.

The corresponding regular grammar will be as follows:

$G = (\{A, B, C, D\}, \{0, 1\}, P, A)$ where

$P = \{A \to 0B|1D|0, B \to 0D|1C|, C \to 0B|1D|0, D \to 0D|1D\}$.

Clearly, $L(M) = L(G) = 0(10)^*$.

4.2   Pumping Lemma for Regular Sets

A language is said to be regular, if it is accepted either by a finite automaton or it has a regular grammar generating it. In order to prove that a language is not regular the most commonly used technique is "pumping lemma." The lemma gives a pumping property that a sufficiently long word has a subword (non-empty) that can be pumped. But the fact that a language satisfies pumping lemma does not mean that it is regular.

Theorem 4.2 (pumping lemma)   *Let L be a regular language over T. Then, there exists a constant k depending on L such that for each $w \in L$ with $|w| \geq k$, there exists $x, y, z \in T^*$ such that $w = xyz$ and*

1. $|xy| \leq k$

2. $|y| > 1$

3. $x\,y^i z \in L$ $\forall i \geq 0$

k is no more than the number of states in the minimum state automaton accepting L.

Proof   Let $M = (K, \Sigma, \delta, q_1, F)$ be a deterministic finite state automaton (DFSA) accepting L. Let $K = \{q_1, \ldots, q_k\}$.
   Let $w = a_1 \ldots a_m \in L$ where $a_i \in \Sigma$, $1 \leq i \leq m$, $m \geq k$.
   Let the transitions on w be as shown below:

$$q_1 a_1 \ldots a_m \vdash a_1 q_2 a_2 \ldots a_m \vdash \cdots \vdash a_1 \ldots a_m q_{m+1}$$

where $q_j \in K$, $1 \leq j \leq m + 1$. Here $a_1 \ldots a_{i-1} q_i a_i \ldots a_m$ means the FSA is in q_i state after reading $a_1 \ldots a_{i-1}$ and the input head is pointing to a_i. Clearly, in the above transitions, $m + 1$ states are visited, but M has only k states. Hence, there exists q_i, q_j such that $q_i = q_j$. Hence for

$$q_1 a_1 \ldots a_m \vdash a_1 q_2 a_2 \ldots a_m \vdash \cdots \vdash (a_1 \ldots a_{i-1} q_i a_i \ldots a_m \ldots$$
$$\vdash a_1 \ldots a_{j-1} q_j a_j \ldots a_m) \vdash \cdots \vdash a_1 \ldots a_m q_{m+1}$$

where the transitions between the brackets start and end at q_i, processing a string α^t for $t \geq 0$. Hence, if $x = a_1 \ldots a_{i-1}$, $y = a_i \ldots a_j$, $z = a_{j+1} \ldots a_m$, $xy^t z \in L$ $\forall t \geq 0$ where $|xy| \leq k$, since q_i is the first state identified to repeat in the transition and $|y| \geq 1$. Hence the lemma.
   The potential application of this lemma is that it can be used to show that some languages are non-regular. We illustrate this with the following example.

Example 4.3   Let $L = \{a^n b^n | n \leq 1\}$. If L is regular, then by the above lemma there exists a constant 'k' satisfying the pumping lemma conditions. Choose $w = a^k b^k$. Clearly $|w| > k$. Then $w = xyz$, $|xy| \leq k$ and $|y| \geq 1$. If $|x| = p$, $|y| = q$, $|z| = r$, $p + q + r = 2k$, and $p + q \leq k$. Hence, xy consists of only a's and since $|y| \geq 1$, $xz \notin L$ as number of a's in x is less than k and $|z|_b = k$. Hence, pumping lemma is not true for $i = 0$ as $xy^i z$ must be in L for $i \geq 0$. Hence L is not regular.

Example 4.4   Show that $L = \{a^i b^j | i, j \geq 1, i \neq j\}$ is not regular.

When we have to use pumping lemma, we have to be careful in choosing the proper word. Suppose L is regular. Then pumping lemma holds. Let n be the constant of the pumping lemma. Now we have to choose a proper string w to show a contradiction. Consider $w = a^n b^{(n+1)!}$. This string belongs to L. w can be written as uvw where u and v contain a's only. We have to choose i properly so that $uv^i w$ is of the form $a^r b^r$.

$$|uv^i w| = 2(n + 1)!$$
$$|uvw| + |v^{i-1}| = 2(n + 1)!$$

$$n + (i - 1)|v| = 2(n + 1)!$$
$$Let\ |v| = k,\ 1 \leq k \leq n$$
$$n + (i - 1)k = 2(n + 1)!$$
$$i = 1 + \frac{2(n+1)!}{k}$$

It can be seen that i is an integer and can be suitably chosen as above. So pump v, i times to get $a^{(n+1)!}b^{(n+1)!}$. We come to the conclusion $a^{(n+1)!}b^{(n+1)!} \in L$, which is a contradiction. Therefore L is not regular.

In the next chapter, we see that there is a simpler proof for this using Myhill-Nerode theorem.

Remarks on Pumping Lemma

One can see that not only regular languages satisfy the pumping lemma property, but also some non-regular languages do so. Hence, the converse of pumping lemma is not true. We can see it in the following example. We use some closure properties of regular languages in Example 4.2.3, which are given in Section 4.3.

Example 4.5 Let $L = \{a^n b^n | n \geq 1\}$. We know L is non-regular. Consider $L_\# = (\#^+ L) \cup \{a, b\}^*$ where $\# \notin \{a, b\}$. $L_\#$ satisfies all the properties of pumping lemma with $k = 1$. For any $w \in \#^+ L$, let $x = \lambda$, $y = \#$ and for any $w \in \Sigma^*$, $x = \lambda$ and y is the first letter of w. However, $L_\#$ is not regular, which can be seen as below. Let h be a homomorphism defined as below: $h(a) = a$ for each $a \in \Sigma$ and $h(\#) = \lambda$. Then $L = h(L_\# \cap \#^+ \Sigma^*)$. Clearly $\#^+ \Sigma^*$ is regular. If $L_\#$ is regular, then $L_\# \cap \#^+ \Sigma^*$ is regular as regular languages are closed under intersection. Also, regular languages are closed under homomorphism and hence L is regular which is a contradiction. Hence $L_\#$ is non-regular. Hence, one requires a stronger version of pumping lemma so that the converse holds (Yu, 1997).

It should also be noted that it is not true that for arbitrarily long strings z in a regular set L, z can be written in the form $uv^i w$ for large i.

Example 4.6 Consider an initial string ab over the alphabet $\Sigma = \{a, b\}$. Use rules $a \rightarrow ab$, $b \rightarrow ba$ to replace a's and b's at every step.

Step 0: $w_0 = ab$
Step 1: $w_1 = abba$
Step 2: $w_2 = abbabaab$
$\vdots$

In step n, we get a string of length 2^{n+1}. It is known that w_n has no substring repeated three times consecutively. $\{w_n\}$ are called cube-free words. So, simple regular languages like $\{a, b\}^*$ contain arbitrarily long words which cannot be written in the form $uv^i w$ for large i.

4.3 Closure Properties

Theorem 4.3 *The family of regular languages is closed under the following operations:* (1) *union* (2) *intersection* (3) *complementation* (4) *catenation* (5) *star, and* (6) *reversal.*

Proof The six closure properties will be proved below either through finite automaton or regular grammars and it has been shown that they are equivalent in Theorem 4.1.1.

1. Union: Let L_1 and L_2 be two regular languages generated by two right linear grammars $G_1 = (N_1, T_1, P_1, S_1)$ and $G_2 = (N_2, T_2, P_2, S_2)$ (say). Without loss of generality let $N_1 \cap N_2 = \phi$. $L_1 \cup L_2$ is generated by the right linear grammar. $G' = (N_1 \cup N_2 \cup \{S\}, T_1 \cup T_2, P_1 \cup P_2 \cup \{S \to S_1, S \to S_2\}, S)$. $L(G') = L(G_1) \cup L(G_2)$ because, the new start symbol of G' is S from which we reach S_1 or S_2 using the rules $S \to S_1$, $S \to S_2$. After this step one can use only rules from P_1 or P_2, hence deriving words in L_1 or L_2 or in both.

2. Intersection: Let L_1, L_2 be any two regular languages accepted by two DFSA's $M_1 = (K_1, \Sigma_1, \delta_1, q_1, F_1)$ and $M_2 = (K_2, \Sigma_2, \delta_2, q_2, F_2)$. Then, the DFSA M constructed as below accepts $L_1 \cap L_2$. Let $M = (K, \Sigma, \delta, q_0, F)$ where $K = K_1 \times K_2$, $q_0 = (q_1, q_2)$, $F = F_1 \times F_2$, $\delta: K \times \Sigma \to K$ is defined by $\delta((p_1, p_2), a) = (\delta_1(p_1, a), \delta_2(p_2, a))$.

One can see that for each input word w, M runs M_1 and M_2 parallely, starting from q_1, q_2, respectively. Having finished reading the input, M accepts only if both M_1, M_2 accept. Hence, $L(M) = L(M_1) \cap L(M_2)$.

3. Complementation: Let L_1 be a regular language accepted by DFSA $M = (K, \Sigma, \delta, q_0, F)$. Then, clearly the complement of L is accepted by the DFSA $M^c = (K, \Sigma, \delta, q_0, K - F)$.

4. Concatenation: We prove this property using the concept of regular grammar. Let L_1 and L_2 and G_1 and G_2 be defined as in proof of union of this theorem. Then, the type 3 grammar G constructed as below satisfies the requirement that $L(G) = L(G_1). L(G_2)$. $G = (N_1 \cup N_2, T_1 \cup T_2, S_1, P_2 \cup P)$ where $P = \{A \to aB/A \to aB \in P_1\} \cup \{A \to aS_2 | A \to a \in P_1\}$. Clearly, $L(G) = L(G_1). L(G_2)$ because any derivation starting from S_1 derives a word $w \in L_1$ and for G, $S_1 \overset{*}{\Rightarrow} wS_2$. Hence, if $S_2 \overset{*}{\Rightarrow} w'$ by G_2, then $S_1 \overset{*}{\Rightarrow} ww'$ by G.

5. Catenation closure: Here also we prove the closure using regular grammar. Let L_1 be a regular grammar generated by $G_1 = (N_1, T_1, P_1, S_1)$. Then, the type 3 grammar $G = (N_1 \cup \{S_0\}, T_1, S_0, \{S_0 \to \varepsilon, S_0 \to S_1\} \cup \{A \to aS_1 | A \to a \in P_1\} \cup P_1)$. Clearly, G generates L_1^*.

6. Reversal: The proof is given using the NFSA model. Let L be a language accepted by a NFSA with ε-transitions which has exactly one final state.

(Exercise: For any NFSA, there exists an equivalent NFSA with ε-transitions with exactly one final state). Let it be $M = (K, \Sigma, \delta, q_0, \{q_f\})$. Then, the reversal automaton $M' = (K, \Sigma, \delta', q_f, \{q_0\})$ where δ' is defined as $\delta'(q, a)$ contains p, if $\delta(p, a)$ contains q for any $p, q \in K, a \in \Sigma \cup \{\varepsilon\}$. One can see that if $w \in L(M)$ then

$w^R \in L(M')$ as in the modified automaton M', each transition takes a backward movement on w. $\qquad\square$

We prove that regular languages are also closed under homomorphism and right quotient.

Theorem 4.4 *Regular languages are closed under homomorphism.*

Proof Let r be the regular expression for the regular languages L and h be the homomorphism. $h(r)$ is an expression obtained by substituting $h(a)$ for each symbol a in r. Clearly, $h(a)$ is a regular expression. Hence, $h(r)$ is a regular expression. For every $w \in L(r)$ the corresponding $h(w)$ will be in $L(h(r))$ and conversely.

Theorem 4.5 *Let L_1 and L_2 be two regular languages. Then L_1/L_2 is also regular.*

Proof Let L_1 be accepted by a *DFSA* $M_1 = (K_1, \Sigma_1, \delta_1, q_1, F_1)$.

Let $M_i = (K_1, \Sigma_1, \delta_1, q_i, F_1)$ be a DFSA with q_i as its initial state, for each $q_i \in K_1$. Construct an automaton $\overline{M}$ that accepts $L_2 \cap L(M_i)$. If there is a successful path from the initial state of this automaton $\overline{M}$ to its final states, then $L_2 \cap L(M_i)$ is not empty. If so add q_i to $\overline{F}$.

Let $\overline{M} = (K_1, \Sigma_1, \delta, q_0, \overline{F})$. One can see that $L(\overline{M}) = L_1/L_2$ for if $x \in L_1/L_2$ whenever for any $y \in L_2$, $\delta_1(q_0, xy) \in F_1$. Hence, $\delta(q_0, x) = q$ and $\delta(q, y) \in F_1$.

Conversely, if $x \in L(\overline{M})$, then $\delta(q_0, x) = q$, $q \in \overline{F}$. By construction there exists a $y \in L_2$ such that $\delta(q, y) \in F_1$, implying $xy \in L_1$ and $x \in L_1/L_2$. Hence the proof. $\qquad\square$

Theorem 4.6 *Let $h: \Sigma_1^* \to \Sigma_2^*$ be a homomorphism. If $L' \subseteq \Sigma_2^*$ is regular, then $h^{-1}(L') = L \subseteq \Sigma_1^*$ will be regular.*

Proof Let $M = (K, \Sigma_2, \delta, q_0, F)$ be a *DFSA* such that $L(M) = L'$. We construct a new *FSA* M' for $h^{-1}(L') = L$ from M as below:

Let $M' = (K, \Sigma_1, \delta', q_0, F)$ be such that K, q_0, F are as in M.
The construction of the transition function δ' is defined as:

$$\delta'(q, a) = \delta(q, h(a)) \quad \text{for } a \in \Sigma_1.$$

i.e., Here $h(a)$ is a string over Σ_2.
For, if $x \in \Sigma_1^*$, and $x = \varepsilon$,

$$\delta'(q, x) = \delta(q, h(x))$$

i.e., $\delta'(q, \varepsilon) = q = \delta(q, h(\varepsilon)) = \delta(q, \varepsilon)$.
If $x \neq \varepsilon$, let $x = x'a$, then

$$\begin{aligned}
\delta'(q, x'a) &= \delta'(\delta'(q, x'), a) \\
&= \delta'(\delta(q, h(x')), a) \\
&= \delta(\delta(q, h(x')), h(a)) \\
&= \delta(\delta(q, h(x')h(a)) \\
&= \delta(q, h(x'a)).
\end{aligned}$$

Hence, one can see that $L(M') = h^{-1}(L(M))$ for any input $x \in \Sigma_1$. i.e.,

$$x \in L(M') \quad \text{iff } \delta'(q_0, x) \in F$$
$$\text{iff } \delta(q_0, h(x)) \in F$$
$$\text{iff } h(x) \in L(M)$$
$$\text{iff } x \in h^{-1}(L(M)).$$

$\square$

Any family of languages which is closed under the six basic operations of union, concatenation, Kleene closure, ε-free homomorphism, intersection with regular sets, and inverse homomorphism is called an abstract family of languages (AFL). The family of regular sets is an AFL. This is seen from the above closure properties. If a family is closed under union, concatenation, Kleene closure, arbitrary homomorphism, intersection with regular sets, and inverse homomorphism, it is called a full AFL. If a family of languages is closed under intersection with regular set, inverse homomorphism and ε-free homomorphism, it is called a trio. If a family of languages is closed under all homomorphisms, as well as inverse homomorphism and intersection with a regular set, then it is said to be a full trio. The family of regular sets is a full trio and a full AFL.

4.4   Decidability Theorems

In this section, we address the basic decidability issues for regular languages. They are membership problem, emptiness problem, and equivalence problems.

Theorem 4.7   *Given a regular language L over T and $w \in T^*$, there exists an algorithm for determining whether or not w is in L.*

Proof   Let L be accepted by a DFSA M (say). Then, for input w one can see whether w is accepted by M or not. The complexity of this algorithm is $O(n)$ where $|w| = n$. Hence, membership problem for regular sets can be solved in linear time.

Theorem 4.8   *There exists an algorithm for determining whether a regular language L is empty, finite or infinite.*

Proof   Let M be a DFSA accepting L. In the state diagram representation of M with inaccessible states from the initial state removed, one has to check whether there is a simple directed path from the initial state of M to a final state. If so, L is not empty. Consider a DFSA M' accepting L, where inaccessible states from the initial state are removed and also states from which a final state cannot be reached are removed.

If in the graph of the state diagram of the DFSA, there are no cycles, then L is finite. Otherwise L is infinite.

One can see that the automaton accepts sentences of length less than n (where n is the number of states of the DFSA), if and only if $L(M)$ is non-empty. One can prove this statement using pumping lemma. That is, $|w| < n$ for if w were the shortest and $|w| \geq n$ then $w = xyz$ and xz is shorter than w that belongs to L.

Also, L is infinite if and only if the automaton M accepts at least one word of length l where $n \leq l < 2n$. One can prove this by using pumping lemma. If $w \in L(M)$, $|w| \geq n$ and $|w| < 2n$, directly from pumping lemma, L is infinite. Conversely, if L is infinite, we show that there should be a word in L whose length is l where $n \leq l < 2n$. If there is no word whose length is l, where $n \leq l < 2n$, let w be the word whose length is at least $2n$, but as short as any word in $L(M)$ whose length is greater than or equal to $2n$. Then by pumping lemma, $w = w_1 w_2 w_3$ where $1 \leq |w_2| \leq n$ and $w_1 w_2 \in L(M)$. Hence, either w was not the shortest word of length $2n$ or more or $|w_1 w_3|$ is between n and $2n-1$, which is a contradiction.

Theorem 4.9 *For any two regular languages L_1 and L_2, there exists an algorithm to determine whether or not $L_1 = L_2$.*

Proof Consider $L = (L_1 \cap \overline{L}_2) \cup (\overline{L}_1 \cap L_2)$. Clearly, L is regular by closure properties of regular languages. Hence, there exists a *DFSA M* which accepts L. Now, by the previous theorem one can determine whether L is empty or not. L is empty if and only if $L_1 = L_2$. Hence the theorem. $\qquad\square$

Problems and Solutions

1. Let Σ be an alphabet. Define I_Σ to be the collection of all infinite languages over Σ. Note that I_Σ does not include any finite language over Σ. Prove or give counter examples to the following:
   a. I_Σ is closed under union
   b. I_Σ is closed under intersection

Solution. a. I_Σ is closed under union. Let L_1 and L_2 be in I_Σ. L_1 and L_2 are infinite sets $L_1 \cup L_2 = \{x | x \in L_1 \text{ or } x \in L_2\}$. $L_1 \cup L_2$ includes L_1 and also L_2. Hence $L_1 \cup L_2$ is infinite.

   b. I_Σ is not closed under intersection. Consider $\Sigma = \{a\}$.
   $L_1 = \{a^{2n} | n \geq 1\}$ is an infinite set.
   $L_2 = \{a^p | p \text{ is a prime}\}$ is an infinite set.
   $L_1, L_2 \in I_\Sigma$
   $L_1 \cap L_2 = \{a^2\}$ which is a finite set and hence it is not in I_Σ.

2. Construct regular grammar equivalent to the following NFSA (Figure 4.2).

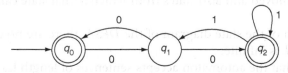

Figure 4.2. State diagram for Problem 2

Solution. Let $G = (N, T, P, S)$ where $N = \{S_0, S_1, S_2\}$, $T = \{0, 1\}$.
P consists of the following rules:

$$S_0 \to 0S_1, \ S_1 \to 0S_2|0S_0|0, \ S_2 \to 1S_1|1S_2|1.$$

3. Construct an equivalent *NFSA* for the following grammar $S \to abS|a$.

Solution.

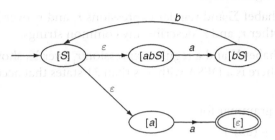

Figure 4.3. Solution to Problem 3

Exercises

1. Let Σ be an alphabet. Define I_Σ to be the collection of all infinite languages over Σ. Note that I_Σ does not include any finite language over Σ. Prove or give counter examples to the following:

   a. I_Σ is closed under complementation

   b. I_Σ is closed under concatenation

   c. I_Σ is closed under Kleene closure

2. If a collection of languages is closed under intersection, does it mean that it is closed under union. Prove or give counter example.

3. If L is accepted by a NFSA, is it necessarily true that all subsets of L are accepted by a NFSA? Prove or give counter examples.

4. Let N_Σ denote the collection of languages such that no $L \in N_\Sigma$ is accepted by a NFSA. Prove or give counter examples to the following:

   a. N_Σ is closed under union

   b. N_Σ is closed under catenation

   c. N_Σ is closed under Kleene closure

5. We have shown that the union of two regular languages is regular. Is the union of a collection of regular languages always regular? Justify your answer.

6. Let M be a DFSA accepting L_1 and G be a regular grammar generating L_2. Using only M and G show that $L_1 \cap L_2$ is regular.

7. Let $P = \{x| \ |x| \text{ is prime}\}$ and let $I(L)$ be defined by $I(L) = L \cap P$. Let D_Σ denote the collection of all languages recognized by a DFSA

   a. Show that D_Σ is not closed under I

   b. Prove or disprove N_Σ is closed under I

8. Given any alphabet Σ and a DFSA M, show that it is decidable whether M accepts even length strings.

9. Given any alphabet Σ and regular expressions r_1 and r_2 over Σ, show that it is decidable whether r_1 and r_2 describe any common strings.

10. Given any alphabet Σ and a regular expression r_1 over Σ, show that it is decidable whether there is a DFSA with less than 31 states that accepts the language described by r_1.

11. Give a regular grammar for:

   a. $(a + b)c^*(d + (ab)^*)$

   b. $(a + b)^*a(a + b)^*$

12. Construct a regular grammar equivalent to each of the following NFSA (Figure 4.4).

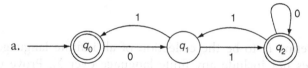

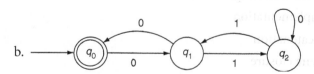

Figure 4.4. State diagrams for Exercise 12

13. Construct an equivalent NFSA for each of the following grammars:

   a. $S \rightarrow abS_1$

      $S_1 \rightarrow abS_1|S_2$

      $S_2 \rightarrow a$

   b. $S \rightarrow abA$

      $A \rightarrow baB$

      $B \rightarrow aA|bb$

5 Finite State Automata with Output and Minimization

In this chapter, we consider Myhill-Nerode theorem, minimization of deterministic finite state automaton (DFSA) and finite state automaton (FSA) with output.

5.1 Myhill-Nerode Theorem

In an earlier chapter, we considered the examples of serial adder, parity machine, acceptor accepting $\{a^n b^m | n, m \geq 1\}$, and many more such examples. Consider the serial adder. After getting some input, the machine can be in 'carry' state or 'no carry' state. It does not matter what exactly the earlier input was. It is only necessary to know whether it has produced a carry or not. Hence, the FSA need not distinguish between each and every input. It distinguishes between classes of inputs. In the above case, the whole set of inputs can be partitioned into two classes – one that produces a carry and another that does not produce a carry. Similarly, in the case of parity checker, the machine distinguishes between two classes of input strings: those containing odd number of 1's and those containing even number of 1's. Thus, the FSA distinguishes between classes of input strings. These classes are also finite. Hence, we say that the FSA has finite amount of memory.

Theorem 5.1 (Myhill-Nerode) *The following three statements are equivalent.*

1. *$L \subseteq \Sigma^*$ is accepted by a DFSA.*
2. *L is the union of some of the equivalence classes of a right invariant equivalence relation of finite index on Σ^*.*
3. *Let equivalence relation R_L be defined over Σ^* as follows: $x R_L y$ if and only if, for all $z \in \Sigma^*$, xz is in L exactly when yz is in L. Then R_L is of finite index.*

Proof   We shall prove (1) $\Rightarrow$ (2), (2) $\Rightarrow$ (3), and (3) $\Rightarrow$ (1).

(1) $\Rightarrow$ (2)

Let L be accepted by a FSA $M = (K, \Sigma, \delta, q_0, F)$. Define a relation R_M on Σ^* such that $x R_M y$ if $\delta(q_0, x) = \delta(q_0, y)$. R_M is an equivalence relation, as seen below.

$\forall x \; x R_M x$, since $\delta(q_0, x) = \delta(q_0, x)$,

$\forall x \; x R_M y \Rightarrow y R_M x \because \delta(q_0, x) = \delta(q_0, y)$ which means $\delta(q_0, y) = \delta(q_0, x)$,

$\forall x, y \; x R_M y$ and $y R_M z \Rightarrow x R_M z$.

For if $\delta(q_0, x) = \delta(q_0, y)$ and $\delta(q_0, y) = \delta(q_0, z)$ then $\delta(q_0, x) = \delta(q_0, z)$.

So R_M divides Σ^* into equivalence classes. The set of strings which take the machine from q_0 to a particular state q_i are in one equivalence class. The number of equivalence classes is therefore equivalent to the number of states of M, assuming every state is reachable from q_0. (If a state is not reachable from q_0, it can be removed without affecting the language accepted). It can be easily seen that this equivalence relation R_M is right invariant, i.e., if

$x R_M y$, $xz R_M yz$ $\forall z \in \Sigma^*$.

$\delta(q_0, x) = \delta(q_0, y)$ if $x R_M y$,

$\delta(q_0, xz) = \delta(\delta(q_0, x), z) = \delta(\delta(q_0, y), z) = \delta(q_0, yz)$. Therefore $xz R_M yz$.

L is the union of those equivalence classes of R_M which correspond to final states of M.

$(2) \Rightarrow (3)$

Assume statement (2) of the theorem and let E be the equivalence relation considered. Let R_L be defined as in the statement of the theorem. We see that $xEy \Rightarrow xR_L y$.

If xEy, then $xzEyz$ for each $z \in \Sigma^*$. xz and yz are in the same equivalence class of E. Hence, xz and yz are both in L or both not in L as L is the union of some of the equivalence classes of E. Hence $xR_L y$.

Hence, any equivalence class of E is completely contained in an equivalence class of R_L. Therefore, E is a refinement of R_L and so the index of R_L is less than or equal to the index of E and hence finite.

$(3) \Rightarrow (1)$

First, we show R_L is right invariant. $xR_L y$ if $\forall z$ in Σ^*, xz is in L exactly when yz is in L or we can also write this in the following way: $xR_L y$ if for all w, z in Σ^*, xwz is in L exactly when ywz is in L.

If this holds $xw R_L yw$.

Therefore, R_L is right invariant.

Let $[x]$ denote the equivalence class of R_L to which x belongs.

Construct a DFSA $M_L = (K', \Sigma, \delta', q'_0, F')$ as follows: K' contains one state corresponding to each equivalence class of R_L. $[\varepsilon]$ corresponds to q'_0. F' corresponds to those states $[x]$, $x \in L$. δ' is defined as follows: $\delta'([x], a) = [xa]$. This definition is consistent as R_L is right invariant. Suppose x and y belong to the same equivalence class of R_L. Then, xa and ya will belong to the same equivalence class of R_L. For,

$$\delta'([x], a) = \delta'([y], a)$$

$$\Downarrow \quad \Downarrow$$

$$[xa] = [ya]$$

if $x \in L$, $[x]$ is a final state in M', i.e., $[x] \in F'$. This automaton M' accepts L. □

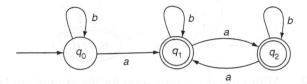

Figure 5.1. FSA accepting $b^*a(a + b)^*$

Example 5.1 Consider the *FSA M* given in Figure 5.1.
The language accepted consists of strings of a's and b's having at least one a.
M divides $\{a, b\}^*$ into three equivalence classes.

1. H_1, set of strings which take M from q_0 to q_0 i.e., b^*.
2. H_2, set of strings which take M from q_0 to q_1, i.e., set of strings which have odd numbers of a's.
3. H_3, set of strings which take M from q_0 to q_2, i.e., set of strings which have even number of a's.

$L = H_2 \cup H_3$ as can be seen.

1. Let $x \in H_1$ and $y \in H_2$. Then, $xb \in H_1$ and $yb \in H_2$. Then, $xb \notin L$ and $yb \in L$. Therefore $x \not{R}_L y$.
2. Let $x \in H_1$ and $y \in H_3$. Then, $xb \in H_1$ and so $xb \notin L$ and $yb \in H_3$ and so $xb \in L$. Therefore $x \not{R}_L y$.
3. Let $x \in H_2$ and $y \in H_3$. Take any string z, xz belongs to either H_2 or H_3 and so in L, yz belongs to either H_2 or H_3 and so in L. Therefore $xR_L y$.

So, if we construct M' as in the proof of the theorem, we have one state corresponding to H_1 and one state corresponding to $L = H_2 \cup H_3$.

Figure 5.2 is the automaton we get as M'. We see that, it accepts $L(M)$. Both M and M' are *DFSA* accepting the same language. But M' has minimum number of states and is called the minimum state automaton.

Theorem 5.2 *The minimum state automaton accepting a regular set L is unique up to an isomorphism and is given by M' in the proof of Theorem* 5.1.

Proof In the proof of Theorem 5.1, we started with M, found equivalence classes for R_M, R_L, and constructed M'. The number of states of M is equal to the index of R_M and the number of states of M' is equal to the index of R_L. Since R_M is a refinement of R_L, the number of states of M' is less than or equal to the number of states of M. If M and M' have the same number of states, then we can find a mapping $h: K \rightarrow K'$ (which identifies each state of K with a state of K') such that if $h(q) = q'$ then for a $\in \Sigma$,

$$h(\delta(q, a)) = \delta'(q', a).$$

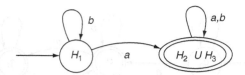

Figure 5.2. Minimum state automaton for the example in Figure 5.1

This is achieved by defining h as follows: $h(q_0) = q'_0$ and if $q \in K$, then there exists a string x such that $\delta(q_0, x) = q$. $h(q) = q'$ where $\delta(q'_0, x) = q'$. This definition of h is consistent. This can be seen as follows: Let $\delta(q, a) = p$ and $\delta'(q', a) = p'$, $\delta(q_0 xa) = p$ and $\delta'(q'_0, xa) = p'$ and hence $h(p) = p'$. □

Minimization of DFSA

In this section, we shall see how we can find the minimum state automaton corresponding to a DFSA.

Let $M = (K, \Sigma, \delta, q_0, F)$ be a DFSA. Let R be an equivalence relation on K such that pRq, if and only if for each input string x, $\delta(p, x) \in F$ if and only if $\delta(q, x) \in F$. This essentially means that if p and q are equivalent, then either $\delta(p, x)$ and $\delta(q, x)$ both are in F or both are not in F for any string x. p is distinguishable from q, if there exists a string x such that one of $\delta(q, x)$, $\delta(p, x)$ is in F and the other is not. x is called the distinguishing string for the pair $< p, q >$.

If p and q are equivalent $\delta(p, a)$ and $\delta(q, a)$ will be equivalent for any a. If $\delta(p, a) = r$ and $\delta(q, a) = s$ and r and s are distinguishable by x, then p and q are distinguishable by ax.

Algorithm to Find Minimum DFSA

We get a partition of the set of states of K as follows:

Step 1 Consider the set of states in K. Divide them into two blocks F and $K - F$. (Any state in F is distinguishable from a state in $K - F$ by ε.) Repeat the following step till no more split is possible.

Step 2 Consider the set of states in a block. Consider the a-successors of them for $a \in \Sigma$. If they belong to different blocks, split this block into two or more blocks depending on the a-successors of the states.

For example, if a block has $\{q_1, \ldots, q_k\}$. $\delta(q_1, a) = p_1$, $\delta(q_2, a) = p_2, \ldots, \delta(q_k, a) = p_k$, and $p_1, \ldots, p_i$ belong to one block, $p_i + 1, \ldots, p_j$ belong to another block and $p_j + 1, \ldots, p_k$ belong to third block, then split $\{q_1, \ldots, q_k\}$ into $\{q_1, \ldots, q_i\}$ $\{q_i + 1, \ldots, q_j\}$ $\{q_j + 1, \ldots, q_k\}$.

Step 3 For each block B_i, consider a state b_i. Construct $M' = (K', \Sigma, \delta', q'_0, F')$ where $K' = \{b_i | B_i$ is a block of the partition obtained in Step 2$\}$.

q_0' corresponds to the block containing q_0. $\delta(b_i, a) = b_j$, if there exists $q_i \in B_i$ and $q_j \in B_j$ such that $\delta(q_i, a) = q_j$. F' consists of states corresponding to the blocks containing states in F.

Example 5.2 Consider the following *FSA M* over $\Sigma = \{b, c\}$ accepting strings which have *bcc* as substrings. A non-deterministic automaton for this will be (Figure 5.3),

Converting to *DFSA* we get *M'* as in Figure 5.4.

where, $p_0 = [q_0]$ $p_1 = [q_0, q_1]$ $p_2 = [q_0, q_2]$ $p_3 = [q_0, q_3]$ $p_4 = [q_0, q_1, q_3]$ $p_5 = [q_0, q_2, q_3]$. Finding the minimum state automaton for *M'*

Step 1 Divide the set o f states into two blocks:

$$\overline{p_0 p_1 p_2} \quad \overline{p_3 p_4 p_5}$$

In $\overline{p_0 p_1 p_2}$, the *b* successors are in one block, the *c* successors of p_0, p_1 are in one block, and p_2 is in another block. Therefore, $\overline{p_0 p_1 p_2}$ is split as $\overline{p_0 p_1}$ and $\overline{p_2}$. The *b* and *c* successors of p_3, p_4, p_5 are in the same block. Now, the partition is $\overline{p_0 p_1}$ $\overline{p_2}$ $\overline{p_3 p_4 p_5}$. Consider $\overline{p_0 p_1}$, the *b* successors of p_0, p_1 are in the same block but the *c* successors of p_0 and p_1 are p_0 and p_2 and they are in different blocks. Therefore, $\overline{p_0 p_1}$ is split into $\overline{p_0}$ and $\overline{p_1}$. Now the partition is $\overline{p_0}$, $\overline{p_1}$, $\overline{p_2}$, and $\overline{p_3 p_4 p_5}$. No further split is possible. The minimum state automaton is given in Figure 5.5.

The minimization procedure cannot be applied to NFSA. For example, consider the NFSA (Figure 5.6),

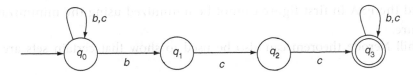

Figure 5.3. NFSA accepting strings containing *bcc* as a substring

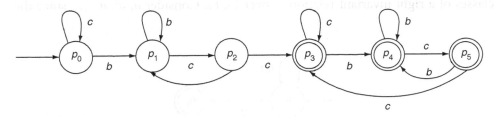

Figure 5.4. The DFSA obtained for the NFSA in Figure 5.3 by subset construction

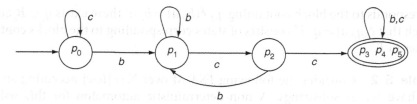

Figure 5.5. The minimum state DFSA for the DFSA in Figure 5.4

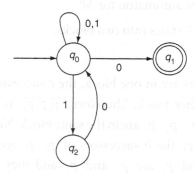

Figure 5.6. NFSA accepting $(0+1)^*0$

The language accepted is represented by the regular expression $(0+1)^*0$ for which NFSA in Figure 5.7 will suffice. But, if we try to use the minimization procedure, $\overline{q_0q_1q_2}$ will be initially split as $\overline{q_0q_2}$ and $\overline{q_1}$. q_0 and q_2 are not equivalent as $\delta(q_0, 0)$, contains a final state while $\delta(q_2, 0)$ does not. So, they have to be split and the FSA in first figure cannot be minimized using the minimization procedure.

Myhill-Nerode theorem can also be used to show that certain sets are not regular.

Example 5.3 We know $L = \{a^n b^n | n \geq 1\}$ is not regular. Suppose L is regular. Then by Myhill-Nerode theorem, L is the union of the some of the equivalence classes of a right invariant relation $\approx$ over $\{a, b\}$. Consider $a, a^2, a^3, \ldots$ since the

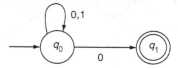

Figure 5.7. Another NFSA accepting $(0+1)^*0$

number o f equivalence classes is finite, for some m and n, $m \neq n$, a^m and a^n must be in the same equivalence class. We write this as $a^m \approx a^n$. Since $\approx$ is right invariant $a^m b^m \approx a^n b^m$. i.e., $a^m b^m$ and $a^n b^m$ are in the same equivalence class. L either contains one equivalence class completely or does not contain that class. Hence, since $a^m b^m \in L$, L should contain this class completely and hence $a^n b^m \in L$ which is a contradiction. Therefore L is not regular.

5.2 Finite Automata with Output

Earlier we considered finite state automata with output like the serial adder. We now consider them formally. The output function can be defined in two ways. If it depends on the state alone, the machine is called a Moore machine. If it depends on both the states and the input, it is called a Mealy machine.

Definition 5.1   *Let $M = (K, \Sigma, \Delta, \delta, \lambda, q_0)$ be a Moore FSA. Here:*

K is a finite set of states
Σ is a finite set of input alphabet
Δ is a finite set of output alphabet
δ, the transition function, is a mapping : $K \times \Sigma \rightarrow K$
λ, the output function, is a mapping : $K \rightarrow \Delta$

q_0 in K is the initial state. Since, we are interested in the output for an input, we do not specify any final state.

   Given an input $a_1 a_2 \ldots a_n$, the machine starts in state q_0, outputs b_0, reads a_1 and goes to q_1 and outputs b_1, reads a_2 and outputs b_2 by going to $q_2 \ldots$ and so on.

   Input: $a_1 a_2 \ldots a_n$
   States: $q_0 q_1 q_2 \ldots q_n$
   Output: $b_0 b_1 b_2 \ldots b_n$

So the output is $b_0 b_1 \ldots b_n$. It should be noted that for an input of length n, we get an output of length $n + 1$.

Example 5.4   Figure 5.8 represents a Moore machine with input alphabet $\{0, 1\}$ and output alphabet $\{y, n\}$. Taking a sample string:

Input: 100110110
States: $q_0 q_1 q_2 q_4 q_4 q_4 q_3 q_2 q_0 q_0$
Output: *ynnnnnnnyy*

Output is y when the binary string read so far represents a number divisible by 5.

Definition 5.2   *Let $M = (K, \Sigma, \Delta, \delta, \lambda, q_0)$ be a Mealy machine. Here K, Σ, Δ, δ, q_0 are as defined for Moore machine. But λ the output function is a mapping $K \times \Sigma \rightarrow K$.*

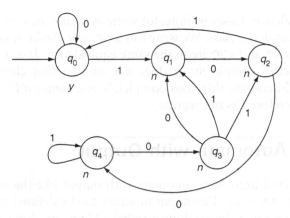

Figure 5.8. A Moore machine

For an input:

Input: $a_1 a_2 \ldots a_n$
States: $q_0 q_1 q_2 \ldots q_n$
Output: $b_1 \ldots b_n$

The output is of length n, if the input is of length n.

Example 5.5 Consider the following Mealy machine.
The machine outputs y if the last two inputs symbols are 01, n, otherwise (Figure 5.9).
For a sample input 001101001, states are $q_0 q_1 q_1 q_2 q_0 q_1 q_2 q_1 q_1 q_2$ and output is
nnynnynny.

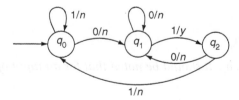

Figure 5.9. A Mealy machine

The Serial adder is an example of a Mealy machine. Since for an input of length n, the output is of length $n + 1$ in the case of Moore machine and of the length n in the case of Mealy machine, we cannot really think of equivalence. But if we ignore the output at time 0, (initial output) for the Moore machine we can talk of equivalence.

Theorem 5.3 *Let M be a Moore machine. Then we can construct a Mealy machine M′ such that for an input $a_1 a_2 \ldots a_n$ if M outputs $b_0 b_1 \ldots b_n$, M′ outputs $b_1 \ldots b_n$.*

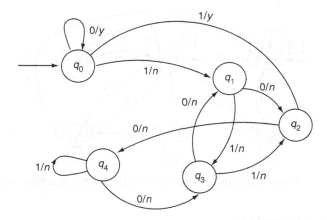

Figure 5.10. Mealy machine equivalent to the Moore machine in Figure 5.8

Proof Let $M = (K, \Sigma, \Delta, \delta, \lambda, q_0)$. Then $M' = (K, \Sigma, \Delta, \delta, \lambda', q_0)$ where $\lambda'(q, a) = \lambda(\delta(q, a))$. It can be easily seen that M and M' are equivalent. □

Example 5.6 Converting the Moore machine in Figure 5.8 into Mealy machine we get, the machine in Figure 5.10.

Theorem 5.4 *Let M' be a Mealy machine. Then, we can construct an equivalent Moore machine M in the sense that if $a_1 a_2 \ldots a_n$ is the input for which M' outputs $b_1 b_2 \ldots b_n$, then M for the same input M' outputs $b_0 b_1 \ldots bn$ where b_0 is chosen arbitrarily from Δ.*

Proof Let $M' = (K', \Sigma, \Delta, \delta', \lambda', q'_0)$ be a Mealy machine. The Moore machine equivalent to M' can be constructed as follows: $M = (K, \Sigma, \Delta, \delta, \lambda, q_0)$ where $K = K' \times \Delta$. Each state in K is an ordered pair $[p, x]$, $p \in K'$, $x \in \Delta$. δ is defined as follows: $\delta([q, b], a) = [\delta'(q, a), \lambda'(q, a)]$ and $\lambda([q, a]) = a$. q'_0 is taken as any one $[q_0, a]$, $a \in \Delta$.

It can be seen that if on input $a_1 a_2 \ldots a_n$ the state sequence of M' is $q_0 q_1 \ldots q_n$ and the output sequence is $b_1 b_2 \ldots b_n$. Then in M, the machine goes through the sequence of states $[q_0, a][q_1, b_1][q_2, b_2] \ldots [q_n, b_n]$ and emits $ab_1 b_2 \ldots b_n$. (First output a should be ignored). □

Example 5.7 Converting the example in Figure 5.9 to Moore machine, we get the machine in Figure 5.11.
The output for each state is shown within a square.

Problems and Solutions

1. Show that $\{a^i b^j | i, j \leq 1, i \neq j\}$ is not regular.

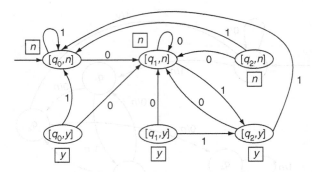

Figure 5.11. Moore machine equivalent to the Mealy machine in Figure 5.9

Solution. As in Example 5.3

$$a^m \approx a^n \ m \neq n$$
$$a^m b^n \approx a^n b^n$$
$$a^m b^n \in L \text{ but } a^n b^n \notin L$$

Therefore, we have a contradiction and the language is not regular.

2. Which of the following languages are regular sets? Prove your answer.

   a. $L_1 = \{xx^R | x \in \{0, 1\}^+\}$
   b. $L_2 = \{xwx^R | x, w \in \{0, 1\}^+\}$
   c. $L_3 = \{xx^R w | x, w \in \{0, 1\}^+\}$

Solution. a. L_1 is not regular.
   Suppose L_1 is regular.
   Let n be the constant of the pumping lemma. Consider $0^n 110^n$. The pump will occur in the first n 0's. So, we shall get strings $0^m 110^n \in L$, $m \neq n$ which is a contradiction.

   b. L_2 is regular.
   L_2 can be represented by the regular expression
   $0(0 + 1)^+ 0 + 1(0 + 1)^+ 1$.

   c. L_3 is not regular. Suppose L_3 is regular, $(01)^n (10)^n 0 \in L$. $x = (01)^n$, $w = 0$.

By Myhill-Nerode theorem, since the number of equivalence classes is finite. (01), $(01)^2$, $(01)^3$,... all cannot belong to different equivalence classes. For some m and n, $m \neq n$ $(01)^m$ and $(01)^n$ will belong to the same equivalence class. We write this as $(01)^m \approx (01)^n$. Let $m < n$. Because of the right invariance,

$$(01)^m (10)^m 0 \approx (01)^n (10)^m 0.$$

Since $(01)^m (10)^m 0 \in L_3$, we conclude $(01)^n (10)^m 0 \in L_3$. But $(01)^n (10)^m 0$ is not of the form $xx^R w$. Hence, we arrive at a contradiction. Therefore, L_3 is not regular.

3. Construct a Mealy machine with $\Sigma = \Delta = \{0, 1\}$. The output is 1 whenever the last four symbols read are 1111. Overlapping sequences are accepted. Output is 0 otherwise.

Solution.

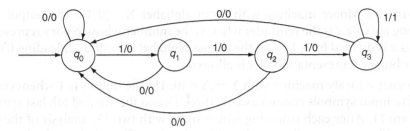

Figure 5.12. Solution to Problem 3

4. Use Myhill-Nerode theorem to show the following language is not regular
   $\{0^i1^j \mid gcd(i, j) = 1\}$

Solution. $L = \{0^i1^j \mid gcd(i, j) = 1\}$ is not regular. Suppose L is regular. Consider the sets of primes $\{p_1, p_2, \ldots\}$. This is an infinite set. Consider the set of strings 0^{P_1}, 0^{P_2}, 0^{P_3}, ... By Myhill-Nerode theorem, all of them cannot be in different equivalence classes. For some p_i and p_j, 0^{P_i} and 0^{P_j} must be in the same equivalence class.

$$0^{P_i} \approx 0^{P_j}$$
$$0^{P_i}1^{P_j} \approx 0^{P_j}1^{P_j}$$
$$0^{P_i}1^{P_j} \in L \text{ whereas } 0^{P_j}1^{P_j} \notin L.$$

Hence, we have a contradiction. L is not regular.

5. Minimize the following DFSA. Indicate clearly which equivalence class corresponds to each state of the new automaton.

		a	b
→	1	6	3
	2	5	6
	③	4	5
	④	3	2
	5	2	1
	6	1	4

Solution. Splitting into non-final and final states $\overline{1256}$, $\overline{34}$.
Considering b successors of $1, 2, 5, 6$ $\overline{1256}$ is split into $\overline{16}$ $\overline{25}$. Further split is not possible. Hence, minimum state automaton is:

		a	b
→	A	A	B
	⑧	B	C
	C	C	A

A corresponds to $\{1, 6\}$.
B corresponds to $\{3, 4\}$.
C corresponds to $\{2, 5\}$.

Exercises

1. Construct a Moore machine with input alphabet $\Sigma = \{0, 1\}$. The output after reading a string x is the reminder when x, the number whose binary representation is x is divided by 3. Hence, the output alphabet $\Delta = \{0, 1, 2\}$ leading 0's in x in the binary representation of x is allowed.

2. Construct a Mealy machine with $\Sigma = \Delta = \{0, 1\}$. The output is 1 whenever the last five input symbols contain exactly three 1's and the 4th and 5th last symbols read are 11. After each substring which starts with two 1's, analysis of the next string will not start until the end of this substring of length five, whether at the end 0 or 1 is output. For example, for input 11110100, output is 00000000. For input 11100110, the output is 00001000.

3. Find a Mealy machine with $\Sigma = \Delta = \{0, 1\}$ satisfying the following condition. The output at time t is 1 if the input at time t is the same as input at time $t - 2$.

4. Find a Mealy machine with $\Sigma = \Delta = \{0, 1\}$ satisfying the following condition: For every input subsequence $x_{3i+1}x_{3i+2}x_{3i+3}$ the output is x_{3i+3} if this substring consisted of 2 or 3 1's. Otherwise it is 0.

5. Find a Mealy machine with $\Sigma = \{a, b, c, d, e\}$ and $\Delta = \{0, 1\}$ satisfying the following condition. The output is 1 if the last three symbols read are in alphabetical order i.e., abc, bcd or cde. Otherwise it is 0.

6. Use Myhill-Nerode theorem to show the following languages are not regular.

   a. $\{a^n bc^n | n \geq 1\}$
   b. $\{a^n b^n c^n | n \geq 1\}$
   c. $\{a^n b^{n2} | n \geq 1\}$
   d. $(ww | w \in \{0, 1\}^+)$
   e. $\{a^n b^m | n \leq m, n, m \geq 1\}$

7. Minimize the following *DFSA*. Indicate clearly which equivalence class corresponds to each state of the new automaton.

		a	b
$\rightarrow$	1	2	3
	2	5	6
	③	1	4
	④	6	3
	5	2	1
	6	5	4

8. Given the following *DFSAs*. Construct minimum state *DFSAs* equivalent to them (Figure 5.13).

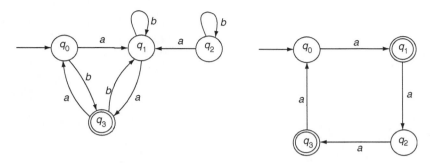

Figure 5.13. State diagrams of DFSA in Exercise 8

9. Given two *DFSAs*, M_1 and M_2 (Figure 5.14). Prove that they are either equivalent or not equivalent.

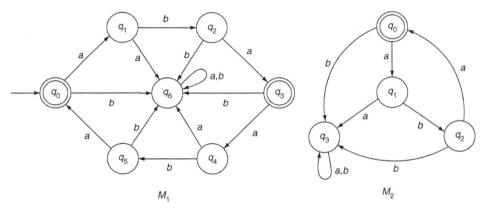

Figure 5.14. State diagrams of DFSA in Exercise 9

10. Using pumping lemma or Myhill-Nerode theorem show that the following languages are not regular.
    a. $L_1 = \{www | w \varepsilon \{a, b\}^*\}$
    b. $L_2 = \{a^{2^n} | n \geq 0\}$
    c. $L_3 = \{w | w$ has equal number of 0's and 1's$\}$
    d. $L_4 = \{x \varepsilon \{a, b, c\}^* |$ length of x is a square$\}$.

11. Given a language L accepted by a *DFSA*, M_1 the minimal *DFSA* accepting L and another machine M_2 for which $L(M_2) = L$, prove that the number of non-final states in the minimal machine M_1 must be less than or equal to the number of non-final states in M_2.

8. Given the following DFSAs. Construct minimum state DFSAs equivalent to them (Figure 5.13).

Figure 5. 13. State diagrams of DFSA in Exercise 8

9. Given two DFSAs, M_1 and M_2 (Figure 5.14). Prove that they are either equivalent or not equivalent.

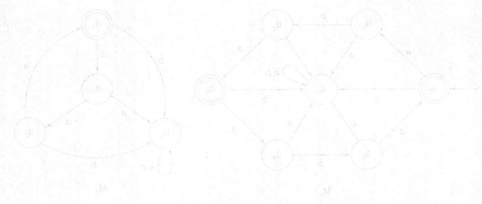

Figure 5. 14. State diagrams of DFSA in Exercise 9

10. Using pumping lemma or Myhill-Nerode theorem show that the following languages are not regular:

   a. $L_1 = \{wwv \mid v \in \{a, b\}^*\}$
   b. $L_2 = \{a^n b^n \mid n > 0\}$
   c. $L_3 = \{w \mid w \text{ has equal number of 0s and 1s}\}$
   d. $L_4 = \{x \times \mid a, b, d\} \text{ length of } x \text{ is a square}\}$

11. Given a language L accepted by a DFSA, M, the minimal DFSA accepting L and another machine M' for which $L(M') = L$, prove that the number of non-final states in the minimal machine M_0 must be less than or equal to the number of non-final states in M'.

CHAPTER
6
Variants of Finite Automata

We have seen that DFSA, NFSA, and NFSA with ε-moves have the same power. They accept the family of regular sets. In this chapter, we consider two generalized versions of FSA. While one of them accepts only regular sets, the other accepts sets, which are not regular. We also have a discussion on probabilistic finite automata and weighted finite automata. These two models have applications in image analysis.

6.1 Two-Way Finite Automata

A two-way deterministic finite automaton (2DFSA) is a quintuple $M = (K, \Sigma, \delta, q_0, F)$ where K, Σ, q_0, F are as in DFSA and δ is a mapping from $K \times \Sigma$ into $K \times \{L, R\}$.

The input tape head can move in both directions. The machine starts on the leftmost symbol of the input in the initial state. At any time, depending on the state and the symbol read, the automaton changes its state, and moves its tape head left or right as specified by the move. If the automaton moves off at the right end of the input tape in a final state, the input is accepted. The input can be rejected in three ways:

1. moving off the right end of the input tape in a non-final state,

2. moving off the left end of the tape and

3. getting into a loop

An instantaneous description (ID) of the automaton is a string in $\Sigma^* K \Sigma^*$. If wqx is an ID, for the input wx and currently the automaton is reading the first symbol of x in state q. If $a_1 \ldots a_{i-1}qa_ia_{i+1} \ldots a_n$ is an ID and $\delta(q, a_i) = (p, R)$ then the next ID is:

$$a_1 \ldots a_{i-1}a_i p a_{i+1} \ldots a_n.$$

If $\delta(q, a_i) = (p, L)$, then the next ID is:

$$a_1 \ldots a_{i-2} p a_{i-1}a_ia_{i+1} \ldots a_n.$$

If, from ID_i the automaton goes to ID_{i+1} in one move, this is represented as $ID_i \vdash ID_{i+1}$. $\vdash^*$ is the reflexive, transitive closure of $\vdash$.

Definition 6.1 *The language accepted by a 2DFSA*

$M = (K, \Sigma, \delta, q_0, F)$ *is defined as:*

$T(M) = \{w \,|\, w \in \Sigma^*, q_0 w \vdash^* w q_f \text{ for some } q_f \in F\}$

Example 6.1 Consider the following 2DFSA:

$M = (\{q_0, q_1, q_2, q_3\}, \{a, b\}, \delta, q_0, \{q_2\})$ where δ is given by the following table.

δ	a	b
$\rightarrow q_0$	(q_1, R)	(q_1, L)
q_1	(q_0, L)	(q_3, R)
$\textcircled{q_2}$	(q_1, L)	(q_2, R)
q_3	(q_2, L)	(q_2, L)

The string *abb* is accepted as follows:

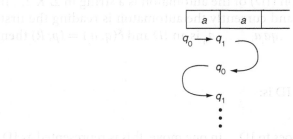

or the sequence of IDs is:

$$q_0 abb \vdash a q_1 bb \vdash ab q_3 b \vdash a q_2 bb \vdash ab q_2 b \vdash abb q_2$$

It can be seen that any string ab^n, $n \geq 2$, will be accepted.

 ab will not be accepted.

 Any string beginning with *aa* will not be accepted.

A string of the form $ab^na \ldots$ cannot be accepted as:

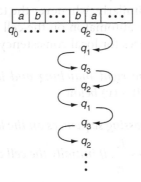

$$T(M) = \{ab^n | n \geq 2\}$$

We have represented in the previous example a useful picture of the behavior of a 2DFSA. This consists of the input, the path followed by the head, and the state; each time the boundary between two tape squares is crossed, with the assumption that the control enters its new state prior to moving the head. The sequence of states below each boundary, between tape cells is termed as a crossing sequence. It should be noted that if a 2DFSA accepts its input, elements of crossing sequence may not have a repeated state with the head moving in the same direction, otherwise, the automaton being deterministic would be in a loop and thus, could never move off the right end of the tape. Another point about crossing sequences is that the first time a boundary is crossed, the head must be moving right. Subsequent crossings must be in alternate directions. Thus, odd-numbered elements of a crossing sequence represent right moves and even-numbered elements represent left moves. If the input is accepted, it follows that, all crossing sequences are of odd length.

A crossing sequence $\begin{matrix} q_1 \\ \vdots \\ q_k \end{matrix}$ is said to be valid if it is of odd length and no two odd-numbered elements or two even-numbered elements are identical. If the 2DFSA has n states, the maximum length of the crossing sequence is therefore $2n - 1$. We show that any set accepted by a 2DFSA is regular by constructing a NFSA, whose states correspond to valid crossing sequences of the 2DFSA.

To proceed further we define the following. Suppose we are given an isolated tape cell holding a symbol a and are also given valid crossing sequences $\begin{matrix} q_1 \\ \vdots \\ q_k \end{matrix}$ and $\begin{matrix} p_1 \\ \vdots \\ p_l \end{matrix}$ at the left and right boundaries of the square.

$$\begin{matrix} & \boxed{a} & \\ q_1 & & p_1 \\ \vdots & & \vdots \\ q_k & & p_l \end{matrix}$$

We can test whether the two sequences are locally compatible as follows: If the tape head moves left from the square holding a in state q_i, restart the automaton on the square in state q_{i+1}. Similarly, whenever the tape head moves right from the square in state p_j, restart the automaton on the cell in state p_{j+1}. This way, we can test the two crossing sequences for local consistency.

Definition 6.2 *We define right matching and left matching pairs of crossing sequences recursively using (i) – (v) below.*

If $\begin{matrix} q_1 \\ \vdots \\ q_k \end{matrix}$ and $\begin{matrix} p_1 \\ \vdots \\ p_l \end{matrix}$ are consistent crossing sequences on the left and right boundary of a cell containing a, $\begin{matrix} q_1 \\ \vdots \\ q_k \end{matrix}$ right matches $\begin{matrix} p_1 \\ \vdots \\ p_l \end{matrix}$, if initially the cell containing a is reached moving right. If it reaches the cell initially moving left, then $\begin{matrix} q_1 \\ \vdots \\ q_k \end{matrix}$ left matches $\begin{matrix} p_1 \\ \vdots \\ p_l \end{matrix}$. The five conditions are:

1. *the null sequence left and right matches the null sequence.*
2. *If $\begin{matrix} q_3 \\ \vdots \\ q_k \end{matrix}$ right matches $\begin{matrix} p_1 \\ \vdots \\ p_l \end{matrix}$ and $\delta(q_1,a) = (q_2,L)$ then $\begin{matrix} q_1 \\ \vdots \\ q_k \end{matrix}$ right matches $\begin{matrix} p_1 \\ \vdots \\ p_l \end{matrix}$.*
3. *If $\begin{matrix} q_2 \\ \vdots \\ q_k \end{matrix}$ left matches $\begin{matrix} p_2 \\ \vdots \\ p_l \end{matrix}$ and $\delta(q_1,a) = (p_1,R)$ then $\begin{matrix} q_1 \\ \vdots \\ q_k \end{matrix}$ right matches $\begin{matrix} p_1 \\ \vdots \\ p_l \end{matrix}$.*
4. *If $\begin{matrix} q_1 \\ \vdots \\ q_k \end{matrix}$ left matches $\begin{matrix} p_3 \\ \vdots \\ p_l \end{matrix}$ and $\delta(p_1,a) = (p_2,R)$ then $\begin{matrix} q_1 \\ \vdots \\ q_k \end{matrix}$ left matches $\begin{matrix} p_1 \\ \vdots \\ p_l \end{matrix}$.*
5. *If $\begin{matrix} q_2 \\ \vdots \\ q_k \end{matrix}$ right matches $\begin{matrix} p_2 \\ \vdots \\ p_l \end{matrix}$ and $\delta(p_1,a) = (q_1,L)$ then $\begin{matrix} q_1 \\ \vdots \\ q_k \end{matrix}$ left matches $\begin{matrix} p_1 \\ \vdots \\ p_l \end{matrix}$.*

We find that 2DFSA accept only regular sets.

Theorem 6.1 *If L is accepted by a 2DFSA, then L is a regular set.*

Proof 1 Let $M = (K, \Sigma, \delta, q_0, F)$ be a 2DFSA. We construct an NFSA M' which accepts $T(M)$.

$$M' = (K', \Sigma, \delta', q_0', F')$$

where:

1. K' contains states which correspond to valid crossing sequences of M.
2. $q_0' = [q_0]$, the crossing sequence of length one having q_0.
3. F' is the set of all crossing sequences of length one containing a state in F. i.e., of the form $[q_f]$, $q_f \in F$.
4. $\delta'(s_c, a) = \{s_d | s_c, s_d$ are states corresponding to valid crossing sequences c and d, respectively and c right matches d on $a\}$.

We now show $T(M) = T(M')$.

1. $T(M) \subseteq T(M')$.

   Let w be in $T(M)$. Consider the crossing sequences generated by an accepting computation of M on w. Each crossing sequence right matches the one at the next boundary, so M' can guess the proper crossing sequences (among other guesses) and accept.

2. $T(M)' \subseteq T(M)$.

   Let w be in $T(M')$. M' has a sequence of states $s_0, s_1, \ldots, s_n$ accepting w. Let $c_0, c_1, \ldots, c_n$ be the crossing sequences of M corresponding to $s_0, \ldots, s_n$, respectively, where $w = a_1 \ldots a_n$.
   $\delta'(s_{i-1}, a_i)$ contains s_i, where each c_{i-1} right matches c_i on a_i.

We can construct an accepting computation of M on input w. We prove by induction on i that M' on reading $a_1 \ldots a_i$ can enter state s_i corresponding to crossing sequence $c_i = \begin{bmatrix} q_1 \\ \vdots \\ q_k \end{bmatrix}$ only if:

1. M started in state q_0 on $a_1 \ldots a_i$ will first move right from position i in state q_1, and

2. for $j = 2, 4, \ldots$, if M is started at position i in state q_j, M will eventually move right from position i in state q_{j+1}. This means k is odd. $\square$

Basis

($i = 0$). As $s_0 = [q_0]$, (1) is satisfied since M begins its computation by moving right from position 0 in state q_0. Since M never moves off at the left end boundary, j cannot be 2 or more. Condition (2) is vacuously satisfied.

Induction

Assume that the hypothesis is true for $i - 1$. M' is in state s_{i-1} corresponding to $\begin{bmatrix} q_1 \\ \vdots \\ q_k \end{bmatrix}$;

after reading $a_1 \ldots a_{i-1}$ and in state s_i corresponding to $\begin{bmatrix} p_1 \\ \vdots \\ p_l \end{bmatrix}$, after reading $a_1 \ldots a_i$; k and ℓ are odd. $\begin{bmatrix} q_1 \\ \vdots \\ q_k \end{bmatrix}$ right matches $\begin{bmatrix} q_1 \\ \vdots \\ q_k \end{bmatrix}$ on a_i. It follows that there must be some odd j such that in state q_j on input a_i, M moves right. Let j_1 be the smallest such j. By definition of "right matches," it follows that $\delta(q_{j1}, a_i) = (p_1, R)$. This proves the condition (1). Also by the definition of "right matches" (rule (iii)) $\begin{bmatrix} q_{j_i + 1} \\ \vdots \\ q_k \end{bmatrix}$ left matches $\begin{bmatrix} p_2 \\ \vdots \\ p_\ell \end{bmatrix}$. If $\delta(p_j, a_i) = (p_{j+1}, R)$ for all even j, then condition (2) is satisfied. In the case that for some smallest even j_2, $\delta(p_{j_2}, a_i) = (q, L)$, then, by the definition of "left

matches" (rule (v)) q must be q_{j_1+1} and $\begin{bmatrix} q_{j_1+2} \\ \vdots \\ q_k \end{bmatrix}$ right matches $\begin{bmatrix} p_{j_2+1} \\ \vdots \\ p_\ell \end{bmatrix}$ on a_i. Now, the

same argument can be repeated for sequences $\begin{bmatrix} q_{j_1+2} \\ \vdots \\ q_k \end{bmatrix}$ and $\begin{bmatrix} p_{j_2+1} \\ \vdots \\ p_\ell \end{bmatrix}$ till condition (2) is

satisfied (which will eventually happen).

Now the induction hypothesis is established for all i. Noting the fact that s_n corresponding to crossing sequence c_n is of the form $[q_f]$ for some $q_f \in F$, we realize that M accepts $a_1 \dots a_n$.

Example 6.2 Let us consider the Example 6.1.1, where $[q_0], [q_1], [q_2], [q_3]$ are some of the valid crossing sequences among others. Let the corresponding NFSA $= (K', \{a, b\}, \delta', [q_0], [q_2])$, where K' corresponds to all valid crossing sequences. Empty sequence right and left matches the empty sequence.
$[q_0]$ right matches $[q_1]$ on a
$[q_1]$ right matches $[q_3]$ on b
$[q_2]$ right matches $[q_2]$ on b from the table. Since $\delta(q_2, b) = (q_2, R)$, empty sequence

left matches $\begin{bmatrix} q_2 \\ q_2 \end{bmatrix}$ on b (rule (iv)). Since, $\delta(q_1, b) = (q_3, R)$, $[q_1]$ right matches $\begin{bmatrix} q_3 \\ q_2 \\ q_2 \end{bmatrix}$

on b (rule (iii)) $[q_2]$ right matches $[q_2]$ on b.

Since, $\delta(q_3, b) = (q_2, L)$, $\begin{bmatrix} q_3 \\ q_2 \\ q_2 \end{bmatrix}$ right matches $[q_2]$ on b (**rule** (ii)).

Though we can consider sequences of length upto seven, in this example these sequences are enough. We get a NFSA as follows:

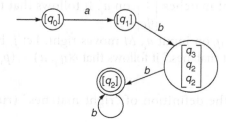

That 2DFSA accept only regular sets that can be proved in another way using Myhill-Nerode theorem, without actually constructing the crossing sequences or NFSA.

Proof 2   Let $M = (K, \Sigma, \delta, q_0, F)$ be a 2DFSA. To show $T(M)$ is regular, consider the relation $R_{T(M)}$ defined in (iii) of Myhill-Nerode theorem. For two strings x_1 and x_2, $x_1 R_{T(M)} x_2$ if $x_1 x$ is in $T(M)$ exactly when $x_2 x$ is in $T(M)$ for any $x \in \Sigma^*$. It is clearly seen that $R_{T(M)}$ is right invariant. If we prove $R_{T(M)}$ is of finite index, then by the third part of the proof of Myhill-Nerode theorem, it will follow that $T(M)$ is regular.

Let $K = \{q_0, \ldots, q_{n-1}\}$ and p be a symbol not in K. For each string $w = a_1 \ldots a_k$, define a function $\tau_w: K \cup \{p\} \to K \cup \{p\}$ as follows: For each state q in K, let $\tau_w(q) = q'$, if M when started on the rightmost symbol of w in state q, ultimately moves off the tape at the right end, going into the state q'. Let $\tau_w(q)$ be p otherwise. (i.e., M started on w does not move off the right end of the tape). Let $\tau(p) = q'$ if M started on the leftmost symbol of w, in state q_0, ultimately moves off the right end of the tape in state q'. Otherwise $\tau_w(p) = p$. (i.e., M started on w at the leftmost symbol in state q_0, does not move off the right end of the tape). Now, we can verify that $x_1 R_{T(M)} x_2$ if $\tau_{x1} = \tau_{x2}$. Consider the strings $x_1 x$ and $x_2 x$.

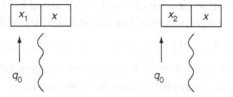

Suppose M is started on $x_1 x$ and moves into the first symbol of x in state r. Then M started on $x_2 x$ will move into the first symbol of x in state r. This is because $\tau_{x1} = \tau_{x2}$. The behavior of M on the x portion is identical for both strings $x_1 x$ and $x_2 x$. When M crosses the boundary between x_1 and x from right to left in state s say, it will do so for $x_2 x$ also. Now, since $\tau_{x1} = \tau_{x2}$ M crosses the boundary between $x_1 x$ and $x_2 x$ from left to right in the same state.

Thus, the crossing sequence at the boundary between x_1 and x is the same as the crossing sequence at the boundary between x_2 and x. Thus, if $x_1 x$ is accepted, so will be $x_2 x$ and vice versa. The number of equivalence classes generated by $R_{T(M)}$ is at most the number of different functions τ_w. Since there are atmost $(n+1)^{(n+1)}$ different functions possible for τ_w (As $\tau_w: K \cup \{p\} \to K \cup \{p\}$), the number of such functions and hence, the number of equivalence classes of $R_{T(M)}$ are finite. Hence, $T(M)$ is regular.

This proves $T(M)$ is regular without actually showing the NFSA accepting it.

6.2   Multihead Finite State Automata

One-way multihead finite automata have been studied in some detail in the literature (Rosenberg, 1996). They have more accepting power than FSA.

Definition 6.3 *A one-way multihead non-deterministic finite automaton* $(k - NFSA)$ *is a device* $M = (k, K, \Sigma, \delta, q_0, \$, F)$, *where* $k \geq 1$ *is the number of input heads, K is the finite set of states, Σ is the finite set of symbols called as alphabet, $q_0 \in K$ is the initial state, $\$ \ (not \ in \ \Sigma)$ is the right end-marker for the inputs, $F \subseteq K$ is the set of final states and δ is a mapping from $K \cup (\Sigma \cup \{\$\})^k$ into the set of subsets of $K \times \{0, 1\}^k$.*

An input to M is a string $a_1 a_2 \ldots a_n$ of symbols in Σ delimited on the right end by the special marker \$. We can think of $a_1 a_2 \ldots a_n \$$ as written on a tape (with each symbol occupying one tape square) and M's heads moving left to right on the tape. A move of M is described as follows: Let M be in the state q with heads $H_1, H_2, \ldots,$ H_k scanning symbols $a_1, \ldots, a_k$ (in $\Sigma \cup \{\$\}$), respectively. Suppose $\delta(q, a_1, \ldots, a_k)$ contains $(p, d_1, \ldots, d_k)$. Then M may move each H_i, d_i squares to the right and enter state p. An instantaneous description ID of M on input $a_1 a_2 \ldots a_n \$$ $(a_i \in \Sigma)$ is given by a $(k + 2)$-tuple $(q, a_1 a_2 \ldots a_n \$, \alpha_1, \alpha_2, \ldots, \alpha_k)$, where q is the state of M and α_i is the distance (i.e., the number of squares) of head H_i from a_1: (Thus, $1 \leq \alpha_i \leq n+1$, where $\alpha_i = 1$, $n + 1$ correspond to H_i being on a_1, \$, respectively.) We define the relation $\vdash$ between ID's as follows: Write $(q, a_1 a_2 \ldots a_n \$, \alpha_1, \alpha_2, \ldots, \alpha_k) \vdash (q', a_1 a_2 \ldots a_n \$,$ $\alpha'_1, \alpha'_2, \ldots, \alpha'_k)$ if from the first ID, M can enter the second ID by a single move. The reflexive-transitive closure of $\vdash$ will be denoted by $\vdash^*$.

A string $a_1 a_2 \ldots a_n$ is accepted (or recognized) by M if:

$$(q_0, a_1 a_2 \ldots a_n \$, 1, \ldots, 1) \vdash^* (q, a_1 a_2 \ldots a_n \$, n +1, \ldots, n +1)$$

for some accepting state q in F. Without loss of generality, we shall assume that $\delta(q, \$, \ldots, \$) = \phi$, i.e., accepting states are halting states.

We say a $k - NFSA$ a simple one-way multihead finite automata, denoted by $k - SNFSA$ if at each transition only one head reads a symbol and moves its head rightwards, i.e., δ is a mapping from $K \cup (\Sigma \cup \{\$\})^k$ into the set of all subsets of $K \times \{0\}^m \times 1 \times \{0\}^n$ where $m + n +1 = k$, $0 \leq m, n \leq k - 1$. We can easily show the equivalence of both $k - NFSA$ and $k - SNFSA$.

Example 6.3 Consider the following 2-head FSA accepting $L = \{a^n b^n | n \geq 1\}$. (Hence, we find non-regular sets are accepted.)

$$M = (2, K, \Sigma, \delta, q_0, \$, F)$$

where $K = \{q_0, q_1, q_2\}$, $\Sigma = \{a, b\}$, $F = \{q_2\}$.

$$\delta(q_0, a, a) = \{(q_0, 1, 0)\}$$
$$\delta(q_0, b, a) = \{(q_1, 1, 1)\}$$
$$\delta(q_1, b, a) = \{(q_1, 1, 1)\}$$
$$\delta(q_1, \$, b) = \{(q_2, 0, 1)\}$$
$$\delta(q_2, \$, b) = \{(q_2, 0, 1)\}$$

The sequence of IDs leading to the acceptance of $aaabbb$ is given below:

$$(q_0, aaabbb\$, 1, 1)$$
$$\vdash (q_0, aaabbb\$, 2, 1)$$

$\vdash (q_0, aaabbb\$, 3, 1)$
$\vdash (q_0, aaabbb\$, 4, 1)$
$\vdash (q_1, aaabbb\$, 5, 2)$
$\vdash (q_1, aaabbb\$, 6, 3)$
$\vdash (q_1, aaabbb\$, 7, 4)$
$\vdash (q_2, aaabbb\$, 7, 5)$
$\vdash (q_2, aaabbb\$, 7, 6)$
$\vdash (q_2, aaabbb\$, 7, 7)$

It can be seen that $\{a^n b^n c^n | n \geq 1\}$, $\{wcw | w \in \{a, b\}^*\}$ can be accepted by multihead FSA. But CFLs like the Dyck set cannot be accepted by multihead FSA.

6.3 Probabilistic Finite Automata

Let $\bar{x} = (x_1, \ldots, x_n)$ be an n-dimensional row stochastic vector, $n \geq 1$. Then, $\bar{x}(i) = x_i, 1 \leq i \leq n, 0 \leq x_i \leq 1, \Sigma x_i = 1$.

Definition 6.4 *A finite probabilistic automaton over a finite alphabet V is an ordered triple PA = (S, s_0, M), where S = $\{s_1, s_2, \ldots, s_n\}$ is a finite set with $n \geq 1$ elements (the set of internal states), s_0 is an n-dimensional stochastic row vector (the initial distribution) and M is a mapping of V into the set of n-dimensional stochastic matrices. For $x \in V$, the (i, j)th entry in the matrix M(x) is denoted by $p_j (s_i, x)$ and referred to as the transient probability of PA to enter into the state s_j, after being in the state s_i after reading the input x.*

As an example, consider the following example $PA_1 = (\{s_1, s_2\}, (1, 0), M)$ over the alphabet $\{x, y\}$ where:

$$M(x) = \begin{vmatrix} 0 & 1 \\ 1 & 0 \end{vmatrix}$$

$$M(y) = \begin{vmatrix} 1/2 & 1/2 \\ 1/2 & 1/2 \end{vmatrix}$$

The initial distribution indicates that s_1 is the initial state. From the matrices M, we see that the state s_1 changes to s_2 with a probability of 1/2 on reading y. This can be indicated in a diagram, with the states being the nodes and the arcs having labels in the form $x(p)$, where x is the symbol, while p is the probability of transition from one node to the other on scanning the symbol x. (Figure 6.1)

For a finite probabilistic automaton, we increase the domain of M from V to V^* as follows:

- $M(\varepsilon) = M$
- $M(wx) = M(w)M(x)$

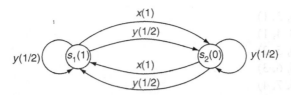

Figure 6.1. State diagram of a probabilistic FSA

Now, for a word w, the $(i, j)th$ entry would denote the probability that the automaton would move to state s_j, if it were initially in state s_i.

Definition 6.5 Let $PA = (\{s_1, \ldots, s_n\}, s_0, M)$ be a finite probabilistic automaton over V and $w \in V^*$. The stochastic row vector $s_0 M(w)$ is termed the distribution of states caused by the word w, and is denoted by $PA(w)$.

We notice that for a word w, the ith entry of $PA(w)$ is the probability that the automaton is in state s_i starting from the initial distribution s_0.

Definition 6.6 Let $\bar{S}_1$ be a n-dimensional column vector, each component of which equals either 0 or 1, and the PA as in the previous definition. Let η be a real number such that $0 \le \eta \le 1$. The language accepted in PA by $\bar{S}_1$ with the cut-point η is defined by: ·

$$L(PA, \bar{S}_1, \eta) = \{w \mid s_0 M(w)\, \bar{S}_1 \ge \eta\}.$$

A language L is η-stochastic for some η.

Clearly there is a one-to-one correspondence between the subsets S_1 of the set $\{s_1, \ldots, s_n\}$ and the column vectors $\bar{S}_1$. To each subset S_1, there corresponds a column vector $\bar{S}_1$ whose ith component equals 1 if and only if $s_i \in S_1$. The language represented by the column vector $\bar{S}_1$ in PA with cut point η consists of all words w such that the sum of the components corresponding to the states of S_1 in the distribution $PA(w)$ is greater than η.

For the example given earlier (Figure 6.1),

$$PA(x^n) = (1, 0)(M(x))^n = (1, 0) \qquad \text{if } n \text{ is even}$$
$$= (0, 1) \text{ if } n \text{ is odd}$$

$$PA(w) = \left(\frac{1}{2}, \frac{1}{2}\right) \text{ if } w \text{ contains at least one } y$$

Thus, if we take $S_1 = \begin{pmatrix} 0 \\ 1 \end{pmatrix}$

i.e., s_2 is a final state and s_1 is not, for $0 \le \eta < \dfrac{1}{2}$ the language accepted is $\Sigma^* - (x^2)^*$;

for $\dfrac{1}{2} \le \eta < 1$ the language accepted is $x(x^2)^*$.

DFSA can be considered as a special case of finite probabilistic automata. If the state set is $\{q_0, \ldots, q_{n-1}\}$ with q_0 as the initial state, initial distribution s_0 is $(1, 0, \ldots, 0)$. For a DFSA $M = (K, \Sigma, \delta, q_0, F)$, a PA can be constructed on the alphabet Σ as follows: $PA = (K, s_0, M)$ $M_x(i, j) = 1$ if $\delta(q_i, x) = q_j$ for $x \in \Sigma$.

Hence, the languages accepted by the PA with cut point η for any $0 < \eta < 1$ is the same as the language accepted by the DFSA M.

Hence, we have the following theorem.

Theorem 6.2   *Every regular language is stochastic. Further, every regular language is η-stochastic for every $0 \leq \eta < 1$.*

Consider a PA over $\{a, b\}$ and $K = \{q_1, q_2, q_3\}$.
Initial distribution π is $(1, 0, 0)$. $S^T = (1, 0, 0)$

$$M(a) = \begin{bmatrix} 1/2 & 1/4 & 1/4 \\ 0 & 0 & 1 \\ 0 & 1/2 & 1/2 \end{bmatrix}$$

$$M(b) = \begin{bmatrix} 0 & 0 & 1 \\ 1/4 & 0 & 3/4 \\ 1 & 0 & 0 \end{bmatrix}$$

$\pi M(a)^2 \overline{S} = 0.25$, $\pi M(a)^3 \overline{S} = 0.125$, $\pi M(b)^3 \overline{S} = 0$.

The strings with probability $\eta = 0.25$ are a^2, $b^{2n}a^2$.

The converse of the above theorem is not true (Salomaa, 1969).

Theorem 6.3   *Every 0-stochastic language is regular.*

Proof   Let $L = L(PA, \overline{S}_1, 0)$ where $PA = (S, s_0, M)$ is a finite probabilistic automaton over Σ. S_1 is an n-dimensional column vector whose components are 0's and 1's.

We construct a set of NFSAs $M_1, \ldots, M_k$ such that $L(PA, \overline{S}_1, 0) = T(M_1) \cup T(M_2) \cup \ldots \cup T(M_k)$. Suppose $S = \{q_1, \ldots, q_n\}$, $s_0 = (a_1, \ldots, a_n)$. Let $a_{i_1}, \ldots, a_{i_k}$ be the non-zero components of s_0.

For each a_{i_j}, $1 \leq j \leq k$, NFSA M_j is constructed as follows:

$$M_j = (K, \Sigma, \delta, q_{i_j}, F)$$

where F corresponds to those elements in $\overline{S}_1$ which are 1's, $\delta(q_i, a)$ contains q_j if $M_{ij}(a)$ is greater than 0. Here M_j is a NFSA with initial state q_{i_j} and final states corresponding to elements of $\overline{S}_1$ which are 1's. δ mapping is the same for all M_j's (only the initial state differs). If there is a transition in the PA with non-zero probability, that is kept in the NFSA.

It is straight forward to see $L(PA, S_1, 0) = T(M_1) \cup \ldots \cup T(M_k)$. $\square$

Similar to regular grammars, regular grammars with probability can be defined, which are counterparts of stochastic finite automata.

Stochastic finite automata have application in syntactic pattern recognition. Consider the following probabilistic automata:

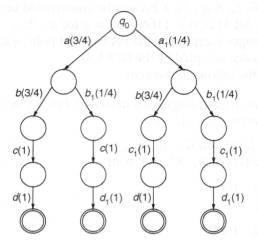

The probabilistic automata given in the above figure accept the quadrilaterals given below. (Figure 6.2)

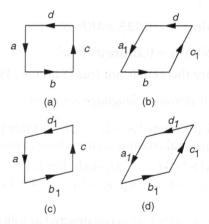

Figure 6.2. Squares and rhombuses generated by PA

Figure (a) is a square while (b), (c), (d) are rhombuses.
Square will be accepted with more probability than the rhombuses.

6.4 Weighted Finite Automata and Digital Images

In this section we consider a variant of finite automata, which is called weighted finite automata (WFA). We give some basic definitions and notations for WFA and the representation of digital images using WFA.

A digital image of finite resolution $m \times n$ consists of $m \times n$ pixels each of which is assigned a value corresponding to its color or grayness. In this section, we consider only square images of resolution $2^n \times 2^n$.

The $2^n \times 2^n$ pixels can be considered to form a bound square on a two dimensional space with x and y orthogonal axes. Thus, the location of each of the $2^n \times 2^n$ pixels can be specified by a tuple (x, y) representing its x and y co-ordinates. Hereafter we will call this tuple as the address of the pixel. The address tuple (x, y) is such that $x \in [0, 2^n - 1]$ and $y \in [0, 2^n - 1]$. Hence, we can specify the x (y) co-ordinate as an n-bit binary number.

In our representation, the address of any pixel at (x, y) is specified as a string $w \in \Sigma^n$, where $\Sigma = \{0, 1, 2, 3\}$. If the n-bits representation of x co-ordinate is $x_{n-1} x_{n-2} \ldots x_1 x_0$ and the n-bits representation of y co-ordinate is $y_{n-1} y_{n-2} \ldots y_1 y_0$, then the address string $w = a_{n-1} a_{n-2} \ldots a_1 a_0$ such that $a_i \in \Sigma$ and $a_i = 2x_i + y_i, \forall i \in [0, 2^n - 1]$. The addresses of the pixels of a 4×4 image are as shown in Figure 6.3.

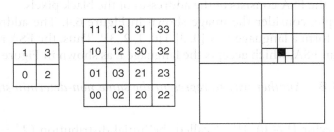

11	13	31	33
10	12	30	32
01	03	21	23
00	02	20	22

1	3
0	2

Figure 6.3. Addressing the subsquares

Another way of getting the same address is to consider a unit square whose subsquares are addressed using 0, 1, 2, 3 as shown in Figure 6.3 and the address of the subsubsquare as a concatenation of the address of the subsquare and the subsubsquare. For example, the address of the darkened square in Figure 6.3 would be 3021. Its co-ordinates are (10, 9) equal to (1010, 1001) in binary. Putting $a_i = 2x_i + y_i$ we get 3021.

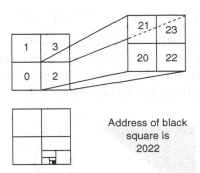

Address of black
square is
2022

6.4.1 Finite Automata and Black-White Images

We give here the representation of black-white images using finite automata (Culik and Kari, 1997).

In order to represent a black-white square image using a finite state automaton, we specify a Boolean function $f\colon \Sigma \to \{0, 1\}$ such that $f(w) = 1$ if the value of the pixel addressed by w is black and $f(w) = 0$ if the value of the pixel addressed by w is white for $w \in \Sigma = \{0, 1, 2, 3\}$.

Definition 6.7   *The FSA representing the $2^n \times 2^n$ resolution black-white image is a non-deterministic FSA, $A = (K, \Sigma, \delta, I, F)$ where*

Q is a finite set of alphabet $\{0, 1, 2, 3\}$.
Σ is a finite set of states.
δ is a transition function as defined for a non-deterministic FSA.
$I \subseteq K$ is a set of initial states. This can be equivalently represented as single initial state q_0 with ε transitions to all states in I.
$F \subseteq K$ is a set of final states.

The language recognized by A, $L(A) = \{w | w \in \Sigma^n, f(w) = 1\}$ i.e., the language recognized by the FSA consists of the addresses of the black pixels.

For example, consider the image shown in Figure 6.4. The addresses of the black squares form a language $L = \{0, 3\}^* 1 \{0, 1, 2, 3\}^*$. Thus, the FSA representing this image is an FSA, which accepts the language L as shown in Figure 6.4.

Definition 6.8   *Another way to represent the same non-deterministic FSA of m states is as:*

1. a row vector $I^A \in \{0, 1\}^{1 \times m}$ called the initial distribution ($I_q^A = 1$ if q is an initial state, 0 otherwise.).

2. a column vector $F^A \in \{0, 1\}^{m \times 1}$ called the final distribution ($F_q^A = 1$ if q is a final state, 0 otherwise.).

3. a matrix $W_a^A \in \{0,1\}^{m \times m}$, $\forall a \in \Sigma$ called the transition matrix ($W_{a_{p,q}}^A = 1$ if $q \in \delta(p, a)$, 0 otherwise.).

This FSA, A, defines the function $f\colon \Sigma^n \to \{0, 1\}$ by:

$$f(a_{n-1} a_{n-2} \dots a_1 a_0) = I^A \cdot W_{a_{n-1}}^A \cdot W_{a_{n-2}}^A \cdot \dots \cdot W_{a_1}^A \cdot W_{a_0}^A \cdot F^A$$

where the operation '$\cdot$' indicates binary multiplication.

We will describe an FSA using diagrams, where states are circles and the transitions are arcs labeled with the alphabet. The initial and final distributions are written inside the circles for each state (see Figure 6.4).

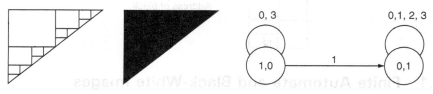

Figure 6.4.   Finite state automaton for a triangle

Next we define a finite state transducer, FST, which represents a transformation such as rotation, translation, etc., on a black-white image. A finite state transducer represents a transformation from an alphabet Σ_1 to another alphabet Σ_2.

Definition 6.9 *An m state finite state transducer FST from an alphabet Σ_1 to an alphabet Σ_2 is specified by:*

1. *a row vector $I \in \{0, 1\}^{1 \times m}$ called the initial distribution;*
2. *a column vector $F \in \{0, 1\}^{m \times 1}$ called the final distribution and*
3. *binary matrices $W_{a,b} \in \{0, 1\}^{m \times m}\ \forall a \in \Sigma_1$ and $b \in \Sigma_2$ called transition matrices.*

Here, we consider only FSTs from Σ to Σ, $\Sigma = \{0, 1, 2, 3\}$. In order to obtain a transformation of an image, we apply the corresponding FST to the FSA representing the image to get a new FSA. The application of an n state FST to an m state FSA $A = (I^A, F^A, W_a^A, a \in \Sigma)$ produces an $n \times m$ state FSA $B = (I^B, F^B, W_b^B, b \in \Sigma)$ as follows:

$$I^B = I \otimes I^A$$

$$F^B = F \otimes F^A$$

$$W_b^B = \sum_{a \in \Sigma} W_{a,b} \otimes W_a^A, \forall b \in \Sigma$$

where the operation $\otimes$ is the ordinary tensor product of matrices. If T and Q are two matrices of size $s \times t$ and $p \times q$ then

$$T \otimes Q = \begin{pmatrix} T_{11}Q & \cdots & T_{1t}Q \\ \vdots & & \vdots \\ T_{s1}Q & \cdots & T_{st}Q \end{pmatrix}$$

We represent the FST in a diagram similar to an FSA. The values in the circles denote the initial and final distributions and the transitions are labeled as 'a/b' as shown in Figure 6.5.

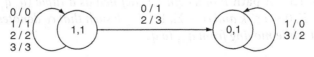

Figure 6.5. Example of a finite state transducer

6.4.2 Weighted Finite Automata and Gray-Scale Images

In this subsection, we present the basic definitions related to the WFA and give the representation of gray-scale images using the WFA.

Definition 6.10 *A **weighted finite automaton** $M = (K, \Sigma, W, I, F)$ is specified by:*

1. *K is a finite set of states.*
2. *Σ is a finite set of alphabets.*
3. *W is the set of weight matrices $W_\alpha: K \times K \rightarrow \Re$ for all $\alpha \in \Sigma \cup \{\varepsilon\}$, the weights of edges labeled α.*
4. *$I: K \rightarrow (-\infty, \infty)$, the initial distribution.*
5. *$F: K \rightarrow (-\infty, \infty)$, the final distribution.*

Here W_α is an $n \times n$ matrix, where $n = |K|$. I is considered to be an $1 \times n$ row vector and F is considered to be an $n \times 1$ column vector. When representing the WFAs as a figure, we follow a format similar to FSAs. Each state is represented by a node in a graph. The initial distribution and final distribution of each state is written as a tuple inside the state. A transition labeled α is drawn as a directed arc from state p to q if $W_\alpha(p, q) \neq 0$. The weight of the edge is written in brackets on the directed arc. For an example of WFA, see Figure 6.6. We use the notation $I_q(F_q)$ to refer to the initial(final) distribution of state q. $W_\alpha(p, q)$ refers to the weight of the transition from p to q. $W_\alpha(p)$ refers to the *pth* row vector of the weight matrix W_α. It gives the weights of all the transitions from state p labeled α in a vector form. Also W_x refers to the product $W_{\alpha_1} \cdot W_{\alpha_2} \dots W_{\alpha_k}$ where $x = \alpha_1 \alpha_2 \dots \alpha_k$.

Definition 6.11 *A WFA is said to be **deterministic** if its underlying FSA is deterministic.*

Definition 6.12 *A WFA is said to be ε-**free** if the weight matrix $W_\varepsilon = 0$ where 0 is the zero matrix of order $n \times n$.*

Hereafter, whenever we use the term WFA, we refer to an ε-free WFA only unless otherwise specified.

A WFA M as in Definition 6.10 defines a function $f: \Sigma^* \rightarrow \Re$, where for all $x \in \Sigma^*$ and $x = \alpha_1 \alpha_2 \dots \alpha_k$,

$$f(x) = I \cdot W_{\alpha_1} \cdot W_{\alpha_2} \cdot \dots \cdot W_{\alpha_k} \cdot F$$

where the operation '$\cdot$' is matrix multiplication.

Definition 6.13 *A **path** P of length k is defined as a tuple $(q_0 q_1 \dots q_k, \alpha_1 \alpha_2 \dots \alpha_k)$ where $q_i \in K, 0 \leq i \leq k$ and $\alpha_i \in \Sigma, 1 \leq i \leq k$ such that α_i denotes the label of the edge traversed while moving from q_{i-1} to q_i.*

Definition 6.14 *The **weight** of a path P is defined as:*

$$W(P) = I_{q_0} \cdot W_{\alpha_1}(q_0, q_1) \cdot W_{\alpha_2}(q_1, q_2) \cdot \dots \cdot W_{\alpha_k}(q_{k-1}, q_k) \cdot F_{q_k}.$$

The function $f: \Sigma^* \rightarrow \Re$ represented by a WFA M can be equivalently defined as follows:

$$f(x) = \sum_{P \text{ is a path of } M \text{ labeled } x} W(P), x \in \Sigma^*$$

Definition 6.15 *A function f: $\Sigma^* \to \Re$ is said to be* **average preserving** *if*

$$f(w) = \frac{1}{m} \sum_{\alpha \in \Sigma} f(w\alpha)$$

for all $w \in \Sigma^*$ where $m = |\Sigma|$.

Definition 6.16 *A WFA M is said to be* **average preserving** *if the function that it represents is average preserving.*

    The general condition to check whether a WFA is average preserving is as follows. A WFA M is average preserving if and only if:

$$\sum_{\alpha \in \Sigma} W_\alpha \cdot F = mF,$$

where $m = |\Sigma|$.

    We also consider the following definitions:

Definition 6.17 *A WFA is said to be* **i-normal** *if the initial distribution of every state is 0 or 1 i.e., $I_{q_i} = 0$ or $I_{q_i} = 1$ for all $q_i \in K$.*

Definition 6.18 *A WFA is said to be* **f-normal** *if the final distribution of every state is 0 or 1 i.e. $F_{q_i} = 0$ or $F_{q_i} = 1$ for all $q_i \in K$.*

Definition 6.19 *A WFA is said to be* **I-normal** *if there is only one state with non-zero initial distribution.*

Definition 6.20 *A WFA is said to be* **F-normal** *if there is only one state with non-zero final distribution.*

Representation of Gray-Scale Images

A gray-scale digital image of finite resolution consists of $2^m \times 2^m$ pixels, where each pixel takes a real grayness value (in reality the value ranges as 0, 1, ... , 256). By a multi-resolution image, we mean a collection of compatible $2^n \times 2^n$ resolution images for $n \geq 0$. Similar to black and white images, we will assign a word $x \in \Sigma^k$ where $\Sigma = \{0, 1, 2, 3\}$ to address each pixel. A word x of length less than k will address a subsquare as in black and white images.

    Then, we can define our finite resolution image as a function $f_i: \Sigma^k \to \Re$, where $f_i(x)$ gives the value of the pixel at address x. A multi-resolution image is a function $f_i: \Sigma^* \to \Re$. It is shown in that for compatibility, the function f_i should be average preserving i.e.,

$$f_I(x) = \frac{1}{4}\left[f_I(x0) + f_I(x1) + f_I(x2) + f_I(x3)\right]$$

    A WFA M is said to represent a multi-resolution image if the function f_M represented by M is the same as the function f_I of the image.

Example 6.4 Consider the 2-state WFA shown in Figure 6.6.

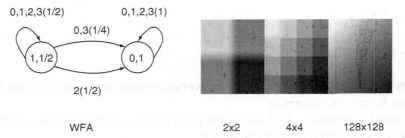

| WFA | | 2x2 | 4x4 | 128x128 |

Figure 6.6. Example: WFA computing linear grayness function

Let $I = (1, 0)$ and $F = \left(\dfrac{1}{2}, 1\right)$, and the weight matrices are $W_0 = \begin{pmatrix} \frac{1}{2} & \frac{1}{4} \\ 0 & 1 \end{pmatrix}$,

$W_1 = \begin{pmatrix} \frac{1}{2} & 0 \\ 0 & 1 \end{pmatrix}, W_2 = \begin{pmatrix} \frac{1}{2} & \frac{1}{2} \\ 0 & 1 \end{pmatrix}, W_3 = \begin{pmatrix} \frac{1}{2} & \frac{1}{4} \\ 0 & 1 \end{pmatrix}.$

$$f(22) = (1,0)\begin{pmatrix} \frac{1}{2} & \frac{1}{2} \\ 0 & 1 \end{pmatrix}\begin{pmatrix} \frac{1}{2} & \frac{1}{2} \\ 0 & 1 \end{pmatrix}\begin{pmatrix} \frac{1}{2} \\ 1 \end{pmatrix}$$

$$= (1,0)\begin{pmatrix} \frac{1}{4} & \frac{3}{4} \\ 0 & 1 \end{pmatrix}\begin{pmatrix} \frac{1}{2} \\ 1 \end{pmatrix}$$

$$= (1,0)\begin{pmatrix} \frac{1}{8}+\frac{3}{4} \\ 1 \end{pmatrix} = \frac{1}{8}+\frac{6}{8} = \frac{7}{8}$$

$$f(11) = (1,0)\begin{pmatrix} \frac{1}{2} & 0 \\ 0 & 1 \end{pmatrix}\begin{pmatrix} \frac{1}{2} & 0 \\ 0 & 1 \end{pmatrix}\begin{pmatrix} \frac{1}{2} \\ 1 \end{pmatrix}$$

$$= (1,0)\begin{pmatrix} \frac{1}{4} & 0 \\ 0 & 1 \end{pmatrix}\begin{pmatrix} \frac{1}{2} \\ 1 \end{pmatrix}$$

$$= (1,0)\begin{pmatrix} \frac{1}{8} \\ 1 \end{pmatrix} = \frac{1}{8}$$

The we can calculate the values of pixels as follows. $f(03) = $ sum of weights of all paths labeled 03.

$$f(03) = \left(1\times\frac{1}{2}\times\frac{1}{2}\times\frac{1}{2}\right)+\left(1\times\frac{1}{2}\times\frac{1}{4}\times1\right)+\left(1\times\frac{1}{4}\times1\times1\right)$$

$$= \frac{1}{8}+\frac{1}{8}+\frac{1}{4} = \frac{1}{2}.$$

Similarly for $f(123)$ we have $f(123) = \dfrac{1}{16} + \dfrac{1}{4} + \dfrac{1}{16} = \dfrac{3}{8}$. The image obtained by this WFA are shown for resolutions 2×2, 4×4 and 128×128 in Figure 6.6.

The RGB format of color images are such that the image in pixel form contains the red, green, and blue values of the pixels. Analogous to gray-scale images, we can use the WFA to represent a color image by extracting the red, green, and blue pixel values and storing the information in a WFA.

6.4.3 Inferencing and De-Inferencing

We described how every digital gray-scale multi-resolution image can be represented by an average-preserving WFA. Algorithms are given for both converting a WFA into a digital image and for inferencing the WFA representing a digital image. The WFA consists of an $I_{1 \times n}$ row vector, $F_{n \times 1}$ column vector and $W_{0_{n \times n}}$, $W_{1_{n \times n}}$, $W_{2_{n \times n}}$, and $W_{3_{n \times n}}$ weight matrices.

De-Inferencing

Assume, we are given a WFA M, $(I, F, W_0, W_1, W_2, W_3)$, and we want to construct a finite resolution approximation of the multi-resolution image represented by M. Let the image to be constructed be $\mathcal{I}$ of resolution $2^k \times 2^k$. Then, for all $x \in \Sigma^k$, we have to compute $f(x) = I \cdot W_x \cdot F$. The algorithm is as follows. The algorithm computes $\phi_p(x)$ for $p \in Q$ for all $x \in \Sigma^i$, $0 \leq i \leq k$. Here, ϕ_p is the image of state p.

Algorithm: De_Infer_WFA

Input   :   WFA $M = (I, F, W_0, W_1, W_2, W_3)$.
Output   : $f(x)$, for all $x \in \Sigma^k$.
           begin

Step 1 :   Set $\phi_p(\varepsilon) \to F_p$ for all $p \in Q$

Step 2 :   for $i = 1, 2, \ldots, k$, *do* the following
           begin

Step 3 :   for all $p \in Q$, $x \in \Sigma^{i-1}$ and $\alpha \in \Sigma$ compute

$$\phi_p(\alpha x) \leftarrow \sum_{q \in Q} W_\alpha(p, q) \cdot \phi_q(x)$$

           end for

Step 4 :   for each $x \in \Sigma^k$, compute

$$f(x) = \sum_{q \in Q} I_q \cdot \phi_q(x).$$

Step 5 :   stop.
           end

The time complexity of the above algorithm is $O(n^2 4^k)$, where n is the number of states in the WFA and $4^k = 2^k \cdot 2^k$ is the number of pixels in the image. We know that $f(x)$ can be computed either by summing the weights of all the paths labeled x or by computing $I \cdot W_x \cdot F$. Finding all paths labeled of length k takes $k \cdot (4k)^n$ time. Since $n \gg k$, we prefer the matrix multiplication over this.

Inferencing

Let $\mathcal{I}$ be the digital gray-scale image of finite resolution $2^k \times 2^k$. In (Culik and Kari, 1994), an iterative algorithm is proposed to obtain the WFA M representing the image $\mathcal{I}$. It is also shown in (Culik and Kari, 1994), that the WFA so obtained is a minimum state WFA. The inference algorithm is given below. In the algorithm Infer_WFA, N is the index of the last state created, i is the index of the first unprocessed state, ϕ_p is the image represented by state p, f_x represents the sub-image at the sub-square labeled x, while $f_{avg}(x)$ represents the average pixel value of the sub-image at the sub-square labeled x, and $\gamma \colon Q \to \Sigma^*$ is a mapping of states to sub-squares.

Algorithm Infer_WFA

Input   :   Image $\mathcal{I}$ of size $2^k \times 2^k$.

Output   :   WFA M representing image $\mathcal{I}$.

             begin

Step 1 :   Set $N \to 0$, $i \leftarrow 0$, $F_{q0} \leftarrow f_{avg}(\varepsilon)$, $\gamma(q_0) \leftarrow \varepsilon$.

Step 2 :   Process q_i, i.e., for $x = \gamma(q_i)$ and each $\alpha \in \{0, 1, 2, 3\}$ do

                begin

Step 3 :   If there are $c_0, c_1, \ldots, c_N$ such that

$$f_{k\alpha} = c_0 \phi_0 + c_1 \phi_1 + \ldots + c_N \phi_N \text{ where } \phi_j = f_{\gamma(q_j)}$$

for $0 \le j \le N$ then set $W_\alpha(q_i, q_j) \leftarrow c_j$ for $0 \le j \le N$.

Step 4 :   else set $\gamma(q_{N+1}) \leftarrow x\alpha$, $F_{q_{N+1}} \leftarrow f_{avg}(x\alpha)$, $W_\alpha(q_i, q_{N+1}) \leftarrow q$

            and $N \leftarrow N + 1$.

              end for

Step 5 :   Set $i \leftarrow i + 1$ and goto Step 2.

Step 6 :   Set $I_{q_0} \leftarrow 1$ and $I_{q_j} \leftarrow 0$ for all $1 \le j \le N$.

            end

Example 6.5   Consider the linearly sloping ap-function f introduced in Example 6.4. Let us apply the inference algorithm to find a minimal ap-WFA generating f.

First, the state q_0 is assigned to the square ε and we define $F_{q_0} = \dfrac{1}{2}$. Consider then the four sub-squares 0, 1, 2, 3. The image in the sub-square 1 can be expressed

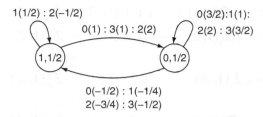

1(1/2) : 2(−1/2)   0(3/2):1(1):
          0(1) : 3(1) : 2(2)   2(2) : 3(3/2)

(1,1/2)   (0,1/2)

0(−1/2) : 1(−1/4)
2(−3/4) : 3(−1/2)

Figure 6.7.   Example: Inference of WFA

as $\dfrac{1}{2}f$ (it is obtained from the original image by decreasing the gray-scale by $\dfrac{1}{2}$)
so that we define $W_1(q_0, q_0) = 0.5$.

The image in sub-square 0 cannot be expressed as a linear combination of f
so that we have to use a second state q_1. Define $W_0(q_0, q_1) = 1$ and $F_{q_1} = \dfrac{1}{2}$ (the

average grayness of sub-square 0 is $\dfrac{1}{2}$). Let f_1 denote the image in sub-square 0 of f.

The image in sub-square 3 is the same as in sub-square 0, so that $W_3(q_0, q_1) = 1$.
In the quadrant 2 we have an image which can be expressed as $2f_1 - \dfrac{1}{2}f$. We

define $W_2(q_0, q_0) = -\dfrac{1}{2}$ and $W_2(q_0, q_1) = 2$. The outgoing transitions from state
q_0 are now ready.

Consider then the images in the square 00, 01, 02 and 03. They can be expressed
as $\dfrac{3}{2}f_1 - \dfrac{1}{2}f, f_1 - \dfrac{1}{4}f, 2f_1 - \dfrac{3}{4}f$ and $\dfrac{3}{2}f_1 - \dfrac{1}{2}f$. This gives us the ap-WFA shown
in Figure 6.7 The initial distribution is $(1, 0)$.

It is shown in Culik and Kari (1997) that in Algorithm Infer_WFA, each state
is independent of the other state, i.e., ϕ_i, where $1 \leq i \leq n$ cannot be expressed as a
linear combination of other states.

$$c_1\phi_1 + c_2\phi_2 + \ldots + c_n\phi_n = 0$$

implies that $c_i = 0$ for all $1 \leq i \leq n$. Hence, the WFA obtained by Algorithm Infer_
WFA is a minimum state WFA.

Now consider Step 3 of Algorithm Infer_WFA. This step asks for finding c_0,
$c_1, \ldots, c_n$ such that $f_\alpha = c_0\phi_0 + c_1\phi_1 + c_2\phi_2 + \cdots + c_n\phi_n$, i.e., to express the sub-image
of the sub-square x_α as a linear combinations of the images represented by the states
so far created. Let the size of the sub-image be $2^k \times 2^k$. Then, the above equation can
be re-stated as follows:

$$\mathcal{I}_{x\alpha,2^k \times 2^k} = c_0 \cdot \mathcal{I}_{0,2^k \times 2^k} + c_1 \cdot \mathcal{I}_{1,2^k \times 2^k} + \cdots + c_n \cdot \mathcal{I}_{n,2^k \times 2^k}$$

where $\mathcal{I}_{i,2^k \times 2^k}$ is the $2^k \times 2^k$ image represented by the state q_i and $\mathcal{I}_{x\alpha,2^k \times 2^k}$ is
the $2^k \times 2^k$ sub-image at the sub-square addressed by $x\alpha$. The equations can be
rewritten as follows:

$$c_0 \mathcal{I}_0(1, 1) + c_1 \mathcal{I}_1(1, 1) + \cdots + c_n \mathcal{I}_n(1, 1) = \mathcal{I}_{x\alpha}(1, 1)$$
$$c_0 \mathcal{I}_0(1, 2) + c_1 \mathcal{I}_1(1, 2) + \cdots + c_n \mathcal{I}_n(1, 2) = \mathcal{I}_{x\alpha}(1, 2)$$
$$\vdots = \vdots$$
$$c_0 \mathcal{I}_0(1, 2^k) + c_1 \mathcal{I}_1(1, 2^k) + \cdots + c_n \mathcal{I}_n(1, 2^k) = \mathcal{I}_{x\alpha}(1, 2^k)$$
$$\vdots = \vdots$$
$$c_0 \mathcal{I}_0(2^k, 1) + c_1 \mathcal{I}_1(2^k, 1) + \cdots + c_n \mathcal{I}_n(2^k, 1) = \mathcal{I}_{x\alpha}(2^k, 1)$$
$$c_0 \mathcal{I}_0(2^k, 2) + c_1 \mathcal{I}_1(2^k, 2) + \cdots + c_n \mathcal{I}_n(2^k, 2) = \mathcal{I}_{x\alpha}(2^k, 2)$$
$$\vdots = \vdots$$
$$c_0 \mathcal{I}_0(2^k, 2^k) + c_1 \mathcal{I}_1(2^k, 2^k) + \cdots + c_n \mathcal{I}_n(2^k, 2^k) = \mathcal{I}_{x\alpha}(2^k, 2^k)$$

This is nothing but a set of linear equations. It can be rewritten in matrix form as $A \cdot C = B$, where A is a $4^k \times (n+1)$ matrix where the *ith* column represents the $2^k \times 2^k = 4^k$ pixels of the image $\mathcal{I}_i$ represented by state q_i. C is an $(n+1) \times 1$ column vector of the coefficients. B is a $4^k \times 1$ vector containing the pixels of the image $I_{x\alpha}$. Thus, Step 3 reduces to solving a set of linear equations.

One well-known method of attacking this problem is using the Gaussian elimination technique. But for using this technique, the rank of the matrix A should be $min(4^k, n)$. But in the general case, $rank(A)$ is found to be $\leq min(4^k, n)$. Hence, this method cannot be used in our case.

Another standard method for solving a set of linear equations is singular value decomposition. This method not only gives the solution, if it exists, but also in the case of non-existing solution, gives us the least mean square approximate solution. The computed coefficients are such that $||B - AC||$ is minimum, where $||M|| = \sqrt{M^T M}$.

Approximate Representation

In image processing applications, it is not always required that the images be exactly represented. We can see that by introducing an error parameter in the above algorithm, the number of states required for representation can be reduced. While solving the linear equations in Step 3 of Algorithm Infer_WFA, we get a solution with least mean square error. We can accept the solution if this error is greater than a positive quantity δ. This way we can represent the image approximately with a smaller automaton.

Compression

In a gray-scale image, eight bits are required per pixel. If the resolution is 512×512, 512×512 bytes are required to store the image. If the number of states is less in a WFA, it can be stored with lesser file space than the image, and we get a compressed representation of the image. It is not difficult to see that any WFA can be made f-normal; further it can be made I-normal since we need not bother about representing images of size 0. Further it was observed that in most cases, the weight matrices obtained are sparse. Hence, it is enough to store only the weights on the edges in a file. This may help to keep an image in compressed form.

Observation

The inference algorithm applied to four images of size 256×256 is given in Figure 6.8. It shows the compression obtained for the images in cases where the error factor was equal to 0%, 5%, 10%, and 15%. The re-constructed images are also shown in Figure 6.8. It can be observed that while error up to 10% does not disturb the figure much, using error of 15% distorts the figure pretty badly. Also, it was observed that the number of states obtained depends on the regularity of the image itself.

The image can perhaps be further compressed by a smarter way of storing the *WFA* in a file. Currently for each edge, four bytes are needed to store the weight (type float). On an average, an n state WFA has $4\frac{n^2}{2} = 2n^2$ edges. The number of bytes used to store an n state WFA is $4(2n^2) = 8n^2$. In order to obtain compression of say 50% for an image of size $2^k \times 2^k$,

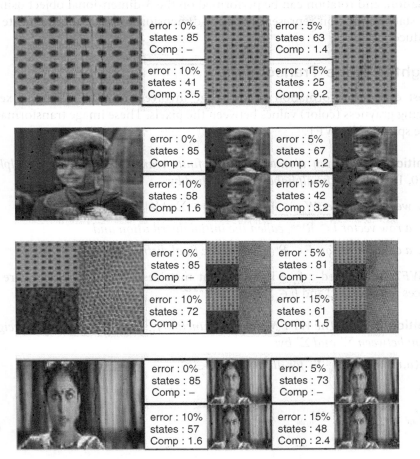

Figure 6.8. Some pictures and their reconstructed images

$$8n^2 \leq \frac{4^k}{2}$$

$$\Rightarrow n^2 \leq \frac{4^k}{16} = 4^{k-2}$$

$$\Rightarrow n \leq 2^{k-2}$$

For a 256×256 image, n should be less than 64 in order to obtain any good compression.

6.4.4 Transformations on Digital Images

Next we give the basic definitions related to the weighted finite transducer (WFT) and show how transformations on the n-WFA, representing the gray-scale and color images, can be done using the WFTs. We also show how 3-dimensional objects can be represented using the FSA and how transformations such as scaling, translation, and rotation can be performed on the 3-dimensional object using the finite state automaton representing the 3-dimensional object and the finite state transducer.

Weighted Finite Transducers

Almost every transformation of an image involves moving (scaling) pixels or changing grayness (color) values between the pixels. These image transformations can be specified by WFT.

Definition 6.21 *An n-state weighted finite transducer M from an alphabet $\Sigma = \{0, 1, 2, 3\}$ into the alphabet Σ is specified by:*

1. *weight matrices $W_{a,b} \in \Re^{n \times n}$ for all $a \in \Sigma \cup \{\varepsilon\}$ and $b \in \Sigma \cup \{\varepsilon\}$;*
2. *a row vector $I \in \Re^{1 \times n}$, called the initial distribution and*
3. *a column vector, $F \in \Re^{n \times 1}$, called the final distribution.*

The *WFT* M is called ε-free if the weight matrices $W_{\varepsilon,\varepsilon}$, $W_{a,\varepsilon}$ and $W_{\varepsilon,b}$ are zero matrices for all $a \in \Sigma$ and $b \in \Sigma$.

Definition 6.22 *The WFT M defines a function $f_M : \Sigma^* \times \Sigma^* \to \Re$, called weighted relation between Σ^* and Σ^* by:*

$$f_M(u,v) = I \cdot W_{u,v} \cdot F, \text{ for all } u \in \Sigma^*, v \in \Sigma^*$$

where

$$W_{u,v} = \sum_{\substack{a_1 \cdots a_k \\ b_1 \cdots b_k}} W_{a_1,b_1} \cdot W_{a_2,b_2} \cdot \ldots \cdot W_{a_k,b_k} \tag{6.1}$$

if the sum converges. (If the sum does not converge, $f_M(u,v)$ remains undefined).

In Equation (6.1), the sum is taken over all decompositions of u and v into symbols $a_i \in \Sigma \cup \{\varepsilon\}$ *and* $b_i \in \Sigma \cup \{\varepsilon\}$, *respectively.*

In the special case of ε-free transducers,

$$f_M(a_1 a_2 \ldots a_k, b_1 b_2 \ldots b_k) = I \cdot W_{a_1, b_1} \cdot W_{a_2, b_2} \cdot \ldots \cdot W_{a_k, b_k} \cdot F,$$

for $a_1 a_2 \ldots a_k \in \Sigma^k$, $b_1 b_2 \ldots b_k \in \Sigma^k$, *and* $f_M(u, v) = 0$, *if* $|u| \neq |v|$.

We recall that WFA defines a multi-resolution function $f : \Sigma^* \to \Re$ *where for all* $x \in \Sigma^*$ *and* $x = \alpha_1, \alpha_2, \ldots \alpha_k$,

$$f(x) = \sum (I \cdot W_{\alpha_1} \cdot W_{\alpha_2} \cdot \ldots \cdot W_{\alpha_k} \cdot F)$$

where the summation is over all possible paths for x and the operation '·' is the matrix multiplication.

Definition 6.23 *Let* $\rho : \Sigma^* \times \Sigma^* \to \Re$ *be a weighted relation and* $f : \Sigma^* \to \Re$, *a multi-resolution function represented by a WFA. The application of ρ to f is the multi-resolution function* $g = \rho(f) : \Sigma^* \to \Re$ *over Σ defined by:*

$$g(v) = \sum_{u \in \Sigma^*} f(u)\rho(u, v), \quad \text{for all } v \in \Sigma^*, \tag{6.2}$$

provided the sum converges. The application $M(f)$ of WFT M to f is defined as the application of the weighted relation f_M to f, i.e. $M(f) = f_M(f)$.

Equation (6.2) defines an application of a WFT to an image in the pixel form. When the image is available in the WFA-compressed form, we can apply a WFT directly to it and compute the re-generated image again from the transformed WFA.

Here, we define the application of the ε-free n-state WFT to a WFA. The application of an ε-free n-state WFT M to an m-state WFA Γ over the alphabet Σ specified by initial distribution I^Γ, final distribution F^Γ and weight matrices W_α^Γ, $\alpha \in \Sigma$, is the mn-state WFA $\Gamma' = M(\Gamma)$ over the alphabet Σ with initial distribution $I^{\Gamma'} = I \otimes I^\Gamma$, final distribution $F^{\Gamma'} = F \otimes F^\Gamma$ and weight matrices

$$W_b^{\Gamma'} = \sum_{a \in \Sigma} W_{a,b} \otimes W_a^\Gamma, \quad \text{for all } b \in \Sigma.$$

Here, $\otimes$ denotes the ordinary tensor product of matrices (called also Kronecker product or direct product), defined as follows: Let T and Q be matrices of sizes $s \times t$ and $p \times q$, respectively. Then, their tensor product is the matrix

$$T \otimes Q = \begin{pmatrix} T_{11}Q & \cdots & T_{1t}Q \\ \vdots & & \vdots \\ T_{s1}Q & \cdots & T_{st}Q \end{pmatrix}$$

of size $sp \times tq$.

Clearly $f_{\Gamma'} = M(f_{\Gamma})$, i.e., the multi-resolution function defined by Γ' is the same as the application of the WFT M to the multi-resolution function computed by the WFA Γ.

We note that every WFT M is a linear operator from $\Re^{\Sigma^*} \rightarrow \Re^{\Sigma^*}$. In other words,

$$M(r_1 f_1 + r_2 f_2) = r_1 M(f_1) + r_2 M(f_2),$$

for all $r_1, r_2 \in \Re$ ft and $f_1, f_2 : \Sigma^* \rightarrow \Re$. More generally, any weighted relation acts as a linear operator.

We give procedures to do transformations such as scaling, translation, and rotation on gray-scale and color images. We give constructions for scaling up the gray-scale image by a factor of 4, scaling down the gray-scale image by a factor of 4, translation of the gray-scale image by units of 2, units of 4, units of 1/2 and units of 1/4 of the gray-scale square image. We also illustrate with examples the above-mentioned transformations on gray-scale and color images.

Scaling

We define how the operation of scaling can be performed on the WFA representing gray-scale images. Consider a gray-scale image of resolution $2^n \times 2^n$. We consider the scaling with respect to the center of the image. So, the co-ordinate axes are shifted to the center of the image. Thus, the new co-ordinate axes are $x' = x - 2^{n-1}$ and $y' = y - 2^{n-1}$.

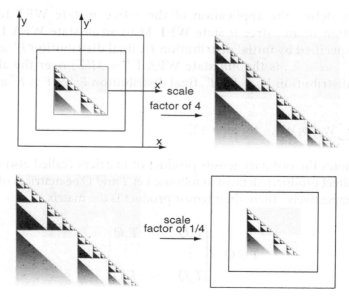

Figure 6.9. Scaling of a gray-scale image.

The operation of scaling by a factor k is defined as follows:

$$x' \leftarrow \frac{x'}{k} \qquad y' \leftarrow \frac{y'}{k}$$

The operation of scaling up by a factor of 4 and scaling down by a factor of 1/4 is illustrated in Figure 6.9. It is seen that the sub-square addressed as 033 in the original gray-scale image becomes the bigger sub-square 0 in the scaled version of the gray-scale image. Similarly, the sub-squares 122, 211, and 300 in the original image are scaled up to form the sub-squares 1, 2 and 3 in the scaled version of the gray-scale image. The *WFA* for the scaled version of the gray-scale image can be obtained from the *WFA* representing the original gray-scale image by introducing a new initial state q'_0 which on reading a 0 (1, 2, 3) makes a transition to the states reachable from the initial states of the original *WFA* by a path labeled 033 (122, 211, 300). The formal construction can be given in a straight-forward manner.

The color images in RGB format are stored in 24 bits per pixel with one byte each for the value of the three primary colors, namely: red, green, and blue. In representing the color image using the *WFA*, we use three functions one each corresponding to the three primary colors. So, the transformation of scaling for color images is same as that mentioned for the gray-scale images except that the *WFA* corresponding to the color image, defines three functions one each for the three primary colors. We illustrate the scaling up of the color image by a factor of 4 and the scaling of the color image by a factor of $\frac{1}{4}$ using an example in Figure 6.10.

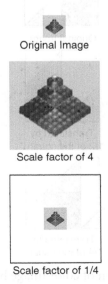

Original Image

Scale factor of 4

Scale factor of 1/4

Figure 6.10. Scaling of the color image (*See color plate on page 417*)

Translation

We define how translations can be performed on WFA representing the gray-scale images using the WFT.

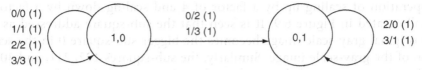

Figure 6.11. WFT for translation

Let Γ be a WFA representing a gray-scale image of resolution $2^n \times 2^n$. Suppose that we want to translate the image from left to right, along the x-axis by one pixel, then the image wraps around on translation i.e., the pixels in the $(2^n - 1)th$ column are moved to the $0th$ column. This is equivalent to adding 1 to the x co-ordinate of the pixels. For example, if the n-bit x co-ordinate of the pixel is $w01^r$, then the x co-ordinate of this pixel after the translation would be $w10^r$, $0 \le r \le n - 1$. The y co-ordinate of the pixel remains unchanged. The WFT for this translation is given in Figure 6.11. The WFA, Γ' representing the translated image can be obtained from the WFA, Γ by applying the WFT to Γ.

As mentioned earlier, the color images are represented by a WFA using three functions, one each for the three primary colors, namely red, green, and blue. So, in order to perform a translation on the color image, we have to apply

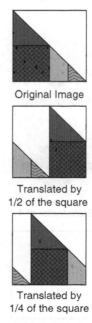

Original Image

Translated by
1/2 of the square

Translated by
1/4 of the square

Figure 6.12. Translation of color image by 1/2 and 1/4 of square
(See color plate on page 417)

the corresponding WFT on all the three functions represented by the WFA. We illustrate the operation of translation on color images with the following example in Figure 6.12.

Rotation also can be done by WFT though the rotated image maybe scaled down by a factor.

Representation of 3-Dimensional Objects

We show how a 3-dimensional object can be represented as an FSA using an alphabet, $\Sigma = \{0, 1, 2, 3, 4, 5, 6, 7\}$. The construction for obtaining the images of the projections of the 3-dimensional object onto the three co-ordinate planes and the construction to obtain the 3-dimensional object from its projections are given in Ramasubramanian and Krithivasan (2000). We see how transformations such as scaling, translation, and rotation can be performed on 3-dimensional objects using the finite state transducers and the FSA representing the object.

A solid object is considered to be a 3-dimensional array. Hence, any point in the solid can be addressed as a 3-tuple (x, y, z). In order to represent the 3-dimensional solid object in the form of a *FSA*, we have to extend the alphabet set Σ, of the *FSA* to $\Sigma = \{0, 1, 2, 3, 4, 5, 6, 7\}$. Now, any string $w \in \Sigma^n$ gives the address of a point in the 3-dimensional space of size $2^n \times 2^n \times 2^n$ enclosing the solid object. If the bit representation of the x co-ordinate is $x_{n-1}x_{n-2} \ldots x_1x_0$, y co-ordinate is $y_{n-1}y_{n-2} \ldots y_1y_0$, z co-ordinate is $z_{n-1}z_{n-2} \ldots z_1z_0$, then the address of the point is the string $w = a_{n-1}a_{n-2} \ldots a_1a_0$ such that

$$a_i = 4x_i + 2y_i + z_i, \quad \forall_i \in [0, n-1]$$

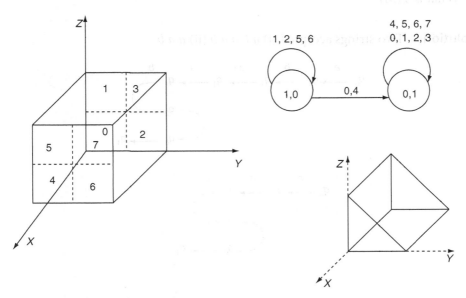

Figure 6.13. Addressing scheme and an example automaton

Figure 6.13 shows how the 8 sub-cubes of a cube are addressed. The figure also gives the FSA which generates the right-angled prism.

Note that whenever we say size of the object, we refer to the 3-dimensional space enclosed by the 3-dimensional object.

Operations like scaling, translation, and rotation can be performed on these 3-dimensional objects using finite state transducers. If the object is solid and convex, in a systematic manner we can find the projections on the three planes. In the other direction, if we are given the projections of an object on the three planes, we can construct the solid object from them. The details are beyond the scope of this book.

Problems and Solutions

1. Consider the following 2DFSA. Give two strings in $T(M)$ and two strings not in $T(M)$ tracing the moves of M.

	a	b
→ q_0	(q_0, R)	(q_1, R)
q_1	(q_1, R)	(q_2, L)
q_2	(q_0, R)	(q_2, L)

What is $T(M)$?

Solution. Two strings accepted (i) $a\,b\,a\,a\,b$ (ii) $a\,a\,b$

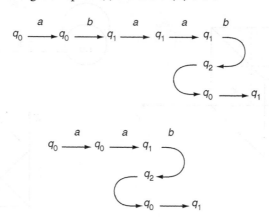

Two strings rejected

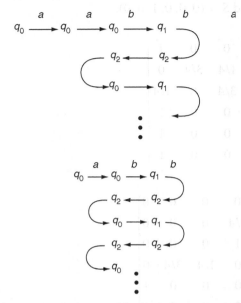

$T(M)$ consists of strings where two b's do not occur consecutively.

2. Consider the PA over the alphabet $\{a, b\}$ with $K = \{q_1, q_2\}$. Initial distribution is $\pi = (1, 0)$ and $\overline{S} = \begin{pmatrix} 0 \\ 1 \end{pmatrix}$.

$$M(a) = \begin{pmatrix} 1/4 & 3/4 \\ 0 & 1 \end{pmatrix}$$

$$M(b) = \begin{pmatrix} 1/2 & 1/2 \\ 1 & 0 \end{pmatrix}$$

Find $\pi M(x) \overline{S}$ where $x \in \{a^2, b^2, ab, a^2b, b^3a^2\}$.

Solution.

$\pi M(a^2) \overline{S} = 0.9375$,
$\pi M(b^2) \overline{S} = 0.25$,
$\pi M(ab) \overline{S} = 0.1250$,
$\pi M(a^2b) \overline{S} = 0.0313$,
$\pi M(b^3a^2) \overline{S} = 0.9609$.

3. Consider the PA over the alphabet $\{a, b\}$ with $K = \{q_1, ..., q_6\}$. Initial distribution is $(1, 0, 0, 0, 0, 0)$ and $S = (0, 0, 0, 1, 0, 0)$.

$$M(a) = \begin{pmatrix} 0 & 0 & 0 & 0 & 0 & 1 \\ 0 & 0 & 0 & 1/4 & 3/4 & 0 \\ 0 & 0 & 0 & 3/4 & 0 & 1/4 \\ 0 & 0 & 0 & 0 & 0 & 1 \\ 0 & 0 & 0 & 0 & 0 & 1 \\ 0 & 0 & 0 & 0 & 0 & 1 \end{pmatrix}$$

$$M(b) = \begin{pmatrix} 0 & 1 & 0 & 0 & 0 & 0 \\ 0 & 1/4 & 3/4 & 0 & 0 & 0 \\ 0 & 0 & 1 & 0 & 0 & 0 \\ 0 & 0 & 0 & 1/4 & 3/4 & 0 \\ 0 & 0 & 0 & 0 & 0 & 1 \\ 0 & 0 & 0 & 0 & 0 & 1 \end{pmatrix}$$

Find $\pi M(x)\,\bar{S}$ where $x \in \{ab, a^2b^2, bab, b^2ab^3, b^4ab\}$. Also, find the language accepted with cut point $\eta = 0.25$.

Solution.

$$\pi M(ab)\,\bar{S} = 0,$$
$$\pi M(a^2b^2)\,\bar{S} = 0,$$
$$\pi M(bab)\,\bar{S} = 0.0625,$$
$$\pi M(b^2ab^3)\,\bar{S} = 0.0098,$$
$$\pi M(b^4ab)\,\bar{S} = 0.1855.$$

For $L(G) = \{b^n a \mid n \geq 1\}$ the cut point η is 0.25.

4. Construct *FSA* over the alphabet $\{0, 1, 2, 3\}$ to represent the following black and white picture.

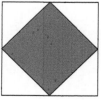

Solution.

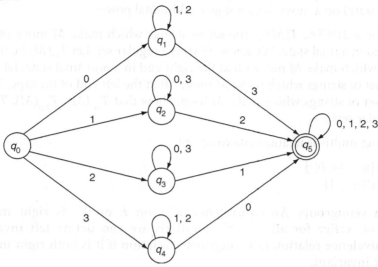

Exercises

1. Consider the following 2DFSA. Give two strings in $T(M)$ and two strings not in $T(M)$ tracing the moves of M.

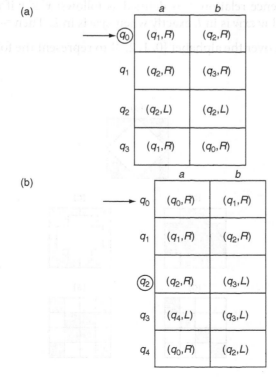

(a)

	a	b
q_0	(q_1,R)	(q_2,R)
q_1	(q_2,R)	(q_3,R)
q_2	(q_2,L)	(q_2,L)
q_3	(q_1,R)	(q_0,R)

(b)

	a	b
q_0	(q_0,R)	(q_1,R)
q_1	(q_1,R)	(q_2,R)
q_2	(q_2,R)	(q_3,L)
q_3	(q_4,L)	(q_3,L)
q_4	(q_0,R)	(q_2,L)

2. Show that adding the capability of 2DFSA to keep its head stationary (and change state) on a move does not give additional power.

3. Let M be a 2DFSA. $T(M)$ is the set of strings which make M move off at the right end in a final state. We know $T(M)$ is a regular set. Let $T_{nf}(M)$ be the set of strings which make M move off at the right end in a non-final state; let $T_{left}(M)$ be the set of strings which make M move off at the left end of the tape. $T_{loop}(M)$ be the set of strings which make M loop. Show that $T_{nf}(M)$, $T_{left}(M)$, $T_{loop}(M)$ are regular sets.

4. Construct multi-head automata to accept:

   i. $\{wcw \mid w \in \{a, b\}^*\}$
   ii. $\{a^n b^n c^n \mid n \geq 1\}$

5. Σ^* is a semigroup. An equivalence relation E on Σ^* is right invariant if $xEy \Rightarrow xzEyz$ for all $z \in \Sigma^*$. Similarly we can define left invariance. An equivalence relation is a congruence relation if it is both right invariant and left invariant.

   Prove that the following three statements about a language $L \subseteq \Sigma^*$ are equivalent:

   a. L is a regular set.
   b. L is the union of some equivalence classes generated, by a congruence relation of finite index over Σ^*.
   c. The congruence relation $\equiv$ is defined as follows: $x \equiv y$ if and only if for all strings z and w zxw is in L exactly when zyw is in L. Then $\equiv$ is of finite index.

6. Construct FSA over the alphabet $\{0, 1, 2, 3\}$ to represent the following black and white pictures.

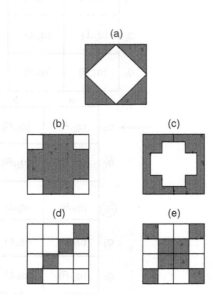

(a)

(b)   (c)

(d)   (e)

Pushdown Automata

In the earlier chapters, we have considered the simplest type of automaton, namely, the FSA. We have seen that a FSA has finite amount memory and hence cannot accept type 2 languages like $\{a^n b^n | n \geq 1\}$. In this chapter, we consider a class of automata, the pushdown automata, which accept exactly the class of context-free (type 2) languages. The pushdown automaton is a finite automaton with an additional tape, which behaves like a stack. We consider two ways of acceptance and show the equivalence between them. The equivalence between context-free grammars (CFG) and pushdown automata is also proved.

7.1 The Pushdown Automaton

Let us consider the following language over the alphabet $\Sigma = \{a, b, c\}$: $L = \{a^n b^m c^n | n, m \geq 1\}$. To accept this, we have an automaton which has a finite control and the input tape which contains the input. Apart from these, there is an additional pushdown tape which is like a stack of plates placed on a spring. Only the top most plate is visible. Plates can be removed from top and added at the top only. In the following example, we have a red plate and a number of blue plates. The machine is initially is q_0 state and initially a red plate is on the stack. When it reads a it adds a blue plate to the stack and remains in state q_0. When it sees the b, it changes to q_1. In q_1, it reads b's without manipulating the stack. When it reads a c it goes to state q_2 and removes a blue plate. In q_2 state, it proceeds to read c's and whenever it reads a c it removes a blue plate. Finally, in q_2 state without reading any input it removes the red plate. The working of the automaton can be summarized by the following table.

State	Top plate	Input		
		a	b	c
q_0	red	add blue plate remain in state q_0	—	—
	blue	add blue plate remain in state q_0	go to q_1	—
q_1	red	—	—	—
	blue	—	remain in state q_1	go to q_2 remove the plate
q_2	red	without waiting for input remove red plate		
	blue	—	—	remain in q_2 remove the plate

Let us see how the automaton treats the input *aabbbaa*.

1. Initially, it is q_0 and reads a *a*. Top plate is red:

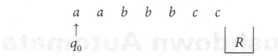

$$a \quad a \quad b \quad b \quad b \quad c \quad c$$

2. When it reads the first *a* in q_0, it adds a blue plate to the stack. Now the situation appears as follows:

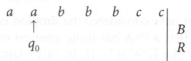

3. When its reads the second *a*, the automaton's instantaneous description (ID) can be represented by:

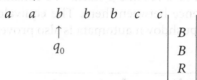

4. In q_0 when it reads a *b* it goes to q_1:

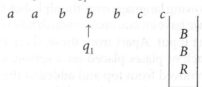

5. In q_1 it reads a *b* without manipulating the stack:

$$a \quad a \quad b \quad b \quad b \quad c \quad c$$

$$\uparrow$$
$$q_1$$

| B |
| B |
| R |

6. In state q_1, when it reads a *c* it removes a blue plate and goes to q_2:

$$a \quad a \quad b \quad b \quad b \quad c \quad c$$

$$\uparrow$$
$$q_1$$

| B |
| B |
| R |

7. In state q_2, when it reads a *c* it removes a blue plate:

$$a \quad a \quad b \quad b \quad b \quad c \quad c$$

$$\uparrow$$
$$q_2$$

| B |
| R |

8. Now, the whole input has been read. The automaton is in q_2 and top plate is red. Now, without looking for the next input it removes the red plate.

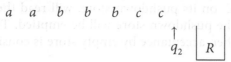

9. The current situation is represented as:

$$a \quad a \quad b \quad b \quad c \quad c$$

The whole input has been read and the stack has been emptied.

The string is accepted by the automaton if the whole input has been read and the stack has been emptied. This automaton can accept in a similar manner any string of the form $a^n b^m c^n$, $n,m \geq 1$.

Now, let us consider the formal definition of a pushdown automaton.

Definition 7.1 *A pushdown automaton (PDA) $M = (K, \Sigma, \Gamma, \delta, q_0, Z_0, F)$ is a 7-tuple where,*

K is a finite set of states
Σ is a finite set of input symbols
Γ is a finite set of pushdown symbols
q_0 in K is the initial state
Z_0 in Γ is the initial pushdown symbol
$F \subseteq K$ is the set of final states

δ is the mapping from $K \times (\Sigma \cup \{\varepsilon\}) \times \Gamma$ into finite subsets of $K \times \Gamma^*$
$\delta(q, a, z)$ contains (p, γ) where $p, q \in K$, $a \in \Sigma \cup \{\varepsilon\}$, $z \in \Gamma$, $\gamma \in \Gamma^*$ which means that when the automaton is ins state q and reading a (reading nothing if $a = \varepsilon$) and the top pushdown symbol is z, it can go to state p and replace z in the pushdown store by the string γ. If $\gamma = z_1 \ldots z_n$; z_1 becomes the new top symbol of the pushdown store. It should be noted that basically the pushdown automaton is non-deterministic in nature.

Definition 7.2 *An instantaneous description (ID) of a PDA is a 3-tuple (q, w, α) where q denotes the current state, w is the portion of the input yet to be read and α denotes the contents of the pushdown store. $w \in \Sigma^*$, $\alpha \in \Gamma^*$ and $q \in K$. By convention, the leftmost symbol of α is the top symbol of the stack.*

If $(q, aa_1 a_2 \ldots a_n, zz_1 \ldots z_n)$ is an ID and $\delta(q, a, z)$ contains $(p, B_1 \ldots B_m)$, then the next ID is $(p, a_1 \ldots a_n, B_1 \ldots B_m z_1 \ldots z_n)$, $a \in \Sigma \cup \{\varepsilon\}$.

This is denoted by $(q, aa_1 \ldots a_n, zz_1 \ldots z_n) \vdash (p, a_1 \ldots a_n, B_1 \ldots B_m z_1 \ldots z_n)$. $\vdash^*$ is the reflexive transitive closure of $\vdash$. The set of strings accepted by the PDA M by emptying the pushdown store is denoted as $Null(M)$ or $N(M)$.

$$N(M) = \{w | w \in \Sigma^*, (q_0, w, Z_0) \vdash^* (q, \varepsilon, \varepsilon) \text{ for some } q \in K\}$$

This means that any string w on the input tape will be accepted by the PDA M by the empty store, if M started in q_0 with its input head pointing to the leftmost symbol of w and Z_0 on its pushdown store, will read the whole of w and go to some state q and the pushdown store will be emptied. This is called acceptance by empty store. When acceptance by empty store is considered, F is taken as the empty set.

There is another way of acceptance called acceptance by final state. Here, when M is started in q_0 with w on the input tape and input tape head pointing to the leftmost symbol of w and with Z_0 on the pushdown store, finally after some moves, reads the whole input and reaches one of the final states. The pushdown store need not be emptied in this case. The language accepted by the pushdown automaton by final state is denoted as $T(M)$.

$$T(M) = \{w \mid w \in \Sigma^*, (q_0, w, Z_0) \vdash^* (q_f, \varepsilon, \gamma) \text{ for some } q_f \in F \text{ and } \gamma \in \Gamma^*\}.$$

Example 7.1 Let us formally define the pushdown automaton for accepting $\{a^n b^m c^n \mid n, m \geq 1\}$ described informally earlier.

$M = (K, \Sigma, \Gamma, \delta, q_0, R, \phi)$ where $K = \{q_0, q_1, q_2\}$, $\Sigma = \{a, b, c\}$, $\Gamma = \{B, R\}$ and δ is given by:

$$\delta(q_0, a, R) = \{(q_0, BR)\}$$
$$\delta(q_0, a, B) = \{(q_0, BB)\}$$
$$\delta(q_0, b, B) = \{(q_1, B)\}$$
$$\delta(q_1, b, B) = \{(q_1, B)\}$$
$$\delta(q_1, c, B) = \{(q_2, \varepsilon)\}$$
$$\delta(q_2, c, B) = \{(q_2, \varepsilon)\}$$
$$\delta(q_2, \varepsilon, R) = \{(q_2, \varepsilon)\}$$

The sequence of *ID's* on input *aabbbcc* is given by:

$(q_0, aabbbcc, R) \vdash (q_0, abbbcc, BR) \vdash (q_0, bbbcc, BBR)$
$\qquad \vdash (q_1, bbcc, BBR) \vdash (q_1, bcc, BBR) \vdash (q_1, cc, BBR)$
$\qquad \vdash (q_2, c, BR) \vdash (q_2, \varepsilon, R) \vdash (q_2, \varepsilon, \varepsilon)$

It can be seen that the above PDA is deterministic. The general definition of PDA is non-deterministic. In order that a PDA is deterministic, two conditions have to be satisfied. At any instance, the automaton should not have a choice between reading a true input symbol or ε; the next move should be uniquely determined. These conditions may be stated formally as follows:

In a deterministic PDA (DPDA),

1. For all q in K, Z in Γ if $\delta(q, \varepsilon, Z)$ is non-empty $\delta(q, a, Z)$ is empty for all $a \in \Sigma$.
2. For all q in K, a in $\Sigma \cup \{\varepsilon\}$, Z in Γ, $\delta(q, a, Z)$ contains at most one element.

In the following sections, we shall show the equivalence of the two modes of acceptance and also the equivalence of non-deterministic PDA with CFG.

Non-deterministic PDA and DPDA are not equivalent. There are languages which can be accepted by non-deterministic PDA but not by DPDA. For example, consider the language $\{ww^R | w \in \{a, b\}^*\}$. Let us informally describe a PDA accepting a string say *abbabbabba*. The pushdown store initially contains a red plate (say). When *a* is read, a blue plate is added and when a *b* is read a green plate is added. This happens, when the PDA reads the first half of the input. During the second half, if a (*a*, blue plate) combination occurs, the blue plate is removed and if a (*b*, green plate) combination occurs, the green plate is removed. Finally, after the whole input is read, the red plate can be removed. Now the question is, how does the automaton know when the second half begins. Whenever *bb* or *aa* occurs in the input, when the automaton looks at the second *b* or *a*, it should consider both possibilities – whether it will be the continuation of the first half or the starting of second half. This language cannot be accepted by any DPDA. It can be seen that any inherently ambiguous context-free language cannot be accepted by DPDA.

7.2 Equivalence between Acceptance by Empty Store and Acceptance by Final State

In this section, we show that acceptance by empty store and acceptance by final state are equivalent.

Theorem 7.1 *L is accepted by a PDA M_1 by empty store, if and only if L is accepted by a PDA M_2 by final state.*

Proof (i) Let L be accepted by a PDA $M_2 = (K, \Sigma, \Gamma, \delta_2, q_0, Z_0, F)$ by final state. Then construct M_1 as follows: $M_1 = (K \cup \{q_0', q_e\}, \Sigma, \Gamma \cup \{X_0\}, \delta_1, q_0', X_0, \phi)$. We add two more states q_0' and q_e and one more pushdown symbol X_0. q_0' is the new initial state and X_0 is the new initial pushdown symbol. q_e is the erasing state.

δ mappings are defined as follows:

1. $\delta_1(q_0', \varepsilon, X_0)$ contains $(q_0, Z_0 X_0)$
2. $\delta_1(q, a, Z)$ includes $\delta_2(q, a, Z)$ for all $q \in K, a \in \Sigma \cup \{\varepsilon\}, Z \in \Gamma$
3. $\delta_1(q_f, \varepsilon, Z)$ contains (q_e, ε) for $q_f \in F$ and $Z \in \Gamma \cup \{X_0\}$
4. $\delta_1(q_e, \varepsilon, Z)$ contains (q_e, ε) for $Z \in \Gamma \cup \{X_0\}$

The first move makes M_1 go to the initial ID of M_2 (except for the X_0 in the pushdown store). Using the second set of mappings M_1 simulates M_2. When M_2 reaches a final state using mapping 3, M_1 goes to the erasing state q_e and using the set of mappings 4, entire pushdown store is erased.

If w is the input accepted by M_2, we have $(q_0, w, Z_0) \underset{M_2}{\overset{*}{\vdash}} (q_f, \varepsilon, \gamma)$. This can happen in M_1 also. $(q_0, w, Z_0) \underset{M_1}{\overset{*}{\vdash}} (q_f, \varepsilon, \gamma)$. M_1 accepts w as follows:

$$(q_0', w, X_0) \vdash (q_0, w, Z_0 X_0) \vdash^* (q_f, \varepsilon, \gamma X_0) \vdash^* (q_e, \varepsilon, \varepsilon) \tag{7.1}$$

Hence, if w is accepted by M_2, it will be accepted by M_1. On the other hand, if M_1 is presented with an input, the first move it can make is using mapping 1 and once it goes to state q_e, it can only erase the pushdown store and has to remain in q_e only. Hence, mapping 1 should be used in the beginning and mapping 3 and 4 in the end. Therefore, mapping 2 will be used in between and the sequence of moves will be as in Equation (7.1).

Hence, $(q_0, w, Z_0 X_0) \vdash_M^* (q_f, \varepsilon, \gamma X_0)$ which means $(q_0, w, Z_0) \vdash_M^* (q_f, \varepsilon, \gamma)$ and w will be accepted by M_2.

(ii) Next, we prove that if L is accepted by M_1 by empty store, it will be accepted by M_2 by final state. Let $M_1 = (K, \Sigma, \Gamma, \delta_1, q_0, Z_0, \phi)$. Then, M_2 is constructed as follows:

$$M_2 = (K \cup \{q_0', q_f\}, \Sigma, \Gamma \cup \{X_0\}, \delta_2, q_0', X_0, \{q_f\})$$

Two more states q_0' and q_f are added to the set of states K. q_0' becomes the new initial state and q_f becomes the only final state. One more pushdown symbol X_0 is added which becomes the new initial pushdown symbol. The δ mappings are defined as follows:

1. $\delta_2(q_0', \varepsilon, X_0)$ contains $(q_0, Z_0 X_0)$
2. $\delta_2(q, a, Z)$ includes all elements of $\delta_1(q, a, Z)$ for $q \in K$, $a \in \Sigma \cup \{\varepsilon\}$, $Z \in \Gamma$
3. $\delta_2(q, \varepsilon, X_0)$ contains (q_f, X_0) for each $q \in K$

Mapping 1 makes M_2 go to the initial ID of M_1 (except for the X_0 in the pushdown store). Then using mapping 2, M_2 simulates M_1. When M_1 accepts by emptying the pushdown store, M_2 has X_0 left on the pushdown store. Using mapping 3, M_2 goes to the final state q_f.

The moves of M_2 in accepting an input w can be described as follows:

$$(q_0', w, X_0) \vdash (q_0, w, Z_0 X_0) \vdash^* (q, \varepsilon, X_0) \vdash (q_f, \varepsilon, X_0)$$

It is not difficult to see that w is accepted by M_2, if and only if w is accepted by M_1.

It should be noted that X_0 is added in the first part for the following reason. M_2 may reject an input w by emptying the store and reaching a nonfinal state. If X_0 were not there, M_1 while simulating M_2 will empty the store and accept the input w. In the second part, X_0 is added because for M_2 to make the last move and reach a final state, a symbol in the pushdown store is required. Thus, we have proved the equivalence of acceptance by empty store and acceptance by final state in the case of non-deterministic PDA. □

Remark The above theorem is not true in the case of DPDA. Any regular set can be accepted by DPDA by final state. The DPDA for a regular set R will behave like a DFSA for R except that throughout the sequence of moves, the pushdown store will contain Z_0 without any change. But even simple regular languages like $\{0\}^*$ cannot be accepted by DPDA by empty store. Suppose we want to accept $\{0\}^*$ by a PDA by empty store. If the initial state is q_0 and the initial pushdown symbol is Z_0, there should be an ε-move for (q_0, Z_0) combination. To read a 'a,' $\delta(q_0, a, Z_0)$ cannot be empty. i.e., both $\delta(q_0, \varepsilon, Z_0)$ and $\delta(q_0, a, Z_0)$ are non-empty and the machine cannot be deterministic.

7.3   Equivalence of CFG and PDA

In this section, we show the equivalence of CFG and non -deterministic PDA.

Theorem 7.2   *If L is generated by a CFG, then L is accepted by a non-deterministic PDA by empty store.*

Proof   Let L be generated by $G = (N, T, P, S)$. Then $M = (\{q\}, T, N \cup T, \delta, q, S, \phi)$ can be constructed to accept $L(G)$. δ is defined as follows.

If $A \rightarrow \alpha$ is a rule in P, $\delta(q, \varepsilon, A)$ contains (q, α). For each α in T, $\delta(q, a, a)$ contains (q, ε).

To see that $L(G) = N(M)$, we note that M simulates a leftmost derivation in G. Suppose

$$S \Rightarrow \alpha_1 \Rightarrow \alpha_2 \Rightarrow \ldots \Rightarrow \alpha_n = w \qquad (7.2)$$

is a leftmost derivation in G. M uses an ε-move if the top pushdown symbol is a non-terminal and reads a true input symbol if the top pushdown symbol is the same as that input symbol and pops it off.

(i) We show if $w \in L(G)$, then $w \in N(M)$.

Consider the derivation in Equation (7.2). Suppose α_i can be written as $x_i \gamma_i$ where x_i is the terminal prefix string and γ_i begins with a non-terminal.

We show by induction on i, the number of steps of derivations in G, that

$$(q, w, S) \vdash^* (q, x_i', \gamma_i) \text{ where } w = x_i x_i' \qquad \square$$

Basis

$i = 0, x_i' = w, \gamma_i = S$

$$(q, w, S) \vdash^* (q, w_i', S)$$

Induction

Suppose the result holds up to i. i.e., $(q, w, S) \vdash^* (q, x_i', \gamma_i)$.

To prove for $i + 1$

$\alpha_i = x_i \gamma_i, \alpha_{i+1} = x_{i+1} \gamma_{i+1}$

and $\alpha_i \Rightarrow \alpha_{i+1}$. The first symbol of γ_i is A say; then we use a rule $A \rightarrow \eta$ to get $\alpha_i \Rightarrow \alpha_{i+1}$.

Now different possibilities arise.

1. η has the form $y_i B \eta_i'$, where $y_i \in T^*$.
2. $\eta \in T^*$ and $\gamma_i = AB\eta_i$, where $B \in N$, $\eta_i \in (N \cup T)^*$.
3. $\eta \in T^*$ and $\gamma_i = Ay'C\eta'_i$, where $y' \in T^*$ and $\eta_i' \in (N \cup T)^*$.

Case (i):   In the first case,

x_i' will be of the form $y_i x_i''$

γ_i will be $A\gamma_i'$

So, we get

$$(q, x_i', \gamma_i) = (q, y_i x_i'', A\gamma_i')$$
$$\vdash (q, y_i x_i'', \eta\gamma_i')$$
$$= (q, y_i x_i'', y_i B\eta_i'\gamma_i')$$
$$\vdash^* (q, x_i'', B\eta_i'\gamma_i')$$

Here $x_i'' = x_{i+1}$ and $\gamma_{i+1} = B\eta_i'\gamma_i'$.

i.e., the PDA uses one ε-move to replace A by $y_i B\eta_i'$ on the stack and matches the symbols of y_i with the symbols on the top of the stack popping them off till B becomes the top of the stack. On the input tape y_i has been read.

Case (ii): $(q, x_i', \gamma_i) = (q, x_i', AB\eta_i)$. Here, x_i' will be of the form $\eta x'_{i+i}$.
$(q, \eta x'_{i+i}, AB\eta_i') \vdash (q, \eta x'_{i+i}, \eta B\eta_i') \vdash^* (q, x'_{i+1}, B\eta_i)$

The symbols of η are matched with the top of the stack and popped off.

Case (iii): $\gamma_i = Ay'C\eta_i'$ where $A, C \in N$, $y' \in T^*$, $\eta_p \in (N \cup T)^*$.
Here x_i' will be of the form $\eta y'x'_{i+1}$.
$(q, \eta y'x'_{i+i}, Ay'C\eta_i') \vdash (q, \eta y'x'_{i+1}, \eta y'C\eta_i')$
$$\vdash^* (q, x'_{i+i}, C\eta_i') = (q, x'_{i+i}, \gamma_{i+1})\ \gamma_{i+1} = C\eta_i'.$$

Finally, $\gamma_n = \varepsilon$; $x_n' = \varepsilon$
$\therefore (q, w, S) \vdash^* (q, \varepsilon, \varepsilon)$

$\therefore w$ will be accepted by M by empty store.

(ii) If $w \in N(M)$, then $w \in L(G)$.

We prove a slightly general result.
If $(q, x, A) \vdash^* (q, \varepsilon, \varepsilon)$ then $A \overset{*}{\Rightarrow} x$.
This can be proved by induction on i, the number of moves of the PDA.

Basis

If $(q, x, A) \vdash (q, \varepsilon, \varepsilon)$,
$\delta(q, x, A)$ contains (q, ε).
x has to be ε by our construction and so $A \to \varepsilon$ is a rule in P.
$A \Rightarrow \varepsilon$. i.e., $A \overset{*}{\Rightarrow} x$.

Induction

Suppose the result is true upto $i - 1$ steps.

Let $(q, x, A) \vdash^* (q, \varepsilon, \varepsilon)$ in i steps. The first step would make use of a mapping of the form $\delta(q, \varepsilon, A)$ contains $(q, B_1 \dots B_m)$. So $(q, x, A) \vdash (q, x, B_1 \dots B_m) \vdash^* (q, \varepsilon, \varepsilon)$. Now x can be written in the form $x_1 x_2 \dots x_m$. After the whole of x is read, stack is emptied (Figure 7.1).

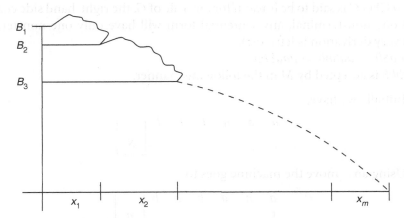

Figure 7.1.   Stack while reading $x_1 x_2 \dots x_m$

Let x_1 be the portion (prefix) of x read at the end of which B_2 becomes the top of the stack (x_1 can be ε).

$\therefore (q, x_1, B_1) \vdash^* (q, \varepsilon, \varepsilon)$.

This should have happened in less than i steps.

$\therefore B_1 \overset{*}{\Rightarrow} x_1$

In a similar manner, we can see that $B_i \overset{*}{\Rightarrow} x_i, 2 \le i \le m$.

Since $(q, x, A) \vdash (q, x, B_1 \dots B_m)$, there should be a mapping $\delta(q, \varepsilon, A)$ contains $(q, B_1 \dots B_m)$ which should have come from the rule $A \rightarrow B_1 \dots B_m$.

Hence, we have

$$A \Rightarrow B_1 \dots B_m \overset{*}{\Rightarrow} x_1 B_2 \dots B_m \overset{*}{\Rightarrow} x_1 x_2 B_3 \dots B_m \Rightarrow \dots$$
$$\overset{*}{\Rightarrow} x_1 x_2 \dots x_{m-1} B_m \overset{*}{\Rightarrow} x_1 x_2 \dots x_{m-1} x_m = x.$$

Now we have to note only that if w is in $N(M)$ $(q, x, S) \vdash^* (q, \varepsilon, \varepsilon)$ and by what we have proved just now $S \overset{*}{\Rightarrow} x$. Hence, $x \in L(G)$.

Having proved this result, let us illustrate with an example.

Example 7.3   Let $G = (\{S\}, \{a, b\}, \{S \rightarrow aSb, S \rightarrow ab\}, S)$ be a CFG.

The corresponding PDA $M = (\{q\}, \{a, b\}, \{S, a, b\}, \delta, q, S, \phi)$ is constructed.

δ is defined as follows:

1. $\delta(q, \varepsilon, S)$ contains (q, aSb)
2. $\delta(q, \varepsilon, S)$ contains (q, ab)
3. $\delta(q, a, a)$ contains (q, ε)
4. $\delta(q, b, b)$ contains (q, ε)

Consider the leftmost derivation of aaabbb (Since the grammar considered is linear – a CFG G is said to be linear if for any rule of G, the right-hand side contains at most one non-terminal, any sentential form will have only one non-terminal and so every derivation is leftmost).

$S \Rightarrow aSb \Rightarrow aaSbb \Rightarrow aaabbb$

aaabbb is accepted by M in the following manner.

1. Initially we have,

$$
\begin{array}{cccccc}
a & a & a & b & b & b \\
\uparrow & & & & &
\end{array}
\quad \boxed{S}
$$

2. Using an ε-move the machine goes to

$$
\begin{array}{cccccc}
a & a & a & b & b & b \\
\uparrow & & & & &
\end{array}
\quad \begin{array}{|c}
a \\
S \\
b
\end{array}
$$

3. a and a are matched using mapping 3 and we get

$$
\begin{array}{cccccc}
a & a & a & b & b & b \\
& \uparrow & & & &
\end{array}
\quad \begin{array}{|c}
S \\
b
\end{array}
$$

4. Using ε-move the next ID becomes

$$
\begin{array}{cccccc}
a & a & a & b & b & b \\
& \uparrow & & & &
\end{array}
\quad \begin{array}{|c}
a \\
S \\
b \\
b
\end{array}
$$

5. a and a are matched. The ID becomes

$$
\begin{array}{cccccc}
a & a & a & b & b & b \\
& & \uparrow & & &
\end{array}
\quad \begin{array}{|c}
S \\
b \\
b
\end{array}
$$

6. Using mapping 2, the next ID becomes

$$a \quad \overset{\uparrow}{a} \quad a \quad b \quad b \quad b \quad \left| \begin{array}{l} a \\ b \\ b \\ b \end{array} \right.$$

In the next four moves, abbb on the input tape are matched with on the stack and symbols on the stack are removed. After reading aaabbb on the input tape, the stack is emptied.

We can also give a diferent proof for Theorem 7.3.

Proof Let us assume that L does not contain ε and $L = L(G)$, where G is in Greibach normal form (GNF). $G = (N, T, P, S)$ where rules in P are of the form $A \rightarrow a\alpha$, $A \in N$, $a \in T$, $\alpha \in N^*$. Then M can be constructed such that $N(M) = L(G)$. $M = (\{q\}, T, N, \delta, q, S \, \phi)$ where δ is defined as follows: If $A \rightarrow a\alpha$ is a rule, $\delta(q, a, A)$ contains (q, ε). M simulates a leftmost derivation in G and the equivalence $L(G) = N(M)$ can be proved using induction. If $\varepsilon \in L$, then we can have a grammar G in GNF with an additional rule $S \rightarrow \varepsilon$ and S will not appear on the right-hand side of any production. In this case, M can have one ε-move defined by $\delta(q, \varepsilon, S)$ contains (q, ε) which will enable it to accept ε. $\qquad \square$

Now, we shall construct a CFG G, given a PDA M such that

$$L(G) = N(M).$$

Theorem 7.3 *If L is accepted by a PDA, then L can be generated by a CFG.*

Proof Let L be accepted by a PDA by empty store.
Construct a CFG $G = (N, T, P, S)$ as follows:

$$N = \{[q, Z, p] | q, p \in K, Z \in \Gamma\} \cup \{S\}.$$

P is defined as follows: $S \rightarrow [q_0, Z_0, q] \in P$ for each q in K.
If $\delta(q, a, A)$ contains $(p, B_1 \dots B_m)$ $(a \in \Sigma \cup \{\varepsilon\})$ is a mapping, then P includes rules of the form:

$[q, A, q_m] \rightarrow a[p, B_1, q_1][q_1, B_2, q_2] \dots [q_{m-1}, B_m, q_m]$ $q_i \in K$, $1 \le i \le m$

If $\delta(q, a, A)$ contains (p, ε) then P includes $[q, A, p] \rightarrow a$

Now, we show that $L(G) = N(M)(= L)$.

It should be noted that the variables and productions in the grammar are defined in such a way that the moves of the PDA are simulated by a leftmost derivation in G.

We prove that:

$$[q, A, p] \overset{*}{\Rightarrow} x \text{ if and only if } (q, x, A) \vdash^* (p, \varepsilon, \varepsilon).$$

That is, if the PDA goes from state q to state p after reading x and the stack initially with A on the top ends with A removed from stack (in between the stack can grow and come down). See Figure 7.1.

This is proved by induction on the number of moves of M.

(i) If $(q, x, A) \vdash^* (p, \varepsilon, \varepsilon)$ then $[q, A, p] \overset{*}{\Rightarrow} x$

Basis

If $(q, x, A) \vdash (p, \varepsilon, \varepsilon)$ $x = a$ or ε, where $a \in \Sigma$ and there should be a mapping δ (q, x, A) contains (p, ε).

In this case, by our construction $[q, A, p] \to x$ is in P.

Hence, $[q, A, p] \Rightarrow x$.

Induction

Suppose the result holds up to $n - 1$ steps.

Let $(q, x, A) \vdash^* (p, \varepsilon, \varepsilon)$ in n steps.

Now, we can write $x = ax'$, $a \in \Sigma \cup \{\varepsilon\}$ and the first move is $(q, ax', A) \vdash (q_1, x', B_1 \ldots B_m)$

This should have come from a mapping $\delta(q, a, A)$ contains $(q_1, B_1 \ldots B_m)$ and there is a rule

$$[q, A, q_{m+1}] \to a[q_1, B_1, q_2][q_2, B_2, q_3] \ldots [q_m, B_m, q_{m+1}] \text{ in } P. \tag{7.3}$$

The stack contains A initially, and is replaced by $B_1 \ldots B_m$. Now, the string x' can be written as $x_1 x_2 \ldots x_m$ such that, the PDA completes reading x_1 when B_2 becomes top of the stack; completes reading x_2 when B_3 becomes the top of the stack and so on.

The situation is described in Figure 7.1.

Therefore, $(q_i, x_i, B_i) \vdash^* (q_{i+1}, \varepsilon, \varepsilon)$ and this happens in less than n steps.

So,

$$(q_i, B_i, q_{i+1}) \overset{*}{\Rightarrow} x_i \text{ by induction hypothesis.} \tag{7.4}$$

Putting $q_{m+1} = p$ in Equation (7.3), we get:

$[q, A, p] \Rightarrow a[q_1, B_1, q_2] \ldots [q_n, B_n, p] \overset{*}{\Rightarrow} ax_1 \ldots x_n = ax' = x$ by Equation (7.4)

Therefore $[q, A, p] \overset{*}{\Rightarrow} x$ in G.

(ii) If $[q, A, p] \overset{*}{\Rightarrow} x$ in G then $(q, x, A) \vdash^* (p, \varepsilon, \varepsilon)$

Proof is by induction on the number of steps in the derivation of G.

Basis

If $[q, A, p] \Rightarrow x$ then $x = a$ or ε where $a \in \Sigma$ and $(q, A, p) \to x$ is a rule in P. This must have come from the mapping $\delta(q, x, A)$ contains (p, ε) and hence $(q, x, A) \vdash (p, \varepsilon, \varepsilon)$.

Induction

Suppose the hypothesis holds up to $(n-1)$ steps and suppose $[q, A, p] \Rightarrow x$ in n steps. The first rule applied in the derivation must be of the form:

$$[q, A, p] \rightarrow a[q_1, B_1, q_2][q_2, B_2, q_3] \dots [q_m, B_m, p] \tag{7.5}$$

and x can be written in the form $x = ax_1 \dots x_m$
such that $[q_i, B_i, q_{i+1}] \overset{*}{\Rightarrow} x_i$.

This derivation must have taken less than n steps and so by the induction hypothesis:

$$(q_i, x_i, B_i) \vdash^* (q_{i+1}, \varepsilon, \varepsilon) \quad 1 \leq i \leq m \text{ and } q_{m+1} = p. \tag{7.6}$$

Equation (7.5) must have come from a mapping $\delta(q, a, A)$ contains $(q, B_1 \dots B_m)$. Therefore,

$$
\begin{aligned}
(q, ax_1 \dots x_m, A) &\vdash (q_1, x_1 \dots x_m, B_1 \dots B_m) \\
&\vdash^* (q_2, x_2 \dots x_m, B_2 \dots B_m) \\
&\vdash^* (q_3, x_3 \dots x_m, B_3 \dots B_m) \\
&\vdots \\
&\vdash^* (q_{m-1}, x_{m-1} x_m, B_{m-1} B_m) \\
&\vdash^* (q_m, x_m, B_m) \\
&\vdash^* (p, \varepsilon, \varepsilon)
\end{aligned}
$$

Hence, $(q, x, A) \vdash^* (p, \varepsilon, \varepsilon)$. Having proved that $(q, x, A) \vdash^* (p, \varepsilon, \varepsilon)$ if and only if $[q, A, p] \overset{*}{\Rightarrow} x$, we can easily see that $S \Rightarrow [q_0, Z_0, q] \overset{*}{\Rightarrow} w$ if and only if $(q_0, w, Z_0) \vdash^* (p, \varepsilon, \varepsilon)$.

This means w is generated by G if and only if w is accepted by M by empty store.

Hence, $L(G) = N(M)$.

Let us illustrate the construction with an example.

Example 7.3 Construct a CFG to generate $N(M)$ where

$$M = (\{p, q\}, \{0, 1\}, \{X, Z_0\} \, \delta, q, Z_0, \phi)$$

where δ is defined as follows:

1. $\delta(q, 1, Z_0) = \{(q, X Z_0)\}$
2. $\delta(q, 1, X) = \{(q, X X)\}$
3. $(q, 0, X) = \{(p, X)\}$
4. $\delta(q, \varepsilon, Z_0) = \{(q, \varepsilon)\}$
5. $\delta(q, 1, X) = \{(p, \varepsilon)\}$
6. $\delta(q, 0, Z_0) = \{(q, Z_0)\}$

It can be seen that:
$$N(M) = \{1^n 0 \, 1^n 0 \mid n \geq 1\}^*$$

The machine while reading 1^n adds X's to the stack and when it reads a 0, changes to state p. In state p, it reads 1^n again removing the X's from the stack. When it reads a 0, it goes to q keeping Z_0 on the stack. It can remove Z_0 by using mapping 4 or repeat the above process several times. Initially, also Z_0 can be removed using mapping 4, without reading any input. Hence, ε will also be accepted.

$G = (N, T, P, S)$ is constructed as follows:

$T = \Sigma$

$N = \{[q, Z_0, q], [q, X, q], [q, Z_0, p], [q, X, p], [p, Z_0, q], [p, X, q], [p, Z_0, p], [p, X, p]\} \cup \{S\}$

Initial rules are:

$r_1.\ S \rightarrow [q, Z_0, q]$
$r_2.\ S \rightarrow [q, Z_0, p]$

Next, we write the rules for the mappings.
Corresponding to mapping 1, we have the rules:

$r_3.\ [q, Z_0, q] \rightarrow 1[q, X, q]\ [q, Z_0, q]$
$r_4.\ [q, Z_0, q] \rightarrow 1[q, X, p]\ [p, Z_0, q]$
$r_5.\ [q, Z_0, p] \rightarrow 1[q, X, q]\ [q, Z_0, p]$
$r_6.\ [q, Z_0, p] \rightarrow 1[q, X, p]\ [p, Z_0, p]$

Corresponding to mapping 2, we have the rules:

$r_7.\ [q, X, q] \rightarrow 1[q, X, q]\ [q, X, p]$
$r_8.\ [q, X, q] \rightarrow 1[q, X, p]\ [p, X, q]$
$r_9.\ [q, X, p] \rightarrow 1[q, X, q]\ [q, X, p]$
$r_{10}.\ [q, X, p] \rightarrow 1[q, X, p]\ [p, X, p]$

Corresponding to mapping 3, we have the rules:

$r_{11}.\ [q, X, q] \rightarrow 0[p, X, q]$
$r_{12}.\ [q, X, p] \rightarrow 0[p, X, p]$

Corresponding to mapping 4, we have the rule:

$r_{13}.\ [q, Z_0, q] \rightarrow \varepsilon$

Corresponding to mapping 5, we have the rule:

$r_{14}.\ [p, X, p] \rightarrow 1$

Corresponding to mapping 6, we have the rule:

$r_{15}.\ [p, Z_0, q] \rightarrow 0[q, Z_0, q]$
$r_{16}.\ [p, Z_0, p] \rightarrow 0[q, Z_0, p]$

So, we have ended up with 16 rules. Let us see whether we can remove some useless non-terminals and rules here.

There is no rule with $[p, X, q]$ on the left-hand side. So, rules involving it can be removed i.e., r_8, r_{11}. Once r_8 and r_{11} are removed, the only rule with $[q, X, q]$ on the left-hand side is r_7 which will create more $[q, X, q]$ whenever applied and the derivation will not terminate. So rules involving $[q, X, q]$ can be removed. *i.e.*, r_3, r_5, r_7, r_9. Now, we are left with rules r_1, r_2, r_4, r_6, r_{10}, r_{12}, r_{13}, r_{14}, r_{15}, r_{16}. If you start with r_2, r_6 can be applied. $[q, Z_0, p]$ will introduce $[p, Z_0, p]$ in the sentential form. Then r_{16} can be applied which will introduce $[q, Z_0, p]$ and the derivation will not terminate. Hence, $[q, Z_0, p]$ and rules involving it can be removed. i.e., rules r_2, r_6, r_{16} can be removed. So, we end up with rules r_1, r_4, r_{10}, r_{12}, r_{13}, r_{14}, r_{15}. Using non-terminals:

A for $[q, z_0, q]$
B for $[q, X, p]$
C for $[p, Z_0, q]$
D for $[p, X, p]$

the rules can be written as:

$S \rightarrow A$
$A \rightarrow 1BC$
$B \rightarrow 1BD$
$B \rightarrow 0D$
$A \rightarrow \varepsilon$
$D \rightarrow 1$
$C \rightarrow 0A$

It can be easily checked that this grammar generates $\{1^n 0 1^n 0 \mid n \geq 1\}^*$.

Problems and Solutions

1. Let $L = \{a^i b^j c^k \mid i, j, k \geq 1 \text{ and } i + j = k\}$

   a. Find a PDA (which accepts via final state) that recognizes L.
   b. Find a PDA (which accepts via empty stack) that recognizes L.

Solution. a. Hint: Push a's and b's into the stack and match them with each c and clear.
The PDA $M = (\{q_0, q_1, q_2, q_3\}, \{a, b, c\}, \{a, b, \$\}, \delta, q_0, \$, \{q3\})$
Transitions are:

$\delta(q_0, a, \$)$ contains $(q_0, a \$)$
$\delta(q_0, a, a)$ contains (q_0, aa)
$\delta(q_0, b, a)$ contains (q_1, ba)
$\delta(q_1, b, b)$ contains (q_1, bb)
$\delta(q_1, c, b)$ contains (q_2, ε)
$\delta(q_2, c, a)$ contains (q_2, ε)
$\delta(q_2, c, b)$ contains (q_2, ε)
$\delta(q_2, \varepsilon, \$)$ contains (q_3, ε)

b. The machine M above is the required PDA, q_3 is the final state and all the transitions remain the same as for (i). This machine accepts L via both by empty stack and final state. Note that this is a DPDA.

2. Find a PDA for $L = \{x \in \{a, b, c\}^* || x|_a + |x|_b = |x|_c\}$.

Solution. This example is slightly different from the previous one as one can have interleaving occurrences of a's, b's and c's.
The transitions are:

$\delta(q_0, a, \$)$ contains $(q_0, a\$)$
$\delta(q_0, b, \$)$ contains $(q_0, b\$)$
$\delta(q_0, c, \$)$ contains $(q_0, c\$)$
$\delta(q_0, a, a)$ contains (q_0, aa)
$\delta(q_0, a, b)$ contains (q_0, ab)
$\delta(q_0, b, a)$ contains (q_0, ba)
$\delta(q_0, b, b)$ contains (q_0, bb)
$\delta(q_0, c, c)$ contains (q_0, cc)
$\delta(q_0, a, c)$ contains (q_0, ε)
$\delta(q_0, b, c)$ contains (q_0, ε)
$\delta(q_0, c, a)$ contains (q_0, ε)
$\delta(q_0, c, b)$ contains (q_0, ε)
$\delta(q_0, \varepsilon, \$)$ contains (q_f, ε)
q_f - final state.

3. Give an example of a finite language that cannot be recognized by any one-state PDA that accepts via final state.

Solution. $L = \{abc\}$

Reason
If abc is accepted in state q_0, then ab, a are also accepted in q_0.

4. Let $L = \{a^n b^n c^m d^m | n, m \geq 1\}$. Find a PDA that accepts L.

Solution. $M = (\{q_0, q_1, q_2, q_3, q_4\}, \{a, b, c, d\}, \{a, c, \$\}, \delta, q_0, \$, \{q_4\})$
Transitions are:

$\delta(q_0, a, \$)$ contains $(q_0, a\$)$
$\delta(q_0, a, a)$ contains (q_0, aa)
$\delta(q_0, b, a)$ contains (q_1, ε)
$\delta(q_1, b, a)$ contains (q_1, ε)
$\delta(q_1, c, \$)$ contains $(q_2, c\$)$
$\delta(q_2, c, c)$ contains (q_2, cc)
$\delta(q_2, d, c)$ contains (q_3, ε)
$\delta(q_3, d, c)$ contains (q_3, ε)

$\delta(q_3, \varepsilon, \$)$ contains (q_4, ε)

This machine accepts L by empty stack. Taking q_4 as the final state L is accepted by final state also.

5. Design a PDA to accept the following language.

  a. The set of all strings of balanced parentheses. i.e., each left parenthesis has a matching right parentheses and pairs of matching parentheses are properly nested.

  b. The set of all non-palindromes over $\{a, b\}$.

Solution.   a. $M = (\{q_0\}, \{(,)\}, \{x, \$\}, \delta, q_0, \$, \phi)$

δ is given by:

$\delta(q_0, (, \$)$ contains $(q_0, X\$)$
$\delta(q_0, (, X)$ contains $(q_0, X X)$
$\delta(q_0,), X)$ contains (q_0, ε)
$\delta(q_0, \varepsilon, \$)$ contains (q_1, ε)

The acceptance is by empty stack.

b. $M = \{(q_0, q_1, q_2), \{a, b\}, \{0, 1, \$\}, \delta, q_0, \$, \phi\}$

  • For one symbol strings, accept by emptying the stack and going to q_2.

$\delta(q_0, a, \$)$ contains (q_2, ε)
$\delta(q_0, b, \$)$ contains (q_2, ε)

  • First half: Push 0 when a is seen and 1 when b is seen.

$\delta(q_0, a, \$)$ contains $(q_0, 0\$)$
$\delta(q_0, a, 0)$ contains $(q_0, 00)$
$\delta(q_0, a, 1)$ contains $(q_0, 01)$
$\delta(q_0, b, \$)$ contains $(q_0, 1\$)$
$\delta(q_0, b, 0)$ contains $(q_0, 10)$
$\delta(q_0, b, 1)$ contains $(q_0, 11)$

  • Guessing the middle of the string:

Change state: For strings with odd length, a symbol is read without changing the stack.
$\delta(q_0, a, 0)$ contains $(q_1, 0)$
$\delta(q_0, a, 1)$ contains $(q_1, 1)$
$\delta(q_0, b, 0)$ contains $(q_1, 0)$
$\delta(q_0, b, 1)$ contains $(q_1, 1)$

  For strings with even length
  Pop 0 when a is seen, pop 1 when b is seen.
$\delta(q_0, a, 0)$ contains (q_1, ε)
$\delta(q_0, b, 1)$ contains (q_1, ε)

- Keep popping for $(a, 0)$ or $(b, 1)$ combination

$\delta(q_1, a, 0)$ contains (q_1, ε)

$\delta(q_1, b, 1)$ contains (q_1, ε)

- If 0 is not found when a is seen or 1 is not found when b is seen, then pop the symbol and change state to q_2. Then continue to clear out all the symbols including $.

$\delta(q_1, a, 1)$ contains (q_2, ε)

$\delta(q_1, b, 0)$ contains (q_2, ε)

$\delta(q_2, a, 0)$ contains (q_2, ε)

$\delta(q_2, b, 0)$ contains (q_2, ε)

$\delta(q_2, a, 1)$ contains (q_2, ε)

$\delta(q_2, b, 1)$ contains (q_2, ε)

- $(q_2, \varepsilon, \$)$ contains (q_2, ε)

6. Find a PDA for

$$L = \{x0y1 \mid x, y \in \{0, 1\}^*, |x| = |y|\}$$

Solution.

$$M = (\{q_0, q_1, q_2\}, \{0, 1\}, \{X, \$\}, \delta, q_0, \$, \phi\}$$

where δ is given by:

$\delta(q_0, 0, \$)$ contains $(q_0, X\$)$

$\delta(q_0, 0, X)$ contains (q_0, XX)

$\delta(q_0, 1, \$)$ contains $(q_0, X\$)$

$\delta(q_0, 1, X)$ contains (q_0, XX)

$\delta(q_0, 0, \$)$ contains $(q_1, \$)$

$\delta(q_0, 0, X)$ contains (q_1, X)

$\delta(q_1, 0, X)$ contains (q_1, ε)

$\delta(q_1, 1, X)$ contains (q_1, ε)

$\delta(q_1, 1, \$)$ contains (q_2, ε)

Acceptance is by empty stack. We can also look at it as acceptance by final state by taking q_2 as the final state.

Exercises

1. Design a PDA which accepts strings of the form $1^*0^n1^n$ and one which accepts strings which contain twice as many zeros as ones.

2. Find a PDAs which accepts set of strings composed of zeros and ones which are:

   a. not of the form ww

   b. of the form 0^n1^n or 0^n1^{2n}

3. Show that the language $\{0^m\,1^n|m \le n \le 2m\}$ is context-free by giving a PDA that accepts it.

4. Let $G = (N, \Sigma, P, S)$ be a CFG with $P = \{S \to aSA|aAA|b, A \to bBBB, B \to b\}$. Construct a PDA which accepts $L(G)$ by final state.

5. Let M be a PDA such that $M = (K, \Sigma, \Gamma, \delta, q_0, Z, F)$ where $K = \{q_0, q_1, q_2, q_3\}$, $\Sigma = \{a, b\}$, $\Gamma = \{A, Z\}$, $F = \phi$

   δ: $\delta\,(q_0, a, Z) = (q_0, AZ)$
   $\delta(q_0, b, A) = (q_1, \varepsilon)$
   $\delta(q_0, a, A) = (q_3, \varepsilon)$
   $\delta(q_1, \varepsilon, Z) = (q_2, \varepsilon)$
   $\delta(q_3, \varepsilon, Z) = (q_0, AZ)$

   Construct a CFG accepting $L(M)$.

6. Construct a DPDA for the following languages.
   a. $\{a^n b^n|n \ge 1\}$
   b. $\{a^n b^m c^{n+m}|n, m > 0\}$

7. Show that if L is a CFL and $\varepsilon \notin L$, then there is a PDA M accepting L by final state such that M has at most two states and makes no ε-moves.

8. A pushdown transducer (PDT) M is an 8-tuple $(K, \Sigma, \Gamma, \Delta, \delta, q_0, Z_0, F)$, where all the symbols have the same meaning as for a PDA except that Δ is a finite output alphabet and δ is a mapping from $K \times (\Sigma \cup \{\varepsilon\}) \times \Gamma\}$ to finite subsets of $K \times \Gamma^* \times \Delta^*$.

   Any configuration of M will be a 4-tuple (q, x, a, y) where q, x, a are as in any PDA and y is the output string at this point of time. The output happens on a separate tape. It never goes back on this tape for any change. The machine may write a string as part of each instruction.

   Design an automaton that changes infix arithmetic expression to postfix expression.

9. The PDA's defined in this chapter make moves on the input tape oneway only. By allowing it to move two-ways on the input tape by having end markers on the input tape, one can define a two-way PDA or 2PDA. Show that the following languages are recognized by a 2PDA.
   a. $\{a^n b^n c^n|n \ge 1\}$
   b. $\{ww|w \in \{0, 1\}^*\}$

10. For a PDA M, let there exist a constant k such that M can never have more than k symbols on its pushdown stack at any time. Show that $L(M)$ is a regular language.

11. Find a grammar generating $L(M)$, $M = (\{q_0, q_1, q_2\}, \{0, 1\}, \{Z_0, A\}, \delta, q_0, Z_0, \{q_2\})$ where δ is given by:

    $\delta(q_0, a, Z_0) = \{(q_1, AZ_0)\}$
    $\delta(q_0, a, A) = \{(q_1, AA)\}$

$$\delta(q_1, a, A) = \{(q_0, AA)\}$$
$$\delta(q_1, \varepsilon, A) = \{(q_2, AA)\}$$
$$\delta(q_2, b, A) = \{(q_2, \varepsilon)\}$$

12. A PDA $M = (Q_1, \Sigma, \Gamma, \delta, q_0, z_0, F)$ is said to be a single-turn PDA if whenever $(q_0, w, z_0) \vdash^* (q_1, w_1, \gamma_1) \vdash^* (q_2, w_2, \gamma_2) \vdash^* (q_3, w_3, \gamma_3)$ and $|\gamma_2| < |\gamma_1|$, then $|\gamma_3| \leq |\gamma_2|$. That is, once the stack starts to de crease in height, it never increases in height.

Show that a language is generated by a linear CFG if and only it is accepted by a single-turn PDA.

CHAPTER

8 Context-Free Grammars–Properties and Parsing

Pumping lemma for regular sets presented in an earlier chapter was used to prove that some languages are non-regular. Now, we give another pumping lemma for context-free languages (CFL) whose application will be to show that some languages are non-context-free. The idea behind this lemma is that longer strings in a CFL, have substrings which can be pumped to get infinite number of strings in the language.

8.1 Pumping Lemma for CFL

Theorem 8.1 *Let L be a CFL. Then there exists a number k (pumping length) such that if w is a string in L of length at least 'k,' then w can be written as $w = uvxyz$ satisfying the following conditions:*

1. $|vy| > 0$
2. $|vxy| \leq k$
3. *For each $i \geq 0$, $uv^i xy^i z \in L$*

Proof Let G be a context-free grammar (CFG) in Chomsky normal form (CNF) generating L. Let 'n' be the number of non-terminals of G. Take $k = 2^n$. Let 's' be a string in L such that $|s| \geq k$. Any parse tree in G for s must be of depth at least n. This can be seen as follows:

If the parse tree has depth n, it has no path of length greater than n; then the maximum length of the word derived is 2^{n-1}. This statement can be proved by induction. If $n = 1$, the tree has structure $\overset{S}{|}$. If $n = 2$, the tree has the structure $\overset{S}{\bigwedge}\overset{}{}$ ... Assuming that the result holds upto $i - 1$, consider a tree with depth i. No path in this tree is of length greater than i. The tree has the structure as in the figure below.

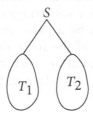

T_1 and T_2 have depth $i - 1$ and the maximum length of the word derivable in each is 2^{i-2}, and so the maximum length of the string derivable in T is $2^{i-2} + 2^{i-2} = 2^{i-1}$.

Choose a parse tree for s that has the least number of nodes. Consider the longest path in this tree. This path is of length at least '$n + 1$.' Then, there must be at least $n + 1$ occurrences of non-terminals along this path. Consider the nodes in this path starting from the leaf node and going up towards the root. By pigeon-hole principle some non-terminal occurring on this path should repeat. Consider the first pair of occurrences of the non-terminal A (say) which repeats while reading along the path from bottom to top. In Figure 8.1, the repetition of A thus identified allows us to replace the subtree under the second occurrence of the non-terminal A with the subtree under the first occurrence of A. The legal parse trees are given in Figure 8.1.

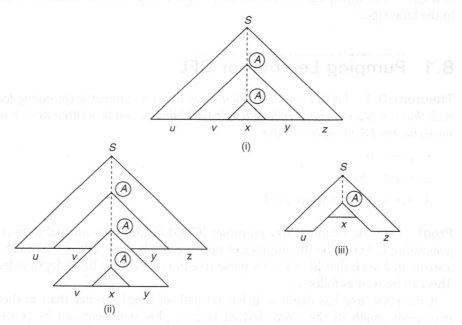

Figure 8.1. Derivation trees showing pumping property

We divide s as $uvxyz$ as in Figure 8.1(i). Each occurrence of A has a subtree, under it generating a substring of s. The occurrence of A near the root of the tree generates the string 'vxy' where the second occurrence of A produces x. Both the occurrences of A produce substrings of s. Hence, one can replace the occurrence of A that produces x by a parse tree that produces vxy as shown in Figure 8.1(ii). Hence, strings of the form uv^ixy^iz, for $i > 0$ are generated. One can replace the subtree rooted at A which produces 'vxy' by a subtree which produced x as in Figure 8.1(iii). Hence, the string 'uxz' is generated. In essence,

$$S \overset{*}{\Rightarrow} u\,Az \overset{*}{\Rightarrow} uv\,Ayz \overset{*}{\Rightarrow} uvxyz$$

We have $A \overset{*}{\Rightarrow} vAy$.

Hence, $A \overset{*}{\Rightarrow} v^i Ay^i$.

Therefore, we have $S \overset{*}{\Rightarrow} u\,Az \overset{*}{\Rightarrow} uv^i Ay^i z \overset{*}{\Rightarrow} uv^i xy^i z$.

Both v and y simultaneously cannot be empty as we consider the grammar in CNF. The lower A will occur in the left or right subtree. If it occurs in the left subtree, y cannot be ε and if it occurs in the right subtree, v cannot be ε.

The length of vxy is at most k, because the first occurrence of A generates vxy and the next occurrence generates x. The number of non-terminal occurrences between these two occurrences of A is less than $n + 1$. Hence, length of vxy is at most $2^n (= k)$. Hence the proof. $\qquad\square$

One can use pumping lemma for showing that some languages are not context-free. The method of proof will be similar to that of application of pumping lemma for regular sets.

Example 8.1 Show that $L = \{a^n b^n c^n | n \geq 0\}$ is not context-free.

Proof Suppose L is context-free. Let p be the pumping length. Choose $s = a^p b^p c^p$. Clearly, $|s| > p$. Then, s can be pumped and all the pumped strings must be in L. But we show that they are not. That is, we show that s can never be divided as $uvxyz$ such that $uv^i xy^i z$ is in L for all $i \geq 0$.

v and y are not empty simultaneously. If v and y can contain more than one type of symbol, then $uv^2 xy^2 z$ may not be of the form $a^n b^n c^n$. If v or y contains only one type of alphabet, then $uv^2 xy^2 z$ cannot contain equal number of a's, b's, and c's or uxz has unequal number of a's, b's, and c's. Thus, a contradiction arises. Hence, L is not a CFL. $\qquad\square$

8.2 Closure Properties of CFL

In this section, we investigate the closure of CFLs under some operations like union, intersection, difference, substitution, homomorphism, and inverse homomorphism etc. The first result that we will prove is closure under substitution, using which we establish closure under union, catenation, catenation closure, catenation +, and homomorphism.

Theorem 8.2 Let L be a CFL over T_Σ and σ be a substitution on T such that $\sigma(a)$ is a CFL for each a in T. Then $\sigma(L)$ is a CFL.

Proof Let $G = (N, T, P, S)$ be a CFG generating L. Since $\sigma(a)$ is a CFL, let $G_a = (N_a, T_a, P_a, S_a)$ be a CFG generating $\sigma(a)$ for each $a \in T$. Without loss of generality, $N_a \cap N_b = \phi$ and $N_a \cap N = \phi$ for $a \neq b$, $a, b \in T$. We now construct a CFG $G' = (N', T', P', S')$ which generates $\sigma(L)$ as follows:

1. N' is the union of N_a's, $a \in T$ and N
2. $T' = \underset{a \in T}{\cup} T_a$
3. P' consists of:
   - all productions in P_a for $a \in T$
   - all productions in P, but for each terminal a occurring in any rule of P, is to be replaced by S_a. i.e., in $A \rightarrow \alpha$, every occurrence of a ($\in T$) in α is replaced by S_a.

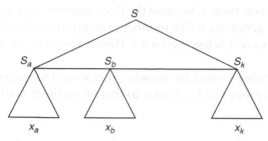

Figure 8.2. A derivation tree showing a string obtained by substitution

Any derivation tree of G' will typically look as in the following figure (Figure 8.2).

Here $ab\ldots k$ is a string of L and $x_a x_b \ldots x_k$ is a string of $\sigma(L)$. To understand the working of G' producing $\sigma(L)$, we have the following discussion:

A string w is in $L(G')$ if and only if w is in $\sigma(L)$. Suppose w is in $\sigma(L)$. Then, there is some string $x = a_1 \ldots a_k$ in L and strings x_i in $\sigma(a_i)$, $1 \leq i \leq k$, such that $w = x_1 \ldots x_k$. Clearly from the construction of G', $S_{a_1} \cdots S_{a_k}$ is generated (for $a_1 \ldots a_k \in L$). From each S_{a_i}, x_is are generated where $x_i \in \sigma(a_i)$. This becomes clear from the above picture of derivation tree. Since G' includes productions of G_{a_i}, $x_1 \ldots x_k$ belongs to $\sigma(L)$.

Conversely for $w \in \sigma(L)$, we have to understand the proof with the help of the parse tree constructed above. That is, the start symbol of G and G' are S. All the non-terminals of G, G_a's are disjoint. Starting from S, one can use the productions of G' and G and reach $w = S_{a_1} \cdots S_{a_k}$ and $w' = a_1 \ldots a_k$, respectively. Hence, whenever w has a parse tree T, one can identity a string $a_1 a_2 \ldots a_k$ in $L(G)$ and string in $\sigma(a_i)$ such that $x_1 \ldots x_k \in \sigma(L)$. Since $x_1 \ldots x_k$ is a string formed by substitution of strings x_i's for a_i's, we conclude $w \in \sigma(L)$. □

Remark One can use the substitution theorem of CFLs to prove the closure of CFLs under other operations.

Theorem 8.3 *CFLs are closed under union, catenation, catenation closure ($*$), catenation $+$, and homomorphism.*

Proof

1. **Union:** Let L_1 and L_2 be two CFLs. If $L = \{1, 2\}$ and $\sigma(1) = L_1$ and $\sigma(2) = L_2$. Clearly, $\sigma(L) = \sigma(1) \cup \sigma(2) = L_1 \cup L_2$ is CFL by the above theorem.
2. **Catenation:** Let L_1 and L_2 be two CFLs. Let $L = \{12\}$. $\sigma(1) = L_1$ and $\sigma(2) = L_2$. Clearly, $\sigma(L) = \sigma(1). \sigma(2) = L_1 L_2$ is CFL as in the above case.

3. **Catenation closure** (∗): Let L_1 be a CFL. Let $L = \{1\}^*$ and $\sigma(1) = L_1$. Clearly, $L_1^* = \sigma(L)$ is a CFL.

4. **Catenation** +: Let L_1 be a CFL. Let $L = \{1\}^+$ and $\sigma(1) = L_1$. Clearly $L_1^+ = \sigma(L)$ is a CFL.

5. **Homomorphism:** This follows as homomorphism is a particular case of substitution. □

Theorem 8.4 *If L is a CFL then L^R is CFL.*

Proof Let $L = L(G)$ be a CFL where $G = (N, T, P, S)$ be a CFG generating L. Let $G^R = (N, T, P^R, S)$ be a new grammar constructed with $P^R = \{A \rightarrow \alpha^R | A \rightarrow \alpha \in P\}$. Clearly, one can show by induction on the length of the derivation that $L(G^R) = L^R$. □

Theorem 8.5 *CFLs are not closed under intersection and complementation.*

Proof Let $L_1 = \{a^n b^n c^m | n, m \geq 1\}$ and $L_2 = \{a^m b^n c^n | n, m \geq 1\}$.

Clearly, L_1 and L_2 are CFLs. (Exercise: Give CFG's for L_1 and L_2).

$L_1 \cap L_2 = \{a^n b^n c^n | n \geq 1\}$ which has been shown to be non-context-free. Hence, CFLs are not closed under ∩.

For non-closure under complementation, if CFL's are closed under complementation, then for any two CFLs L_1 and L_2, $L_1 \cap L_2 = (L_1^c \cup L_2^c)^c$ which is a CFL. Hence, we get CFLs are closed under intersection, which is a contradiction. □

Remark CFLs are not closed under difference i.e., $L_1 - L_2$ need not be a CFL for all CFLs L_1 and L_2. If for all CFLs L_1 and L_2 if $L_1 - L_2$ where a CFL, then taking L_1 as Σ^* we get $\Sigma^* - L_2$ is a CFL for all CFL's L_2, which we know is not true.

Even though intersection of two CFLs need not be context-free, an attempt is made to look for the closure under intersection of a CFL with a regular language. This is a weaker claim.

Theorem 8.6 *If L is a CFL and R is a regular language, then $L \cap R$ is a CFL.*

Proof Let $M = (K, \Sigma, \Gamma, \delta, q_0, Z_0, F)$ be a pushdown automata (PDA) such that $T(M) = L$ and let $A = (\bar{K}, \Sigma, \bar{\delta}, \bar{q}_0, \bar{F})$ be a DFSA such that $T(A) = R$. A new PDA M' is constructed by combining M and A such that the new automaton simulates the action of M and A on an input parallely. Hence, the new PDA M' will be as follows: $M' = (K \times \bar{K}, \Sigma, \Gamma, \delta', [q_0, \bar{q}_0], Z_0, F \times \bar{F})$ where $\delta'([p, q], a, X)$ is defined as follows: $\delta'([p, q], a, X)$ contains $([r, s], \gamma)$ where $\bar{\delta}(q, a) = s$ and $\delta(p, a, X)$ contains (r, γ).

Clearly for each move of the PDA M', there exists a move by the PDA M and a move by A. The input a may be in Σ or $a = \varepsilon$. When a is in Σ, $\bar{\delta}(q, a) = s$ and when $a = \varepsilon, \bar{\delta}(q, a) = q$, i.e., A does not change its state while M' makes a transition on ε.

To prove $L(M') = L \cap R$. We can show that $(q_0, w, Z_0) \overset{*}{\underset{M}{\vdash}} (q_f, \varepsilon, \gamma)$ if and only if $([q_0, \overline{q}_0], w, Z_0) \overset{*}{\underset{M}{\vdash}} ([q_f, p], \varepsilon, \gamma)$ where $\overline{\delta}(\overline{q}_0, w) = p$. The proof is by induction on the number of derivation steps and is similar to that of closure of regular languages with respect to intersection. If $q_f \in F$ and $p \in \overline{F}$, then w belongs to both L and R. Therefore M' accepts $L \cap R$. $\qquad\qquad\square$

Remark Since $L \cap R$ is context-free where L is a CFL and R being regular, $L - R = L \cap \overline{R}$ is also a CFL.

Theorem 8.7 *Family of CFLs is closed under inverse homomorphism.*

Proof Let L be a CFL over Σ'. Let h be a homomorphism from Σ to Σ'. To prove $h^{-1}(L)$ is CFL. We give the proof using PDA which accepts $h^{-1}(L)$. Let $M = (K, \Sigma', \Gamma, \delta, q_0, Z_0, F)$ be a PDA such that $T(M) = L$. We now construct a PDA M' such that $T(M') = h^{-1}(L)$. Let $M' = (K', \Sigma, \Gamma, \delta', (q_0, \varepsilon), Z_0, F \times \{\varepsilon\})$ where

1. $K' = \{(q, x)\ q \in K, x$ is a suffix (need not be proper) of some string $h(a)$ for $a \in \Sigma\}$.

2. δ' is defined to simulate δ and action of h.

    a. $\delta'((q, \varepsilon), a, X) = \{(q, h(a)), X)\}$ for all $a \in \Sigma$, all states $q \in K, X \in \Gamma$. Here a cannot be ε.

    b. If $\delta(q, b, X)$ contains (p, γ) where $b \in \Sigma$ or $b = \varepsilon$, then $\delta'(q, bx), \varepsilon, X)$ contains $((p, x), \gamma)$.

    c. The set of accepting states are of the form (f, ε) where $f \in F$.

From the construction of M', one can see that, for the new PDA M,

    a. a buffer is added to the finite state set.

    b. Whenever the buffer is empty, it can be filled with $h(a)$, where a is the next input symbol, keeping the stack and the state of M in tact.

    c. Whenever the buffer is not empty the PDA M's non-ε-moves can be performed on the frontmost element of the buffer, thereby removing that element from the buffer.

    d. The PDA M's ε-moves can always be performed without affecting the buffer.

Hence, we can see that $(q_0, h(w), Z_0) \overset{*}{\underset{M}{\vdash}} (p, \varepsilon, \gamma)$ if and only if $((q_0, \varepsilon), w, Z_0) \overset{*}{\underset{M}{\vdash}} ((p, \varepsilon), \varepsilon, \gamma)$. The proof that $T(M') = h^{-1}(L)$ follows from the above argument. The whole action of M' having M as its part can be depicted pictorially as shown:

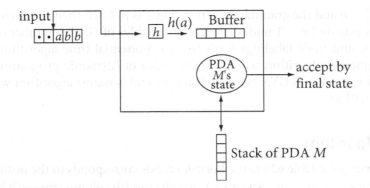

Hence the theorem. □

Since the family of CFL is closed under the six basic operations of union, concatenation, Kleene closure, arbitrary homomorphism, intersection with regular sets, and inverse homomorphism, the family of CFL is a full abstract family of languages (AFL). It is also a full trio.

8.3 Decidability Results for CFL

The three decision problems that we studied for regular languages are emptiness, finiteness, and membership problems. The same can be studied for CFLs also. The discussion of the results under this section is based on either the representation of a CFL as in a PDA form or in simplified CFG form. Hence, we will be using CFG in CNF or a PDA which accepts by empty stack or final state.

Theorem 8.8 *Given a CFL L, there exists an algorithm to test whether L is empty, finite or infinite.*

Proof To test whether L is empty, one can see whether the start symbol S of the CFG $G = (N, T, S, P)$ which generates L is useful or not. If S is a useful symbol, then $L \neq \phi$.

To see whether the given CFL L is infinite, we have the following discussion. By pumping lemma for CFL, if L contains a word of length t, with $|t| > k$ for a constant k (pumping length), then clearly L is infinite.

Conversely, if L is infinite it satisfies the conditions of the pumping lemma, otherwise L is finite. Hence, we have to test whether L contains a word of length greater than k. □

Membership Problem for CFL

Given a CFL L and a string w, one wishes to have a procedure to test whether w is in L or not. One can approach for the result directly using derivation trees.

That if $|w| = n$ and the grammar G generating L is in CNF, then the derivation tree for w uses exactly $2n - 1$ nodes labeled by variables of G. The number of possible trees for w and node labelings leads to an exponential time algorithm. There is another efficient algorithm which uses the idea of "dynamic programming." The algorithm is known as CYK (Cocke, Younger, and Kasami) algorithm which is an $O(n^3)$ algorithm.

CYK Algorithm

We fill a triangular table where the horizontal axis corresponds to the positions of an input string $w = a_1 \, a_2 \ldots a_n$. An entry X_{ij} which is an ith column entry will be filled by a set of variables A such that $A \overset{*}{\Rightarrow} a_i a_{i+1} \ldots a_j$. The triangular table will be filled row wise in upward fashion. For Example, if $w = a_1 a_2 a_3 a_4 a_5$, the table will look like:

$$
\begin{array}{lllll}
X_{15} & & & & \\
X_{14} & X_{25} & & & \\
X_{13} & X_{24} & X_{35} & & \\
X_{12} & X_{23} & X_{34} & X_{45} & \\
X_{11} & X_{22} & X_{33} & X_{44} & X_{55} \\
\hline
a_1 & a_2 & a_3 & a_4 & a_5
\end{array}
$$

Note by the definition of X_{ij}, bottom row corresponds to a string of length one and top row corresponds to a string of length n, if $|w| = n$. The computation of the table is as below.

First row (from bottom): Since the strings beginning and ending position is i, they are simply those variables for which we have $A \rightarrow a_i$, and listed in X_{ii}. We assume that the given CFG in CNF generates L.

To compute X_{ij} which will be in $(j - i + 1)th$ row, we fill all the entries in the rows below. Hence, we know all the variables which give strings $a_i a_{i+1} \ldots a_j$. Clearly, we take $j - i > 0$. Any derivation of the form $A \overset{*}{\Rightarrow} a_i a_{i+1} \ldots a_j$ will have a derivation step like $A \overset{*}{\Rightarrow} BC \overset{*}{\Rightarrow} a_i a_{i+1} \ldots a_j$. B derives a prefix of $a_i a_{i+1} \ldots a_j$ and C derives a suffix of $a_i a_{i+1} \ldots a_j$, i.e., $B \overset{*}{\Rightarrow} a_i a_{i+1} \ldots a_k$, $k < j$ and $C \overset{*}{\Rightarrow} a_{k+1} a_{k+2} \ldots a_j$. Hence we place A in X_{ij} if, for a k, $i \leq k < j$, there is a production $A \rightarrow BC$ with $B \in X_{ik}$ and $C \in X_{k+1j}$. Since X_{ik} and X_{k+1j} entries are already known for all k, $1 \leq k \leq j$, X_{ij} can be computed.

The algorithm terminates once an entry X_{1n} is filled where n is the length of the input. Hence we have the following theorem.

Theorem 8.8 *The algorithm described above correctly computes X_{ij} for all i and j. Hence $w \in L(G)$, for a CFL $L = L(G)$ if and only if $S \in X_{1n}$.*

Example 8.2 Consider the CFG G with the following productions:

$$S_0 \rightarrow AB|SA$$
$$S \rightarrow AB|SA|a$$

$A \rightarrow AB|SA|a|b$

$B \rightarrow SA$

We shall test the membership of aba in $L(G)$ using CYK algorithm. The table thus produced on application of CYK algorithm is as below:

S_0, S, A, B		
S_0, S, A, B	ϕ	
S, A	A	S, A
a	b	a

Since X_{13} has S_0, *aba* is in $L(G)$.

8.4   SubFamilies of CFL

In this section, we consider the special cases of CFLs.

Definition 8.1   *A CFG $G = (N, T, P, S)$ is said to be linear if all rules are of the form $A \rightarrow xBy$ or $A \rightarrow x$, $x, y \in T^*$, $A, B \in N$. i.e., the right-hand side consists of at most one non-terminal.*

Example 8.3 $G = (\{S\}, \{a, b\}, P, S)$ where $P = \{S \rightarrow aSb, S \rightarrow ab\}$ is a linear CFG generating $L = \{a^n b^n \mid n \geq 1\}$.

Definition 8.2   *For an integer $k \geq 2$, a CFG, $G = (N, T, P, S)$ is termed k-linear if and only if each production in P is one of the three forms, $A \rightarrow xBy$, $A \rightarrow x$, or $S \rightarrow \alpha$, where α contains at most k non-terminals and S does not appear on the right-hand side of any production, $x, y \in T^*$.*
   A CFL is k-linear if and only if it is generated by a k-linear grammar.

Example 8.4 $G = (\{S, X, Y\}, \{a, b, c, d, e\}, P, S)$ where $P = \{S \rightarrow XcY, X \rightarrow aXb, X \rightarrow ab, Y \rightarrow dYe, Y \rightarrow de\}$ generates $\{a^n b^n cd^m e^m \mid n, m \geq 1\}$. This is a 2-linear grammar.

Definition 8.3   *A grammar G is metalinear if and only if there is an integer k such that G is k-linear. A language is metalinear if and only if it is generated by a metalinear grammar.*

Definition 8.4   *A minimal linear grammar is a linear grammar with the initial letter S as the only non-terminal and with $S \rightarrow a$, for some terminal symbol a, as the only production with no non-terminal on the right side. Furthermore, it is assumed that a does not occur in any other production.*

Example 8.5 $G = (\{S\}, \{a, b\}, \{S \to aSa, S \to b\})$ is a minimal linear grammar generating $\{a^n b a^n \mid n \geq 0\}$.

Definition 8.5   *An even linear grammar is a linear grammar where all productions with a non-terminal Y on the right-hand side are of the form $X \to uYv$ where $|u| = |v|$.*

Definition 8.6   *A linear grammar $G = (N, T, P, S)$ is deterministic linear if and only if all production in P are of the two forms.*

$$X \to aYv \quad X \to a, a \in T, \ v \in T^*$$

and furthermore, for any $X \in N$ and $a \in T$, there is at most one production having 'a' as the first symbol on the right-hand side.

Definition 8.7   *A CFG $G = (N, T, P, S)$ is sequential if and only if an ordering on symbols of N can be imposed $\{X_1, \ldots, X_n\}$ where $S = X_1$ and for all rules $X_i \to \alpha$ in P, we have $\alpha \in (V_T \cup \{X_j \mid i \leq j \leq n\})^*$.*

Example 8.6 $G = (\{X_1, X_2\}, \{a, b\}, P, X_1)$ where
$P = \{X_1 \to X_2 X_1, X_1 \to \varepsilon, X_2 \to aX_2 b, X_2 \to ab\}$ is sequential generating L^* where $L = \{a^n b^n \mid n \geq 1\}$.

Definition 8.8   *The family of languages accepted by deterministic PDA are called deterministic CFL (DCFL).*

Definition 8.9   *A PDA $M = (K, \Sigma, \Gamma, \delta, q_p, Z_0, F)$ is called a k-turn PDA, if and only if the stack increases and decreases (makes a turn) at most k times. If it makes just one-turn, it is called a one-turn PDA. When k is finite, it is called finite-line PDA. It should be noted that for some CFL number of turns of the PDA cannot be bounded.*

   We state some results without giving proofs.

Theorem 8.9   *The family of languages accepted by one-turn PDA is the same as the family of linear languages.*

Theorem 8.10   *The class of regular sets forms a subclass of even linear languages.*

Definition 8.10   *A CFG $G = (N, T, P, S)$ is said to be ultralinear (sometimes called non-terminal bounded) if and only if there exists an integer k such that any sentential form α with, $S \overset{*}{\Rightarrow} \alpha$, contains at most k-non-terminals (whether leftmost, rightmost or any derivation is considered). A language is ultralinear (non-terminal bounded) if and only if it is generated by an ultralinear grammar.*

Theorem 8.11   *The family of ultralinear languages is the same as the family of languages accepted by finite-turn PDA.*
For Example, consider the CFL:

$L = \{w | w \in \{a, b\}^+, w \text{ has equal number of } a\text{'s and } b\text{'s}\}.$

For accepting arbitrarily long strings, the number of turns of the PDA cannot be bounded by some k.

Definition 8.11 Let $G = (N, T, P, S)$ be a CFG. For a sentential form α, let $\#_N(\alpha)$ denote the number of non-terminals in α. Let D be a derivation of a word w in G.

$D: S = \alpha_0 \Rightarrow \alpha_1 \Rightarrow \alpha_1 \cdots \Rightarrow \alpha_r = w$

The index of D is defined as:

$ind(D) = \max_{0 \le j \le r} \#_N(\alpha_j)$

For a word w in L(G), there may be several derivations, leftmost, rightmost etc. Also if G is ambiguous, w may have more than one leftmost derivation.
For a word $w \in L(G)$, we define:

$ind(w, G) = \min_D ind(D)$

where D ranges over all derivations of w in G. The index of G, ind(G), is the smallest natural number u such that for all $w \in L(G)$, $ind(w, G) \le u$. If no such u exists, G is said to be of infinite index. Finally, the index of a CFL L is defined as $ind(L) = \min_G ind(G)$ where G ranges over all the CFGs generating L.

We say that a CFL is of finite index, then the index of L is finite. The family of CFL with finite index is denoted as $\mathcal{FI}$. Sometimes, this family is also called the family of derivation-bounded languages.

Example 8.7 Let $G = (\{X_1, X_2\}, \{a, b\}, P, X_1)$ where

$P = \{X_1 \rightarrow X_2 X_1, X_1 \rightarrow \varepsilon, X_2 \rightarrow aX_2b, X_2 \rightarrow ab\}$

is of index 2. The language consists of strings of the form $a^{n_1}b^{n_1}a^{n_2}b^{n_2} \ldots a^{n_r} b^{n_r}$. In a leftmost derivation, the maximum number of non-terminals that can occur is 2 whereas in a rightmost derivation it is r and keeps increasing with r. This grammar is not a non-terminal bounded grammar but it is of finite index.

Example 8.8 L = Dyck set = well-formed strings of parentheses is generated by $\{S \rightarrow SS, S \rightarrow aSb, S \rightarrow ab\}$ $(a = (, b =))$. Here, we find that as the length of the string increases, and the level of nesting increases the number of non-terminals in a sentential form keeps increasing and cannot be bounded. This CFG is not of finite index. L is not of finite index.

Definition 8.12 A CFG $G = (N, T, P, S)$ is termed non-expansive if there is no non-terminal $A \in N$ such that $A \overset{*}{\Rightarrow} \alpha$ and α contains two occurrences of A. Otherwise G is expansive. The family of languages generated by non-expansive grammars is denoted by $\mathcal{NE}$.

Theorem 8.12 $\mathcal{NE} = \mathcal{FI}$.

8.5 Parikh Mapping and Parikh's Theorem

We present in this section a result which connects CFLs to semi-linear sets.

Semi-linear Sets

Let N denote the set of non-negative integers. For each integer $n \geq 1$, let

$$N^n = N \times N \times \ldots \times N \ (n \text{ times})$$

If $x = (x_1, \ldots, x_n)$, and $y = (y_1, \ldots, y_n) \in N^n$, they are called vectors of order n or n-vectors. We can talk about linear dependence, linear independence of such vectors.

$$x + y = (x_1 + y_1, x_2 + y_2, \ldots, x_n + y_n)$$

$cx = (cx_1, cx_2, \ldots, cx_n)$ where c is a constant $c \in N$.

Definition 8.13 *Given subsets C and P of N^n, let $L(C; P)$ denote the set of all elements in N^n which can be represented in the form $c_0 + x_1 + \ldots + x_m$ for some c_0 in C and some (possibly empty) sequence $x_1, \ldots, x_m$ of elements of P. C is called the set of constants and P the set of periods of $L(C; P)$.*

Thus, $L(C; P)$ is the set of all elements x in N^n of the form $x = c_0 + \sum_1^m k_i x_i$ with c_0 in C, $x_1, \ldots, x_m$ in P, and $k_1, \ldots, k_m$ in N. If C consists of exactly one element c_0, $C = \{c_0\}$, then we write $L(C; P)$ as $L(c_0; P)$.

Definition 8.14 *$L \subseteq N^n$ is said to be a linear set if $L = L(c_0; P)$ where $c_0 \in N^n$ and P is a finite set of elements from N^n. $P = \{P_1, \ldots, P_s\}$. In this case, $L(c_0; P)$ can be written as $L(c_0; P_1, \ldots, P_s)$.*

Example 8.9 Let $c_0 = (0, 0, 1)$, $P_1 = (2, 0, 0)$, $P_2 = (0, 2, 0)$.
Then $L((0, 0, 1); (2, 0, 0), (0, 2, 0))$ is a linear set. It has elements of the form $(0, 0, 1) + k_1(2, 0, 0) + k_2(0, 2, 0)$ i.e., $(2k_1, 2k_2, 1)$ where $k_1, k_2 \in N$.

A linear set can be represented in more than one way. If $L(c_0; P_1, \ldots, P_s)$ is a linear set, it can also be represented by $L(c_0; P_1, \ldots, P_s, P_1 + P_2)$ etc. The only condition on P is that it should be finite.

Definition 8.15 *A subset of N^n is said to be semi-linear if it is a finite union of linear sets.*
   Let $L_1 = ((0, 0, 1); (2, 0, 0), (0, 2, 0))$ *be a linear set having elements of the form $(2k_1, 2k_2, 1)$.*
   $L_2 = ((0, 0, 2); (1, 1, 0))$ *be another linear set having elements of the form $(k_3, k_3, 2)$ where $k_1, k_2, k_3 \in N$.*
   Then $L_1 \cup L_2$ is a semi-linear set having elements of the form $(2k_1, 2k_2, 1)$ or $(k_3, k_3, 2)$.

Parikh Mapping

Let $\Sigma = \{a_i \mid 1 \leq i \leq n\}$ be an alphabet. That is, we are considering an ordering among the elements of Σ.

Definition 8.16 *Let* $\Sigma = \{a_i \mid 1 \leq i \leq n\}$. *The mapping* $\psi: \Sigma^* \to N^n$ *is defined by* $\psi(z) = (n_{a_1}(z), n_{a_2}(z), \ldots, n_{a_n}(z))$ *where* $n_{a_i}(z)$ *denotes the number of occurrences of* a_i *in Z.*

Thus $\psi(\varepsilon) = (0, \ldots, 0)$ *and* $\psi(z_1 z_2 \ldots z_r) = \displaystyle\sum_{i=1}^{r} \psi(z_i)$. ψ *is called Parikh mapping. If L is a language,*

$$\psi(L) = \bigcup_{z \in L} \psi(z)$$

Example 8.10 *Let* $\Sigma = \{a, b, c\}$

$z = aabbaaccb$

Then $\psi(z) = (4, 3, 2)$.

The definition of Parikh mapping was given by Parikh in 1961, and also he proved a result connecting CFLs to semi-linear sets.

Theorem 8.13 *If L is a CFL, then* $\psi(L)$ *is semi-linear.*

Proof Without loss of generality, let $\varepsilon \notin L$. Let $G = (N, T, P, S)$ be an ε-free grammar generating L. (If we add ε to L, we need to add only a linear set containing $(0, \ldots, 0)$ alone). Again without loss of generality, we assume G has no unit-productions.

Let N' be a subset of N containing S and let $t = \#(N')$. Consider the subset L' of L which consists of strings w in L having the property that in some derivation tree of $S \overset{*}{\Rightarrow} w$, the non-terminals which are node names are exactly the elements in N'. Since L is the union of all such L' and there are only a finite number of subsets of N and hence only a finite number of such L', it is enough if we show $\psi(L')$ is semi-linear. From that it will follow $\psi(L)$ is semi-linear.

For every element X in N', we define two sets A_X and B_X. A word α in $(N \cup T)^*$ is in A_X if the following conditions are satisfied.

1. α contains exactly one occurrence of X.
2. α contains no other non-terminal.
3. There is a derivation tree of $X \overset{*}{\Rightarrow} \alpha$, containing nodes, whose node names are in N', such that no non-terminal occurs more than $t + 2$ times in any path of the tree.

A word w is in B_X if the following two conditions are satisfied:

4. w is in T^*.
5. There is a derivation tree of $X \overset{*}{\Rightarrow} w$ such that each non-terminal in N', and no other non-terminal, is a node name in the tree. Also no non-terminal occurs more than $t + 2$ times in any path of the tree.

Since there are only a finite number of trees satisfying conditions (3) and (5), A_X and B_X are finite sets.

Extend ψ from $T^* \to N^n$ to $(N \cup T)^k \to N^n$ such that

$$\psi(X) = (0, \ldots, 0)$$

for each X in N' and

$$\psi(z_1, \ldots, z_k) = \sum_1^k \psi(z_i), \quad z_i \in N' \cup T.$$

For Example, if $N' = \{X, Y\}$, $T = \{a, b, c\}$

$$\psi(aabXcYbb) = (2, 3, 1)$$

For each variable X in N' let

$$PA = \{\psi(\alpha) | \alpha \text{ in } A_X\} = \{v_1^X, \ldots, v_{rX}^X\}$$
$$PB = \{\psi(w) \mid w \text{ in } B_S\} = \{u_1 \ldots, u_h\}$$

For each j, $1 \leq j \leq h$, let

$$C_j = \left\{ u_j + \sum_{x \text{ in } N'} \sum_{i=1}^{rX} k_i^X v_i^X \middle| k_i^X \text{ in } N \right\}$$

Each C_j is linear.

To show that $\psi(L')$ is semi-linear it is enough to show that:

$$\psi(L') = \bigcup_{j=1}^h C_j$$

First, we show $\psi(L') \subseteq \bigcup_{j=1}^h Cj$.

Let w be an element of L' and τ (see Figure 8.3) a derivation tree of $S \overset{*}{\Rightarrow} w$ such that the node names in τ which are non-terminals are exactly the elements in N'. Suppose no non-terminal occurs more than $t + 2$ times in any path; then w is in B_s, so that $\psi(w)$ is in $\bigcup_1^h C_j$.

Suppose that some non-terminal occurs more than $t + 2$ times in any path. For each node r in τ, let τ_r be the subtree of τ generated by r. There exists a subtree τ_{β_0} in τ containing $t + 3$ nodes $\beta_0, \beta_1, \cdots, \beta_{t+2}$ with node name X, each β_{i+1} is a descendant of β, such that no proper subtree of τ_{β_0} contains more than $t + 2$ nodes with the same label. For each $i \geq 1$, let $D\left(T_{\beta_i}, T_{\beta_{i+1}}\right)$ be the set of those non-terminals which are node names in T_{β_1}, but not in $T_{\beta_{i+1}}$. Let $p \geq 1$ be the smallest integer such that:

(6) $D\left(T_{\beta_p}, T_{\beta_{p+1}}\right) = \phi$.

If (6) were not true for any p, $1 \leq p \leq t + 1$, then τ would contain at least $t + 1$ different node labels which are non-terminals, a contradiction. Thus, the existence of p is proved. Let τ' be the tree obtained from τ by deleting τ_{β_p} and replacing it with $T_{\beta_{p-1}}$. By (6) the node names which are non-terminals in T' are exactly the non-terminals in N'. Also τ' has fewer nodes than τ. Let U be the part of T_{β_b} from

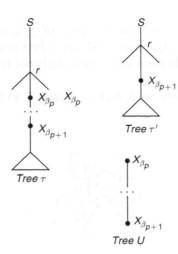

Figure 8.3. Cutting and rejoining of trees

which $T_{\beta_{p-1}}$ has been deleted, but node β_{p+1} remains. Then, U is the derivation tree of a derivation $X \overset{*}{\Rightarrow} w'$ where w contains one occurrence of X. i.e., w' is in A_X. This process of cutting of subtrees can be done for different nodes in τ till a tree with root S occurs such that $S \overset{*}{\Rightarrow} w$ and $\psi(w) = u_j$ for some u_j is in B_S. Whenever this cutting and replacing process takes place, we have removed a portion of τ corresponding to the derivation $X \overset{*}{\Rightarrow} \alpha'$, where α' contains exactly one X and no other non-terminal.

Thus, $\alpha' \in A_X$. Thus, if w is the result of the derivation $S \overset{*}{\Rightarrow} w$ for which τ is the derivation tree, then $\psi(w) \in C_j$. This is because, each cutting and replacing contributes one v_c^X and there will be a finite number of cutting and replacing and final reduced tree τ attributes to u_j. Thus, $\tau(w) \in C_j$. Hence, we get $\psi(L') \subseteq \bigcup_{j=1}^{h} C_j$.

Now, we have to show $\bigcup_{j=1}^{h} C_j \subseteq \psi(L')$.

Let v be in some C_j. Suppose $v = u_j$. Then, $v = \psi(w)$ for some w in B_S and so w is in L'. It is enough, if we show that if v is in $C_j \cap \psi(L')$, then $v + v_i^X$ is in $\psi(L')$, for each v_i^X, X in N' . It will follow that $u_j + \sum_{all\ i, X} k_i^X v_i^X$, k_i^X in N, v_i^X in A_X, is in $\psi(L')$. Thus, $C_j \subseteq \psi(L')$ and the result follows.

Now to show if v is in $C_j \cap \psi(L')$, $v + v_i^X$ is in $\psi(L')$ for each v_i^X, let there be a word $w \in T^*$ such that $S \overset{*}{\Rightarrow} w$ and $\psi(w) = v$ and let τ be the corresponding derivation tree. The non-terminals which are node names in τ are exactly the elements in N'.

By definition of v_i^X, there is a derivation tree τ' of $X \overset{*}{\Rightarrow} w'$ of some word w' such that conditions (1), (2), and (3) are satisfied. Let β_1 be a node in τ whose node name is X. β_1 exists, since the node names in τ are exactly the non-terminals in N'. Let τ be cut at β_1.

This gives rise to two portions T_1 and T_2. Attach T_1 to τ' at β_1 and attach T_2 to τ' at the node β with label X.

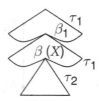

Let τ'' be the tree thus obtained. Then, the result of τ'' is a word w'' in L' such that $\psi(w'') = \psi(w) + v_i^X = v + v_i^X$. Thus $v + v_i^X$ is in $\psi(L')$.

Hence, $\bigcup_{j=1}^{h} C_j = \psi(L')$

Since L is the union of a finite number of such L' and each $\psi(L')$ is semi-linear, $\psi(L)$ is semi-linear.

Example 8.11 $L = \{a^n b^n | n \geq 1\}$

$\psi(L) = L(C; P)$
$C = (1, 1) \quad P = (1, 1)$
$\psi(a^n b^n) = (n, n)$

which can be represented as:

$(1, 1) + (n - 1)(1, 1)$.

We can also see that the grammar for L is $S \rightarrow aSb, S \rightarrow ab$. The constant comes from $S \rightarrow ab$, $(1, 1)$ being $\psi(ab)$.

The period comes from $S \rightarrow aSb$ as $S \overset{*}{\Rightarrow} aSb$ and $\psi(aSb) = (1, 1)$.

Example 8.12 The Parikh mapping for $L = \{wcw^R | w \in \{a, b\}^*\}$ is $L(C; P_1, P_2)$ where

$C = (0, 0, 1)$
$P_1 = (2, 0, 0)$
$P_2 = (0, 2, 0)$

The grammar is $S \rightarrow aSa, S \rightarrow bSb, S \rightarrow c$.
Constant comes from $S \rightarrow c$.
Period P_1 comes from $S \rightarrow aSa$.
Period P_2 comes from $S \rightarrow bSb$.

Application of Parikh's Theorem

Parikh Theorem can be used to show certain languages are not CFL.

Example 8.13 $L = \{a^{n^2} \mid n \geq 1\}$ is not a CFL.

The Parikh mapping of L is $\{(n^2)\}$ which cannot be expressed as a semi-linear set.

If the Parikh mapping of a language L is not semi-linear, we can conclude that L is not context-free. But if the Parikh mapping of L is semi-linear, we cannot conclude L is a CFL. For example, consider $\{a^n b^n c^n \mid n \geq 1\}$. The Parikh mapping can be expressed as $L(c; p)$ where $c = (1, 1, 1)$ and $p = (1, 1, 1)$. But, we know $\{a^n b^n c^n \mid n \geq 1\}$ is not a CFL. Thus, the converse to Parikh's theorem is not true.

In an earlier chapter, we have seen that if a CFL is a bounded CFL, whether it is inherently ambiguous or not, is decidable. The algorithm which does this, is based on Parikh's theorem. We also get the results similar to the one given below as a consequence of Parikh's theorem.

Example 8.14 Let $L = \{w \mid w \in \{a, b\}^*, |w| = n^2 \text{ for an integer } n\}$. Then, L is not context-free.

If L is context-free, by closure under homomorphism, $h(L)$ is context-free for any homomorphism h. Define h from $\{a, b\}^* \to c^*$ as follows:

$h(a) = h(b) = c.$

Then, $h(L) = \{c^{n^2} \mid n \geq 1\}$ which has been shown to be non-context-free by Parikh's theorem. Hence, L cannot be context-free.

8.6 Self-embedding Property

In this section, we consider the self-embedding property which makes CFL more powerful than regular sets. Pumping lemma for CFL makes use of this property. By this property, it is possible to pump equally on both sides of a substring which is lacking in regular sets.

Definition 8.17 *Let $G = (N, T, P, S)$ be a CFG. A non-terminal $A \in N$ is said to be self-embedding, if $A \overset{*}{\Rightarrow} xAy$ where $x, y \in (N \cup T)^+$. A grammar G is self-embedding if it has a self-embedding non-terminal.*

A *CFG* is non-self-embedding if none of its non-terminals are self-embedding. Any right linear grammar is non-self-embedding, as the non-terminal occurs as the rightmost symbol in any sentential form. Hence, a regular set is generated by a non-self-embedding grammar. We have the following result:

Theorem 8.14 *If a CFG G is non-self-embedding, then $L(G)$ is regular.*

Proof Let $G = (N, T, P, S)$ be a non-self-embedding CFG. Without loss of generality we can assume that $\varepsilon \notin L(G)$ and G is in GNF. (While converting a

CFG to Greibach normal form (GNF), the self-embedding or non-self-embedding property does not get affected). Let k be the number of non-terminals in G and l be the maximum length of the right-hand side of any production in G. Let $w \in L(G)$ and consider a leftmost derivation of w in G. Every sentential form is of the form $x\alpha$ where $x \in T^*$ and $\alpha \in N^*$. The length of α can be at most kl. This can be seen as follows. Suppose there is a sentential form $x\alpha$ where $|\alpha| > kl$. Consider the corresponding derivation tree which is of the form given in figure.

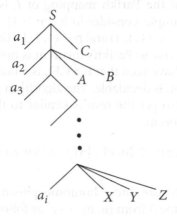

Consider the path from S to X, the leftmost non-terminal in α. Consider the nodes in this path where non-terminals are introduced to the right of the nodes. Since the maximum number of nodes introduced on the right is $l - 1$, there must be more than k such nodes as $|\alpha| > kl$. So two of such nodes will have the same label say A and we get $A \stackrel{*}{\Rightarrow} x'A\beta$, $x' \in T^+$, $\beta \in N^+$. Hence, A is self-embedding and G is not non-self-embedding as supposed. Hence, the maximum number of non-terminals which can occur in any sentential form in a leftmost derivation in G is kl.

Construct a right linear grammar $G' = (N', T', P', S')$ such that $L(G') = L(G')$. $N' = \{[\alpha] | \alpha \in N^+, |\alpha| \le kl\}$.
$S' = [S]$
P' consists of rules of the following form.
If $A \to aB_1 \ldots B_m$ is in P, then
$[A\beta] \to a[B_1 \ldots B_m\beta]$ is in P' for all possible $\beta \in N^*$ such that $|A\beta| \le kl$, $|B_1 \ldots B_m\beta| \le kl$. So, if there is a derivation in G.

$$S \Rightarrow a_1\alpha_1 \Rightarrow a_1a_2\alpha_2 \Rightarrow \cdots \Rightarrow a_1 \cdots a_{n-1}\alpha_{n-1} \Rightarrow a_1 \cdots a_n$$

there is a derivation in G' of the form:

$$[S] \Rightarrow a[\alpha_1] \Rightarrow a_1a_2[\alpha_2] \Rightarrow \cdots \Rightarrow a_1 \cdots a_{n-1}[\alpha_{n-1}] \Rightarrow a_1 \cdots a_n$$

and vice versa. Hence, $L(G) = L(G')$ and $L(G)$ is regular.

Theorem 8.15 *Every CFL over a one-letter alphabet is regular. Thus, a set $\{a^i | i \in A\}$ is a CFL if and only if A is ultimately periodic.*

Proof   Let $L \subseteq a^*$ be a CFL. By pumping lemma for CFL, there exists an integer k such that for each word w in L such that $|w| > p$, w can be written as $vvxyz$ such that

$|vxy| \leq k$, $|vy| > 0$ and $uv^i xy^i z \in L$ for all $i \geq 0$, w is in a^*. Hence, u, v, x, y, z all are in a^*. So, $uxz(vy)^*$ is in L for all $i > 0$. Let $vy = a^j$. So $uxz(a^j)^i$ is in L for all $i \geq 0$. Let $n = k(k-1) \ldots 1 = k!$. Then $w(a^n)^m$ is in L, because $w(a^n)^m$ can be written as $w(a^j)^i$ for $i = m \times \frac{k!}{j}, 1 \leq j \leq k$. $w(a^n)^* \subseteq L \subseteq a^*$ for each word w in L such that $|w| > k$.

For each i, $1 \leq i \leq n$, let $A_i = a^{k+i}(a^n)^* \cap L$. If $A_i \neq \phi$, let w_i be the word in A_i of minimum length. If $A_i = \phi$, let w_i be undefined. Then w is in $\bigcup_i w_i(a^n)^*$ for each w in L with $|w| > k$. Let B be the set of strings in L of length $\leq k$. Then $L = B \cup \bigcup_{i=1}^n w_i(a^n)^*$. B is a finite set represented by $u_1 + \ldots + u_r$ (say). Then L is represented by $(u_1 + \ldots + u_r) + (w_1 + \ldots + w_n)(a^n)^*$. Therefore, L is regular.

Example 8.15 As seen earlier, it immediately follows that $\{a^{n^2} \mid n \geq 1\}$, $\{a^{2^n} \mid n \geq 0\}$, $\{a^p \mid p$ is a prime$\}$ are not regular and hence they are not context-free.

8.7 Homomorphic Characterization

Earlier, we saw that the family of CFL is a full AFL. For an AFL $\mathcal{F}$, if there exists a language $L_0 \in \mathcal{F}$, such that any language L in $\mathcal{F}$ can be obtained from L_0 by means of some of these six operations, then L_0 is called a generator for the AFL $\mathcal{F}$. Any regular set is a generator for the family of regular sets. Let R be any regular set. Any other regular set R' can be got by $(\Sigma^* \cup R) \cap R'$. Next, we show that the Dyck set is a generator for the family of CFL.

Definition 8.18 *Consider the CFG*
$$G = (\{S\}, T, S, \{S \to \varepsilon, S \to SS, S \to a_1 Sa'_1, S \to a_2 Sa'_2, \cdots, S \to a_n Sa'_n\}),$$
$T = \{a_1, a_2, \ldots, a_n, a'_1, a'_2, \ldots, a'_n\}$, $n \geq 1$. *The language $L(G)$ is called the Dyck set over T and usually denoted by D_n.*

Example 8.16 Let $G = (\{S\}, T, S, \{S \to aSa', S \to bSb'\})$, $T = \{a, b, a', b'\}$. The set D_2 consists of matching nested parentheses if:
a stands for (,
b stands for [,
a' stands for),
b' stands for].

The set D_n has the following properties:

1. For w_1, $w_2 \in D_n$, $w_1 w_2 \in D_n$.
2. For $w_1 \in D_n$, $a_i w_1 a'_i \in D_n$ for $i = 1, 2, \ldots, n$.
3. Each word $w \neq \varepsilon$ in D_n is of the form $a_i w_1 a'_i w_2$, for some w_1, $w_2 \in D_n$ for some $i \in \{1, 2, \ldots, n\}$.
4. If $a_i a'_i w \in D_n$, then $w \in D_n$.

One can see that all the above properties are satisfied for D_n and this can be proved from the definition of Dyck set. We have the following result for CFLs.

Theorem 8.15 *Every CFL can be represented as a homomorphic image of the intersection of a regular language and a Dyck language.*

Proof Let L be a CFL. Without loss of generality let $\varepsilon \notin L$. If $\varepsilon \in L$, then $L - \{\varepsilon\}$ can be expressed in the form $h(D \cap R)$ where R is a regular language, D is a Dyck language. Then, $L = h(D \cap (R \cup \{\varepsilon\}))$ where $h(\varepsilon) = \varepsilon$. Hence, we can assume that L is ε-free and is generated by a CFG $G = (N, T, P, S)$ which is in CNF. Let $T = \{a_1, \dots, a_t\}$ and let P contain productions of the form $A_i \to B_i C_i$, $i = 1, 2, \dots, m$ and terminal rules of the form $A \to a_i$, $A \in N$, $a_i \in T$. Let D_{t+m} be a Dyck language over $T' = \{a_1, a_2, \dots, a_{t+m}, a_1', a_2', \dots, a_{t+m}'\}$. Let R be the regular language generated by the right linear grammar.

$$G' = (N, T', P', S),$$

where
$P' = \{A \to aa' | a \in T, A \to a \in P\} \cup \{A \to aa'a_{t+i}' C_i | a \in T, A \to a \in P, i \in \{1, \dots, m\}\} \cup \{A_i \to a_{t+i} B_i | 1 \le i \le m\}$.

Having defined the Dyck set D_{t+m} and R, we define the homomorphism h as follows so that $h(D_{t+m} \cap R)$ is L.

h is a homomorphism from T' to T given by:

$$h(a_i) = a_i, \quad \text{for } i = 1, \dots, t$$
$$h(a_i) = h(a_j') = \varepsilon, \text{ for}$$
$$i = t+1, t+2, \dots, t+m,$$
$$j = 1, \dots, t+m.$$

Now to prove $L = h(D_{t+m} \cap R)$.

i. $L \subseteq h(D_{t+m} \cap R)$.

To prove this let us prove a general result as below.

If $A = w_0 \underset{G}{\Rightarrow} w_1 \underset{G}{\Rightarrow} w_2 \underset{G}{\Rightarrow} \dots \underset{G}{\Rightarrow} w_k = w$, where $A \in N$, $w \in T^*$, is a derivation in G, there is a word w_q in D_{m+r} such that $A \underset{G'}{\overset{*}{\Rightarrow}} w_q$ and $w = h(w_q)$.

To prove that $A \underset{G'}{\overset{*}{\Rightarrow}} \alpha$, and $w = h(\alpha)$.

The proof is by induction on the number of derivation steps.

For $k = 1$, and $w \in T$ means that $A \to w$ is a rule in P. By G', for this rule there has to be a rule $A \to ww'$ in P' and hence $ww' \in D_{t+m}$ and $w = h(ww')$.

Assume the result to be true for all derivations n, $n \ge 1$ and let,
$A_i = w_0 \Rightarrow w_1 \Rightarrow w_2 \Rightarrow \dots \Rightarrow w_{n+1} = w$, for $A_i \in N$, $w_{n+1} = w \in T^+$ be a derivation according to G. Since G is in Chomsky normal form, clearly w_1 will be $B_i C_i$, $1 \le i \le m$.

Clearly, $w = \alpha_1 \alpha_2$ where $B_i \overset{*}{\underset{G'}{\Rightarrow}} \alpha_1$ and $C_i \overset{*}{\underset{G'}{\Rightarrow}} \alpha_2$ in less than n number of steps. Then by our inductive assumption, there are words w_1, w_2 in D_{t+m} such that:

$$\alpha_1 = h(w_1), \quad \alpha_2 = h(w_2), \quad B_i \overset{*}{\underset{G'}{\Rightarrow}} w_1 \text{ and } C_i \overset{*}{\underset{G'}{\Rightarrow}} w_2$$

Hence,

$$A_i \underset{G'}{\Rightarrow} a_{t+i} B_i \overset{*}{\underset{G'}{\Rightarrow}} a_{t+i} w_1 a'_{t+i} C_i$$

$$\overset{*}{\underset{G'}{\Rightarrow}} a_{t+i} w_1 a'_{t+i} w_2$$

Now, choose $\alpha = a_{t+i} w_1 a'_{t+i} w_2$ such that $h(\alpha) = h(w_1)\, h(w_2) = \alpha_1 \alpha_2 = w_{n+1} = w$.

Hence for any derivation $S \overset{*}{\underset{G}{\Rightarrow}} w$, there exists word $\alpha \in D_{t+m}$ and $S \overset{*}{\underset{G'}{\Rightarrow}} \alpha$ such that $h(\alpha) = w$.

ii. To show $h(D_{t+m} \cap R) \subseteq L$, we proceed as before by simulating the derivations of G' by derivations in G. Let

$$A = \alpha_0 \Rightarrow \alpha_1 \Rightarrow \ldots \alpha_n = \alpha,$$

where $A \in N$, $\alpha \in D_{t+m}$ be a derivation according to G'. Then $A \overset{*}{\underset{G}{\Rightarrow}} h(\alpha)$.

For $n = 1$, $\alpha = aa'$ for some $a \in T$ and $A \to a$ is the rule which is used.

Hence, $A \overset{*}{\underset{G_1}{\Rightarrow}} h(\alpha)$ and $h(\alpha) = a$, a will be in L by a terminal rule of G, $A \to a$.

Assume the result to be true for all $k \leq n$ in the above type of derivations. Consider

$$A = \alpha_0 \Rightarrow \alpha_1 \Rightarrow \alpha_2 \ldots \Rightarrow \alpha_{n+1} = \alpha \tag{8.1}$$

where $A \in N$, $\alpha \in D_{t+m}$ be a derivation of G'. Since $n \geq 1$, $n+1 \geq 2$, the rules of G' of the form $A \to aa'$, $a \in T$ and $A \to aa'a'_{t+i} C_i$ are not used in the beginning of the derivation. These applications will produce words that cannot appear in D_{t+m}. Hence, for some α_j, $1 \leq j \leq t$, $\alpha_1 = a_{m+j} B_j$ is used in the derivation in the beginning of the derivation. But the derivation from A_j deriving α'_{n+1}, is such that $\alpha = a_{t+i} \alpha'_{n+1}$ where $\alpha'_{n+1} \in D_{t+m}$.
That is,

$$B_j \underset{G_1}{\Rightarrow} \alpha'_2 \underset{G_1}{\Rightarrow} \alpha'_3 \underset{G_1}{\Rightarrow} \ldots \underset{G_1}{\Rightarrow} \alpha'_{n+1} \tag{8.2}$$

Hence, α will be of the form $a_{t+j} \alpha' \alpha'_{t+j} \alpha''$ where $\alpha', \alpha'' \in D_{t+m}$. Hence α'_k, in the above derivation of Equation (8.2) from B_j, must be of the form $\alpha'_k = \alpha' \alpha'_{t+j} C_j$, $2 \leq k \leq n$. Hence, the rule that is used in $(k-1)th$ step must be $B \to aa'a_{t+j} C_j$, $a \in T$, $B \in N$ and for $B \to a$ in P the corresponding rule in P' is $B \to aa'$. Hence, using this rule in the $(k-1)th$ step of derivation of Equation (8.2), we obtain $B_j \overset{*}{\underset{G'}{\Rightarrow}} \alpha'$ in less than n steps. Likewise, we argue for $C_j \overset{*}{\underset{G'}{\Rightarrow}} \alpha''$ through the applications of production of G'. Hence, for derivation of Equation (8.1), the actual details are:

$$A = X_j = B_j C_j \;\overset{*}{\underset{G}{\Rightarrow}}\; h(\alpha')h(\alpha'')$$
$$= h(a_{t+j}\alpha'a'_{t+j}\alpha'')$$
$$= h(\alpha)$$

Hence the result. ☐

Problems and Solutions

1. Prove that the following languages are not context-free.

   a. $L_1 = \{a^p \mid p \text{ is a prime}\}$.
   b. $L_2 = \{a,b\}^* - \{a^n b^{n^2} \mid n \geq 0\}$

Solution.

a. $L_1 = \{a^p \mid p \text{ is a prime}\}$.

Suppose L_1 is context-free.

Then, by pumping lemma there exists k such that for all $z \in L_1$ and $|z| \geq k$. z can be written in the form $uvxyz$ such that $uv^ixy^iz \in L$ for all $i \geq 0$. Consider some $p > k$. $a^p \in L_1$

$$a^p = uvxyz$$

Now $u, v, x, y, z \in a^*$. Therefore, by pumping lemma:

$$uxz(vy)^i \in L_1 \text{ for all } i \geq 0$$

Let $|vy| = r$

$$uxz(a^r)^i \in L_1 \text{ for all } i \geq 0$$

or

$$z(a^r)^{i-1} \in L_1 \quad \text{for all } i \geq 0$$
$$a^{p+r(i-1)} \in L_1 \quad \text{for all } i \geq 0$$

Choose i such that $p + r(i-1)$ is not a prime. Select $i - 1 = p$. Therefore, $i = p + 1$.

$a^{p+rp} \in L_1$.

But, $a^{p+rp} = a^{p(r+1)}$.

$p(r+1)$ is not a prime. So, we come to the conclusion that a^s where s is not a prime belong to L_1. This is a contradiction.

Therefore, L_1 is not context-free.

b. $L_2 = \{a,b\}^* - \{a^n b^{n^2} \mid n \geq 0\}$.

Suppose L_2 is context-free.

Since the family of context-free languages is closed under intersection with regular sets. $L_2 \cap a^*b^*$ is context-free.

This contains strings of the form $L_3 = \{a^n b^m \mid m \neq n^2\}$.

We shall show this is not context-free. If L_3 is context-free, then by pumping lemma there is a constant k which satisfies the conditions of pumping lemma. Choose $z = a^n b^m$ where $n > k$, $m \neq n^2$.

$z = uvxyz$ where $|vxy| \leq k$, $|vy| \geq 1$ such that $uv^i xy^i z \in L_3$ for all $i \geq 0$. If v or y consists of both a and b, then by pumping we shall get a string which is not of the form $a^i b^j$. If $v \in a^*$, $y \in b^*$, then we have to show by pumping that we can get a string not in L_3. Let $v = a^p$ and $y = b^q$. Then $a^{n-p} b^{m-q} \in L$ ($i = 0$).

Choose $m = (n - p)^2 + q$. i.e., we started with $a^n b^{(n-p)^2 + q}$. Then
$$a^{n-p} b^{(n-p)^2 + q - q} = a^{(n-p)} b^{(n-p)^2} \in L_3.$$
This is a contradiction.

L_3 is not context-free and hence L_2 is not context-free.

2. Which of the following sets are context-free and which are not? Justify your answer.

a. $L_1 = \{a^n b^m c^k \mid n, m, k \geq 1 \text{ and } 2n = 3k, \text{ or } 5n = 7m\}$.
Solution.

$S \rightarrow A$	$S \rightarrow BD$
$A \rightarrow a^3 Ac^2$	$D \rightarrow cD$
$A \rightarrow a^3 Cc^2$	$D \rightarrow c$
$C \rightarrow bC$	$B \rightarrow a^7 Bb^5$
$C \rightarrow b$	$B \rightarrow a^7 b^5$

This CFG generates L_1.

b. $L_2 = \{a^i b^j c^k d^l, i, j, k, l \geq 1, i = l, j = k\}$.
Solution. L_2 is CFL generated by:
$S \rightarrow aSd$
$S \rightarrow aAd$
$A \rightarrow bAc$
$A \rightarrow bc$

c. $L_3 = \{x \in \{a, b, c\}^* \mid \#_a x = \#_b x = \#_c x\}$.

Solution. L_3 is not context-free.
Suppose L_3 is context-free.
Then, since the family of CFL is closed under intersection with regular sets
$L_3 \cap a^* b^* c^*$ is regular.
This is $\{a^n b^n c^n \mid n \geq 0\}$.
We have shown that this is not context-free
L_3 is not context-free.

d. $L_4 = \{a^m b^n \mid n, m \geq 0, 5m - 3n = 24\}$.
Solution. It can be seen that:
$a^6 b^2 \in L_4$
$a^9 b^7 \in L_4$
$a^{12} b^{12} \in L_4$
$a^{15} b^{17} \in L_4$

$S \to a^3Sb^5$, $S \to a^6b^2$ which generates L_4.

e. $L_5 = \{a^mb^n \mid n \neq m\}$.
Solution. Worked out earlier in Chapter 2.

3. Let $\mathcal{NL}_2$ be the set of non-context-free languages. Determine whether or not.

   a. $\mathcal{NL}_2$ is closed under union.
   Solution. No.
   $L_1 = \{a^p \mid p \text{ is a prime}\}$.
   $L_2 = \{a^p \mid p \text{ is not a prime}\}$.
   $L_1 \cup L_2 = \{a^n \mid n \geq 1\}$ is CFL whereas L_1 and L_2 are not.
   b. $\mathcal{NL}_2$ is closed under complementation.
   Solution. No.
   $L = \{x \mid x \in \{a, b\}^*\}$ and not of the form ww is CFL.
   $\overline{L} = \{ww \mid w \in \{a,b\}^*\}$ is not a CFL.
   c. $\mathcal{NL}_2$ is closed under intersection.
   Solution. No.
   $L_1 = \{a^p \mid p \text{ is a prime}\}$.
   $L_2 = \{a^{2^n} \mid n \geq 0\}$.
   L_1 and L_2 are not CFL. $L_1 \cap L_2 = \{a^2\}$ is a singleton and hence a CFL.
   d. $\mathcal{NL}_2$ is closed under catenation.
   Solution. No.
   $L_1 \quad = \{a^p \mid p \text{ is a prime}\}$.
   $L_2 \quad = \{a^p \mid p \text{ is not a prime}\}$.
   $L_1 \quad = \{a^2, a^3, a^5, a^7, a^{11}, \ldots\}$.
   $L_2 \quad = \{a, a^4, a^6, a^8, a^9, a^{10}, a^{12}, \ldots\}$.
   $L_1L_2 = \{a^3, a^4, a^6, a^7, a^8, a^9, a^{10}, a^{11}, \ldots\}$
   $\qquad = a^* - \{a, a^2, a^5\}$ is CFL.
   e. $\mathcal{NL}_2$ is closed under Kleene closure.
   Solution. No.
   L_1^* is CFL.
   L_2^* is CFL.

4. Is the language $\{x^my^n \mid m, n \in N, m \leq n \leq 2m\}$ context-free? Justify your answer.
   Solution. Yes.
   $S \to xSy$
   $S \to xSyy$
   $S \to \varepsilon$

5. Is the union of a collection of context-free languages always context-free? Justify your answer.

   Solution. Finite union of CFL is CFL.
   $L_1, L_2, L_3, \ldots, L_k$ are CFL.
   Let L_i be generated by $G_i = (N_i, T, P_i, S_i)$ and let $N_i \cap N_j = \phi$ for $i \neq j$
   $G = (\{S\} \underset{i}{\cup} \cup N_i, T, \underset{i}{\cup} P_i \underset{i}{\cup} \{S \to S_i\}, S)$

generates $L_1 \cup L_2 \cup \ldots L_k$.
Infinite union of CFL is not CFL
$L_i = \{a^i | i \text{ is a particular prime}\}$.
L_i are CFL.
But $\bigcup_i L_i$ is not a CFL.

6. Consider the following context-free grammar:

$S \rightarrow AA|AS|b$

$A \rightarrow SA|AS|a$

For strings *abaab* and *bab*, *bbb*.
Construct the CYK parsing table.
Are these strings in $L(G)$?
Solution.

S, A		
A	S, A	
S	A	S
b	a	b

$bab \in L$

ϕ		
ϕ	ϕ	
S	S	S
b	b	b

$bbb \notin L$

S, A				
A, S	S, A			
S, A	S	S, A		
S, A	A	S	S, A	
A	S	A	A	S
a	b	a	a	b

$abaab \in L$

Exercises

1. Consider $L = \{y \in \{0, 1\}^* \mid |y|_0 = |y|_1\}$. Prove or disprove that L is context-free.

2. Let G be the following grammar:

$S \rightarrow CF|DE|AB$
$D \rightarrow BA|0$
$E \rightarrow SD$
$A \rightarrow AA|1$
$B \rightarrow BB|0$
$C \rightarrow FS$
$F \rightarrow AB|1$

Use CYK algorithm to determine which of the following strings are in $L(G)$.
10110, 0111010, 0110110.
For each of the above strings present the final table, state if the string is in $L(G)$ and if it is, then give the derivation.

3. Let G be defined $S \rightarrow AS|b$, $A \rightarrow SA|a$. Construct CYK parsing tables for:
   a. *bbaab*
   b. *ababab*
   c. *aabba*
   Are these strings in $L(G)$?

4. $S \rightarrow SS|AA|b$, $A \rightarrow AS|AA|a$

   Give CYK parsing tables for:
   aabb, and *bbaba*.
   Are these strings in $L(G)$?

5. For the CFG
   $S \rightarrow AB|BC$
   $A \rightarrow BA|a$
   $B \rightarrow CC|b$
   $C \rightarrow AB|a$
   Construct CYK parsing tables for:
   a. *ababb*
   b. *bbbaaa*

6. Let DCFL be the collection of languages accepted by a deterministic PDA. Given Examples to show that even if L_1 and L_2 are in DCFL:
   $L_1 \cdot L_2$ need not be in DCFL
   $L_1 - L_2$ need not be in DCFL

7. Given a DPDA M show that it is decidable whether $L(M)$ is a regular set.

8. Let L be in DCFL and R a regular set. Show that it is decidable whether R is contained in L.

9. Using a cardinality argument show that there must be languages that are not context-free.

10. Let LIN be a family of linear languages. Pumping lemma for linear languages can be stated as follows:

Let $L \subseteq \Sigma^*$ be in LIN. Then, there exists a constant $p > 0$ such that for all words z in L with $|z| \geq p$ can be expressed as $z = uxwyv$ for some $u, v, x, y, w \in \Sigma^*$ such that:

1. $|uxyv| < p$
2. $|xy| \geq 1$
3. for all $i \geq 0$, $ux^i wy^i v \in L$
   i. Prove the LIN language pumping lemma.
   ii. Using the LIN language pumping lemma, prove that the following languages are not linear.
   a. $\{a^i b^i c^j d^j | i, j \geq 1\}$
   b. $\{x | x$ is in $\{a, b\}^*$ and $\#_a(x) = \#_b(x)\}$
   c. $\{a^i b^i c^i | i \geq 1\}$

11. Prove or disprove the following claims:
    a. Family of deterministic context-free languages (DCF) is closed under complementation.
    b. Family of DCF is closed under union.
    c. Family of DCF is closed under regular intersection.
    d. Family of DCF is closed under reversal.
    e. Family of LIN is closed under union.
    f. Family of LIN is closed under intersection.
    g. Family of LIN is closed under reversal.

12. A language L consists of all words w over the alphabet $\{a, b, c, d\}$ which satisfy each of the following conditions:
    a. $\#_a(w) + \#_b(w) = 2(\#_c(w) + \#_d(w))$.
    b. aaa is a subword of w but abc is not a subword of w.
    c. The third letter of w is not c.
    Prove that L is context-free.

13. Compare the family of minimal linear languages with the family regular languages. Characterize the languages belonging to the intersection of these two families.

14. Prove that there is a linear language which is not generated by any deterministic linear grammar.

15. A Parikh mapping ψ depends on the enumeration of the basic alphabet; another enumeration gives a different mapping ψ'. Prove that if $\psi(L)$ is semi-linear for some ψ, then $\psi'(L)$ is semi-linear for any ψ'.

16. Consider languages over a fixed alphabet T with at least two letters. Prove that, for any natural number n, there is a CFL L_n which is not generated by any type-2 grammar containing fewer than n non-terminals.

17. Consider the grammar G determined by the productions:

$X_0 \rightarrow adX_1 da | aX_0 a | aca,$

$X_1 \rightarrow bX_1 b | bdX_0 db.$

Prove that $L(G)$ is not sequential. This shows that not all linear languages are sequential. Conversely, give an Example of a sequential language which is not metalinear.

18. Let G be a CFG with the production $S \to AB$, $A \to a$, $B \to AB|b$. Run the CYK algorithm for the string aab.

19. a. Modify the CYK algorithm to count the number of parse trees of a given string and to construct one if the number is non-zero.

  b. Test your algorithm of part (i) above on the following grammar:
     $S \to ST|a$
     $T \to BS$
     $B \to +$
     and string $a + a + a$.

20. Use closure under union to show that the following languages are CFL.

  a. $\{a^m b^m | m \neq n\}$
  b. $\{a, b\}^* - \{a^n b^n | n \geq 0\}$
  c. $\{w \in \{a, b\}^* | w = w^R\}$
  d. $\{a^m b^n c^p d^q | n = q \text{ or } m \leq p \text{ or } m + n = p + q\}$

21. Prove the following stronger version of the pumping lemma.
    Let G be a CFG. Then, there are numbers K and k such that any string $w \in L(G)$ with $|w| \geq K$ can be re-written as $w = uvxyz$ with $|vxy| \leq k$ in such a way that either v or y is non-empty and $uv^n xy^n z \in L(G)$ for every $n \geq 0$.

22. Show that the class of DCFL is not closed under homomorphism.

Turing Machines

We have seen earlier that FSA have finite amount of memory and hence cannot do certain things. For example, no FSA can accept $\{a^n b^n | n \geq 1\}$. Though, it is possible to have FSA for adding two arbitrarily long binary numbers, we cannot have an FSA which can multiply two arbitrarily long binary numbers. Hence the question arises. What happens when we leave this restriction of finite memory? What problems can be solved by mechanical process with unlimited memory? By mechanical process, it is meant a procedure so completely specified that a machine can carry it out. Are there processes that can be precisely described yet still cannot be realized by a machine (computer)?

Programming — the job of specifying the procedure that a computer is to carry out — amounts to determining in advance, everything that a computer will do. In this sense, a computer's program can serve as a precise description of the process the machine can carry out, and in this same sense it is meaningful to say that anything that can be done by a computer can be precisely described.

Often, one also hears a kind of converse statement to the effect that "any procedure which can be precisely described, can be programmed to be performed by a computer." This statement is the consequence of the work of Alan M. Turing and is called Turing's thesis or Church—Turing thesis or Turing hypothesis. A. M. Turing put forth his concept of computing machine in his famous 1936 paper, which was an integral part of the formalism of the theory of computability. These machines are called Turing machines (TM) and are still the subject of research in computer science.

As an explication of the concept of algorithm, the concept of TM is particularly helpful in offering a clear and realistic demarcation of what constitutes a single step of execution. The problem of how to separate the steps from one another in a step-by-step procedure is clearly specified when it is put into the form of a TM table.

To start with, we may specify an effective procedure as follows: An effective procedure is a set of rules which tell us, from moment to moment, precisely how to behave. With this in mind, Turing's thesis may be stated as follows: Any process which could naturally be called an effective procedure can be realized by a TM.

One cannot expect to prove Turing's thesis, since the term 'naturally' relates rather to human dispositions than to any precisely defined quality of a process. Support must come from intuitive arguments. Hence, it is called Turing's hypothesis or Church—Turing thesis and not as Turing's theorem.

Perhaps, the strongest argument in favor of Turing's thesis is the fact that, over the years, all other noteworthy attempts to give precise yet intuitively satisfactory definitions of "effective procedure" have turned out to be equivalent to Turing's concept. Some of these are Church's "effective calculability", Post's canonical systems, and Kleene's general recursive function.

Turing also stated the halting problem for TMs and showed that it is undecidable. The concept of 'undecidability' was one of the major breakthroughs in mathematics (theoretical computer science) in the first half of twentieth century. After this, many problems like the Hilbert's 10th problem have been seen to be undecidable and the long search for an algorithm for these problems was given up. But, it also became clear that problems like Fermat's last theorem were decidable, even though at that time nobody could prove or disprove it. Recently, in the last decade, this conjecture has been proved to be true.

Till today, TM is taken as the model of computation. Whenever a new model of computation (like DNA computing, membrane computing) is defined, it is the practice to show that this new model is as capable as the TM. This proves the power of the new model of computation.

In this chapter, we see the basic definition of TMs with examples and some techniques for TM construction. In the next three chapters, we will learn more about this model and related concepts.

9.1 TM as an Acceptor

The TM can be considered as an accepting device accepting sets of strings. Later, we shall see that TM accept the family of languages generated by type 0 grammars. The set accepted by a TM is called a recursively enumerable set.

When we consider the TM as an accepting device, we usually consider a one-way infinite tape. In the next chapter, we shall see that by having a two-way infinite tape, the power does not change. The TM consists of a one-way infinite read/write tape and a finite control (Figure 9.1).

The input $a_1 \ldots a_n$ is placed at the left end of the tape. The rest of the cells contain the blank symbol $\not{b}$. Initially, the tape head points to the leftmost cell in the initial state q_0. At any time, the tape head will point to a cell and the machine will be in a particular state. Suppose the machine is in state q and pointing to a cell containing the symbol a, then depending upon the δ mapping (transition function) of the TM it will change state to p and write a symbol X replacing a and move its tape head one cell to the left or to the right. The TM is not allowed to move-off the

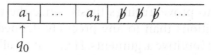

Figure 9.1. Initial configuration

left end of the tape. When it reaches a final state it accepts the input. Now, we will consider the formal definition.

Definition 9.1 *A TM* $M = (K, \Sigma, \Gamma, \delta, q_0, F)$ *is a 6-tuple, where*

- *K is a finite set of states;*
- *Σ is a finite set of input symbols;*
- *Γ is a finite set of tape symbols, $\Sigma \subseteq \Gamma$, $\not{b} \in \Gamma$ is the blank symbol;*
- *q_0 in K is the initial state;*
- *$F \subseteq K$ is the set of final states; and*
- *δ is a mapping from $K \times \Gamma$ into $K \times \Gamma \times \{L, R\}$.*

Note

a. Turing machine mapping is defined in such a way that it is deterministic. In the next chapter, we see that non-deterministic TM can also be defined. Though they have the same power as far as accepting power is concerned, the number of steps may exponentially increase if a deterministic TM tries to simulate a non-deterministic TM.

b. In some formulations the head remaining stationary is allowed. i.e., δ: $K \times \Gamma \rightarrow K \times \Gamma \times \{L, S, R\}$. But we shall stick to $\{L, R\}$ as remaining stationary can be achieved by two moves, first moving right and then moving back left.

Next, we consider an instantaneous description (ID) of a TM.

Definition 9.2 *An ID of a TM is a string of the form $\alpha_1 q \alpha_2$, $\alpha_1, \alpha_2 \in \Gamma^*$, $q \in K$.*
This means that at that particular instance $\alpha_1 \alpha_2$ is the content of the tape of the TM. q is the current state and the tape head points to the first symbol of α_2. See Figure 9.2.

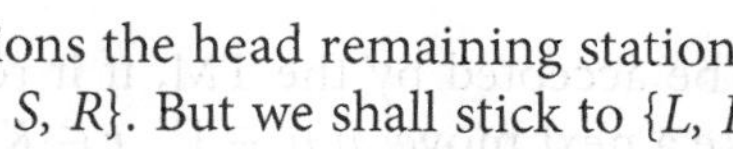

Figure 9.2. Contents of tape and head position for ID $\alpha_1 q \alpha_2$

The relationship between IDs can be described as follows:
If $X_1 \ldots X_{i-1} q X_i X_{i+1} \ldots X_m$ is an ID and $\delta(q, X_i) = (p, Y, R)$ then the next ID will be $X_1 \ldots X_{i-1} Y p X_{i+1} \ldots X_m$.
If $\delta(q, X_j) = (p, Y, L)$ then the next ID will be $X_1 \ldots X_{i-2} p X_{i-1} Y X_{i+1} \ldots X_m$.
We denote this as:

$$X_1 \ldots X_{i-1} q X_i X_{i+1} \ldots X_m \vdash X_1 \ldots X_{i-2} p X_{i-1} Y X_{i+1} \ldots X_m.$$

$q_0 X_1 \ldots X_m$ is the initial ID. Initially, the tape head points to the leftmost cell containing the input. If $q X_1 \ldots X_m$ is an ID and $\delta(q, X_1) = (p, Y, L)$, machine halts. i.e., moving off the left end of the tape is not allowed. If $X_1 \ldots X_m q$ is an ID, q is reading the leftmost blank symbol. If $\delta(q, \not b) = (p, Y, R)$ next ID will be $X_1 \ldots X_m Y p$. If $\delta(q, \not b) = (p, Y, L)$ next $I\Delta$ will be $X_1 \ldots X_{m-1} p X_m Y$. $\vdash^*$ is the reflexive, transitive closure of $\vdash$. i.e., $ID_0 \vdash ID_1 \vdash \ldots \vdash ID_n$ is denoted as $ID_0 \vdash^* ID_n$, $n \geq 0$. An input will be accepted if the *TM* reaches a final state.

Definition 9.3 *A string w is accepted by the* TM, $M = (K, \Sigma, \Gamma, \delta, q_0, F)$ *if* $q_0 w \vdash^* \alpha_1 q_f \alpha_2$ *for some* $\alpha_1, \alpha_2 \in \Gamma^*$, $q_f \in F$. *The language accepted by the* TM *M is denoted as:*

$$T(M) = \{w | w \in \Sigma^*, q_0 w \vdash^* \alpha_1 q_f \alpha_2 \text{ for some } \alpha_1, \alpha_2 \in \Gamma^*, q_f \in F\}$$

Note

a. It should be noted that, by definition, it is not necessary for the TM to read the whole input. If $w_1 w_2$ is the input and the TM reaches a final state after reading w_1, $w_1 w_2$ will be accepted; for that matter any string $w_1 w_j$ will be accepted. Usually, while constructing a TM we make sure that the whole of the input is read.

b. Usually, we assume that after going to a final state, the TM halts, i.e., it makes no more moves.

c. A string w will not be accepted by the TM, if it reaches an ID $\eta_1 r \eta_2$ from which it cannot make a next move; $\eta_1 \eta_2 \in \Gamma^*$, $r \in K$ and r is not a final state or while reading w, the TM gets into a loop and is never able to halt.

Having given the formal definition of TM as an acceptor, let us consider some examples.

Example 9.1 Let us consider a TM for accepting $\{a^i b^j c^k | i, j, k \geq 1, i = j + k\}$.

The informal description of the TM is as follows. Consider Figure 9.3 which shows the initial ID.

The machine starts reading a 'a' and changing it to a X; it moves right; when it sees a 'b,' it converts it into a Y and then starts moving left. It matches a's and b's. After that, it matches a's with c's. The machine accepts when the number of a's is equal to the sum of the number of b's and the number of c's.

Formally, $M = (K, \Sigma, \Gamma, \delta, q_0, F)$
$K = \{q_0, q_1, q_2, q_3, q_4, q_5, q_6, q_7, q_8\}$ $F = \{q_8\}$
$\Sigma = \{a, b, c\}$
$\Gamma = \{a, b, c, X, Y, Z, \not b \}$

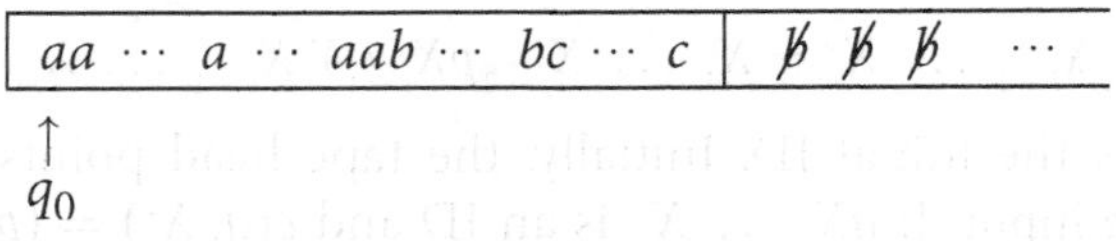

Figure 9.3. Initial configuration of the TM for Example 9.1

δ is defined as follows:

$\delta(q_0, a) = (q_1, X, R)$

In state q_0, it reads a 'a' and changes it to X and moves right in q_1.

$\delta(q_1, a) = (q_1, a, R)$

In state q_1, it moves right through the 'a's.

$\delta(q_1, b) = (q_2, Y, L)$

When it sees a 'b,' it changes it into a Y.

$\delta(q_2, a) = (q_2, a, L)$

$\delta(q_2, Y) = (q_2, Y, L)$

In state q_2, it moves left through the 'a's and Y's.

$\delta(q_2, X) = (q_0, X, R)$

When it sees a X, it moves right in q_0 and the process repeats.

$\delta(q_1, Y) = (q_3, Y, R)$

$\delta(q_3, Y) = (q_3, Y, R)$

$\delta(q_3, b) = (q_2, Y, L)$

After scanning the 'a's, *it moves through the* Y's till it sees a 'b,' then it converts it into a Y and moves left.

$\delta(q_3, c) = (q_4, Z, L)$

When no more 'b's remain it sees a 'c' in state q_3, changes that into Z and starts moving left in state q_4. The process repeats. After matching 'a's and 'b's, the TM tries to match 'a's and 'c's.

$\delta(q_4, Y) = (q_4, Y, L)$

$\delta(q_4, a) = (q_4, a, L)$

$\delta(q_4, X) = (q_0, X, R)$

$\delta(q_3, Z) = (q_5, Z, R)$

$\delta(q_5, c) = (q_4, Z, L)$

$\delta(q_5, Z) = (q_5, Z, R)$

$\delta(q_4, Z) = (q_4, Z, L)$

When no more 'a's remain it sees a Y in state q_0 checks that all 'b's and 'c's have been matched and reaches the final state q_8.

$\delta(q_0, Y) = (q_6, Y, R)$

$\delta(q_6, Y) = (q_6, Y, R)$

$\delta(q_6, Z) = (q_7, Z, R)$

$\delta(q_7, Z) = (q_7, Z, R)$

$\delta(q_7, b) = (q_8, b, halt)$

Let us consider the move of the TM on an input *aaabcc*.

The sequence of moves is given below:

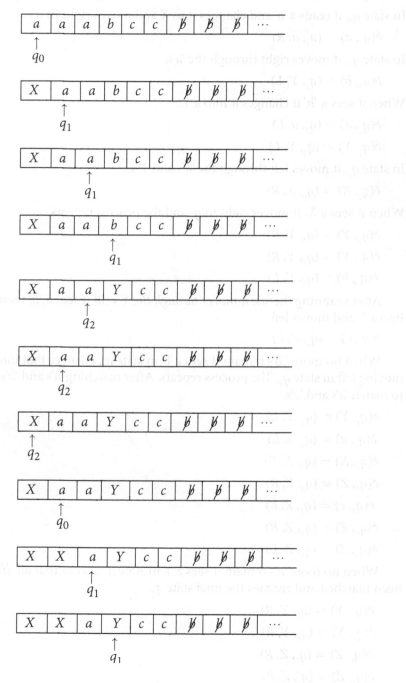

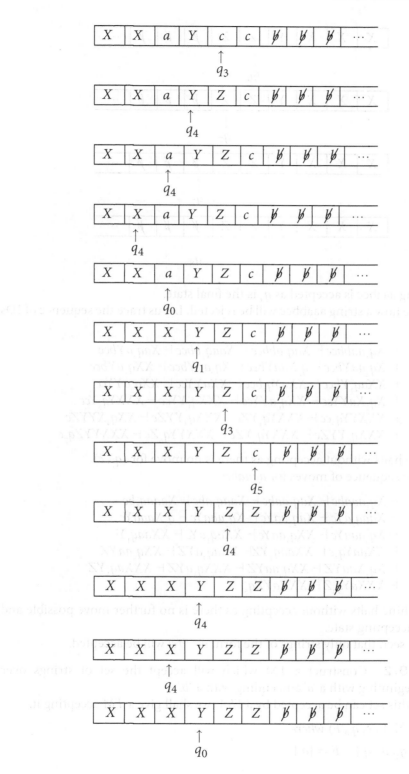

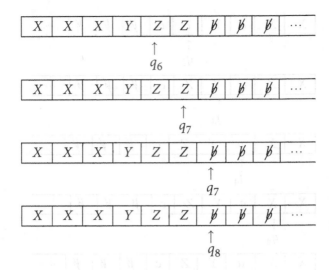

The string aaabcc is accepted as q_8 is the final state.

Let us see how a string aaabbcc will be rejected. Let us trace the sequence of IDs on *aaabbcc*

$$q_0aaabbcc \vdash Xq_1aabbcc \vdash Xaq_1abbcc \vdash Xaaq_1bbcc \vdash Xaq_2aYbcc$$
$$\vdash Xq_2aaYbcc \vdash q_2XaaYbcc \vdash Xq_0aaYbcc \vdash XXq_1aYbcc$$
$$\vdash XXaq_1Ybcc \vdash XXaYq_3bcc \vdash XXaYYcc \vdash XXq_2aYYcc$$
$$\vdash Xq_2XaYYcc \vdash XXq_0aYYcc \vdash XXXq_1YYcc \vdash XXXYq_3Ycc$$
$$\vdash XXXYYq_3cc \vdash XXXYq_4YZc \vdash XXXq_4YYZc \vdash XXq_4XYYZc$$
$$\vdash XXXq_0YYZc \vdash XXXYq_6YZc \vdash XXXYYq_6Zc \vdash XXXYYZq_7c$$

The machine halts without accepting as there is no move for (q_7, c).

Let us see the sequence of moves for *aaaabc*:

$$q_0aaaabc \quad \vdash Xq_1aaabc \vdash Xaq_1aabc \vdash Xaaq_1abc \vdash Xaaaq_1bc$$
$$\vdash Xaaq_2aYc \vdash Xaq_2aaYc \vdash Xq_2aaaYc \vdash q_2XaaaYc$$
$$\vdash Xq_0aaaYc \vdash XXq_1aaYc \vdash XXaq_1aYc \vdash XXaaq_1Yc$$
$$\vdash XXaaYq_3c \vdash XXaaq_4YZ \vdash XXaq_4aYZ \vdash XXq_4aaYZ$$
$$\vdash Xq_4XaaYZ \vdash XXq_0aaYZ \vdash XXXq_1aYZ \vdash XXXaq_1YZ$$
$$\vdash XXXaYq_3Z \vdash XXXaYZq_5$$

The machine halts without accepting as there is no further move possible and q_5 is not an accepting state.

It can be seen that only strings of the form $a^{i+j}b^ic^j$ will be accepted.

Example 9.2 Construct a TM which will accept the set of strings over $\Sigma = \{a, b\}$ beginning with a '*a*' and ending with a '*b.*'

Though this set can be accepted by a *FSA*, we shall give a *TM* accepting it.

$M = (K, \Sigma, \Gamma, \delta, q_0, F)$ *where*

$K = \{q_0, q_1, q_2, q_3\} \quad F = \{q_3\}$

$\Sigma = \{a, b\}\ \Gamma\ \{a, b, X, \not{b}\ \}$

δ is defined as follows:

$\delta(q_0, a) = (q_1, X, R)$

$\delta(q_1, a) = (q_1, X, R)$

$\delta(q_1, b) = (q_2, X, R)$

$\delta(q_2, a) = (q_1, X, R)$

$\delta(q_2, b) = (q_2, X, R)$

$\delta(q_2, \not{b}\ ) = (q_3, \not{b}, halt)$

Let us see how the machine accepts *abab*.

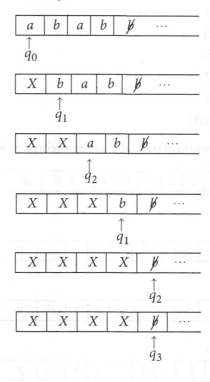

It can be seen that after initially reading '*a*,' the machine goes to state q_1. Afterwards, if it sees a '*a*' it goes to state q_1; if it sees a '*b*' it goes to q_2. Hence, when it sees the leftmost blank symbol, if it is in state q_2 it accepts as this means that the last symbol read is a '*b*.'

Example 9.3 Construct a TM which will accept strings over $\Sigma = \{(,), \#\}$, which represent well-formed strings of parentheses placed between $\#$'s. Input is of the form $\#w\#$ where w is a well-formed string of parentheses. The TM $M = (K, \Sigma, \Gamma, \delta, q'_0, F)$ accepts this set, where

$K = \{q_0', q_0, q_1, q_2, q_3, q_4, q_5\} \quad F = \{q_5\}$

$\Sigma = \{(,), \#\}$

$\Gamma = \{(,), X, \#, \not{b}\}$

δ is defined as follows:

$\delta(q_0', \#) = (q_0, \#, R)$

$\delta(q_0, () = (q_0, (, R)$

$\delta(q_0,)) = (q_1, X, L)$

$\delta(q_1, X) = (q_1, X, L)$

$\delta(q_1, () = (q_0, X, R)$

$\delta(q_0, X) = (q_0, X, R)$

$\delta(q_0, \#) = (q_2, \#, R)$

$\delta(q_2, \not{b}) = (q_3, \not{b}, L)$

$\delta(q_3, \#) = (q_4, \#, L)$

$\delta(q_4, X) = (q_4, X, L)$

$\delta(q_4, \#) = (q_5, \#, halt)$

The sequence of moves on $\#(((())()))\#$ is represented as follows:

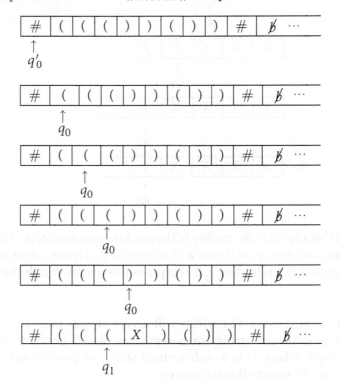

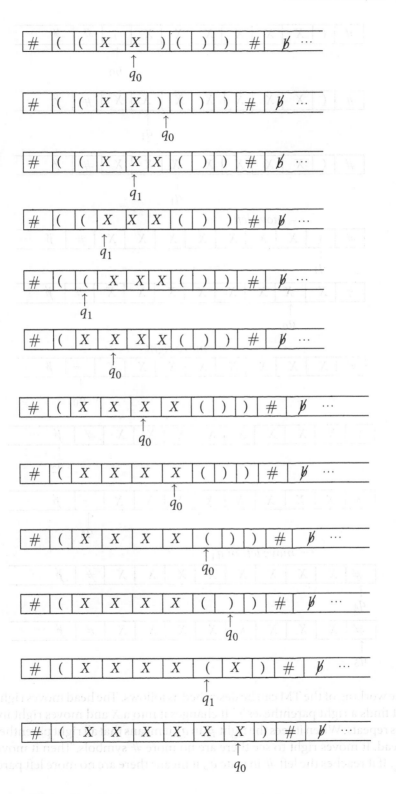

The machine of the TM in the above figure works as follows. The head moves right in state q_0 till it finds a right parenthesis. It changes it into an X and moves right in state q_1. The process repeats... ...has been read, it moves right in state q_0 to ignore X symbols, then it moves left in state q_1. If it reads centre left ... ...the ... stops if there are no more left parentheses.

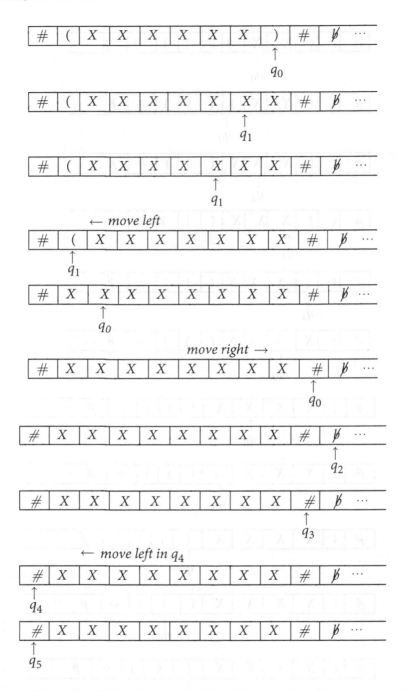

The working of the TM can be described as follows. The head moves right in state q_0 till it finds a right parentheses ').' It changes it into a X and moves right in q_0. This process repeats. When it sees the right # in q_0, it means that all right parentheses have been read. It moves right to see there are no more # symbols. Then it moves left in state q_4. If it reaches the left # in state q_4, it means there are no more left parentheses left. Hence, all left and right parentheses have been matched. The machine accepts by going to state q_5. It will be on the left $\#$ in state q_1, if there is a right parenthesis for which there is no left parenthesis and will halt without accepting. In state q_3 if it sees left parenthesis, it means there is a left parenthesis for which there is no matching right parenthesis. The machine will halt without accepting.

9.2 Turing Machine as a Computing Device

In the last section, we have viewed TM as an acceptor. In this section, we consider the TM as a computing device. It computes functions which are known as partial-recursive functions. In this section, we consider the tape of the TM as infinite in both directions. We can make this assumption without loss of generality as in the next chapter, we shall prove the equivalence of one-way and two-way infinite tapes. The machine is started with some non-blank portion on the tape, with the rest of the tape containing blanks only. This is taken as the input. After making some moves, when the machine halts, the non-blank portion of the tape is taken as the output. For some inputs, the machine may get into a loop in which case the output is not defined. Hence, the function computed will be a partial function. While considering the TM as a computing device we do not bother about the final states. Initial tape head position has to be specified.

Example 9.4 (Unary to binary converter)   The input is a string of a's which is taken as the unary representation of an integer; a^i represents integer i. The output is of the form $b_i X^i$ where b_i is a binary string which is the binary representation of integer i. The mapping for the TM which does this is given below. The tape symbols are $\{ \not{b}, a, X, 0, 1 \}$. The machine has two states q_0 and q_1. q_0 is the initial state and a right moving state. q_1 is a left moving state.

$$\delta(q_0, a) = (q_1, X, L)$$
$$\delta(q_1, X) = (q_1, X, L)$$
$$\delta(q_1, \not{b}) = (q_0, 1, R)$$
$$\delta(q_1, 0) = (q_1, 1, R)$$
$$\delta(q_1, 1) = (q_1, 0, L)$$
$$\delta(q_0, X) = (q_0, X, R)$$
$$\delta(q_0, \not{b}) = (q_2, \not{b}, halt)$$

The machine works like a binary counter. When it has converted j 'a's into X's, it prints binary number j to the left of the position where it started. Let us consider the working of the machine on $aaaaa$. *It should output* $101XXXXX$.

	$\not{b}$	$\not{b}$	$\not{b}$	a	a	a	a	a	$\not{b}$	

$\uparrow$
q_0

The machine starts in state q_0 on the leftmost a.

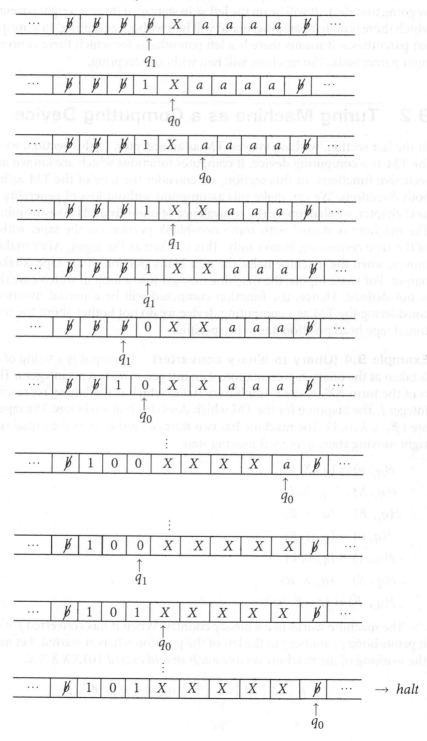

$\rightarrow$ *halt*

Example 9.5 (Copy machine) Given an input $\#w\#$, where w is a string of a's and b's, the machine makes a copy of w and halts with $\#w\#w\#$. The machine starts in state q_0, the initial state on the leftmost symbol of w.

It reads a 'a', changes that into a X and moves right in state q_a. When it sees the first blank symbol, it prints a 'a' and moves left in state q_1. If it sees a 'b' in q_0, it changes that into a Y and moves right in state q_b. When it sees the first blank symbol, it prints a 'b' and moves left in state q_1. In state q_1 it moves left till it sees a 'X' or a 'Y' and the process repeats. When no more 'a' or 'b' remains to be copied, the machine goes to q_2, prints a $\#$ after the copy it has made and moves left in q_3. In q_3, it moves left till the $\#$ symbol. Then, moving left it converts the 'X's and 'Y's into 'a's and 'b's respectively, and halts when it sees the leftmost $\#$ symbol. q_a and q_b are used to remember the symbol the machine has read.

The state set is $\{q_0, q_a, q_b, q_1, q_2, q_3, q_4, q_5\}$.

Tape symbols are $\{\#, a, b, X, Y, \not b\}$

δ mappings are given by:

$$\delta(q_0, a) = (q_a, X, R)$$
$$\delta(q_a, a) = (q_a, a, R)$$
$$\delta(q_0, b) = (q_b, Y, R)$$
$$\delta(q_b, a) = (q_b, a, R)$$
$$\delta(q_a, b) = (q_a, b, R)$$
$$\delta(q_a, \#) = (q_a, \#, R)$$
$$\delta(q_a, \not b) = (q_1, a, L)$$
$$\delta(q_b, b) = (q_b, b, R)$$
$$\delta(q_b, \#) = (q_b, \#, R)$$
$$\delta(q_b, \not b) = (q_1, b, L)$$
$$\delta(q_1, a) = (q_1, a, L)$$
$$\delta(q_1, b) = (q_1, b, L)$$
$$\delta(q_1, \#) = (q_1, \#, L)$$
$$\delta(q_1, X) = (q_0, X, R)$$
$$\delta(q_1, Y) = (q_0, Y, R)$$
$$\delta(q_0, \#) = (q_2, \#, R)$$
$$\delta(q_2, a) = (q_2, a, R)$$
$$\delta(q_2, b) = (q_2, b, R)$$
$$\delta(q_2, \not b) = (q_3, \#, L)$$
$$\delta(q_3, a) = (q_3, a, L)$$
$$\delta(q_3, b) = (q_3, b, L)$$
$$\delta(q_3, \#) = (q_4, \#, L)$$

$$\delta(q_4, X) = (q_4, a, L)$$
$$\delta(q_4, Y) = (q_4, b, L)$$
$$\delta(q_4, \#) = (q_5, \#, halt)$$

The sequence of moves in input $\#abb\#$ can be described as follows:

$$\#q_0abb\# \vdash \#Xq_abb\# \vdash^* \#Xbb\#q_a \vdash \#Xbbq_1 \#a \vdash^* \#q_1Xbb\#a$$
$$\vdash \#Xq_0bb\#a \vdash \#XYq_bb\#a \vdash^* \#XYb\#aq_b \vdash \#XYb\#q_1ab$$
$$\vdash^* \#XYq_0b\#ab \vdash \#XYYq_b\#ab \vdash^* \#XYY\#abq_b \vdash^* \#XYY\#aq_1bb$$
$$\vdash^* \#XYY\,q_0\#abb \vdash \#XYY\#q_2abb \vdash^* \#XYY\#abbq_2 \vdash \#XYY\#abq_3b\#$$
$$\vdash^* \#XYYq_3\#abb\# \vdash \#XYq_4Y\#abb\# \vdash^* q_4\#abb\#abb\#$$
$$\vdash q_5\#abb\#abb\#.$$

Example 9.6 To find the reversal of a string over $\{a, b\}$.

Input is $\#w\#$, $w \in \{a, b\}^+$.

Output is $\#w^R\#$.

The set of states is $\{q_0, q_1, q_2, q_3, q_4, q_a, q_b\}$.

The tape symbols are $\{\#, a, b, \not{b}\}$.

Initial tape head position is on the last symbol of w

δ is given by:

$$\delta(q_0, a) = (q_a, X, R)$$
$$\delta(q_0, b) = (q_b, X, R)$$
$$\delta(q_a, \#) = (q_a, \#, R)$$
$$\delta(q_b, \#) = (q_b, \#, R)$$
$$\delta(q_a, a) = (q_a, a, R)$$
$$\delta(q_a, b) = (q_a, b, R)$$
$$\delta(q_b, a) = (q_b, a, R)$$
$$\delta(q_b, b) = (q_b, b, R)$$
$$\delta(q_a, X) = (q_a, X, R)$$
$$\delta(q_b, X) = (q_b, X, R)$$
$$\delta(q_a, \not{b}) = (q_1, a, L)$$
$$\delta(q_b, \not{b}) = (q_1, b, L)$$
$$\delta(q_1, a) = (q_1, a, L)$$
$$\delta(q_1, b) = (q_1, b, L)$$
$$\delta(q_1, \#) = (q_0, \#, L)$$
$$\delta(q_0, X) = (q_0, X, L)$$

$\delta(q_0, \#) = (q_2, \cancel{b}, R)$

$\delta(q_2, X) = (q_2, \cancel{b}, R)$

$\delta(q_2, \#) = (q_2, \#, R)$

$\delta(q_2, a) = (q_2, a, R)$

$\delta(q_2, b) = (q_2, b, R)$

$\delta(q_2, \cancel{b}) = (q_3, \#, R)$

$\delta(q_3, \cancel{b}) = (q_4, \cancel{b}, halt)$

If the input is  the machine proceeds

to copy the symbols one by one after the second # in the reverse order, changing the original symbols into X's.

When it realizes that it has finished copying the symbols in the reverse order, it erases the first # and the X's, moves right and after the sequence of a's and b's, prints a # and halts.

It should be noted the reversed string appears after the second #. It would be an interesting exercise to reverse the string in place. i.e., if $\#w\#$ is the input, the machine halts with $\#w^R\#$ in the same location.

Example 9.7 Given two integers i and j, $i > j$, to compute the quotient and reminder when i is divided by j.

The input is

	#	a^i	#	b^j	#	

with the tape head positioned on the leftmost 'b' in the initial state q_0.

The output is

	#	X^i	#	b^j	#	c^k	#	d^l	#	

where k is the quotient when i is divided by j and l is the remainder. The TM which does this is described as follows:

The TM converts the b's into Y's and a's into X's one by one. When it sees no more b's it prints a 'c' after the # meaning j has been subtracted from i once.

...	#	X^j	a^{i-j}	#	b^j	#	c	...

This repeats as many times as possible. Each time a 'c' is printed. Finally, when the number of a's which have to be converted to X's is less than j, the TM while trying to convert a 'a' into a 'X,' will not find a 'a.' At this stage, it would have converted $(i \bmod j + 1)$ b's into Y's. The TM prints a # after c's and prints $(i \bmod j +1)$ d's. It does this by changing a Y into a 'b' and printing a 'd' after rightmost # and d's. When all the Y's have been converted into b's, we have $(i \bmod j + 1)$ d's after the rightmost #. The TM erases the last d and prints a # and halts. The set of states are $\{q_0, \ldots, q_{21}\}$. The tape symbols are $\{ \not{b}, \#, a, b, c, d, X, Y\}$. The mappings are given by:

$$\delta(q_0, b) = (q_1, Y, L)$$

changes 'b' to Y and moves left.

$$\delta(q_1, Y) = (q_1, Y, L)$$
$$\delta(q_1, \#) = (q_2, \#, L)$$
$$\delta(q_2, a) = (q_2, a, L)$$

moves left.

$$\delta(q_2, \#) = (q_3, \#, R)$$
$$\delta(q_2, X) = (q_3, X, R)$$

when the leftmost # or an X is seen, the head starts moving right.

$$\delta(q_3, a) = (q_4, X, R)$$

one 'a' is changed into X

$$\delta(q_4, a) = (q_4, a, R)$$
$$\delta(q_4, \#) = (q_5, \#, R)$$
$$\delta(q_5, Y) = (q_5, Y, R)$$

moves right

$$\delta(q_5, b) = (q_1, Y, L)$$

process starts repeating

$$\delta(q_5, \#) = (q_6, \#, R)$$

all 'b's have been converted to Y's

$$\delta(q_6, c) = (q_6, c, R)$$
$$\delta(q_6, \not{b}) = (q_7, c, L)$$

one 'c' is printed

$$\delta(q_7, c) = (q_7, c, L)$$
$$\delta(q_7, \#) = (q_8, \#, L)$$

moves left

$$\delta(q_8, Y) = (q_8, b, L)$$

Y's are changed back to 'b's

$$\delta(q_8, \#) = (q_0, \#, R)$$

process starts repeating

$$\delta(q_3, \#) = (q_9, \#, R)$$

all 'a's have been changed. Now the number of 'c's represents the quotient. Y's represent the remainder.

$$\delta(q_9, Y) = (q_9, Y, R)$$

$$\delta(q_9, b) = (q_9, b, R)$$

$$\delta(q_9, \#) = (q_{10}, \#, R)$$

$$\delta(q_{10}, c) = (q_{10}, c, R)$$

moves right

$$\delta(q_{10}, \cancel{b}) = (q_{11}, \#, L)$$

$\#$ is printed after the 'c's

$$\delta(q_{11}, c) = (q_{11}, c, L)$$

$$\delta(q_{11}, \#) = (q_{12}, \#, L)$$

$$\delta(q_{12}, b) = (q_{12}, b, L)$$

$$\delta(q_{12}, Y) = (q_{13}, b, R)$$

$$\delta(q_{13}, b) = (q_{13}, b, R)$$

$$\delta(q_{13}, \#) = (q_{14}, \#, R)$$

$$\delta(q_{14}, c) = (q_{14}, c, R)$$

$$\delta(q_{14}, \#) = (q_{15}, \#, R)$$

$$\delta(q_{15}, d) = (q_{15}, d, R)$$

$$\delta(q_{15}, \cancel{b}) = (q_{16}, d, L)$$

$$\delta(q_{16}, d) = (q_{16}, d, L)$$

$$\delta(q_{16}, \#) = (q_{11}, \#, L)$$

Y's are copied as 'd's

$$\delta(q_{12}, \#) = (q_{17}, \#, R)$$

after all Y's have been copied as 'd's the process starts finishing

$$\delta(q_{17}, b) = (q_{17}, b, R)$$

$$\delta(q_{17}, \#) = (q_{18}, \#, R)$$

$$\delta(q_{18}, c) = (q_{18}, c, R)$$

$$\delta(q_{18}, \#) = (q_{19}, \#, R)$$

$$\delta(q_{19}, d) = (q_{19}, d, R)$$

$$\delta(q_{19}, \cancel{b}) = (q_{20}, \cancel{b}, L)$$

$$\delta(q_{20}, d) = (q_{21}, \#, halt)$$

The move of a TM can be represented as a state diagram:

means the TM when in state p and reading X, prints a Y over X, goes to state q and moves right.

The state diagram for Example 9.2.2 (copy) can be represented as:

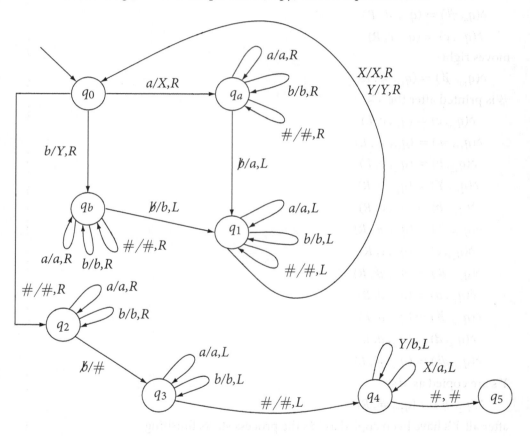

9.3 Techniques for TM Construction

Designing a TM to solve a problem is an interesting task. It is somewhat similar to programming. Given a problem, different TMs can be constructed to solve it. But, we would like to have a TM which does it in a simple and efficient manner. Like we learn some techniques of programming to deal with alternatives, loops etc, it is helpful to understand some techniques in TM construction, which will help in designing simple and efficient TM. It should be noted that we are using the word 'efficient' in an intuitive manner here, though later in Chapter 12, we shall deal with it formally. Next, we consider some techniques.

1. Considering the state as a tuple.

In Example 9.2.2, we considered a *TM* which makes a copy of a given string over $\Sigma = \{a, b\}$. After reading a 'a,' the machine remembers it by going to q_a and after reading a 'b,' it goes to q_b. In general, we can represent the state as $[q, x]$ where $x \in \Sigma$ denoting that it has read a 'x.'

2. Considering the tape symbol as a tuple.

Sometimes, we may want to mark some symbols without destroying them or do some computation without destroying the input. In such cases, it is advisable to have multiple tracks on the tape. This is equivalent to considering the tape symbol as a tuple.

. . .		A			. . .
. . .		B			. . .
. . .		C			. . .

↑

There is only one tape head. In the above figure, there are three tracks. The head is pointing to a cell which contains A on the first track, B on the second track, and C on the third track. The tape symbol is taken a 3-tuple $[A, B, C]$. Some computation can be done in one track by manipulating the respective component of the tape symbol. This is very useful in checking off symbols.

3. Checking off symbols.

We use one track of the tape to mark that some symbols have been read without changing them.

Example 9.8   Consider a TM for accepting

$w\#w\#w, w \in \{a, b\}^*$

A tape having two tracks is considered.

. . .	a	b	b	$\#$	a	b	b	$\#$	a	b	b	. . .
. . .												. . .

The first track contains the input. When the *TM* reads the first a in state q_0, it stores it in its memory (by taking the state as a pair), checks off 'a' by printing a $\sqrt{}$ in the second track below a, moves right and after the $\#$ symbol checks whether the symbol is a 'a.' If so, marks it by putting a $\sqrt{}$ in the second track, moves right and again checks the first symbol after $\#$ is a 'a' and if so it marks also. It then moves left and repeats the process with each unmarked leftmost symbols in each block. When all the symbols in the first block match with the second and third blocks, the machine halts accepting the string.

The mappings can be defined as follows:

$$\delta(q_0, [a, \cancel{b}]) = ([q, a], [a, \checkmark\,], R)$$
$$\delta(q_0, [b, \cancel{b}]) = ([q, b], [b, \checkmark\,], R)$$

The machine reads the leftmost symbol, marks it and remembers whether it is a 'a' or 'b' by storing it in the state:

$$\delta([q, a], [a, \cancel{b}]) = ([q, a], [a, \cancel{b}], R)$$
$$\delta([q, a], [b, \cancel{b}]) = ([q, a], [b, \cancel{b}], R)$$
$$\delta([q, b], [a, \cancel{b}]) = ([q, b], [a, \cancel{b}], R)$$
$$\delta([q, b], [b, \cancel{b}]) = ([q, b], [b, \cancel{b}], R)$$

The head passes through symbols in the first block to the right:

$$\delta([q, a], [\#, \cancel{b}]) = ([p, a], [\#, \cancel{b}], R)$$
$$\delta([q, b], [\#, \cancel{b}]) = ([p, a], [\#, b], R)$$

When the head encounters a $\#$ in the first track, the first component of the state is changed to p.

$$\delta([p, a], [a, \checkmark\,]) = ([p, a], [a, \checkmark\,], R)$$
$$\delta([p, a], [b, \checkmark\,]) = ([p, a], [b, \checkmark\,], R)$$
$$\delta([p, b], [a, \checkmark\,]) = ([p, b], [a, \checkmark\,], R)$$
$$\delta([p, b], [b, \checkmark\,]) = ([p, b], [b, \checkmark\,], R)$$
$$\delta([p, a], [a, \cancel{b}]) = ([r, a], [a, \checkmark\,], R)$$
$$\delta([p, b], [b, \cancel{b}]) = ([r, b], [b, \checkmark\,], R)$$

When it encounters a first unchecked symbol it marks it by putting a $\checkmark$ in the second track and changes the first component of the state to r.

$$\delta([r, a], [a, \cancel{b}]) = ([r, a], [a, \cancel{b}], R)$$
$$\delta([r, b], [a, \cancel{b}]) = ([r, b], [a, \cancel{b}], R)$$
$$\delta([r, a], [b, \cancel{b}]) = ([r, a], [b, \cancel{b}], R)$$
$$\delta([r, b], [b, \cancel{b}]) = ([r, b], [b, \cancel{b}], R)$$

The head moves through the second block without changing symbols, when the first component of the state is r:

$$\delta([r, a], [\#, \cancel{b}]) = ([s, a], [\#, \cancel{b}], R)$$
$$\delta([r, b], [\#, \cancel{b}]) = ([s, b], [\#, \cancel{b}], R)$$

When it encounters a $\#$ in the first track it moves right into the third block changing the first component of the state to s.

$\delta([s, a], [a, \checkmark]) = ([s, a], [a, \checkmark], R)$

$\delta([s, a], [b, \checkmark]) = ([s, a], [b, \checkmark], R)$

$\delta([s, b], [a, \checkmark]) = ([s, b], [a, \checkmark], R)$

$\delta([s, b], [b, \checkmark]) = ([s, b], [b, \checkmark], R)$

It moves right looking for the unchecked symbol:

$\delta([s, b], [b, \not{b}]) = (t, [b, \checkmark], L)$

$\delta([s, a], [a, \not{b}]) = (t, [a, \checkmark], L)$

When it encounters an unchecked symbol in the third block it marks it by putting a $\checkmark$ in the second track and starts moving left.

$\delta(t, [a, \checkmark]) = (t, [a, \checkmark], L)$

$\delta(t, [b, \checkmark]) = (t, [b, \checkmark], L)$

$\delta(t, [\#, \not{b}]) = (t', [\#, \not{b}], L)$

It moves into the second block in state t':

$\delta(t', [a, \not{b}] = (t', [a, \not{b}], L)$

$\delta(t', [b, \not{b}] = (t', [b, \not{b}], L)$

$\delta(t', [a, \checkmark]) = (t', [a, \checkmark], L)$

$\delta(t', [b, \checkmark]) = (t', [b, \checkmark], L)$

It moves left in the second block.

$\delta(t', [\#, \not{b}]) = (t'', [\#, b], L)$

It moves left into the first block in state t''.

$\delta(t'', [a, \not{b}]) = (t'', [a, \not{b}], L)$

$\delta(t'', [b, \not{b}]) = (t'', [b, \not{b}], L)$

It moves left in the first block through unchecked symbols.

When it encounters a checked symbol, it moves right in state q_0 and the whole process repeats.

$\delta(t'', [a, \checkmark]) = (q_0, [a, \checkmark], R)$

$\delta(t'', [b, \checkmark]) = (q_0, [b, \checkmark], R)$

This way the machine checks for same symbols in the first, second, and third blocks. When the machine encounters a $\#$ in the first track in state q_0, it means it has checked all symbols in the first block. Now, it has to check that there are no more symbols in the second and third block.

$$\delta(q_0, [\#, \not b]) = (q_1, [\#, \not b], R)$$
$$\delta(q_1, [a, \checkmark]) = (q_1, [a, \checkmark], R)$$
$$\delta(q_1, [b, \checkmark]) = (q_1, [b, \checkmark], R)$$

If it encounters an unchecked symbol, it halts without accepting:

$$\delta(q_1, [a, \not b]) = (q_n, [a, \not b], R)$$
$$\delta(q_1, [b, \not b]) = (q_n, [b, \not b], R)$$

If it finds all symbols are checked in the second block, it moves to the third block in state q_2:

$$\delta(q_1, [\#, \not b]) = (q_2, [\#, \not b], R)$$

In the third block, it checks whether all symbols have already been checked. If so, it halts in accepting state q_y. Otherwise, halts in non-accepting state q_n.

$$\delta(q_2, [a, \checkmark]) = (q_2, [a, \checkmark], R)$$
$$\delta(q_2, [b, \checkmark]) = (q_2, [b, \checkmark], R)$$
$$\delta(q_2, [a, \not b]) = (q_n, [a, \not b], R)$$
$$\delta(q_2, [b, \not b]) = (q_n, [b, \not b], R)$$
$$\delta(q_2, [\not b, \not b]) = (q_y, [\not b, \not b], R)$$

If the input has more symbols in the first block (than second block), it moves in the second block in state $[p, a]$ or $[p, b]$ and encounters $[\#, \not b]$. Then it halts rejecting the input:

$$\delta([p, a], [\#, \not b]) = (q_n, [\#, \not b], R)$$
$$\delta([p, b], [\#, \not b]) = (q_n, [\#, \not b], R)$$

If the input has equal symbols in the first and second block but less symbols in the third block, the machine encounters $[\not b, \not b]$ in state $[s, b]$ or $[s, a]$ and halts without accepting:

$$\delta([s, a], [\not b, \not b]) = (q_n, [\not b, \not b], R$$
$$\delta([s, b], [\not b, \not b]) = (q_n, [\not b, \not b], R)$$

Thus, we find that having two tracks and using the second track to check off symbols is a useful technique.

When we consider a single tape multi-track TM, we really take the tape symbol as a tuple. This need not be considered as a variation of TM.

4. Shifting over.

Sometimes, we may have to shift symbols on the tape to the right or left to allow for some symbols to be written. Suppose the contents of the tape are $a_1 \ldots a_{i-1} A a_{i+1} \ldots a_n$ at some instant. A has to be replaced by $abcd$ say. Then, $a_{i+1} \ldots a_n$ have to be shifted three cells to the right and then in the space created $abcd$ can be printed. We can use the state as a tuple to store some information and shift symbols. Suppose the head is reading a_{i+1} in state q and the shifting process has to start. Then, the TM reads a_{i+1} and goes to a state $[q, -, -, a_{i+1}]$ and prints X over a_i.

The ID

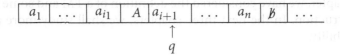

| a_1 | $\ldots$ | a_{i1} | A | a_{i+1} | $\ldots$ | a_n | b | $\ldots$ |

$\uparrow$
q

changes to

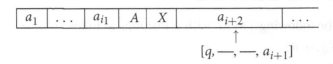

| a_1 | $\ldots$ | a_{i1} | A | X | a_{i+2} | $\ldots$ |

$\uparrow$
$[q, -, -, a_{i+1}]$

Next, the *TM* reads a_{i+2}, storing it in the fourth component, and shifting a_{i+1} from fourth component to the third component.

$$\delta([q, -, -, a_{i+1}], a_{i+2}) = ([q, -, a_{i+1}, a_{i+2}], X, R)$$

Similarly, $\delta([q, -, a_{i+1}, a_{i+2}], a_{i+3}) = ([q, a_{i+1}, a_{i+2}, a_{i+3}]X, R)$
When it reads a_{i+4}, it deposits a_{i+1} in that cell

$$\delta([q, a_{i+1}, a_{i+2}, a_{i+3}], a_{i+4}) = ([q, a_{i+2}, a_{i+3}, a_{i+4}], a_{i+4}, R)$$

In general:

$$\delta([q, a_j, a_{j+1}, a_{j+2}], a_{j+3}) = ([q, a_{j+1}, a_{j+2}, a_{j+3}], a_j, R) \ i+1 \le j \le n$$

where $a_{n+1}, a_{n+2}, a_{n+3}$ is blank symbol b. Finally, it starts moving left $\delta([q, a_n, b, b], b) = (q', a_n, L)$.

In q', it moves left till it finds $AXXX$ and replaces it by *abcd*. A similar method can be used for shifting symbols to the left. Thus, storing some information in some components of the state and cyclically moving the components helps in the technique of shifting off symbols.

5. Subroutines.

Just as a computer program has a main procedure and subroutines, the TM can also be programmed to have a main TM and TMs which serve as subroutines. Suppose we have to make n copies of a word w. Input is $\#w\#$ and the output is $\#w\# \underbrace{www \ldots w}_{n \text{ times}}$.

In this case, we can write the mappings for a TM M_{sub} which when started on $\#w\#x$ ends up with $\#w\#xw$. The main TM will call this M_{sub} n times. Similarly, for multiplying two unary numbers m and n, n has to be copied on m times. We can write a subTM for copying and main TM will call this m times.

In order that a TM M_1 uses another TM M_2 as a subroutine, the states of M_1 and M_2 have to be disjoint. Also, when M_1 wants to call M_2, from a state of M_1, the control goes to the initial state of M_2. When the subroutine finishes and returns to M_1, from the halting state of M_2, the machine goes to some state of M_1. Note that a subroutine TM call another TM as its subroutine. This technique helps to construct a TM in a topdown manner dividing the work into tasks and writing a TM for each task and combining them.

In this chapter, we have considered the definition of a TM and some techniques for TM construction. In the next three chapters, we shall study more about TMs and computability.

Problems and Solutions

1. Consider the following TM M' with transitions as follows:

$\delta(q_0, 1) = (q_1, 0, R)$

$\delta(q_1, 1) = (q_1, 1, R)$

$\delta(q_1, 0) = (q_2, 1, R)$

$\delta(q_2, 0) = (q_3, 0, L)$

$\delta(q_3, 0) = (q_0, 0, R)$

$\delta(q_3, 1) = (q_3, 1, L)$

q_0 is the initial state and 0 is taken as blank symbol.

a. Trace the sequence of moves when the machine is started on

...0 0 1̲ 1 1 1 1 0 0 0 1 1 0 0...

b. What happens when it is started on:

1. ...0 0 1̲ 1 0 0 0 1 1 1 0 0 1 1 1 1 0 0 0...

2. ...0 0 0 0 1̲ 1 1 0 0 0 0...

3. ...0 0 0 1 1 1̲ 1 1 1 0 0 0 1 1 1 0 0...

4. ...0 0 0 1 1 1̲ 1 1 0 0 0...

Solution.

a.

q_0 1 1 1 1 0 0 0 1 1

0 q_1 1 1 1 0 0 0 1 1

0 1 q_1 1 1 0 0 0 1 1

0 1 1 q_1 1 0 0 0 1 1

0 1 1 1 q_1 0 0 0 1 1

0 1 1 1 1 q_2 0 0 1 1

0 1 1 1 q_3 1 0 0 1 1

0 1 1 q_3 1 1 0 0 1 1

0 1 q_3 1 1 1 0 0 1 1

0 q_3 1 1 1 1 0 0 1 1

q_3 0 1 1 1 1 0 0 1 1

0 q_0 1 1 1 1 0 0 1 1

0 0 q_1 1 1 1 0 0 1 1

0 0 1 q_1 1 1 0 0 1 1

0 0 1 1 q_1 1 0 0 1 1

0 0 1 1 1 q_1 0 0 1 1

0 0 1 1 1 1 q_2 0 1 1

0 0 1 1 1 q_3 1 0 1 1

0 0 1 1 q_3 1 1 0 1 1

0 0 1 q_3 1 1 1 0 1 1

0 0 q_3 1 1 1 1 0 1 1

0 q_3 0 1 1 1 1 0 1 1

0 0 q_0 1 1 1 1 0 1 1

0 0 0 q_1 1 1 1 0 1 1

0 0 0 1 q_1 1 1 0 1 1

0 0 0 1 1 q_1 1 0 1 1

0 0 0 1 1 1 q_1 0 1 1

0 0 0 1 1 1 1 q_2 1 1

No move for (q_2, 1); machine halts with output … 0 0 0 1 1 1 1 1 1 ….

The first block of 1's is shifted step by step to the right till it becomes adjacent to the second block of 1's.

b.

1. … 0 0 1 1 0 0 0 1 1 1 0 0 1 1 1 1 0 0 0 …
   ↑
   q_0

It will halt when the *ID* is as below:

… 0 0 0 0 0 1 1 1 1 1 0 0 1 1 1 1 0 0 0 …
   ↑
   q_2

First block of 1's will be shifted to the right till it is adjacent to the second block; but third block of 1's is not affected.

2. … 0 0 0 0 1 1 1 0 0 0 0 …
   ↑
   q_0

When there is only one block of 1's it gets shifted one cell to the right and the process repeats. It never stops as there is no second block of 1's.

3. … 0 0 0 1 1 1 1 1 0 0 0 1 1 1 0 0 0 …
   ↑
   q_0

1 1 q_0 1 1 1 0 0 0 1 1 1

1 1 0 q_1 1 1 0 0 0 1 1 1

$1\ 1\ 0\ 1\ q_1\ 1\ 0\ 0\ 0\ 1\ 1\ 1$

$1\ 1\ 0\ 1\ 1\ q_1\ 0\ 0\ 0\ 1\ 1\ 1$

$1\ 1\ 0\ 1\ 1\ 1\ q_2\ 0\ 0\ 1\ 1\ 1$

$1\ 1\ 0\ 1\ 1\ q_3\ 1\ 0\ 0\ 1\ 1\ 1$

$1\ 1\ 0\ 1\ q_3\ 1\ 1\ 0\ 0\ 1\ 1\ 1$

$1\ 1\ 0\ q_3\ 1\ 1\ 1\ 0\ 0\ 1\ 1\ 1$

$1\ 1\ q_3\ 0\ 1\ 1\ 1\ 0\ 0\ 1\ 1\ 1$

$1\ 1\ 0\ q_0\ 1\ 1\ 1\ 0\ 0\ 1\ 1\ 1$

$\vdots$

$\dots 0\ 0\ 0\ 1\ 1\ 0\ 0\ 0\ 1\ 1\ \underset{\substack{\uparrow \\ q_2}}{1}\ 1\ 1\ 0\ 0\dots$

Since the machine starts with the third 1 in the first block, the portion of the first block from this point is shifted to the right till it becomes adjacent to the second block.

4. $\dots 0\ 0\ 0\ 1\ 1\ \underset{\substack{\uparrow \\ q_0}}{1}\ 1\ 1\ 0\ 0\ 0\dots$

There is only one block of 1's. The portion of the block from the initial position is shifted one cell to the right and this process starts repeating and never stops as there is no second block 1's. The portion of the block of 1's to the left of the initial tape head position is unaffected.

2. Construct a TM with three characters 0, 1, and # which locates a '1' under the following conditions. There is only one # on the tape and somewhere to the right of it is a '1.' The rest of the tape is blank. The head starts at or to the left of the #. When the TM halts, the tape is unchanged and head stops at the '1.' Zero is taken as the blank symbol.

Solution. The transition table is as follows. Here q_3 is the (halt or) final state:

	0	1	#
q_0	$(q_0, 0, R)$	$(q_0, 1, R)$	$(q_1, \#, R)$
q_1	$(q_1, 0, R)$	$(q_2, 1, R)$	—
q_2	$(q_3, 0, L)$	—	—
q_3	—	—	—

3. Construct a TM over an alphabet {0, 1, #}, where 0 indicates blank, which takes a non-null string of 1's and #'s and transfers the rightmost symbol to the left-hand end. Thus, $\dots 000\#1\#1\#1000\dots$ becomes $\dots 0001\#1\#1\#000\dots$. The head is initially at the leftmost non-blank symbol.

Solution. The machine mainly has to move to the right-hand end, read the character, to identify the rightmost 1 or #. Then, move it to the leftmost end and halt. The transitions are:

	0	1	#
q_0	$(q_1, 0, L)$	$(q_0, 1, R)$	$(q_0, \#, R)$
q_1	$(q_4, 0, R)$	$(q_2, 0, L)$	$(q_3, 0, L)$
q_2	$(q_4, 1, L)$	$(q_2, 1, L)$	$(q_2, \#, L)$
q_3	$(q_4, \#, L)$	$(q_3, 1, L)$	$(q_3, \#, L)$
q_4	$(q_5, 0, R)$	—	—

4. Design a *TM* with one track, one head, and three characters 0, 1, # to compute the following functions. Input and output are to be in binary form as follows. Zero is represented as # # and 7 is represented as # 1 1 1 #. That is the binary string represented by '*n*' is enclosed between two #'s on left and right of it. ♭ is the blank symbol.
   a. $f(n) = n + 1$
   b. $g(n) = 2n$.
   Input is #n#
   Output is #n + 1# in (a) and #2n# in (b)

Solution.
   a. The function to be computed is $f(n) = n + 1$.

Input is $\flat\,\flat\,\flat\,\#\overbrace{\cdots}^{n}\#\,\flat\,\flat$
$$\underset{q_0}{\uparrow}$$

Output is $\#\overbrace{\cdots}^{n+1}\#\,\flat\,\flat$

The transition table is given below:

	0	1	#	♭
q_0	—	—	$(q_1, \#, L)$	—
q_1	$(q_4, 1, L)$	$(q_2, 0, L)$	$(q_3, 1, L)$	—
q_2	$(q_4, 1, L)$	$(q_2, 0, L)$	$(q_3, 1, L)$	—
q_3	—	—	—	$(q_4, \#, L)$
q_4	—	—	—	—

b. The function to be computed is $g(n) = 2n$.

Input is $\not b \not b \# \overset{n}{\overbrace{1 \cdots}} \# \not b \not b$
$\underset{q_0}{\uparrow}$

Output is $\not b \not b \# \overset{2n}{\overbrace{1 \cdots}} \# \not b \not b$
$\underset{q_0}{\uparrow}$

	0	1	#	$\not b$
q_0	$(q_0, 0, R)$	$(q_0, 1, R)$	$(q_1, 0, R)$	—
q_1	—	—	—	$(q_2, \#, L)$
q_2	—	—	—	—

Exercises

1. Draw a state diagram for a *TM* accepting each of the following languages:
   a. $\{x \in \{0, 1\}^* | \#_1(x) = 2\#_0(x) + 1\}$.
   b. The language of all non-palindromes over $\{a, b\}$.

2. Consider the *TM* whose state transition is given below:
   $\delta(q_0, 1) = (q_1, 0, R)$
   $\delta(q_1, 0) = (q_2, 1, R)$
   $\delta(q_2, 1) = (q_3, 0, L)$
   $\delta(q_3, 0) = (q_0, 1, R)$
   $\delta(q_0, 0) = (q_0, 0, R)$
   $\delta(q_1, 1) = (q_1, 1, R)$
   $\delta(q_2, 0) = (q_2, 0, R)$
   $\delta(q_3, 1) = (q_3, 1, L)$

   Here, q_0 is the start state and q_2 is a final state.

   a. For each of the initial tape configurations, determine the final tape pattern that the machine will produce and indicate the final head position.
      i. $\ldots \underline{0}1110111110\ldots$
      ii. $\ldots \underline{0}1110110\ldots$
      Here '$\underline{B}$' means the head is presently reading that symbol 'B.'

   b. What effect will the machine have on an arbitrary initial pattern of the form $\ldots 01^m01^n0 \ldots$, where m and n are positive integers. Explain briefly how the machine works. What is the final position of the reading head?

   c. Show how to modify the given transitions so that the machine will always halt at its starting position.

3. Consider the *TM* described by the following state diagram.

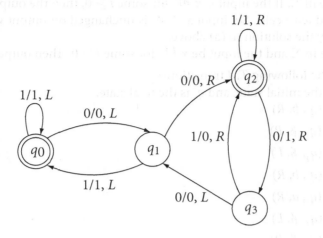

a. Determine the behavior of the machine for each of the following initial configurations:

    i.   ...000000000000...

    ii. ...00000100101100...

    iii. ...011000100000000...

b. Describe as clearly and concisely as you can the initial tape configurations for which the machine will eventually halt.

4. Design a TM for the following job. When started anywhere on a tape that is blank except for a single 1, the machine eventually halts with that 1 under its reading head. The remainder of the tape is to be blank when the machine halts.

5. Design a TM that behaves as follows:

    When presented with a tape containing an arbitrary string of 1's and 2's (preceded and followed by blanks) and made to scan the first symbol in the string, the machine is to reverse the string. Thus, if presented with the tape pattern,

    ...00121121200...

the machine should eventually produce the tape pattern,

    ...00212112100...

and halt as indicated. The final pattern is to occupy the same region of the tape as the initial pattern. A solution using between six and nine states is reasonable.

6. Construct a TM to carry out the following operations:

a. A left shift of its input by one cell.

b. A cyclic left shift of its input by one cell.

c. Let c be in Σ (the input alphabet). If the input word $x = x_1 c x_2$ where x_1 is in $(\Sigma - \{c\})^*$, then produce $c x_2$ as output.

d. A duplication of its input. i.e., if the input is w, the output should be ww.

e. Let 1 be in Σ. If the input is $x\ \cancel{b}1^i$ for some $i \geq 0$, then the output should be x shifted left i cells. So, input $x\ \cancel{b}\ \cancel{b}$ is unchanged on output while $x\ \cancel{b}1$ is given by the solution to (a) above.

f. Let 1 be in Σ and the input be $x\ \cancel{b}1^i$ for some $i \geq 0$. Then output x^i.

7. Consider the following *TM* transitions:
Here, q_0 is the initial state, and q_2 is the final state.

$\delta(q_0, a) = (q_1, b, R)$

$\delta(q_0, b) = (q_3, \cancel{b}, R)$

$\delta(q_0, \cancel{b}) = (q_2, \cancel{b}, L)$

$\delta(q_1, a) = (q_1, b, R)$

$\delta(q_1, b) = (q_1, a, R)$

$\delta(q_1, \cancel{b}) = (q_2, \cancel{b}, L)$

$\delta(q_3, a) = (q_4, \cancel{b}, R)$

$\delta(q_3, b) = (q_3, b, R)$

$\delta(q_4, a) = (q_1, b, R)$

a. Give four words accepted by the TM together with their configuration sequences.

b. Give four words that are not accepted by the TM and in each case explain why not.

8. Design a *TM* that when started on any tape pattern of the form:

$$\ldots 01^n 01^x 00 \ldots \ (n > 0, x \geq 0)$$

eventually halts with the pattern

$$\ldots 01^n 01^{x\,+\,n} 00 \ldots$$

on its tape. The new pattern is to start in the same square as the given pattern.

9. Using the *TM* of problem (8) as a submachine, design a new TM that behaves as follows. When started on any pattern of the form:

$$\ldots \underline{0}1^m 01^n 00 \ldots \ (m, n > 0)$$

the machine is eventually to halt with the pattern

$$\ldots 01^{mn}0 \ldots$$

on its tape. The location of this final pattern may be chosen to make the design of the machine as simple as possible.

10. For each of the following languages, construct a TM that recognizes the language:

a. $\{xyx | x$ and y are in $\{a, b\}^*$ and $|x| > 1\}$

b. $\{a^i b^i c^j d^j | i \neq j\}$

c. $\{aba^2 b^2 a^3 b^3 \ldots a^n b^n | n \geq 0\}$

11. Consider the *TM* with input alphabets $\{a, b\}$, start state q_0 with the following transitions:

$\delta(q_0, \not b) = (q_1, \not b, R)$

$\delta(q_1, a) = (q_1, a, R)$

$\delta(q_1, b) = (q_1, b, R)$

$\delta(q_1, \not b) = (q_2, \not b, L)$

$\delta(q_2, a) = (q_3, \not b, R)$

$\delta(q_2, b) = (q_5, \not b, R)$

$\delta(q_2, \not b) = (q_2, \not b, N)$

$\delta(q_3, \not b) = (q_4, a, R)$

$\delta(q_4, a) = (q_4, a, R)$

$\delta(q_4, b) = (q_4, b, R)$

$\delta(q_4, \not b) = (q_7, a, L)$

$\delta(q_5, \not b) = (q_6, b, R)$

$\delta(q_6, a) = (q_6, a, R)$

$\delta(q_6, b) = (q_6, b, R)$

$\delta(q_6, \not b) = (q_7, b, L)$

$\delta(q_7, a) = (q_7, a, L)$

$\delta(q_7, b) = (q_7, b, L)$

$\delta(q_7, \not b) = (q_2, \not b, L)$

   a. What is the final configuration if the input is $\not b ab \not b$?

   b. What is the final configuration if the input is $\not b \not b baa \not b$?

   c. Describe what the TM does for an arbitrary input string in $\{a, b\}^*$.

12. Construct a TM to accept the language $\{a^i b^j | i < j\}$.

13. Construct a TM to accept the language

   $\{w \in \{a, b\}^* | w \text{ contains the same number of } a'\text{s and } b'\text{s}\}$

14. Construct a TM to accept the language $\{w \in \{a, b\}^* | w = w^R\}$.

15. Construct a TM to compute the following functions. Let the input x be represented in unary notation:

   a. $f(x) = x + 2$

   b. $f(x) = 2x$

   c. $f(x) = x \bmod 2$.

16. Give informal arguments which explain why *TMs* are more powerful than PDAs.

10 Variations of Turing Machines

In Chapter 9, we defined the computability model called "Turing Machine" (TM). This model is one of the most beautiful, simple, and an useful abstract model. We had elaborate discussion of this model through various examples. One can think of variations of the basic model in many ways. For example, one can work with two tapes, instead of a single tape. These models are got by adding extra components and power to the control and hence, appear to be more powerful than the basic model, but they are not. We could also consider some restricted version of the basic model. In this chapter we are considering such variants and discuss their computing capabilities. We note that the power is not increased by adding extra components and not decreased by considering the restricted versions.

10.1 Generalized Versions

In this section, we consider the following generalized versions of the basic model and show that they are equivalent to the basic model as far as accepting power is concerned. The variants are:

1. Turing machines with two-way infinite tapes
2. Multitape TM
3. Multihead TM
4. Non-deterministic TMs
5. Turing machines with 2-dimensional tapes

10.1.1 Two-Way Infinite Tape TM

A two-way infinite tape Turing machine (TTM) is a TM with its input tape infinite in both directions, the other components being the same as that of the basic model. We observe from the following theorem that the power of TTM is no way superior of that of the basic TM.

That a one-way TM M_0 can be simulated by a two-way TM M_D can be seen easily. M_D puts a $\#$ to the left of the leftmost nonblank and moves its head right and simulates M_0. If M_D reads $\#$ again, it halts rejecting the input as this means M_0 tries to move off the left end of the tape.

Theorem 10.1 *For any TTM $M_D = (K, \Sigma, \Gamma, \delta, q_0, F)$ there exists an equivalent TM $M_{D'}$.*

Proof The tape of the M_D at any instance is of the form

⊭	$\cdots$	a_{-2}	a_{-1}	a_0	a_1	a_2	$\cdots$	a_n	⊭

where a_0 is the symbol in the cell scanned by M_D initially. M_0 can represent this situation by two tracks:

a_0	a_1	a_2	$\cdots$
#	a_{-1}	a_{-2}	$\cdots$

When M_D is to the right of a_0, the simulation is done on the upper track. When M_D is to the left of a_0, the simulation is done in M_0 on the lower track. The initial configuration would be:

a_0	a_1	$\cdots$	a_n
⊭	⊭	⊭	⊭

$M_0 = (K', \Sigma', \Gamma', \delta', q_0', F')$ where

$K' = \{q_0'\} \cup (K \times \{1, 2\})$

$\Sigma' = \Sigma \times \{⊭\}$

$\Gamma' = \Gamma \times (\Gamma \cup \{\#\})$

$F' = \{[q, 1], [q, 2] | q \in F\}$

δ' is defined as follows:

If $\delta(q, a) = (q', c, L/R)$ and if the head of M_D is to the right of a_0 we have: $\delta([q, 1], [a, b]) = ([q', 1], [c, b], L/R)$; simulation is done on the upper track 1.

If M_D is to the left of the initial position, simulation is done on the lower track. If $\delta(q, b) = (q', c, L/R)$

$\delta'([q,2],[a,b]) = ([q', 2],[a,c], R/L)$

The initial move will be:

$\delta'(q_0', [a_0, ⊭]) = ([q, 1], [A, \#], R)$

if $\delta(q_0, a_0) = (q, A, R)$.

$\delta'(q_0', [a_0, ⊭]) = ([q, 2], [A, \#], R)$

if $\delta(q_0, a_0) = (q, A, L)$.

When reading the leftmost symbol M_D behaves as follows:

If $\delta(q, a) = (p, A, R)$

$\quad \delta'([q, 1/2], [a, \#]) = ([p, 1], [A, \#], R)$.

If $\delta(q, a) = (p, A, L)$

$\quad \delta'([q, 1/2], [a, \#]) = ([p, 2], [A, \#], R)$.

while simulating a move when M_D is to the left of the initial position, M_0 does it in the lower track always moving in a direction opposite to that of M_D. If M_D reaches an accepting state q_f, M_0 reaches $[q_f, 1]$ or $[q_f, 2]$ and accepts the input.

10.1.2 Multi-tape TM

Definition 10.1 *A multi-tape TM is a TM, with n tapes each having a separate tape head. The move of this TM will depend on the state and symbol scanned by each head. In each tape, a symbol is printed on the cell scanned and each head moves left or right independently depending on the move.*

Suppose we have a 3-tape TM (Figure 10.1).

The symbols scanned by the heads are A, B and C respectively. Then, the mapping will be of the form:

$\quad \delta(q, A, B, C) = (q', (A', L), (B', R), (C', R))$

The state changes to q.

In the first tape, A' is printed over A and the tape head moves left. In the second tape, B' is printed over B and the tape head moves right while in the third tape C' is printed over C, the tape head moving right.

Theorem 10.2 *A multi-tape TM can be simulated by a single tape TM.*

Proof Let $M = (K, \Sigma, \Gamma, \delta, q_0, F)$ be a k-tape TM. It can be simulated by a single tape TM M' having $2k$ tracks. Odd numbered tracks contain the contents of M's tapes.

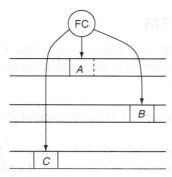

Figure 10.1. TM with three tapes

		...	A	...	
		...	X	...	
		...		...	B
		...		...	X
C	...			...	
X	...			...	

Figure 10.2. TM with one tape having six tracks

Even-numbered tracks contain the blank symbols excepts in one position where it has a marker X. This specifies the position of the head in the corresponding M's tape. The situation in Figure 10.1 is represented by a 6-track TM as given in Figure 10.2.

To simulate a move of the multi-tape TM M, the single tape TM M' makes two sweeps, one from left to right and another from right to left. It starts on the leftmost cell, which contains a X in one of the even tracks. While moving from left to right, when it encounters a X, it stores the symbol above it in its finite control. It keeps a counter as one of the component of the state to check whether it has read the symbols from all the tapes. After the left to right move is over, depending on the move of M determined by the symbols read, the single tape TM M' makes a right to left sweep changing the corresponding symbols on the odd tracks and positioning the X's properly in the even-numbered tracks. To simulate one move of M, M' roughly takes (it may be slightly more depending on the left or right shift of X) a number of steps equal to twice the distance between the leftmost and the rightmost cells containing a X in an even-numbered track. When M' starts all X's will be in one cell. After i moves the distance between the leftmost and rightmost X can be at most $2i$. Hence, to simulate n moves of M, M' roughly takes $\sum_{i=1}^{n} 2(2i) = \sum_{i=1}^{n} 4i = O(n^2)$ steps. If M reaches a final state, M' accepts and halts. $\qquad\square$

An off-line TM is a multi-tape TM with a read only input tape. In this tape, input w is placed with end markers as $\mathord{\text{\textcent}}w\$$ and symbols cannot be rewritten on this tape.

10.1.3 Multi-head TM

Definition 10.2 *A multi-head TM is a single tape TM having k heads reading symbols on the same tape. In one step, all the heads sense the scanned symbols and move or write independently.*

Theorem 10.3 *A multi-head TM M can be simulated by a single head TM M'.*

Proof Let M have k heads. Then, M' will have $k + 1$ tracks on a single tape. One track will contain the contents of the tape of M and the other tracks are used to mark the head positions. One move of M is simulated by M' by making a left to right sweep followed by a right to left sweep. The simulation is similar to the one given in Theorem 10.2. One fact about which one has to be careful here is the time when two heads scan the same symbol and try to change it differently. In this case, some priority among heads has to be used.

10.1.4   Non-deterministic Turing Machine (NTM)

One can define a NTM by the following transition function:

$$\delta: K \times \Gamma \to \mathbb{P}(K \times \Gamma \times \{L, R\})$$

where δ is a mapping from $K \times \Gamma$ to the power set of $K \times \Gamma \times \{L, R\}$. The computation of any input will be in several directions and the input is accepted if there is at least one sequence of moves, which accepts it.

A NTM is $N = (K, \Sigma, \Gamma, \delta, q_0, F)$ where $K, \Sigma, \Gamma, q_0, F$ as in the definition of TM. δ is defined as above.

Theorem 10.4 *Every NTM can be simulated by a deterministic TM (basic model).*

Proof   The computation of a NTM is a tree whose branches correspond to different possibilities for the machine movement on the given input. If some branch of the computation leads to the accept state, then, the machine accepts the input. The root of the tree would be the start configuration and each node is a possible continuation from the root node.

Computation of a NTM 'N' on any input w is represented as a tree. Each branch is a branch of nondeterminism. Each node is a configuration of N. Root will be the start configuration. One has to traverse the whole tree in a 'breath-first' manner to search for a successful path. One cannot proceed by 'depth-first' search as the tracing may lead to an infinite branch while missing the accepting configurations of some other branches.

Using a multi-tape TM one can simulate N on a given input. For each path of the tree, simulation is done on a separate tape. The paths are considered one-by-one in the increasing order of depth and among paths of equal length, the paths are considered from left to right.

Let us see how the implementation works on a DTM with the tapes. There is an input tape containing input which is never altered. Second tape will be a simulation tape which contains a copy of N's tape content on some branch of its non-deterministic computation. The third tape keeps track of the location of the DTM in NTM's computation tree. The three tapes may be called as input tape, simulation tape, and address tape.

Suppose every node in the tree has at most b children. Let every node in the tree has address, which is a string over the alphabet $\Sigma_b = \{1, 2, \ldots, b\}$ (say). To obtain a node with address 145, start at the root going to its child numbered 1, move to its 4th child and then move to the nodes that corresponds to its 5th child. Ignore addresses that are meaningless. Then, in a breath-first manner check the nodes (configurations) in canonical order as ε, 1, 2, 3,..., b, 11, 12, 13,..., $1b$, 21, 22,..., $2b$, ..., 111, 112, ... (if they exist). Then, DTM on input $w = a_1 \ldots a_n$ works as follows. Place w on the input tape and the others are empty. Copy the contents of the input tape to simulation tape. Then, simulate NTM's one non-deterministic branch on the simulation tape. On each choice, consult the address tape for the next move. Accept if the accepting configuration is reached. Otherwise abort this branch of simulation. The abortion will take place for the following reasons.

- symbols on address tape are all used;
- rejecting configurations encountered; and
- non-deterministic choice is not a valid choice.

Once the present branch is aborted, replace the string on the address tape with the next string in canonical order. Simulate this branch of the NTM as before. □

10.1.5 Two-Dimensional TM

The TM can have 2-dimensional tapes. When the head is scanning a symbol, it can move left, right, up or down. The smallest rectangle containing the non-blank portion is $m \times n$, then it has m rows and n columns. A 1-dimensional TM, which tries to simulate this 2-dimensional TM will have two tapes. On one tape, this m rows of n symbols each will be represented as m blocks of size n each separated by markers. The second tape is used as scratch tape. When the 2-dimensional TM's head moves left or right, it is simulated in a block of the 1-dimensional TM. When the 2-dimensional TM's head moves up or down, the 1-dimensional TM's head moves to the previous block or the next block. To move to the correct position in that block, the second tape is used. If m or n increases, number of blocks or the size of the blocks is increased.

10.2 Restricted TMs

In this section we can discuss some more variations of TMs, which are in the form of restrictions. For example, we have an offline TM that has a restriction on the input tape. One can view the development of TM from finite state automata in a hierarchical way. When viewed as language recognizers FSA, PDA models could not recognize some languages, whereas a TM can do so. One can view the tape of the basic TM as input tape, output tape, and processing space. For example, a PDA is equivalent to a NTM with input tape, resembling the input tape of the PDA, the storage tape resembling the stack of the PDA. Now the processing of NTM can simulate the processing of the PDA. Hence, any computing can be simulated by a TM. But there are some standard ways a TM can be restricted leading to multi-stack TMs, counter machines, etc, without losing out on accepting power.

Definition 10.3 *A deterministic TM with read only input and two storage tape is called a deterministic two stack Turing machine (DTSTM). When the head of the DTSTM tries to move left on the tapes, a blank symbol b will be printed.*

One can easily simulate a TM with a DTSTM. At any point of time, one can see the symbol being scanned by the head of the TM, placed on the top of one stack, the symbols to its left on this stack below the symbols scanned, placing the symbols closer to the present head position, closer to the top of the stack. Similar exercise is done for the symbols to the right of the present head position by placing them in the second stack. Hence, clearly a move of the TM has a corresponding action on the input and stacks of the DTSTM and the simulation can be done.

Theorem 10.5 *There exists a DTSTM that simulates the basic TM on any given input.*

The next variant is a 'counter' machine. A 'counter' machine can store finite number of integers each counter storing a number. The counters can be either increased or decreased and cannot cross a 'stack' or 'counter' symbol 'Z.' In other words, it is a machine with stacks having only two stack symbols Z and b (blank). Every stack will have Z as its initial symbol. A stack may hold a string of the form $b^i Z$, $i \geq 0$, indicating that the stack holds an integer i in it. This stack can be increased or decreased by moving the stack head up or down. A counter machine with 2-stacks is illustrated in the following figure.

Theorem 10.6 *For a basic TM, there exists an equivalent 4-counter TM.*

Proof The equivalence is shown between a 2-stack TM (DTSTM) and a 4-counter machine. We have already seen that a DTSTM and basic TM are equivalent.

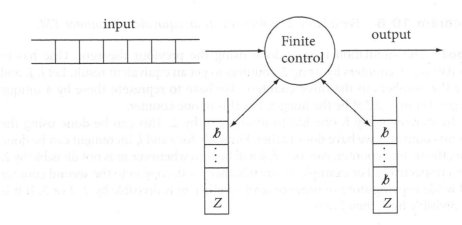

We now see how to simulate each stack with two counters. Let $X_1, X_2, \ldots, X_{t-1}$ be the $(t - 1)$ stack symbols. Each stack content can be uniquely represented by an integer in base 't.' Suppose $X_{i_1} X_{i_2} \ldots X_{i_n}$ is the present stack content with X_{i_n} on the top in DTSTM. Then, the integer count will be

$$k = i_n + t i_{n-1} + t^2 i_{n-2} + \ldots + t^{n-1} i_1 .$$

For example, if the number of stack symbols used is 3, and an integer for the stack content $X_2 X_3 X_1 X_2$ will be:

$$k = 2 + 4 + 4^2.3 + 4^3.2 = 172.$$

Suppose X_r is to be put on the top of the stack, then the new integer counter has to be $kt + r$. The first counter contains k and the second counter contains zero at this point. To get $kt + r$ in the second counter, the counter machine has to move the first counter head to the left by one cell and move the head of the second counter t cells to the right. Thus, when the first counter head reaches 'Z' the second counter contains kt. Now add r to the second counter to get $kt + r$.

If it is a clear move of the stack, X_{i_k} is to be cleared. Then k has to be reduced to $\lfloor k/t \rfloor$, the integer part of k/t . Now, the adjustment is decrementing the count of the first counter in steps and increment the second counter by one. This repeats till the first counter becomes zero.

Now by the above exercise, one is able to identify the stack symbol on the stack from the two counters thus designed. That is $k \bmod t$ is the index i_n and hence, X_{i_n} is the top symbol of the stack.

The above theorem can be improved and hence, we have the following theorems.

Theorem 10.7 *For a basic TM, there exists an equivalent 3-counter TM.*

Proof The idea of the simulation is similar to the previous theorem. Instead of having two counters for adjusting the two counters that correspond to two stacks, one common counter is used to adjust the operation of pop, push or change of the stack symbols. □

Theorem 10.8 *For a basic TM, there exists an equivalent 2-counter TM.*

Proof The simulation is now done using the previous theorem. One has to simulate the 3-counters by using 2-counters to get an equivalent result. Let $i, j,$ and k be the numbers in the three counters. We have to represent these by a unique integer. Let $m = 2^i 3^j 5^k$ be the integer. Put this in one counter.

To increment say i, one has to multiply m by 2. This can be done using the second counter as we have done earlier. Similarly for j and k increment can be done using the second counter. Any of i, j, k will be zero whenever m is not divisible by 2, 3 or 5 respectively. For example, to say whether $j = 0$, copy m to the second counter and while copying store in finite control whether m is divisible by 2, 3 or 5. If it is not divisible by 3, then $j = 0$.

Finally to decrease i, j, k, divide m by 2, 3, 5, respectively. This exercise is also similar to the previous one except that the machine will halt whenever m is not divisible by a constant by which we are dividing. □

A TM can be restricted by reducing the tape alphabet or by reducing the number of states. One can also aim at reducing the number of tape symbols to achieve universality. There exists a TM with three states, one tape but any amount of tape symbols to recognize recursively enumerable languages. Following is one such characterization.

Theorem 10.9 *There exists a TM with one tape and tape alphabet $\{0, 1, \not{b}\}$ to recognize any recursively enumerable language L over $\{0, 1\}$.*

Proof Let $M = (K, \{0, 1\}, \Gamma, \delta, q_0, F)$ be a TM recognizing L. Now the tape alphabet Γ can be anything. Our aim is to construct an equivalent TM with $\Gamma = \{0, 1, \not{b}\}$. For that we encode each symbol of Γ. Suppose Γ has 't' symbols. We use binary codes to code each symbol of Γ by 'k' bits where $2^{k-1} < t < 2^k$.

We now have to design another TM M' with $\Gamma = \{0, 1, \not{b}\}$. The tape of M' will consists of coded symbols of Γ and the input over $\{0, 1\}$. The simulation of one move of M by k moves of M' is as follows. The tape head of M' is initially at the leftmost symbol of the coded input. M' has to scan the next $k - 1$ symbols to its right to make a decision of change of state or overwrite or move left or right as per M. The TM M' stores in its finite control the state of M and the head position of M' which is a number between 0 to $k - 1$. Hence, M' clearly indicates at the end of a block of moves whether one move of M is made or not. Once the finite control indicates '0' as head position, it means this is time for the change on the tape, state as per M's instruction. If the thus changed state is an accepting state of M, M' accepts.

One observation is that on the tape of M', there has to be code for the blank symbol of M. This is essential for simulating the blank of M by M'. Second observation is that any tape symbol of M is directly coded in terms of 0s and 1s and as any string w is placed on the tape of M, the codes for each symbol of w is concatenated and placed on the tape of M'. □

One can see from the previous result that even if the input for L is not over $\{0, 1\}$, the above TM construction will work, because the input of L over some other alphabet will be now coded and placed as input for a TM with tape alphabet $\{0, 1, \not{b}\}$.

Also one can see that one can construct a multi-tape TM that uses only two symbols 0 and 1 as tape alphabet to simulate any TM. One has to keep the input tape fixed with the input. There will be a second tape with tape symbols coded as binary symbols. This simulates moves of the original TM. The newly constructed TM must have positions on the tape to indicate the present head position, cells to indicate that the binary representation of the symbol under scan is already copied. Each ID is copied on the third tape after simulation of one move. If we take the input alphabet $\{0, 1\}$, we start with the second tape (first tape is not necessary). In the third tape, IDs are copied one by one without erasing. Thus, we have the following result.

Theorem 10.10 *Any TM can be simulated by an offline TM having one storage tape with two symbols 0 and 1 where 0 indicates blank. A blank (0) can be retained as 0 or replaced by 1 but a '1' cannot be rewritten at a cell with '0'.*

10.3 Turing Machines as Enumerators

The languages accepted by the TM are recursively enumerable sets. One can think of a TM as generating a language. An enumerator is a TM variant which generates a recursively enumerable language. One can think of such a TM to have its output on a printer (an output tape). That is, the output strings are printed by the output device printer. Thus, every string that is processed freshly, is added to the list, thereby printing it also.

The enumerator machine has an input tape, which is blank initially, an output device which may be a printer. If such a machine does not halt, it may perform printing of a list of strings infinitely. Let M be an enumerator machine and $G(M)$ be the list of strings appearing on output tape. We have the following theorem for M.

Theorem 10.11 *A language L is recursively enumerable if and only if there exists an enumerator M such that $G(M) = L$.*

Proof Let M be an enumerator such that $L = G(M)$. To show that there exists a TM $\overline{M}$ recognizing L. Let w be an input for $\overline{M}$. Perform the following two steps on w.

1. Run M and compare each output string of M with w.

2. If w appears on the output tape of M, accept w.

That is, $\overline{M}$ accepts only those strings that appear on the output tape of M. Hence $T(\overline{M}) = G(M)$.

Conversely let $\overline{M}$ be a TM such that $L = T(\overline{M})$. We construct an enumerator M that prints every string of L as follows.

Let Σ be the alphabet of L and $w_1, w_2, w_3, w_4, \ldots$ be all possible strings over Σ. The enumerator machine M will do the following for any input from Σ^*.

1. Repeat the following for $i = 1, 2, 3, \ldots$

2. Run $\overline{M}$ for i steps on each input $w_1, w_2, \ldots, w_i$.

3. If $\overline{M}$ accepts any string w_i print the corresponding string w_i.

Clearly, if any string w is accepted by $\overline{M}$, it will be output by the enumerator M. In the above procedure, one can see that there will be repeated printing of a string w. It is straightforward to see $G(M) = L = T(\overline{M})$.

If L is a recursive set (a set accepted by a TM which halts on all inputs), then there exists an enumerator M for L which will print the strings in L in canonical order.

10.4 Equivalence Between TMs and Type 0 Languages

In this section, we prove the equivalence between Type-0 grammars and TM. That is, any recursively enumerable set can be generated by a type 0 grammar and it can also be recognized by a TM.

Theorem 10.12 *If L is the language generated by an unrestricted grammar $G = (N, T, P, S)$, then L is recognized by a TM.*

Proof   For G, we construct a TM M with two tapes such that on one tape we put the input w and the other tape is used to derive w using P. Each time a rule from P is applied, compare the two tapes for acceptance or rejection of w. Initially put w on one tape. Then, M initially places S on the second tape. Nondeterministically select a rule $S \to \alpha$ from P, replace S by α on the second tape. Now compare the tapes, if they agree accept w. Otherwise, from the present string α, choose a location 'i' nondeterministically such that β is a subword occurring in α from position i. Choose a rule $\beta \to \gamma$ again nondeterministically. Apply to α, by inserting γ at the position of β. Now, let the present tape content be α_I. If $\alpha_I = w$, then accept w, otherwise continue the procedure.   □

Theorem 10.13 *If L is accepted by a TM M, then there exists an unrestricted grammar generating L.*

Proof   Let L be accepted by a TM $M = (K, \Sigma, \Gamma, q_0, \delta, F)$. Then, G is constructed as follows. Let $G = (N, \Sigma, P, S_1)$ where $N = ((\Sigma \cup \{\varepsilon\} \times \Gamma) \cup \{S_1, S_2, S_3\})$. P consists of the following rules:

1. $S_1 \to q_0 S_2$
2. $S_2 \to (a, a)S_2$ for each $a \in T$.
   That is, G produces every time two copies of symbols from Σ.
3. $S_2 \to S_3$
4. $S_3 \to (\varepsilon, \varepsilon)S_3$
5. $S_3 \to \varepsilon$
6. $q(a, X) \to (a, Y)p$
   if $\delta(q, X) = (p, Y, R)$ for every a in $\Sigma \cup \{\varepsilon\}$, each $q \in Q$, $X, Y \in \Gamma$. This rule simulates the action of M on the second component of the symbols (α, β).
7. $(b, Z)q(a, X) \to p(b, Z)(a, Y)$
   if $\delta(q, X) = (p, Y, L)$ for each $a, b \in \Sigma \cup \{\varepsilon\}$, each $q \in Q$, $X, Y, Z \in \Gamma$. This rule does the same job as rule 6.
8. $[a, X]q \to qaq$, $q[a, X] \to qaq$ and $q \to \varepsilon$ for each $a \in \Sigma \cup \{\varepsilon\}$, $X \in \Gamma$ and $q \in F$.

These rules bring out w from the pair if the second component of the input pair is properly accepted by M.

Hence, we see from the rules that the constructed grammar "nondeterministically" generates two copies of w in Σ^* using rules (1) and (2) and simulates M through the rules 6 and 7. Rule 8 brings out w if it is accepted by M. The equivalence that if $w \in L(G)$, then $w \in L(M)$ and conversely can be proved by induction on the number of derivation steps and on the number of moves of the TM. Hence the theorem. $\qquad\square$

10.5 Linear-Bounded Automata

A linear-bounded automata (LBA) is a NTM with a bounded, finite-input tape. That is, input is placed between two special symbols $\cent$ and $\$$.

$\cent$	a_1	a_2	$\cdots$	a_n	$\$$	

But, all the other actions of a TM are allowed except that the read/write head cannot fall off on left of $\cent$ and right of $\$$. Also, $\cent$ and $\$$ are not altered. One can say that this is a restricted version of TM.

Definition 10.4 *A LBA is a 8-tuple* $M = (K, \Sigma, \Gamma, \delta, q_0, \cent, \$, F)$ *where* $K, \Sigma,$ $\Gamma, q_0,$ F *and* δ *are as in any TM. The language recognized by M is* $L(M) = \{w|w \in \Sigma^*$ *and* $q_0 \cent w \$ \overset{*}{\vdash} p\beta$ *for some* $p \in F\}$.

One can show that the family of languages accepted by a LBA is exactly CSL.

Theorem 10.14 *If L is a CSL, then L is accepted by a LBA.*

Proof For L, one can construct a LBA with 2-track tape. The simulation is done as in Theorem 10.13 where we place w on the first track and produce sentential forms on the second track, every time comparing with contents on the first track. If $w = \varepsilon$, the LBA halts without accepting. $\qquad\square$

Theorem 10.15 *If L is recognized by a LBA, then L is generated by a context-sensitive grammar.*

Proof Let $M = (K, \Sigma, \Gamma, q_0, \delta, \cent, \$, F)$ be a LBA such that $L(M) = L$. Then, one can construct a CSG, $G = (N, \Sigma, P, S_1)$ as below.

N consists of nonterminals of the form (a, β) where $a \in \Sigma$ and β is of the form x or qx or $q\cent x$ or $x\$$ or $qx\$$ where $q \in K, x \in \Gamma$.

P consists of the following productions:

1. $S_1 \rightarrow (a, q_0 \mathbb{c} a) S_2$;
2. $S_1 \rightarrow (a, q_0 \mathbb{c} a\$)$;
3. $S_2 \rightarrow (a, a) S_2$; and
4. $S_2 \rightarrow (a, a\$)$ for all $a \in \Sigma$.

   The above four rules generate a sequence of pairs whose first components form a terminal string $a_1 a_2 \ldots a_t$ and the second components form the LBA initial ID.

   The moves of the LBA are simulated by the following rules in the second component.

5. If $\delta(q, X) = (p, Y, R)$ we have rules of the form $(a, qX)(b, Z) \rightarrow (a, Y)(b, pZ)$
   $(a, q \mathbb{c} X)(b, Z) \rightarrow (a, \mathbb{c} Y)(b, pZ)$ where $a, b \in \Sigma, p, q \in K, X, Y, Z \in \Gamma$.

6. If $\delta(q, X) = (p, Y, L)$ we have rules of the form $(b, Z)(a, qX) \rightarrow (b, pZ)(a, Y)$
   $(b, Z)(a, qX\$) \rightarrow (b, pZ)(a, Y\$)$ where $a, b \in \Sigma, p, q \in K, X, Y, Z \in \Gamma$.

7. $(a, q\beta) \rightarrow a$ if q is final, for all $a \in \Sigma$.

8. $(a, \alpha)b \rightarrow ab$
   $b(a, \alpha) \rightarrow ba$ for any $a \in \Sigma$ and all possible α.

Clearly, all the productions are context-sensitive. The simulation leads to a stage where the first components emerge as the string generated if the second components representing LBA ID has a final state.

ε will not be generated by the grammar whether or not it is in $T(M)$. □

We have already seen that $\varepsilon \notin L$, if L is context-sensitive by definition. To include ε, we must have a new start symbol S' and include $S' \rightarrow \varepsilon$, making sure S' does not appear on the right-hand side of any production by adding $S' \rightarrow \alpha$ where $S \rightarrow \alpha$ is a rule in the original CSG with S as the start symbol.

10.6 Gödel Numbering

In the construction of counter automata, we have used the concept of Gödel numbering. Let us consider this topic more formally.

Perhaps the most famous and most important of the several deep theorems about mathematical logic proved by Kurt Gödel (1931) was his incompleteness theorem: for any sound logical axiomatic system that is sufficiently rich to contain the theory of numbers, there must be number-theoretic statements that can neither be proved nor disproved in the system. Gödel's theorem is one of the most significant discoveries made in the twentieth century, since it places a limit on the efficacy of mathematical reasoning itself. During proving his result, Gödel used a numbering scheme which is called Gödel numbering.

10.6.1 Gödel Numbering of Sequences of Positive Integers

The first class of objects to which we shall assign Gödel numbers is the class of finite sequences of positive integers. Let us consider the primes in the increasing order of magnitude. Prime(0) is 2, Prime(1) is 3, Prime(2) is 5 and so on.

Definition 10.5 *The Gödel number of the finite sequence of positive integers is* $i_1, i_2, ..., i_n$ *is*

$$2^{i_1} * 3^{i_2} * 5^{i_3} * ... * (Prime\ (n-1))^{i_n}$$

Example 10.1 The Gödel number of the sequence 2, 1, 3, 1, 2, 1 is

$$2^2 * 3^1 * 5^3 * 7^1 * 11^2 * 13^1 = 16,516,500.$$

From the Gödel number, the sequence can be got back. For example, if the Gödel number is 4200, the sequence is 3, 1, 2, 1. This is obtained as follows. Divide 4200 by 2 as many times as possible $\dfrac{4200}{2} = \dfrac{2100}{2} = \dfrac{1050}{2} = 525$. So the first number in the sequence is 3. Divide 525 by 3 as many times as possible. $\dfrac{525}{3} = 175$. 175 is not divisible by 3. Hence the second number in the sequence is 1. Divide 175 by 5 as many times as possible. $\dfrac{175}{5} = \dfrac{35}{5} = 7$. So third number in the sequence is 2 and the last number is 1 as 7 is divisible by 7 once. So the sequence is 3, 1, 2, 1.

10.6.2 Gödel Number of Strings

Once we have a method of finding the Gödel number of a sequence of positive integers, it is not difficult to find a method of assigning Gödel numbers to any written piece of English text. First, assign a positive integer to every distinguishable character including blanks, small letters, capital letters, and each punctuation sign. One possible way is as follows: blank 1, small a through z, 2 through 27; capital A through Z, 28 through 53; period 54; comma 55; and so on. The Gödel number of any piece of text is simply the Gödel number of the corresponding sequence of integers. For example, the Gödel number of the word 'book' is $2^3 * 3^{16} * 5^{16} * 7^{12}$.

10.6.3 Gödel Number of Undirected Graphs

An undirected graph consists of nodes and edges. The procedure of assigning to a graph a suitable Gödel numbering begins with an assignment of a distinct prime number to each node of the graph. This assignment is made arbitrarily. We then note that once we have the information about how many nodes there are and which nodes are connected to which by edges, we have complete information about the graph. Supposing the nodes have been numbered $P_0, ..., P_n$, we take a Gödel number of the graph to be the number

$P_0^{K_0} * P_1^{K_1} * \cdots * P_n^{K_n}$, where, for each i, K_i is the product of all those $P_j^{x_j}$ such that the node numbered P_i is connected by x_j edges to the node numbered P_j; Thus $K_i = 1$ if the node numbered P_i is not connected to any other node.

Consider the following graph, where the nodes are assigned prime numbers

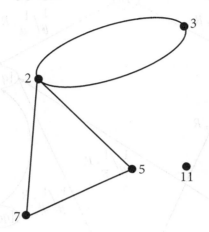

The Gödel numbering for this graph is

$$2^{K_0} * 3^{K_1} * 5^{K_2} * 7^{K_3} * 11^{K_5}$$

where

$K_0 = 3^2 * 5 * 7$
$K_1 = 2^2$
$K_2 = 2 * 7$
$K_4 = 2 * 5$ and
$K_5 = 1$

i.e., the Gödel number is given by

$$2^{3^2 * 5 * 7} * 3^{2^2} * 5^{2*7} * 7^{2*5} * 11^1$$

From the Gödel numbering, the graph can be obtained. This idea can be extended to labeled graphs, directed graphs, suitably.

Problems and Solutions

1. For the following two-way infinite TM, construct an equivalent one-way TM.

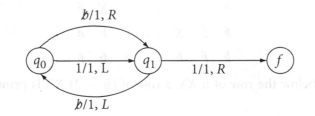

Solution.

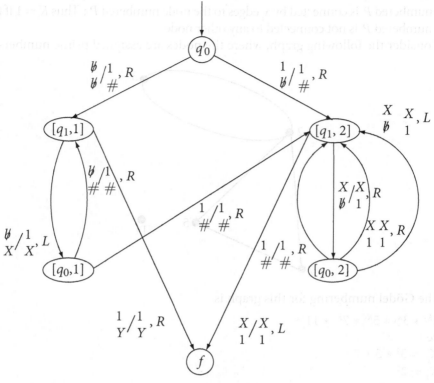

$X \in \{1, b\}$

$Y \in \{1, b, \#\}$

2. Construct a TM M with a 2-dimensional tape. M starts with initial ID:

$$
\begin{array}{cccccccccc}
b & b & b & b & \ldots & b & b & b & b \\
b & X & X & X & \ldots & X & X & X & b \\
b & b & b & b & \ldots & b & b & b & b
\end{array}
$$

i.e., a row of n X's surrounded by blanks. It has to halt with the final ID.

$$
\begin{array}{ccccccc}
b & b & b & \ldots & b & b & b \\
b & b & X & \ldots & X & b & b \\
b & X & & \ldots & & X & b \\
b & b & X & \ldots & X & b & b \\
b & b & b & \ldots & b & b & b
\end{array}
$$

i.e., above and below the row of n X's, a row of $(n - 2)$ X's is printed, centrally adjusted.

Solution.

$$K = \{q_0, \ldots, q_{11}\}$$
$$\Gamma = \{X, Y, \not{b}\}$$

δ is given by:

$$\delta(q_0, X) = (q_1, Y, R)$$
$$\delta(q_1, X) = (q_2, Y, U)$$
$$\delta(q_2, \not{b}) = (q_3, X, D)$$
$$\delta(q_3, Y) = (q_4, Y, D)$$
$$\delta(q_4, \not{b}) = (q_5, X, U)$$
$$\delta(q_5, Y) = (q_1, Y, R)$$
$$\delta(q_1, \not{b}) = (q_6, \not{b}, L)$$
$$\delta(q_6, Y) = (q_7, Y, U)$$
$$\delta(q_7, X) = (q_8, \not{b}, D)$$
$$\delta(q_8, Y) = (q_9, Y, D)$$
$$\delta(q_9, X) = (q_{10}, \not{b}, U)$$
$$\delta(q_{10}, Y) = (q_{10}, X, L)$$
$$\delta(q_{10}, \not{b}) = (q_{11}, \not{b}, \text{halt})$$

Exercises

1. Consider the following TM with two-way infinite tape.

   $$M = (\{q_0, q_1, q_2, q_3\}, \{0, 1\}, \{0, 1\}, \delta, q_0, \{q_3\})$$

   where δ is given by:

   $$\delta(q_0, 0) = (q_1, 1, R)$$
   $$\delta(q_1, 1) = (q_2, 0, L)$$
   $$\delta(q_2, 0) = (q_0, 1, R)$$
   $$\delta(q_1, 0) = (q_3, 0, R)$$

   Construct an equivalent one-way infinite tape TM.

2. It is desired to design a TM that copies patterns of 1's and 2's in accordance with the following format:

   Initial tape pattern : ... $A\,1\,2\,1\,1\,2\,1\,2\,2\,0$ ... $B\,0\,0\,0\,0\,0\,0\,0\,0\,0$ ...
   　　　　　　　　　　　　　　↑

   Final tape pattern : ... $A\,1\,2\,1\,1\,2\,1\,2\,2\,0$ ... $B\,1\,2\,1\,1\,2\,1\,2\,2\,0$ ...
   　　　　　　　　　↑

   a. First, design the machine as a 2-track machine. Assume that the given pattern is initially written in the top track and that the bottom track is initially blank. Let the machine use the bottom track to mark each symbol in the given pattern with an X as it is copied. Give the state diagram of the machine.

b. Now, convert the 2-track machine of (a) into an equivalent one-track machine by assigning single symbols to ordered pairs of upper and lower-track symbols. Choose this assignment so that the resulting machine meets the format specified at the beginning of the problem. How many tape symbols does the 1-track machine use? What are their roles?

3. It is desired to design a 2-tape TM that behaves as follows. The machine's first tape is initially inscribed with a pattern of the form

$$\ldots 0\,1^{n_1}\,0\,1^{n_2}\,0\ldots 0\,1^{n_k}\,0\ldots \quad (\text{where } k \geq 1)$$
$$\uparrow$$

and the second tape is left blank. The machine is to determine which of the given blocks of 1's is the longest and is to halt with a copy of that block on its second tape. The original pattern is to be left unchanged on the first tape. The machine is to halt scanning the 0 to the right of the given pattern on its first tape and the 0 to the left of the block formed on the second tape.

Design an appropriate machine, using the symbol alphabet $\{0, 1\}$ for each tape. Describe your machine graphically, using the same conventions used for ordinary TM, except that: (1) the symbols scanned and written on the machine's first and second tapes are to be represented by symbol pairs of the form $\frac{s1}{s2}$, as in the case of two-track machines; and (2) each state is to be labeled with a pair of direction symbols of the form $\frac{D1}{D2}$ to indicate the directions that the machine is to move on its first and second tapes when it enters that state. Each of D_1 and D_2 may be either L, R, or $-$, where the symbol $-$ indicates that the machine does not shift the tape head in question.

4. Let M be any TM that operates on a doubly infinite tape. Show that there exists another doubly infinite machine $\hat{M}$ that duplicates each of M's computations in at most half as many steps as M, as long as $\hat{M}$'s initial and final tape patterns are properly encoded.

Describe a typical step in $\hat{M}$'s computation. Hint: Let the squares of M's tape be represented on three tracks of $\hat{M}$'s tape according to the following scheme.

M's tape:

-5	-4	-3	-2	-1	0	1	2	3	4	5

$\hat{M}$'s tape:

-11	-9	-7	-5	-3	-1	1	3	5	7	9
-10	-8	-6	-4	-2	0	2	4	6	8	10
-9	-7	-5	-3	-1	1	3	5	7	9	11

5. Construct a TM with two-dimensional tape which gives the following output for the given input.

a. Input is
$$\underbrace{\begin{matrix} b & b & b & b \dots b & b \\ b & X & X & X \dots X & b \end{matrix}}_{n}$$
$$b \quad b \quad b \quad b \dots b \quad b$$

Output is :
$$\begin{matrix} b & & \cdots & & b \\ & \boxed{\begin{matrix} n \times n \\ \text{square of} \\ X's \end{matrix}} & \\ \vdots & & & & \vdots \\ b & & \cdots & & b \end{matrix}$$

Output is an array of X's surrounded by blanks.

b. Input is.
$$\underbrace{\begin{matrix} b & b & b & b \dots b & b \\ b & X & X & X \dots X & b \end{matrix}}_{2n+1}$$
$$b \quad b \quad b \quad b \dots b \quad b$$

Output is
$$\begin{matrix} b & b & b & & \cdots & & b & b & b \\ b & X & X & & \cdots & & X & X & b \\ b & b & X & & \cdots & & X & b & b \\ b & b & b & X & \cdots & X & b & b & b \\ & & & & \vdots & & & & \\ b & b & \cdots & b & X & b & \cdots & b & b \\ b & b & \cdots & & & & \cdots & b & b \end{matrix}$$
$(2n+1)$ of X's

6. Give type 0 grammar for the TM,
    a. given in Exercise 1.
    b. given in Exercise 7, Chapter 9.

Universal Turing Machine and Decidability

In this chapter, we consider universal turing machine (TM), the halting problem, and the concept of undecidability.

11.1 Encoding and Enumeration of Turing Machines

The TM is specified by a 6-tuple $M = (K, \Sigma, \Gamma, \delta, q_0, F)$ (refer Definition 9.1). $\cancel{b}$ in Γ is a special symbol. The TM can be encoded as a binary string. Without loss of generality, we can take the state set as $(q_1, q_2, ..., q_s\}$ where q_1 is the initial state and q_2 is the final state. The tape symbol set can be taken as $\{\cancel{b}, 0, 1\}$. A move of the TM is represented as:

$$\delta(q_j, X_j) = (q_k, X_r, d_l)$$

Note that we are considering deterministic TMs. This move means that the TM while reading X_j in state q_i, goes to state q_k, prints X_r over X_j and moves left or right as specified by d_l. This can be represented as a binary string $0^i 10^j 10^k 10^r 10^l$. Note that $1 \leq i, k \leq s, 1 \leq j, r \leq 3, \ell = 1$ or 2. 0^i denotes state q_i; 0^j denotes tape symbol X_j; $j = 1$ denotes $\cancel{b}$; $j = 2$ denotes 0; $j = 3$ denotes 1; 0^k denotes state q_k and 0^r denotes symbol X_r. If $\ell = 1$, move is to the left; if $\ell = 2$, move is to the right. Thus, each move of the TM can be represented as a binary string. Suppose the moves of the TM are given by $m_1, m_2, ..., m_n$. The encoding of these moves are given by the binary strings $d_{m_1}, d_{m_2}, ..., d_{m_n}$. A binary string $111d_{m_1} 11d_{m_2} 11 ... 11d_{m_n} 111$ specifies an encoding of the TM moves one separated from another by two 1's and the encoding begins with three 1's and ends with three 1's. Note that any permutation of $m_1, ..., m_n$ also represents the same TM and hence, different encodings may represent the same TM.

Enumeration of TMs

The binary encoding of a TM can be looked at as the binary representation of an integer p. So, we can say that the binary representation of integer p represents the TM T_p. Thus, we have an enumeration $T_1, T_2, T_3, ..., T_p, ...$ of TMs. Some of these representations may not be proper encodings. For example, strings not beginning with three 1's are not proper encodings. We take them as representing TM with no moves and hence accepting the empty set ϕ.

11.2 Recursive and Recursively Enumerable Sets

We have seen that the language accepted by a TM is a type 0 language. It is also called a recursively enumerable (RE) set. A TM accepts a string by going to a final state and halting. It can reject a string by halting in a non-final state or getting into a loop. A TM when started on an input may get into a loop and never halt.

We have also seen that a TM corresponds to an effective procedure. An effective procedure is one where at each step, the next step is specified. An effective procedure need not halt. For example,

$i = 1$
while true do
begin
   print i
   $i = i + 1$
end.

is an effective procedure which will keep on printing integers one by one and will never halt. An algorithm is an effective procedure which always halts and gives an answer. Hence, an algorithm corresponds to a TM which halts on all inputs. While the set of strings accepted by a TM is called a RE set, the set of strings which is accepted by a TM which halts on all inputs is called a recursive set.

Theorem 11.1 *The complement of the recursive set is recursive.*

Proof Let L be a recursive set accepted by a TM M which halts on all inputs.

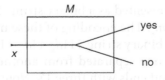

$\overline{L}$ will be accepted by $\overline{M}$, given by:

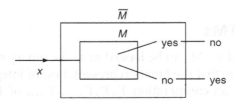

Hence, $\overline{L}$ is recursive. $\qquad\qquad\qquad\qquad\qquad\qquad\square$

Theorem 11.2   *The union of two recursive sets is recursive.*

Proof   Let L_1 and L_2 be recursive sets accepted by TMs M_1 and M_2, respectively. $L_1 \cup L_2$ will be accepted by:

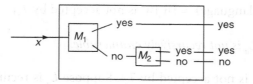

Theorem 11.3   *If L_1 and L_2 are recursively enumerable sets, then $L_1 \cup L_2$ is recursively enumerable.*

Proof   Let L_1 and L_2 be accepted by TMs M_1 and M_2 (which need not always halt), respectively. $L_1 \cup L_2$ will be accepted by:

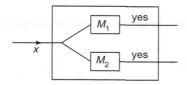

Theorem 11.4   *If L and $\bar{L}$ are both recursively enumerable, then L is recursive.*

Proof   Let L be accepted by M and $\bar{L}$ be accepted by $\bar{M}$. Given w, w will either be accepted by M or $\bar{M}$. L can be accepted by a TM M' which halts on all inputs as follows:

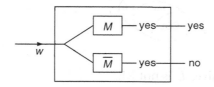

We have seen that the set of all TMs over the tape alphabets $\{0, 1, \not{b}\}$ can be enumerated and the set of strings over $\{0, 1\}$ can be enumerated. So, we can talk about the *ith* TM and the *jth* string over $\{0, 1\}$. Consider an infinite Boolean matrix.

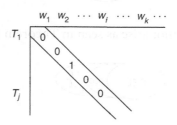

The entry on the jth row and ith column is 1 if w_i is accepted by T_j and 0 if w_i is not accepted by T_j. Consider the diagonal elements of this infinite Boolean matrix. Take those w_i which correspond to 0 elements in the matrix. Define:

L_d(the diagonal language) $= \{w_i | w_i$ is not accepted by $T_i\}$

Theorem 11.5 *L_d is not recursively enumerable.*

Proof $L_d = \{w_i | w_i$ is not accepted by $T_i\}$. Suppose L_d is recursively enumerable. Then, there exists a TM T_j accepting it. If w_j is accepted by T_j, then by definition of L_d, $w_j \notin L_d$. But since T_j accepts L_d, $w_j \in L_d$. This is a contradiction. Therefore, L_d is not *RE*. $\square$

Theorem 11.6 *There exists a language which is not recursively enumerable.*

We have shown that L_d is not RE. Later, we show that $\overline{L_d}$ is RE but not recursive.

It should be noted that for a language L and its complement, three possibilities exist.

1. L and $\overline{L}$ are recursive.

2. L and $\overline{L}$ are not RE.

3. L is *RE* but not recursive. $\overline{L}$ is not RE.

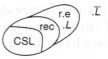

The following situation cannot arise as seen in Theorem 11.4.

11.3 Universal TM

A Universal TM is a TM which can simulate any other TM including itself. Let us denote a universal TM by U. Without loss of generality, we are considering TMs with tape alphabets $\{0,1,\beta\}$. The encoding of such a TM T is a binary string d_T. U has three tapes. The first tape is presented with $d_T\ t$; i.e., the encoding of T and the input t to T. It will be of the form:

111	... 11	...	...	111 t ...

Note that t is a string over $\{0, 1\}$. The second tape initially has a 0. Without loss of generality, we can assume that T has states $\{q_1, \ldots, q_k\}$ where q_1 is the initial state, and q_2 is the final state. The second tape contains the information about the state. If at any instant T is supposed to be in state q_i, U while simulating T will have 0^i in tape 2. Tape 3 is used for simulation. Pictorially, U can be represented by the following figure.

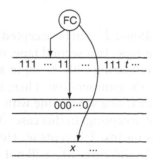

U first checks whether the prefix of the input is a proper encoding of a TM. i.e., it checks whether the portion between the first 111 and the second 111 is divided into blocks by 11 and the code within one 11 and the next 11 is of the form $0^i 10^j 10^k 10^r 10^l$, $1 \leq j, r \leq 3, \ell = 1$ or 2. If so, it proceeds. Otherwise, it halts rejecting the input.

If it finds that the string between the first 111 and the second 111 is a proper encoding of a TM, then it copies the portion of the input after the second 111 onto the third tape and positions the head of the third tape on the leftmost non-blank symbol. The second tape initially contains 0 denoting that the state is q_1 initially. At any instance, the second tape will contain 0^i denoting that the current state is q_i. The third tape head will be positioned on the symbol being read as (X_j say). Then, U will store i and j in its memory and scan the encoding of T in the first tape looking for a block of the form $0^i 10^j 10^k 10^r 10^l$. If it does not find one, U halts without accepting. If it finds one, then it replaces 0^i in the second tape by 0^k, rewrites the symbol X_j scanned by the third tape head to X_r and moves the third tape head left or right depending on whether $\ell = 1$ or 2. It should be noted that U may take more than one step to simulate one step of T. If at any time T reaches the final state q_2, 00 will be the content of tape 2 and U halts accepting the input. If T halts on t without accepting, U also halts without accepting. If T when started on t gets into a loop, U also gets into a loop. The language accepted by U is L_u and consists of strings of the form $d_T t$ where T accepts t.

Even though U has used three tapes, we can have a universal TM $\overline{U}$ with a single tape simulating U. It is known that there is a universal TM with a single tape, 5 states, and 7 symbols.

Earlier, we have seen that L_d is not RE. Now, we show $\overline{L_d}$ is RE but not recursive.

Theorem 11.7 $\overline{L_d}$ *is recursively enumerable but not recursive.*

Proof   It is easy to see $\overline{L_d}$ is not recursive. If it were recursive, the complement L_d will be recursive. We have seen that the complement L_d is not even RE. Hence, $\overline{L_d}$ is not recursive.

That $\overline{L_d}$ is RE can be seen as follows: $\overline{L_d}$ can be accepted by a multi-tape TM $\overline{M_d}$ as follows: $\overline{M_d}$ has w on its input tape. In a second tape, it generates strings $w_1, w_2, \ldots$ in canonical order each time comparing with the input and stops this process when it finds $w = w_i$, the ith string in the enumeration. Then, it generates the encoding of T_i on another tape. Next, it calls U as a subroutine with $d_T w_i$ as input. U has three possibilities: (i) It halts without accepting. In this case, $\overline{M_d}$ halts without accepting w_i; (ii) U halts accepting . This means, T_i accepts w_i. Hence, $\overline{M_d}$ halts and accepts w_i; and (iii) U gets into a loop. In this case, $\overline{M_d}$ will not come out of the subroutine and will not halt.

It is easy to see that $\overline{M_d}$ accepts a string $w = w_i$ if and only if w_i is accepted by T_i. Since we are able to have a TM for $\overline{L_d}$, it is RE. □

Theorem 11.8 L_u *is recursively enumerable but not recursive.*

Proof   Since we have a TM $\overline{U}$ for L_u, it is RE.

Next, we show it is not recursive. Suppose L_u were recursive, then $\overline{L_d}$ becomes recursive. We can have a TM M for $\overline{L_d}$ which halts on all inputs. M works as follows: Given w as input, it generates strings $w_1, w_2, \ldots$ until it finds $w_i = w$. i.e., the given string is the ith string in the enumeration. Then it calls $\overline{U}$ with $d_T w_i$. $\overline{U}$ will halt either accepting $d_T w_i$ or rejecting $d_T w_i$. If it accepts, M accepts and halts. If it rejects, M rejects and halts. Thus, M accepts $\overline{L_d}$, and always halts. Thus, we have to conclude $\overline{L_d}$ is recursive. We have earlier seen that $\overline{L_d}$ is not recursive. Hence, we arrive at a contradiction. Therefore, L_u is not recursive. □

By the property of a language L and its complement $\overline{L}$ we discussed earlier, we note that:

Theorem 11.9 $\overline{L_u}$ *is not recursively enumerable.*

The Halting Problem

The halting problem for TMs was shown to be undecidable by Turing. This was a major breakthrough and many problems were shown to be undecidable after this.

The halting problem for TMs can be stated as follows: Given a TM in an arbitrary configuration, will it eventually halt? We shall show that there cannot exist an algorithm which takes as input a TM in a configuration and tells whether it will halt or not. Thus, we say that the halting problem is recursively unsolvable or undecidable. It should be noted that this does not mean that for a particular TM in a specified configuration, we cannot tell whether it will halt or not. We may be able to say for this particular instance whether it will halt or not. We shall see subsequently, what a problem and an instance of a problem mean.

Theorem 11.10 *The halting problem for Turing machines is recursively undecidable.*

Proof 1 The proof is by contradiction. Suppose the halting problem is decidable. Then, there is an algorithm to solve this and hence a corresponding TM (which we call as 'Halt').

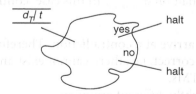

This TM 'Halt' takes as an input, an encoding d_T of a TM T and input t. Finally, it halts saying 'yes' if T on t halts and 'no' if T on t does not halt. Note that 'Halt' always halts and says either 'yes' or 'no.'

Now, let us modify this TM 'Halt' a little and have a TM 'copyhalt' as follows: The input to 'copyhalt' is the encoding d_T of a TM. Note that d_T is a binary string. Given d_T 'copyhalt' makes a copy of d_T as $d_T d_T$ and calls 'Halt'. i.e., it calls 'Halt' as a subroutine with $d_T | d_T$.

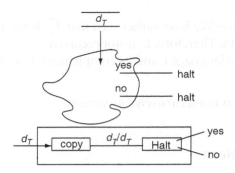

It halts and says 'yes' if T on d_T halts. It halts and says 'no' if T on d_T does not halt. If it is possible to have 'Halt', it is possible to have 'copyhalt'.

Now, modify 'copyhalt' a little to get a TM 'contradict'. We add two states at the 'yes' exit of 'copyhalt' to make the machine oscillate.

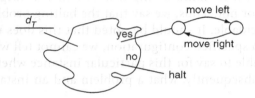

If it is possible to have 'copyhalt', it is possible to have 'contradict',

Now, what happens if you give the encoding of 'contradict' as input to 'contradict'?

There are two possibilities:

1. $d_{contradict}$ halts on $d_{contradict}$ → In this case 'contradict' takes the 'yes' exit and gets into a loop and never halts.

2. $d_{contradict}$ does not halt on $d_{contradict}$. In this case 'contradict' takes the 'no' exit and halts.

Hence, in both cases we arrive at a contradiction. Therefore, our assumption that a TM 'Halt' exists is not correct. i.e., there cannot exist an algorithm which solves the halting problem for TMs. □

We can present a slightly different argument.

Proof 2 We show that if the halting problem is decidable, we can have a TM M accepting L_d. M is constructed as follows: Given w as input, M finds out that $w = w_i$ or w is the *ith* string in the enumeration. Then, it generates the encoding of the *ith* TM T_i and calls 'Halt' (which solves the halting problem) with T_i and w_i as input. Halt will come out with one of the following answers.

1. T_i on w_i does not halt. In this case T_i does not accept w_i. Therefore, M halts and accepts $w = w_i$.

2. T_i on w_i halts. In this case, M calls U as a subroutine with T_i and w_i and finds out whether T_i accepts w_i or not. If T_i accepts w_i, M halts and rejects w_i. If T_i does not accept w_i, M halts and accepts w_i. Thus, we find that M accepts L_d and M always halts. Therefore, we should conclude L_d is recursive. But, we know that L_d is not even RE. Hence, the assumption that 'Halt' exists is not correct. In other words, the halting problem is undecidable. □

11.4 Problems, Instances, and Languages

A decision problem is a problem for which the answer is 'yes' or 'no.' For example, satisfiability problem means to find out whether a Boolean expression is satisfiable or not. We call this as SAT. Also AMB is the ambiguity problem for CFG – i.e., finding out whether a CFG is ambiguous or not. A particular CFG is an instance of the problem. If this particular CFG G is ambiguous, it is an 'yes' instance of the problem. If it is not ambiguous, it is a 'no' instance of the problem. Similarly, a particular Boolean expression is an instance of SAT problem. If it is satisfiable, it is an 'yes' instance of the problem. If it is not satisfiable, it is a 'no' instance of the problem. In contrast to these problems, problems like finding a Hamiltonian circuit in a graph are called optimization problems. Whether a graph has a Hamiltonian circuit or not is a decision problem. Finding one is an optimization problem. We shall consider more of this concept in the next chapter.

Any instance of a problem can be encoded as a string. A Boolean expression can be looked at as a string. For example, $(x_1 + x_2)(\overline{x}_1 + \overline{x}_2)$ can be written as $(x1 + x2)(\neg x1 + \neg x2)$ – a string from the alphabet $\{(,), x, +, \neg, 0,1,\ldots, 9\}$. A CFG $G = (N, T, P, S)$ can be looked at as a string over $N \cup T \cup \{(,), \{,\}, \rightarrow ,\}$. For example, the grammar $(\{S\}, \{a, b\}, P, S)$ where P consists of $S \rightarrow aSb$, $S \rightarrow ab$ can be looked at as a string $(\{S\}, \{a, b\}, \{S \rightarrow aSb, S \rightarrow ab\}, S)$. It is to be noted that generally integers are represented as decimal or binary and not as unary. The problem can be reformulated as one recognizing the language consisting of the 'yes' instances of the problem.

L_u is the language for the problem 'Does M accept w?' It consists of strings $d_M w$ where d_M is the encoding of M and M accepts w.

11.5 Rice's Theorem

Let us recall that a language accepted by a TM is called a recursively enumerable (RE) language. Without loss of generality we consider TMs over the input alphabet $\{0, 1\}$ and tape alphabet $\{0,1,b\}$.

Let $\mathcal{F}$ be a set of RE languages. Each language is over the alphabets $\{0, 1\}$. $\mathcal{F}$ is said to be a property of the RE languages. A language L has the property

$\mathcal{F}$, if $L \in \mathcal{F}$. For example, $\mathcal{F}$ may denote the set $\{L|L$ is recursive$\}$. $\mathcal{F}$ is a trivial property if $\mathcal{F}$ is empty or $\mathcal{F}$ contains all RE languages. Let $L_{\mathcal{F}}$ denote the set $\{d_M|L(M)$ is in $\mathcal{F}\}$ where M is a TM, $L(M)$ is the language accepted by it and d_M is the encoding of M.

Theorem 11.11 (Rice's Theorem (for recursive index sets)) *Any nontrivial property $\mathcal{F}$ of the recursively enumerable languages is undecidable.*

Proof In essence we want to show $L_{\mathcal{F}}$ is not recursive.

Without loss of generality we assume that ϕ is not in $\mathcal{F}$. Otherwise, we have to consider the family RE $- \mathcal{F}$, where RE is the family of RE languages.

Since $\mathcal{F}$ is a non-trivial property, $\mathcal{F}$ must contain at least one L. Let a specific language $L \in \mathcal{F}$ and M_L be the TM accepting L. Suppose this property $\mathcal{F}$ is decidable, then $L_{\mathcal{F}}$ must be recursive. There must be a TM $M_{\mathcal{F}}$ which halts on all inputs which accepts $L_{\mathcal{F}}$. We use M_L and $M_{\mathcal{F}}$ to show that L_u is recursive as follows:

Construct a TM M' as follows given a TM M and input w.

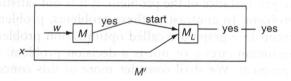

It is straightforward to have an algorithm A to construct M' given M, w and M_L. M' works as follows: It ignores its input x and simulates M on w. If M accepts w, it starts M_L on x. x will be accepted by M_L if $x \in L$. So, if M accepts w, M' accepts L. If M does not accept w, then M' does not accept any string. $L(M') = \phi$. Now, we know that $\phi \notin \mathcal{F}$ and $L \in \mathcal{F}$. If $L_{\mathcal{F}}$ is recursive there should be a TM $M_{\mathcal{F}}$ accepting it and halting on all inputs. Give the encoding of M' as input to $M_{\mathcal{F}}$.

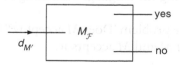

If it comes out of 'yes' exit, then $L(M')$ is in $\mathcal{F}$. i.e., $L(M') = L$ which can happen only if M accepts w. If it comes out of the 'no' exit then $L(M')$ is not in $\mathcal{F}$. i.e., $L(M') = \phi$ which happens only if M does not accept w.

So, depending on whether $M_{\mathcal{F}}$ takes the 'yes' exit or 'no' exit, we can say whether M accepts w or M does not accept w. i.e., we are able to have a TM for L_u which halts on all inputs. The structure of that TM is given in the following figure.

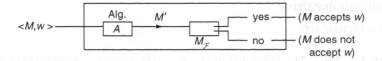

Hence, we see L_u is recursive. But, we have already seen L_u is not recursive. Hence, there is contradiction. This contradiction is due to the assumption of the TM $M_{\mathcal{F}}$ which halts on all inputs. Hence, $M_{\mathcal{F}}$ cannot exist. Therefore, $\mathcal{F}$ is undecidable. □

We state the following results which follow from the above theorem.

Theorem 11.12   *The following properties of recursively enumerable sets are not decidable.*

1. *emptiness (Is L empty?)*
2. *finiteness (Is L finite?)*
3. *regularity (Is L regular?)*
4. *context-freedom (Is L context-free?)*
5. *nonemptiness (Is L nonempty?)*
6. *recursiveness (Is L recursive?)*
7. *nonrecursiveness (Is L nonrecursive?)*

We found that if $\mathcal{F}$ is a non-trivial property, $L_{\mathcal{F}}$ is not recursive. Under what conditions $L_{\mathcal{F}}$ is RE is given by another theorem of Rice. We state this theorem without proof.

Theorem 11.13 (Rice's theorem for recursively enumerable index sets)

$L_{\mathcal{F}}$ *is recursively enumerable if and only if $\mathcal{F}$ satisfies the following three conditions:*

1. *If L is in $\mathcal{F}$ and $L \subseteq L'$ for some recursively enumerable language L', then L' is in $\mathcal{F}$ (the containment property).*
2. *If L is an infinite language in $\mathcal{F}$, then there is a finite subset of L which is in $\mathcal{F}$.*
3. *The set of finite languages in $\mathcal{F}$ is enumerable.*

Because of the above theorem, we have the following results.

Theorem 11.14   *The following properties of recursively enumerable languages are not recursively enumerable.*

1. $L = \phi$
2. $L = \Sigma^*$
3. *L is recursive*
4. *L is nonrecursive*

5. *L has only one string*

6. *L is a regular set*

Theorem 11.15 *The following properties of recursively enumerable languages are recursively enumerable.*

1. $L \neq \phi$

2. *L contains at least eight members*

3. *w is in L for some fixed w (membership problem)*

11.6 Reduction of Problems to Show Undecidability

In the last section, we have shown that any non-trivial problem of RE sets is undecidable. This theorem helps to prove many problems to be undecidable. Consider the problem: 'Will a TM started on a blank tape halt?' This is equivalent to the problem does $\varepsilon \in T(M)$? and hence undecidable by Rice's theorem. But for problems about TMs, there is no simple theorem which can be applied. Each problem has to be looked at separately.

Example 11.1 Consider the question, "Does machine T ever print the symbol S_0 when started on tape t?" This is undecidable. There does not exist a TM which will take $d_T t$ as input and say whether the symbol S_0 will be printed or not, for all (T, t).

For, we may take each machine T which does not ordinarily use the symbol S_0 and alter the machine so that before it halts, 'it prints S_0 and halts.' Then, the 'printing problem' for the new machine is the same as the halting problem for the old machine. Since any machine that does use S_0 can first be converted to one that does not (by renaming S_0) and then altered as above, solution of the printing problem would give solution to all halting problems, and we know that this cannot be done.

Example 11.2 It is decidable whether a single-tape TM started on blank tape scans any cell three or more times. If the tape does not scan any cell three or more times, the crossing sequence on the left and right boundary of a cell can be at most two. The crossing sequence is a sequence of states $q_1, q_2, q_3, \cdots, q_k$ where if the machine enters a cell in q_1 from one direction, it leaves the cell after sometime in q_2 in the reverse direction. There are only a finite number of crossing sequences of length two. So considering these possibilities, either the tape head will stay within a bounded region or get into a periodic repeating pattern. But either way, it will be possible to find out whether it scans a cell three times or not.

After the halting problem for TMs was proved to be undecidable, many problems for which researchers were trying to find algorithms were shown to be undecidable. For proving the new problem undecidable, a known undecidable problem has to be reduced to it. Let P_{new} be the problem which is to be shown to be undecidable and let P_{known} be the known undecidable problem. Then, the argument to be given is that if P_{new} were decidable, P_{known} will be decidable. Since we know P_{known} is undecidable, P_{new} has to be undecidable. This process we term as reducing P_{known} to P_{new}.

Many problems can be proved undecidable by reducing the halting problem to it. But many problems related to formal languages can be proved by reducing a problem known as PCP to them. The PCP is a well-known undecidable problem. We consider this in the next section.

11.7   Post's Correspondence Problem

Let Σ be an alphabet having at least two elements.

Definition 11.1   *Given two ordered sets of strings $w_1,\ldots,w_k$ and $x_1,\ldots,x_k$ over Σ, is it possible to find integers $i_1,\ldots,i_n$, $1 \le i_j \le k$ such that $w_{i_1}\ldots w_{i_n} = x_{i_1}\ldots x_{i_n}$? This is called Post's Correspondence Problem (PCP). If integers $i_1,\ldots,i_n$ can be found, for an instance of a problem, that instance of PCP has a solution. If no such integers can be found, then that instance does not have a solution.*

Example 11.3   Consider the sets of strings:

	w	x
1.	bbab	a
2.	ab	abbb
3.	baa	aa
4.	b	bbb

2, 1, 4, 3, is a solution for this instance of PCP as:
$w_2 w_1 w_4 w_3 = x_2 x_1 x_4 x_3 = abbbabbbaa$

Example 11.4   Consider the following sets:

	w	x
1.	aab	aba
2.	bb	bba
3.	aaaa	b

If this instance has a solution, it has to begin with 2. Since the third pair has different first letters and the first pair has different second letters. Beginning the solution with 2, we have:

w: bb
x: bba

To proceed we have to select only the first pair, since second and third pair will give different w and x strings. Selecting 1, we continue to find a solution (Now, we have 21):

w: bbaab
x: bbaaba

w matches with x upto the fifth letter, but x has six symbols. To continue the solution by a similar argument, we have to select only the first pair. Now the processed strings are:

w: bbaabaab
x: bbaabaaba

Again, we get the same situation. If we try to get the same string, we have to select the first pair only and we always get w and x where $|x| = |w| + 1$ and w matches with x but for the last symbol. At no point, we will be able to get $x = w$ and hence this instance of PCP has no solution.

Note that we may be able to look at a particular instance of a problem and give an answer. When we say a problem is undecidable, we mean that there is no algorithm which will take an arbitrary instance of the problem and will give a solution.

Modified PCP (MPCP)

We consider a slightly different variation of PCP.

Definition 11.2 *Given two ordered sets of strings $w_1,\ldots,w_k$ and $x_1,\ldots,x_k$, can we find a sequence of integers $i_1,i_2,\ldots,i_n$ $1 \le i_j \le k$, such that*

$$w_1 w_{i_1} w_{i_2} \ldots w_{i_n} = x_1 x_{i_1} \ldots x_{i_n}$$

Note that in MPCP we are fixing the first pair.

Theorem 11.16 *If PCP were decidable, then MPCP would be decidable.*

Proof We are reducing MPCP to PCP. Given an instance of MPCP over Σ, we construct an instance of PCP over $\Sigma \cup \{\#, \$\}$ as follows:

Let $w_1,\ldots,w_k$ and $x_1,\ldots,x_k$ be the sets for MPCP. For PCP, we have two sets $y_0, y_1,\ldots,y_k, y_{k+1}$, and $z_0, z_1,\ldots,z_k, z_{k+1}$. y_i is obtained from w_i by putting a $\#$ symbol after each symbol of w_i. z_i is obtained from x_i by putting the $\#$ symbol before each symbol of x_i. $y_0 = \# y_1$ and $z_0 = z_1$; $y_{k+1} = \$$ and $z_{k+1} = \# \$$. □

Example 11.5 Let us consider the instance MPCP.

	w	x
1.	ab	abbb
2.	bbab	a
3.	baa	aa
4.	b	bbb

This has solution as 1, 2, 4, and 3.
The corresponding PCP we construct is as follows.

	y	z
1.	#a#b#	#a#b#b#b
2.	a#b#	#a#b#b#b
3.	b#b#a#b#	#a
4.	b#a#a#	#a#a
5.	b#	#b#b#b
6.	$	#$

If the instance of PCP, we have, constructed has a solution, it has to be begin with the 0th pair and end with the $(k + 1)th$ pair because only the first pair has the same first symbol and the $(k + 1)th$ pair has the same last symbol.

It is straightforward to see that if 1, $i_1, \ldots, i_n$ is a solution of the MPCP, then 0, $i_1, \ldots, i_n$, k +1 is a solution of the PCP and vice versa. In the example considered above, 0, 2, 4, 3, 5 will be a solution of PCP generating the string,

$$\#a\#b\#b\#b\#a\#b\#b\#b\#a\#a\#\$.$$

Thus, if there is an algorithm to solve PCP, any instance of MPCP can be converted to an instance of PCP by the above method and solved. Hence, if the PCP were decidable, MPCP would be decidable or in otherwords, MPCP can be reduced to PCP.

Next, we prove that if MPCP were decidable, then L_u becomes recursive or the problem whether a TM M accepts a string w becomes decidable (which we know is not decidable).

Theorem 11.17 *If* MPCP *were decidable, then the problem whether a Turing machine accepts a string becomes decidable.*

Proof Given a TM M and an input w, we construct an instance of MPCP as follows:

Let M be given by $(K, \Sigma, \Gamma, \delta, q_0, F)$ where $K = \{q_0, \ldots, q_{r-1}\}$. Without loss of generality, we can assume that when M reaches the final state it halts and accepts. The MPCP we want to construct will be over the alphabets $K \cup \Gamma \cup \{\cent\}$.
First pair is:

$\cent$ $\cent q_0 w \cent$

We know that $q_0 w$ is the initial ID. The other pairs are grouped as follows:
Group I: X X $X \in \Gamma$

$\cent$ $\cent$

Group II: Pairs for moves.
If $\delta(q, a)$ contains (p, A, R) we have the pair:

qa Ap

If $\delta(q, a)$ contains (p, A, L)
we have a set of pairs:

Xqa pXA $X \in \Gamma$

If there are m symbols in Γ, we have m pairs

If $\delta(q, \cancel{b}) = (p, C, R)$
we have:

$q\cent$ $Cp\cent$

If $\delta(q, \cancel{b}) = (p, C, L)$
we have a set of pairs:

$Xq\cent$ $pXC\cent$ $X \in \Gamma$

Group III: Consuming pairs
If q is a final state, we have:

aqb q
aq q
qb q $a, b \in \Gamma$

Group IV: Ending pairs

$q\cent\cent$ $\cent$

We show that the instance of MPCP, we have constructed, has a solution if and only if M accepts w.
If M accepts w, then there is a sequence of IDs $q_0 w \vdash \cdots \vdash \alpha_1 q_f \alpha_2$ where q_f is a final state.

The instance of MPCP, we have constructed, will try to generate these IDs successively and finally consuming some symbols will generate the same string with both the ordered sets.

The initial strings will be:

$$\overline{W} : \text{\textcent}$$
$$\overline{X} : \text{\textcent}q_0 w \text{\textcent}$$

To proceed with the solution, we must get $q_0 w \#$ in the first string. While we do that we get the second ID in the next string. At any instance, the partial solution will be of the form:

$$\overline{W} : \text{\textcent}\text{ID}_0\text{\textcent}\text{ID}_1\text{\textcent}\ldots\text{\textcent}\text{ID}_{n-1}\text{\textcent}$$
$$\overline{X} : \text{\textcent}\text{ID}_0\text{\textcent}\text{ID}_1\text{\textcent}\ldots\text{\textcent}\text{ID}_{n-1}\text{\textcent}\text{ID}_n\text{\textcent}$$

Once the final state is reached, strings from Group III will be used in consuming the symbols and we shall get the same string in $\overline{W}$ and $\overline{X}$. Thus, the constructed instance of MPCP has a solution if and only if M accepts w. ☐

Theorem 11.18: *PCP is not decidable.*

Proof   Given M and w, by the above method we can construct an instance of MPCP. If MPCP were decidable, we can find out whether this instance of MPCP has a solution. If it has a solution, M accepts w. If it does not have a solution, M does not accept w. Thus, the problem whether M accepts w becomes decidable. But we know that this is not decidable. (L_u is not recursive). Hence, MPCP is not decidable.

By the previous theorem if PCP were decidable, MPCP would be decidable. But, we have just proved that MPCP is not decidable. Therefore, PCP is not decidable. ☐
We shall illustrate the construction given in Theorem 11.17 with an example.

Example 11.6   Consider the following TM with the alphabets $\{0, 1, \text{\textit{b}}\}$ and state set $\{q_0, q_1, q_2, q_3, q_4\}$. q_0 is the initial state and q_4 is the final state. The mappings are given by:

	0	1	$\text{\textit{b}}$
q_0	$(q_1, 0, R)$	–	–
q_1	$(q_2, 0, R)$	–	–
q_2	$(q_3, 1, R)$	$(q_3, 1, L)$	$(q_3, 1, R)$
q_3	$(q_2, 1, L)$	$(q_4, 1, R)$	$(q_2, 1, L)$
q_4	–	–	–

On input 00, the sequence of IDs are given by:

$$q_0 00 \vdash 0q_1 0 \vdash 00q_2 \vdash 001q_3 \vdash 00q_2 11 \vdash 0q_3 011 \vdash q_2 0111 \vdash 1q_3 111 \vdash 11q_4 11$$

The two sets of strings of the MPCP to be constructed are given by:

		W	$\overline{X}$
First pair		1. ¢	¢$q_0$00¢
Group I:		2. 0	0
		3. 1	1
		4. ¢	¢
Group II:			
for $\delta(q_0, 0) = (q_1, 0, R)$		5. $q_0$0	0q_1
for $\delta(q_1, 0) = (q_2, 0, R)$		6. $q_1$0	0q_2
for $\delta(q_2, 0) = (q_3, 1, R)$		7. $q_2$0	1q_3
for $\delta(q_2, 1) = (q_3, 1, L)$		8. 0$q_2$1	0$q_3$01
		9. 1$q_2$1	$q_3$11
for $\delta(q_2, b) = (q_3, 1, R)$		10. q_2¢	1q_3¢
for $\delta(q_3, 0) = (q_2, 1, L)$		11. 0$q_3$0	$q_2$01
		12. 1$q_3$0	$q_2$11
for $\delta(q_3, 1) = (q_4, 1, R)$		13. $q_3$1	1q_4
for $\delta(q_3, b) = (q_2, 1, L)$		14. 0q_3¢	$q_2$01¢
		15. 1q_3¢	$q_2$11¢
Group III:		16. 0$q_4$0	q_4
		17. 1$q_4$1	q_4
		18. 0$q_4$1	q_4
		19. 1$q_4$0	q_4
		20. 1q_4	q_4
		21. 0q_4	q_4
		21. $q_4$1	q_4
		22. $q_4$0	q_4
Last pair		23. q_4¢¢	¢

$\overline{W}$ and $\overline{X}$ strings are constructed step by step as follows:

$\overline{W}$ ¢

$\overline{X}$ ¢$q_0$00¢

using 5, 2, 4

$\overline{W}$ $\text{¢}q_0 00\text{¢}$

$\overline{X}$ $\text{¢}q_0 00\text{¢}0q_1 0\text{¢}$

using 2, 6, 4

$\overline{W}$ $\text{¢}q_0 00\text{¢}0q_1 0\text{¢}$

$\overline{X}$ $\text{¢}q_0 00\text{¢}0q_1 0\text{¢}00q_2\text{¢}$

using 2, 2, 10

$\overline{W}$ $\text{¢}q_0 00\text{¢}0q_1 0\text{¢}00q_2\text{¢}$

$\overline{X}$ $\text{¢}q_0 00\text{¢}0q_1 0\text{¢}00q_2\text{¢}001q_3\text{¢}$

using 2, 2, 15

$\overline{W}$ $\text{¢}q_0 00\text{¢}0q_1 0\text{¢}00q_2\text{¢}001q_3\text{¢}$

$\overline{X}$ $\text{¢}q_0 00\text{¢}0q_1 0\text{¢}00q_2\text{¢}001q_3\text{¢}00q_2 11\text{¢}$

using 2, 8, 3, 4

$\overline{W}$ $\text{¢}q_0 00\text{¢}0q_1 0\text{¢}00q_2\text{¢}001q_3\text{¢}00q_2 11\text{¢}$

$\overline{X}$ $\text{¢}q_0 00\text{¢}0q_1 0\text{¢}00q_2\text{¢}001q_3\text{¢}00q_2 11\text{¢}0q_3 011\text{¢}$

using 11, 3, 3, 4

$\overline{W}$ $\text{¢}q_0 00\text{¢}0q_1 0\text{¢}00q_2\text{¢}001q_3\text{¢}00q_2 11\text{¢}0q_3 011\text{¢}$

$\overline{X}$ $\text{¢}q_0 00\text{¢}0q_1 0\text{¢}00q_2\text{¢}001q_3\text{¢}00q_2 11\text{¢}0q_3 011\text{¢}q_2 0111\text{¢}$

using 7, 3, 3, 3, 4

$\overline{W}$ $\text{¢}q_0 00\text{¢}0q_1 0\text{¢}00q_2\text{¢}001q_3\text{¢}00q_2 11\text{¢}0q_3 011\text{¢}q_2 0111\text{¢}$

$\overline{X}$ $\text{¢}q_0 00\text{¢}0q_1 0\text{¢}00q_2\text{¢}001q_3\text{¢}00q_2 11\text{¢}0q_3 011\text{¢}q_2 0111\text{¢}1q_3 111\text{¢}$

using 3, 13, 3, 3, 4

$\overline{W}$ $\text{¢}q_0 00\text{¢}0q_1 0\text{¢}00q_2\text{¢}001q_3\text{¢}00q_2 11\text{¢}0q_3 011\text{¢}q_2 0111\text{¢}1q_3 111\text{¢}$

$\overline{X}$ $\text{¢}q_0 00\text{¢}0q_1 0\text{¢}00q_2\text{¢}001q_3\text{¢}00q_2 11\text{¢}0q_3 011\text{¢}q_2 0111\text{¢}1q_3 111\text{¢}11q_4 11\text{¢}$

Now, we start consuming symbols
using 3, 17, 3, 4

$\overline{W}$ $\text{¢}q_0 00\text{¢}0q_1 0\text{¢}00q_2\text{¢}001q_3\text{¢}00q_2 11\text{¢}0q_3 011\text{¢}q_2 0111\text{¢}1q_3 111\text{¢}11q_4 11\text{¢}$

$\overline{X}$ $\text{¢}q_0 00\text{¢}0q_1 0\text{¢}00q_2\text{¢}001q_3\text{¢}00q_2 11\text{¢}0q_3 011\text{¢}q_2 0111\text{¢}1q_3 111\text{¢}11q_4 11\text{¢}1q_4 1\text{¢}$

using 17, 4

$\overline{W}$ $\text{¢}q_0 00\text{¢}0q_1 0\text{¢}00q_2\text{¢}001q_3\text{¢}00q_2 11\text{¢}0q_3 011\text{¢}q_2 0111\text{¢}1q_3 111\text{¢}11q_4 11\text{¢}1q_4 1\text{¢}$

$\overline{X}$ $\text{¢}q_0 00\text{¢}0q_1 0\text{¢}00q_2\text{¢}001q_3\text{¢}00q_2 11\text{¢}0q_3 011\text{¢}q_2 0111\text{¢}1q_3 111\text{¢}11q_4 11\text{¢}1q_4 1\text{¢}q_4\text{¢}$

using 23

$$\overline{W} \quad \text{¢}q_000\text{¢}0q_10\text{¢}00q_2\text{¢}001q_3\text{¢}00q_211\text{¢}0q_3011\text{¢}q_20111\text{¢}1q_3111\text{¢}11q_411\text{¢}1q_41\text{¢}q_4\text{¢}\text{¢}$$

$$\overline{X} \quad \text{¢}q_000\text{¢}0q_10\text{¢}00q_2\text{¢}001q_3\text{¢}00q_211\text{¢}0q_3011\text{¢}q_20111\text{¢}1q_3111\text{¢}11q_411\text{¢}1q_41\text{¢}q_4\text{¢}\text{¢}$$

We get the same string in $\overline{W}$ and $\overline{X}$.

Note that successive IDs appear between ¢'s and once the final state is reached, symbols are consumed to make both strings equal.

We can make use of PCP to prove many problems in formal language theory to be undecidable.

Theorem 11.19 *The ambiguity problem for CFG is undecidable.*

Proof We reduce PCP to the ambiguity problem of CFG. Given an instance M of PCP, we construct a CFG G such that M has a solution if and only if G is ambiguous.

Let the two sets of strings of M be $W = \{w_1, \ldots, w_k\}$ and $X = \{x_1, x_2, \ldots, x_k\}$ over the alphabet Σ. Let $\Sigma' = \{a_1, \ldots, a_k\}$, $\Sigma' \cap \Sigma = \phi$. Construct a CFG G with non-terminal alphabet $\{S, S_A, S_B\}$ and terminal alphabet $\Sigma \cup \Sigma'$. The productions of G are given by:

$$S \rightarrow S_A$$
$$S \rightarrow S_B$$
$$S_A \rightarrow w_i S_A a_i$$
$$S_B \rightarrow x_i S_B a_i$$
$$S_A \rightarrow w_i a_i$$
$$S_B \rightarrow x_i a_i, \quad 1 \le i \le k$$

S is the start symbol.

If M has a solution $i_1, \ldots, i_n$ then, $w_{i_1} w_{i_2} \ldots w_{i_n} = x_{i_1} \ldots x_{i_n}$. Then, the string $w_{i_1} \ldots w_{i_n} a_{i_n} a_{i_{n-1}} \ldots a_{i_2} a_{i_1}$ has two derivations in G, one starting with rule $S \rightarrow S_A$ and another starting with rule $S \rightarrow S_B$ and G is ambiguous.

On the other hand, let G be ambiguous. Any string derived starting with $S \rightarrow S_A$ can have only one derivation tree as the symbols from Σ' dictate which rules have to be applied. A similar argument holds if the derivation starts with $S \rightarrow S_B$. If G is ambiguous, there should be a string for which we can have two derivation trees. One should start with $S \rightarrow S_A$ and another should start with $S \rightarrow S_B$. In this case, the string derived will be $w_{i_1} w_{i_2} \ldots w_{i_n} a_{i_n} \ldots a_{i_1} = x_{i_1} x_{i_2} \ldots x_{i_n} a_{i_n} \ldots a_{i_1}$ and deleting the suffix $a_{i_n} \ldots a_{i_1}$ we get:

$$w_{i_1} \ldots w_{i_n} = x_{i_1} \ldots x_{i_n},$$

i.e., $i_1, \ldots, i_n$ is a solution for M. Hence, M has a solution if and only if G is ambiguous. If there were an algorithm for the ambiguity problem, then given an instance of PCP, we can construct the corresponding CFG and find out whether it is ambiguous or not by the algorithm for the ambiguity problem. From this, we can find out if the given instance of PCP has a solution or not. Here, PCP would become decidable. But we know that PCP is not decidable. Hence, we have to conclude ambiguity problem for CFG is not decidable. □

11.8 Computable Functions

In an earlier chapter, we have looked at a TM as a computing device. It computes a function. The TM M starts with input 1^n. It halts in an accepting state h_a and at that time if the contents of the tape is $1^{f(n)}$, if f is defined at n. It halts at a non-accepting state or goes into a loop if $f(n)$ is not defined at n. The partial function f is computed by M. A function which can be computed by a TM is called a Turing computable function. Here, we are restricting ourselves where the domain and range of the functions are tuples of integers. The focus on numerical function values is not as restrictive as it might sound, because any function from strings to strings can be described by encoding both arguments and values of the function as numbers.

Primitive Recursive Function

Definition 11.3 (Initial Functions)   *The initial functions are the following:*

1. *Constant functions: For each $k \geq 0$ and each $a \geq 0$, the constant function $C_a^k : \mathbb{N}^k \to \mathbb{N}$ is defined by the formula:*

   $C_a^k(X) = a$ *for every $X \in \mathbb{N}^k$*

   In the case $k = 0$, we may identify the function C_a^k with the number a.

2. *The successor functions: $\mathbb{N} \to \mathbb{N}$ is defined by the formula:*

   $s(x) = x+1$

3. *Projection functions: For each $k \geq 1$ and each i with $1 \leq i \leq k$, the projection function $p_i^k : \mathbb{N}^k \to \mathbb{N}$ is defined by the formula:*

   $p_i^k(x_1, x_2, \ldots, x_i, \ldots, x_k) = x_i$

Definition 11.4 (Composition)   *Suppose f is a partial function from $\mathbb{N}^k$ to $\mathbb{N}$, and for each i with $1 \leq i \leq k$, g_i is a partial function from $\mathbb{N}^m$ to $\mathbb{N}$. The partial function obtained from f and $g_1, g_2, \ldots, g_k$ by composition is the partial function h from $\mathbb{N}^m$ to $\mathbb{N}$ defined by the formula:*

   $h(X) = f(g_1(X), g_2(X), \ldots, g_k(X))\ (X \in \mathbb{N}^m)$

Definition 11.5 (The Primitive Recursion Operation) *Suppose $n \geq 0$, and g and h are functions of n and $n + 2$ variables, respectively. The function obtained from g and h by the operation of primitive recursion is the function $f : \mathbb{N}^{n+1} \to \mathbb{N}$ defined by the formulas:*

$$f(X, 0) = g(X)$$
$$f(X, k+1) = h(X, k, f(X, k))$$

for every $X \in \mathbb{N}^n$ and every $k \geq 0$.

Definition 11.6 (Primitive Recursive Functions) *The set PR of primitive recursive functions is defined as follows:*

1. *All initial functions are elements of PR.*
2. *For any $k \geq 0$ and $m \geq 0$, if $f: \mathbb{N}^k \to \mathbb{N}$ and $g_1, g_2, ..., g_k: \mathbb{N}^m \to \mathbb{N}$ are elements of PR, then the function $f(g_1, g_2, ..., g_k)$ obtained from f and $g_1, g_2, ..., g_k$ by composition is an element of PR.*
3. *If $g: \mathbb{N}^n \to \mathbb{N}$ and $h: \mathbb{N}^{n+2} \to \mathbb{N}$ are primitive recursive then $f: \mathbb{N}^{n+1} \to \mathbb{N}$ obtained by primitive recursion (as in Definition 11.5) is in PR.*
4. *starting from the initial functions all functions obtained by the application of composition and primitive recursion are in PR.*

Example 11.7 Let us consider sum and production functions.
sum: $\mathbb{N} \times \mathbb{N} \to \mathbb{N}$ sum $(x, y) = x + y$
product: $\mathbb{N} \times \mathbb{N} \to \mathbb{N}$ product $(x, y) = x * y$
($*$ denotes multiplication here)
It can be seen that sum is primitive recursive, as it can be defined as follows:

$$\text{sum}(x, 0) = g(x) = C_x^1$$
$$\text{sum}(x, K+1) = h(x, K, \text{sum}(x, K))$$
$$= s(p_3^3(x, K, \text{sum}(x, K)))$$

It can also be seen that multiplication is primitive recursive, as it can be defined as follows:

$$\text{product}(x, 0) = 0 = C_0^1$$
$$\text{product}(x, K+1) = x * (K+1)$$
$$= \text{sum}(x, \text{product}(x, K))$$
$$= \text{sum}(p_1^3(x, K, \text{product}(x, K)), p_3^3(x, K, \text{product}(x, K)))$$

It is straightforward to see that:

Theorem 11.20 *Every primitive recursive function is a computable total function.*

Primitive Recursive Predicates

An arbitrary function may be defined as:

$$f(X) = \begin{cases} f_1(X) & \text{if } P_1(X) \text{ is true} \\ f_2(X) & \text{if } P_2(X) \text{ is true} \\ \dots \\ f_K(X) & \text{if } P_K(X) \text{ is true} \end{cases}$$

where $P_1, P_2, \dots, P_K$ are conditions.

A condition P depending on the variable $X \in \mathbb{N}^n$, makes $P(X)$ either true or false. This is called a predicate. When it has n arguments, it is called a n-place predicate.

The associated characteristic function $\chi_P : \mathbb{N}^n \to \{0,1\}$ is defined by:

$$\chi_P(X) = \begin{cases} 1 & \text{if } P(X) \text{ is true} \\ 0 & \text{otherwise} \end{cases}$$

If X_p is a primitive recursive function, χ_p is called primitive recursive predicate.

Theorem 11.21 *Suppose $f_1, f_2, \dots, f_k$ are primitive recursive functions from $\mathbb{N}^m$ to $\mathbb{N}$, P_1, $P_2, \dots, P_k$ are primitive recursive n-place predicates, and for every $X \in \mathbb{N}^n$, exactly one of the conditions $P_1(X), \dots, P_k(X)$ is true. Then, the function $f : \mathbb{N}^n \to \mathbb{N}$ defined by:*

$$f(X) = \begin{cases} f_1(X) & \text{if } P_1(X) \text{ is true} \\ f_2(X) & \text{if } P_2(X) \text{ is true} \\ \dots \\ f_K(X) & \text{if } P_K(X) \text{ is true} \end{cases}$$

is primitive recursive.

Definition 11.7 (Bounded Minimalization) *For an $(n+1)$-place predicate P, the bounded minimalization of P is the function $m_P : \mathbb{N}^{n+1} \to \mathbb{N}$ defined by:*

$$m_P(X,k) = \begin{cases} min\{y \mid 0 \le y \le k \text{ and } P(X,y)\} & \text{if this set is not empty,} \\ k+1 & \text{otherwise} \end{cases}$$

The symbol μ is often used for the minimalization operator, and we sometimes write:

$$m_P(X,k) = \mu^k y \left[P(X,y) \right]$$

An important special case is that in which $P(X, y)$ is $(f(X, y) = 0)$, for some $f : \mathbb{N}^{n+1} \to \mathbb{N}$. In this case, m_p is written m_f and referred to as the bounded minimalization of f.

Theorem 11.22 *If P is a primitive recursive $(n + 1)$-place predicate, its bounded minimalization m_p is a primitive recursive function.*

There are functions which can be precisely described but not primitive recursive. Ackermann's function is defined as:

For $m, n \in \mathbb{N}$

$$A(n, 0) = n + 1$$
$$A(0, m + 1) = A(1, m)$$
$$A(n + 1, m + 1) = A(A(n, m + 1), m)$$

This function is not primitive recursive.

Definition 11.8 (Unbounded Minimalization) *If P is an $(n+1)$-place predicate, the unbounded minimalization of P is the partial function $M_p : \mathbb{N}^n \to \mathbb{N}$ defined by:*

$$M_p(X) = min\{y | P(X, y) \text{ is true}\}$$

$M_p(X)$ *is undefined at any $X \in \mathbb{N}^n$ for which there is no y satisfying $P(X, y)$.*

The notation $\mu y[P(X, y)]$ is also used for $M_p(X)$. In the special case in which $P(X, y) = (f(X, y) = 0)$, we write $M_p = M_f$ and refer to this function as the unbounded minimalization of f.

Definition 11.9 (μ-Recursive Functions) *The set $\mathcal{M}$ of μ-recursive, or simply recursive, partial functions is defined as follows:*

1. *Every initial function is an element of $\mathcal{M}$.*
2. *Every function obtained from elements of $\mathcal{M}$ by composition or primitive recursion is an element of $\mathcal{M}$.*
3. *For every n ≥ 0 and every total function $f : \mathbb{N}^{n+1} \to \mathbb{N}$ in $\mathcal{M}$, the function $M_f : \mathbb{N}^n \to \mathbb{N}$ defined by:*

   $$M_f(X) = \mu y[f(X, y) = 0]$$

   is an element of $\mathcal{M}$.
4. *No other functions are in the set $\mathcal{M}$.*

Theorem 11.23 *All μ-recursive partial functions are computable.*

The equivalence between μ-recursive functions and Turing computable functions can be shown. The proof is fairly lengthy and is beyond the scope of this book.

We next show that there exist functions which can be specified properly but are not μ-recursive.

The Busy Beaver Problem

Consider a TM with two-way infinite tape, an input alphabet equal to $\{1\}$, and a tape alphabet equal to $\{1, b\}$. How many 1's can there be when the empty word is accepted? Since 1 is the only non-blank symbol, this is equivalent to asking if it halts when given the blank tape as input, then how many non-blank cells can there be?

This is called busy beaver game because of the similarity of 1's to twigs and the activity of the machine to the industrious activity of beavers.

The maximum number of non-blank cells that can be obtained by such an n-state TM is denoted by $\Sigma(n)$. A n-state machine that produces $\Sigma(n)$ non-blank cells is called a busy beaver. $\Sigma(1) = 1, \Sigma(2) = 4, \Sigma(3) = 6, \Sigma(4) = 13$, respectively. 1-state and 2-state busy beavers are shown below:

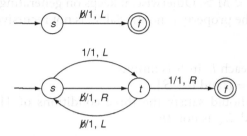

$\Sigma(5)$ is at least 1915 and $\Sigma(n)$ grows very fast.

We next show $\Sigma(n)$ is not a Turing computable function.

Let us define this function slightly differently. Let $\sigma: \mathbb{N} \to \mathbb{N}$ be defined as follows: $\sigma(0) = 0$. For $n > 0$, $\sigma(n)$ is obtained by considering TMs having n non-halting states and tape alphabet $\{1, 0\}$ (0 is taken as blank). We can take the non-halting set of states as $\{q_0, \ldots, q_{n-1}\}$ with q_0 as the initial state. Since the number of non-halting states and number of tape symbols are finite, there are only a finite number of TMs of this type. We restrict our attention to those which halt on input 1^n. $\sigma(n)$ denotes the largest number of 1's that can be printed when any of these machines halt.

We show that $\sigma(n)$ cannot be computed by a TM. Suppose σ is Turing computable. Then, it is possible to find a TM T_σ having tape alphabets $\{1, 0\}$ that computes it. This is possible as we have seen (Theorem 10.10).

Let $T = T_\sigma T_1$, where T_1 is a TM having tape alphabets $\{0,1\}$ that moves its tape head to the first square to the right of its starting position in which there is a 0 writes a 1 there and halts. T simulates T_σ first and when T_σ halts, T continues simulating with T_1. Let m be the number of states of T. By definition of σ, no TM with m states and tape alphabets $\{0, 1\}$ can end up with more than $\sigma(m)$ 1's on the tape if it halts on input 1^m. But T is a machine of this type that halts with output $1^{\sigma(m)+1}$. This is a contradiction. Hence, σ is not Turing computable.

Problems and Solutions

1. Which of the following properties of RE sets are themselves RE?

   a. L contains at least two strings.

   b. L is infinite.

Solution.   a. This is RE.

Let $S = \{L_1, L_2, \ldots\}$ each L in S contains at least two strings. $L_S = \{<M> \mid T(M) = L$ and $L \in S\}$.

L_S will be accepted by a TM M_S which halts accepting $<M>$ if $<M>$ is in L_S but may not halt if $<M>$ is not in L_S. M_S takes as input $<M>$ and uses a pair generator and simulates the behavior of M on string x_i for j steps. It also keeps a counter, which initially contains 0.

If M accepts x_i in j steps, it increases the counter by 1. If the counter reads 2, M_S halts and accepts $<M>$. Otherwise, it keeps on generating pair after pair and keeps testing. Since the property is nontrivial. L_S is not recursive.

b. This is not RE.

Let $S = \{L_1, L_2, \ldots\}$ each L in S is infinite.
$L_S = \{<M> \mid T(M) = L$ and $L \in S\}$.

If L_S is RE, it should satisfy the three conditions of Theorem 11.13. But condition 2 is violated. L_S is not RE.

2. Which of the following decision problems are decidable?
Let T_i denote the *ith* TM.

   a. Given x, determine whether $x \in S$, where the set S is defined inductively as follows: $0 \in S$, if $u \in S$, then $u^2 + 1$, $3u + 2$ and $u!$ are all members of S.

   b. Given x_1, x_2, and x_3 determine whether $f(x_1) = \pi^2(x_2, x_3)$, where f is a fixed non-total recursive function (π^2 is Cantor numbering).

Solution.   a. This is decidable.

Construct a TM T halting on all inputs which stops saying 'yes' if $x \in S$ or stops saying 'no' if $x \notin S$.

T has one input tape which initially contains x. It has six more tapes $T_u, T_1, T_2, T_3, T_0, T_{list}$.
T_u initially contains nothing (blank meaning 0)
T_1 initially contains 1
T_2 initially contains 2
T_3 initially contains 1

T_{list} contains in the increasing order a list of numbers separated by #'s. Initially, it contains $\# 1 \# 2 \#$.

T_0 is the output tape which is initially blank. When u is in T_u, T computes $u^2 + 1$ on T_1, $3u + 2$ on T_2 and $u!$ on T_3, it then compares x with the contents of T_1, T_2 and T_3. If there is a match, T outputs 'yes' in T_0 and halts. If there is no match, the contents of T_1, T_2, and T_3 are added to the list in T_{list} in the proper place. Next string from T_{list} is taken and placed on T_u and the process repeats. The process stops if a match between the input and the contents of T_1 or T_2 or T_3 is found at any time with output 'yes.' If the contents of T_1, T_2, and T_3 are greater than x (input) the process stops outputting 'no.' This is possible as the three functions computed are monotonically increasing. Hence, the problem is decidable.

   b. This problem is undecidable.

f is a non-total function and π^2 is a total function.

   Any algorithm to solve the problem with inputs x_1, x_2, and x_3 should have two subroutines one computing $f(x_1)$ and another computing $\pi^2(x_2, x_3)$. Since f is nontotal for some arguments, the algorithm will not come out of the subroutine for computing $f(x_1)$ and will not be able to halt. Hence, the problem is undecidable.

3. Fermat's last theorem, until recently one of the most-famous unproved statements in mathematics, asserts that there are no integer solution (x, y, z, n) to the equation $x^n + y^n = z^n$ satisfying $x, y > 0$ and $n > 2$. Show how a solution to the halting problem would allow you to determine the truth or falsity of the statement.

Solution. Suppose the halting problem is decidable. Construct a *TM T* which will solve Fermat's last theorem as follows:

   TM T has four tapes. In tape T_1, it systematically generates ordered quadruples (x, y, z, n), $x \geq 1, y \geq 1, z \geq 1, n \geq 3$. Initial one is $(1, 1, 1, 3)$.

   In T_2, it computes $x^n + y^n$.

   In T_3, it computes z^n.

   It compares contexts of T_2 and T_3 and if they match, outputs 'yes' in T_4. If there is no match, next quadruple is generated in T_1 and the process repeats. If there is no solution for Fermat's last theorem, T will not halt and will go on forever. Now if 'Halt' is the algorithm for the halting problem, give T and the first quadruple as input. If 'Halt' says 'yes', then Fermat's last theorem has a solution. If 'Halt' says 'no', then Fermat's last theorem has no solution.

Exercises

1. Suppose the tape alphabets of all TMs are selected from some infinite set of symbols $a_1, a_2, \ldots$. Explain how each TM may be encoded as a binary string.

2. Which of the following properties of RE sets are themselves RE.

   a. L is a context-free language.

   b. $L = L^R$

3. Which of the following decision problems are decidable?
Let T_i denote the *ith* TM

   a. Given i and n, determine whether T_i visits more than n squares after being started on blank tape.

   b. Given i, determine whether T_i ever writes the same symbol during two consecutive moves after being started on blank tape.

c. Given i, determine whether there exists a TM with fewer states that computes the same one-variable function as T_i.

4. Show that the following functions are primitive recursive.

a. exponentiation

b. factorial function

c. predecessor function

d. proper subtraction

$$x - y = \begin{cases} x - y & \text{if } x \geq y \\ 0 & \text{if } x < y \end{cases}$$

e. absolute difference $|x - y|$

f. Sign function

$$Sg(y) = \begin{cases} 1 & \text{if } y \geq 0 \\ 0 & \text{if } y = 0 \end{cases}$$

$$\overline{Sg}(y) = \begin{cases} 0 & \text{if } y \geq 0 \\ 1 & \text{if } y = 0 \end{cases}$$

g. comparison function

$$ls(x, y) = \begin{cases} 1 & \text{if } x < y \\ 0 & \text{if } x \geq y \end{cases}$$

$$gr(x, y) = \begin{cases} 1 & \text{if } x > y \\ 0 & \text{if } x \leq y \end{cases}$$

$$eqs(x, y) = \begin{cases} 1 & \text{if } x = y \\ 0 & \text{if } x \neq 0 \end{cases}$$

5. For each decision problem given, determine whether it is solvable or unsolvable and prove your answer.

a Given a TM T, does it ever reach a state other than its initial state when it starts with a blank tape?

b. Given a TM T and a non-halting state q of T, does T ever enter state q when it begins with a blank tape?

c. Given a TM T and a non-halting state q of T, is there an input string x that would cause T eventually to enter state q?

d. Given a TM T, does it accept the string ε in an even number of moves?

e. Given a TM T, is there a string which it accepts in an even number of moves?

f. Given a TM T and a string w, does T loop forever on input w?

g. Given a TM T, are there any input strings on which T loops forever?

h. Given a TM T and a string w, does T reject input w?

i. Given a TM T, are there any input strings rejected by T?

j. Given a TM T, does T halt within ten moves on every string?

k. Given a TM T, is there a string on which T halts within 10 moves?

l. Given TMs T_1 and T_2, is $L(T_1) \subseteq L(T_2)$ or $L(T_2) \subseteq L(T_1)$?

6. Which of the following problems about CFGs and their languages are decidable, and which of these are not decidable? Prove.

a. the problem of determining whether an arbitrary string belongs to the language generated by a given CFG.

b. the problem of determining whether a CFG generates a non-empty language.

c. the problem of determining whether the languages generated by two CFGs have any strings in common.

d. the problem of determining whether two CFGs generate the same language.

e. given two CFGs G_1 and G_2, $L(G_1) \subseteq L(G_2)$.

f. given CFG G and a regular set R determine whether $L(G) = R$.

g. given CFG G and a regular set R determine whether $R \subseteq L(G)$.

h. given CFG G determine whether $\overline{L(G)}$ is a CFL.

i. given two CFGs G_1 and G_2 determine whether $L(G_1) \cap L(G_2)$ is a CFL.

CHAPTER

12

Time and Space Complexity

In the earlier chapters, we considered the Turing machine (TM) and its acceptance power. By Church–Turing hypothesis, we realize that whatever could be done by a computer can be achieved by a TM. Also, while considering the variations of TMs, we found that even though all of them have the same accepting power, the number of steps could be very much increased in some cases. We also noted earlier that a procedure corresponds to a TM and an algorithm corresponds to a TM, which halts on all inputs. When we study algorithms for problems, we are also interested in finding efficient algorithms. Hence, it becomes essential to study the time and tape (space) complexity of TMs. In this chapter, we study some of these results.

12.1   The RAM Model

The standard model of computation which will represent the action of a modern computer is the family of random access machines (RAM). They are also referred to as register machines sometimes. There are several variations of this model. We consider the following model. It consists of a central processor and an unbounded number of registers. The processor carries out instructions from a given limited set on these registers. Each register can store an arbitrarily large integer. The program is not stored in these registers. It immediately follows that a RAM program cannot modify itself. In this way, it is different from the stored program concept. Also, at any time, the RAM program can refer to only a fixed number of registers, even though it has unbounded number of registers. When the machine starts, the input data is stored in a few registers. When it stops, the result of the computation is stored in a few registers. Let us consider the simplest RAM model which uses only four instructions, viz, increment, decrement, jump on zero, and halt. To add two numbers stored in R_1 and R_2 and store the result in R_1, the following program can be executed.

loop: Jump on zero, R_2, done
  Decrement R_2
  Increment R_1
  done: Halt.

It may look as though RAM model is more efficient compared to TMs, when such operations like addition or subtraction are considered. But for string operations like concatenating two strings x and y, TM may look more efficient.

In fact, we shall see that one can be simulated by the other, where the time could be cubed and the order of the space is the same.

We would also like to consider addition and subtraction, though including them as complicate things.

Assume that we assign unit cost to the four instructions mentioned earlier. Increment is the one instruction, where space may increase. It should be noted that for charging for space, we can either use the maximum number of bits used in all the registers or in any register as any program uses only a fixed number of registers and the two will only differ by a constant factor. We would like the space measure not to exceed the time measure. Since, increment instruction can result in increasing the space by one, we realize:

Space = O (input size + time)

We also assume register transfers can be done at unit cost. We also assume that addition and subtraction can be done at unit cost. Under these assumptions also, the relationship between space and time is preserved.

Involving multiplication makes the space increase exponentially. Hence, we shall use a RAM model without multiplication.

Here, we are not using indexing capability or indirect addressing used in computers. But allowing these techniques it can be easily proved that the relationship between SPACE and TIME becomes:

$$\text{SPACE} = O(\text{TIME}^2)$$

Comparison of RAM and TM

When we talk about computation which model should we consider? The RAM or the TM? How does SPACE and TIME get affected when we consider one model rather than the other? We prove below that our two models are equivalent in terms of computability and that the choice of model causes only a polynomial change in complexity measures. The proof consists simply of simulating one machine by the other and vice versa. This also establishes the equivalence of the two models from the point of view of computability.

Simulation of RAM by a TM

At any time, only a finite number of registers of RAM are used. Let the registers be numbered as 1, 2, ..., m, containing u_1, u_2, ..., u_m. Then, the simulating TM has in its tape #1 $*$ u_1#2 $*$ u_2#3 $*$ u_3 ... #m $*$ u_m# where the block #i $*$ u_i# denotes the fact that the ith register of RAM contains the integer u_i. Note that i and u_i can be represented in binary. Any operation like 'increment' or 'decrement' is transfered to the finite state control of the TM and executed. The change in register i from u_i to v_i is simulated by changing the block #i $*$ u_i# to #i $*$ v_i#. When this is done, shifting of symbols to the left or right is done if necessary.

Our simulation is efficient in terms of space: the space used by the TM is at most a constant multiple of the space used by the RAM,

$$\text{SPACE}_{TM} = \Theta\ (\text{SPACE}_{RAM})$$

But, more time is required as the TM has to scan and find the correct block and shift symbols if necessary. Nevertheless, for one step of RAM, the TM may scan the non-blank portion of the tape a finite number of times (maximum k say). Hence, $\text{TIME}_{TM} = O(\text{TIME}_{RAM}.\text{SPACE}_{RAM})$.

Simulation of TM by RAM

Simulating a TM with a RAM requires representing the state of the TM, as well as the contents of its tape and the position of tape head only in registers. The state can be kept in one register and the RAM program can decrement this register and use jump on zero to simulate a move of the TM. The symbol scanned by the tape head will be kept in one register. The symbols of the TM can be taken as $X_1, \ldots, X_{k-1}$, and if the current symbols scanned is X_i, integer i will be stored in that register. In the next move, the tape head will move left or right and scan X_j say. Then, the contents of this register will be changed to integer j. This can be done using 'decrement' and 'increment' operations of the RAM. The ID of the TM is given by $\alpha_1 q \alpha_2$ or

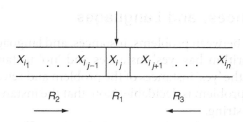

$X_{i_1} X_{i_2} \ldots X_{i_{j-1}} q X_{i_j} \ldots X_{i_n}$, where X_{i_j} is the symbol scanned by the tape head. To store this and the symbol read, three registers R_1, R_2, and R_3 can be used.

R_1 contains i_j.

R_2 contains $i_{j-1} + k i_{j-2} + k^2 i_{j-3} + \ldots + k^{j-2} i_1$,

R_3 contains $i_{j+1} + k i_{j+2} + k^2 i_{j+3} + \ldots + k^{n-j-1} i_n$.

If X_a is read and X_b is to be printed in the cell and the move is left the mapping will be $\delta(q, X_a) = (q', X_b, L)$. This is simulated by the RAM using the following instructions:

$R_1 \leftarrow b$

$R_3 \leftarrow k.R_3 + R_1$

$R_1 \leftarrow R_2 \bmod k$

$R_2 \leftarrow R_2 \div k \left(\left\lfloor \dfrac{R_2}{k} \right\rfloor \right)$

In order to simulate a right move:

$$\delta(q, X_a) = (q', X_b, R)$$

the following steps are executed by RAM:

$$R_1 \leftarrow b$$
$$R_2 \leftarrow k. R_2 + R_1$$
$$R_1 \leftarrow R_3 \bmod k$$
$$R_3 \leftarrow R_3 \div k$$

Except for the division, all operations can be carried out in constant time by the RAM model. The multiplication by d can be done with a constant number of additions. Division requires more time. It can be accomplished by building the quotient, digit by digit in time proportional to the square of the number of digits of the operand – or equivalently in time proportional to the square of the space used by the TM.

Hence, we have:

$$SPACE_{RAM} = \Theta (SPACE_{TM})$$
$$TIME_{RAM} = O(TIME_{TM} \cdot SPACE^2_{TM})$$

We can conclude that any TM can be simulated on RAM with at most cubic increase in time and linear increase in space.

Problems, Instances, and Languages

Recall the connection between problems, instances, and languages given in Section 11.4. A decision algorithm has 'yes' instances and 'no' instances. A TM can be constructed to accept the 'yes' instances of the problem and reject the 'no' instances of the problem, if the problem is decidable. Note that the instance of the problem is encoded suitably as a string.

When we talk about an algorithm, we talk about its efficiency. i.e., the amount of time it will take or the memory it will use as a measure of the size of the input. When we talk about solving a problem with an algorithm, intuitively, we think of the computer for executing it, i.e., RAM will be a suitable model. We call an algorithm efficient if it has polynomial-time complexity. Since the TM can simulate a RAM with time complexity increasing by a cubic factor, equivalently we can think about the TMs, which accept the 'yes' instances and their time complexity. Hence, we shall consider the time and tape (space) complexity of TMs and formulate our study.

12.2 Time and Tape Complexity of TMs

Space Complexity

Consider the offline TM M. It has a read-only input tape and the input is placed within end markers # and $. It has k storage tapes infinite in one direction. If for every input word of length n, M scans at most $S(n)$ cells on any storage tape, then M is said to be an $S(n)$ space bounded TM, or of space complexity $S(n)$. The language recognized by M, is also said to be of space complexity $S(n)$. It should be noted that symbols on the input tape cannot be rewritten and only the cells used in storage tapes count towards space complexity. This way of looking at the TM helps to consider space bounds less than $O(n)$. For example, log n. If the symbols on the input tape can be written, then minimum space complexity will be n, as we need to look at whole of the input.

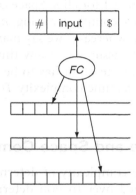

Figure 12.1. Multi-tape TM with read only input tape

Time Complexity

For considering the time complexity, we look at the following variation of the TM. The TM M has k two-way infinite tapes. One of them initially contains the input. Symbols in all tapes can be rewritten.

If for every input word of length n, M makes at most $T(n)$ moves before halting, then M is said to be a $T(n)$ time-bounded TM or of time complexity $T(n)$. The language recognized by M is said to be of time complexity $T(n)$.

The two different models for time and space complexity are considered for making the proofs simpler. Also, time complexity will be different if we use a single tape TM. In Chapter 10, we have seen that when we simulate a multi-tape TM by a single tape, number of steps may be squared. Consider the following example. We would like to have a TM for accepting strings of the form $wcwcw$. In a single tape, we can have two tracks, check off the symbols moving the tape head left and right several times. If $|w| = n$, the machine may make n left sweeps and n right sweeps. Hence, the time complexity will be $O(n^2)$. If we use three tapes, where one tape initially contains $wcwcw$, the tape head on this tape moves right reading w and copying it on the second tape and when it encounters a c, copies the portion after the first c till the second c w onto the third tape, moves the second and third heads to the leftmost non-blank symbols and moves all the heads right checking that the symbols read under the three heads are the same i.e., the input string is of the form *wcwcw*.

The length of the input is $3n + 2$.

Number of steps is $2n + 2 + n + n = 4n + 2$.

Hence, time complexity is $O(n)$.

Assumptions

It should be clear that every TM uses atleast one cell on all inputs, so if $S(n)$ is a space complexity measure, $S(n) \geq 1$ for all n. Space complexity $S(n)$ really means $\max(1, \lceil S(n) \rceil)$. Suppose the space complexity is $\log_2 n$, this does not make sense if input is of size 1 or 0 (string ε), whereas if we say $\max(1, \lceil S(n) \rceil)$ it makes sense.

Similarly, it is reasonable to assume that any time complexity measure $T(n)$ is atleast $n + 1$, as the whole of the input has to be read and to realize that the first blank has to be read. Hence, time complexity $T(n)$ really means $\max(n + 1, \lceil T(n) \rceil)$.

Non-deterministic Time and Space Complexity

The concept of time and tape complexity of deterministic TMs which we just now considered, can be carried over to non-deterministic TMs also. A non-deterministic TM is of time complexity $T(n)$, if no sequence of choices of moves of the machine on input of size n, causes the machine to make more than $T(n)$ moves. It is of space complexity $S(n)$, if no sequence of choices of moves on input of size n, enables it to scan more than $S(n)$ cells on any tape.

Complexity Classes

The family of languages accepted by deterministic TMs of space complexity $S(n)$ is denoted by $DS(S(n))$. The family of languages accepted by non-deterministic TMs with space complexity $S(n)$ is denoted by $NS(S(n))$. The family of languages accepted by deterministic (non-deterministic) TMs of time complexity $T(n)$ is denoted by $DT(T(n))$ $(NT(T(n)))$.

If we do not put bound on the number of states and number of tape symbols, some information can be stored in state and tape symbols can be taken as tuples to hold the information in some (say k) consecutive cells. This may help to get linear speed up in $S(n)$. We state some results without giving proofs. The proofs involve detailed constructions.

1. If L is accepted by an $S(n)$ space-bounded TM with k storage tapes, then for any $c > 0$, L is accepted by a $cS(n)$ space bounded TM.

2. If a language L is accepted by a TM with k storage tapes with space complexity $S(n)$, it is accepted by a TM with a single tape with the same space complexity $S(n)$.

3. Linear speed-up like in 1 above can be given for time complexity also.

4. If L is accepted by a multi-tape TM with time complexity $T(n)$, it is accepted by a single tape TM with time complexity $(T(n))^2$.

Space Hierarchy

What complexity functions are considered as 'well behaved'? For this we define 'space constructible,' 'fully space constructible,' 'time constructible,' 'fully time constructible' functions.

When we say 'space complexity is $S(n)$,' we mean that on an input of size n, the TM uses at most $S(n)$ space. It need not use $S(n)$ space on all inputs of size n (can use less). $S(n)$ is said to be space constructible, if there is some TM M that is $S(n)$ tape bounded, and for each n, there is some input of length n on which M actually uses $S(n)$ tape cells. It should be noted that M need not use $S(n)$ space on all inputs of length n. If for all n, M uses exactly $S(n)$ cells on any input of length n, then we say $S(n)$ is fully space constructible. n^k, 2^n, $n!$ (k an integer) are fully space constructible functions.

A function $T(n)$ is said to be time constructible if there exists a $T(n)$ time-bounded multi-tape TM M such that for each n there exists some input of length n on which M actually makes $T(n)$ moves. We say that $T(n)$ is fully time constructible if there is a TM, which uses $T(n)$ time on all inputs of length n. Most common functions are fully time constructible.

Some Results on Complexity Classes

We state some results without proof.

1. If $S_2(n)$ is a fully space constructible function and $\inf\limits_{n \to \infty} \dfrac{S_1(n)}{S_2(n)} = 0$ and $S_1(n), S_2(n) \geq \log_2 n$, then there is a language in $DS(S_2(n))$ which is not in $DS(S_1(n))$.

2. If $T_2(n)$ is a fully time constructible function and $\inf\limits_{n \to \infty} \dfrac{T_1(n) \log T_1(n)}{T_2(n)} = 0$, then there is a language in $DT(T_2(n))$ but not in $DT(T_1(n))$.

3. If L is in $DT(f(n))$, then L is in $DS(f(n))$.

4. Savitch's Theorem: If L is in $NS(S(n))$, then L is in $DS(S^2(n))$ provided $S(n)$ is fully space constructible and $S(n) \geq \log_2 n$.

Polynomial Time and Space

Whenever an algorithm can be solved in deterministic polynomial-time, we consider it as an efficient algorithm. When this cannot be done, we call such problems as intractable problems.

The languages recognizable in deterministic polynomial-time form a natural and important class and we denote it as $\mathcal{P}$.

$$\mathcal{P} = \cup_{i \geq 1} \mathrm{DT}(n^i)$$

There are a number of well-known problems which do not appear to be in $\mathcal{P}$ but have efficient non-deterministic polynomial-time algorithms. They are denoted as $\mathcal{NP}$:

$$\mathcal{NP} = \cup_{i \geq 1} \mathrm{NT}(n^i)$$

A deterministic algorithm corresponds to finding a solution by searching the solution space sequentially, whereas a non-deterministic algorithms corresponds to guessing a solution and verifying it. Consider the problem of finding whether a graph has clique of size k. Clique is a complete subgraph. A deterministic algorithm will take one by one subsets of the vertex set of size k and will check whether the induced subgraph on these k vertices forms a clique. If there are n vertices in the original graph, there are $_nC_k$ ways of selecting k vertices and one by one we have to check for each of these subsets. On the other hand a non-deterministic algorithm guesses a k subset and verifies whether the induced subgraph on these k vertices is a complete graph. Thus, the difference between $\mathcal{P}$ and $\mathcal{NP}$ is analogous to the difference between efficiently finding a proof of a statement (such as "this graph has a Hamiltonian circuit") and efficiently verifying a proof. (i.e., checking that a particular circuit is Hamiltonian). Intuitively, verifying looks easier, but we do not know for sure. Whether $\mathcal{P} = \mathcal{NP}$ is still an open problem, though evidences lead us to believe they are not equal.

Other important classes are:

$$\mathcal{PSPACE} = \cup_{i \geq 1} \mathrm{DS}(n^i)$$
$$\mathcal{NSPACE} = \cup_{i \geq 1} \mathrm{NS}(n^i)$$

By Savitch's Theorem, $\mathrm{NS}(n^i) \subseteq \mathrm{DS}(n^{2i})$ and hence, $\mathrm{PSPACE} = \mathrm{NSPACE}$.

Obviously, $\mathcal{P} \subseteq \mathcal{NP} \subseteq \mathrm{PSPACE}$, yet it is not known whether any these containments is proper.

Because of space hierarchy results, we have:

$$\mathrm{DS}(\log n) \subsetneq \mathcal{PSPACE}$$

We know that:

$$\mathrm{DS}(\log n) \subseteq \mathcal{P} \subseteq \mathcal{NP} \subseteq \mathcal{PSPACE} \qquad (12.1)$$

Hence, atleast one of the containment in Equation (12.1) is proper.

Intractable Problems

We have already seen the connection between problems and languages. Time complexity of an algorithm is measured in terms of the size of the input to the algorithm. Looking at from the point of view of TMs and languages accepted, we have seen that the time complexity is measured in terms of the length of the input string. Exponential time algorithms are not considered as "good" algorithms. Most exponential time algorithms are merely variation on exhaustive search, whereas polynomial-time algorithms generally are made possible only through the gain of some deeper insight into the structure of the problem. Generally, people agree that a problem is not "well-solved" until a polynomial-time algorithm is known for it. Hence, we shall refer to a problem as intractable if it is so hard that no polynomial-time algorithm can possibly solve it.

There are two different causes for intractability. The first one is that the problem is so difficult that an exponential amount of time is needed to find a solution. The second is that the solution itself is required to be so extensive that it cannot be described with an expression having length bounded by a polynomial function of the input length. For example, if the input is a sequence of m distinct integers $i_1, i_2, \ldots, i_m$ and we want to output all possible permutations of them; the length of the output itself cannot be a polynomial function of the length of the input and so cannot be computed in polynomial-time. The existence of this sort of intractability is mostly apparent from the problem definition. So, we shall consider the first type of intractability, i.e., we shall consider only problem for which the solution length is bounded by a polynomial function of the input length.

The earliest intractability results were by A. M. Turing, when he proved some problems to be undecidable. (We have considered this concept in the last chapter.) After the undecidability of the halting problem of TM was proved, a variety of other problems were proved to be undecidable, including Hilbert's 10th problem (solvability of polynomial equations in integers) and some problems of 'tiling the plane.'

The interest hence is on 'decidable' intractable problems. Some problems from automata theory have been proved to be intractable. For example, it has been shown that the problem whether an extended regular expression (including Boolean operators $\cap$ and $\neg$ apart from concatenation, $(+)$ union, and $(*)$ star) denoting the empty set requires exponential space.

When theoreticians try to find powerful methods for proving problems intractable, they try to focus on learning more about the ways in which various problems are interrelated with respect to their difficulty.

The principal technique used for demonstrating that two problems are related is that of "reducing" one to the other, by giving a constructive transformation that maps any instance of the first problem into an equivalent instance of the second. Such a transformation provides the means for converting any algorithm that solves the second problem into a corresponding algorithm for solving the first problem. (We have seen this type of reduction in the last chapter.) When we want to show a new problem to be 'undecidable,' we reduce a known undecidable problem to it.

In the study of NP-complete problems, we are trying to identify problems which are hardest in the class $\mathcal{NP}$. The foundations of the theory of NP-completeness were laid in a paper by Stephen Cook (1971) in which he introduced the idea of 'polynomial-time reducibility' and proved the Boolean satisfiability problem is NP-complete. Once this problem has been proved NP-complete, several other problems were proved NP-complete, by reducing this problem to them. Satisfiability problem has the property that every problem in $\mathcal{NP}$ can be polynomially reduced to it. If the satisfiability problem can be solved with a polynomial-time algorithm, then so can every problem in $\mathcal{NP}$ and if any problem in $\mathcal{NP}$ is intractable, then the satisfiability problem must also be intractable. Thus, in a sense, the satisfiability problem is the 'hardest' problem in $\mathcal{NP}$.

The question of whether or not the NP-complete problems are intractable is now considered to be one of the foremost open questions in theoretical computer science. Though many believe that NP-complete problems are intractable, no proof has been given yet. Neither has it been disproved. Apart from the interest in proving the connection between NP-completeness and intractability, proving some problems to be NP-complete is important by itself. Because, once we know a problem to be NP-complete, one can stop trying to find deterministic algorithms for the problem and either consider approximate or randomized algorithms for the problem or concentrate on restricted versions of the problem which may have polynomial deterministic algorithms.

Noting the connection between decision problems and languages (Section 11.4), we now formulate the study of NP-completeness in terms of languages.

Reducibility and Complete Problems

Definition 12.1 *We say that a language L' is polynomial-time reducible to L if there is a deterministic polynomial-time bounded TM that for each input x produces an output y that is in L if and only if x is in L'.*

Theorem 12.1 *Let L' be polynomial-time reducible to L. Then*

    a. *L' is in $\mathcal{NP}$ if L is in $\mathcal{NP}$.*

    b. *L' is in $\mathcal{P}$ if L is in $\mathcal{P}$.*

Proof Proofs of (a) and (b) are similar.

Proof for (b). Assume that the reduction of L' to L is done by a TM with time complexity $P_1(x)$ where P_1 is a polynomial. Let L be accepted by a $P_2(n)$ time-bounded TM where P_2 is a polynomial. Then L' can be accepted in polynomial time as follows: Given input x of length n, produce y by $P_1(n)$ time reduction. As at most one symbol can be printed per move, it follows that $|y| \leq P_1(x)$. Give y as input to the TM accepting L. In time $P_2(P_1(n))$, it will tell whether y is in L or not. Then, the total time to test whether x is in L' is $P_1(n) + P_2(P_1(n))$ which is a polynomial in x. Hence L' is in $\mathcal{P}$. $\qquad\square$

Theorem 12.2 *If L_1 is polynomial-time reducible to L_2 and L_2 is polynomial-time reducible to L_3, then L_1 is polynomial-time reducible to L_3.*

Proof Let Σ_1, Σ_2, and Σ_3 be the alphabets of the languages L_1, L_2, and L_3, respectively. Let $f: \Sigma_1^* \to \Sigma_2^*$ be a polynomial-time transformation from L_1 to L_2, i.e., there is a DTM M_1 which takes x_1 as input and outputs x_2 in time $P_1(|x_1|)$ such that x_1 is in L_1 if and only if x_2 is in L_2. Similarly, let $f_2: \Sigma_2^* \to \Sigma_3^*$ be a polynomial transformation from L_2 to L_3. i.e., there is a DTM M_2 which takes x_2 as input and outputs x_3 in time $P_2(|x_2|)$ such that x_2 is in L_2 if and only if x_3 is in L_3. Here P_1 and P_2 are polynomials. Then, the function $f: \Sigma_1^* \to \Sigma_3^*$ defined by $f(x) = f_2(f_1(x))$ for all $x \in \Sigma$ is the desired transformation from L_1 to L_3. A DTM (which is a combination of M_1 and M_2) first converts x_1 to x_2 in $P_1(|x_1|)$ time, $|x_2| \le P_1(|x_1|)$. Then, x_2 is converted to x_3 by $P_2(|x_2|) = P_2(P_1(|x_1|))$ time. It is easy to see x_3 is in L_3 if and only if x_1 is in L_1 and this transformation is achieved in time $P_1(|x|) + P_2(P_1(|x|))$ which is a polynomial. □

Next we define log-space reducibility, though we shall not use this concept further in this chapter.

Definition 12.2 *A log-space transducer is an off-line TM that always halts, having log n scratch storage and a write-only output tape on which the head never moves left. We say that L' is log-space reducible to L if there is a log-space transducer that given an input x, produces an output string y that is in L if and only if x is in L'.*

We say that two languages L_1 and L_2 are polynomially equivalent if L_1 is polynomial-time reducible to L_2 and vice versa.

By Theorem 12.2, we see that this is a reasonable legitimate equivalence relation. The relationship "polynomial-time reduces" imposes a partial order on the resulting equivalence classes of languages. The class P forms the 'least' equivalence class under this partial order and can be viewed as consisting of the 'easiest' languages. The class of *NP*-complete languages (problems) will form another such equivalence class. It contains the "hardest" languages in $\mathcal{NP}$.

Definition 12.3 *Let C be a class of languages.*

1. *We say that a language L is complete for C with respect to polynomial-time reductions if L is in C, and every language in C is polynomial-time reducible to L.*

2. *We say L is hard for C with respect to polynomial-time reductions if every language in C is polynomial-time reducible to L, but L is not necessarily in C.*

We can also define complete and hard problems with respect to log-space reductions. The following definitions follow:

Definition 12.4 *A language L is defined to be NP-complete, if:*

1. *$L \in \mathcal{NP}$*
2. *any language $L' \in \mathcal{NP}$ is polynomial-time reducible to L.*

We can also define this in terms of decision problems.

Definition 12.5 *A decision problem Π is NP-complete if:*

1. $\Pi \in \mathcal{NP}$

2. *any other decision problem $\Pi' \in \mathcal{NP}$ is polynomial-time reducible to Π.*

Thus $\mathcal{NP}$-complete problems can be identified as 'the hardest problems in $\mathcal{NP}$.' If any single $\mathcal{NP}$-complete problem can be solved in polynomial-time, then all problems in $\mathcal{NP}$ can be solved in deterministic polynomial-time. If any problem in $\mathcal{NP}$ is proved intractable, then so are all the $\mathcal{NP}$-complete problems. If Π is an $\mathcal{NP}$-complete problem, correspondingly if L is a $\mathcal{NP}$-complete language, then if $\mathcal{P} \neq \mathcal{NP}, L \in \mathcal{NP} - \mathcal{P}$.

If $\mathcal{P} \neq \mathcal{NP}$ (which is still open), the following figure gives the relationship between these sets.

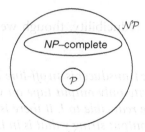

How do we show that a given problem is $\mathcal{NP}$-complete? In the last chapter, we saw that to show a new problem to be undecidable, we reduce a known undecidable problem to it. Similarly, to show a new problem (language) to be $\mathcal{NP}$-complete, we reduce (polynomial-time) a known $\mathcal{NP}$-complete problem (language) to it.

Theorem 12.3 *If L_1 and L_2 are in $\mathcal{NP}$, L_1 is $\mathcal{NP}$-complete, and L_1 is polynomial-time reducible to L_2, then L_2 is $\mathcal{NP}$-complete.*

To show that L_2 is NP-complete, two conditions have to be satisfied.

1. L_2 is in $\mathcal{NP}$ (This is given) and

2. any L in $\mathcal{NP}$ is polynomial-time reducible to L_2.

Any L in $\mathcal{NP}$ is polynomial-time reducible to L_1 as L_1 is $\mathcal{NP}$-complete. It is given that L_1 is polynomial-time reducible to L_2. Hence, by Theorem 12.2, any L in $\mathcal{NP}$ is polynomial-time reducible to L_2. Therefore, L_2 is $\mathcal{NP}$-complete. $\square$

Therefore, to show a problem Π to be $\mathcal{NP}$-complete, we have to show $\Pi \in \mathcal{NP}$, and a known $\mathcal{NP}$-complete problem Π_0 is polynomial-time reducible to Π.

Satisfiability-Cook's Theorem

A Boolean expression is an expression composed of variables, parentheses, and the operators $\wedge$ (logical AND), $\vee$ (logical OR) and $\neg$ (negation). The order of precedence among this is $\neg$, $\wedge$, $\vee$. Variables take on values 0 (false) and 1 (true); so do expressions. The truth table for AND, OR, NOT are given below. Here E_1 and E_2 are expressions.

E_1	E_2	$E_1 \wedge E_2$	$E_1 \vee E_2$	$\neg E_1$
0	0	0	0	1
0	1	0	1	1
1	0	0	1	0
1	1	1	1	0

Suppose E is a Boolean expression involving variables $\{x_1, \ldots, x_m\}$. Each variable can be assigned value 0 or 1. Hence, there are 2^m possible assignments of the variables. The satisfiability problem is that whether there is an assignment of the variables which makes the expression take the value 1 (true).

We may represent the satisfiability problem as a language L_{sat} as follows. Let the variables of some Boolean expression be $x_1, \ldots, x_m$ for some m. Encode variable x_i as the symbol x followed by i written in binary. So, the alphabet for L_{sat} is $\{\wedge, \vee, \neg, (,), x, 0, 1\}$. Each x_i may take $[\log m] + 1$ symbols. An expression:

$$(x_1 \vee x_2) \wedge (\neg x_1 \vee \neg x_2) \tag{12.2}$$

will be coded as:

$$(x1 \vee x10) \wedge (\neg x1 \vee \neg x10). \tag{12.3}$$

If an expression of the form of Equation (12.2) is of length n its coded version will be of length at most $O(n\log n)$. Without our argument getting affected, we can take the expression in form of Equation (12.2) as the log n factor is not going to affect the polynomial-time reducibility.

A Boolean expression is satisfiable if it evaluates to 1 for some assignment of the variables. It is unsatisfiable if it evaluates to 0 for all assignments of the variables. $(x_1 \vee x_2)$ is satisfiable for assignment $x_1 x_2$: 10, 01, 11; $x_1 \wedge \neg x_1$ is unsatisfiable as it evaluates to 0 whether $x_1 = 0$ or 1.

A Boolean expression is said to be in conjunctive normal form (CNF) if it is of the form $E_1 \wedge E_2 \wedge \ldots \wedge E_k$, and each E_j, called a clause is of the form $\alpha_{i_1} \vee \alpha_{i_2} \cdots \vee \alpha_{i_r}$, where each α_{i_j} is a literal, that is, either x or $\neg x$, for some variable x. $(x_1 \vee x_2) \wedge (x_1 \vee \neg x_2 \vee x_3)$ is in CNF. The expression is said to be in 3-CNF if each clause has exactly three distinct literals.

We next state Cook's theorem.

Theorem 12.4 *The satisfiability problem is NP-complete.*

Proof The decision problem is 'Is a Boolean expression satisfiable or not?'. Consider the language L_0 consisting of all strings representing satisfiable Boolean expressions. i.e., the 'yes' instances of the problem. We claim that L_0 is in $\mathcal{NP}$. A non-deterministic algorithm to accept L_0 guesses a satisfying assignment of 0's and 1's to the Boolean variables and evaluates the expression to verify if it evaluates to 1.

The evaluation can be done in time proportional to the length of the expression by a number of parsing algorithms. Even a naive method should not take more than $O(n^2)$ steps. In one pass, try to evaluate the innermost subexpressions. In the next passes repeat the same process. Even in the worst case it may not require more than n passes. Hence, there is a non-deterministic polynomial-time algorithm for this and the non-deterministic TM accepting L_0 will do it in $O(n^2)$ time in the worst case.

The first condition for NP-completeness is satisfied. Next, we have to show that any L in $\mathcal{NP}$ is polynomial-time reducible to L_0. Consider a language L in $\mathcal{NP}$. Let M be a non-deterministic TM of polynomial-time complexity that accepts L, and let w be the input to M. From M and w, we can construct a Boolean expression w_0 such that w_0 is satisfiable if and only if M accepts w. We show that for each M, w_0 can be constructed from w in polynomial-time. The polynomial will depend on M.

Without loss of generality, assume M has a single tape and has state set $\{q_1, q_2, \ldots q_s\}$ and tape alphabet $\{X_1, \ldots, X_m\}$. q_1 is taken as the initial state and q_2 as the final state. X_1 is taken as the blank symbol. Let $p(x)$ be the time complexity of M.

Suppose M has an input w of length n. M accepts w in less than or equal to $p(n)$ moves. Let $ID_0 \vdash ID_1 \vdash \ldots \vdash ID_q$ be a sequence of moves accepting w. $q \leq p(n)$ and in each ID the non-blank portion of the tape has no more than $p(n)$ cells.

Now, we construct a Boolean expression w_0 that "simulates" a sequence of ID's entered by M. Each assignment of true(1) and false(0) to the variables of w_0 represents at most one sequence of ID's of M. It may or may not be a legal sequence. The Boolean expression w_0 will take on the value true(1) if and only if the assignment to the variables represents a valid sequence $ID_0 \vdash ID_1 \vdash \ldots \vdash ID_q$ of ID's leading to acceptance. i.e., w_0 is satisfiable if and only if M accepts w, $q \leq p(n)$.

In forming the Boolean expression, the following variables are used. We also mention how we have to interpret them.

1. $A\langle i,j,t\rangle$ – this is 1 if the ith cell of the TM M's tape contains the jth tape symbol X_j at time t. We can see that $1 \leq i \leq p(n)$, $1 \leq j \leq m$, $0 \leq t \leq p(n)$. Hence, there are $O(p^2(n))$ such variables.

2. $S\langle k, t\rangle$ – this is 1 if and only if M is in state q_k at time t. Here $1 \leq k \leq s$, $0 \leq t \leq p(n)$.

   $S\langle 1, 0\rangle$ should be 1 as M is in the initial state q_1 at time 0. There are $O(p(n))$ such variables.

3. $H\langle i, t\rangle$ - this is 1 if and only if at time t, the tape head is scanning tape cell i. Here $1 \leq i \leq p(n)$, $0 \leq t \leq p(n)$. Therefore, there are $O(p^2(n))$ such variables. $H\langle 1, 0\rangle$ should be 1 as the tape head of M starts on cell 1 initially.

Thus w_0 uses $O(p^2(n))$ variables. If they are represented using binary numbers, each variable may require $c \log n$ for some constant c. c will depend on p. This $c \log n$ factor will not affect the polynomial complexity and hence without loss of generality, we can assume that each Boolean variable can be represented by a single symbol.

From the Boolean variables mentioned above, we construct the expression w_0 to represent a sequence of IDs.

It will be useful to use the following Boolean expression to simplify the notation:

$$\psi(x_1,\ldots,x_r)=(x_1\vee\ldots\vee x_r)\prod_{\substack{i,j\\i\neq j}}(\neg x_i \vee \neg x_j) \qquad (12.4)$$

$\psi(x_1, \ldots , x_r) = 1$ when exactly one of $x_1, \ldots , x_r$ is true. If none of $x_1, \ldots , x_r$ is true, the first factor $x_1 \vee \ldots \vee x_r$ will be 0. If two or more $x_1, \ldots , x_r$ is 1, then atleast one of the factors $(\neg x_i \vee \neg x_j)$ will be 0 and ψ will be 0. There are $\dfrac{r(r-1)}{2}$ factors of the form $(\neg x_i \vee \neg x_j)$ and so there are $\dfrac{r(r-1)}{2}+1$ factors in ψ. Hence, the length of ψ is $O(r^2)$.

If M accepts w, then there is a valid sequence of IDs, $\text{ID}_0 \vdash \ldots \vdash \text{ID}_q, q \leq p(n)$. In each ID, the non-blank portion of the tape is less than or equal to $p(n)$.

To have uniformity, we assume that M runs upto time $p(n)$ taking each ID after ID_q identical with ID_q. We also consider upto $p(n)$ cells in the tape in each ID. The non-blank portion cannot exceed $p(n)$ cells but can be less than $p(n)$ cells. In that case, we consider blank cells upto the $p(n)$th cell.

There are certain conditions that should be satisfied by the IDs. We put them together to get the expression w_0. These conditions can be mentioned as follows:

1. The tape head scans exactly one cell in each ID.
2. In each ID, each tape cell contains exactly one tape symbol.
3. The machine is in one state at each instance of time or in other words each ID has only one state.
4. The modification of the content of the tape takes place only in the cell scanned by the tape head when the machine moves from one ID to the next ID.
5. Depending on the state and the symbol read, the move of M defines (nondeterministically) the next state, symbol to be printed on the cell scanned by the tape head, and the direction of the move of the tape head.
6. The first ID, ID_0 is the initial ID.
7. The final ID should have final state. (Note that we have taken q_1 as the initial state and q_2 as the final state.)

We now write Boolean expressions $E_1, E_2, \ldots , E_7$ to denote these conditions.

1. The first condition is translated into the Boolean expression

$$E_1 = A_0 A_1 \ldots A_{p(n)}$$

$$A_t = \psi(H\langle 1, t\rangle, \ldots, H\langle p(n), t\rangle)$$

A_t tells that at time instant t, the head is scanning only one cell. Length of A_t is $O(p^2(n))$ and hence, length of E_1 is $O(p^3(n))$ and E_1 can be written in that time.

2. At time instant t, the ith cell contains only one symbol. This can be written as:

$$B_{it} = \psi(A\langle i, 1, t\rangle, A\langle i, 2, t\rangle, \ldots, A\langle i, m, t\rangle)$$

$$E_2 = \prod_{i,t} B_{it}$$

Length of B_{it} is $O(m^2)$ where m is a constant. Considering the range of i and t $(1 \leq i \leq p(n), 0 \leq t \leq p(n))$ E_2 is of length $O(p^2(n))$ and can be written down in that time.

3. The fact that M can be in only one state at any instant t can be written by the expression:

$$C_t = \psi(S\langle 1, t\rangle, S\langle 2, t\rangle, \ldots, S\langle s, t\rangle)$$

$$E_3 = C_0 C_1 C_2 \ldots C_{p(n)}$$

Length of C_t is $O(s^2)$ where s is a constant. Hence, length of E_3 is $O(p(n))$.

4. From one ID to the next ID, only the symbol scanned by the head can be changed:

$$D_{ijt} = (A\langle i, j, t\rangle \equiv A\langle i, j, t+1\rangle \vee H\langle i, t\rangle)$$

and $E_4 = \prod_{i,j,t} D_{ijt}$

D_{ijt} means the head is scanning the ith cell at time t or the contents of the ith cell at time $t+1$ is the same as its content at time t. Length of D_{ijt} is constant and hence, length of E_4 is $O(p^2(n))$ considering the range of $i, j,$ and t.

5. The next condition says that the change from one ID to the next ID is effected by a move of M. This is represented by:

$$E_{ijkt} = \neg A\langle i, j, t\rangle \vee \neg H\langle i, t\rangle \vee \neg S\langle k, t\rangle$$
$$\vee \sum_l (A\langle i, j_l, t+1\rangle \wedge S\langle k_l, t+1\rangle \wedge H\langle i_l, t+1\rangle)$$

Here, l ranges over all possible moves of M. (M is nondeterministic and may have many choices for the next move.)

This expression means either the ith cell is not containing the jth symbol at time t or the head is not scanning the ith cell at time t or the state is not q_k at time t or else (the state is q_k, ith cell contains X_j, and the head scans the ith cell), the next move is one of the possible choices of $\delta(q_k, X_j)$. If $\delta(q_k, X_j) = \bigcup_l \langle q_{k_l}, X_{j_l}, d_l\rangle$.

In E_{ijkt}, $i_l = i - 1$ if $d_l = L$ and

$i_l = i + 1$ if $d_l = R$

$$E_5 = \prod_{i,j,k,t} E_{ijkt}$$

Length of each E_{ijkt} is constant and hence, length of E_5 is $O(p^2(n))$.

6. In the initial ID, the state is q_1, the head scans the first cell and the first n cells contain the input while the remaining cells contain blank symbol.

Remembering the fact that X_1 represents the blank symbol:

$$E_6 = S\langle 1,0 \rangle \wedge H\langle 1,0 \rangle \wedge \prod_{1 \leq i \leq n} A\langle i, j, 0 \rangle \wedge \prod_{n < i \leq p(n)} A\langle i, 1, 0 \rangle$$

E_6 is of length $O(p(n))$.

7. In the final ID, the state is q_2 which is given by $E_7 = S\langle 2, p(n) \rangle$.

The Boolean expression w_0 is $E_1 \wedge E_2 \wedge \ldots \wedge E_7$. E_1 is of length $O(p^3(n))$ while other E_i's are less than that. Hence, w_0 is of length $O(p^3(n))$. This holds if each variable is looked at as a single symbol. Otherwise, there will be one more $(\log n)$ factor. w_0 will be $O(p^3(n)\log n)$ and hence $O(np^3(n))$. Length of w_0 is a polynomial function of length of w. w_0 can be written down in time proportional to its length.

It is straightforward to see that given an accepting sequence of ID's $\mathrm{ID}_0 \vdash \mathrm{ID}_1 \vdash \ldots \vdash \mathrm{ID}_{p(n)}$, we can assign values 0 and 1 to the variables such that w_0 becomes 1. Conversely, if there is an assignment of values 0 and 1 to the variables, which makes w_0 equal to 1, this will represent a valid sequence of moves of M leading to the acceptance of w. Thus, w_0 is satisfiable if and only if M accepts w.

We have taken an arbitrary non-deterministic TM M. M accepts L and hence L is in $\mathcal{NP}$. From any string w in L, w_0 can be written down in polynomial time. Thus, any L in $\mathcal{NP}$ is polynomial-time reducible to the satisfiability problem. Therefore, satisfiability problem is NP-complete. $\qquad\square$

It is a known fact that any Boolean expression of finite length can be converted to CNF and the length may increase at most by a constant factor.

In Theorem 12.4, we considered expressions $E_1, \ldots E_7$. E_1, E_2, E_3 are in CNF. E_6 and E_7 contain conjunction of single literals and hence, trivially in CNF.

E_4 is the conjunction of expressions of the form $(x_1 \equiv x_2) \vee x_3$. $x_1 \equiv x_2$ means $(x_1 \wedge x_2) \vee (\neg x_1 \wedge \neg x_2)$.

$(x_1 \equiv x_2) \vee x_3$ can be written as:

$(x_1 \wedge x_2) \vee (\neg x_1 \wedge \neg x_2) \vee x_3$ which can be written as $(x_1 \vee \neg x_2 \vee x_3) \wedge (\neg x_1 \vee x_2 \vee x_3)$ which is in CNF.

E_5 is the product of E_{ijkt} where each E_{ijkt} is of finite length and can be converted to CNF, when the length of the expression can be increased at most by a constant factor.

So, w_0 can be converted to w_0' in CNF where the length of w_0 may increase by a constant factor. Hence, w_0' can be written down in polynomial-time of the length of w. Hence, we have the following theorem.

Theorem 12.5 *The satisfiability problem for Boolean expressions in CNF is NP-complete (CNF - satisfiability is NP-complete).* □

Theorem 12.6 *3-SAT is NP-complete.*

Proof A CNF is said to be in 3-SAT form if each of the clauses has exactly three literals. We have already seen by the previous theorem that Boolean expression w_0' can be written in CNF such that M accepts w if and only if w_0' is satisfiable; length of w_0' is a polynomial function of w and this polynomial depends on M. w_0' can be written down in time proportional to its length. Now, we show that from w_0' we can write an expression w_0'' by introducing some more variables and w_0'' is satisfiable if and only if w_0' is satisfiable. The length of w_0'' will be a constant multiple of the length of w_0'.

We do this as follows:

Each clause in w_0' is of the form $(x_1 \vee x_2 \ldots \vee x_k)$. If $k = 3$, we leave the clause as it is. If $k = 1$, then introduce new variables y_1 and y_2 and replace x_1 by $(x_1 \vee y_1 \vee y_2) \wedge (x_1 \vee \neg y_1 \vee y_2) \wedge (x_1 \vee y_1 \vee \neg y_2) \wedge (x_1 \vee \neg y_1 \vee \neg y_2)$. Whatever value we give for y_1 and y_2 one of the above four clauses will have two literals (apart from x_1) false and to make the clause evaluate to 1, x_1 has to be 1. If $k = 2$, $x_1 \vee x_2$ is replaced by $(x_1 \vee x_2 \vee y_1) \wedge (x_1 \vee x_2 \vee \neg y_1)$ by introducing new variable y_1. One of the above two clauses will have the literal apart from x_1 and x_2 as 0 whether $y_1 = 0$ or 1. Hence, to make the expression evaluate to 1, $x_1 \vee x_2$ must evaluate to 1. □

If $k \geq 4$, $x_1 \vee x_2 \ldots \vee x_k$ is replaced by:

$$(x_1 \vee x_2 \vee y_1) \wedge (x_3 \vee \neg y_1 \vee y_2) \wedge (x_4 \vee \neg y_2 \vee y_3) \ldots$$
$$\wedge (x_i \vee \neg y_{i-2} \vee y_{i-1}) \wedge \ldots$$
$$\wedge (x_{k-2} \vee \neg y_{k-4} \vee y_{k-3}) \wedge (x_{k-1} \vee x_k \vee \neg y_{k-3}) \quad (12.5)$$

We have introduced new variables $y_1, \ldots, y_{k-3}$. We show that $x_1 \vee x_2 \ldots \vee x_k$ evaluates to 1 if and only if Equation (12.5) evaluates to 1 for some assignment of the new variables.

Suppose $x_1 \vee \ldots \vee x_k$ evaluates to 1. Then, let x_i be 1. Then, assign $y_1 = y_2 = \ldots = y_{i-2} = 1$ and $y_{i-1} = y_i = \ldots = y_{k-3} = 0$. Then, each clause in Equation (12.5) becomes 1 and Equation (12.5) evaluates to 1.

Next, we show if Equation (12.5) evaluates to 1 for some assignment of $x_1, \ldots, x_k$, $y_1, \ldots y_{k-3}$, then $x_1 \vee \ldots \vee x_k$ evaluates to 1. Suppose x_1 or x_2 is 1, then $x_1 \vee \ldots \vee x_k = 1$. Hence, consider the case when $x_1 = 0$ and $x_2 = 0$. In this case $y_1 = 1$ to make Equation, (12.5) evaluate to 1. Similarly, if x_{k-1} or $x_k = 1$, $x_1 \vee \ldots \vee x_k = 1$. Hence, consider the case when $x_{k-1} = x_k = 0$. In this case, y_{k-3} should be 0 to make the last clause equal to 1. So, in the case when $x_1 = x_2 = x_{k-1} = x_k = 0$ $y_1 = 1$ and $y_{k-3} = 0$. So, for some i, $y_i = 1$ and $y_{i+1} = 0$. In this case, in order that the clause $(x_{i+2} \vee \neg y_i \vee y_{i+1})$ becomes 1, x_{i+2} must be 1. Hence, $x_1 \vee \ldots \vee x_k$ evaluates to 1.

So, given a clause $z = x_1 \vee \ldots \vee x_k$ in CNF $k \geq 4$, we can introduce new variables $y_1, \ldots, y_{k-3}$ and write an expression z' in 3-CNF such that, if there is an assignment of variables which makes $z = 1$, there is an assignment of variables which makes

$z' = 1$ and vice versa. Also the length of z' is at most a constant multiple of z. Hence, we conclude 3-SAT is NP-complete.   □

When we want to show a new problem Π (corresponding language L) to be NP-complete, we have to show that Π (L) is in $\mathcal{NP}$ and that some known NP-complete problem $\Pi_0(L_0)$ is polynomial-time reducible to Π (L). Suppose $L_0 \subseteq \Sigma_1^*$ and $L \subseteq \Sigma_2^*$. There is a polynomial-time DTM, which converts a string x in Σ_1^* to a string y in Σ_2^* such that $y \in L$ if and only if $x \in L_0$.

We next show that the clique problem is NP-complete by showing that CNF satisfiability is polynomial-time reducible to the clique problem. A clique is a complete subgraph of a graph. Clique problem may be stated as follows "Does an undirected graph G have a clique of size k?". We have to represent the graph G as a string. This can be done by listing the edges of G. k is also an input. If d_G is an encoding of G, $k\#d_G$ is an encoding of the clique problem.

Theorem 12.7   *Clique problem is NP-Complete.*

Proof   1.   Clique problem is in $\mathcal{NP}$.

We can have a NTM which nondeterministically selects k vertices of G and checks whether edges exist between every pair of these k vertices. It is straightforward to see that this checking can be done in polynomial time. Hence, clique problem is in $\mathcal{NP}$.

2. Next, we show that CNF-satisfiability is polynomial-time reducible to the clique problem. Given an instance of expression in CNF with k clauses, we construct a graph, which has a clique of size k if and only if the CNF expression is satisfiable. Let $e = E_1 \ldots E_k$ be a Boolean expression in CNF. Each E_i is of the form $(x_{i_1} \vee \cdots \vee x_{i_{k_i}})$ where x_{i_j} is a literal. Construct an undirected graph $G = (V, E)$ whose vertices are represented by pairs of integers $[i, j]$ where $1 \leq i \leq k$ and $1 \leq j \leq k_i$. The number of vertices of G is equal to the number of literals in e. Each vertex of the graph corresponds to a literal of e. The edges of G are these pairs $[i, j], [k, l]$ where $i \neq k$ and $x_{ij} \neq \neg x_{kl}$ i.e., x_{ij} and x_{kl} are such that if one is variable y the other is not $\neg y$. If one is y and the other is $\neg y$, we cannot assign values independently to x_{ij} and x_{kl}. To enable independent assignment of values to x_{ij} and x_{kl} we have the condition that $x_{ij} \neq \neg x_{kl}$.

The number of vertices of G is less than the length of e and the number of edges will be almost the square of it. Thus, G can be encoded as a string whose length if bounded by a polynomial in the length of e and can be computed in time bounded by a polynomial in the length of e. We next show that G has a clique of size k if and only if e is satisfiable.

1. If e is satisfiable, then G has a clique of size k. If e is satisfiable, there is a literal in each clause which takes the value 1. Consider the subgraph of G whose vertices correspond to these literals. The k vertices have their first

components 1, ... , k. (No two of them will have the same first component). We see that these vertices $[i, m_i]$ $1 \le i \le k$ form a clique. If not, there must be two vertices $[i, m_i]$ $[j, m_j]$ $i \ne j$ such that there is no edge between them. This can happen only if $x_{i_{m_i}} = \neg x_{j_{m_j}}$. If $x_{i_{m_i}} = 1$, $x_{j_{m_j}} = 0$ and vice versa. But, we have chosen $x_{i_{m_i}}$ and $x_{j_{m_j}}$, such that each is equal to 1. Hence $x_{i_{m_i}} = \neg x_{j_{m_j}}$ is not possible and there are edges between every pair of vertices of this set.

2. If G has a clique of size k, then e is satisfiable. Let $[i, m_i]$, $1 \le i \le k$, form a clique. By our construction, the vertices will have such labels. No two of them will have the same first component. The vertex $[i, m_i]$ corresponds to a literal x_{m_i} in the ith clause. This literal may be a variable y or the negation of a variable $\neg y$. If x_{m_i} is a variable assign the value 1 to it. If x_{m_i} is the negation of a variable, assign the value 0 to it. As there is an edge between every pair of vertices, $x_{i_{m_i}} \ne \neg x_{j_{m_j}}$. So, we can consistently assign values to these variables. This will make the literal x_{m_i} 1 and each clause will evaluate to 1 and so will e. So e will be satisfiable.

Thus, we have a polynomial-time reduction of the CNF-satisfiability problem to the clique problem. Therefore, the clique problem is NP-complete. □

Example 12.1 Let us illustrate the construction in the above theorem with an example. Let e be $(p_1 \vee p_2 \vee p_3) \wedge (\neg p_1 \vee \neg p_3) \wedge (\neg p_2 \vee \neg p_3)$. The corresponding graph G will be:

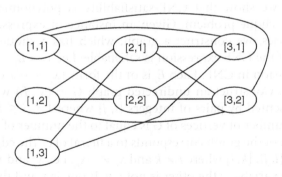

$p_1 = 1$ $p_2 = 1$ $p_3 = 0$ *is an assignment which satisfies the given expression.* [1, 1], [2, 2], [3, 2] *correspondingly form a clique of size 3.*

So far, thousands of problems have been proved to be NP-complete. Still more and more problems are being proved to be NP-complete. They are from different fields like automata theory, graph theory, set theory, and so on. We list a few of them (without proof).

Some NP-complete problems:

1. Vertex cover: Let $G = (V, E)$ be a graph. A vertex cover of G is a subset $S \subseteq V$ such that each edge of G is incident upon some vertex in S.
   Problem: Does an undirected graph have a vertex cover of size k?

2. Hamiltonian circuit: A Hamiltonian circuit is a cycle of G containing every vertex of V.
   Problem: Does an undirected graph have a Hamiltonian circuit?

3. Set cover: Given a family of sets $S_1, S_2, \ldots, S_n$ does there exist a subfamily of k sets $S_{i_1}, S_{i_2}, \ldots, S_{i_k}$ such that:
   $$\cup_{j=1}^{k} S_{i_j} = \cup_{j=1}^{n} S_j ?$$

4. Regular expression inequivalence: Given two regular expressions E_1 and E_2 over the alphabet Σ, do E_1 and E_2 represent different languages?

5. 3-Dimensional matching: Given a set $M \subseteq W \times X \times Y$ where W, X, and Y are disjoint sets having the same number q of elements, does M contain a subset M' of q elements and no two elements of M' agree in any coordinate?

6. Integer programming: Given a finite set X of pairs $(\overline{x}, b)$ where $\overline{x}$ is an m-tuple of integers, and b is an integer, an m-tuple $\overline{c}$ of integers, and an integer B, is there an m-tuple $\overline{y}$ of integers such that:

   $\overline{x}, \overline{y} \leq b$ for all $(\overline{x}, b) \in X$ and $c.y \geq B$

   (If $\overline{x} = (x_1, \ldots, x_m)$ and $\overline{y} = (y_1, \ldots, y_m)$, $\overline{x}.\overline{y} = x_1 y_1 + x_2 y_2 + \ldots + x_m y_m$).

Beyond NP-completeness

We next see some hierarchy of problems. Let NPC denote the family of NP-complete problems.

Definition 12.6 *A problem is NP-hard if every problem in NP is polynomial-time reducible to it. It is NP-easy if it is polynomial-time reducible to some problem in NP.*

Definition 12.7 *The class* co − NP *is composed of the complements of the problem in NP.*

   co − NP = $\{\Sigma^* - L: L$ *is over the alphabet* Σ *and* $L \in NP\}$

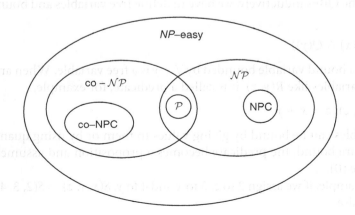

Let Co-NPC denote the family of Co-NP-complete problems.
Similar to NP-complete problems, we can define *co*-NP-complete problems. The hierarchy of problems can be represented by the previous figure.
NPC and co-NPC represent the set of NP-complete and co-NP-complete problems, respectively.

It is believed that $co - \mathcal{NP} \neq \mathcal{NP}$. This is a stronger conjecture than $\mathcal{P} \neq \mathcal{NP}$. This is because $\mathcal{NP} \neq co - \mathcal{NP}$ implies $\mathcal{P} \neq \mathcal{NP}$, while we can have $\mathcal{NP} = co - \mathcal{NP}$ and still we can have $\mathcal{P} \neq \mathcal{NP}$.

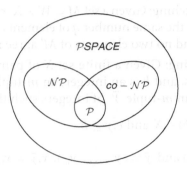

We know that PSPACE = NSPACE by Savitch's theorem. Considering the hierarchy with respect to PSPACE, we have,

Definition 12.8 *A language L is PSPACE complete if*

  1. *L is in PSPACE and*

  2. *any language in PSPACE is polynomial-time reducible to L.*

We state a few results without proof.

Quantified Boolean formulas (QBF) are built from variables, the operators $\wedge$, $\vee$ and $\neg$, parentheses, and the quantifiers $\forall$ (for all) and $\exists$ (there exists). When defining the QBFs inductively, we have to define free variables and bound variables. Consider:

$$\forall x (P(x) \wedge Q(y))$$

Here, x is a bound variable bounded by $\forall x$, y is a free variable. When an expression has free variables like $R(y, z)$, it is called a predicate, for example,

$$S(x, y, z): z = x + y$$

The variables can be bound by giving values to them or by using quantifiers. If all variables are bound, the predicate becomes a proposition and assumes value true (1) or false (0).

For example, if we assign 2 to z, 3 to x and 4 to y, $S(x, y, z) = S(2, 3, 4): 2 = 3 + 4$ which is false.

$\forall x \forall y \exists z, S(x, y, z)$ is a proposition where all variables are bound by quantifiers. This means for all x and for all y (taking the underlying set as the set of integers), there is z such that $z = x + y$. This is true. The QBF problem is to determine whether a QBF with no free variables has the value true.

Theorem 12.8 *QBF is in PSPACE and is a PSPACE complete problem.*

Context-sensitive recognition problem is stated as: Given a CSG G and a string w, is w in $L(G)$?

Theorem 12.9 *The CSL recognition problem is PSPACE complete.*

Some problems have been proved to require exponential amount of time for their solution.

Definition 12.9 *An extended regular expression over an alphabet Σ is defined as follows:*

1. *ε, ϕ and a, for a in Σ are extended regular expressions denoting $\{\varepsilon\}$, the empty set and $\{a\}$, respectively.*

2. *If R_1 and R_2 are extended regular expressions denoting the languages L_1 and L_2, respectively, then $(R_1 + R_2)$, $(R_1 . R_2)$, (R_1^*), $(R_1 \cap R_2)$ and $(\neg R_1)$ are extended regular expressions denoting $L_1 \cup L_2$, $L_1 L_2$, L_1^*, $L_1 \cap L_2$ and $\Sigma^* - L_1$, respectively.*

Redundant pairs of parentheses may be deleted from extended regular expressions if we assume the operators have the following increasing order of precedence.

$+ \cap \neg . *$

Definition 12.2.10 *Let us define the function $g(m, n)$ by:*

1. $g(0, n) = n$
2. $g(m, n) = 2^{g(m-1, n)}$ *for* $m > 0$

$g(1, n) = 2^n$, $g(2, n) = 2^{2^n}$ *and*

$g(m, n) = 2^{2^{2^{\cdots^n}}}$

A function $f(n)$ is elementary if it is bounded above for all but a finite set of n's by $g(m_0, n)$ for some fixed m_0.

Theorem 12.10 *Let $S(n)$ be any elementary function. Then, there is no $S(n)$ space bounded (hence $S(n)$ time bounded) deterministic TM to decide whether an extended regular expression denotes the empty set.*

Many more complexity classes can be defined and this leads to the introduction of 'complexity theory.' Oracle computations have also been defined. 'Complexity Theory' is a field of study by itself and is beyond the scope of this book.

Problems and Solutions

1. Show that $DT(2^{2^n+2n})$ properly includes $DT(2^{2^n})$.

Solution.

$$\underset{n\to\infty}{Lt}\frac{2^{2^n}\log(2^{2^n})}{2^{2^n+2n}}=\underset{n\to\infty}{Lt}\frac{(2^{2^n}2^n)}{2^{2^n}2^n.2^n}=0$$

By result 2 mentioned in "Some Results on Complexity Classes," $DT(2^{2^n+2n})$ properly includes $DT(2^{2^n})$.

2. What is the relationship between:
   a. $DS(n^2)$ and $DS(n^3)$?
   b. $DT(2^n)$ and $DT(3^n)$?
   c. $NS(2^n)$ and $DS(5^n)$?

Solution.

a. $\underset{n\to\infty}{Lt}\dfrac{n^2}{n^3}=0$

By result 1 mentioned in "Some Results on Complexity Classes," $DS(n^3)$ properly includes $DS(n^2)$.

b. $\underset{n\to\infty}{Lt}\dfrac{2^n\log(2^n)}{3^n}=\underset{n\to\infty}{Lt}\dfrac{n}{(3/2)^n}=0$

By result 2 $DT(2^n)$ is properly included in $DT(3^n)$.

c. (c) $NS(2^n)$ is included in $DS((2^n)^2) = DS(4^n)$ (result 4) $DS(4^n)$ is properly included in $DS(5^n)$ (result 1) Therefore, $NS(2^n)$ is properly included in $DS(5^n)$.

3. Show that the following problem is NP-complete. One-in-Three-3SAT (1in3SAT) has the same description as 3SAT, except that a satisfying truth assignment must set exactly one literal to true in each clause.

Solution.

One-in-Three-3SAT (1in3SAT)

   Is the given Boolean expression, given in 3SAT, satisfiable with the additional condition that the truth assignment must set exactly one literal to true in each clause.

   1in3SAT is in NP, as we can non-deterministically give a truth assignment and evaluate the expression and also check the additional condition on truth assignment in polynomial time.

   We next reduce 3SAT to 1in3SAT. Let w_0 be a Boolean expression in 3SAT form. From this, construct a Boolean expression w_0' for the 1in3SAT problem as follows. To each clause

$$(x_1 + x_2 + x_3) \tag{12.6}$$

of w_0 introduce new variables a, b, c, d and convert this to:

$$(\overline{x}_1 + a + b)(b + x_2 + c)(c + d + \overline{x}_3) \tag{12.7}$$

If Equation (12.6) is not satisfiable $x_1 = x_2 = x_3 = 0$. In this case, looking at Equation (12.7) as lin3SAT problem $\overline{x}_1 = 1 = \overline{x}_3$. Hence, $a = b = c = d = 0$. Since $x_2 = 0$. $(b + x_2 + c)$ becomes 0. Equation (12.7) is not satisfiable or in otherwords, if Equation (12.7) is satisfiable, Equation (12.6) is satisfiable.

To prove the other way round, let Equation (12.6) be satisfiable.

If $x_2 = 1$, then make $b = 0 = c$, $a = x_1$, $d = x_3$.

Then, Equation (12.7) satisfies the additional restriction and is satisfiable.

If $x_2 = 0$, then if $x_1 = x_3 = 1$ make $a = 1$, $b = 0$, $c = 1$, $d = 0$.

If $x_1 = 1$, $x_2 = 0$, $x_3 = 0$ make $a = 0$, $b = 1$, $c = 0$, $d = 0$.

If $x_1 = 0$, $x_2 = 0$, $x_3 = 1$ make $a = 0$, $b = 0$, $c = 1$, $d = 0$.

In all cases if Equation (12.6) is satisfiable Equation (12.7) is satisfiable.

If w_0 has k clauses and n variables, w_0' has $3k$ clauses and $n + 4k$ variables. w_0 can be converted to w_0' in polynomial time.

Hence, the known NP-complete problem 3SAT is polynomial-time reducible to lin3SAT problem. Hence, lin3SAT is NP-complete.

4. Positive lin3SAT problem is the lin3SAT problem, where none of the literals are negated. Show that it is NP-complete.

Solution.
Positive 3SAT problem is: Given a Boolean expression in 3SAT form, where none of the literals are negated, is the expression satisfiable?

This is a trivial problem as the assignment giving values 1 to all the variables makes the expression satisfiable.

It is straightforward to see that positive lin3SAT problem is in NP. It can be shown to be NP-complete by reducing the lin3SAT problem to it.

Let $w_0 = c_1 \ldots c_k$ be a Boolean expression in 3SAT form. From this, we construct an expression w in 3SAT form where none of the literals are negated such that w_0 is satisfiable with the lin3 condition if and only if w is satisfiable with the lin3 condition.

Also, given w_0, w can be constructed in polynomial time.

Let $x_1, \ldots, x_n$ be the variables used in w_0. There are k clauses in w_0. In w, we use variables $x_1, \ldots, x_n$ and also variables $y_1, \ldots, y_n$ and $z_1, \ldots, z_k$, $z'_1, \ldots, z'_k$, $z''_1, \ldots, z''_k$.

We shall now give the method of constructing w from w_0.

For each clause c_i in w_0 some clauses c'_i are constructed.

1. If c_i is of the form $(x_k + x_l + x_m)$ with no literal negated, this is kept as it is in c'_i

2. If c_i is of the form $(\neg x_k + x_l + x_m)$ with one literal negated, c'_i consists of $(y_k + x_l + x_m)(y_k + x_k + z_i)(x_1 + z'_i + z_i)(x_m + z''_i + z_i)$ (y_k in essence refers to $\neg x_k$). If $(\neg x_k + x_l + x_m)$ is satisfiable with the 1in3 condition, then c'_i is satisfiable with the 1in3 condition and vice versa. It should be noted that one of y_k or x_k will be 0 and the other 1 and z_i has to be 0. The values of z'_i, z''_i can be properly chosen to satisfy the 1in3 condition.

3. If c_i is of the form $(\neg x_k + \neg x_l + x_m)$ with two of the literals negated, c'_i consists of $(y_k + y_l + x_m)(y_k + x_k + z_i)(y_l + x_l + z_i)(x_m + z'_i + z_i)$.

   Again, it can be checked that if c_i is satisfiable with the 1in3 condition then c'_i is satisfiable with the 1in3 condition and vice versa. Note that one of y_k, x_k is 0 and the other 1 as also one of y_l, x_l is 0 and the other 1 and $z_i = 0$. z'_i assumes suitable value to satisfy the 1in3 condition.

4. If c_i is of the form $(\neg x_k + \neg x_l + \neg x_m)$ will all three literals negated, c'_i consists of $(y_k + y_l + y_m)(y_k + x_k + z_i)(y_l + x_l + z_i)(y_m + x_m + z_i)$. Again, it can be checked that if c_i is satisfiable with the 1in3 condition c'_i is satisfiable with the 1in3 condition and vice versa. Also $z_i = 0$ and one of y_j, x_j $(j = k, l, m)$ is 0 and the other 1, $w = c'_1 \ldots c'_k$ and it is straightforward to see that w' can be constructed from w_0 in polynomial time. Hence, positive 1in3SAT is NP-complete.

5. Exact cover by three-sets (X3C): Given a set with $3n$ elements for some natural number n and a collection of subsets of the set, each of which contains exactly three elements, do there exist in the collection n subsets that together cover the set?
   Show that this problem is NP-complete.

Solution.
Membership in NP is obvious. Select a set of n three-sets and check whether they cover the given set. To show X3C is NP-complete, we reduce positive 1in3SAT to it. Let us consider an instance of positive 1in3SAT with n variables and k clauses. This instance of positive 1in3SAT will be converted to a X3C instance with $18k$ elements and $15k$ three-sets such that positive 1in3SAT instance is satisfiable if and only if the X3C instance has a 'yes' answer. i.e., an exact cover with n three-sets is present.

For each clause $c = (x + y + z)$ we set up six elements $x_c, y_c, z_c, t_c, f'_c, f''_c$. The first three will represent the three literals, while the other three will distinguish the true literal from the two false literals. For each variable, we construct a component with two attaching points (one corresponding to true and the other to false) for each of its occurrences. See Figure 12.2.

Let variable x occur n_x times in the Boolean expression. We set up $4n_x$ elements of which $2n_x$ will be used as attaching points while the other will ensure consistency. Call the attaching points X^i_i and X^j_i for $1 \leq i \leq n_x$; call the other point p^i_x, $1 \leq i \leq 2n_x$. Now, we construct three-sets. The component associated with variable x has $2n_x$ sets:

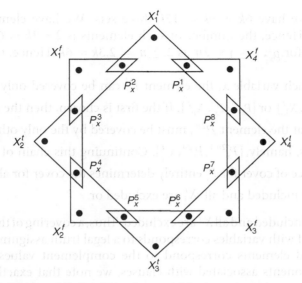

Figure 12.2. x is the variable occuring 4 times

$$\{P_x^{2i-1}, P_x^{2i}, X_i^t\} \text{ or } 1 \leq i \leq n_x$$

$$\{P_x^{2i}, P_x^{2i+1}, X_i^f\} \text{ for } 1 \leq i \leq n_x \text{ and}$$

$$\{P_x^{2n_x}, P_x^1, X_{n_x}^f\}$$

Suppose there are n variables $x_1, \ldots, x_n$, x_i occurs n_{x_i} times say. Then, $n_{x_1} + n_{x_2} + \ldots + n_{x_n} = 3k$ as there are k clauses. So the number of three-sets formed is $2(n_{x_1} + \ldots + n_{x_n}) = 6k$.

Also, corresponding to each clause $c = (x + y + z)$, we make nine three-sets, three for each literal. The first of these sets, if picked for the cover indicates that the associated literal is the one set to true in the clause; for literal x in clause c, this set is $\{x_c, t_c, X_i^t\}$ for some attaching point i. If one of the other two is picked, the associated literal is set to false; for literal x, they are $\{x_c, f_c', X_i^f\}, \{x_c, f'', X_i^f\}$.

So for $(x + y + z)$ we have:

$$(x_c, t_c, X_i^t), (y_c, t_c, Y_j^t), (z_c, t_c, Z_k^t)$$

$$(x_c, f_c', X_i^f), (y_c, f_c', Y_j^f), (z_c, f_c', Z_k^f),$$

$$(x_c, f_c'', X_i^f), (y_c, f_c'', Y_j^f), (z_c, f_c'', Z_k^f)$$

for some i, j, k.

So, totally we have $6k + 9k = 15k$ three sets. We have element x_i^t and x_i^f for $1 \leq i \leq n_x$. Hence, the number of such elements is $2 * 3k = 6k$. Number of elements of the for p_x^j, $1 \leq j \leq 2n_x$ is 2. $\sum n_x = 2.3k = 6k$. Hence, totally we have $18k$ elements.

Note that, for each variable x, the element P_x^1 can be covered only by one of the two sets $\{P_x^1, P_x^1, X_1^t\}$ or $\{P_x^{2n}, P_x^1, X_{n_x}^f\}$. If the first is chosen, then the second cannot be chosen, so that the element P^{2n}, must be covered by the only other three-set in which it appears, namely, $\{P_x^{2n-1}, P_x^{2n}, x_{n_x}^t\}$. Continuing this chain of reasoning, we see that the choice of cover for P_x^1 entirely determines the cover for all P_x^i. In this,

   i. all X_i^f are included and all X_i^t are excluded or

   ii. all X_i^t are included and all X_i^f are excluded. Thus, a covering of the components associated with variables corresponds to a legal truth assignment, where the concerned elements correspond to the complement values. Considering the components associated with clauses, we note that exactly three of the nine sets must be selected for the cover. Whichever set is selected to cover the element, t_c must include a true literal, thereby ensuring that at least one literal per clause is true. The other two sets chosen cover f'_c and f''_c and thus, contain one false literal each, ensuring that at most one literal per clause is true. It can be seen that the construction of the sets can be done in polynomial time, given an instance of positive 1in3SAT.

Note that there are $18k$ elements and $15k$ three-sets. Out of the $15k$ three-sets, we must select $6k$ to get an exact cover. For each clause, 3 three-sets are chosen amounting to $3k$ three-sets. For each variable x occurring n_x times, n_x three-sets are chosen involving elements of the form p_x^i. The number of such three-sets is $\sum_x n_x = 3k$. Hence, totally we select $3k + 3k = 6k$ three-sets and by our choice they are disjoint and hence form an exact cover.

Exercises

1. The notion of a crossing sequence – the sequence of states in which the boundary between two cells is crossed – was introduced in Chapter 6 with regard to two-way FSA. The notion can be extended to TM. Prove the following about crossing sequences.

   a. The time taken by single-tape TM M on input w is the sum of the lengths of the crossing sequences between each two cells of M's tape.

   b. Suppose M is a single tape TM which accepts an input after reading the whole input and reaches the accepting state when the tape is in a cell to the right of the cells where the input was originally placed. Show that if M accepts input $w_1 w_2$, and the crossing sequence between w_1 and w_2 is the same as that between x_1 and x_2 when M is given input x_1, x_2, then M accepts $x_1 w_2$.

2. Discuss how many steps a single-tape TM will require to accept
   a. $\{wcw^R | w \in \{a, b\}^*\}$
   b. $\{wcw | w \in \{a, b\}^*\}$

3. Show that the following functions are fully time and space constructible
   a. n^2
   b. 2^n
   c. $n!$

4. Show that the following problems are NP-complete. Let $G = (V, E)$ be an undirected graph.
   a. A vertex cover of G is a subset $S \subseteq V$ such that each edge of G is incident upon some vertex in S.
      Does an undirected graph have a vertex cover of size k, $|S| = k$?
   b. A Hamilton circuit is a cycle of G containing every vertex of V. Does an undirected graph have a Hamilton circuit?
   c. G is k-colorable if there exists an assignment of the integers $1, 2, ..., k$, called "colors," to the vertices of G such that no two adjacent vertices are assigned the same color. The chromatic number of G is the smallest integer k such that G is k-colorable. Is an undirected graph k-colorable?

Let $G'' = (V', E')$ be a directed graph.
   a. A feedback vertex set is a subset $S' \subseteq V'$ such that every cycle of G' contains a vertex in S'.
      Does a directed graph have a feedback vertex set with k members?
   b. A feedback edge set is a subset $F' \subseteq E'$ such that every cycle of G' contains a edge in F'.
      Does a directed graph have a feedback edge set with k members?
   c. A directed Hamilton circuit is a cycle containing every vertex of V.
      Does a directed graph have a directed Hamilton circuit?

5. Consider the following problems:
   a. Not-all-equal 3SAT(NAE3SAT) has the same description as 3SAT, except that a satisfying truth assignment may not set all three literals of any clause to true. This constraint results in a symmetric problem: the complement of a satisfying truth assignment is a satisfying truth assignment.
   b. Maximum cut (MxC): Given an undirected graph and a positive integer bound, can the vertices be partitioned into two subsets such that the number of edges with endpoints in both subsets is no smaller than the given bound?
   c. Partition: Given a set of elements, each with a positive integer size, and such that the sum of all element sizes is an even number, can the set be partitioned into two subsets such that the sum of the sizes of the elements of one subset is equal to that of the other subset?

d. Art Gallery (AG): Given a simple polygon, P, of n vertices and a positive integer bound, $B \leq n$, can at most B "guards" be placed at vertices of the polygon in such a way that every point in the interior of the polygon is visible to at least one guard? (A simple polygon one with a well-defined interior; a point is visible to a guard if and only if the line segment joining the two does not intersect any edge of the polygon).

Show that these problems are NP-complete.

13 Recent Trends and Applications

13.1 Regulated Re-writing

In a given grammar, re-writing can take place at a step of a derivation by the usage of any applicable rule in any desired place. That is, if A is a nonterminal occurring in any sentential form say $\alpha A \beta$, the rules being $A \rightarrow \gamma$, $A \rightarrow \delta$, then any of these two rules are applicable for the occurrence of A in $\alpha A \beta$. Hence, one encounters nondeterminism in its application. One way of naturally restricting the nondeterminism is by regulating devices, which can select only certain derivations as correct in such a way that the obtained language has certain useful properties. For example, a very simple and natural control on regular rules may yield a non-regular language.

While defining the four types of grammars in Chapter 2, we put restrictions in the form of production rules to go from type 0 to type 1, then to type 2 and type 3. In this chapter, we put restrictions on the manner of applying the rules and study the effect. There are several methods to control re-writing. Some of the standard control strategies will be discussed below.

Matrix Grammar

A matrix grammar is a quadruple $G = (N, T, P, S)$ where N, T, and S are as in any Chomsky grammar. P is a finite set of sequences of the form:

$$m = [\alpha_1 \rightarrow \beta_1, \, \alpha_2 \rightarrow \beta_2, \, ..., \, \alpha_n \rightarrow \beta_n]$$

$n \geq 1$, with $\alpha_i \in (N \cup T)^+$, $\beta_p \in (N \cup T)^*$, $1 \leq i \leq n$. m is a member of P and a 'matrix' of P.

G is a matrix grammar of type i, where $i \in \{0, 1, 2, 3\}$, if and only if the grammar $G_m = (N, T, m, S)$ is of type i for every $m \in P$. Similarly, G is ε-free if each G_m is ε-free.

Definition 13.1 *Let $G = (N, T, P, S)$ be α matrix grammar. For any two strings $u, v \in (N \cup T)^+$, we write $u \underset{G}{\Rightarrow} v$ (or $u \Rightarrow v$ if there is no confusion on G), if and only if there are strings $u_0, u_1, u''_2, ..., u_n$ in $(N \cup T)^+$ and a matrix $m \in M$ such that $u = u_0$, $u_n = v$ and*

$$u_{i-1} = u'_{i-1} x_i u''_{i-1}, \, u_i = u'_{i-1} y_i u''_{i-1}$$

for some u'_{i-1}, u''_{i-1} for all $0 \leq i \leq n - 1$ and $x_i \rightarrow y_i \in m, 1 \leq i \leq n$.

Clearly, any direct derivation in a matrix grammar G corresponds to an n-step derivation by $G_m = (N, T, m, S)$. That is, the rules in m are used in sequence to reach v. $\overset{*}{\Rightarrow}$ is the reflexive, transitive closure of $\Rightarrow$ and

$$L(G) = \{w/w \in T^*, S \overset{*}{\Rightarrow} w\}$$

Definition 13.2 *Let $G = (N, T, P, S)$ be a matrix grammar. Let F be a subset of rules of M. We now use the rules of F such that, the rules in F can be passed over if they cannot be applied, whereas the other rules in any matrix $m \in P$, not in F must be used. That is, for $u, v \in (N \cup T)^+$, $u \Rightarrow v$, if and only if there are strings $u_0, u_1, ..., u_n$ and a matrix $m \in M$ with rules $\{r_1, \overset{m}{r_2}, ..., r_n\}$ (say), with r_i: $x_i \rightarrow y_i, 1 \leq i \leq n$. Then, either $u_{i-1} = u'_{i-1}x_iu''_{i-1}, u_i = u'_{i-1}y_iu''_{i-1}$ or the rule $x_i \rightarrow y_i \in F$. Then $u_i = u_{i-1}$.*

This restriction by F on any derivation is denoted as $\underset{ac}{\Rightarrow}$, where 'ac' stands for 'appearance checking' deviation mode. Then,

$$L(G, F) = \{w/S \underset{ac}{\overset{*}{\Rightarrow}} w, \ w \in T^*\}$$

Let $\mathcal{M}(\mathcal{M}_{ac})$ denote the family of matrix languages without appearance checking (with appearance checking) of type 2 without ε-rules.

Let $\mathcal{M}^\lambda(\mathcal{M}_{ac}^\lambda)$ denote the family of matrix languages without appearance checking (with appearance checking) of type 2 with ε-rules.

Example 13.1 Let $G = (N, T, P, S)$ be a matrix grammar where

$N = \{S, A, B, C, D\}$
$T = \{a, b, c, d\}$
$P = \{P_1, P_2, P_3, P_4\}$, where
$P_1: [S \rightarrow ABCD]$
$P_2: [A \rightarrow aA, B \rightarrow B, C \rightarrow cC, D \rightarrow D]$
$P_3: [A \rightarrow A, B \rightarrow bB, C \rightarrow C, D \rightarrow dD]$
$P_4: [A \rightarrow a, B \rightarrow b, C \rightarrow c, D \rightarrow d]$

Some sample derivations are:

$$S \underset{P_1}{\Rightarrow} ABCD \underset{P_2}{\Rightarrow} aABcCD \underset{P_4}{\Rightarrow} aabccd$$

$$S \underset{P_1}{\Rightarrow} ABCD \underset{P_2}{\Rightarrow} aABcCD \underset{P_3}{\Rightarrow} aAbBcCdD \underset{P_4}{\Rightarrow} aabbccdd$$

We can see that the application of matrix P_2 produces an equal number of a's and c's, application of P_3 produces an equal number of b's and d's. P_4 terminates the derivation. Clearly, $L(G) = \{a^n b^m c^n d^m | n, m \geq 1\}$.

The rules in each matrix are context-free, but the language generated is context-sensitive and not context-free.

Example 13.2 Let $G = (N, T, P, S)$ be a matrix grammar with

$N = \{S, A, B, C\}$
$T = \{a, b\}$
$P = \{P_1, P_2, P_3, P_4, P_5\}$,
where
$P_1: [S \to ABC]$
$P_2: [A \to aA, B \to aB, C \to aC]$
$P_3: [A \to bA, B \to bB, C \to bC]$
$P_4: [A \to a, B \to a, C \to a]$
$P_5: [A \to b, B \to b, C \to b]$

Some sample derivations are:

$$S \underset{P_1}{\Rightarrow} ABC \underset{P_2}{\Rightarrow} aAaBaC \underset{P_3}{\Rightarrow} abAabBabC \underset{P_4}{\Rightarrow} abaabaaba$$

$$S \underset{P_1}{\Rightarrow} ABC \underset{P_3}{\Rightarrow} bAbBbC \underset{P_2}{\Rightarrow} baAbaBbaC \underset{P_5}{\Rightarrow} babbabbab$$

Clearly, $L(G) = \{www | w \in \{a, b\}^+\}$.

Programmed Grammar

A programmed grammar is a 4-tuple $G = (N, T, P, S)$, where N, T, and S are as in any Chomsky grammar. Let R be a collection of re-writing rules over $N \cup T$, $lab(R)$ being the labels of R. σ and φ are mappings from $lab(R)$ to $2^{lab}(R)$

$$P = \{(r, \sigma(r), \varphi(r)) | r \in R\}$$

Here, G is said to be type i, or ε-free if the rules in R are all type i, where $i = 0, 1, 2, 3$ or ε-free, respectively.

Definition 13.3 *For any x, y over $(N \cup T)^*$, we define derivation as below:*

(i) *$(u, r_1) \Rightarrow (v, r_2)$ if and only if $u = u_1 x u_2$, $v = u_1 y u_2$ for u_1, u_2 are over $N \cup T$ and $(r_1 : x \to y, \sigma(r_1), \varphi(r_1)) \in P$ and $r_2 \in \sigma(r_1)$ and*

(ii) *$(u, r_1) \underset{ac}{\Rightarrow} (v, r_2)$ if and only if $(u, r_1) \Rightarrow (v, r_2)$ holds, or else $u = v$ if r_1: $(x \to y, \sigma(r_1), \varphi(r_1))$ is not applicable to u, i.e., x is not a subword of u and $r_2 \in \varphi(r_1)$. Thus, $\Rightarrow$ only depends on φ.*

Here, $\sigma(r)$ is called the $\overset{ac}{\text{success}}$ field as the rule with label r is used in the derivation step. $\varphi(r)$ is called the failure field as the rule with label r cannot be applied and we move on to a rule with label in $\varphi(r)$. $\overset{*}{\Rightarrow}$, $\overset{*}{\underset{ac}{\Rightarrow}}$ are the reflexive and transitive closures of $\Rightarrow$, and $\underset{ac}{\Rightarrow}$, respectively.

The language generated is defined as follows:

$$L(G, \sigma) = \{w | w \in T^*, (S_1, r_1) \overset{*}{\underset{ac}{\Rightarrow}} (w, r_2) \text{ for some } r_1, r_2 \in lab(P)\}.$$

$$L(G, \sigma, \varphi) = \{w | w \in T^*, (S_1, r_1) \underset{ac}{\overset{*}{\Rightarrow}} (w, r_2) \text{ for some } r_1, r_2 \in lab(P)\}.$$

Let $\mathcal{P}(\mathcal{P}_{ac})$ denote the family of programmed languages without (with) appearance checking of type 2 without ε-rules.

Let $\mathcal{P}^\lambda(\mathcal{P}_{ac}^\lambda)$ denote the family of programmed languages without (with) appearance checking of type 2 with ε-rules.

Example 13.3   Let $G = (N, T, P, S)$ be a programmed grammar with

$N = \{S, A, B, C, D\}$
$T = \{a, b, c, d\}$
P:

	r	$\sigma(r)$	$\varphi(r)$
1.	$S \rightarrow ABCD$	2, 3, 6	ϕ
2.	$A \rightarrow aA$	4	ϕ
3.	$B \rightarrow bB$	5	ϕ
4.	$C \rightarrow cC$	2, 3, 6	ϕ
5.	$D \rightarrow dD$	2, 3, 6	ϕ
6.	$A \rightarrow a$	7	ϕ
7.	$B \rightarrow b$	8	ϕ
8.	$C \rightarrow c$	9	ϕ
9.	$D \rightarrow d$	ϕ	ϕ

Let $lab(F) = \{1, 2, 3, 4, 5, 6, 7, 8, 9\}$.
Some sample derivations are:

$$S \underset{1}{\Rightarrow} ABCD \underset{6}{\Rightarrow} aBCD \underset{7}{\Rightarrow} abCD \underset{8}{\Rightarrow} abcD \underset{9}{\Rightarrow} abcd$$

$$S \underset{1}{\Rightarrow} ABCD \underset{2}{\Rightarrow} aABCD \underset{4}{\Rightarrow} aABcCD \underset{6}{\Rightarrow} aaBcCD \underset{7}{\Rightarrow} aabcCD \underset{8}{\Rightarrow} aabccD \underset{9}{\Rightarrow}$$
$aabccd$.

$L(G) = \{a^n b^m c^n d^m | n, m \geq 1\}$

Example 13.4   Let $G = (N, T, P, S)$ be a programmed grammar with:

$N = \{S, A, B, C\}$
$T = \{a, b\}$
P:

	r	σ	φ
1.	$S \rightarrow ABC$	2, 5, 8, 11	ϕ
2.	$A \rightarrow aA$	3	ϕ
3.	$B \rightarrow aB$	4	ϕ
4.	$C \rightarrow aB$	2, 5, 8, 11	ϕ
5.	$A \rightarrow bA$	6	ϕ

6.	$B \rightarrow bB$	7	ϕ
7.	$C \rightarrow cB$	2, 5, 8, 11	ϕ
8.	$A \rightarrow a$	9	ϕ
9.	$B \rightarrow a$	10	ϕ
10.	$C \rightarrow a$	ϕ	ϕ
11.	$A \rightarrow b$	12	ϕ
12.	$B \rightarrow b$	13	ϕ
13.	$C \rightarrow b$	ϕ	ϕ

$L(G) = \{www | w \in \{a, b\}^+\}$.

Random Context Grammar

A random context grammar has two sets of nonterminals X, Y where the set X is called the permitting context and Y is called the forbidding context of a rule $x \rightarrow y$.

Definition 13.4 $G = (N, T, P, S)$ *is a random context grammar where N, T, S are as in any Chomsky grammar, where*

$P = \{(x \rightarrow y, X, Y) | x \rightarrow y$ *is a rule over $N \cup T$, X, Y are subsets of N*$\}$.
We say $u \Rightarrow v$ if and only if $u = u'xu''$, $v = u'yu''$ for u', u'' over $N \cup T$ and $(x \rightarrow y, X, Y) \in P$ such that all symbols X appear in $u'u''$ and no symbol of Y appears in $u'u''$. $\overset{*}{\Rightarrow}$ is the reflexive, transitive closure of $\Rightarrow$.

$$L(G) = \{w : S \overset{*}{\Rightarrow} w, w \in T^*\}.$$

As before, L is of type i, whenever G with rules $x \rightarrow y$ in P are of type i, $i = 0, 1, 2, 3$, respectively.

Example 13.5   Consider the random context grammar $G = (N, T, P, S)$, where:

$N = \{S, A, B, C\}$
$T = \{a\}$
$P = \{(S \rightarrow AA, \phi, \{B, D\}),$
$(A \rightarrow B, \phi, \{S, D\}),$
$(B \rightarrow S, \phi, \{A, D\}),$
$(A \rightarrow D, \phi, \{S, B\}),$
$(D \rightarrow a, \phi, \{S, A, B\})\}$.
Some sample derivations are:
$S \Rightarrow AA \Rightarrow DA \Rightarrow DD \Rightarrow aD \Rightarrow aa$
$S \Rightarrow AA \Rightarrow BA \Rightarrow BB \Rightarrow SB \Rightarrow SS$

$\qquad \Rightarrow AAS \Rightarrow AAAA \overset{*}{\Rightarrow} a^4$
$L(G) = \{a^{2n} | n \geq 1\}$.

Time-Varying Grammar

Given a grammar G, one can think of applying set of rules only for a particular period. That is, the entire set of rules in P is not available at any step of a derivation. Only a subset of P is available at any time 't' or at any i-th step of a derivation.

Definition 13.5 *A time-varying grammar of type i, $0 \leq i \leq 3$, is an ordered pair (G, ϕ) where $G = (N, T, P, S)$ is a type i grammar, and ϕ is a mapping of the set of natural numbers into the set of subsets of P. $(u, i) \Rightarrow (v, j)$ holds if and only if:*

1. *$j = i + 1$ and*

2. *there are words u_1, u_2, x, y over $N \cup T$ such that $u = u_1 x u_2$, $v = u_1 y u_2$ and $x \rightarrow y$ is a rule over $N \cup T$ in $\phi(i)$.*

$\overset{*}{\Rightarrow}$ *be the reflexive, transitive closure of $\Rightarrow$ and*

$$L(G, \phi) = \{w \mid (S, 1) \overset{*}{\Rightarrow} (w, j) \text{ for some } j \in N, w \in \text{'}$$

A language L is time varying of type i if and only if for some time-varying grammar (G, ϕ) is of type i with $L = L(G, \phi)$.

Definition 13.6 *Let (G, ϕ) be a time-varying grammar. Let F be a subset of the set of productions P. A relation $\underset{ac}{\Rightarrow}$ on the set of pairs (u, j), where u is a word over $N \cup T$ and j is a natural number which is defined as follows:*

$(u, j_1) \Rightarrow (v, j_2)$ *holds, if*
$(u, j_1) \underset{ac}{\Rightarrow} (v, j_2)$ *holds, or else,*
$j_2 = j_1 + 1$, *$u = v$, and for no production*
$x \rightarrow y$ *in $F \cap \phi(j_1)$, x is a subword of u.*

$\underset{ac}{\overset{*}{\Rightarrow}}$ *is the reflexive, transitive closure of $\Rightarrow$. Then, the language generated by (G, ϕ) with appearance checking for productions in F is defined as:*

$$L_{ac}(G, \phi, F) = \{w \mid w \in T^* \mid (S, 1) \underset{ac}{\overset{*}{\Rightarrow}} (w, j) \text{ for some } j\}$$

The family of languages of this form without appearance checking when the rules are context-free (context-free and ε-free) and ϕ is a periodic function are denoted as $\mathcal{I}^\lambda$ and $\mathcal{I}$, respectively. With appearance checking, they are denoted as $\mathcal{T}_{ac}^\lambda$ and $\mathcal{I}_{ac}$, respectively.

Example 13.6 Let (G, ϕ) be a periodically time-varying grammar with

$G = (N, T, P, S)$, where
$N = \{S, X_1, Y_1, Z_1, X_2, Y_2, Z_2\}$
$T = \{a, b\}$
$P = \phi(1) \cup \phi(2) \cup \phi(3) \cup \phi(4) \cup \phi(5) \cup \phi(6)$ where
$\phi(1) = \{S \rightarrow a X_1 a Y_1 a Z_1, \ S \rightarrow b X_1 b Y_1 b Z_1, \ X_1 \rightarrow X_1, \ Z_2 \rightarrow Z_2\}$

$\phi\,(2) = \{X_1 \rightarrow aX_1,\ X_1 \rightarrow bX_2, X_2 \rightarrow aX_1, X_2 \rightarrow bX_2,\ X_1 \rightarrow \varepsilon, X_2 \rightarrow \varepsilon\}$

$\phi\,(3) = \{Y_1 \rightarrow aY_1,\ Y_1 \rightarrow bY_2,\ Y_2 \rightarrow aY_1, Y_2 \rightarrow bY_2,\ Y_1 \rightarrow \varepsilon,\ Y_2 \rightarrow \varepsilon\}$

$\phi\,(4) = \{Z_1 \rightarrow aZ_1,\ Z_1 \rightarrow bZ_2,\ Z_2 \rightarrow aZ_1,\ Z_2 \rightarrow bZ_2,\ Z_1 \rightarrow \varepsilon,\ Z_2 \rightarrow \varepsilon\}$

$\phi\,(5) = \{X_2 \rightarrow X_2, Y_1 \rightarrow Y_1\}$

$\phi\,(6) = \{Y_2 \rightarrow Y_2, Z_1 \rightarrow Z_1\}$

Some sample derivations are:

$(S, 1) \Rightarrow (aX_1 aY_1 aZ_1,\ 2) \Rightarrow (aaY_1 aZ_1,\ 3) \Rightarrow (aaaZ_1,\ 4) \Rightarrow (aaa, 5)$

$(S, 1) \Rightarrow (bX_1 bY_1 bZ_1,\ 2) \Rightarrow (baX_1 bY_1 bZ_1,\ 3) \Rightarrow (baX_1 baY_2 bZ_1,\ 4)$

$\Rightarrow (baX_1 baY_1 baZ_1,\ 5) \Rightarrow (baX_1 baY_1 baZ_1,\ 6) \Rightarrow (baX_1 baY_1 baZ_1,\ 7)$

$\Rightarrow (baX_1 baY_1 baZ_1,\ 8) \Rightarrow (babaY_1 baZ_1,\ 9) \Rightarrow (bababaZ_1,\ 10) \Rightarrow (bababa, 11)$

Here, $L(G, \phi) = \{www | w \in \{a, b\}^+\}$.

Example 13.7   Let (G, ϕ) be a periodically time-varying grammar with

$G = (N, T, P, S)$, where:

$N = \{A, B, C, D, S, A_1,\ A_2,\ B_1,\ B_2,\ C_1,\ C_2,\ D_1,\ D_2\}$

$T = \{a, b, c, d\}$

$P: \bigcup_{i=1}^{8} \phi\,(i)$, where

$\phi\,(1) = \{S \rightarrow aAbBcCdD, D_1 \rightarrow D, A_2 \rightarrow A\}$

$\phi\,(2) = \{A \rightarrow aA_1, A_1 \rightarrow A_2, A \rightarrow \varepsilon\}$

$\phi\,(3) = \{B \rightarrow B_1, B \rightarrow bB_2, B \rightarrow \varepsilon\}$

$\phi\,(4) = \{C \rightarrow cC_1, C \rightarrow C_2, C \rightarrow \varepsilon\}$

$\phi\,(5) = \{D \rightarrow D_1, D \rightarrow dD_2, D \rightarrow \varepsilon\}$

$\phi\,(6) = \{A_1 \rightarrow A, B_2 \rightarrow B\}$

$\phi\,(7) = \{B_1 \rightarrow B, C_2 \rightarrow C\}$

$\phi\,(8) = \{C_1 \rightarrow C, D_2 \rightarrow D\}$

$L(G, \phi) = \{a^n b^m c^n d^m | n, m \geq 1\}$.

Regular Control Grammars

Let G be a grammar with production set P and $lab(P)$ be the labels of productions of P. To each derivation D, according to G, there corresponds a string over $lab(P)$ (the so-called control string). Let C be a language over $lab(P)$. We define a language L generated by a grammar G such that every string of L has a derivation D with a control string from C. Such a language is said to be a controlled language.

Definition 13.7   *Let $G = (N, T, P, S)$ be a grammar. Let $lab(P)$ be the set of labels of productions in P. Let F be a subset of P. Let D be a derivation of G and K be word over $lab(P)$. K is a control word of D, if and only if one of the following conditions are satisfied:*

1. *for some string u, v, u_1, u_2, x, y over $N \cup T$, D: $u \Rightarrow v$ and $K = f$, where $u = u_1 x u_2$, $v = u_1 y u_2$ and $x \rightarrow y$ has a label f.*

2. *for some u, x, y, D is a derivation of a word 'u' only and K = ε or else K = f, where x→y has a label f ∈ F and x is not a subword of u.*

3. *for some* u, v, w, K_1, K_2, D *is a derivation* $u \overset{*}{\Rightarrow} v \overset{*}{\Rightarrow} w$, *where* $K = K_1 K_2$ *and u* $\overset{*}{\Rightarrow} v$ *uses* K_1 *as control string and* $v \overset{*}{\Rightarrow} w$ *uses* K_2 *as control string.*

Let C be a language over the alphabet lab(P). The language generated by G with control language C with appearance checking rules F is defined by:

$$L_{ac}(G, C, F) = \{w \in T^* \mid D: S \overset{*}{\Rightarrow} w, D \text{ has a control word } K \text{ of } C\}$$

If $F = \phi$, the language generated is without appearance checking and denoted by $L(G, C)$.

Whenever C is regular and G is of type i, where $i = 0, 1, 2, 3$, then G is said to be a regular control grammar of type i.

Let $\mathcal{L}(i, j, k)$ denote a family of type i languages with type j control with $k = 0, 1$. $k = 0$ denotes without appearance checking; $k = 1$ denotes with appearance checking.

Example 13.8 Let $G = (N, T, P, S)$ be a regular control grammar where

$N = \{A, B, C, D, S\}$
$T = \{a, b, c, d\}$
P:

1. $S \rightarrow ABC$
2. $A \rightarrow aA$
3. $B \rightarrow bB$
4. $C \rightarrow cC$
5. $D \rightarrow dD$
6. $A \rightarrow a$
7. $B \rightarrow b$
8. $C \rightarrow c$
9. $D \rightarrow d$

Then, $lab(P) = \{1, 2, 3, 4, 5, 6, 7, 8, 9\}$
Let $K = 1(24)^*(35)^*6789$. Clearly, K is regular. Then,

$$L(G, K) = \{a^n b^m c^n d^m \mid n, m \geq 1\}$$

Some sample derivations are:
For $u = 124356789 \in K$,

$$S \underset{1}{\Rightarrow} ABCD \underset{2}{\Rightarrow} aABCD \underset{4}{\Rightarrow} aABcCD \underset{3}{\Rightarrow} aAbBcCD \underset{5}{\Rightarrow} aAbBcCdD \underset{6}{\Rightarrow}$$

$$aabBcCdD \underset{7}{\Rightarrow} aabbcCdD \underset{8}{\Rightarrow} aabbccdD \underset{9}{\Rightarrow} aabbccdd.$$

If $u = 124246789 \in K$,

$$S \underset{1}{\Rightarrow} ABCD \underset{2}{\Rightarrow} aABCD \underset{4}{\Rightarrow} aABcCD \underset{2}{\Rightarrow} aaABcCD \underset{4}{\Rightarrow} aaABccCD \underset{6}{\Rightarrow}$$

$$aaaBccCD \underset{7}{\Rightarrow} aaabccCD \underset{8}{\Rightarrow} aaabcccD \underset{9}{\Rightarrow} aaabcccd$$

Example 13.9 Let $G = (N, T, P, S)$ be a grammar with:

$N = \{S, A, B, C\}$
$T = \{a, b\}$
P:

  1. $S \to ABC$
  2. $A \to aA$
  3. $B \to aB$
  4. $C \to aC$
  5. $A \to bA$
  6. $B \to bB$
  7. $C \to bC$
  8. $A \to a$
  9. $B \to a$
 10. $C \to a$
 11. $A \to b$
 12. $B \to b$
 13. $C \to b$
and $lab(P) = \{1, 2, \ldots, 13\}$.
Let $K = 1(234 + 567)^*(89(10) + (11)(12)(13))$ be a regular control on G.

$$L(G, K) = \{www | w \in \{a, b\}^+\}$$

Theorem 13.1 *The family of languages generated by type i grammars, with regular control and with appearance checking is equal to $\mathcal{L}_i$, for $i = 0, 3$.*

The following table consolidates the inclusion relation among the families of regular control languages.

i	$\mathcal{L} = \mathcal{L}(i, 3, 0)$	$\mathcal{L} = \mathcal{L}(i, 3, 1)$
0	$\mathcal{L} = \mathcal{L}_0$	$\mathcal{L} = \mathcal{L}_0$
1	$\mathcal{L} = \mathcal{L}_1$	$\mathcal{L} = \mathcal{L}_1$
2	$\mathcal{L}_2 \subseteq \mathcal{L}$	$\mathcal{L} = \mathcal{L}_0$
3	$\mathcal{L} = \mathcal{L}_3$	$\mathcal{L} = \mathcal{L}_3$

We state some results without proof.

Theorem 13.2 *The family of languages generated (with appearance checking) by type i matrix grammars, the family of languages generated (with appearance* *checking) by type i periodically, time-varying grammars and the family of languages generated (with appearance checking) by type i programmed grammars are equal to the family of languages $\mathcal{L}_i$ of type i for $i = 0, 1, 3$.*

As we have seen earlier, $\mathcal{M}_{ac}^\lambda$, $\mathcal{M}_{ac}$, $\mathcal{M}^\lambda$, and $\mathcal{M}$ denote the family of context-free matrix languages with appearance checking and ε-rules, without appearance checking and but with ε-rules, and without appearance checking and without ε-rules. $\mathcal{T}_{ac}^\lambda$, $\mathcal{T}_{ac}$, $\mathcal{T}^\lambda$, and $\mathcal{T}$ denote the corresponding families of context-free periodically time-varying languages. $\mathcal{P}_{ac}^\lambda$, $\mathcal{P}_{ac}$, $\mathcal{P}^\lambda$, and $\mathcal{P}$ denote the corresponding families of programmed languages.

Let

$$\mathcal{R}_{ac}^\lambda = \mathcal{L}(2,3,1)$$
$$\mathcal{R}_{ac} = \mathcal{L}(2-\lambda,3,1)$$
$$\mathcal{R}^\lambda = \mathcal{L}(2,3,0)$$
$$\mathcal{R} = \mathcal{L}(2-\lambda,3,0)$$

Theorem 13.3

$$\mathcal{M}_{ac}^\lambda = \mathcal{P}_{ac}^\lambda = \mathcal{T}_{ac}^\lambda = \mathcal{R}_{ac}^\lambda = \mathcal{L}_0$$
$$\mathcal{M}^\lambda = \mathcal{P}^\lambda = \mathcal{T}^\lambda = \mathcal{R}^\lambda$$
$$\mathcal{M}_{ac} = \mathcal{P}_{ac} = \mathcal{T}_{ac} = \mathcal{R}_{ac}$$
$$\mathcal{M} = \mathcal{P} = \mathcal{T} = \mathcal{R}$$

Indian Parallel Grammars

In the definition of matrix, programmed, time-varying, regular control, and random context grammars, only one rule is applied at any step of derivation. In this section, we consider parallel application of rules in a context-free grammars (CFG).

Definition 13.8 *An Indian parallel grammar is a 4-tuple $G = (N, T, P, S)$ where the components are as defined for a CFG. We say that $x \Rightarrow y$ holds in G for strings x, y over $N \cup T$, if*

$x = x_1 A x_2 A \dots A x_n A x_{n+1}$, $A \in N$, $x_i \in (N \cup T) - \{A\})^*$ for $1 \leq i \leq n+1$.
$y = x_1 w x_2 w \dots w x_n w x_{n+1}$, $A \rightarrow w \in P$.
i.e., if a sentential form x has n occurrences of the nonterminal A, and if $A \rightarrow w$ is to be used it is applied to all A's in x simultaneously. $\overset{*}{\Rightarrow}$ is the reflexive, transitive closure of $\Rightarrow$.

$$L(G) = \{w \mid w \in T^*, S \overset{*}{\Rightarrow} w\}$$

Example 13.10 We consider the Indian parallel grammar:

$$G = (\{S\}, \{a\}, \{S \to SS, S \to a\}, S).$$

Some sample derivations are:

$S \Rightarrow a$,

$S \Rightarrow SS \Rightarrow aa$,

$S \Rightarrow SS \Rightarrow SSSS \Rightarrow aaaa$ and

$L(G) = \{a^{2^n}/n \geq 0\}$.

It is clear from this example that some non-context-free languages can be generated by Indian parallel grammars.

The other way round, the question is: Can all context-free languages (CFL) be generated by Indian parallel grammars? Since the first attempt to solve this was made in (Siromoney and Krithivasan, 1974), this type of grammar is called an Indian parallel grammar. We state the following theorem without proof.

Theorem 13.4 *The Dyck language (which is a CFL) cannot be generated by an Indian parallel grammar.*

13.2 Marcus Contextual Grammars

Marcus defined the contextual grammars in 1969. The implicit motivation for these new generative devices were in the concepts of descriptive linguistics. S. Marcus introduced first what are known as 'external contextual grammars (ECG)' and other variants like 'internal contextual grammars (ICG)'; total contextual grammars were developed later. The power of contextual grammars is compared with Chomskian grammars, and some other grammars (Păun, 1997). The research on this branch of formal language theory is well developed now.

In a CFG, rules are always of the form $A \to \alpha$. One understands that the application of the rules to any word containing A does not depend on the context. That is, any word of the form $w_1 A w_2$ will yield $w_1 \alpha w_2$ on application of $A \to \alpha$ once, whereas a CFG will contain rules of the form $w_1 A w_2 \to w_1 \alpha w_2$, which are understood to be sensitive to the contexts w_1 and w_2. That is, one cannot apply this rule to any word containing A as in the case of context-free rule. Thus, in the above-said Chomskian models of re-writing, contexts may or may not play a role for re-writing.

One can see that one can derive a collection of strings from a specified set of rules by means of grammars. That is, grammars are used to compute strings or words. There are various models to generate a set of strings. Contextual grammars are one such models to compute a specified set of strings. In this model, strings are attached to the existing strings to generate longer strings.

13.2.1 Definitions and Examples

Here, we will introduce basic definitions of contextual grammars and illustrate the models with examples.

Definition 13.9 *A contextual grammar with choice is a construct:*

$$G = (V, A, C, \psi),$$

where V is an alphabet, A is a finite language over V, C is a finite subset of $V^* \times V^*$ and $\psi: V^* \to 2^C$.

The strings in A are called the axioms, the elements of C are of the form (u, v) called as contexts. ψ is a selection or choice mapping.

For $x, y \in V^*$, we define:

$x \underset{ex}{\Rightarrow} y$, *if and only if $y = uxv$ for a context $(u, v) \in \psi(x)$ and*

$x \underset{in}{\Rightarrow} y$, *if and only if $x = x_1 x_2 x_3$, $y = x_1 u x_2 v x_3$ and for $x_1, x_2, x_3 \in V^*$, $(u, v) \in \psi(x_2)$*

$\underset{ex}{\Rightarrow}$ *means that the derivation of y from x is direct and external in G. That is the context (u, v) is adjoined externally to x to reach y, provided $\psi(x)$ contains (u, v).*
$\underset{in}{\Rightarrow}$ *means that the derivation of y from x is direct and internal in G. That is, the context (u, v) is inserted as specified by ψ. That is, if $\psi(x_2)$ contains (u, v), if $x = x_1 x_2 x_3$, then y will be $x_1 u x_2 v x_3$.*
As in the derivations of strings in Chomsky grammars, $\underset{ex}{\overset{*}{\Rightarrow}}$, $\underset{in}{\overset{*}{\Rightarrow}}$ are reflexive, transitive closure of $\underset{ex}{\Rightarrow}$, $\underset{in}{\Rightarrow}$ respectively.

$$L(G) = \{x \in V^* \mid w \overset{*}{\underset{\alpha}{\Rightarrow}} x, \text{ for any } w \in A \text{ where } \alpha \in \{ex, in\}\}$$

That is, $L_{ex}(G)$ is the language generated by G in the external mode. Here, G may be called ECG. $L_{in}(G)$ is the language generated by G in the internal mode. Here, G may be called ICG.

Example 13.11 *Consider the grammar $G = (\{a, b\}, \{a\}, \{(a, b)\}, \psi)$, where $\psi(a) = (a, b) = \psi(b)$. Then, the words generated by G as ECG will be: $L_{ex}(G) = \{a, aab\}$ and $L_{in}(G) = \{a, aab, aabab, aaabb, ...\}$. Some sample derivations are:*

$\underset{a}{\uparrow} a \underset{b}{\uparrow} \underset{in}{\Rightarrow} a \underset{a}{\uparrow} a \underset{a}{\uparrow} b \underset{in}{\Rightarrow} aaabb$

$a \underset{in}{\Rightarrow} \underset{a}{\uparrow} a \underset{b}{\uparrow} ab \underset{in}{\Rightarrow} aaba \underset{a}{\uparrow} b \underset{b}{\uparrow} \underset{in}{\Rightarrow} aabaabb$

Remark In the above example, one can see that the same grammar has been taken to act on two different derivation modes. Hence, the languages generated are different.

One can understand that re-writing that happens in contextual grammar depends on the selection mapping ψ. Suppose $\psi(x) = (u, v)$, one can understand that the string x is re-written as uxv. Hence, the contextual grammar can be represented as a 3-tuple $G' = (V, A, P)$, where V and A are as before, P is a finite set of pairs (S, C), where $S \subseteq V^*$, $S \neq \phi$ and C a finite subset of $V^* \times V^*$, called the contexts. The pair (S, C) is called a contextual production or rule. G' is now said to be in modular form. Any contextual grammar has an equivalent modular form and vice versa. The grammar $G' = (V, A, P)$ is said to be the canonical modular variant of a contextual grammar G.

Definition 13.10 *A total contextual grammar is a construct $G = (V, A, C, \psi)$, where V, A, C as in the above definition of contextual grammar. ψ is a mapping $V^* \times V^* \times V^* \to 2^C$.*

$\Rightarrow$ *relation is defined as below:*
$x \Rightarrow y$ iff $x = x_1 x_2 x_3$; $y = x_1 u x_2 v x_3$ where $(u, v) \in \psi(x_1, x_2, x_3)$.
$\overset{*}{\Rightarrow}$ *is the reflexive transitive closure of* $\Rightarrow$.

$$L(G) = \{x \in V^* | w \overset{*}{\Rightarrow} x, w \in A\}.$$

An ECG is a total contextual grammar with $\psi(x_1, x_2, x_3) = \phi$ for all $x_1, x_2, x_3 \in V^*$ with $x_1 x_3 \neq \varepsilon$. If $\psi(x_1, x_2, x_3) = \psi(x'_1, x_2, x'_3)$ for all $x_1, x'_1, x_2, x_2, x_3, x'_3 \in V^*$, in a total contextual grammar, then G is an ICG.

Example 13.12 Let $G = (\{a, b\}, \{aba\}, \{(a, a)\}, \psi)$ be a total contextual grammar, where $\psi(a, b, a) = \{(a, a)\}$, $\psi(x_1, x_2, x_3) = \phi$ where $x_1 \neq a \neq x_3, x_2 \neq b$. Then, some sample derivations are:

$a_\uparrow b_\uparrow a \Rightarrow aa \uparrow b \uparrow aa \Rightarrow aaabaaa.$
Hence, $L(G) = \{a^n ba^n | n \geq 1\}.$

Definition 13.11 *A contextual grammar $G = (V, A, C, \psi)$ is said to be without choice if $\psi(x) = C$ for all $x \in V^*$.*

In such a case, ψ can be ignored and the contextual grammar is simply $G = (V, A, C)$. $\Rightarrow$ and $\overset{*}{\Rightarrow}$ are defined as below:
$\underset{ex}{\Rightarrow} : x \underset{ex}{\Rightarrow} y$ if and only if $y = uxv$ for any $(u, v) \in C$

$\underset{in}{\Rightarrow} : x \underset{in}{\Rightarrow} y$ if and only if $x = x_1 x_2 x_3$; $y = x_1 u x_2 v x_3$ for any $(u, v) \in C$.

Example 13.13 *Consider the contextual grammar $G = (\{a, b\}, \{\varepsilon\}, \{a, b\})$. Clearly, G is a grammar without choice.*

$L_{ex}(G) = \{a^n b^n | n \geq 0\}$
whereas $L_{in}(G) = D_{\{a, b\}}$, the Dyck language over $\{a, b\}$. For G, in the external mode, the context (a, b) is always attached outside a word w derived previously. Hence, $L_{ex}(G) = \{a^n b^n | n \geq 0\}$.

For G, in the internal mode, (a, b) is inserted anywhere in the word derived so far.

Notations. Let us represent the languages of contextual grammars in the following way:

1. TC = the family of languages generated by total contextual grammars with choice.
2. $ECC(EC)$ = the family of languages generated by contextual grammars in the external mode with choice (without choice).
3. $ICC(IC)$ = the family of languages generated by contextual grammars in the internal mode with choice (without choice).
4. The families of finite, regular, linear, context-free, context-sensitive, and recursively enumerable-languages are denoted by FIN, REG, LIN, CF, CS, RE, respectively.

13.2.2 Generative Capacity

In this section, we prove some basic results that show the generative power of contextual grammars. In other words, we obtain the relations between families of contextual languages with families in the Chomskian hierarchy.

Theorem 13.5 *Every finite language is a contextual language in (EC).*

Proof Let L be a finite language over an alphabet V. Then, a contextual grammar (V, L, P) with $P = \phi$ generates L.
Converse of the above proposition is not true, as we can see this from some of the previous examples. □

Theorem 13.6 *There exists a contextual language in EC which is not regular.*

Proof Consider the language $L = \{a^n b^n | n \geq 1\}$. Then, the contextual grammar $G = (V, A, P)$, where $V = \{a, b\}$, $A = \{ab\}$, $P = (\phi, (a, b))$ generates L in the external mode. L is not regular but a contextual language in EC. □

Theorem 13.7 *Every ECL is a CFL.*

Proof If L is a contextual language and L is finite, L is in REG.

Suppose L is contextual and L is infinite. Then, there exists a contextual grammar $G = (V, A, P)$ such that $A \neq \phi$, P contains contexts of the form (S_i, C_i), C_i is a non-null context. That is, if $C_i = (u_i, v_i)$ then at least one of u_i, v_i is not ε. Clearly, $S_i = \phi$. Let $C_i = (u_i, v_i)$, $1 \leq i \leq n$ be such contexts.
Let $G' = (N, V, S, P)$ be the CFG with $N = \{S\}$ such that:

1. for $A = \{x_1, \ldots, x_k\}$, P contains the following rules:

$$S \to x_1$$
$$S \to x_2$$
$$\vdots$$
$$S \to x_k$$

2. for $C_i = (u_i, v_i)$, $1 \leq i \leq n$, P contains:

$$S \rightarrow u_1 S v_1$$
$$S \rightarrow u_2 S v_2$$
$$\vdots$$
$$S \rightarrow u_n S v_n$$

Clearly, G' is context-free.

To prove $L(G') \subseteq L(G)$, let $w \in L(G)$. Then, w will be of the form $u_{i_1}^{j_1} u_{i_2}^{j_2} \cdots u_{i_p}^{j_p} X_l u_{i_p}^{j_p} \cdots u_{i_1}^{j_1}$. The contexts (u_{i_1}, u_{i_1}) are, applied j_1 times, (u_{i_2}, u_{i_2}) are applied j_2 times, and so on, $X_l \in A$. Start with rule $S \rightarrow u_{i_1} S u_{i_1}$, apply j_1 times, $S \rightarrow u_{i_2} S u_{i_2}$ apply j_2 times, and so on, and finally apply $S \rightarrow X_l$ once to get w. By re-tracing the argument from the CFG G' to G, one can see that $L(G) \subseteq L(G')$. Hence, $L(G) = L(G')$. □

Remark If L is a CFL and L is infinite, the set of integers which represent the lengths of the strings in L contains an infinite arithmetic progression. The sequence $\{n^2\}$, $n = 1, 2, \cdots$ contains no subsequence which is an infinite arithmetic progression. Hence, $\{a^{n^2} \mid n \geq 1\}$ is not context-free and hence non-external contextual language (non-EC).

Converse of the above theorem is not true.

Theorem 13.8 *There exists a language $L \in REG$ which is not in EC.*

Proof Consider $L = \{a b^m c a b^n \mid n, m \geq 1\}$. It is not difficult to see L being in REG. But L is not in EC. Let there be an ECG $G = (V, A, P)$ generating L in external manner. For $P = \{(S_i, C_i) \mid 1 \leq i \leq n\}$, $S_i = \phi$. Any word generated by G will be of the form:

$$w = u_{i_1}^{j_1} u_{i_2}^{j_2} \ldots u_{i_n}^{h_n} X v_{i_n}^{j_n} \ldots v_{i_1}^{j_1},$$

where $X \in A$, $j_1, j_2, \ldots, j_n$ are positive integers and (u_{i_j}, v_{i_j}) are contexts. Since in any word $w \in L$, c occurs only once and a occurs only twice, they must be in the axiom and the intermediate terms between the two a's belong to X. Hence, X will be of the form:

$$X = Y \, a b^m c a Z,$$

where $Y = \varepsilon$ and Z is of the form b^k. Hence,

$$X = a b^m c a b, \quad m > 0.$$

This implies that A is infinite, which cannot happen. Hence, L is not in EC. □

It follows from Theorem 13.8.

Theorem 13.9 *There exists a CFL which is not in EC.*

In order to compare the variants of contextual grammar among themselves, we need to understand the structure of the strings generated by them. Rather, we would like to discuss some necessary conditions that a contextual language must satisfy. We will first understand such properties. This will also help us to compare the variants of contextual languages among themselves.

Property 1   Let L be a language over V^*. L is said to have external bounded step (*EBS*) property, if there is a constant p such that for each $x \in L$, $|x| > p$, there is a 'y' such that $x = uyv$, and $0 < |uv| \leq p$.

Example 13.14   Let $L = \{a^n b^n | n \geq 1\}$.
Here $p = 2$. Suppose $x = a^n b^n$, then x can be put as $a(a^{n-1} b^{n-1})b$ where $uv = ab$. Hence, L satisfies EBS property.

Property 2   Let L be a language over V. Then L satisfies internal bounded step (*IBS*) property, if there is a constant p such that for each $x \in L$, $|x| > p$, there is $y \in L$ such that $x = x_1 ux_2 vx_3$, $y = x_1 x_2 x_3$ and $0 < |uv| \leq p$.

Example 13.15   Let $L = \{a^n b^m | n, m \geq 1\}$. For $x = a^n b^m = a^{n-2}a(ab)bb^{m-2}$, $y = a^{n-2}(ab)b^{m-2} = a^{n-1}b^{m-1} \in L$, and $p = 2$. Hence, L satisfies IBS property.

Property 3   Let L be a language over V. L is said to satisfy 'bounded length increase' (*BLI*) property, if there is a constant p such that for each $x \in L$, $|x| > p$, there is a $y \in L$ with $0 < |x| - |y| \leq p$.

Example 13.16   Let $L = \{a^n b^n c^n d^n e^n | n \geq 1\}$. This language has a BLI property. For $x = a^n b^n c^n d^n e^n$, $y = a^{n-1}b^{n-1}c^{n-1}d^{n-1}e^{n-1}$ with $|x| - |y| = 5$, and $p = 5$ here.

Remark   If L is a language satisfying both *EBS* and *IBS* property, then it also satisfies *BLI* property. But by our previous example, one can see that the converse need not be true.

Theorem 13.10   *All contextual languages in ICC satisfy IBS property.*

Proof   Let $L \subseteq V^*$ have a contextual grammar $G = (V, A, P)$.
Let $p = \max\{|x| | x \in A\}$, $p' = \max\{|uv| | (u, v) \in C\}$.
Then $\psi(x) = \{(u, v) \in C_i | x_1 ux_2 vx_3 \in L, x_1, x_2, x_3 \in V^*, x \in S_j\}$,
where $(S_j, C_i) \in P$.
Choose $p = \max\{p, p'\}$.
For any $z \in L(G)$, with
$|z| > p$, $z = x'_1 uxvx'_2$ for some
$(u, v) \in C_i$ and $x \in S_i$ such that $(S_i, C_i) \in P$.
Hence, all languages in *ICC* satisfies *IBS* property. $\square$

Example 13.17   Let $L = \{a^n b^n | n \geq 1\}$. Suppose L is in *IC*. Then, there is a contextual grammar without choice mapping. Let it be $G = (\{a, b\}, A, C)$ where C is a collection of contexts. Since $A \subset L$, suppose $ab \in A$. The elements of C must be of the form (a, b) so that inserting this into 'ab' in internal mode we get $a^2 b^2$. In order to get $a^3 b^3$ from this, we can use the same context.

$$i.e., aa_1 b_1 b \underset{in}{\Rightarrow} a^3 b^3$$

Since G is without choice, we get $_\uparrow a_\uparrow abb \Rightarrow a^2 bab^2$ which is not in L. One can attach $(a^2, b^2) \in C$ to get $a^3 b^3$ and also other words like $a^3 ba^2 b^3 \notin L$ are obtained. That is, it is not possible to split a word w as $x_1 x_2 x_3$ such that $x_1 x_2 x_3 = a^n b^n$ and $x_1 ax_2 bx_3 = a^{n+1} b^{n+1}$. Hence, $\{a^n b^n | n \geq 1\} \notin IC$.

Example 13.18   Consider the contextual grammar $G = (\{a, b\}, \{ab\}, P)$, where $P = (S, C)$ with $S = ab$, $C = (a, b)$. The typical internal mode derivatives are:

$$_\uparrow ab_\uparrow \underset{in}{\Rightarrow} a_\uparrow ab_\uparrow b \Rightarrow a^2_\uparrow ab_\uparrow b^2 \Rightarrow aaaabbbb$$

Hence, $L = \{a^n b^n | n \geq 1\} \in ICC$.

Theorem 13.11 $IC \subsetneq ICC$

Proof   Inclusion follows from definitions. For proper inclusion, one can see that $L = \{a^n b^n | n \geq 1\} \notin IC$ but in ICC.   □

Theorem 13.12 $L = \{a^n | n \geq 1\} \cup \{b^n | n \geq 1\}$ is not in EC.

Proof   Suppose L be in EC. Then, there exists a contextual grammar $G = (V, A, C)$ without choice such that $L(G) = L$. Clearly, $V = \{a, b\}$. Since L is infinite, there has to be a recursion, through C generating L. Since A is finite, without loss of generality we may assume $A = \{a, b\}$. To get a^+ from a by external mode, we need contexts like (ε, a) or (a, ε). But as it is a contextual grammar without choice, we get other strings like ba, ab, aba etc., that are not in L. Similar argument holds for b^+. Hence, L cannot be in EC.   □

Example 13.19   Let $G = (V, A, P)$ be a contextual grammar with $V = \{a, b\}$, $A = \{a, b\}$. $P = \{(a^i, (\varepsilon, a)), (b^i, (\varepsilon, b))\}$, for $i \geq 1$ be the choice mapping. That $\psi(a^i) = (\varepsilon, a)$, $i \geq 1$, $\psi(b^i) = (\varepsilon, b)$, $i \geq 1$.

Clearly, in the external mode, $L(G) = \{a^+ \cup b^+\}$.
Some sample derivations are:

$$a \Rightarrow aa \underset{ex}{_\uparrow \Rightarrow} aaa \underset{ex}{_\uparrow \Rightarrow} aaaa$$

$$b \Rightarrow bb \underset{ex}{_\uparrow \Rightarrow} bbb \underset{ex}{_\uparrow \Rightarrow} bbbb$$

Hence, $L(G) \in ECC$.

Theorem 13.13 $EC \subsetneq ECC$.

Proof   Inclusion follows from definition. For proper inclusion, we see that $L = \{a^+ \cup b^+\} \in ECC$ but not EC.   □

Theorem 13.14 $L = \{a^n b^n c^n | n \geq 1\} \notin ICC$.

Proof Suppose $L \in ICC$. Then, there exists an *ICG* G with choice such that $L(G) = L$. Let $G = (V, A, P)$ be such that $V = \{a, b, c\}$. Without loss of generality, let $A = \{abc\}$. P must be constructed suitably to generate $a^n b^n c^n$. That, any word in L is of the form $a^n b^n c^n$ which has to be split suitably so that one can identify the choice word, on both sides of which the context is inserted. Suppose $w = a^n b^n c^n = x_1 x_2 x_3$, such that $x_1 u x_2 v x_3 \in L$ and $x_1 u x_2 v x_3 = a^{n+1} b^{n+1} c^{n+1}$, for $(u, v) \in \psi(x_2)$. But, this implies $x_1 u^i x_2 v^i x_3 \in L$ which is not true for any choice mapping. □

Example 13.20 Consider the *TC* grammar $G = (\{a, b, c\}, A, P)$, where $A = \{abc\}$, $P = (S_i, C_i)$ where $S_i = (a^i, b^i, c^i)$, $C_i = (ab, c)$ for $i \geq 1$. Some sample derivations are: $a_1 b_1 c \Rightarrow aa_1 bb_1 cc \Rightarrow aaabbbccc$.

Clearly, $L(G) = \{a^n b^n c^n | n \geq 1\}$.

Theorem 13.15 $ICC \subsetneq TC$.

Proof Inclusion follows from definitions. For proper inclusion, we can see that $L = \{a^n b^n c^n | n \geq 1\}$ is in TC but not in ICC. □

Theorem 13.16 $L = \{ab^n a | n \geq 1\} \notin ECC$.

Proof Suppose L is in ECC. Then, there exists an ECG $G = (V, A, P)$ with choice generating L. Clearly, $V = \{a, b\}$. Without loss of generality $A = \{aba\}$. Since L is infinite, there exists a word $w \in L$ such that $w = uw'v$ such that $(u, v) \in \psi(w')$ and $w' \in L$. For if $w = ab^n a$, w' has to be chosen such that $w' \in L$ and $uw'v = ab^n a$. This means w' is also of the form $ab^m a$. In such case, w cannot be in L. Hence, L is not in ECC. □

Example 13.21 Consider the *TC* grammar $G = (V, A, P)$, where $V = \{a, b\}$, $A = \{aba\}$, P contains $((a, b, a), (\varepsilon, b))$, $((a, b, b), (\varepsilon, b))$. Then, $L(G) = \{ab^n a | n \geq 1\}$.
Some sample derivations are:

$$a_1 b_1 a \Rightarrow a_1 b_1 ba \Rightarrow a_1 b_1 bba \Rightarrow abbba .$$

Theorem 13.17 $ECC \subsetneq TC$.

Proof Inclusion follows from definitions. For proper inclusion, we see that $\{ab^+ a\}$ is in TC but not in ECC. □

13.2.3 Closure and Decidability Properties of Contextual Languages

We study the closure properties of contextual languages IC, EC, ICC, ECC, and TC. One observes that since the contextual grammars defined do not use nonterminals, these families are not closed under all the operations. Let us first see the statement of a positive result of *TC* without proof (păun, 1997).

Theorem 13.18   *TC is closed under substitution.*

Using this theorem, one can say that *TC* is closed under union, catenation, Kleene +, finite substitution, and morphism. One can see that for a language $L_1 = \{1, 2\}$, $L_2 = \{1, 2\}$, and $L_3 = 1^+$ are in *TC*. Hence, if σ is a substitution with $\sigma(1) = L$, $\sigma(2) = L'$, where L and L' are any arbitrary *TC* languages, $\sigma(L_1) = L \cup L'$, $\sigma(L_2) = LL'$ and $\sigma(L_3) = L^+$. By the above theorem, all these are in *TC*. Closure under morphism follows from the definition of substitution.

Theorem 13.19   *EC, IC, ICC are not closed under union and substitution.*

Proof   Consider $L_1 = \{a^n | n \geq 1\}$ and $L_2 = \{b^n | n \geq 1\}$. $L_1, L_2 \in EC$ (IC). But, we have seen previously, that $L_1 \cup L_2 \notin EC(IC)$.

For non-closure of *ICC*, consider $L_3 = \{a^n b^n | n \geq 1\} \in ICC$. $L_1 \cup L_3 = \{a^n | n \geq 1\} \cup \{a^n b^n | n \geq 1\} \notin ICC$. Since *EC, IC,* and *ICC* are not closed under union, for $L_0 = \{1, 2\}$, with $\sigma(1) = L_1$, $\sigma(2) = L_2$, we get $\sigma(L_0) = L_1 \cup L_2 \notin EC(IC)$. Similarly for *ICC*.   □

One can generate examples to see that none of the families *EC, IC, ICC,* and *ECC* are closed under concatenation. All the closure properties are listed in Table 13.1 and we have given the proof for selected ones.

We consider some basic decidability results of contextual languages.

For all contextual grammars $G = (V, A, P)$ as $L(G)$ includes A, $L(G) \neq \phi$, if and only if A is not empty. Hence, we have:

Table 13.1

	IC	EC	ICC	ECC	TC
Union	No	No	No	Yes	Yes
Intersection	No	No	No	No	No
Complement	No	No	No	No	No
Concatenation	No	No	No	No	Yes
Kleene+	No	No	No	No	Yes
Morphisms	No	Yes	No	Yes	Yes
Finite substitution	No	Yes	No	Yes	Yes
Substitution	No	No	No	No	Yes
Intersection with regular languages	No	No	No	No	No
Inverse morphisms	No	No	No	No	No
Shuffle	No	No	No	No	No
Mirror image	Yes	Yes	Yes	Yes	Yes

Theorem 13.20   *Emptiness problem is decidable for all contextual languages.*

For any external/internal contextual grammar without choice $G = (V, A, P)$, we have seen that if $L(G)$ is infinite then the contexts (α, β) in $C \in P$ must satisfy the condition that at least one of the contexts α, β is not ε, and $A = \phi$. Hence, we have:

Theorem 13.21 *The finiteness problem is decidable for grammars corresponding to languages of IC and EC.*

Theorem 13.22 *The membership problem is decidable for grammars corresponding to languages of IC and EC.*

Proof Let $G = (V, A, P)$ with contexts in P are of the form (ψ, C), where $C = (u, v)$ (say) be an external/internal contextual grammar. $\qquad \square$
Let us construct the following sets recursively.

$K_0(G) = A$
$K_i(G) = \{x \in V^* / w \Rightarrow x \text{ for some } w \in K_{i-1}(G)\} \cup K_{i-1}(G), i \geq 1$.

For a given x over V^*, $x \in L(G)$, if and only if $x \in K_{|x|}(G)$, where $|x|$ is the length of x. Such a computation can be done in a finite number of steps. Hence the result.

One can see from the definitions of *ECC*, *ICC*, and *TC*, the grammars generating them have a choice of mapping which may or may not be computable. Hence, we have:

Theorem 13.23 *The membership problem is undecidable for grammars with arbitrary selection mapping.*

13.3 Lindenmayer Systems

L-systems were defined by Lindenmayer in an attempt to describe the development of multi-cellular organisms. In the study of developmental biology, the important changes that take place in cells and tissues during development are considered. *L*-systems provide a framework within which these aspects of development can be expressed in a formal manner. *L*-systems also provide a way to generate interesting classes of pictures by generating strings and interpreting the symbols of the string as the moves of a cursor.

From the formal language theory point of view, *L*-systems differ from the Chomsky grammars in the following three ways:

(i) Parallel re-writing of symbols is done at every step. This is the major difference.
(ii) There is no distinction between nonterminals and terminals (In extended *L*-system, we try to introduce the distinction).
(iii) Starting point is a string called the axiom.

Definition 13.12 *A 0L system is an ordered triple $\pi = (V, w_0, P)$ where V is an alphabet, w_0 a non-empty word over V which is called the axiom or initial word;*

and P is a finite set of rules of the form $a \rightarrow \alpha$, $a \in V$ and $\alpha \in V^*$. Furthermore, for each $a \in V$, there is at least one rule with a on the left-hand side (This is called the completeness condition).

The binary relation $\Rightarrow$ is defined as follows: If $a_1 \ldots a_n$ is a string over V and $a_i \rightarrow w_i$ are rules in P,

$$a_1 \ldots an \Rightarrow w_1 \ldots w_n$$

$\overset{*}{\Rightarrow}$ is the reflexive transitive closure of $\Rightarrow$. The language generated by the 0L system is:

$$L(\pi) = \{w | w \in V^*, w_0 \overset{*}{\Rightarrow} w\}$$

Definition 13.13 A 0L system $\pi = (V, w_0, P)$ is deterministic if for every $a \in V$, there is exactly o n e rule in P with a on the left-hand side. It is propagating (ε-free), if ε is not on the right-hand side of any production. Notations DOLS, P0LS, and DP0LS are used for these systems.

The languages generated by these systems are called DOL, P0L, and DP0L languages, respectively.

Example 13.22 Consider the following DP0L system:

$$\pi_1 = (\{a, b\}, ab, \{a \rightarrow aa, b \rightarrow bb\})$$

The derivation steps are:
$ab \Rightarrow aabb \Rightarrow aaaabbbb \Rightarrow \cdots$
$L(\pi_1) = \{a^{2^n} b^{2^n} | n \geq 0\}$

Example 13.23 Consider the following DP0L system:

$$\pi_2 = (\Sigma, 4, P),$$

where $\Sigma = \{0, 1, 2, \ldots, 9, (,)\}$
P has rules:
$0 \rightarrow 10$
$1 \rightarrow 32$
$2 \rightarrow 3(4)$
$3 \rightarrow 3$
$4 \rightarrow 56$
$5 \rightarrow 37$
$6 \rightarrow 58$
$7 \rightarrow 3(9)$
$8 \rightarrow 50$
$9 \rightarrow 39$
$(\rightarrow ($
$) \rightarrow)$

The 10 steps in the derivation are given below:

1   4
2   56
3   3758
4   33(9)3750
5   33(39)33(9)3710
6   33(339)33(39)33(9)3210
7   33(3339)33(339)33(39)33(4)3210
8   33(33339)33(3339)33(339)33(56)33(4)3210
9   33(333339)33(33339)33(3339)33(3758)33(56)33(4)3210
10 33(3333339)33(333339)33(33339)33(33(9)3750)33(3758)33(56)33(4)3210

If the symbols are interpreted as steps, cells with the portion within ( ) representing a branch, we get the following growth pattern for each step.

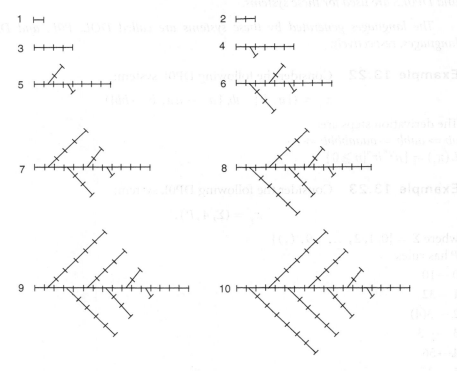

The following hierarchy can be easily seen as:

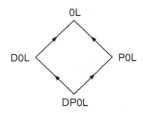

It can be seen that the family of $0L$ languages is not closed under any of the usual operation (*AFL* operation) union, concatenation, Kleene closure, ε-free, homomorphism, intersection with regular sets, and inverse homomorphism. For example, even though $\{a\}$ and $\{aa\}$ are $0L$ languages generated by $0L$ systems with appropriate axioms and rule $a \rightarrow a$, we find their union $\{a, aa\}$ is not a $0L$ language. If it is a $0L$ language, the $0L$ system generating it will have as axiom either a or aa. If a is the axiom, to generate aa, there must be a rule $a \rightarrow aa$, in which case other strings will also be generated. If aa is the axiom, to generate a, we must have $a \rightarrow a$ and $a \rightarrow \varepsilon$, in which case ε will also be generated. In a similar manner, we can give examples for nonclosure under other operations.

This also shows that there are finite languages which are not $0L$.

Theorem 13.24 *Every P0L language is context-sensitive.*

Proof Let $\pi = (V, w_0, P)$ be a *P0L* system. Then, construct a *CSG* to generate: $\{XwX \mid w \in L(\pi), \text{ where } X \notin V\}$.

Let G be the type 1 grammar required, where
$G = (N, T, P, S)$
$N = \{X_0\} \cup \{<a, L>, <a, R> \mid a \in V\} \cup \{<R, X>\}$
$S = X_0$ and P consists of the following rules:

$$
\begin{aligned}
X_0 &\rightarrow Xw_0X \\
Xa &\rightarrow X <a, L> \\
<a, L> b &\rightarrow w_a <b, L> \qquad a \rightarrow w_a \in P \\
<a, L> X &\rightarrow w_a <R, X> \\
a <R, X> &\rightarrow <a, R> X \\
b <a, R> &\rightarrow <b, R> a \\
X <b, R> &\rightarrow Xb
\end{aligned}
$$

Initially, Xw_0X is generated. In one left to right sweep, each symbol in w_0 is replaced by a right-hand side. When the marker L reaches the right X, it changes to R, and by making a right to left sweep, it reaches the left X and the process repeats.

We have shown that if $L \subseteq V^*$ is a *P0L* language, then L' is a type 1 language where $L' = \{XwX \mid w \in L\}$ and $X \notin V$. It can be easily seen that if L' is a *CSL*, then so is L. This follows from a result known as workspace theorem (Salomaa, 1973). $\square$

The following result can be proved even though the proof is slightly more involved.

Theorem 13.25 *Every 0L language is context-sensitive.*

The development rules describing the growth of an organism need not be the same always. For example, the growth of a plant maybe described by a set of rules in daytime and by a different sets of rules during night. There maybe different sets of rules for summer, for winter etc. Hence, this concept is used in tabled systems.

Definition 13.14 *A Tabled 0L (T0L) system is an ordered triple $T\pi = (V, w_0, P)$, where V is an alphabet, w_0 is the axiom and P is a finite set of tables. Each* *table contains rules of the form $a \to \alpha$ for $a \in V$. Each table will have at least one rule with a on the left-hand side for each $a \in V$ (completeness condition). If $\alpha \neq \beta$ is a derivation step $\alpha = a_1 \ldots a_n$, $\beta = \beta_1 \ldots \beta_{ni} a_i \to \beta_i \in t$, where t is a table in P. i.e., in one step only, rules from the same table should be used. $\overset{*}{\Rightarrow}$ is the reflexive transitive closure of $\Rightarrow$. The language generated is:*

$$L(T\pi) = \{w \,|\, w \in V^*, \; w_0 \overset{*}{\Rightarrow} w\}$$

Example 13.24 Consider the *T0L* system:

$T\pi = (\{a\}, \, a, \, \{\{a \to a^2\}, \{a \to a^3\}\})$.
$L(T\pi) = \{a^i \,|\, i = 2^m 3^n \text{ for } m, n \geq 0\}$

A *T0L* system is deterministic, if each table has exactly one rule for each $a \in V$. It is propagating if ε-rules are not allowed. We can hence talk about *DT0L* systems, *PT0L* systems, *DPT0L* systems, and the corresponding languages.

Extended System:
Nondistinction between nonterminals and terminals affected the closure properties. From formal-language theory point of view, extended systems are defined which make the families defined closed under many operations. Here, the system has two sets of symbols, terminals and nonterminals, or total alphabet, and target alphabet.

Definition 13.15 *An E0L system is defined as a 4-tuple $G = (V, \Sigma, w_0, P)$ where (V, w_0, P) is a 0L system and $\Sigma \subseteq V$ is the target alphabet. $\Rightarrow$ and $\overset{*}{\Rightarrow}$ are defined in the usual manner. The language generated is defined as:*

$$L(G) = \{w \,|\, w \in \Sigma^*, \; w_0 \overset{*}{\Rightarrow} w\}.$$

In a similar manner, ET0L systems can be defined by specifying the target alphabet.

Example 13.25 Let G be $(\{S, a\}, \{a\}, S, \{S \to a, \, S \to aa, \, a \to a\})$ be an *E0L* system. The language generated is $\{a, aa\}$ which is not a 0L language.

Systems with Interactions

Definition 13.16 *A 2L system is an ordered 4-tuple $H = (V, w_0, P, \$)$, where V and w_0 are as in 0L system. $\$ \notin V$ is the input from environment and P is a finite set of rules of the form $< a, \, b, \, c > \to w$, $b \in V$, $a, \, c \in V \cup \{\$\}$, $w \in V^*$. $\Rightarrow$ is defined as follows:*

$a_1 \ldots a_n$ is a sentential form and $a_1 \ldots a_n \Rightarrow \alpha_1 \ldots \alpha_n$ if $(a_{i-1}, a_i, a_{i+1}) \to \alpha_i$, is in P for $2 \leq i \leq n-1$, ($\$, a_1, a_2) \to \alpha_1$, $(a_{n-1}, a_n, \$) \to \alpha_n \in P$.

$\overset{*}{\Rightarrow}$ is the reflexive transitive closure of $\Rightarrow$. i.e., for re-writing a symbol, the left and right neighbors are also considered. The language generated is defined as

$L(H) = \{w|w \in V^*, \ w_0 \overset{*}{\Rightarrow} w\}$. *If only the right neighbor (or left neighbor) is considered, it is called a 1L system. i.e., A 2L system is a 1L system if and only if one of the following conditions hold.*

1. *for all a, b, c, d in V, P contains $(a, b, c) \to \alpha$ if and only if P contains $(a, b, d) \to \alpha$ for all $d \in V \cup \{\$\}$ or*
2. *$(a, b, c) - \alpha$ is in P if and only if for all $d \in V \bigcup \{\$\}(d, b, c) \to \alpha$ is in P.*

The corresponding languages are called 2L and 1L languages.

Example 13.26 Consider 2L system:

$$H_2 = (\{a, \ b\}, a, \ P, \ \$)$$

where P is given by:

$$(\$, \ a, \ \$) \to a^2 | a^3 | a^3 b | ba^3$$
$$(x, \ b, \ y) \to b | b^2$$

$$(a, \ a, \ a) \to a$$
$$(a, \ a, \ b) \to a$$
$$(\$, \ a, \ a) \to a$$
$$x, \ y \in \{a, \ b, \ \$\}$$

$$L(H_2) = \{a, \ a^2, \ a^3, \ a^3 b^*, \ b^* a^3\}$$

The hierarchy of the language families generated is shown in the below figure.

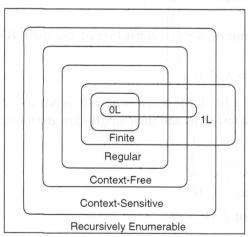

Deterministic 0L systems are of interest because they generate a sequence of strings called *D0L* sequence. The next step generates a unique string. The lengths of the sequence of the strings may define a well-known function. Such a function is called a growth function. Consider the following example.

Example 13.27 Consider the following 0L systems:

1. $S = (\{a\}, a, \{a \to a^2\})$, we have:

   $L(S) = \{a^{2^n} | n \geq 0\}$.

The above language is a $DP0L$-language. The growth function is $f(n) = 2^n$.

2. $S = (\{a, b\}, a, \{a \to b, b \to ab\})$, the words in $L(S)$ are:

   $a, b, ab, bab, abbab, bababbab,\ldots$

The lengths of these words are the Fibonacci numbers.

3. $S = (\{a, b, c\}, a, \{a \to abcc, b \to bcc, c \to c\})$, the words in $L(S)$ are:

   $a, abcc, abccbcccc, abccbccccbccccc,\ldots$

The lengths of these words are the squares of natural numbers.

4. $S = (\{a, b, c\}, a, \{a \to abc, b \to bc, c \to c\})$, the words in $L(S)$ are:

   $a, abc, abcbcc, abcbccbccc, abcbccbcccbcccc,\ldots$

The lengths of these words are the triangular numbers.

5. $S = (\{a, b, c, d\}, a, \{a \to abcd^5, b \to bcd^5, c \to cd^6, d \to d\})$, the words in $L(S)$ are:

   $a, abcd^5, abcd^5bcd^5cd^6d^5,\ldots$

The lengths of these words are the cubes of natural numbers.

Two $D0L$ systems are growth equivalent, if they have the same growth function. Let $\pi = (V, w_0, P)$ be a $D0L$ system. Then, let there be a n-dimensional row vector which is the Parikh mapping of w_0. $M(P)$ is a $n \times n$ matrix whose ith row is the Parikh mapping of α_i, where $a_i \to \alpha_i \in P$. η

is a n-dimensional column vector $\begin{pmatrix} 1 \\ \vdots \\ 1 \end{pmatrix}$ consisting of 1's. Then, $f(n)$, the growth

function is given by $f(n) = \pi M^n \eta$.

Example 13.28 $\pi = (\{a, b, c\}, a, \{a \to abcc, b \to bcc, c \to c\})$.
The strings generated in a few steps and their lengths are given below.

w_0	a	1
step 1	$abcc$	4
step 2	$abccbcccc$	9
step 3	$abccbccccbccccc$	16

It is obvious that $f(n) = (n + 1)^2$
π is $(1, 0, 0)$

M is $\begin{pmatrix} 1 & 1 & 2 \\ 0 & 1 & 2 \\ 0 & 0 & 1 \end{pmatrix}$, η is $\begin{pmatrix} 1 \\ 1 \\ 1 \end{pmatrix}$

$$\pi\, M\eta \ \ is = (1,0,0) \begin{pmatrix} 1 & 1 & 2 \\ 0 & 1 & 2 \\ 0 & 0 & 1 \end{pmatrix} \begin{pmatrix} 1 \\ 1 \\ 1 \end{pmatrix}$$

$$= (1\,0\,0) \begin{pmatrix} 4 \\ 3 \\ 1 \end{pmatrix} = 4$$

$\pi\, M^2 \eta = 9$ and so on.

The growth function $f(n)$ is termed as malignant, if and only if there is no polynomial $p(n)$ such that $f(n) \le p(n)$ for all n.

Applications

L-systems are used for a number of applications in computer imagery. It is used in the generation of fractals, plants, and for object modeling in three dimensions. Applications of L-systems can be extended to reproduce traditional art and to compose music.

Two-Dimensional Generation of Patterns

Here, the description of the pattern is captured as a string of symbols. An L-system is used to generate this string. This string of symbols is then viewed as commands controlling a LOGO-like turtle. The basic commands used are move forward, make right turn, make left turn etc. Line segments are drawn in various directions specified by the symbols to generate the straight-line pattern. Since most of the patterns have smooth curves, the positions after each move of the turtle are taken as control points for B-spline interpolation. We see that this approach is simple and concise.

Fractals Generated by L-systems

Many fractals can be thought of as a sequence of primitive elements. These primitive elements are line segments. Fractals can be coded into strings. Strings that contain necessary information about a geometric figure can be generated by L-systems. The graphical interpretation of this string can be described based on the motion of a LOGO-like turtle.

A state of the turtle is defined as a triplet (x, y, A), where the Cartesian coordinates (x, y) represent the position of the turtle and angle A, called the turtle's heading, is interpreted as the direction in which the turtle is facing. Given the step size d and the angle δ, the turtle can move with respect to the following symbols.

f: Move forward a step length d. The state of the turtle changes to (x', y', A), where $x' = x + d * \cos(A)$ and $y' = y + d * \sin(A)$. A line is drawn between the points (x, y) and (x', y').

F: Move forward as above but without drawing the line.

+: Turn the turtle left by an angle δ. The next state of the turtle will be $(x, y, A + \delta)$. Positive orientation of the angle is taken as anti-clockwise.

−: Turn the turtle as above but in clockwise direction.

Interpretation of a String

Let *S* be a string and (x_0, y_0, A_0) be the initial state of the turtle, and step size *d*, angle increment δ are the fixed parameters. The pattern drawn by the turtle corresponding to the string *S* is called the turtle interpretation of the string *S*.

Consider the following *L* system.

Axiom: $w : f + f + f + f$

production: $f \rightarrow f + f - f - ff + f + f - f$

The above *L*-system is for 'Koch island.'

The images corresponds to the string generated for different derivation steps $n = 0, 1, 2$ is shown in Figure 13.1. The angle increment δ is 90°. The step size *d* could be any positive number. The size of the 'Koch island' depends on the step size and the number of derivation steps.

Koch constructions are a special case of *L*-systems. The initiator corresponds to the axiom in the *L*-system. The generator is represented by the single production.

Interpolation

Consecutive positions of the turtle can be considered as control points specifying a smooth interpolating curve. *B*-spline interpolation is used for most of the kolam patterns (Figure 13.2)

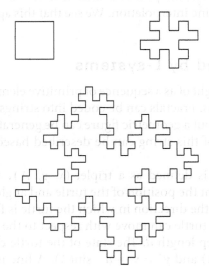

Figure 13.1.   Fractals generated by *L*-system

Figure 13.2. Kolam patterns generated by *L*-system

Candies

Figure 13.2 shows the kolam pattern 'Candies' which can the generated by the following *L*-system.
Axiom: $(-D--D)$
Productions:

$$A \rightarrow f++ffff--f--ffff++f++ffff--f$$
$$B \rightarrow f--ffff++f++ffff--f--ffff++f$$
$$C \rightarrow BfA--BfA$$
$$D \rightarrow CfC--CfC$$

Angle increment = 45°

Generation of Plant Structure

For generating living organisms like plants, a three-dimensional turtle is used. A three-dimensional turtle is different in some respects, compared to the two-dimensional one. It has additional parameters for width and color and is represented by a 6-tuple $< P, H, L, U, w, c>$ where the position vector P represents the turtle's position in cartesian coordinates, and vectors H, L, and U represent the turtle's orientation. w represents the width of the line drawn by the turtle. c corresponds to the color of the lines drawn.

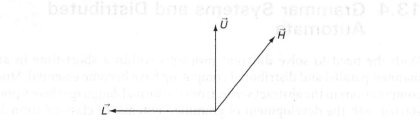

For generating plant-like structures, some special L-systems are used. They are bracketed 2L-systems and stochastic L-system. In bracketed L-systems, brackets are used to separate the branches from the parent stem. In stochastic L-systems, probabilities are attached to the rules which can capture the variations in plant development.

Figure 13.3 gives a few images of plants formed by L-systems.

Figure 13.3.   Some pictures of plants generated by L-systems
(*See color plate on page 418*)

13.4 Grammar Systems and Distributed Automata

With the need to solve different problems within a short-time in an efficient manner, parallel and distributed computing have become essential. Study of such computations in the abstract sense, from the formal-language theory point of view, started with the development of grammar systems. In classical formal-language theory, a language is generated by a single grammar or accepted by a single automaton. They model a single processor or we can say the devices are centralized. Though multi-tape Turing machines (TMs) try to introduce parallelism in a small way, the finite control of the machine is only one. The introduction of distributed computing useful in analyzing computation in computer networks, distributed databases etc., has led to the notions such as distributed parallelism, concurrency, and communication. The theory of grammar systems and the distributed automata are formal models for distributed computing, where these notions could be formally defined and analyzed.

Grammar Systems

A grammar system is a set of grammars working in unison, according to a specified protocol, to generate one language. These are studied to model distribution, to increase the generative power, to decrease the complexity etc. The study of grammar systems probes into the functioning of such system under specific protocols and the influence of various protocols on various properties of the system are considered.

Grammar system can be sequential or parallel. A co-operating distributed (CD) grammar system is sequential. Here, all grammars work on one sentential form. At any instant only one grammar is active. This is called a 'blackboard' model. Suppose a problem is to be solved in a class. The teacher asks one student to start working on the problem on the blackboard. The student writes a few steps, then goes back. Another student comes and continues working on the problem. On his return, a third student comes and continues. The process continues till the problem is solved. Now, the question arises. At what time does one student return and the next one starts? There may be several ways for defining this. Correspondingly, in the CD grammar system, they are different modes of co-operation. The student may return when he is not able to proceed further (terminating mode); he may return at any time ($*$-mode); he may return after doing k-steps ($= k$-mode); he may return after doing k steps or less ($\leq k$-mode); he may return after k or more steps ($\geq k$-mode). The power and properties of CD grammar systems under these different protocols are studied.

A parallel communicating (PC) grammar system is basically a parallel generation of strings by different grammars and putting them together by communication. This is called the "classroom" model. There is a problem which a group of students have to solve. Each student has his own 'notebook' containing the description of a particular subproblem of the given problem. Each student operates only on his own notebook. The leader (master) has the description of the whole problem and decides when the problem is solved. The students communicate on request the contents of their 'notebooks.' The students may communicate with each other either in each step (non-centralized mode) or when the leader requests it (centralized mode). The whole problem is solved is this way. Hence, in PC grammar system each grammar has its own sentential form and communicates it with others on request.

13.4.1 CD Grammar Systems

Definition 13.17 *A CD grammar system of degree $n \geq 1$, is a construct:*

$$GS = (N, T, S, P_1, ..., P_n),$$

where N and T are disjoint alphabets (non-terminals and terminals); $S \in N$ is the start symbol and $P_1, ... P_n$ are finite sets of rewriting rules over $N \cup T$. $P_1, ..., P_n$ are called components of the system.

Another way of specifying a CD grammar system is:

$$GS = (N, T, S, G_1, ..., G_n),$$

where $G_i = (N, T, P_i, S), 1 \leq i \leq n$.

Definition 13.18 *Let $GS = (N, T, S, P_1, ..., P_n)$ be a CD grammar system. We now define different protocols of co-operation:*

1. *Normal mode (∗ mode): $\underset{P_i}{\overset{*}{\Rightarrow}}$ is defined by, $x \underset{P_i}{\overset{*}{\Rightarrow}} y$ without any restriction. The student works on the blackboard as long as he wants.*

2. *Terminating mode (t mode): For each $i \in \{1, ..., n\}$, the terminating derivation by the ith component, denoted by $\underset{P_i}{\overset{t}{\Rightarrow}}$, is defined by $x \underset{P_i}{\overset{t}{\Rightarrow}} y$ if and only if $x \underset{P_i}{\overset{*}{\Rightarrow}} y$ and there is no $z \in (N \cup T)^*$ with $y \underset{P_i}{\Rightarrow} z$.*

3. *$= k$ mode: For each $i \in \{1, ..., n\}$, the k-steps derivation by the ith component, denoted by $\underset{P_i}{\overset{=k}{\Rightarrow}}$, is defined by $x \underset{P_i}{\overset{=k}{\Rightarrow}} y$ if and only if there are $x_1, ..., x_{k+1} \in (N \cup T)^*$ such that $x = x_i, y = x_{k+1}$ and for each $j, 1 \leq j \leq k$*

$$x_j \underset{P_i}{\Rightarrow} x_{j+1}.$$

4. *$\leq k$ mode: For each component P_i, the $\leq k$-steps derivation by the ith component denoted by $\underset{P_i}{\overset{\leq k}{\Rightarrow}}$, is defined by:*

$$x \underset{P_i}{\overset{\leq k}{\Rightarrow}} y \text{ if and only if } x \underset{P_i}{\overset{=k'}{\Rightarrow}} y \text{ for some } k' \leq k.$$

5. *$\geq k$ mode: The $\geq k$ steps of derivation by the ith component, denoted as $\underset{P_i}{\overset{\geq k}{\Rightarrow}}$, is defined by:*

$$x \underset{P_i}{\overset{\geq k}{\Rightarrow}} y \text{ if and only if } x \underset{P_i}{\overset{=k'}{\Rightarrow}} y \text{ for some } k' \geq k.$$

Let $D = \{*, t\} \cup \{\leq k, \geq k, = k | k \geq 1\}$.

Definition 13.19 *The language generated by a CD grammar system $GS = (N, T, S, P_1, ..., P_n)$ in derivation mode $f \in D$ is:*

$$L_f(GS) = \{w \in T^* | S \underset{P_{i_1}}{\overset{f}{\Rightarrow}} \alpha_1 \underset{P_{i_2}}{\overset{f}{\Rightarrow}} \alpha_2 ... \underset{P_{i_m}}{\overset{f}{\Rightarrow}} \alpha_m = w, m \geq 1, 1 \leq i_j \leq n, 1 \leq j \leq m\}.$$

Example 13.29

1. Consider the following CD grammar system:

   $GS_1 = (\{S, X, X', Y, Y'\}, \{a, b, c\}, S, P_1 P_2)$, where

   $P_1 = \{S \to S, S \to XY, X' \to X, Y' \to Y\}$

   $P_2 = \{X \to aX', Y \to bY'c, X \to a, Y \to bc\}$

   If $f = *$ mode, the first component derives $S \Rightarrow XY$, the second component derives from Y, $bY'c$, it can switch to first component or derive $a\,X'$ from X.

   In the first component, X' can be changed to X or Y' can be changed to Y or both. The derivation proceeds similarly.

   It is not difficult to see that the language generated is $\{a^m b^n c^n \backslash m, n \geq 1\}$. The same will be true for t mode, $= 1$ mode, ≥ 1 mode, $\leq k$ mode for $k \geq 1$.

   But, if we consider $= 2$ mode, each component should execute two steps. In the first component, $S \Rightarrow S \Rightarrow XY$. In the second component, $XY \Rightarrow aX'Y \Rightarrow aX'bY'c$. Then, control goes back to component one where X' and Y' are changed to X and Y in two steps. The derivation proceeds in a similar manner. It is easy to see that the language generated by GS_1 in the $= 2$ mode is $\{a^n b^n c^n | n \geq 1\}$. A similar argument holds for ≥ 2-mode also and the language generated is the same.

   At most, two steps of derivation can be done in each component. Hence, in the case of $= k$ or $\geq k$ mode where $k \geq 3$, the language generated is the empty set.

2. $GS_2 = (\{S, A\}, \{a\}, S, P_1, P_2, P_3)$

   $P_1 = \{S \to AA\}$

   $P_2 = \{A \to S\}$

   $P_3 = \{A \to a\}$

   In the $*$ mode, $\{a^n | n \geq 2\}$ is generated as the control can switch from component to component at any time.

   A similar result holds for ≥ 1, $\leq k$ ($k \geq 1$) modes. For $= 1$, $= k$, $\geq k$ ($k \geq 2$), the language generated is empty as $S \to AA$ can be used only once in P_1 and $A \to a$ can be used once in P_3.

   In the t mode, in P_1, $S \Rightarrow AA$ and if the control goes to P_3 from AA, aa is derived. If the control goes to P_2 from AA, SS is derived. Now, the control has to go to P_1 to proceed with the derivation $SS \Rightarrow AAAA$, and if the control goes to P_2, S^4 is derived; if it goes to P_3, a^4 is derived. It is easy to see that the language generated in t mode is $\{a^{2^n} | n \geq 1\}$.

3. $GS_3 = (\{S, X_1, X_2\}, \{a, b\}, S, P_1, P_2, P_3)$, where

   $P_1 = \{S \to S, S \to X_1 X_1, X_2 \to X_1\}$

   $P_2 = \{X_1 \to aX_2, X_1 \to a\}$

   $P_3 = \{X_1 \to bX_2, X_1 \to b\}$

   In $*$ mode, $= 1$, ≥ 1 mode, $\leq k$ mode ($k \geq 2$), t mode the language generated will be $\{w | w \in \{a, b\}^*, |w| \geq 2\}$. In $= 2$ mode, each component has to execute two steps, so the language generated will be $\{ww | w \in \{a, b\}^+\}$.

A similar argument holds for ≥ 2 steps. For $= k$ or $\geq k$ modes ($k \geq 3$), the language generated is empty, as each component can use at most two steps before transferring the control.

We state some results about the generative power without giving proof. The proofs are fairly simple, and can be tried as exercise. It can be easily seen that for CD grammar systems working in any of the modes defined having regular, linear, context-sensitive, or type 0 components, respectively, the generative power does not change; i.e., they generate the families of regular, linear, context-sensitive, or recursively enumerable languages, respectively. But by the example given, we find that CD grammar systems with context-free components can generate context-sensitive languages. Let $CD_n(f)$ denote the family of languages generated by CD grammar systems with ε-free context-free components, the number of components being at most n. When the number of components is not limited, the family is denoted by $CD_\infty(f)$. If ε-rule are allowed the corresponding families are denoted by $CD_n^\varepsilon(f)$ and $CD_\infty^\varepsilon(f)$, respectively.

Theorem 13.26   a. $CD_\infty(f) = CF$, for all $f \in \{=1, \geq 1, {}^*\} \cup \{\leq k | k \geq 1\}$

        b. $CF = CD_1(f) \subseteq CD_2(f) \subseteq CD_r(f) \subseteq CD_\infty(f) \subseteq MAT$, for all $f \in \{= k, \geq k | k \geq 2\}$, $r \geq 3$, where MAT is the family of context-free matrix languages without ε-rules and appearance checking.

        c. $CD_r(= k) \subseteq CD_r(= sk)$, for all k, r, $s \geq 1$.

        d. $CD_r(\geq k) \subseteq CD_r(\geq k + 1)$, for all r, $k \geq 1$.

        e. $CD_\infty(\geq) \subseteq CD_\infty(=)$.

        f. $CF = CD_1(t) = CD_2(t) \subset CD_3(t) = CD_\infty(t) = ET0L$, where $ET0L$ is the family of languages defined by extended, tabled-0L systems.

        g. Except for the inclusion $CD_\infty(f) \subseteq MAT$ all the previous relations are also true for CD grammar system with ε-rules

$$CD_\infty^\varepsilon(f) \subseteq MAT^\varepsilon,$$

where MAT^ε is the family of context-free matrix languages without appearance checking allowing for ε-rules.

The proofs are straight-forward (and not given here).

13.4.2 PC Grammar Systems

Definition 13.20   *A PC grammar system of degree n, $n \geq 1$, is an $(n + 3)$-tuple:*

$$GP = (N, K, T, (S_1, P_1), \ldots, (S_n, P_n)),$$

where N is a non-terminal alphabet, T is a terminal alphabet, $K = \{Q_1, Q_2, \ldots, Q_n\}$ are query symbols. N, T, K are mutually disjoint. P_i is a finite set of rewriting rules over $N \cup K \cup T$, and $S_i \in N$, for all $1 \leq i \leq n$.
Let $V_{GP} = N \cup K \cup T$.

The sets P_i, are called components of the system. The index i of Q_i points to the ith component P_i of GP.

An equivalent representation for GP is $(N, K, T, G_1, \ldots G_n)$, where $G_i = (N \cup K, T, S_i, P_i)$, $1 \leq i \leq n$.

Definition 13.21   *Given a PC grammar system*

$$GP = (N, K, T, (S_1, P_1), \ldots, (S_n, P_n)),$$

as above, for two n-tuples $(x_1, x_2, \ldots, x_n)$, $(y_1, \ldots, y_n)$, with $x_i, y_i \in V_{GP}^*$, $1 \leq i \leq n$, where $x_1 \notin T^*$, we write $(x_1, \ldots, x_n) \Rightarrow (y_1, \ldots, y_n)$ if one of the following two cases holds.

1. *For each i, $1 \leq i \leq n$, $|x_i|_K = 0$ (i.e., no query symbol in x_i), and either $x_i \Rightarrow y_i$ by a rule in P_i or $x_i = y_i \in T^*$.*

2. *There is i, $1 \leq i \leq n$, such that $|x_i|_K > 0$. (i.e., x_i has query symbols). Let for each such i, $x_i = z_1 Q_{i_1} z_2 Q_{i_2} \cdots z_t Q_{i_t} z_{t+1}$, $t \geq 1$ for $z_j \in (N \cup T)^*$, $1 \leq j \leq t + 1$. If $|x_{i_j}|_K = 0$, for all j, $1 \leq j \leq t$, then $y_i = z_1 x_{i_1} z_2 x_{i_2} \cdots z_t x_{i_t} z_{t+1}$ and $y_{i_j} = S_j$ (in returning mode) and $y_{i_j} = x_{i_j}$ (in non-returning mode) $1 \leq j \leq t$. If for some j, $1 \leq j \leq t$, $|x_{i_j}|_K \neq 0$, then $y_i = x_i$. For all i, $1 \leq i \leq n$, such that y_i is not specified above, we have $y_i = x_i$.*
   An n-tuple $(x_1, \ldots, x_n)$ with $x_i \in V_{GP}^*$ is called an instantaneous description (ID) (of GP).
   *Thus an ID $(x_1, \ldots, x_n)$ directly gives rise to an ID $(y_1, \ldots, y_n)$, if either
   (a) component-wise derivation: No query symbol appears in $x_1, \ldots, x_n$; then we have $x_i \Rightarrow y_i$ using a rule in P_i, if x_i has a non-terminal. If $x_i \in T^*$, $y_i = x_i$.
   (b) communication step: Query symbols occur in some x_i. Then, a communication step is performed. Each occurrence of Q_j in x_i is replaced by x_j, provided x_j does not contain query symbols. In essence, a component x_i containing query symbols is modified only when all occurrences of query symbols in it refer to strings without occurrences of query symbols. In this communication step, x_j replaces the query symbol Q_j. After that, G_j resumes starting from axiom (this is called returning mode) or continues from where it was (this is called non-returning mode). Communication has priority over rewriting. No rewriting is possible as long as one query symbol is present in any component. If some query symbols in a component cannot be replaced in a given communication step, it may be possible that they can be replaced in the next step. When the first component (master) has a terminal string derivation stops. $\Rightarrow$ is used to represent both rewriting and communication steps. $\stackrel{*}{\Rightarrow}$ is the reflexive transitive closure of $\Rightarrow$. We write $\Rightarrow_r$ for returning mode. $\Rightarrow_{nr}$ for non-returning mode.*

Definition 13.22 *The language generated by a PC grammar system GP*

1. *in returning mode is:*

$$L_r(GP)\{x \in T^* \mid (S_1, \ldots, S_n) \underset{r}{\overset{*}{\Rightarrow}} (x, \alpha_2, \ldots, \alpha_n), \alpha_p \in V_{GP}^*, 2 \leq i \leq n\}$$

2. *in non-returning mode is:*

$$L_{nr}(GP)\{x \in T^* \mid (S_1, \ldots, S_n) \underset{nr}{\overset{*}{\Rightarrow}} (x, \alpha_2, \ldots, \alpha_n), \alpha_i \in V_{GP}^*, 2 \leq i \leq n\}$$

If a query symbol is present, rewriting is not possible in any component. If circular query occurs, communication will not be possible and the derivation halts without producing a string for the language. Circular query means something like the following: component i has query symbol Q_j; component j has query symbol Q_k; and component k has query symbol Q_i; this is an example of a cycle query.

The first component is called the master and the language consists of terminal strings derived there.

Generally, any component can introduce the query symbols. This is called non-centralized system. If only the first component is allowed to introduce query symbols, it is called a centralized system.

A PC grammar system is said to be regular, linear, context-free, and context-sensitive, depending on the type of rules used in components.

There are a number of results on the hierarchy of PC grammar systems. Csuhaj-Varju et al., (1994) and Dassow and Păun, (1997) give a detailed description of these systems.

Examples 13.30

1. Let $GP_1 = (\{S_1, S_1', S_2, S_3\}, \{Q_1, Q_2, Q_3\}, \{a, b\}, (S_1, P_1), (S_2, P_2), (S_3, P_3)), P_1$ consists of rules:

   1. $S_1 \rightarrow abc$
   2. $S_1 \rightarrow a^2 b^2 c^2$
   3. $S_1 \rightarrow aS_1'$
   4. $S_1 \rightarrow a^3 Q_2$
   5. $S_1' \rightarrow aS$
   6. $S_1' \rightarrow a^3 Q_2$
   7. $S_2 \rightarrow b^2 Q_3$
   8. $S_3 \rightarrow c$

   $P_2 = \{S_2 \rightarrow bS_2\}$

   $P_3 = \{S_3 \rightarrow cS3\}$

$L_r(GP_1) = L_{nr}(GP_1) = \{a^n b^n c^n \mid n \geq 1\}$

This can be seen as follows:

$$\frac{G_1}{S_1} \qquad \frac{G_2}{S_2} \qquad \frac{G_3}{S_3}$$

abc	bS_2	cS_3

- derivation stops abc $\in L_r(GP_1)$, $L_{nr}(GP_1)$

S_1	S_2	S_3
$a^2b^2c^2$	bS_2	cS_3

$a^2b^2c^2 \in L_r(GP_1)$, $L_{nr}(GP_1)$

G_1	G_2	G_3	
S_1	S_2	S_3	
a^3Q_2	bS_2	cS_3	
$a^3b\,S_2$	S_2	$c\,S_3$	
$a^3bb^2Q_3$	bS_2	c^2S_3	
$a^3b^3c^2S_3$	bS_2	S_3	
$a^3b^3c^3$	b^2S_2	cS_3	in returning mode

S_1	S_2	S_3	
a^3Q_2	bS_2	cS_3	
a^3bS_2	bS_2	cS_3	
$a^3bb^2Q_3$	b^2S_2	c^2S_3	
$a^3b^3c^2S_3$	b^2S_2	c^2S_3	
$a^3b^3c^3$	b^3S_2	c^3S_3	in non-returning mode

$a^3b^3c^3 \in L_r(GP_1)$, $L_{nr}(GP_1)$

G_1	G_2	G_3	
S_1	S_2	S_3	
aS_1	bS_2	cS_3	
aa^3Q_3	b^2S_2	c^2S_3	
$a^4b^2S_2$	S_2	c^2S_3	
$a^4b^2b^2Q_3$	bS_2	c^3S_3	
$a^4b^4c^3S_3$	bS_2	S_3	in returning mode
$a^4b^4c^4$	b^2S_2	cS_3	

S_1	S_2	S_3	
aS_1	bS_2	cS_3	
aa^3Q_2	b^2S_2	c^2S_3	
$a^4b^2S_2$	b^2S_2	c^2S_3	
$a^4b^2b^2Q_3$	b^3S_2	c^3S_3	
$a^4b^4c^3\,S_3$	b^3S_2	c^3S_3	in non-returning mode
$a^4b^4c^4$	b^4S_2	c^4S_3	

$a^4b^4c^4 \in L_1(GP_1), L_{nr}(GP_1)$.

2. Let $GP_2 = (\{S_1, S_2\}, \{Q_1, Q_2\}, \{a, b\}, (S_1, P_1,) (S_2, P_2))$, where

$P_1 = \{S_1 \to S_1, S_1 \to Q_1 Q_2\}$
$P_2 = \{S_2 \to aS_2, S_2 \to bS_2, S_2 \to a, S_2 \to b\}$
$L_r(GP_2) = L_{nr}(GP_2) = \{ww | w \in \{a, b\}^+\}$

We see how *abbabb* is derived.

$\dfrac{G_1}{S_1}$	$\dfrac{G_2}{S_2}$	
S_1	aS_2	
S_1	abS_2	
$Q_2 Q_2$	abb	
abbabb	S_2	in returning mode
abbabb	*abb*	in non-returning mode

However, $abbabb \in L_r(GP_1)$, $L_{nr}(GP_1)$

This type of communication is called communication by request. There is also another way of communication known as communication by command (Dassow and Păun, 1997). A restricted version of this communication by command is found useful in characterizing the workload in computer networks (Arthi *et al.*, 2001).

13.4.3 Distributed Automata*

Formal-language theory and automata theory are twins, in the sense that the development of one triggers the other one, so as to make them as close to each other as possible. Hence, we study co-operative distributed automata here. We restrict ourselves to the blackboard or sequential model here (Krithivasan *et al.*, 1999), though there is work on the parallel model also.

Distributed Nondeterministic FSA

Definition 13.23 *An n-FSA is a 5-tuple* $\Gamma = (K, V, \Delta, q_0, F)$ *where,*

1. K *is an n-tuple* $(K_1, K_2, \ldots, K_n)$, *where each* K_i *is a set of states (of the ith component)*
2. V *is the finite set of alphabet*
3. Δ *is an n-tuple* $(\delta_1, \delta_2, \ldots, \delta_n)$ *of state transition functions where each* $\delta_i: K_i \times (V \cup \{\varepsilon\}) \to 2^{K^{union}}, 1 \le i \le n$
4. $q_0 \in K_{union}$ *is the initial state*
5. $F \subseteq K_{union}$ *is the set of final accepting states.*

*The contents of this section originally appeared in "Distributed Processing in Automata" by Kamala Krithivasan, M. Sakthi Balan and Prahlad Harsha, *IJFCS*, Vol. 10, No. 4, 1999, pp 443–463. © World Scientific Company. Reproduced with permission.

where $K_{union} = \cup_i K_i$. This notation is followed throughout this section.

Each of the component FSA of the n-FSA is of the form $M_i = (K_i, V, \delta_i)$, $1 \le i \le n$. Note that here K_i's need not be ¹disjoint. In this system, we can consider many modes of acceptance depending upon the number of steps the system has to go through in each of the n components. The different modes of acceptance are t-mode, *-mode, $\le k$-mode, $\ge k$-mode, and $= k$-mode. Description of each of the above modes of acceptance is as follows:

t-mode acceptance:

Initially, the automaton which has the initial state begins the processing of input string. Suppose that the system starts from the component i. In component i, the system follows its transition function as any "stand alone" FSA. The control is transfered from the component i to component j only if the system arrives at a state $q \notin K_i$ and $q \in K_j$. The selection of j is nondeterministic if q belongs to more than one K_j. The process is repeated and we accept the strings if the system reaches any one of the final states. It does not matter which component the system is in.

If, for some $i(1 \le i \le n)$ $K_i = K_{union}$, then by no way the system can go out of the ith component. In this case, ith component acts like a "sink."

Definition 13.24 *The ID of the n-FSA, (ID) is given by a 3-tuple (q, w, i) where $q \in K_{union}, w \in V^*, 1 \le i \le n$.*

In this ID of the n-FSA, q denotes the current state of the whole system, w the portion of the input string yet to be read, and i the index of the component in which the system is currently in.
The transition between the ID's is defined as follows:

1. $(q, aw, i) \vdash (q', w, i)$ iff $q' \in \delta_i(q, a)$, where $q \in K_i$, $q' \in K_{union}$, $a \in V \cup \{\varepsilon\}$, $w \in V^*$, $1 \le i \le n$
2. $(q, w, i) \vdash (q, w, j)$ iff $q \in K_j - K_i$

Let $\vdash^*$ be the reflexive and transitive closure of $\vdash$.

Definition 13.25 *The language accepted by the n-FSA $\Gamma = (K, V, \Delta, q_0, F)$ working in t-mode is defined as follows:*

$$L_t(\Gamma) = \{w \in V^* | (q_0, w, i) \vdash (q_f, \varepsilon, j) \text{ for some } q_f \in F, 1 \le j, i \le n \text{ and } q_0 \in K_i\}$$

*-mode acceptance:

Initially, the automaton which has the initial state begins the processing of the input string. Suppose the system starts the processing from the component i. Unlike the termination mode, here there is no restriction. The automaton can transfer the control to any of the component at any time if possible, i.e, if there is some j, such that $q \in K_j$ then the system can transfer the control to the component j. The selection is done nondeterministically, if there is more than one j.

The ID and the language accepted by the system in $*$-mode can be defined analogously. The language accepted in $*$-mode is denoted as $L*(\Gamma)$.

$= k$-mode ($\leq k$-mode, $\geq k$-mode) acceptance:

Initially, the component which has the initial state begins the processing of the input string. Suppose the system starts the processing from the component i. The system transfers the control to the other component j, only after the completion of exactly k ($k'(k' \leq k)$, $k'(k' \geq k)$) number of steps in the component i, i.e., if there is a state $q \in K_j$, then the transition from component i to the component j takes place only if the system has already completed $k(k'(k' \leq k)$, $k'(k' \geq k))$ steps in component i. If there is more than one choice for j, the selection is done nondeterministically.

The ID of an n-FSA in the above three modes of derivations and the language generated by them are defined as follows,

Definition 13.26 *The ID of the n-FSA is given by a 4-tuple (q, w, i, j), where $q \in K_{union}$, $w \in V^*$, $1 \leq i \leq n$, j is a non-negative integer.*

In this ID of the n-FSA, q denotes the current state of the whole system, w the portion of the input string yet to be read; i the index of the component in which the system is currently in, and j denotes the number of steps for which the system has been in, in the ith component. The system accepts the strings only if the n-FSA is in the final state in some component i after reading the string and provided, it has completed k-steps in the component i in the case of $= k$-mode of acceptance (it has completed some $k'(k' \leq k)$ steps in the component i in the case of $\leq k$-mode of acceptance or it has completed some $k'(k' \geq k)$ steps in the component i in the case of $\geq k$-mode of acceptance). The languages accepted by the respective modes are denoted as $L_{=k}$, $L_{\leq k}$, and $L_{\geq k}$.

Power of Acceptance of Different Modes

We find that, whatever maybe the mode of co-operation, it does not increase the acceptance power if the n components are FSA.

Theorem 13.27 *For any n-FSA Γ working in t-mode, we have $L_t(\Gamma) \in REG$.*

Proof Let $\Gamma = (K, V, \Delta, q_0, F)$ be an n-FSA working in t-mode, where $\Delta = (\delta_1, \delta_2, ..., \delta_n)$ and the components have states $K_1, K_2, ..., K_n$. Consider the FSA $M = (K', V, \delta, q'_0, F')$ where,

$K' = \{[q, i] | q \in K_{union}, 1 \leq i \leq n\} \cup \{q'_0\}$

$F' = \{[q_f, i] | q_f \in F, 1 \leq i \leq n\}$

δ contains the following transitions:
for each $q_k \in \delta_i(q_j, a)$, $q_j \in K_i$, $a \in V \cup \{\varepsilon\}$, $1 \leq i \leq n$,

1. $[q_0, i'] \in \delta(q'_0, \varepsilon)$, such that $q_0 \in K_{i'}$

2. if $q_k \in K_i$, then $[q_k, i] \in \delta([q_j, i], a)$
3. if $q_k \in K_j - K_i$, then $[q_k, j] \in \delta([q_j, i], a)$, $1 \leq j \leq n$

This construction of FSA clearly shows that $L(M) = L(\Gamma)$ and so $L(\Gamma) \in REG$. □

Theorem 13.28 *For any n-FSA Γ working in ∗-mode, we have $L*(\Gamma) \in REG$.*

Proof Let $\Gamma = (K, V, \Delta, q_0, F)$ be an n-FSA working in ∗-mode, where $\Delta = (\delta_1, \delta_2, ..., \delta_n)$ and the components have states $K_1, K_2, ..., K_n$. Consider the FSA $M = (K', V, \delta, q_0', F')$ where,

$$K' = \{[q, i] \,/q \in K_{\text{union}}, 1 \leq i \leq n\} \cup \{q_0'\}$$

$$F' = \{[q_f, i] \,/q_f \in F, 1 \leq i \leq n\}$$

δ contains the following transitions:

1. $[q_0, i] \in \delta(q_0', \varepsilon)$ such that $q_0 \in K_i$, $1 \leq i \leq n$,
2. for each $q_y \in \delta_i(q_s, a)$, $q_s \in K_i$, $a \in V \cup \{\varepsilon\}$, $1 \leq i \leq n$,
   $\{[q_y, j]\} \subseteq \delta([q_s, i], a)$, $1 \leq j \leq n$ and $q_y \in K_j$.

This construction of FSA clearly shows that, $L(M) = L(\Gamma)$ and so $L(\Gamma) \in REG$. □

Theorem 13.29 *For any n-FSA Γ, $n \geq 1$ working in $= k$-mode, we have $L_{=k} \in REG$.*

Proof Let $\Gamma = (K, V, \Delta, q_0, F)$ be an n-FSA working in $= k$-mode where $\Delta = (\delta_1, \delta_2, ..., \delta_n)$ and the components have states $K_1, K_2, ..., K_n$. Consider the FSA $M = (K', V, \delta, q_0', F')$ where,

$$K' = \{[q, i, j] \mid q \in K_{\text{union}}, 1 \leq i \leq n, 0 \leq j \leq k\}$$

$$F' = \{[q_f, i, k] \mid q_f \in F, 1 \leq i \leq n\}$$

δ contains the following transitions:
for each $q_y \in \delta_i(q_s, a)$, $q_s \in K_i$, $a \in V \cup \{\varepsilon\}$, $1 \leq i \leq n, 0 \leq j \leq k$

1. $[q_0, i', 0] \in \delta(q_0', \varepsilon)$ such that $q_0 \in K_i$,
2. if $j < k$ then $[q_y, i, j] \in \delta([q_s, i, j-1], a)$
3. if $j = k$ then $[q_s, j', 0] \in \delta([q_s, i, k], \varepsilon)$, $1 \leq j' \leq n$ and $q_s \in K_{j'}$.

This construction of FSA clearly shows that, $L(M) = L(\Gamma)$ and so, $L(\Gamma) \in REG$. □

Theorem 13.30 *For any n-FSA Γ in $\leq k$-mode, we have $L_{\leq k}(\Gamma) \in REG$.*

Proof Let $\Gamma = (K, V, \Delta, q_0, F)$ be a n-FSA working in $\leq k$-mode where $\Delta = (\delta_1, \delta_2, ..., \delta_n)$ and the component states $K_1, K_2, ..., K_n$. Consider the FSA $M = (K', V, \delta, q_0', F')$ where,

$$K' = \{[q, i, j] \mid q \in K_{\text{union}}, 1 \leq i \leq n, 0 \leq j \leq k\}$$
$$q_0 = [q_0, i', 0] \text{ s.t. } q_0 \in K_{i'}, 1 \leq i' \leq n$$

$$F' = \{[q_f, i, k'] \mid q_f \in F, 1 \leq i \leq n, 1 \leq k' \leq k\}$$

δ contains the following transitions and nothing more
for each $q_y \in \delta_i(q_s, a), q_s \in K_i, a \in V \cup \{\varepsilon\}, 1 \leq i \leq n, 0 \leq j \leq k+1$

1. if $j - 1 < k$ then:
   a. $\{[q_y, i, j]\} \in \delta([q_s, i, j-1], a)$ where $q_y \in K_i, 1 \leq i \leq n$
   b. $\{[q_y, i'', 0]\} \in \delta([q_s, i, j-1], a)$ where $q_y \in K_{i''}, 1 \leq i'' \leq n, i \neq i''$
2. if $j - 1 = k$ then $[q_s, j', 0] \in \delta([q_s, i, j - 1], \varepsilon), 1 \leq j' \leq n$ and $q_s \in K_{j'}$.

This construction of FSA clearly shows that, $L(M) = L(\Gamma)$. So $L(\Gamma) \in REG$. □

Theorem 13.31   *For any n-FSA Γ in $\geq k$-mode, we have* $L_{\geq k}(\Gamma) \in REG$.

Proof   Let $\Gamma = (K, V, \Delta, q_0, F)$ be a n-FSA in $\geq k$-mode, where $\Delta = (\delta_1, \delta_2, ..., \delta_n)$ and the component states $K_1, K_2, ..., K_n$.
Consider the FSA $M = (K', V, \delta, q_0', F')$ where,

$$K' = \{[q, i, j] \mid q \in K_{union}, 1 \leq i \leq n, 0 \leq j \leq k\} \cup \{[q, i] \mid q \in U_i K_i, 1 \leq i \leq n\}$$
$$q_0 = [q_0, i', 0] \text{ s.t. } q_0 \in K_{i'}, 1 \leq i' \leq n$$
$$F' = \{[q_f, i] \mid q_f \in F, 1 \leq i \leq n\}$$

δ contains the following transitions and nothing more
for each $q_y \in \delta_i(q_s, a), q_s \in K_i, a \in V \cup \{\varepsilon\}, 1 \leq i \leq n, 0 \leq j \leq k+1$

1. if $j-1 < k$ then $[q_y, i, j] \in \delta([q_s, i, j-1], a)$
2. if $j-1 = k$ then:
   a. $\{[q_y, i]\} \in \delta([q_s, i, j-1], a), q_y \in K_i$
   b. $\{[q_y, j', 0]\} \in \delta([q_s, i, j-1], a), 1 \leq j' \leq n, j' \neq i$, and $q_y \in K_{j'}$
3. $\{[q_y, i]\} \in \delta([q_s, i], a), q_y \in K_i$
4. $\{[q_y, j', 0]\} \in \delta([q_s, i], a), 1 \leq j' \leq n, j' \neq i$, and $q_y \in K_{j'}$

This construction of FSA clearly shows that, $L(M) = L(\Gamma)$. So $L(\Gamma) \in REG$.

Thus, we find for n-FSA the different modes of acceptance are equivalent and n-FSA accept only regular sets. Basically, the model we have defined is nondeterministic in nature. Restricting the definition to deterministic n-FSA, will not decrease the power as any regular set can be accepted by a 1-DFA. □

Distributed Nondeterministic Pushdown Automata

Next we define distributed PDA and consider the language accepted in different modes. We find that the power of distributed PDA is greater than the power of a single "centralized" PDA. Distributed PDA with different modes of acceptance have equal power, equal to that of a TM. In the case of PDA, usually two types of acceptance viz. acceptance by empty store and acceptance by final state are considered. Initially, we consider only acceptance by final state. Towards the end, we show the equivalence to acceptance by empty store.

Definition 13.27   *An n-PDA is a 7-tuple $M = (K, V, \Gamma, \Delta, q_0, Z, F)$ where,*

1. *K is an n-tuple $(K_1, K_2, \ldots, K_n)$, where each K_i is the finite set of states for component i.*
   $$K_{union} = \underset{i}{U} K_i$$

2. *V is the finite set of input alphabet.*

3. *Γ is an n-tuple $(\Gamma_1, \Gamma_2, \ldots, \Gamma_n)$, where each Γ_i is a finite set of stack symbols for component i.*

4. *Δ is an n-tuple $(\delta_1, \delta_2, \ldots, \delta_n)$ of state transition functions where each*
   $$\delta_i : K_i \times \left(V \cup \{\varepsilon\}\right) \times \Gamma_i \to 2^{K_{union} \times \Gamma_i^*}, 1 \leq i \leq n$$

5. *$q_0 \in K_{union}$ is the initial state.*

6. *Z is an n-tuple $(Z_1, Z_2, \ldots, Z_n)$ where each $Z_i \in \Gamma_i$ $(1 \leq i \leq n)$ is the start symbol of stack for the ith component.*

7. *$F \subseteq K_{union}$ is the set of final accepting states.*

Each of the component PDAs of the n-PDA is of the form
$M_i = (K_i, V, \Gamma_i, \delta_i, Z_i)$, $1 \leq i \leq n$. Here, $K'_i s$ need not be disjoint. As in the case of distributed FSA, we can have several modes of acceptance.

t-mode acceptance:

Initially, the component which has the initial state begins the processing of the input string. Suppose the component i has the start state. The ith component starts the processing with the stack having the start symbol Z_i. The processing proceeds in the component i as in a stand alone PDA. Suppose in the component i the system arrives at a state q where $q \notin K_i$ the system goes to the jth component $(1 \leq j \leq n)$ provided $q \in K_j$. If there is more than one choice for j, we choose any one of them nondeterministically. After choosing a particular jth component, the automaton remains in this component until it reaches a state outside the domain of its transition function and the above procedure is repeated. The string is accepted if the automaton reaches any one of the final states. It does not matter which component the system is in, or the stacks of the components are empty or not. The presence of multi-stacks increases the generative capacity of the whole system.

∗-mode acceptance:

Initially, the automaton which has the initial state begins the processing of the input string. Suppose the system starts the processing from the component i. Unlike the termination mode, here there is no restriction. The automaton can transfer the control to any of the component at any time if possible, i.e, if there is some j such that $q \in K_j$ then the system can transfer the control to the component j. The selection is done nondeterministically if there is more than one j. The stacks for each component is maintained separately.

=k-mode($\leq$ k-mode, $\geq$ k-mode) acceptance:

Initially, the component which has the initial state begins the processing of the input string. Suppose the system starts the processing from the component i. The system transfers the control to the other component j only after the completion of exactly $k(k'(k' \leq k), k'(k' \geq k))$ number of steps in the component i, i.e., if there is a state $q \in K_j$ then the transition from component i to the component j takes place only if the system has already completed $k(k'(k' \leq k), k'(k' \geq k))$ steps in component i. If there is more than one choice for j, the selection is done nondeterministically.

Definition 13.28 *The ID of the n-PDA working in t-mode is given by a $n+3$ - tuple $(q, w, \alpha_1, \alpha_2, \ldots, \alpha_n, i)$ where $q \in K_{union}$, $w \in V^*$, $\alpha_k \in \Gamma_k^*$, $1 \leq i, k \leq n$.*

In this ID of the n-PDA, q denotes the current state of the whole system, w the portion of the input string yet to be read and i the index of the component in which the system is currently in and $\alpha_1, \alpha_2, \ldots, \alpha_n$ are the contents of the stacks of the components, respectively.

The transition between the ID's in t-mode is defined as follows:

- $(q, aw, \alpha_1, \alpha_2, \ldots, X\alpha_p, \ldots, \alpha_n, i) \vdash (q', w, \alpha_1, \alpha_2, \ldots, \beta\alpha_p, \ldots, \alpha_n, i)$
  if $(q', \beta) \in \delta_i(q, a, X)$
  and

- $(q, w, \alpha_1, \alpha_2, \ldots, X\alpha_p, \ldots, \alpha_n, i) \vdash (q', w, \alpha_1, \alpha_2, \ldots, \beta\alpha_p, \ldots, \alpha_n, j)$
  if $(q', \beta) \in \delta_i(q, a, X)$ and $q' \in K_j - K_p$
  where
  $q \in K_p, q' \in K_{union}, a \in V \cup \{\varepsilon\}, w \in V^*, 1 \leq i \leq n, \alpha_j \in \Gamma_j^*, 1 \leq j < n, \beta \in \Gamma_i^*,$
  $X \in \Gamma_i$.

Let $\vdash^*$ be the reflexive and transitive closure of $\vdash$

Definition 13.29 *The language accepted by the n-PDA $M = (K, V, \Gamma, \Delta, q_0, Z, F)$ in the t-mode is defined as follows:*

$L_t(M) = \{w \in V^* \mid (q_0, w, Z_1, Z_2, \ldots, Z_n, i') \vdash^* (q_f, \varepsilon, \alpha_1, \alpha_2, \ldots, \alpha_n, i)$ *for some* $q_f \in F$, $1 \leq i, i' \leq n, \alpha_i \in \Gamma_i^*$ *and* $q_0 \in K_{i'}\}$

Definition 13.30 *The ID of the n-PDA working in $= k$-mode is given by a $n+4$- tuple $(q, w, \alpha_1, \alpha_2, \ldots, \alpha_n, i, j)$, where $q \in K, w \in V^*, \alpha_{i'} \in \Gamma_{j'}^*, 1 \leq i, i' \leq n, 0 \leq j \leq k$.*

In this ID of the n-PDA, q denotes the current state of the whole system, w the portion of the input string yet to be read, and i the index of the component in which the system is currently in and $\alpha_1, \alpha_2, \ldots, \alpha_n$ are the contents of the stacks of the components, respectively and j denotes the number of steps completed in the component i.

The transition between the ID's in $= k$-mode is defined as follows:

- $(q, aw, \alpha_1, \alpha_2, \ldots, X\alpha_p, \ldots, \alpha_n, i, j) \vdash (q', w, \alpha_1, \alpha_2, \ldots, \beta\alpha_p, \ldots, \alpha_n, i, j+1)$
  if $(q', \beta) \in \delta_i(q, a, X), j < k-1,$

where

$q \in K_i$, $q' \in K_{union}$, $a \in V \cup \{\varepsilon\}$, $w \in V^*$, $1 \leq i \leq n$, $\alpha_j \in \Gamma_j^*$, $1 \leq j \leq n$, $\beta \in \Gamma_i^*$, $X \in \Gamma_i$.

and if $q' \in K_j (j \neq i)$

- $(q', w, \alpha_1, \alpha_2, \ldots, X\alpha_i, \ldots, \alpha_n, i, k) \vdash (q', w, \alpha_1, \alpha_2, \ldots, X\alpha_i, \ldots, \alpha_n, j, 0)$

Let $\vdash^*$ be the reflexive and transitive closure of $\vdash$.

Definition 13.31 *The language accepted by the n-PDA $M = (K, V, \Gamma, \Delta, q_0, Z, F)$ in the $= k$-mode is defined as follows:*

$L_{=k}(M) = \{ w \in V^* \mid (q_0, w, Z_1, Z_2, \ldots, Z_n i', 0) \vdash^* (q_f, \varepsilon, \alpha_1, \alpha_2, \ldots, \alpha_n, i, k)$ *for some* $q_f \in F$, $1 \leq i$, $i' \leq n$, $\alpha_i \in \Gamma_i^*$ *and* $q_0 \in K_{i'} \}$

The instantaneous description and the language accepted for the other modes of acceptance are similarly defined.

Example 13.31 Consider the $= 2$-mode 2-PDA

$M = ((K_1, K_2), V, (\Gamma_1, \Gamma_2), (\delta_1, \delta_2), \{q_0\}, (Z_1, Z_2), \{q_f\})$,

where

$K_1 = \{q_0, q_1, q_p, q_{p'}, q_s, q_z, q_c, q_{c'}\}$
$K_2 = \{q_1, q_2, q_c, q_b, q_f\}$
$V = \{a, b, c\}$
$Z_1 = Z$
$Z_2 = Z$
$F = \{q_f\}$
$\Gamma_1 = \{Z, a\}$
$\Gamma_2 = \{Z, b\}$

δ_1 and δ_2 are defined as follows, with the assumption that $X \in \{Z, a\}$ and $Y \in \{Z, b\}$.

$$\delta_1(q_0, \varepsilon, Z) = \{(q_1, Z)\} \tag{13.1}$$
$$\delta_1(q_1, a, X) = \{(q_1, aX)\} \tag{13.2}$$
$$\delta_2(q_1, \varepsilon, X) = \{(q_2, X)\} \tag{13.3}$$
$$\delta_2(q_2, a, Z) = \{(q_p, Z)\} \tag{13.4}$$
$$\delta_1(q_p, \varepsilon, X) = \{(q_{p'}, aX)\} \tag{13.5}$$
$$\delta_1(q_{p'}, \varepsilon, X) = \{(q_1, X)\} \tag{13.6}$$
$$\delta_2(q_2, b, Y) = \{(q_s, bY)\} \tag{13.7}$$
$$\delta_1(q_s, \varepsilon, a) = \{(q_2, \varepsilon)\} \tag{13.8}$$
$$\delta_1(q_z, \varepsilon, Z) = \{(q_c, \varepsilon)\} \tag{13.9}$$
$$\delta_1(q_z, \varepsilon, a) = \{(q_1, a)\} \tag{13.10}$$
$$\delta_2(q_c, c, b) = \{(q_b, \varepsilon)\} \tag{13.11}$$
$$\delta_2(q_b, \varepsilon, Z) = \{(q_f, \varepsilon)\} \tag{13.12}$$
$$\delta_2(q_b, \varepsilon, b) = \{(q_c, b)\} \tag{13.13}$$

$$\delta_1(q_c, \varepsilon, Z) = \{(q_{c'}, Z)\} \tag{13.14}$$
$$\delta_1(q_{c'}, \varepsilon, Z) = \{(q_c, Z)\} \tag{13.15}$$

The above 2-*PDA* working in =2-mode accepts the following language:

$$L = \{a^n b^n c^n \mid n \geq 1\}$$

Explanation:

The first component starts the processing. When it uses the first two transitions, it should have read an a. Then, it switches the control to the second component where it is in the state q_1. After using the ε-transition to go to the state q_2, it can either read a a or b. Suppose it reads an a, then the system will be in the state q_p. The state q_p is used here to put the already read a on to the first-component stack. This task is carried out by rules 13.5 and 13.6. Suppose when in the second component it reads a b, then the system will be in the state q_s, which is used to see whether there is one a for each b. This task is carried out by rules 13.8, 13.9, and 13.10. Immediately, after seeing there is no more a's in the first component's stack then it realizes that number of b's is equal to number of b's and it goes to the state q_c, which is used to read c's. This task is carried out by rule 13.9. After reading each and every c through rule 13.11, it will erase a b. When there is no b left in the stack, the system will be in the final state q_f. If there are more b's left in the second component stack, then the system will be in the state q_c. Then, it uses the last two ε-rules in the first component and repeats the above procedure until it arrives at the state q_f.

Example 13.32 Consider the *t-mode* 2-*PDA*:

$$M = ((K_1 \, K_2), V, (\Gamma_1, \Gamma_2), (\delta_1, \delta_2), \{q_0\}, (Z_1, Z_2), \{q_f\}),$$
where

$$K_1 = \{q_0, q_a, q_b, q_T\}$$
$$K_2 = \{q_{a'}, q_{b'}, q_s, q_f, q_e\}$$
$$V = \{a, b\}$$
$$F = \{q_f\}$$
$$\Gamma_1 = \{Z, a, b\}$$
$$\Gamma_2 = \{Z, a, b\}$$
$$\Delta = (\delta_1, \delta_2),$$

where δ_1 and δ_2 are defined as follows, with the assumption that $X \in \{Z_1, a, b\}$, and $Y \in \{Z_2, a, b\}$.

$$\delta_1(q_0, a, Z_1) = \{(q_a, aZ_1)\} \tag{13.16}$$
$$\delta_1(q_0, b, Z_1) = \{(q_b, bZ_1)\} \tag{13.17}$$
$$\delta_1(q_a, b, X) = \{(q_a, bX)\} \tag{13.18}$$
$$\delta_1(q_b, a, X) = \{(q_b, aX)\} \tag{13.19}$$
$$\delta_1(q_a, a, X) = \{(q_T, X), (q_a, aX)\} \tag{13.20}$$

$$\delta_1(q_b, b, X) \quad = \{(q_T, X), (q_b, bX)\} \tag{13.21}$$
$$\delta_1(q_T, \varepsilon, a) \quad = \{(q_a, \varepsilon)\} \tag{13.22}$$
$$\delta_1(q_T, \varepsilon, b) \quad = \{(q_b, \varepsilon)\} \tag{13.23}$$
$$\delta_2(q_a, \varepsilon, Y) \quad = \{(q_T, aY)\} \tag{13.24}$$
$$\delta_2(q_b, \varepsilon, Y) \quad = \{(q_T, bY)\} \tag{13.25}$$
$$\delta_1(q_T, \varepsilon, Z_1) \quad = \{(q_e, Z_1)\} \tag{13.26}$$
$$\delta_2(q_e, \varepsilon, \{a, b\}) = \{(q_s, \varepsilon)\} \tag{13.27}$$
$$\delta_2(q_s, a, a) \quad = \{(q_s, \varepsilon)\} \tag{13.28}$$
$$\delta_2(q_s, b, b) \quad = \{(q_s, \varepsilon)\} \tag{13.29}$$
$$\delta_2(q_s, \varepsilon, Z_2) = \{(q_f, Z_2)\} \tag{13.30}$$

The above 2-*PDA* in *t-mode* accepts the following language *L*:

$$L = \{ww \mid w \in \{a, b\}^*\}.$$

Explanation:

From q_0, the first component either reads a or b and stores the information that the first alphabet is a or b by entering the state q_a or q_b, respectively. It also stacks the first alphabet already read. This is done by rules 13.16 and 13.17. From q_a or q_b, it reads b or a and stacks the read alphabet in the first-component stack. This is done by rules 13.18, 13.19, 13.20, and 13.21. In $q_x(x \in \{a, b\})$, if the first component reads x then it could be the start of the string identical to the string read. So, in order to check this, the stacked up alphabets in the first component are transfered to the second-component stack. This is done by the rules 13.22, 13.23, 13.24, and 13.25. After transferring the stack, the system will be in the state q_e. The second component in state q_e erases the top alphabet, since it has already checked that the first alphabet matches. This is carried out by the rule 13.27. Rules 13.28, 13.29, and 13.30 check whether the read alphabet matches with the top-stack alphabet, i.e., second half of the input is the same as the first half.

Acceptance Power of NPDA

As in the case of NFSA, we can show the equivalence between different modes of co-operation in the case of NPDA also. We know that a two-stack machine can simulate a TM. Hence, it is straightforward to see that a 2-PDA is as powerful as a TM.

Acceptance by Empty Store

Definition 13.32   *The language accepted by the n-PDA*

$M = (K, V, \Gamma, \Delta, q_0, Z, F)$ *by "empty store acceptance" is defined as follows:*

$$N(M) = \{w \in V^* \mid (q_0, w, Z_1, Z_2, \ldots, Z_n, i') \vdash^* (q, \varepsilon, \varepsilon, \varepsilon, \ldots, \varepsilon \ (n \ times), i)$$

$$for \ some \ q \in K_i, \ 1 \leq i, i' \leq n, \ and \ q_0 \in K_{i'}\}$$

Equivalence

The equivalence of acceptance by final state and empty store in a n-PDA in t-mode is proved by the following theorems:

Theorem 13.32 *If L is $L(M_2)$ for some n-PDA M_2, then L is $N(M_1)$ for some n-PDA M_1, where the acceptance mode is t-mode both for M_1 and M_2.*

Proof Let $M_2 = (K, V, \Gamma, \Delta, q_0, Z, F)$ be a n-PDA in t-mode, where the acceptance is by final state. Let,

$$K = (K_1, K_2, \ldots, K_n)$$
$$\Gamma = (\Gamma_1, \Gamma_2, \ldots, \Gamma_n)$$
$$\Delta = (\delta_1, \delta_2, \ldots, \delta_n)$$
$$Z = (Z_1, Z_2, \ldots, Z_n)$$

The n-PDA $M_1 = (K', V, \Gamma', \Delta', q_0, Z', \phi)$ in t-mode, where the acceptance is by empty store is constructed as follows: $K' = (K'_1, K'_2, \ldots, K'_n)$ and $\Delta' = (\delta'_1, \delta'_2, \ldots, \delta'_n)$

1. $K'_i = K_i \cup \{q_i\}, 1 \leq i \leq n$
2. $\Gamma'_i = \Gamma_i \cup \{Z'_i\}$
3. For each i $\delta'_i(q, a, X)$, includes all elements of $\delta_i(q, a, X)$ $\forall q \in K_i, a \in V, X \in \Gamma_i$
4. $\delta'_i(q, \varepsilon, Z'_i)$ contains $(q, Z_i Z'_i)$
5. For all $i (1 \leq i \leq n)$ if $q \in F \cap K_i$ then $\delta'_i(q, \varepsilon, X)$ contains (q_1, X)
6. For $1 \leq i \leq n - 1$,
   a. $\delta'_i(q_i, \varepsilon, X)$ contains $(q_i, \varepsilon), X \in \Gamma_i$
   b. $\delta'_i(q_i, \varepsilon, Z_i)$ contains (q_{i+1}, ε)
7. $\delta'_n(q_n, \varepsilon, Z'_n)$ contains (q_n, ε)

Whenever the system enters a final state, string read by the system should be accepted by the system, i.e., the stacks of the components should be emptied. For this, as soon as the system enters the final state it has the possibility of going to the first component through the state q_1. When in the state q_1, the system empties the first-component stack and enters the second component through the state q_2 and the procedure is repeated. In the state q_n, the system empties the stack of the nth component. It is straightforward to prove that $L(M_2) = N(M_1)$. $\quad\square$

Theorem 13.33 *If L is $N(M_1)$ for some n-PDA M_1 in t-mode, then L is $L(M_2)$ for some n + 1-PDA M_2 in t-mode.*

Proof Let $M_1 = (K, V, \Gamma, \Delta, q_0, Z, \phi)$ be a n-PDA in t-mode. Let,

$$K = (K_1, K_2, \ldots, K_n),$$
$$\Gamma = (\Gamma_1, \Gamma_2, \ldots, \Gamma_n),$$
$$\Delta = (\delta_1, \delta_2, \ldots, \delta_n),$$

$Z = (Z_1, Z_2, \ldots, Z_n).$

The $n + 1$-PDA $M_2 = (K', V, \Gamma', \Delta', q_0, Z', \{q_f\})$, where

$K' = (K'_1, K'_2, \ldots, K'_n, K'_{n+1}),$

$\Gamma' = (\Gamma'_1, \Gamma'_2, \ldots, \Gamma'_n, \Gamma'_{n+1}),$

$\Delta' = (\delta'_1, \delta'_2, \ldots, \delta'_n, \delta'_{n+1})$ and

$Z' = (Z'_1, Z'_2, \ldots, Z'_n, Z'_{n+1})$ is constructed as follows:

1. $K'_i = K_i \cup \{r'_{qi} \mid q \in K_i\} \cup \{q_i\}, 1 \le i \le n$
2. $K'_{n+1} = \{r_{qi} \mid q \in K_{union}\} \cup \{q_f, q_g\}$
3. $\Gamma'_i = \Gamma_i \cup \{Z'_i\}, 1 \le i \le n$
4. $\Gamma'_{n+1} = \{Z_{qi} \mid q \in K_{union}\} \cup \{Z'_{n+1}\}$
5. $\delta'_i (q, \varepsilon, Z'_i)$ contains $(q, Z_i Z'_i)$
6. $\delta'_i (q, a, X)$ includes all elements of $\delta'_i (q, a, X) \, \forall q \in K_i, a \in V, X \in \Gamma_i$
7. For $1 \le i \le n$, $\delta'_i (q, \varepsilon, Z'_i)$ contains (r_{qi}, Z'_i)
8. $\delta'_{n+1} (r_{qi}, \varepsilon, Z'_{n+1})$ contains $(q_i, Z_{qi} Z_{n+1})$
9. $\delta'_i (q_i, \varepsilon, Z'_i)$ contains $(q_{i+1}, Z'_i), 1 \le i \le n - 1$
10. $\delta'_i (q_i, \varepsilon, X)$ contains $(q_g, X), 1 \le i \le n, X \in \Gamma_i$
11. $\delta'_n \delta(q_n, \varepsilon, Z'_n)$ contains (q_f, ε)
12. $\delta'_{n+1} (q_g, \varepsilon, Z_{qi})$ contains (r'_{qi}, ε)
13. $\delta'_i (r'_{qi}, \varepsilon, X)$ contains $(q, X), 1 \le i \le n, X \in \Gamma_i$

Whenever the system's stacks are empty, the system enters the new final state q_f included in the newly added component K'_{n+1}. For this, if the system in the state q in the component i sees its stack is empty, the system enters the state r_{qi} which is only in the newly added state set K'_{n+1}. In the component K'_{n+1} in state r_{qi}, Z_{qi} is put into its stack to store the information, which state and which component the system has to go, if the system sees that some stacks are non-empty. After stacking the Z_{qi}, the system uses the states q_j to see whether the stack of the component j is empty or not. If it is empty, it goes to the next component to check the emptiness of the next component. If not, it enters the state q_g which is in the component $n + 1$ to get the information from which state and component it has to continue the processing. This work is done by the state r'_{qi}.

It is straightforward to prove that $L(M_2) = N(M_1)$. $\square$

The equivalence of the "empty store acceptance" and the "final state acceptance" in the other modes can be proved similarly.

Distributed k-turn PDA

In this section, we consider only $*$-mode acceptance. Also, $K = K_1 = K_2 = \cdots = K_n$. In this restricted version of distributed PDA, the stacks of the component PDAs can perform at most a k number of turns while accepting a string. A n-PDA in which the stack of each of the components can perform at most k-turns each is called a *k-turn n-pushdown automata* (*k*-turn *n*-PDA). If *n* is not explicitly mentioned, then the system is called *k-turn distributed* PDA and is denoted by the symbol *k*-turn $*$-PDA. The following corollary immediately follows from this definition of *k*-turn *n*-PDA and the fact that the family of languages accepted by *k*-turn PDAs is the family of non-terminal bounded languages. The proofs are omitted here.

Theorem 13.34   *For any k-turn $*$-PDA M_1, there exists a 1-turn $*$-PDA M_2 such that $L(M_1) = L(M_2)$.*

This theorem tells us that we can restrict our attention to 1-turn $*$-PDA as far as analyzing accepting power is concerned.

Theorem 13.35   *The family of languages accepted by 1-turn $*$-PDAs is closed under the following operations:*

1. *Morphism*
2. *Intersection with regular sets*

The following result is well known (Păun *et al.*, 1998).

Theorem 13.36   *Each language $L \in RE$, $L \subseteq T^*$, can be written in the form $L = pr_T(EQ(h_1, h_2) \cap R)$, where $R \subseteq V_1^*$ is a regular language and $h_1, h_2: V_1^* \to V_2^*$ are two ε-free morphisms, $T \subseteq V_1$.*

Here, $EQ(h_1, h_2)$ means the following:
For two morphisms $h_1, h_2: V_1^* \to V_2^*$, the set $EQ(h_1, h_2) = \{w \in V_1^* | h_1(w) = h_2(w)\}$ is called the equality set of h_1, h_2.

We say that a homomorphism h is a projection (associated to V_1) and denote it by pr_{V_1} if $h: (V_1 \cup V_2)^* \to V_1^*$, $h(a) = a$ for $a \in V_1$ and $h(a) = \varepsilon$, otherwise.

The following theorem shows that equality sets are accepted by 1-turn 2-PDAs.

Theorem 13.37   *For any 2-morphisms $h_1, h_2: V_1^* \to V_2^*$, there exists a 1-turn 2-PDA M such that $L(M) = EQ(h_1, h_2)$.*

This theorem coupled with the characterization of *RE* by equality sets (Theorem 13.36) and the closure properties under morphism and intersection with regular sets (Theorem 13.35), proves that the family of languages accepted by 1-turn 2-PDA includes the whole of *RE*, where *RE* is the family of recursively enumerable languages (family of languages accepted by Turning machines). Coupled with Church's hypothesis, we have:

Theorem 13.38   *For each $L \in RE$, there exists a 1-turn 2-PDA M such that $L(M) = L$ and conversely, for each 1-turn 2-PDA M, we have $L(M) \in RE$.*

New Models of Computation

14.1 DNA Computing

Mathematical biology is a highly interdisciplinary area of research that lies at the intersection of mathematics and biology. So far, in this area, mathematical results have been used to solve biological problems. The development of stochastic processes and statistical methods are examples of such a development. In contrast, an instance of the directed Hamilton path problem was solved solely by manipulating DNA strings by Leonard Adleman. Hence, one can see that biological technique is used to solve a mathematical problem, thus paving way for a new line of research 'DNA computing.' The resemblance between mathematics and biology is that in both, simple operations are applied to initial information to obtain a result. Hence, the use of biology to solve a mathematical problem was demonstrated by a mathematician with adequate knowledge in biology, to bring together these two fields. Adleman thought that DNA strings can be used to encode an information while enzymes can be employed to simulate simple computations.

Molecules that play central roles in molecular biology and genetics, are DNA, RNA, and the polypeptides. The recombinant behaviors of double-stranded DNA molecules is made possible by the presence of restricted enzymes. Hence, DNA computing is a fast-growing research area concerned with the use of DNA molecules for the implementation of computational processes.

Even before the first experiment was performed by Adleman in 1994, in 1987 itself, Tom Head studied the recombinant behavior of DNA strands from formal language theory point of view. Culik connected this behavior of DNA strands to semigroup of dominoes.

The theory developed here does not require a concern for its origins in molecular biology. We present only the details of 'splicing rules' and hence 'splicing systems.' We provide a new generative device called 'splicing system' that allows a close simulation of molecular recombination processes by corresponding generative processes acting on strings. Here, first we start a brief discussion on double stranded form of DNA and 'splicing operation.'

DNA molecules may be considered as strings over the alphabet consisting of the four compound "two-level" symbols,

A C G T
T G C A.

Any DNA strand, for example, will consist of double strands like the one given below:

A A A A A G A T C A A A G G
T T T T T C T A G T T T C C.

Here, A, G, C, T stand for deoxyribonucleotide adenine, guanine, cytosine and thymine, respectively. A always bonds with T (double hydrogen bond) and C always bonds with G (triple hydrogen bond). One can look at (A, T) as complements and as also (C, G).

Let us first explain what a splicing rule is. Any splicing rule recognizes critical subwords in the double stranded DNA molecule. For example in

A A A A A A A,   G A T C,   A A A A A A A
T T T T T T T,   C T A G,   T T T T T T T

the strands between the comma's indicate critical subwords in the molecule.

For example, when DpnI encounters a segment in any DNA molecule having the 4-letter subword,

G A T C
C T A G

it cuts (in both strands of) the DNA molecule between A and T.

The ligase enzyme has the potential to bind together pairs of these molecules. For example if:

Molecule 1

A A A A A A A G A T C A A A A A A A
T T T T T T T C T A G T T T T T T T

Molecule 2

C C C C C T G G C C A C C C C C
G G G G G A C C G G T G G G G G

then if the enzymes DpnI, which cuts between A and T and BalI, which cuts between G and C act on molecules 1 and 2, to obtain

A A A A A A A G A   T C A A A A A A A
T T T T T T T C T   and   A G T T T T T T T

and

C C C C C T G G   C C A C C C C C
G G G G G A C C   and   G G T G G G G G.

The ligase enzyme is put in the solution containing the above 'cut positions' to recombine. Hence, one can see that new molecule 3 is formed.

Molecule 3

A A A A A A A G A C C A C C C C C
T T T T T T T C T G G T G G G G G

Several possible molecules can be formed by the ligase. But we have given molecule 3, which is got from the recombination of the first cut portion of molecule 1 with the second cut portion of molecule 2. Molecule 3 thus cannot be cut further by DpnI and BalI further.

Suppose u and v represent critical subwords in molecule 1 and u' and v' represent critical subwords in molecule 2 where uv is the underlying subword in molecule 1, $u'v'$ is the underlying subword in molecule 2. Then, the action of the enzymes on molecule 1: $xuvy$ (say) and molecule 2: $x'u'v'y'$ results in,

1. xu	2. vy
3. $x'u'$	4. $v'y'$.

Then, the presence of an appropriate ligase in the aqueous solution results in molecule 3 which is $xuv'y'$. The whole operation defined above is known as splicing operation.

Hereafter we can refer DNA strands as strings over the alphabet $\Sigma = \{A, G, C, T\}$. Splicing system has been conceived as a generative mechanism, thus paving way for the study of recombinant behavior of DNA molecules by means of formal language theory. 'Splicing system' was proposed by Tom Head. The action of enzymes and a ligase is represented by a set of splicing rules acting on the strings. The language of all possible strings that may be generated by the splicing process serves as a representation of the set of all molecules that may be generated by the recombination process. In the description so far, we have omitted the chemical aspects of molecular interaction.

Splicing Operation

In this section, we consider splicing systems with uniterated and iterated modes.

Let V be an alphabet. $\#$, $\$$ be two symbols not in V. A splicing rule over V is a string of the form:

$$r = u_1 \# u_2 \$ u_3 \# u_4,$$

where $u_i \in V^*$, $1 \leq i \leq 4$.

If $x, y \in V^*$ such that $x = x_1 u_1 u_2 x_2$, $y = y_1 u_3 u_4 y_2$, then $(x, y) \vdash z$ by rule r to yield $z = x_1 u_1 u_4 y_2$. We say that on applying the splicing rule 'r' to x, y, one gets z. In x and y, $u_1 u_2$, $u_3 u_4$ are called the sites of the splicing and x, the first term and y, the second term of the splicing operation. When understood from the context, we omit the specification of r and we write $\vdash$ instead of $\underset{r}{\vdash}$.

When we build computability models, in order to keep these models as close as possible to the reality, we shall consider the operation of the form:

$$(x, y) \overset{r}{\vDash} (z, w) \text{ iff } x = x_1 u_1 u_2 x_2,$$
$$y = y_1 u_3 u_4 y_2,$$
$$z = x_1 u_1 u_4 y_2,$$

$$w = y_1 u_3 u_2 x_2,$$
for some $x_1, x_2, y_1, y_2 \in V^*$,

where $r = u_1 \# u_2 \$ u_3 \# u_4$ is a splicing rule.

Example 14.1 Let $V = \{a, b, c\}$. Let $r = a\#b\$c\#a$. Let $x = a^{10}b$ and $y = ca^5$. Applying r to x and y,

$$(a^{10}b, ca^5) \vdash_r a^{15}.$$

In general for $x = a^m b$, $y = ca^n$,

$$(a^m b, ca^n) \vdash_r a^{m+n}.$$

This rule produces, for a suitable input of two integers m and n (represented in unary) $m + n$ (in unary).

The following figure illustrates the result z by the application of the splicing rule r to x and y.

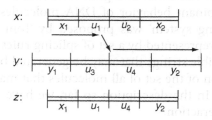

An H-scheme is a pair $\sigma = (V, R)$ where V is an alphabet and $R \subseteq V^* \# V^* \$ V^* \# V^*$ is a set of splicing rules.

R can be infinite and hence depending on the nature of R (in Chomskian class of languages), we can classify σ. That is, if R belongs to REG, then we say that σ is of REG type or an REG H-scheme. Thus, $\sigma(L) = \{z \in V^* | (x, y) \vdash z$ for some $x, y \in L, r \in R\}$.

Example 14.2 Suppose $\sigma = (\{a, b\}, R)$ where $R = \{a\#b\$b\#a\}$. For $L = \{a^n b^n, b^n a^n | n \geq 1\}$, $\sigma(L)$ is computed as follows:

$$(ab, ba) \vdash_r aa$$
$$(a^2 b^2, ba) \vdash_r a^3$$
$$\vdots$$
$$(a^n b^n, ba) \vdash_r a^{n+1}$$
$$(a^n b^n, b^m a^m) \vdash_r a^{n+m}$$

Hence $\sigma(L) = \{a^n | n \geq 2\}$ which is regular.

Example 14.3 Suppose $\sigma = (\{a, b, c\}, R)$ where
$R = \{a^n\#b\$b\#c^n \mid n \geq 1\}$
Let $L_1 = \{a^nb \mid n \geq 1\}$, $L_2 = \{bc^n \mid n \geq 1\}$
For $x \in L_1, y \in L_2, (x, y) \vdash a^nc^n$.
Hence $\sigma(L = L_1 \cup L_2) = \{a^nc^m \mid n, m \geq 1\}$.

Example 14.4 Let $\sigma = (\{a, b\}, R)$ where
$R = \{w\#\$\#w^R \mid w \in \{a, b\}^+\}$
For $x \in L_1 = \{w \mid w \in \{a, b\}^+\}$ and $y \in L_1^R$,
where $L_1^R = \{w^R \mid w \in L\}.(x, y) \vdash ww^R$.
Hence $\sigma(L = L_1 \cup L_2) = \{ww^R \mid w \in \{a, b\}^+\}$.

Remarks

1. From the splicing scheme, one can see that a splicing rule is applicable to any two strings having the subwords that can be subjected to splicing. Hence, the site of cutting is to be present in the two strings. In such a case, the whole strings that are considered need not be over the alphabet of splicing rule. But, the alphabet of a splicing rule is a subset of the alphabet of the strings to be spliced.

2. The scheme defined above considers a language L of strings subject to splicing. That is, σ is defined as a unary operation with languages. One can also think σ as binary operation. That is:

$$\sigma(L_1, L_2) = \{z \in V^* \mid (x, y) \vdash_r z, x, y \in L_1, r \in L_2\}$$

Given any two families of languages F_1 and F_2 over V, we define
$$S(F_1, F_2) = \{\sigma(L) \mid L \in F_1, \sigma = (V, R), \text{ with } R \in F_2\}$$

3. One can see that each set of splicing rules is a language over the basic alphabet and $\{\#, \$\}$. We say that F_1 is closed under σ of F_2-type if $S(F_1, F_2) \subseteq F_1$. Hence, we try to investigate the power of F_2-type splicing by investigating $S(F_1, F_2)$ for various F_1. Here, F_1, F_2 will belong to {FIN, REG, LIN, CF, CS, RE}. In all the results, the families of languages considered are supposed to contain atleast the finite languages.

Lemma 14.1 *if $F_1 \subseteq F_1'$ and $F_2 \subseteq F_2'$ then $S(F_1, F_2) \subseteq S(F_1', F_2')$ for all F_1, F_1', F_2, F_2'.*

Proof is obvious from the definitions. For example, if $F_1 = \text{REG}$, $F_1' = \text{CF}$, $F_2 = \text{REG}$, $F_2' = \text{CF}$, then $S(\text{REG}, \text{REG}) \subseteq S(\text{CF}, \text{CF})$.

Lemma 14.2 *If F_1 is a family of languages closed under concatenation with symbols, then $F_1 \subseteq S(F_1, F_2)$ for all F_2.*

Proof Let $L \subseteq V^*, L \in F_1$ and $c \notin V$. Suppose $L' = \{wc \mid w \in L\} \in F_1$. Then $\sigma = (V \cup \{c\}, \{\#c\$c\#\})$ generates L, where $L \in S(F_1, F_2)$. $\square$

Lemma 14.3 *If F_1 is a family of languages closed under union, catenation with symbols and* FIN *splicing, then F_1 is closed under concatenation.*

Proof   Let $L_1, L_2 \in F_1, L_1, L_2 \subseteq V^*$. Let $C_1, C_2 \notin V$ and $\sigma = (V \cup \{C_1, C_2\}, \{\#C_1\$C_2\#\})$. Clearly $\sigma(L_1 C_1 \cup C_2 L_2) = L_1 L_2$. $L_1 C_1, C_2 L_2 \in F_1$ as F_1 is closed under concatenation with symbols. $L_1 C_1 \cup C_2 L_2 \in F_1$ as F_1 is closed under union. $\sigma(L_1 C_1 \cup C_2 L_2) \in F_1$ as F_1 is closed under FIN splicing. Therefore $L_1 L_2 \in F_1$. $\square$

Theorem 14.1 $S(\text{REG}, \text{REG}) \subseteq \text{REG}$.

Proof   By the above lemma, since REG languages are closed under catenation and arbitrary gsm mapping, REG is closed under REG splicing $\square$

Since REG languages are closed under catenation with symbols we have REG $\subsetneq$ $S(\text{REG}, F_2)$ for any $F_2 \in (\text{FIN}, \text{REG}, \text{CF}, \text{CS}, \text{RE})$. Hence, we have,

Theorem 14.2 $S(\text{REG}, \text{REG}) = \text{REG}$.

Table 14.1 Families obtained by non-iterated splicing

$S(F_1, F_2)$	FIN	REG	LIN	CF	CS	RE
FIN	FIN	FIN	FIN	FIN	FIN	FIN
REG	REG	REG	REG, LIN	REG, CF	REG, RE	REG, RE
LIN	LIN, CF	LIN, CF	RE	RE	RE	RE
CF	CF	CF	RE	RE	RE	RE
CS	RE	RE	RE	RE	RE	RE
RE	RE	RE	RE	RE	RE	RE

Table 14.1 gives power of splicing on Chomskian languages. In the table, the rows are marked for F_1 and columns are marked for F_2 in $S(F_1, F_2)$. The intersection of the row and column entries indicate the power of $S(F_1, F_2)$. If there are two entries like F_3, F_4 it means $F_3 \subsetneq S(F_1, F_2) \subsetneq F_4$. All the assertions are proved in the literature (Păun *et al.*, 1998).

Iterated Splicing

Let $\sigma = (V, R)$ be a splicing scheme where $R \subseteq V^* \# V^* \$ V^* \# V^*$, one can apply σ to a language $L \subseteq V^*$ iteratively. That is:

$$\sigma^0(L) = L$$
$$\sigma^1(L) = \sigma^0(L) \cup \sigma(L)$$
$$\sigma^2(L) = \sigma^1(L) \cup \sigma(\sigma^1(L))$$
$$\vdots$$
$$\sigma^{i+1}(L) = \sigma^i(L) \cup \sigma(\sigma^i(L))$$
$$\sigma^*(L) = \bigcup_{i \geq 0} \sigma^i(L)$$

$\sigma^*(L)$ is the smallest language L' which contains L and is closed under the splicing with respect to σ, $\sigma(L') \subseteq L'$. Also for two languages L_1 and L_2, we can define $H(L_1, L_2) = \sigma^*(L)$ where $\sigma = (V, R)$, $L = L_1$, $R = L_2$. That is for any family of languages F_1 and F_2,

$$H(F_1, F_2) = \{\sigma^*(L) | L \in F_1 \text{ and } \sigma = (V, R) \text{ with } R \in F_2\}.$$

Example 14.5 Let $\sigma = (\{a, b\}, R)$ be a splicing scheme. Let $L = \{aba, abba\}$, $R = \{r_1: a\#b\$b\#ba, r_2: b\#a\$b\#ba\}$.

Consider,

$$(a \,|\, ba, ab \,|\, ba) \vdash_{r_1} aba \,.$$

Here, the vertical line '$|$' indicates the position at which the splicing rule r_1 is used.
Consider,

$$(ab \,|\, a, ab \,|\, ba) \vdash_{r_2} abba \,.$$

Here,

$$L = \{aba, abba\}$$
$$\sigma^0(L) = \{abba, aba\}$$
$$\sigma^1(L) = \{aba, abba, abbba\}$$
$$\sigma^i(L) = \{ab^n a \,|\, 1 \le n \le i+2\} \text{ for } i \ge 1$$

Hence $\sigma^*(L) = \{ab^n a | n \ge 1\}$.

We now state a few simple lemmas.

Lemma 14.4 If $F_1 \subseteq F_1'$ and $F_2 \subseteq F_2'$, then $H(F_1, F_2) \subseteq H(F_1', F_2')$ for all families F_1, F_1', F_2, F_2'.

Proof follows from definition.

Definition 14.1 Let $\sigma = (V, R)$ be a H-scheme with R finite. The radius of σ is defined as:

$$\text{rad}(\sigma) = \max\{|x| \,|\, x = u_i, 1 \le i \le 4, \text{ for some } u_1\#u_2\$u_3\#u_4 \in R\}.$$

$S(F, p)$ for $p \ge 1$, denote the family of languages $\sigma(L)$ for some $L \in F$ and σ, an H-scheme with radius less than or equal to p.

In Example 14.5, $\text{rad}(\sigma) = 2$. The important observation made for radius is that:

$$S(F, 1) \subseteq S(F, p) \text{ for all } p \ge 1.$$

Here, $F \in \{\text{FIN, REG, CF, CS, RE}\}$.

Lemma 14.5 $F \subseteq H(F, 1)$ for all $F \in \{\text{FIN, REG, CF, CS, RE}\}$.

Proof Let $L \subseteq \Sigma^*$ be given. Let $c \notin V$ and the H-scheme $\sigma = V \cup \{c\}, \{\#c\$c\#\}$. We clearly have $\sigma^i(L) = L$, for all $i \ge 1$ and $\sigma^*(L) = L$. $\square$

Theorem 14.3 (**The regularity preserving lemma**) $H(REG, FIN) \subseteq REG$.

Proof is lengthy and is not included here.

Theorem 14.4 $FIN \subset H(FIN, 1) \subset H(FIN, 2) \subset \ldots \subset H(FIN, FIN) \subset REG$.

Proof Inclusions follow from definitions and from the previous lemmas and theorem. For proper inclusion, we have the following example.
Consider the language:

$L_n = \{a^{2n}b^{2n}a^k b^{2n}a^{2n}| k \geq 2n + 1\}$.

Consider the H-scheme $\sigma = (\{a, b\}, a^{n+1}\#a^n\$a^{n+1}\#a^n\})$, $L'_n = \{a^{2n}b^{2n}a^{2n+2}b^{2n}a^{2n}\}$. Clearly $L_n = \sigma^*(L'_n)$.

L_n cannot be generated by any H-scheme $\sigma_1 = (V, R)$ with $rad(\sigma_1) \leq n$. Suppose it is possible to do so. This means there exist a H-scheme $\sigma_2 = (V, R)$ where $rad(\sigma_2) \leq k$ such that $L_n = \sigma_2^*(L''_n)$. Let $r = u_1\#u_2\$u_3\#u_4 \in R$ such that $|u_1u_2| \leq 2n$. Clearly if $u_1u_2 \in a^*$, then it is a subword of a^{2n} occurring in $x = a^{2n}b^{2n}a^k b^{2n}a^{2n}$, $k \geq 2n + 1$; similarly for y.

$(a^n \mid a^n b^{2n}a^k b^{2n}a^{2n}, a^{2n}b^{2n}a^k b^{2n}a^n \mid a^n) \vdash_r a^{2n}$ is not in L_n.

There are also other ways for identifying u_1, u_2, u_3, u_4 in x and y so that $(x, y) \vdash z$ and z is not of the form $a^{2n}b^{2n}a^k b^{2n}a^{2n}$, $k \geq 2n + 1$. We arrive at strings not in L_n. Hence the result. $\square$

Lemma 14.6 Every language L in RE, $L \subseteq \Sigma^*$, can be written as $L = \Sigma^* \cap L'$ for $L' \in H(FIN, REG)$.

Proof Let $G = (N, \Sigma, P, S)$ be a type 0 grammar such that $L(G) = L$. Let $\sigma = (V, R)$ be a H-scheme such that:

$V = N \cup \Sigma \cup \{X, X', B, Y, Z\} \cup \{Y_\alpha | \alpha \in N \cup \Sigma \cup \{B\}\}$.
$L_0 = \{XBSY, XZ, ZY\} \cup \{ZvY | u \to v \in P\} \cup \{ZY_\alpha, X'\alpha Z | \alpha \in N \cup \Sigma \cup \{B\}\}$.

That is, L_0 is the initial set of strings (axiom) available for splicing.
R contains the following group of rules:

I. $Xw\#uY\$Z\#vY$ for $u \to v \in P$ and $w \in (N \cup \Sigma \cup \{B\})^*$.

This set of rules is used to simulate rules in P. That is, they indicate the application of the rule $u \to v \in P$ for a string containing 'u.'

II. Next we have to simulate any sentential form w of G by a string $XBwY$ produced by σ and conversely if Xw_1Bw_2Y is produced by σ, then, w_2w_1 is a sentential form of G. For this we have the following set of rules.

$$
\left.
\begin{array}{l}
\text{1. } Xw\#\alpha Y\$Z\#Y_\alpha \\
\text{2. } X'\alpha\#Z\$X\#wY_\alpha \\
\text{3. } X'w\#Y_\alpha\$Z\#Y
\end{array}
\right\}
\text{ for } \alpha \in N \cup \Sigma \cup \{B\}, w \in (N \cup \Sigma \cup \{B\})^*.
$$

4. $X\#Z\$X'\#wY$ for $w \in (N \cup \Sigma \cup \{B\})^*$.

These rules move symbols from the right-hand end of the current string to the left-hand end. The presence of B indicates the beginning of the corresponding sentential form. For, if the current string in σ is of the form $\beta_1 w_1 B w_2 \beta_2$ for some β_1, β_2 markers of type X, X', Y, Y_α, $\alpha \in N \cup \Sigma \cup \{B\}$, w_1, $w_2 \in (N \cup \Sigma)^*$, then $w_2 w_1$ is a sentential form of G.

The starting string will be $XBSY$ where S is the axiom of G.

Let us actually see how the above rules simulate the sentential forms. If:

$$(Xw\alpha Y, ZY_\alpha) \vdash XwY_\alpha$$

by rule 1. Y_α indicates the erasing of α which is to the right of w. Now to XwY_α, the only applicable rule is rule 2. i.e.,

$$(X'\alpha Z, XwY_\alpha) \vdash X'\alpha wY_\alpha.$$

This indicates the shifting of α to the left of w. The only possible rule to be applied is rule 3. Hence,

$$(X'\alpha wY_\alpha, ZY) \vdash X'\alpha wY.$$

Now the application of rule 4, produces:

$$(XZ, X'\alpha wY \vdash X\alpha wY).$$

Hence, we started with $Xw\alpha Y$ and reached $X\alpha wY$ by the application of above set of rules. This can be repeated as long as we want.

III. Now, the strings thus produced by σ must contain only symbols from Σ. Hence, we have the following set of rules.

1. $\#ZY\sigma XB\#wY$ for $w \in \Sigma^*$
2. $\#Y\$XZ\#$.

Clearly, XB can be removed only if the string produced by r has Y, the string between X and Y is over Σ, the symbol B is at the left-hand position. That is, the string must be of the form $XBwY$, $w \in \Sigma^*$. After removing XB, we can remove Y using rule 2 above. i.e.,

$$(wY, XZ) \vdash w.$$

Hence, for $w \in L(G)$, $w \in \sigma^*(L_0) \cap \Sigma^*$,

Clearly, $\sigma^*(L_0) \cap \Sigma^* \subseteq L(G)$ and conversely if $w \in L(G)$, it can be produced by the above said way by σ giving $w \in \sigma^*(L_0) \cap \Sigma^*$. Thus $L(G) = \sigma^*(L_0) \cap \Sigma^*$. $\square$

We state a result by means of Table 14.2 which gives the hierarchy among various families of $H(F_1, F_2)$, where $F_1, F_2 \in \{FIN, REG, LIN, CF, CS, RE\}$.

Here the intersection of the row marked F_1 with the column marked F_2, there appears $H(F_1, F_2)$ or two families F_1, F_2 such that $F_3 \subset H(F_1, F_2) \subset F_4$.

Next, we define a system called extended H-system (EH). A EH-system is a quadruple $\gamma = (V, T, A, R)$ where V is an alphabet, $T \subseteq V$ is a set of terminal alphabet, $A \subseteq V^*$ is its axiom set, R is a set of splicing rules. Here $\sigma = (V, R)$ is the underlying splicing scheme or H-scheme. We are now familiar about usage of σ^j for given set of input strings.

The language generated by γ is defined to be $L(\gamma) = \Sigma^*(A) \cap T^*$. For any two families of languages F_1, F_2, let $EH(F_1, F_2)$ denote the family of languages $L(\gamma)$ generated by EH-system γ where $A \in F_1$ and $R \in F_2$.

Table 14.2. Generative power of H-systems

$H(F_1, F_2)$	FIN	REG	LIN	CF	CS	RE
FIN	FIN, REG	FIN, RE	FIN, RE	FIN, RE	FIN, RE	FIN, RE
REG	REG	REG, RE	REG, RE	REG, RE	REG, RE	REG, RE
LIN	LIN, CF	LIN, RE	LIN, RE	LIN, RE	LIN, RE	LIN, RE
CF	CF	CF, RE	CF, RE	CF, RE	CF, RE	CF, RE
CS	CS, RE	CS, RE	CS, RE	CS, RE	CS, RE	CS, RE
RE	RE	RE	RE	RE	RE	RE

For any two families F_1, F_2 we denote $EH(F_1, F_2)$ to be the family of languages $L(\gamma)$ generated by an EH-system γ, where $A \in F_1$, $R \in F_2$. The generative power of EH-systems is given by Table 14.3. We state two important results without proof.

Theorem 14.5 $EH(FIN, FIN) = REG$

Theorem 14.6 $EH(FIN, REG) = RE$

Example 14.6 Let $\gamma = (V, T, A, R)$ be an EH-system where

$V = \{B, a, b\}$ $T = \{a, b\}$ $A = \{a, b, aB, Bb\}$
$R = \{a\#B\ \$B\ \#b,$
$\quad a\#\$\#aB,$
$\quad a\#B\$\#a,$
$\quad Bb\#\$\#b,$
$\quad b\#\$B\#b\}.$
$L(\gamma) = \{a^n | n \geq 1\} \cup \{b^m | m \geq 1\} \cup \{a^n b^m | n, m \geq 1\}.$

We see that from splicing scheme, one can define a splicing system with a well-defined collection of input. This splicing system actually resembles a generative grammar. Formally, it is a system $\gamma = (V, L, R)$ where (V, R) is a splicing scheme.

Table 14.3. The generative power of extended H-systems

$EH(F_1, F_2)$	FIN	REG	LIN	CF	CS	RE
FIN	REG	RE	RE	RE	RE	RE
REG	REG	RE	RE	RE	RE	RE
LIN	LIN, CF	RE	RE	RE	RE	RE
CF	CF	RE	RE	RE	RE	RE
CS	RE	RE	RE	RE	RE	RE
RE	RE	RE	RE	RE	RE	RE

Definition 14.2   *A simple H-system is a triple $\gamma = (V, A, M)$ where V is the total alphabet, A is a finite language over V and $M \subseteq V$. The elements of A are called axioms and those of M are called markers. When simple H-systems were introduced, four ternary relations on the language V^* were considered corresponding to splicing rules of the form*

$$a\#\$a\#, \ \#a\$\#a, \ a\#\$\#a, \ \#a\$a\#$$

where a is an arbitrary element of M. The rules listed above correspond to splicing rules of type $(1, 3)$, $(2, 4)$, $(1, 4)$ and $(2, 3)$, respectively. Clearly, rules of types $(1, 3)$ and $(2, 4)$ define the same operation for $x, y, z \in V^*$ and $a \in M$. We obtain:

$$(x, y) \vdash^a_{(1, 3) or (2, 4)} z \text{ iff } x = x_1 a x_2, y = y_1 a y_2, z = x_1 a y_2$$
$$\text{for some } x_1, x_2, y_1, y_2 \in V^*.$$

For the $(1, 4)$ and the $(2, 3)$ types, we have

$$(x, y) \vdash^a_{(1,4)} z \text{ iff } x = x_1 a x_2, y = y_1 a y_2, z = x_1 a a y_2$$
$$\text{for some } x_1, x_2, y_1, y_2 \in V^*.$$
$$(x, y) \vdash^a_{(2, 3)} z \text{ iff } x = x_1 a x_2, y = y_1 a y_2, z = x_1 y_2$$
$$\text{for some } x_1, x_2, y_1, y_2 \in V^*.$$

Similar to H-systems, we define iterated splicing for simple H-systems; for a language $L \subseteq V^*$ and $(i, j) \in \{(1, 3), (2, 4), (1, 4), (2, 3)\}$. We denote:

$$\sigma_{(i, j)}(L) = \{z \mid z \in V^*, (x, y) \vdash^a_{(i, j)} z \text{ for } x, y \in L, a \in M\}.$$

Define

$$\sigma^0_{(i, j)}(L) = L,$$
$$\sigma^{k+1}_{(i, j)}(L) = \sigma^k_{(i, j)}(L) \cup \sigma_{(i, j)}(\sigma^k_{(i, j)}(L)), k \geq 0,$$
$$\sigma^*_{(i, j)}(L) = \bigcup_{k \geq 0} \sigma^k_{(i, j)}(L).$$

The language generated by γ with splicing rules of type (i, j) is defined as:

$$L_{(i, j)}(\gamma) = \sigma^*_{(i, j)}(A).$$

Note that SH-systems are of radius one.

Example 14.7   Let $\gamma = (\{a, b, c\}, A, M = \{a\})$ be a simple H-system. Let $a\#\$a\#$ be the splicing rule. This is a $(1, 3)$ SH-system. Let $A = \{abc, aabc, aaabc\}$.

$$L_{(1, 3)}(\gamma) = \{a^n bc \mid n \geq 1\}.$$

Definition 14.3   *An EH-system with permitting contexts is a quadruple $\gamma = (V, T, A, R)$ where V, T, A are the same as defined earlier and R is a finite set of triples $p = (r = u_1 \# u_2, \$ u_3 \# u_4, C_1, C_2)$, where $C_1, C_2 \subseteq V$ and r is a usual splicing rule.*
   In this case, $(x, y) \vdash_p w$ iff $(x, y) \vdash_r w$ and all symbols of C_1 appear in x and all symbols of C_2 occur in y.
   An EH-system with forbidding contexts is a quadruple $\gamma = (V, T, A, R)$ where V, T, A are the same as defined earlier and R is a finite set of triples $p = (r = u_1 \# u_2 \$ u_3 \# u_4, C_1, C_2)$ where $C_1, C_2 \subseteq V$ and r is a usual splicing rule.

In this case, $(x, y) \vdash_p w$ iff $(x, y) \vdash_r w$ and no symbol of C_1 appears in x and no symbol of C_2 occurs in y.

EH (FIN, $p[k]$) refers to the family of languages generated by EH- systems with permitting contexts, finite set of axioms and rules with maximum radius equal to k for $k \geq 1$. In a similar fashion, one can define EH(FIN, $f[k]$) to be the family of languages generated by EH-systems with forbidding contexts, finite set of axioms, and rules with maximum radius equal to k.

We state some results without proof.

Theorem 14.7 $EH_2(FIN, p[2]) = RE.$

Theorem 14.8 $EH_2(FIN, p[1]) = CF.$

There are several models of splicing systems. Some of them are studied by splicing graphs, arrays, etc. In each model, the power of splicing is explored from formal language theory point of view. Other aspects of splicing like circular splicing, self-assembly are some of the topics of recent research.

14.2   Membrane Computing

Membrane computing is a new computability technique which is inspired from biochemistry. The model used for any computation here resembles a membrane structure and it is a highly parallel, distributed computing model. Several cell-like membranes are recurrently placed inside a unique membrane called "skin" membrane. The structure of this model may be placed as a Venn diagram without intersected sets and with unique superset. Hence, the structure or compartment of the computing model can be diagrammatically represented as below:

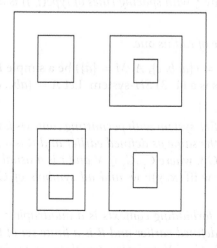

The name or the representation of the whole diagram will be called a membrane structure. In the regions delimited by the membranes, the objects or data structure are placed. These objects evolve by evolution rules. After evolution, the developed new data structure may remain in the same membrane or may move from one compartment to another. Starting with a certain number of objects in certain membranes, let the system evolve. If it halts, then the computation is finished. The result can be viewed either in some membrane region or outside skin membrane. If the development of the system goes forever, then the computation fails to produce an output.

The new method of computation is proposed by Păun in 1998 and hence, this system of computation is also called as P system. In the regions delimited by membranes, objects are placed. Hence, the object of evolution may be strings, multisets etc. These evolve based on rules placed in the regions. By varying the evolving objects and evolution rules, several variants of P systems or membrane systems have been developed. In any variant, the objects are assumed to evolve; each object can be transformed into other objects, can pass through a membrane, or can dissolve the membrane in which it is placed. A priority relation between the rules is also permitted. The evolution is done in parallel for all objects which can evolve.

A *multiset* over a set X is a mapping $M: X \to N \cup \{\infty\}$. For $a \in X$, $M(a)$ is called the multiplicity of a in the multiset M. The *support* of M is the set $supp(M) = \{a \in X \mid M(a) > 0\}$. We can write a multiset M of finite support, $supp(M) = \{a_1, \ldots, a_n\}$ in the form $\{(a_1, M(a_1)), \ldots, (a_n, M(a_n))\}$. We can also represent this multiset by the string $w(M) = a_1^{M(a_1)} \ldots a_n^{M(a_n)}$, as well as by any permutation of $w(M)$. Conversely, having a string $w \in V^*$, we can associate with it the multiset $M(w): V \to N \cup \{\infty\}$ defined by $M(w)(a) = |w|_a$, $a \in V$.

For two multisets M_1, M_2 over the same set X we say that M_1 is included in M_2, and we write $M_1 \subseteq M_2$ if $M_1(a) \leq M_2(a)$ for all $a \in X$. The union of M_1, M_2 is the multiset $M_1 \cup M_2$ defined by $(M_1 \cup M_2)(a) = M_1(a) + M_2(a)$. We define here the difference $M_2 - M_1$ of two multisets only if $M_1 \subseteq M_2$ and this is the multiset defined by $(M_2 - M_1)(a) = M_2(a) - M_1(a)$.

Operations with Strings and Languages

The Boolean operations (with languages) are denoted as usual: $\cup$ for union, $\cap$ for intersection, and c for complementation.

P Systems with Labeled Membranes

We start from the observation that life "computes" not only at the genetic level, but also at the cellular level. At a more specific level with respect to the models we are going to define, important to us is the fact that the parts of a biological system are well delimited by various types of *membranes*, in the broad sense of the term, starting from the membranes, which delimit the various intra-cell components, going to the cell membrane and then to the skin of organisms, and ending with more or less virtual "membranes," which delimit, for instance, parts of an ecosystem. In very practical terms, in biology and chemistry one knows membranes which keep together certain chemicals and allow other chemicals to pass, in a selective manner, sometimes only in one direction (for instance, through protein channels placed in membranes).

Formalizing the previous intuitive ideas, we now introduce the basic structural ingredient of the computing devices we will define later: membrane structures.

Let us consider first the language MS over the alphabet $\{[,]\}$, whose strings are recurrently defined as follows:

1. $[\ ] \in MS$;
2. If $\mu_1, \ldots, \mu_n \in MS, n \geq 1$, then $[\mu_1 \ldots \mu_n] \in MS$;
3. nothing else is in MS.

Consider now the following relation over the elements of MS: $x \sim y$ if and only if we can write the two strings in the form $x = \mu_1\mu_2\mu_3\mu_4, y = \mu_1\mu_3\mu_2\mu_4$, for $\mu_2\mu_3 \in MS$ and $\mu_2, \mu_3 \in MS$(two pairs of parentheses, which are neighbors at the same level are interchanged, together with their contents). We also denote by $\sim$ the reflexive and transitive closure of the relation $\sim$. This is clearly an equivalence relation. We denote by $\overline{MS}$ the set of equivalence classes of MS with respect to this relation. The elements of $\overline{MS}$ are called *membrane structures*.

Each matching pair of parentheses [,] appearing in a membrane structure is called a *membrane*. The number of membranes in a membrane structure μ is called the *degree* of μ and is denoted by $deg(\mu)$ while the external membrane of a membrane structure μ is called the *skin* membrane of μ. A membrane, which appears in $\mu \in \overline{MS}$ in the form [ ](no other membrane appears inside the two parentheses) is called an *elementary* membrane.

The *depth* of a membrane structure μ, denoted by $dep(\mu)$ is defined recurrently as follows:

1. If $\mu = [\ ]$, then $dep(\mu) = 1$;
2. If $\mu = [\mu_1 \ldots \mu_n]$, for some $\mu_1, \ldots, \mu_n \in MS$,
   then $dep(\mu) = \max\{dep(\mu_i) \mid 1 \leq i \leq n\} + 1$.

A membrane structure can be represented in a natural way as a Venn diagram. This makes clear that the order of membrane structures of the same level in a larger membrane structure is irrelevant; what matters is the topological structure, the relationship between membranes.

The Venn diagram representation of a membrane structure μ also makes clear the notion of a *region* in μ: any closed space delimited by membranes is called a region of μ. It is clear that a membrane structure of degree n contains n internal regions, one associated with each membrane. By the *outer* region, we mean the whole space outside the skin membrane. Figure 14.1 illustrates some of the notions mentioned above.

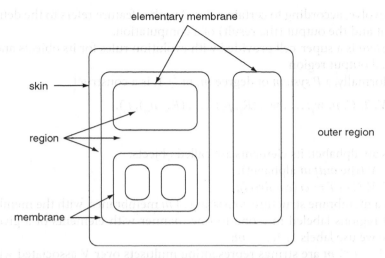

Figure 14.1. A membrane structure

We now make one more step towards the definition of a computing device, by adding objects to a membrane structure. Let U be a finite set whose elements are called objects. Consider a membrane structure μ of degree n, $n \geq 1$, with the membranes labeled in a one-to-one manner, for instance, with the numbers from 1 to n. In this way, the regions of μ are also identified by the numbers from 1 to n. If a multiset $M_i: U \to \mathbf{N}$ is associated with each region i of μ, $1 \leq i \leq n$, then we say that we have a *super-cell* (note that we do not allow infinite multiplicities of objects in U).

Any multiset M_i mentioned above can be empty. In particular, all of them can be empty, that is, any membrane structure is a super-cell. On the other hand, each individual object can appear in several regions, and in several copies.

Several notions defined for membrane structures are extended in the natural way to super-cells: degree, depth, region etc.

The multiset corresponding to a region of a super-cell (in particular, it can be an elementary membrane) is called *the contents* of this region. The total multiplicities of the elements in an elementary membrane m (the sum of their multiplicities) is called *the size* of m and is denoted by $size(m)$.

If a membrane m' is placed in a membrane m such that m and m' contribute to delimiting the same region (namely, the region associated with m), then all objects placed in the region associated with m are said to be *adjacent* to membrane m' (so, they are immediately "outside" membrane m' and "inside" membrane m).

A super-cell can be described by a Venn diagram where both the membranes and the objects are represented (in the case of objects, taking care of their multiplicities).

We are now ready to introduce the subject of our investigation, a computing mechanism essentially designed as a distributed parallel machinery, having as the underlying structure a super-cell. The basic additional feature is the possibility of objects to evolve, according to certain rules. Another feature refers to the definition of the input and the output (the result) of a computation.

A *P system* is a super-cell provided with evolution rules for its objects and with a designated output region.

More formally, a *P system* of degree m, $m \geq 1$, is a construct

$$\Pi = (V, T, C, \mu, w_1, \ldots, w_m, (R_1, \rho_1), \ldots, (R_m, \rho_m), i_0),$$

where:

1. V is an alphabet; its elements are called objects;
2. $T \subseteq V$ (the *output* alphabet);
3. $C \subseteq V, C \cap T = \phi$ (catalysts);
4. μ is a membrane structure consisting of m membranes, with the membranes and regions labeled in a one-to-one manner with elements of a given set; here we use labels $1, 2, \ldots, m$;
5. $w_i, 1 \leq i \leq m$ are strings representing multisets over V associated with the regions $1, 2, \ldots, m$ of μ;
6. $R_i, 1 \leq i \leq m$, are finite sets of *evolution rules* over V associated with the regions $1, 2, \ldots, m$ of μ; ρ_i is a partial order relation over $R_i, 1 \leq i \leq m$, specifying a *priority relation* among rules of R_i.
   An evolution rule is a pair (u, v), which we usually write in the form of $u \rightarrow v$, where u is a string over V and $v = v'$ or $v = v'\delta$, where v' is a string over

   $$\{a_{here}, a_{out}, a_{in_j} \mid a \in V, 1 \leq j \leq m\},$$

   and δ is a special symbol not in V. The length of u is called *the radius* of the rule $u \rightarrow v$. (The strings u, v are understood as representations of multisets over V, in the natural sense.)
7. i_0 specifies the *output* membrane of Π if it is a number between 1 and m. If it is equal to ∞, it indicates that the output is read in the outer region.

When presenting the evolution rules, the indication "here" is in general omitted. It may be remembered that the multiset associated with a string w is denoted by $M(w)$.

If Π contains rules of radius greater than one, then we say that Π is a system *with co-operation*. Otherwise, it is a *non-cooperative* system. A particular class of co-operative systems is that of catalytic systems: the only rules of radius greater than one are of the form $ca \rightarrow cv$, where $c \in C, a \in V - C$, and v contains no catalyst; moreover, no other evolution rules contain catalysts (there is no rule of the form $c \rightarrow v$ or $a \rightarrow v_1 c v_2$, for $c \in C$). A system is said to be *propagating* if there is no rule, which diminishes the number of objects in the system (note that this can be done by "erasing" rules, but also by sending objects out of the skin membrane).

Of course, any of the multisets $M(w_1), \ldots, M(w_n)$ can be empty (that is, any w_i can be equal to ϕ) and the same is valid for the sets $R_1, \ldots, R_n$ and their associated priority relations ρ_i.

The components μ and $w_1, \ldots, w_n$ of a P system define a super-cell. Graphically, we will draw a P system by representing its underlying super-cell, and also adding the rules to each region, together with the corresponding priority relation. In this way, we can have a complete picture of a P system, much easier to understand than a symbolic description.

The $(m + 1)$—tuple $(\mu, w_1, \ldots, w_m)$ constitutes the *initial configuration* of Π. In general, any sequence $(\mu', w'_{i_1}, \ldots, w'_{i_k})$, with μ', a membrane structure obtained by removing from μ all membranes different from $i_1, \ldots, i_k$ (of course, the skin membrane is not removed), with w'_j strings over V, $1 \leq j \leq k$, and $\{i_1, \ldots, i_k\} \subseteq \{1, 2, \ldots, m\}$, is called a *configuration* of Π.

It is important to note that the membranes preserve the initial labeling in all subsequent configurations; in this way, the correspondence between membranes, multisets of objects, and sets of evolution rules is well specified by the subscripts of these elements.

For two configurations:

$$C_1 = (\mu', w'_{i_1}, \ldots, w'_{i_k}), C_2 = (\mu'', w''_{j_1}, \ldots, w''_{j_l}),$$

of Π we write $C_1 \Rightarrow C_2$ and we say that we have a *transition* from C_1 to C_2, if we can pass from C_1 to C_2 by using the evolution rules appearing in $R_{i_1}, \ldots, R_{i_k}$ in the following manner:

Consider a rule $u \to v$ in a set R_{i_t}. We look to the region of μ' associated with the membrane i_t. If the objects mentioned by u, with the multiplicities specified by u appear in w'_{i_t} (that is, the multiset $M(u)$ is included in $M(w'_{i_t})$), then, these objects can evolve according to the rule $u \to v$. The rule can be used only if no rule of a higher priority exists in R_{i_t} and can be applied at the same time with $u \to v$. More precisely, we start to examine the rules in the decreasing order of their priority and assign objects to them. A rule can be used only when there are copies of the objects whose evolution it describes and which are not "consumed" by rules of a higher priority. Moreover, there is no rule of a higher priority, irrespective of which rules it involves, which is applicable at the same step. Therefore, all objects to which a rule *can* be applied *must* be the subject of a rule application. All objects in u are "consumed" by using the rule $u \to v$, that is, the multiset $M(u)$ is subtracted from $M(w'_{i_t})$.

The result of using the rule is determined by v. If an object appears in v in the form a_{here}, then it will remain in the same region i_t. If an object appears in v in the form a_{out}, then a will exit the membrane i_t and will become an element of the region immediately outside it (thus, it will be adjacent to the membrane i_t from which it was expelled). In this way, it is possible that an object leaves the system. If it goes outside the skin of the system, then it never comes back. If an object appears in the form a_{in_q}, then a will be added to the multiset $M(w'_q)$, providing that a is adjacent to the membrane q. If a_{in_q} appears in v and membrane q is not one of the membranes delimiting "from below" the region i_t, then the application of the rule is not allowed.

If the symbol δ appears in v, then membrane i_t is removed (we say *dissolved*) and at the same time the set of rules R_{i_t} (and its associated priority relation) is removed. The multiset $M(w'_{i_t})$ is added (in the sense of multisets union) to the multiset associated with the region which was immediately external to membrane i_t. We do not allow the dissolving of the skin, because this means that the super-cell is lost and we no longer have a correct configuration of the system.

All these operations are performed in parallel, for all possible applicable rules $u \to v$, for all occurrences of multisets u in the region associated with the rules, for all regions at the same time. No contradiction appears because of multiple membrane dissolving, or because simultaneous appearance of symbols of the form a_{out} and δ. If at the same step, we have a_{in_i} outside a membrane i and δ inside this membrane, then, because of the simultaneity of performing these operations, again no contradiction appears: we assume that a is introduced in membrane i at the same time when it is dissolved, thus a will remain in the region placed outside membrane i; that is, from the point of view of a, the effect of a_{in_i} in the region outside membrane i and δ in membrane i is a_{here}.

A sequence of transitions between configurations of a given P system Π is called a *computation* with respect to Π. A computation is *successful* if and only if it halts, that is, there is no rule applicable to the objects present in the last configuration. If the system is provided with an output region $i_0 \neq \infty$, then the membrane i_0 is present as an elementary one in the last configuration of the computation. Note that the output membrane was not necessarily an elementary one in the initial configuration. The result of a successful computation can be the total number of objects present in the output membrane of a halting configuration, or $\psi_T(w)$, where w describes the multiset of objects from T present in the output membrane in a halting configuration (ψ_T is the Parikh mapping associated with T), or a language, as it will be defined immediately. The set of vectors $\psi_T(w)$ for w describing the multiset of objects present in the output membrane of a system Π in a halting configuration is denoted $P_s(\Pi)$ (from "Parikh set") and we say that it is *generated* by Π in the *internal mode*. When we are interested only in the number of objects present in the output membrane in the halting configuration of Π, we denote by $N(\Pi)$ the set of numbers "generated" in this way.

When no output membrane is specified ($i_0 = \infty$), we observe the system from outside and collect the objects ejected from the skin membrane, in the order they are ejected. Using these objects, we form a string. When several objects are ejected at the same time, any permutation of them is considered. In this way, a string or a set of strings is associated with each computation, that is, a language is associated with the system.

We denote by $L(\Pi)$ the language computed by Π in the way described above. We say that it is *generated* by Π *in the external mode*.

We now illustrate with an example, the functioning of a P system.

Example 14.8   Consider the P system of degree 3

$$\Pi = (V, T, C, \mu, w_1, w_2, w_3, (R_1, \rho_1), (R_2, \rho_2), (R_3, \rho_3), 3),$$
$$V = \{a, b, c, d, x\},$$
$$T = \{x\},$$

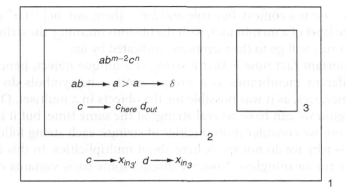

Figure 14.2. *P* system generating product *mn*

$$C = \phi,$$
$$\mu = [1[2]2[3]3]1,$$
$$w_1 = \phi, R_1 = \left\{c \to x_{in_3}, d \to x_{in_3}\right\}, \rho_1 = \phi,$$
$$w_2 = \{ab^{m-2}c^n\}, R_2 = \{ab \to a, a \to \delta, c \to c_{here}d_{out}\},$$
$$\rho_2 = \{ab \to a > a \to \delta\},$$
$$w_3 = \phi, R_3 = \phi, \rho_3 = \phi.$$

The initial configuration of the system is presented in Figure 14.2.

In this example, there are no objects present in membrane 1 and 3, hence, no rule can be applied here. We start in membrane 2, using the objects *a*, *b*, *c* present in membrane 2, the rules $ab \to a, c \to c_{here}d_{out}$, applied $m - 2$ times reduces ab^{m-2} to a and c^n remains in membrane 2. $m - 2$ copies of *d* are sent out and then membrane 2 dissolves. At this time $x^{n(m-2)}$ is available in membrane 3. When membrane 2 dissolves $c^n d^n$ are in membrane 1, and sent to membrane 3 as x^{2n} in the next step. Hence $N(\pi) = \{mn | n \geq 1, m \geq 2\}$.

Rewriting *P* Systems

Now, we consider objects which can be described by finite strings given over a finite alphabet, instead of objects of an atomic type. The evolution of an object then corresponds to a transformation of the string. The transformations take place in the form of rewriting steps. Consequently, the evolution rules are given as rewriting rules.

Assume that we have an alphabet *V*. A usual rewriting rule is a pair (u, v) of words over *V*. For $x, y \in V^*$ we write $x \Rightarrow y$ iff $x = x_1 u x_2$ and $y = x_1 v x_2$, for some strings $x_1, x_2 \in V^*$. The rules are also provided with indications on the target membrane of the produced string. Here, the membrane dissolving action is not considered as it is not required for obtaining computational completeness. Always we use context-free rules of the form:

$$X \to (v, tar)$$

where $X \rightarrow v$ is a context-free rule and $tar \in \{here, out, in_j\}$ ("tar" comes from target, j is the label of a membrane), with the obvious meaning: the string produced by using this rule will go to the membrane indicated by tar.

The important fact now is that a string is a unique object, hence, it passes through different membranes as a unique entity, its symbols do not follow different itineraries, as it was possible for the objects in a multiset. Of course, in the same region we can have several strings at the same time, but it is irrelevant whether or not we consider multiplicities of strings: each string follows its own "fate." That is why we do not speak here about multiplicities. In this framework, the catalysts are meaningless. Now, we discuss some basic variants of rewriting P systems.

P Systems with Sequential Rewriting

A *sequential rewriting P system* (or rewriting P systems, for short) (Păun, 1998) is a language-generating mechanism of the form:

$$\Pi = (V, T, \mu, L_1, \ldots, L_n, (R_1, \rho_1), \ldots (R_n, \rho_n), i_0),$$

where V is an alphabet, $T \subseteq V$ is the output alphabet, μ is a membrane structure consisting of n membranes labeled with $1, 2, \ldots, n$, $L_1, L_2, \ldots, L_n$ are finite languages over V associated with the regions $1, 2, \ldots, n$ of μ, $R_1, \ldots, R_n$ are finite sets of context-free evolution rules and $\rho_1, \ldots, \rho_n$ are partial order relations over $R_1, \ldots, R_n$. i_0 is the output membrane if $1 \leq i_0 \leq n$, otherwise $i_0 = \infty$. In the former case, the output is read within the system, and in the latter case, the output is read in the outer region.

The language generated by a system Π is denoted by $L(\Pi)$ and it is defined as explained in the previous chapter with the differences specific to an evolution based on rewriting: we start from an initial configuration of the system and proceed iteratively, by transition steps performed using the rules in parallel, to all strings which can be rewritten, obeying the priority relations, and collecting the terminal strings generated in a designated membrane, the output one.

Note that each string is processed by one rule only, the parallelism refers here to processing simultaneously all available strings by all applicable rules. If several rules can be applied to a string, maybe in several places each, then we take only one rule and only one possibility to apply it and consider the obtained string as the next state of the object described by the string. It is important to have in mind that the evolution of strings is not independent of each other, but interrelated in two ways:

Case 1: There exists a priority relation among the rules

A rule r_1 applicable to a string x can forbid the use of another rule r_2, for rewriting another string y, which is present at that time in the same membrane. After applying the rule r_1, if r_1 is not applicable to y or to the string x' obtained from x by using r_1, then it is possible that the rule r_2 can now be applied to y.

Case 2: There is no priority relation among the rules

Even without priorities, if a string x can be rewritten forever in the same membrane or on an itinerary through several membranes, then all strings are lost, because the computation never stops irrespective of the strings collected in the output membrane and which cannot evolve further.

The family of all languages $L(\Pi)$ generated by sequential rewriting P systems with atmost m membranes, using priorities and having internal (external) output can characterize RE. In fact to show this a system with two membranes is sufficient.

P Systems based on Sequential Rewriting with Membranes of Variable Thickness

A variant of sequential rewriting P systems with no priorities, by allowing the membranes to be permeable only under certain conditions is a P system with variable thickness. The concentration difference in neighboring regions plays an important role in this variant. This is motivated biologically from the fact that in real cells, molecules can pass through membranes mainly because of concentration difference in neighboring regions, or by means of electrical charges (ions can be transported in spaces of opposite polarization).

The control of membrane permeability is achieved as follows: besides the action of dissolving a membrane, (indicated by introducing the symbol δ) we also use the action of making a membrane thicker (this is indicated by the symbol τ). Initially, all membranes have thickness one. If a rule $X \to \upsilon\tau$ is applied in a membrane of thickness one, introducing the symbol τ, then the membrane thickness becomes two. A membrane of thickness two does not become thicker by using further rules that introduce the symbol τ, but no object can enter or exit it. If a rule $X \to \upsilon\delta$, which introduces the symbol δ is used in a membrane of thickness one, then the membrane is dissolved; if the membrane had thickness two, then it returns to thickness one. The following points should be noted:

1. If rules which introduce both δ and τ are applied in a single step in a membrane, then the membrane does not change its thickness.
2. If two or more rules involving τ are applied in a membrane in a single step, the membrane becomes non-permeable.
3. If two or more rules involving δ are applied in a single step in a non-permeable membrane or a membrane of thickness two or one, the membrane dissolves.

The actions of symbols δ, τ are illustrated in Figure 14.3.

A P system based on *sequential rewriting, with external output and membranes of variable thickness* is a construct:

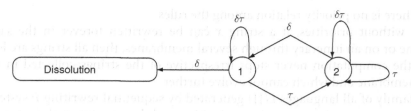

Figure 14.3. The effect of actions δ, τ

$$\Pi = (V, T, \mu, L_1, L_2, \ldots, L_n, R_1, R_2, \ldots, R_n, \infty)$$

where V is the total alphabet of the system; $T \subseteq V$ is the terminal alphabet; μ is a membrane structure consisting of n membranes labeled with 1, 2, ... , n; $L_1, \ldots, L_n$ are finite languages over V, associated with the regions 1, 2, ... , n of μ and $R_1, R_2, \ldots, R_n$ are sets of evolution rules for the regions of μ. The rules are of the following form:

$$X \to (v', tar), X \in V, v' = v \text{ or } v\delta \text{ or } v\tau, v \in V^*, tar \in \{here, out, in\}$$

The meaning of these rules are obvious: if a rule $X \to (v\tau, tar)$ is applied in a membrane i, the string replaces X by v and moves to the membrane indicated by tar,
—increasing its thickness, if it is of thickness one
—making it non-permeable if it is of thickness two.
Similarly, the rule $X \to (v\delta, tar)$ applied in a membrane i reduces the thickness of the target membrane if it is of thickness two and dissolves the target membrane if it is of thickness one. The effect of δ, τ are also carried to the target membrane along with the string. It should be noted that this is the only variant where the effect of actions δ, τ are carried over to the target membrane. In all the other variants, the effects of these actions are pertained to the membranes where the symbols δ, τ are introduced through rules.

The language generated by the system consists of all strings over T^* coming out of the skin membrane, after a complete computation. The way of rewriting the strings is the same as that of sequential rewriting P systems. Here, we do not have priorities, but we have the membrane dissolving and thickening actions. It is seen that these two controls are sufficient for obtaining computational completeness with no priorities and no bound on the number of membranes.

P Systems with Replicated Rewriting

A variant of rewriting P systems, which is capable of solving hard problems is introduced in this section. For solving hard problems with P systems which use rewriting rules, we need to replicate strings, in order to get an exponential space in a linear time. Hence, we consider rules which replicate the strings at the same time when rewriting them.

A P system based on *replicated rewriting* is a construct

$$\Pi = (V, T, \mu, L_1, L_2, \ldots, L_m, R_1, R_2, \ldots, R_m, \infty)$$

where V is the total alphabet; $T \subseteq V$ is the terminal alphabet; μ is a membrane structure consisting of m membranes labeled with $1, 2, \ldots, m$; $L_1, \ldots, L_m$ are finite languages over V, associated with the regions of μ and $R_1, R_2, \ldots, R_m$ are finite sets of developmental rules of the form:

$$X \to (v_1, tar_1)\|(v_2, tar_2)\| \ldots \|(v_n, tar_n), n \geq 1$$

where $tar_i \in \{here, out\} \cup \{in_j, \mid 1 \leq j \leq m\}, X \in V, v_i \in V^*, 1 \leq i \leq n$. If $n > 1$, then the rule is a replicated rewriting rule, otherwise, it is just a rewriting rule.

When a rule $X \to (v_1, tar_1)\|(v_2, tar_2)\| \ldots \|(v_n, tar_n)$ is used to rewrite a string $x_1 X x_2$, we obtain n strings $x_1 v_i x_2$ which are sent to the regions indicated by tar_i, $1 \leq i \leq n$, respectively. When $tar_i = here$, the string remains in the same region, when $tar_i = out$, the string exits the current membrane and when $tar_i = in_j$, the string is sent to membrane j, providing that it is directly inside the membrane where the rule is applied; if there is no such membrane j inside the membrane we work, then the rule cannot be applied.

A computation is defined as follows: we start from the strings present in an initial configuration and proceed iteratively, by transition steps laid down by using the rules in parallel, in each membrane to all strings which can be rewritten by local rules; the result is collected outside the system, at the end of halting computations. We do not consider here further features such as priorities among the rules or the possibility of dissolving membranes.

The language generated by a replicated rewriting P system Π is denoted $L(\Pi)$ and it consists of all strings over T^* sent out of the system at the end of a halting configuration.

Solving SAT and HPP

We see that the satisfiability of propositional formulas in the conjuctive normal form (SAT) problem and the Hamiltonian path problem (HPP) can be solved in a linear time using replicated rewriting P systems. The time is estimated here as the number of steps the system works. This means, we have a parallel time where each unit is the time of a "biological" step in the system, the time of using any rule, supposing that all rules take the same time to be applied.

The SAT is probably the most known NP-complete problem. It asks whether or not for a given formula in the conjunctive normal form there is a truth-assignment of the variables for which the formula assumes the value *true*. A formula as above is of the form:

$$\gamma = C_1 \wedge C_2 \wedge \ldots \wedge C_m,$$

where each C_i, $1 \leq i \leq n$, is a *clause* of the form of a disjunction

$$C_i = y_1 \vee y_2 \vee \ldots \vee y_r,$$

with each y_j being either a propositional variable, x_s, or its negation, $\neg\, x_s$. (Thus, we use the variables $x_1, x_2, \ldots$ and the three connectives $\vee, \wedge, \neg$: *or, and, negation*). For example, let us consider the propositional formula:

$$\beta = (x_1 \vee x_2) \wedge (\neg\, x_1 \vee \neg\, x_2)$$

We have two variables, x_1, x_2, and two clauses. It is easy to see that it is satisfiable: any of the following truth-assignments makes the formula *true*:

$$(x_1 = true,\, x_2 = false),\, (x_1 = false,\, x_2 = true).$$

We give below two theorems without proof.

Theorem 14.9 *The SAT problem can be solved by using replicated rewriting P systems in a time linear in the number of variables and number of clauses.*

Theorem 14.10 *The Hamiltonian path problem can be solved by P systems with replicated rewriting in a time linear in the number of nodes of the given graph.*

P Systems with Active Membranes

A natural possibility is to let the number of membranes also to increase during a computation, for instance, by division, as is well known in biology. Actually, the membranes from biochemistry are not at all passive, like those in the models cited above. For example, the passing of a chemical compound through a membrane is often done by a direct interaction with the membrane itself (with the so-called *protein channels* or *protein gates* present in the membrane). During this interaction, the chemical compound passing through the membrane, as well as the membrane itself, can be modified.

These observations were made use of, to form a new class of *P* systems where the central role in the computation is played by the membranes. Evolution rules were associated both with objects and membranes, while the communication through membranes was performed with the direct participation of the membranes; moreover, the membranes could not only be dissolved, but they also could multiply by *division*. An elementary membrane could be divided by means of an interaction with an object from that membrane. Each membrane was supposed to have an "electrical polarization" (we will say *charge*), one of the three possible: *positive, negative,* or *neutral*. If a membrane had two immediately lower membranes of opposite polarizations, one *positive* and one *negative*, then that membrane could also divide in such a way that the two membranes of opposite charge were separated; all membranes of neutral charge and all objects were duplicated and a copy of each of them was introduced in each of the two new membranes. The skin was never divided.

In this way, the number of membranes could grow, even exponentially. By making use of this increased parallelism, one could compute faster. It was proved that this is the case, indeed: the SAT problem, one of the basic NP-complete problems, could be solved in this framework in linear time. Moreover, the model was shown to be computationally universal: any recursively enumerable set of (vectors of) natural numbers could be generated by these systems.

An important application of this class of P systems is that these systems are capable of solving a real-world problem, viz., breaking DES.

We now directly define the variant of P systems.

Let $d \geq 1$ be a natural number. A *P system with active membranes and d-bounded membrane division* (in short, we say a *P system with active membranes*) is a construct

$$\Pi = (V, T, H, \mu, w_1, \ldots, w_m, R),$$

where:

1. $m \geq 1$;
2. V is an alphabet (the *total alphabet* of the system);
3. $T \subseteq V$ (the *terminal* alphabet);
4. H is a *finite set* of *labels* for the membranes;
5. μ is a *membrane structure*, consisting of m membranes, labeled (not necessarily in a one-to-one manner) with elements of H; all membranes in μ are supposed to be neutral;
6. $w_1, \ldots, w_m$ are strings over V, describing the *multisets of objects* placed in the m regions of μ;
7. R is a finite set of *developmental rules*, of the following forms:

   (a) $\left[{}_h a \to u \right]_h^\alpha$, for $h \in H$, $a \in V$, $v \in V^*$, $\alpha \in \{+, -, 0\}$ (object evolution rules),

   (b) $a \left[{}_h \; \right]_h^{\alpha_1} \to \left[{}_h b \right]_h^{\alpha_2}$, where $a, b \in V$, $h \in H$, $\alpha_1, \alpha_2 \in \{+, -, 0\}$ (an object is introduced in the membrane),

   (c) $\left[{}_h a \right]_h^{\alpha_1} \to \left[{}_h \; \right]_h^{\alpha_2} b$, for $h \in H$, $\alpha_1, \alpha_2 \in \{+, -, 0\}$, $a, b \in V$ (an object is sent out),

   (d) $\left[{}_h a \right]_h^\alpha \to b$, for $h \in H$, $\alpha \in \{+, -, 0\}$, $a, b \in V$ (dissolving rules),

   (e) $\left[{}_h a \right]_h^\alpha \to \left[{}_h a_1 \right]_h^{\alpha_1} \left[{}_h a_2 \right]_h^{\alpha_2} \ldots \left[{}_h a_n \right]_h^{\alpha_n}$,

   for $\alpha, \alpha_i \in \{+, -, 0\}$, $a \in V$, $a_i \in V^*$, $i = 1, \ldots, n$, $h \in H$, and $n \leq d$ (division rules for elementary membranes),

   (f)
   $$\left[{}_{h_0} \left[{}_{h_1} \; \right]_{h_1}^{\alpha_1} \cdots \left[{}_{h_k} \; \right]_{h_k}^{\alpha_k} \left[{}_{h_{k+1}} \; \right]_{h_{k+1}}^{\alpha_{k+1}} \cdots \left[{}_{h_n} \; \right]_{h_n}^{\alpha_n} \right]_{h_0}^{\alpha_0}$$
   $$\to \left[{}_{h_0} \left[{}_{h_1} \; \right]_{h_1}^{\beta_1} \cdots \left[{}_{h_k} \; \right]_{h_k}^{\beta_k} \right]_{h_0}^{\gamma_0} \left[{}_{h_0} \left[{}_{h_{k+1}} \; \right]_{h_{k+1}}^{\beta_{k+1}} \cdots \left[{}_{h_n} \; \right]_{h_n}^{\beta_n} \right]_{h_0}^{\gamma_n},$$

   for $k \geq 1$, $n > k$, $h_i \in H$, $0 \leq i \leq n$, $n \leq d$, and there exist i, j, $1 \leq i, j \leq n$, such that $\alpha_i, \alpha_j \in \{+, -\}$; moreover, $\beta_j, \gamma_j \in \{+, -, 0\}$, $1 \leq j \leq n$ (division of non-elementary membranes).

Note that in all rules of types (a) − (e), the objects do not directly interact. In rule (a), an object is transformed into a string of objects, and in the rest of the rules, an object is replaced with another one.

These rules are applied according to the following *principles:*

1. All the rules are applied in parallel: in a step, the rules of type (a) are applied to all objects to which they can be applied, all other rules are applied to all membranes to which they can be applied; an object can be used by only one rule, non-deterministically chosen (there is no priority relation among rules), but any object which can evolve by a rule of any form, should evolve.

2. If a membrane is dissolved, then all the objects in its region are left free in the region immediately above it. Because all rules are associated with membranes, the rules of a dissolved membrane are no longer available in subsequent steps. The skin membrane is never dissolved.

3. Note that in a rule of type (f) at least two membranes in its left-hand side should have opposite polarization. All objects and membranes not specified in a rule and which do not evolve are passed unchanged to the next step. For instance, if a membrane with the label h is divided by a rule of type (e) which involves an object a, then all other objects in membrane h which do not evolve are introduced in each of the resulting membranes h. Similarly, when dividing a membrane h by means of a rule of type (f), the contents of each membrane is reproduced unchanged in each copy, providing that no rule is applied to their objects.

4. If at the same time a membrane h is divided by a rule of type (e) and there are objects in this membrane which evolve by means of rules of type (a), then in the new copies of the membrane we introduce the result of the evolution. That is, we may suppose that first the evolution rules of type (a) are used, changing the objects, and then the division is produced, so that in the new membranes with label h we introduce copies of the changed objects. Of course, this process takes only one step. The same assertions apply to the division by means of a rule of type (f): always we assume that the rules are applied "from bottom-up". We first apply the rules of the innermost region and then proceed level by level until the region of the skin membrane is reached.

5. The rules associated with a membrane h are used for all copies of this membrane, irrespective whether or not the membrane is an initial one or it is obtained by division. At one step, a membrane h can be the subject of only one rule of types (b) − (f).

6. The skin membrane can never divide. As any other membrane, the skin membrane can be "electrically charged."

The membrane structure of the system at a given time, together with all multi-sets of objects associated with the regions of this membrane structure is the *configuration* of the system at that time. The $(m + 1)$-tuple $(M, w_1, \ldots, w_m)$ is the *initial configuration.* We can pass from a configuration to another by using the rules from R according to the principles given above. We say that we have a (direct) *transition* among configurations.

A sequence of transitions which starts from the initial configuration is called a *computation* with respect to Π. A computation is *complete* if it cannot be continued: there is no rule which can be applied to objects and membranes in the last configuration.

Note that during a computation, the number of membranes (hence the degree of the system) can increase and decrease but the labels of these membranes are always among the labels of membranes present in the initial configuration (by division we only produce membranes with the same label as the label of the divided membrane).

During a computation, objects can leave the skin membrane (by means of rules of type (c)). The terminal symbols, which leave the skin membrane are collected in the order of their expelling from the system, so, a string is associated to a complete computation; when several terminal symbols leave the system at the same time, then any ordering of them is accepted (thus, with a complete computation we possibly associate a set of strings, due to this "local commutativity" of symbols which are observed outside the system at the same time). In this way, a language is associated with Π, denoted by $L(\Pi)$, consisting of all strings which are associated with all complete computations in Π.

Two facts are worth emphasizing: (1) the symbols not in T that leave the skin membrane as well as all symbols from T, which remain in the system at the end of a halting computation are not considered in the generated strings and (2) if a computation goes for ever, then it provides no output, it does not contribute to the language $L(\Pi)$.

Generally, to solve NP-complete problems, which can be solved deterministically in exponential time, the following steps can be used.

1. Start with a linear membrane structure. The central membrane is always divided into an exponential number of copies.
2. In the central "parallel engine" one generates, making use of the membrane division, a "data pool" of an exponential size; due to the parallelism, this takes only a linear time. In parallel with this process, a "timer" is simultaneously ticking, in general, for synchronization reasons.
3. After finishing the generation of the "data pool", one checks whether or not any solution of our problem exists.
4. A message is sent out of the system at a precise moment telling whether or not the problem has a solution.

Solving SAT in Linear Time

We illustrate the usefulness of P systems with 2-bounded division by solving the SAT problem in linear time. The time is estimated here as the number of steps the system works. This means, we have a parallel time where each unit is the time of a "biological" step in the system, the time of using any rule, supposing that all rules take the same time to be applied. Figure 14.4 illustrates the shape of P system that solves a NP-complete problem.

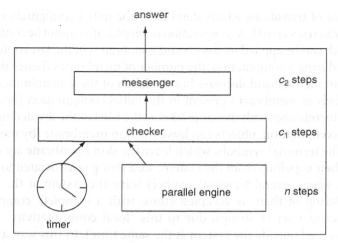

Figure 14.4. The shape of P systems solving NP-complete problems

Theorem 14.11 *The SAT problem can be solved by a P system with active membranes and two bounded division in a time, which is linear in the number of variables and the number of clauses.*

14.3 Tissue *P* Systems

The tissue P system, a variant of P system is mainly concerned with two things, intercellular communication (of chemicals, energy, information) by means of complex networks of protein channels, and the way the neurons co-operate, processing impulses in the complex net established by synapses.

The computing model tissue P system, in short, tP system, consists of several cells, related by protein channels. In order to preserve the neural intuition, we will use the shorter and suggestive name of synapses for these channels. Each cell has a state from a given finite set and can process multi-sets of objects (chemical compounds in the case of cells, impulses in the case of the brain), represented by symbols from a given alphabet. The standard rules are of the form $sM \rightarrow s'M'$, where s, s' are states and M, M' are multisets of symbols. Some of the elements of M' may be marked with "go," and this means that they have to immediately leave the cell and pass to the cells to which they have direct links through synapses. This communication (transfer of symbol-objects) can be done in a replicative manner (the same symbol is sent to all adjacent cells), or in a non-replicative manner; in the second case we can send all the symbols to only one neighboring cell, or we can distribute them nondeterministically. One more choice appears in using the rules $sM \rightarrow s'M'$: we can apply such a rule only to one occurrence of M (one mode), or all occurrences of M in a parallel way (parallel mode); or we can apply a maximal package of rules of the form $sM_i \rightarrow s'M'$, $1 \leq i \leq k$, that is, involving the same states s, s', which can be applied to the current multiset (the maximal mode).

By the combination of the three modes of processing objects and the three modes of communication among cells, we get nine possible behaviors of tP system.

This model starts from a given initial configuration (that is, initial states of cells and initial multisets of symbol-objects placed in them) and proceeds until reaching a halting configuration, where no further rule can be applied, and then associates a result with this configuration. Because of the non-deterministic behavior of a tP system, starting from the given initial configuration we can get arbitrarily many outputs. Output will be defined by sending symbols out of the system. For this purpose, one cell will be designated as the output cell, and in its rules $sM \rightarrow s'M'$ the symbols from M' are marked with the indication "out"; such a symbol will immediately leave the system, contributing to the result of the computation.

We now formally define this computing model.

A tissue P system, of degree m, $m \geq 1$, is a construct:

$$\Pi = (O, \sigma_1, \sigma_2, \ldots, \sigma_m, syn, i_{out}),$$

where:

- O is a finite non-empty alphabet (of objects);
- $syn \subseteq \{1, \ldots, m\} \times \{1, \ldots, m\}$ (synapses among cells);
- $i_{out} \in \{1, \ldots, m\}$ indicates the *output cell*;
- σ_i, $1 \leq i \leq m$, are cells, where each $\sigma_i = (Q_i, s_{i,0}, w_{i,0}, P_i)$, with:
  - Q_i is a finite set of states;
  - $s_{i,0} \in Q_i$ is the initial state;
  - $w_{i,0}$ is the initial multiset of objects;
  - P_i is a finite set of rules of the form $sw \rightarrow s'xy_{go}z_{out}$, where $s, s' \in Q_i$, w, $x \in O^*$, $y_{go} \in (O \times \{go\})^*$ and $Z_{out} \in (O \times \{out\})^*$, with the restriction that $z_{out} = \lambda$ for all $i \in \{1, 2, \ldots, m\}$ different from i_{out}.

A tP system is said to be co-operative if it contains at least a rule $sw \rightarrow s'w'$ such that $|w| > 1$, and non-cooperative in the opposite case. The objects which appear in the left-hand multiset w of a rule $sw \rightarrow s'w'$ are sometimes called impulses, while those in w' are also called excitations.

Remark 1. Note that rules of the forms $s \rightarrow s'$, $s \rightarrow s'w'$ are not allowed.

Remark 2. Synapses of the form (i, i), $1 \leq i \leq m$, are not allowed.

Any m-tuple of the form $(s_1 w_1, \ldots, s_m w_m)$, with $s_i \in Q_i$ and $w_i \in O^*$, for all $1 \leq i \leq m$, is called a configuration of Π; thus, $(s_{1,0} w_{1,0} \ldots, s_{m,0} w_{m,0})$ is the initial configuration of Π.

Using the rules from the sets P_i, $1 \leq i \leq m$, we can define transitions among the configurations of the system. For this purpose, we first consider three *modes of processing the impulse-objects* and three *modes of transmitting excitation-objects* from one cell to another cell.

Let us denote $O_{go} = \{(a, go) \mid a \in O\}$, $O_{out} = \{(a, out) \mid a \in O\}$, and $O_{tot} = O \cup O_{go} \cup O_{out}$.

For $s, s' \in Q$, $x \in O^*$, $y \in O^*_{tot}$, we write:

$sx \Rightarrow_{min} s'y$ iff $sw \rightarrow s' \in P_i$, $w \subseteq x$, and $y = (x - w) \cup w'$;

$sx \Rightarrow_{par} s'y$ iff $sw \rightarrow s'w' \in P_i$, $w^k \subseteq x$, $w^{k+1} \not\subseteq x$,

for some $k \geq 1$ and $y = (x - w^k) \cup w'^k$;

$sx \Rightarrow_{max} s'y$ iff $sw_1 \rightarrow s' w_1, \ldots, sw_k \rightarrow s'w'_k \in P_i$, $k \geq 1$, such that

$w_1 \ldots w_k \subseteq x$, $y = (x - w_1 \ldots w_k) \cup w'_1 \ldots w'_k$,

and there is no $sw \rightarrow s'w' \in P_i$ such that

$w_1 \ldots w_k w \subseteq x$.

Intuitively, in the min mode, only one occurrence of the left-hand side symbol of a rule is processed (replaced by the string from the right-hand side of the rule, at the same time changing the state of the cell). In the *par* mode, a maximal change is performed with respect to a chosen rule, in the sense that as many as possible copies of the multiset from the left-hand side of the rule are replaced by the corresponding number of copies of the multiset from the right-hand side. In the max mode, the change is performed with respect to all rules, which use the current state of the cell and introduce the same new state after processing the multisets.

Now, remember that the multiset w' from a rule $sw \rightarrow s'w'$ contains symbols from O, but also symbols of the form (a, go) (or, in the case of the cell i_{out}, of the form (a, out)). Such symbols will be sent to the cells related by synapses to the cell σ_i where the rule $sw \rightarrow s'w'$ is applied, according to the following three transmitting modes, *repl, one,* and *spread:*

- *repl:* each symbol a, for (a, go) appearing in w', is sent to each of the cells σ_j such that $(i, j) \in syn$;
- *one:* all symbols a appearing in w' in the form (a, go) are sent to one for the cells σ_j such that $(i, j) \in syn$, nondeterministically chosen;
- *spread:* the symbols a appearing in w' in the form (a, go) are nondeterministically distributed among the cells σ_j such that $(i, j) \in syn$.

If we have at most two cells, three modes of transmitting the processed multisets from a cell to another cell are coincide.

During any transition, some cells can do nothing: if no rule is applicable to the available multisets in the current state, a cell waits until new multisets are sent to it from its ancestor cells. It is also worth noting that each transition lasts one time unit, and that the work of the net is synchronized, the same clock marks the time for all cells.

A sequence of transitions among configurations of the system Π is called a computation of Π. A computation which ends in a configuration where no rule in any cell can be applied is called an *halting computation*. During a halting computation the tP system Π sends out, through the cell $\sigma_{i_{out}}$, the multiset z. We say that the vector $\Psi_O(z)$, representing the multiplicities of objects from z, is computed by Π.

We denote by $N_{\alpha,\beta}(\Pi)$, for $\alpha \in \{min, par, max\}$, $\beta \in \{repl, one, spread\}$, the set of all natural numbers computed in this way by a system Π, in the mode(α, β). The family of all sets $N_{\alpha,\beta}(\Pi)$, computed by all co-operative tissue P systems with at most $m \geq 1$ cells, each of them using at most $r \geq 1$ states, is denoted by $NtP_{m,r}$ (Coo, α, β); when non-cooperative systems are used, we write $NtP_{m,r}$ (nCoo, α, β) for the corresponding family of sets of numbers. When any of the parameters m, r is not bounded we replace it with $*$.

Example 14.9 (**Tissue *P* Systems as Generative Devices**) Consider first a simple *tP* system: $\Pi_1 = (O, \sigma_1, \sigma_2, \sigma_3, syn, i_{out})$,

$O = \{a\}$,
$\sigma_1 = (\{s\}, s, a^2, \{sa \rightarrow s(a, go), sa \rightarrow s(a, out)\})$,
$\sigma_2 = (\{s\}, s, \lambda, \{sa \rightarrow s(a, go)\})$,
$\sigma_3 = (\{s\}, s, \lambda, \{sa \rightarrow s(a, go)\})$,
$syn = \{(1, 2), (1, 3), (2,1), (3,1)\}$,
$i_{out} = 1$.

A *tP* system can be graphically represented (Figure 14.5) with Π_1, with ovals associated with the cells (these ovals contain the initial state, the initial multiset, and the set of rules, and will be labeled with $1, 2, \ldots, m$), with arrows indicating the synapses, and with an arrow leaving from the output cell.

The system is presented in Figure 14.5.

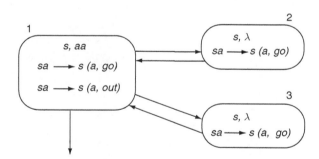

Figure 14.5. An example of a tP system

$N_{min, repl}(\Pi_1) = \{(n) \mid n \geq 1\}$,
$N_{min, \beta}(\Pi_1) = \{1,2\}$, for $\beta \in \{one, spread\}$,
$N_{par, repl}(\Pi_1) = \{(2^n) \mid n \geq 1\}$,
$N_{par, \beta}(\Pi_1) = \{2\}$, for $\beta \in \{one, spread\}$,
$N_{max, repl}(\Pi_1) = \{(n) \mid n \geq 1\}$,
$N_{max, \beta}(\Pi_1) = \{1, 2\}$, for $\beta \in \{one, spread\}$,

Indeed, in the non-replicative mode of communication, no further symbol is produced, hence, we only generate the vector $\{1, 2\}$. In the replicative case, the symbols produced by the rule $sa \rightarrow s(a, go)$ from cell 1 are doubled by communication. When the rules are used in the parallel mode, then all symbols are processed at the same time by the same rule, which means that all symbols present in the system are doubled from a step to the next one, therefore, the powers of 2 are obtained. When the rules are used in the minimal mode, the symbols are processed or sent out one by one, hence, all natural numbers can be obtained. In the maximal mode, we can send copies of symbol a at the same time to cells 2 and 3, and outside the system, hence, again any number of symbols can be sent out.

There are several variants of P systems in the literature. Some of them are splicing P systems, contextual P systems, tissue P systems, etc. Issues like complexity, decidability were also discussed. One of the directions of research, which is being investigated more in recent times is spiking neural P systems. The details of the above can be seen in "http://ppage.psystems.eu." There are also attempts to make practical use of this theoretical computing model.

Multiple Choice Questions (Set I)

In each of the following questions, choose the correct answer from the four choices provided.

1. The following grammar
   $G = (N, T, P, S)$
   $N = \{S, A, B\}$
   $T = \{a, b, c\}$
   $P : S \rightarrow aSa$
   $\quad\; S \rightarrow aAa$
   $\quad\; A \rightarrow bB$
   $\quad\; B \rightarrow bB$
   $\quad\; B \rightarrow c$ is

   a. is type 3
   b. is type 2 but not type 3
   c. is type 1 but not type 2
   d. is type 0 but not type 1

2. The following grammar
   $G = (N, T, P, S)$
   $N = \{S, A, B, C, D, E\}$
   $T = \{a, b, c\}$
   $P : S \rightarrow aAB$
   $\quad\;\; AB \rightarrow CD$
   $\quad\;\; CD \rightarrow CE$
   $\quad\;\; C \;\rightarrow aC$
   $\quad\;\; C \;\rightarrow b$
   $\quad\;\; bE \;\rightarrow bc$ is

   a. is type 3
   b. is type 2 but not type 3
   c. is type 1 but not type 2
   d. is type 0 but not type 1

3. The following grammar
   $G = (N, T, P, S)$
   $N = \{S, A, B, C\}$
   $T = \{a, b, c\}$

$P : S \rightarrow aS$
$A \rightarrow bB$
$B \rightarrow cC$
$C \rightarrow a$ is

a. is type 3
b. is type 2 but not type 3
c. is type 1 but not type 2
d. is type 0 but not type 1

4. The following grammar
$G = (N, T, P, S)$
$N = \{S, A, B, C, D, E\}$
$T = (a, b, c)$
$P : S \rightarrow ABCD$
$\quad BCD \rightarrow DE$
$\quad D \quad \rightarrow aD$
$\quad D \quad \rightarrow a$
$\quad E \quad \rightarrow bE$
$\quad E \quad \rightarrow c$ is

a. is type 3
b. is type 2 but not type 3
c. is type 1 but not type 2
d. is type 0 but not type 1

5. Consider the following CFG
$S \rightarrow aB \qquad S \rightarrow bA$
$B \rightarrow b \qquad A \rightarrow a$
$B \rightarrow bS \qquad A \rightarrow aS$
$B \rightarrow aBB \qquad A \rightarrow bAA$
Consider the following derivation
$S \Rightarrow aB$
$\quad \Rightarrow aaBB$
$\quad \Rightarrow aaBb$
$\quad \Rightarrow aabSb$
$\quad \Rightarrow aabbAb$
$\quad \Rightarrow aabbab$
This derivation is

a. a leftmost derivation
b. a rightmost derivation
c. both leftmost and rightmost derivation
d. neither leftmost nor rightmost derivation

6. Consider the following language
   $L = \{a^n b^n c^n d^n | n \geq 1\}$
   L is

   a. CFL but not regular
   b. CSL but not CFL
   c. regular
   d. type 0 language but not type 1

7. Consider the following language
   $L = \{a^n b^n | n \geq 1\}$
   L is

   a. CFL but not regular
   b. CSL but not CFL
   c. regular
   d. type 0 language but not type 1

8. Consider the following language
   $L = \{a^n b^m c^p d^q | n, m, p, q \geq 1\}$
   L is

   a. CFL but not regular
   b. CSL but not CFL
   c. regular
   d. type 0 language but not type 1

9. The following CFG is in
   $S \rightarrow AB$
   $B \rightarrow CD$
   $B \rightarrow AD$
   $B \rightarrow b$
   $D \rightarrow AD$
   $D \rightarrow d$
   $A \rightarrow a$
   $C \rightarrow a$

   a. Chomsky normal form but not strong Chomsky normal form
   b. Weak Chomsky normal form but not Chomsky normal form
   c. Strong Chomsky normal form
   d. Greibach normal form

10. The following CFG is in
    $S \rightarrow aBB$
    $B \rightarrow bAA$

$A \rightarrow a$

$B \rightarrow b$

    a. Chomsky normal form but not strong Chomsky normal form

    b. Weak Chomsky normal form but not Chomsky normal form

    c. Strong Chomsky normal form

    d. Greibach normal form

11. Which of the following CF language is inherently ambiguous?

    a. $\{a^n b^n c^m d^m | n, m \geq 1\}$

    b. $\{a^n b^m c^p d^q | n = p \text{ or } m = q, n, m, p, q \geq 1\}$

    c. $\{a^n b^m c^p d^q | n \neq m \wedge p \neq q\}$

    d. $\{a^n b^m c^p d^q | n \neq m \vee p \neq q\}$

12. Which string is not accepted by the following FSA?

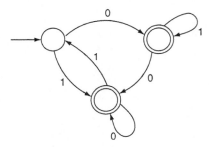

    a. 00111

    b. 01010

    c. 00110

    d. 11010

13. Which string is accepted by the following FSA?

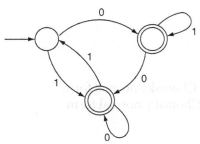

    a. 00111

    b. 11011

    c. 01101

    d. 0101

14. Can a DFSA simulate a NFSA

   a. No
   b. Yes
   c. sometimes
   d. depends on NFA

15. Which of the following is true for an arbitrary language L.

   a. $L^* = \bigcup_{i=1}^{\infty} L^i$
   b. $L^* = L^+ \cup \{\lambda\}$
   c. $L^* = L^+$
   d. $L^* = L^+ - \{\lambda\}$

16. The concept of FSA is much used in this part of the compiler

   a. lexical analysis
   b. parser
   c. code generation
   d. code optimization

17. The concept of grammar is much used in this part of the compiler

   a. lexical analysis
   b. parser
   c. code generation
   d. code optimization

18. $(a + b)(cd)^*(a + b)$ denotes the following set

   a. $\{a(cd)^n b | n \geq 1\}$
   b. $\{a(cd)^n a | n \geq 1\} \cup \{b(cd)^n b / n \geq 1\}$
   c. $\{a(cd)^n a | n \geq 0\} \cup \{a(cd)^n b / n \geq 0\} \cup \{b(cd)^n a / n \geq 0\} \cup \{b(cd)^n b / n \geq 0\}$
   d. $\{ac^n d^n b | n \geq 1\}$

19. baa^*c denotes the set

   a. $\{b^n a^m c^p | n, m, p \geq 1\}$
   b. $\{ba^n c | n \geq 0\}$
   c. $\{ba^n c | n \geq 1\}$
   d. $\{w | w$ is a string of $a, b, c\}$

20. The set of all strings over the alphabet $\Sigma = \{a, b\}$ (including ε) is denoted by

   a. $(a + b)^*$
   b. $(a + b)^+$
   c. $a^+ b^+$
   d. $a^* b^*$

21. Palindromes can't be recognized by any FSA because

    a. FSA cannot remember arbitrarily large amount of information
    b. FSA cannot deterministically fix the midpoint
    c. Even if the mid point is known an FSA cannot find whether the second half of the string matches the first half
    d. all of the above

22. Let $\Sigma = \{a, b, c, d, e\}$. The number of strings in Σ^* of length 4 such that no symbol is used more than once in a string is

    a. 360
    b. 120
    c. 35
    d. 36

23. Which of the following denotes Chomskian hiearchy?

    a. $REG \subset CFL \subset CSL \subset type0$
    b. $CFL \subset REG \subset type0 \subset CSL$
    c. $CSL \subset type0 \subset REG \subset CFL$
    d. $CSL \subset CFL \subset REG \subset type0$

24. A language L is accepted by a FSA iff it is

    a. CFL
    b. CSL
    c. recursive
    d. regular

25. Which of the following regular expressions denotes a language comprising of all possible strings over $\Sigma = \{a, b\}$ of length n where n is a multiple of 3.

    a. $(a + b + aa + bb + aba + bba)^*$
    b. $(aaa + bbb)^*$
    c. $((a + b)(a + b)(a + b))^*$
    d. $(aaa + ab + a) + (bbb + bb + a)$

26. A language is represented by a regular expression $(a)^*(a + ba)$. Which of the following string does not belong to the regular set represented by the above expression.

    a. aaa
    b. aba
    c. ababa
    d. aa

27. Which of the following is not primitive recursive but partially recursive?

    a. McCarthy's function
    b. Riemann function
    c. Ackermann's function
    d. Bounded function

28. Consider the following right-linear grammar $G = (N, T, P, S)$ $N = \{S\}$
    $P : S \rightarrow aS|aA$ $T = \{a, b\}$
    $A \rightarrow bA|b$
    Which of the following regular expression denotes $L(G)$?

    a. $(a + b)^*$
    b. $a(ab)^*b$
    c. aa^*bb^*
    d. a^*b^*

29. Which of the following strings is not generated by the following grammar?
    $S \rightarrow SaSbS|\varepsilon$

    a. aabb
    b. abab
    c. aababb
    d. aaabb

30. Consider the following NFSA

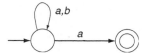

    The automaton accepts

    a. all words of the form $\{(ab)^n a|n \geq 1\}$
    b. all words that end with a and ε
    c. all words that end with a and not ε
    d. all words containing substring ba

31. Consider a language L for which there exists a Turing machine (TM), T, that accepts every word in L and either rejects or loops for every word that is not in L. The language L is

    a. NP hard
    b. NP complete
    c. recursive
    d. recursively enumerable

32. Consider the following statements
    (I) Recursive languages are closed under complementation
    (II) Recursively enumerable languages are closed under union
    (III) Recursively enumerable languages are closed under complementation
    Which of the above statement are TRUE?

    a. I only
    b. I and II
    c. I and III
    d. II and III

33. Which of the following statement is wrong?

    a. Any regular language can be generated by a context-free grammar
    b. Some non-regular languages cannot be generated by any CFG
    c. the intersection of a CFL and regular set is a CFL
    d. All non-regular languages can be generated by CFGs.

34. Recursively enumerable languages are not closed under

    a. union
    b. homomorphism
    c. complementation
    d. concatenation

35. Which of the following problem is undecidable?

    a. membership problem for CFL
    b. membership problem for regular sets
    c. membership problem for CSL
    d. membership problem for type 0 languages

36. Recursive languages are

    a. a proper superset of CFL
    b. always recognized by PDA
    c. are also called type 0 languages
    d. always recognized by FSA

37. R_1 and R_2 are regular sets. Which of the following is not true?

    a. $R_1 \cap R_2$ neet not be regular
    b. $\Sigma^* - R_1$ is regular
    c. $R_1 \cup R_2$ is regular
    d. R_1^* is regular

38. Which of the following regular expression identity is true?

    a. $r(^*) = r^*$
    b. $(r^*s^*)^* = (r+s)^*$
    c. $(r+s)^* = r^* + s^*$
    d. $r^*s^* = r^* + s^*$

39. Which one of the following statement is FALSE?

    a. context-free languages are closed under union
    b. context-free languages are closed under concatenation
    c. context-free languages are closed under intersection
    d. context-free languages are closed under Kleene closure

40. Which of the following conversion is not possible (algorithmically)?

    a. regular grammar to context-free grammar
    b. nondeterministic FSA to deterministic FSA
    c. nondeterministic PDA to deterministic PDA
    d. nondeterministic TM to deterministic TM

Answers

1. b	11. b	21. d	31. d
2. c	12. a	22. b	32. b
3. a	13. b	23. a	33. d
4. d	14. b	24. d	34. c
5. d	15. b	25. c	35. d
6. b	16. a	26. c	36. a
7. a	17. b	27. c	37. a
8. c	18. c	28. c	38. b
9. c	19. c	29. d	39. c
10. d	20. a	30. c	40. c

Multiple Choice Questions (Set II)

In each of the following questions, choose the correct answer from the four choices provided.

1. Consider three decision problems P_1, P_2 and P_3. It is known that P_1 is decidable and P_2 is undecidable. Which one of the following is TRUE?

    a. P_3 is decidable if P_1 is reducible to P_3
    b. P_3 is undecidable if P_3 is reducible to P_2
    c. P_3 is undecidable if P_2 is reducible to P_3
    d. P_3 is decidable if P_3 is reducible to P_2's complement

2. Consider three problems P_1, P_2 and P_3. It is known that P_1 has polynomial time solution and P_2 is NP-complete and P_3 is in NP. Which one of the following is true.

    a. P_3 has polynomial time solution if P_1 is polynomial time reducible to P_3
    b. P_3 is NP complete if P_3 is polynomial time reducible to P_2
    c. P_3 is NP complete if P_2 is reducible to P_3
    d. P_3 has polynomial time complexity and P_3 is reducible to P_2

3. Consider the FSA M

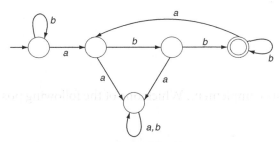

    The language recognized by M is

    a. $\{w \in \{a, b\}^* \mid$ every a in w is followed by exactly two b's$\}$
    b. $\{w \in \{a, b\}^* \mid$ every a in w is followed by atleast two b's$\}$
    c. $\{w \in \{a, b\}^* \mid w$ contains the substring 'abb'$\}$
    d. $\{w \in \{a, b\}^* \mid w$ does not contain 'aa' as substring$\}$

4. Let N_f and N_p denote the classes of languages accepted by nondeterministic FSA and nondeterministic PDA, respectively. Let D_f and D_p denote the classes of languages accepted by deterministic FSA and PDA respectively. Which of the following is TRUE?

Some of these questions have appeared in GATE examinations.

a. $D_f \subset N_f \quad D_p \subset N_p$
b. $D_f \subset N_f \quad D_p = N_p$
c. $D_f = N_f \quad D_p \subset N_p$
d. $D_f = N_f \quad D_p = N_p$

5. Consider the languages
   $L_1 = \{a^n b^n c^m | n, m > 0\}$ and $L_2 = \{a^n b^m c^m | n, m > 0\}$
   Which one of the following statements is false?

   a. $L_1 \cap L_2$ is a CFL
   b. $L_1 \cup L_2$ is a CFL
   c. $L_1 \cup L_2$ is inherently ambiguous
   d. $L_1 \cap L_2$ is a CSL

6. Consider the languages
   $L_1 = \{a^n b^m c^n d^p | n, m, p > 0\}$ and $L_2 = \{a^n b^m c^p d^m | n, m, p > 0\}$
   Which one of the following statements is false?

   a. $L_1 \cap L_2$ is a CFL
   b. $L_1 \cup L_2$ is a CFL
   c. $L_1 \cup L_2$ is inherently ambiguous
   d. $L_1 \cap L_2$ is a CSL

7. Consider the languages
   $L_1 = \{a^n b^m c^m d^n | n, m > 0\}$ and $L_2 = \{a^n b^n c^m d^m | n, m > 0\}$
   Which one of the following statements is false?

   a. $L_1 \cup L_2$ is a CFL
   b. $L_1 \cap L_2$ is a CFL
   c. L_1 and L_2 are CFL
   d. $L_1 \cap L_2$ is a CSL

8. Let L and $\bar{L}$ be a language and its complement. Which one of the following possibilities will not hold?

   a. L and $\bar{L}$ are recursive
   b. L is recursively enumerable but not recursive $\bar{L}$ is not recursively enumerable
   c. L and $\bar{L}$ are not recursively enumerable
   d. L and $\bar{L}$ are recursively enumerable but not recursive

9. Let L_1 be a recursive language and let L_2 be a recursively enumerable language which is not recursive. Which one of the following is TRUE?

   a. $\bar{L}_1$ is recursive, $\bar{L}_2$ is recursively enumerable.
   b. $\bar{L}_1$ is recursive, $\bar{L}_2$ is not recursively enumerable.

c. $\overline{L_1}$ and $\overline{L_2}$ are recursively enumerable.

d. $\overline{L_1}$ is recursively enumerable and $\overline{L_2}$ is recursive.

10. Consider the languages

$L_1 = \{ww^R | w \in \{0,1\}^*\}$

$L_2 = \{wcw^R | w \in \{0,1\}^*\}$

$L_3 = \{ww | w \in \{0,1\}^*\}$

Which one of the following is TRUE?

a. L_1 is deterministic CFL

b. L_2 is deterministic CFL

c. L_3 is a CFL but not a deterministic CFL

d. L_3 is deterministic CFL

11. Let S be a NP–complete problem and Q and R be two other problems not known to be in NP. Q is polynomial time reducible to S and S is polynomial time reducible to R. Which one of the following statements is TRUE?

a. R is NP complete

b. R is NP hard

c. Q is NP complete

d. Q is NP hard

12. $L_1 = \{a^{n+m} b^n c^m | n, m \geq 0\}$

$L_2 = \{a^{n+m} b^{n+m} c^m | n, m \geq 0\}$

$L_3 = \{a^{n+m} b^{n+m} c^{m+n} | n, m \geq 0\}$

Which of these languages are not CF.

a. L_1 only

b. L_3 only

c. L_1 and L_2

d. L_2 and L_3

13. If s is a string over $(0+1)^*$ then let $m_0(s)$ denote the number of 0's in s and $n_1(s)$ the number of 1's in s. Which one of the following languages is not regular?

a. $L = \{s \in (0+1)^* | n_0(s) \text{ is a 3-digit prime}\}$

b. $L = \{s \in (0+1)^* | \text{for every prefix } s' \text{ of } s, |n_0(s') - n_1(s')| \leq 2\}$

c. $L = \{s \in (0+1)^* | |n_0(s) - n_1(s)| \leq 4\}$

d. $L = \{s \in (0+1)^* | n_0(s) \bmod 7 = n_1(s) \bmod 5 = 0\}$

14. For $s \in (0+1)^*$ let $d(s)$ denote the decimal value of s (eg. $D(|0|) = 5$).

Let $L = \{s \in (0+1)^* | d(s) \bmod 5 = 2 \text{ and } d(s) \bmod 7 \neq 4\}$

Which one of the following statements is TRUE?

    a. L is recursively enumerable but not recursive
    b. L is recursive, but not context-free
    c. L is context-free, but not regular
    d. L is regular

15. Let FHAM be the problem of finding a Hamiltonian cycle in a graph G and DHAM be the problem of determining if a Hamiltonial cycle exists in a graph. Which one of the following is TRUE?

    a. Both FHAM and DHAM are NP-hard
    b. FHAM is NP hard, but DHAM is not
    c. DHAM is NP hard, but FHAM is not
    d. Neither FHAM nor DHAM is NP hard

16. Consider the following statements about the context-free grammar
$G = \{S \rightarrow SS, S \rightarrow ab, S \rightarrow ba, S \rightarrow c\}$
    (I) G is ambiguous
    (II) G produces all strings with equal number of a's and b's
    (III) G can be accepted by a deterministic PDA
Which combination below expresses all the true statements about G?

    a. I only
    b. I and III only
    c. II and III only
    d. I, II and III

17. Let L_1 be a regular language and L_2 a deterministic CFL. L_3 is recursively enumerable but not recursive. Which one of the following statement is FALSE?

    a. $L_1 \cap L_2$ is a DCFL
    b. $L_3 \cap L_1$ is recursive
    c. $L_1 \cup L_2$ is context-free
    d. $L_1 \cap L_2 \cap L_3$ is recursively enumerable

18. Consider the regular language $L = (111 + 11111)^*$. The minimum number of states in any DFA accepting the language is

    a. 3
    b. 5
    c. 8
    d. 9

19. Which one of the following grammars generates the language $L = \{a^i b^j | i \neq j\}$.

    a. $S \rightarrow AC|CB$
       $C \rightarrow aCb|a|b$
       $A \rightarrow aA|\varepsilon$
       $B \rightarrow Bb|\varepsilon$

b. $S \rightarrow aS|Sb|a|b$
c. $S \rightarrow AC|CB$
   $C \rightarrow aCb|\varepsilon$
   $A \rightarrow aA|\varepsilon$
   $B \rightarrow Bb|\varepsilon$
d. $S \rightarrow AC|CB$
   $C \rightarrow aCb|\varepsilon$
   $A \rightarrow aA|a$
   $B \rightarrow bB|b$

20. In the above correct grammar what is the minimum length of the derivation (number of steps starting from S) to generate the string $a^l\, b^m$ with $l \ne m$?

   a. $\max(l, m) + 2$
   b. $l + m + 2$
   c. $l + m + 3$
   d. $\max(l, m) + 3$

21. Consider $S \rightarrow SS|a$.
    What is the number of different derivation trees for $aaaaa$

   a. 3
   b. 5
   c. 7
   d. 14

22. Which one of the following grammar generates $L = \{a^i\, b^j\, c^k | i \ne k, i, j, k \ge 1\}$

   a. $S \rightarrow AC|CB$
      $A \rightarrow aA|a$
      $B \rightarrow Bc|c$
      $C \rightarrow aCc|bD|b$
      $D \rightarrow bD|b$
   b. $S \rightarrow aS|aA$
      $A \rightarrow bA|bB$
      $B \rightarrow cB|c$
   c. $S \rightarrow AB$
      $A \rightarrow aAb|ab$
      $B \rightarrow bBc|bc$
   d. $S \rightarrow AC|CB$
      $A \rightarrow aA|\varepsilon$
      $B \rightarrow Bc|\varepsilon$
      $C \rightarrow aCc|\varepsilon|bD$
      $D \rightarrow bD|b|\varepsilon$

23. A minimum state deterministic automaton accepting the language $L = \{w|w \in \{0,1\}^*$, the number of 0's and 1's in w are divisible by 3 and 5 respectively$\}$ has

    a. 15 states
    b. 11 states
    c. 10 states
    d. 9 states

24. The language $L = \{0^i21^i / i \geq 0\}$ over the alphabet $\{0, 1, 2\}$ is

    a. not recursive
    b. is recursive and is a deterministic CFL
    c. is a regular language
    d. is not a deterministic CFL but a CFL

25. Which of the following languages is regular?

    a. $\{ww^R|w \in \{0, 1\}^+\}$
    b. $\{ww^Rx|w, x \in \{0, 1\}^+\}$
    c. $\{w x w^R|w, x \in \{0, 1\}^+\}$
    d. $\{xww^R|w, x \in \{0, 1\}^+\}$

26. Let $\Sigma = \{0, 1\}$, $L_1 = \Sigma^*$ and $L_2 = \{0^n 1^n|n \geq 1\}$ then the languages $L_1 \cup L_2$ and L_2 are respectively

    a. regular, regular
    b. regular, not regular
    c. not regular, regular
    d. not regular, not regular

27. Which of the following statements is false?

    a. The halting problem for Turing machines is undecidable
    b. determining whether a context-free grammar is ambiguous is un-decidable
    c. given two arbitrary context-free grammar, G_1 and G_2, it is undecidable with $L(G_1) = L(G_2)$
    d. given two regular grammars G_1 and G_2, it is undecidable whether $L(G_1) = L(G_2)$

28. Two of the following four regular expressions are equivalent. Which two?
    (i) $(00)^* (0 + \varepsilon)$ (ii) $(00)^*$ (iii) 0^* (iv) $0(00)^*$

    a. (i) and (ii)
    b. (ii) and (iii)
    c. (i) and (iii)
    d. (iii) and (iv)

29. Let $L \subseteq \Sigma^*$ where $\Sigma = \{a, b\}$. Which of the following is true?

   a. $L = \{x | x \text{ has an equal number of } a\text{'s and } b\text{'s }\}$ is regular
   b. $L = \{a^n b^n \mid n \geq 1\}$ is regular
   c. $L = \{a^m b^n \mid m, n \geq 1\}$ is regular
   d. $L = \{x | x \text{ has more } a\text{'s than } b\text{'s}\}$ is regular

30. Define for a CFL L, $init\ (L) = \{u \mid uv \in L \text{ for some } v \in \{0, 1\}^*\}$. In other words $init\ (L)$ is the set of prefixes of L. Let $L = \{w | w \in \{0, 1\}^+, w \text{ has equal number of } 0\text{'s and } 1\text{'s}\}$. Then $init\ (L)$ is

   a. the set of all binary strings with unequal number of 0's and 1's
   b. the set of all binary stings including ε
   c. the set of all binary strings with exactly one more 0 than the number of 1's or one more 1 than the number of 0's.
   d. none of the above

31. If L_1 and L_2 are CFL and R a regular set, one of the languages below is not necessarily a CFL. Which one?

   a. $L_1 L_2$
   b. $L_1 \cup L_2$
   c. $L_1 \cap L_2$
   d. $L_1 \cap R$

32. The grammar whose productions are
   $\langle stmt \rangle \rightarrow$ if $\langle id \rangle$ then $\langle stmt \rangle$
   $\langle stmt \rangle \rightarrow$ if $\langle id \rangle$ then $\langle stmt \rangle$ else $\langle stmt \rangle$
   $\langle stmt \rangle \rightarrow \langle id \rangle := \langle id \rangle$
   $\langle id \rangle \rightarrow a|b|c|d|f$
   is ambiguous because

   a. the sentence if a then if b then $c:= d$ has more than one derivation trees
   b. the leftmost and rightmost derivation of the sentence if a then if b then $c := d$ give rise to different parse trees
   c. the sentence if a then if b then $c := d$ else $c := f$ has more than two parse trees
   d. the sentence if a then if b then $c := d$ else $c := f$ has two parse trees

33. Which one of the following regular expressions over $\{0, 1\}$ denotes the set of all strings not containing 100 as a substring?

   a. $0^*(11^*0)^*$
   b. 0^*1010^*
   c. 0^*1^*01
   d. $0^*(10 + 1)^*$

34. Which one of the following is not decidable?

    a. given a Turing machine M, a string s, and an integer k, M accepts s with k steps
    b. equivalence of two given Turing machines
    c. language accepted by a given DFSA is nonempty
    d. language generated by a CFG is nonempty

35. Which of the following languages over $\{a, b, c\}$ is accepted by a deterministic PDA?

    a. $\{wbw^R | w \in \{a, c\}^*\}$
    b. $\{ww^R | w \in \{a, b, c\}^*\}$
    c. $\{a^n b^n c^n | n \geq 1\}$
    d. $\{w | w$ is a palindrome over $\{a, b, c\}\}$

36. Which of the following instances of the post correspondence problem has a viable sequence (a solution)?

    a. $\{(b, bb), (bb, bab), (bab, abb), (abb, babb)\}$
    b. $\{(ab, aba), (baa, aa), (aba, baa)\}$
    c. $\{(ab, abb), (ba, aaa), (aa, a)\}$
    d. none of the above

37. It is undecidable, whether

    a. an arbitrary TM has 15 states
    b. an arbitrary TM halts after 10 steps
    c. an arbitrary TM ever prints a specific letter
    d. an arbitrary TM accepts a string w in 5 steps

38. Let $r = 1(1+0)^*$, $s = 11^*0$ and $t = 1^*0$ be three regular expressions and R, S, T the regular sets corresponding to them. Which of the following is true?

    a. $S \subset R$
    b. $R \subset S$
    c. $T \subset S$
    d. $R \subset T$

39. Which one of the following is the strongest correct statement about a finite language L over a finite alphabet Σ?

    a. L is undecidable
    b. L is recursive
    c. L is a CSL
    d. L is a regular set

40. Which of the following statements is TRUE?

    a. infinite union of regular sets is regular
    b. infinite union of finite sets is regular
    c. finite union of finite sets is regular
    d. complement of a finite set need not be regular

Answers

1. c	11. b	21. d	31. c
2. c	12. d	22. a	32. d
3. b	13. c	23. a	33. d
4. c	14. d	24. b	34. b
5. a	15. a	25. c	35. a
6. a	16. b	26. b	36. c
7. b	17. b	27. d	37. c
8. d	18. d	28. c	38. a
9. b	19. a	29. c	39. d
10. b	20. a	30. b	40. c

Bibliography

Aho, AV and MJ Corasick (1975). 'Efficient string matching: an aid to bibliographic search'. *Comm. ACM* **18**: 6, 333–340.

Aho, AV, JE Hopcroft and JD Ullman (1974). *The Design and Analysis of Computer Algorithms*. Reading, Mass: Addison-Wesley.

Aho, AV, and JD Ullman (1970). 'A characterization of two-way deterministic classes of languages'. *J. Comput. Syst. Sci.* **4**: 6, 523–538.

Aho, AV, and JD Ullman (1972). *The Theory of Parsing, Translation and Compiling*, Vol. I: *Parsing*. Englewood Cliffs, New Jersey: Prentice Hall.

Aho, AV, and JD Ullman (1972). *The Theory of Parsing, Translation and Compiling*, Vol. II: *Compiling*. Englewood Cliffs, New Jersey: Prentice Hall.

Aho, AV, and JD Ullman (1977). *Principles of Compiler Design*. Reading, Massachussets: Addison-Wesley.

Arthi, K, K Krithivasan and SV Raghavan (2001). 'A generative model for capturing user behaviour in computer networks'. *Proc. of SCI 2001*, Orlando, USA, Vol. 5, pp. 162–167.

Backus, JW (1959). 'The syntax and semantics of the proposed international algebraic language of the Zøurich ACM-GAMM conference'. *Proc. International Conference on Information Processing*, pp. 125–132, UNESCO.

Bar-Hillel, Y, M Perles and E Shamir (1961). 'On formal properties of simple phrase structure grammars'. *Z. Phonetik. Sprachwiss. Kommunikationsforsch.* **14**, 143–172.

Blattner, M (1973). 'The unsolvability of the equality problem for sentential forms of context-free grammars'. *J. Comput. Syst. Sci.* **7**: 5, 463–468.

Book, RV [1972]. 'On languages accepted in polynomial time'. *SIAM J. Comput.* **1**: 4, 281–287.

Book, RV (1974). 'Comparing complexity classes'. *J. Comput. Syst. Sci.* **9**: 2, 213–229.

Book, RV (1976). 'Translational lemmas, polynomial time, and $(logn)^j$ space'. *Theor. Comput. Sci.* **1**: 3, 215–226.

Book, RV, SA Greibach and B Wegbreit (1970). 'Time-and tape-bounded Turing acceptors and AFL's'. *J. Comput. Syst. Sci.* **4**: 6, 606–621.

Borscev, VB (1967). 'Okrestnostyne grammatiki'. *Naučno-Techničeskaja Informacija*, Ser. 2, 11, 39–41.

Brainerd, WS and LH Landweber (1974). *Theory of Computation*, New York: John Wiley and Sons.

Brzozowski, JA (1962). 'A survey of regular expressions and their applications'. *IEEE Trans. Electron. Comput.* **11**: 3, 324–335.

Brzozowski, JA (1964). 'Derivations of regular expressions'. *J. ACM* **11**: 4, 481–494.

Calude, CS and Gh. Păun (2001). 'Computing with Cells and Atoms, An Introduction to Quantum, DNA and Membrane computing'. London: Taylor and Francis.

Cantor, DC (1962). 'On the ambiguity problem of Backus systems'. *J. ACM* **9**: 4, 477–479.

Chomsky, N (1959). 'On certain formal properties of grammars'. *Inform. Contr.* **2**: 2, 137–167.

Chomsky, N (1962). 'Context-free grammars and pushdown storage'. *In Quarterly Program Report. No. 65*, pp. 187–194, Cambridge, Massachussets: MIT Res. Lab. Elect.

Chomsky, N (1963). 'Formal properties of grammars'. *In Handbook of Mathematical Psychology*, Vol. 2, pp. 323–418, New York: John Wiley and Sons.

Chomsky, N and GA Miller (1958). 'Finite state languages'. *Inform. Contr.* **1**: 2, 91–112.

Chomsky, N and MP Schutzenberger (1963). 'The algebraic theory of context free languages'. In F. Broffort and D. Hirschberg (eds.), *In Computer Programming and Formal Systems*, pp. 118–161, Amsterdam: North Holland.

Cook, SA (1973). 'A hierarchy for nondeterministic time complexity'. *J. Comput. Syst. Sci.* **7**: 4, 343–353.

Cremers, A and S Ginsburg (1975). 'Context-free grammar forms'. *J. Comput. Syst. Sci.* **11**: 1, 86–117.

Csuhaj-Varju, E, J Dassow, J Kelemen and Gh Păun (1994). 'Grammar Systems: A Grammatical Approach to Distribution and Cooperation'. London: Gordon and Breach.

Cudia, DF (1970). 'General problems of formal grammars'. *J. ACM* **17**: 1, 31–43.

Cudia, DF and WE Singletary (1968). 'Degrees of unsolvability in formal grammars'. *J. ACM* **15**: 4, 680–692.

Culik II, K and J Kari (1993). 'Image compression using weighted finite automata'. *Comput. Graph.* **15**: 3, 305–313.

Culik II, K and J Kari (1994). 'Inference algorithms for wfa and image compression'. In Yuval Fisher (ed.), *Fractal Image Compression, Theory and Application*, Chap. 13, 243–258. New York: Springer-Verlag.

Culik II, K and J Kari (1997). 'Digital images and formal languages'. In G. Rozenberg and A. Salomaa, (eds.), *Handbook of Formal Languages*, Vol. **3**. Chap. 10, 599–616. New York: Springer-Verlag.

Dassow, J and Gh Păun (1989). *Regulated Rewriting in Formal Language Theory*. Berlin, Heidelberg: Springer-Verlag.

Dassow, J and Gh Păun (1997). 'Grammar systems'. In G. Rozenberg and A. Salomaa (eds.), *Handbook of Formal Languages*, Vol. **2**. Chap. 4, 155–214. New York: Springer-Verlag.

Davis, M (1958). *Computability and Unsolvability*. New York: McGraw-Hill.

De Remer, FL (1969). 'Generating parsers for BNF grammars,' *Proc. of the 1969 Spring Joint Computer Conference*, pp. 793–799, Montvale, New Jersey: AFIPS Press.

De Remer, FL (1971). 'Simple *LR(k)* grammars'. *Comm. ACM* **14**: 7, 453–460.

Earley, J (1970). 'An efficient context-free parsing algorithm'. *Comm. ACM* **13**: 2, 94–102.

Ehrenfeucht, A, Gh Păun and G Rozenberg (1997). 'Contextual grammars and formal languages'. In G. Rozenberg and A. Salomaa (eds.), *Handbook of Formal Languages*, Vol. **2**. Chap. 6, 237–294. New York: Springer-Verlag.

Eilenberg, S and CC Elgot (1970). *Recursiveness*. New York: Academic Press.

Fischer, MJ (1969). 'Two characterizations of the context-sensitive languages'. *Proc. of the Tenth Annual IEEE Symposium on Switching and Automata Theory*, pp. 157–165, Waterloo, Canada, Oct. 15–17.

Fischer, PC (1963). 'On computability by certain classes of restricted Turing machines'. *Proc. of the Fourth Annual IEEE Symp. on Switching Circuit Theory and Logical Design*, pp. 23–32, Chicago, *Illinois*, Oct. 20–30.

Fischer, PC (1965). 'On formalisms for Turing machines'. *J. ACM* **12**: 4, 570–588.

Fischer, PC (1966). 'Turing machines with restricted memory access'. *Inform. Contr.* **9**: 4, 364–379.

Fischer, PC, AR Meyer and AL Rosenberg (1968). 'Counter machines and counter languages'. *Math. Syst. Theor.* **2**: 3, 265–283.

Fischer, PC, AR Meyer and AL Rosenberg (1972). 'Real-time simulation of multi-head tape units'. *J. ACM* **19**: 4, 590–607.

Floyd, RW (1967). 'Nondeterministic algorithms'. *J. ACM* **14**: 4, 636–644.

Friedman, A (1975). *Logical Design of Digital Systems*, Potomac, Maryland: Computer Science Press.

Friedman, EP (1977). 'The equivalence problem for deterministic context-free languages and monadic recursion schemes'. *J. Comput. Syst. Sci.* **14**: 3, 344–359.

Fu, KS (1982). *Syntactic Pattern Recognition and Applications*. New Jersey: Prentice-Hall, Inc.

Garey, MR, RL Graham and DS Johnson (1976). 'Some NP-complete geometric problems'. *Proc. of the Eighth Annual ACM Symposium on the Theory of Computing*. pp. 10–22, Hersley, Pennsylvania.

Garey, MR and DS Johnson (1978). *Computers and Intractability: A Guide to the Theory of NP-Completeness*. San Francisco: H. Freeman.

Garey, MR, DS Johnson and RE Tarjan (1976). 'The planar Hamilton circuit problem is NP-complete'. *SIAM J. Comput.* **5**: 4, 704–714.

Ginsburg, S (1966). *The Mathematical Theory of Context-Free Languages*. New York: McGraw Hill.

Ginsburg, S (1975). *Algebraic and Automata-Theoretic Properties of Formal Languages*. Amsterdam: North Holland.

Ginsburg, S and SA Greibach (1966). 'Deterministic context-free languages'. *Inform. Contr.* **9**: 6, 563–582.

Ginsburg, S and SA Greibach (1966). 'Mappings which preserve context-sensitive languages'. *Inform. Contr.* **9**: 6, 563–582.

Ginsburg, S and SA Greibach (1969). 'Abstract families of languages'. *Studies in Abstract Families of Languages*, pp. 1–32, Memoir No. 87, Providence, Rhode Island: American Mathematical Society.

Ginsburg, S and EH Spanier (1966). 'Finite turn pushdown automata'. *SIAM J. Control.* **4**: 3, 429–453.

Ginsburg, S and JS Ullian (1966). 'Ambiguity in context-free languages'. *J. ACM* **13**: 1, 62–88.

Ginsburg, S and JS Ullian (1966). 'Preservation of unambiguity and inherent ambiguity in context free languages'. *J. ACM* **13**: 3, 364–368.

Gray, JN, MA Harrison and O Ibarra (1967). 'Two-way pushdown automata'. *Inform. Control.* **11**: 1–2, 30–70.

Greibach, SA (1965). 'A new normal form theorem for context-free phrase structure grammars'. *J. ACM* **12**: 1, 42–52.

Greibach, SA and JE Hopcroft (1969). 'Independence of AFL operations'. *Studies in Abstract Families of Languages*, pp. 33–40, Memoir No. 87, Providence, Rhode Island: American Mathematical Society.

Head, T (1987). 'Formal language theory and DNA: An analysis of the generative capacity of specific recombinant behaviors'. *B. Math. Biol.*, **49**, 737–759.

Hennie, FC (1977). *Introduction to Computability.* Reading, Massachussets: Addison-Wesley.

Herman, GT and G Rozenberg (1975). *Developmental Systems and Languages.* Amsterdam: North Holland.

Hopcroft, JE and JD Ullman (1969). 'Some results on tape-bounded Turing machines'. *J. ACM* **16**: 1, 168–177.

Hopcroft, JE and JD Ullman (1969). *Formal Languages and Their Relation to Automata,* Reading, Massachussets: Addison-Wesley.

Hopcroft, JE, R. Motwani and JD Ullman (2001). *Introduction to Automata Theory, Langauges, and Computation.* Asia: Pearson Education.

Hunt, HB, III and DJ Rozenkrantz (1974). 'Computational parallels between the regular and context-free languages'. *Proc. of the Sixth Annual ACM Symposium on the Theory of Computing,* pp. 64–74, Seattle, Washington.

Hunt, HB, III and DJ Rozenkrantz (1977). 'On equivalence and containment problems for formal languages'. *J. ACM* **24**: 3, 387–396.

Hunt, HB, III, DJ Rozenkrantz and TG Szymanski (1976). 'On the equivalence, containment and covering problems for regular expressions'. *J. Comput. Syst. Sci.* **12**: 2, 222–268.

Hunt, HB, III and TG Szymanski (1975). 'On the complexity of grammar and related problems'. *Proc. of the Seventh Annual ACM Symposium on the Theory of Computing,* pp. 54–65, Albuquerque, New Mexico.

Jones, ND (1973). *Computability Theory: An Introduction.* New York: Academic Press.

Kari, L (2000). 'DNA computing in vitro and vivo', In *Future Generation Computer Systems,* 776, 1–12, Amsterdam: Elsevier Science.

Kasami, T (1965). 'An efficient recognition and syntax algorithm for context-free languages'. *Scientific Report AFCRL-65-758,* Bedford, Massachussets: Air Force Cambridge Research Lab.

Kasami, T and K Torii (1969). 'A syntax analysis procedure for unambiguous context-free grammars'. *J. ACM* **16**: 3, 423–431.

Kleene, SC (1956). *Automata Studies,* Princeton, NJ: Princeton Univ. Press.

Knuth, DE (1965). 'On the translation of languages from left to right'. *Inform. Control* **8**: 6, 607–639.

Knuth, DE, JH Morris, Jr. and VR Pratt (1977). 'Fast pattern matching in strings'. *SIAM J. Comput.* **6**: 2, 323–350.

Kohavi, Z (1970). *Switching and Finite Automata Theory.* New York: McGraw- Hill.

Korenjak, AJ (1969). 'A practical method for constructing $LR(k)$ processors'. *Comm. ACM* **12**: 11, 613–623.

Kosaraju, SR (1974). 'Regularity preserving functions'. *SIGACT News* **6**: 2, 16–17.

Kosaraju, SR (1975). 'Context-free preserving functions'. *Math. Syst. Theor.* **9**: 3, 193–197.

Krithivasan, K, M Sakthi Balan and P Harsha (1999). 'Distributed processing in automata'. *Int. J. Found. Comput. Sci.* **10**: 4, 443–464.

Kuroda, SY (1964). 'Classes of languages and linear bounded automata'. *Inform. Control* **7**: 2, 207–223.

Ladner, RE (1975). 'On the structure of polynomial time reducibility'. *J. ACM* **22**: 1, 155–171.

Ladner, RE, N Lynch and A Selman (1974). 'Comparison of polynomial time reducibilities'. *Proc. of the Sixth Annual ACM Symposium on the Theory of Computing,* pp. 110–121, Seattle, Washington.

Landweber, PS (1963). 'Three theorems on phrase structure grammars of type 1'. *Inform. Control* **6**: 2, 131–136.

Landweber, PS (1964). 'Decision problems of phrase structure grammars'. *IEEE Trans. Electron. Comput.* **13**, 354–362.

Lesk, ME (1975). 'LEX - a lexical analyzer generator'. CSTR 39, Murray Hill, New Jersey: Bell Laboratories.

Lewis, PM, II, DJ Rosenkrantz and RE Stearns (1976). *Compiler Design Theory,* Reading, Massachussets: Addison-Wesley.

Lewis, PM, II and RE Stearns (1968). 'Syntax directed transduction'. *J. ACM* **15**: 3, 465–488.

Lindenmayer, A (1968). 'Mathematical models for cellular interactions in development, parts I and II'. *J. Theor. Biol.* **18**, 280–315.

Lindenmayer, A (1971). 'Developmental systems without cellular interaction, their languages and grammars'. *J. Theor. Biol.* **30**, 455–484.

Maibaum, TSE (1974). 'A generalized approach to formal languages'. *J. Comput. Syst. Sci.,* **8**: 3, 409–439.

Marcus, S (1969). 'Contextual grammars'. *Rev. Roum. Math. Pures App.,* **14**, 1525–1534.

McNaughton, R and H Yamada (1960). 'Regular expressions and state graphs for automata'. *IEEE T. Electron. Comput.* **9**: 1, 39–47.

Mealy, GH (1955). 'A method for synthesizing sequential circuit'. *Bell Syst. Tech. J.* **34**: 5, 1045–1079.

Meyer, AR and LJ Stockmeyer (1973). 'The equivalence problem for regular expressions with squaring requires exponential space'. *Proc. of the Thirteenth Annual IEEE Symposium on Switching and Automata Theory*, pp. 125–129, Univ. of Maryland.

Minsky, ML (1961). 'Recursive unsolvability of Post's problem of 'tag' and other topics in the theory of Turing machines'. *Ann. Math.*, **74**: 3, 437–455.

Minsky, ML (1967). *Computation: Finite and Infinite Machines*. Englewood Cliffs, New Jersey: Prentice Hall.

Moore, EF (ed.) (1964). *Sequential Machines: Selected Papers*, Reading, Massachussets: Addison-Wesley.

Moret, BM (2002). *The Theory of Computation*. Asia: Pearson Education.

Myhill, J (1957). 'Finite automata and the representation of events'. WADD TR–57–624, pp. 112–137, Ohio: Wright Patterson AFB.

Myhill, J (1960). 'Linear bounded automata'. WADD TR–60–165, pp. 60–165, Ohio: Wright Patterson AFB.

Parikh, RJ (1966). 'On context-free languages'. *J. ACM* **13**: 4, 570–581.

Paull, MC and SH Unger (1968). 'Structural equivalence of context-free grammars'. *J. Comput. Syst. Sci.* **2**: 4, 427–468.

Păun, Gh (1997). 'Marcus Contextual Grammar'. The Netherlands: Kluwer Academic Publishers.

Păun, Gh (2002). '*Membrane Computing: An Introduction*'. New York: Springer.

Păun, Gh, Rozenberg and A Salomaa (1998). '*DNA Computing New Computing Paradigms*'. New York: Springer.

Paz, A (1971). *Introduction to Probabilistic Automata*, Washington: Academic Press.

Pisanti, N (1998). 'DNA computing: a survey'. *Bull. EATCS*, **64**, February, 188–216.

Prusinkiewics, P, K Krithivasan (1988). 'Algorithmic generation of South Indian folk art patterns'. *Proc. of INCOCG*, Singapore, September, 323–335.

Rabin, MO (1963). 'Real-time computation'. *Israel J. Math.* **1**: 4, 203–211.

Rabin, MO and D Scott (1959). 'Finite automata and their decision problems'. *IBM J. Res.* **3**: 2, 115–125.

Ramasubramanian, SV (1999). 'Finite Automata and Digital Images'. B. Tech. Project, IIT Madras: Dept. of Comp. Sci. & Engg.

Ramasubramanian, SV and Kamala Krithivasan (2000). "Finite automata and digital images'. *IJPRAI*, **14**: 4, 501–524.

Rice, HG (1953). 'Classes of recursively enumerable sets and their decision problems'. *Trans. AMS* **89**, 25–59.

Rice, HG (1956). 'On completely recursively enumerable classes and their key arrays'. *J. Symbolic Logic* **21**, 304–341.

Rosenberg, A (1996). On multihead finite automata'. *IBM J. Res. Devel* **10**, 388–394.

Rozenberg, G and A Salomaa (1980). *'The Mathematical Theory of L Systems'*. New York: *Academic Press.*

Rozenberg, G and A Salomaa (1997). *Handbook of Formal Languages.* Vol. 1, 2, 3, New York: Springer.

Rozenkrantz, DJ and RE Stearns (1970). 'Properties of deterministic top-down grammars'. *Inform. Control* **17**: 3, 226–256.

Sakthi Balan, M (2000). 'Distributed processing in automata'. M.S. Thesis, IIT Madras: Dept. of Comp. Sci. & Engg.

Salomaa, A (1969). *Theory of Automata,* Amsterdam: Pergamon Press.

Salomaa, A (1973). *Formal Languages,* New York: Academic Press.

Savitch, WJ (1970). 'Relationships between nondeterministic and deterministic tape complexities'. *J. Comput. Syst. Sci.* **4**: 2, 177–192.

Scheinberg, S (1960). 'Note on the Boolean properties of context-free languages'. *Inform. Control* **3**: 4, 372–375.

Schutzenberger, MP (1963). 'On context-free languages and pushdown automata'. *Inform. Control* **6**: 3, 246–264.

Seiferas, JI, M Fischer and AR Meyer (1973). 'Refinements of non-deterministic time and space hierarchies'. *Proc. of the Fourteenth Annual IEEE Symposium on Switching and Automata Theory,* pp. 130–137, New York.

Seiferas, JI and R McNaughton (1976). 'Regularity preserving relations'. *Theor. Comput. Sci.* **2**: 2, 147–154.

Shannon, CE and J McCarthy (eds.) (1956). *Automata Studies.* Princeton, New Jersey: Princeton Univ. Press.

Sheperdson, JC (1959). 'The reduction of two-way automata to one-way automata'. *IBM J. Res.* **3**: 2, 198–200.

Sipser, M (1997). *Introduction to the Theory of Computation.* Singapore: Brooks/Cole, Thomson Learning.

Siromoney, R and K Krithivasan (1974). 'Parallel context-free languages'. *Inform. Control,* **24**, 155–162.

Sivasubramanyam, Y (2002). 'Studies in weighted automata with application to image processing'. M.S. Thesis, IIT Madras: Department of Computer Science and Engineering.

Skyum, S (1974). 'Parallel context-free languages'. *Inform. Control,* **26**, 280–285.

Stanley, RJ (1965). 'Finite state representations of context-free languages'. *Quarterly Prog. Rept. No. 76,* 276–279, MIT Res. Lab. Elect., Massaschussets: Cambridge.

Stearns, RE (1967). 'A regularity test for pushdown machines'. *Inform. Control* **11**: 3, 323–340.

Stearns, RE and J Hartmanis (1963). 'Regularity preserving modifications of regular expressions'. *Inform. Control* **6**: 1, 55–69.

Stockmeyer, LJ (1976). 'The polynomial time hierarchy'. *Theor. Comput. Sci.* **3**: 1, 1–22.

Sudborough, IH (1975). 'A note on tape-bounded complexity classes and linear context-free languages'. *J. ACM* **22**: 4, 499–500.

Sudborough, IH (1975). 'On tape-bounded complexity classes and multihead finite automata'. *J. Comput. Syst. Sci.* **10**: 1, 62–76.

Turing, AM (1936). 'On computable numbers with an application to the Entscheidungs-problem'. *Proc. of the London Mathematical Societies*, **2**: 42, 230–265. A correction, *ibid.*, **43**, pp. 544–546.

Valiant, LG (1975). 'General context-free recognition in less than cubic time'. *J. Comput. Syst. Sci.* **10**: 2, 308–315.

Wise, DS (1976). 'A strong pumping lemma for context-free languages'. *Theor. Comput. Sci.* **3**: 3, 359–370.

Wood, D (1987). *Theory of Computation*. New York: Harper & Row Publishers.

Younger, DH (1967). 'Recognition and parsing of context-free languages in time n^3'. *Inform. Control* **10**: 2, 189–208.

Yu, S (1997). 'Regular languages'. In G. Rozenberg and A. Salomaa, (eds). *Handbook of Formal Languages*, Vol. 1. Chap. 2, 41–110, New York: Springer-Verlag.

Illustrations

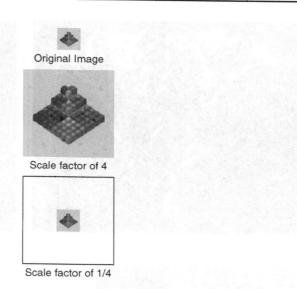

Original Image

Scale factor of 4

Scale factor of 1/4

Figure 6.10. Scaling of the color image

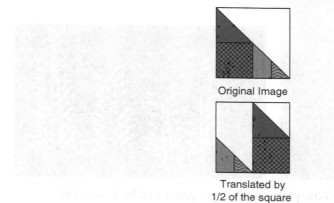

Original Image

Translated by
1/2 of the square

Translated by
1/4 of the square

Figure 6.12. Translation of color image by 1/2 and 1/4 of square

Figure 13.3. Some pictures of plants generated by *L*-systems

Index